# Harmony in Conflict

Active Adaptation to Life in Present-day Chinese Society

衝突中求和諧

Volume 1

by

Richard W. Hartzell

**CAVES BOOKS, LTD.**
Taipei, Taiwan, Republic of China

Published by
# CAVES BOOKS, LTD.
103 Chungshan N. Rd., Sec. 2, Taipei, Taiwan, R.O.C.

Tel: 541—4754, 537—1666

有著作權◇不准翻印
台內著字第 75949 號

發行人：周　　政
發行所：敦煌書局股份有限公司
地　址：台北市中山北路2段103號
電　話：(02) 537·1666（總機）
郵　撥：0014103—1
印刷所：聯和印製廠有限公司
新聞局登記證局版台業字0269號
中華民國80 年 2 月　　日第3版

© 1988 Richard W. Hartzell
USA Copyright TX 2-467-893

Library of Congress Cataloging in Publication Data

Hartzell, Richard W.
　Harmony in Conflict

1. Chinese studies—acculturological sinology.　2. Acculturation.
3. Communication—intercultural communication.　4. Culture conflict—USA and China.
　　　I. Title　II. Hartzell, Richard W.

First Printing: September 1988
Second Printing: August 1989

Thirdth Printing: Febuary 1991

ISBN 957-606-001-X

# PREFACE

This is a book about adaptation, or more properly acculturation, into Chinese society. It discusses a large number of difficulties and pitfalls which the foreigner will come across in such a process of adaptation, and offers some strategies for dealing with them, in a fashion which will enable him to maintain his mental equilibrium.

Much has been written about China. Yet for the most part, books about the "Middle Kingdom" emphasize the collection and study of historical data, elaborate on the philosophy in a highly theoretical manner, or examine the prominent literary works produced by different ages as means to understanding the Chinese people. Others deal with highly specialized topics such as religious rituals, medical treatment, superstituous practices, holidays and festivals, family and clan structure, development of art in different regions, peculiar customs in various provinces, or political trends over the millennia. These pages, by contrast, concern themselves with the more directly relevant side of Chinese society now as it is lived by the Chinese people of today, discussing basic considerations underlying eating, uses of money, employment, friendship, business dealings, social relations, etc. Herein are offered a number of insights as to why the Chinese will say one thing, and then do something else.

Foreigners who come to China are involved in a wide variety of occupations and endeavors. There are tourists, students, diplomats, engineers, doctors, lawyers, businessmen, and businesswomen of every description, and others who fit into no convenient category. Adaptation to life in this new culture, whether on a short-term or long-term basis, is an ongoing process. For this reason, one might suspect that the collected and dissected experiences of some particular foreigners in China, being too specific in regard to their own endeavors, might lack reference value to other foreigners. This would certainly be true if the writers did not have a broad grasp of basic cultural fundamentals.

In assembling the data presented in this volume, I have consciously tried to pick out representative examples of Chinese behavior and thinking. Often I have found it desirable to outline some suggested discussion questions, to help the reader come to grips with his own evaluation of the matter at hand, and reach what he feels is a valid conclusion. Especially important is that it has frequently been possible to take the extra step and develop a method for perceiving and dealing with a vast array of related situations. By the use of some simple perceptual tools, the foreigner will be able to see how many seemingly unrelated happenings actually fit quite closely together, and will learn to examine many types of situations from the Chinese point of view. This I believe will enable him to deal with the present-day Chinese more effectively and harmoniously, both now and in the future.

RICHARD W. HARTZELL

# INTRODUCTION
## Approaches to Understanding the Chinese

For a number of years I wrote for a variety of Chinese newspapers and magazines for a living. I wrote in Chinese. My typical article would deal with a westerner's view of many facets of Chinese society, and generally try to find some humor even in the most trying situation. I frequently had daily conversations with Chinese editors, reporters, cartoonists, new writers, and established novelists, talking about the goings on in society, the information printed in the newspaper, and the stories which, for some reason or another, did not get printed. They would of course comment on my own expositions and reporting, and this gave me a good deal of insight into their thinking. I obtained further reaction on my work, and the westernized views I was expounding, from the Chinese reading public, both by mail and by telephone. As my contacts expanded, I became familiar with a wide range of Chinese people in the publishing, broadcasting, advertising and other fields.

I often wondered if there might be some efficient way for the interested foreigner to gain an understanding of Chinese thinking and behavior, without going through the endless trial-and-error which all of my foreign acquaintances seemed to be engaged in, with every group of new arrivals making many of the same mistakes. In the bookstores were (and are) a variety of books about China, discussing the history, philosophy, ethical thought, customs, religion, and other topics. However, even a thorough reading of each of these books several times had not to my knowledge helped any significant number of foreigners in dealing with a variety of problem areas which did, like clockwork, tend to crop up when westerners and Chinese lived, worked, and played together. I do not deny that these books are useful and valuable, however they did not address the specific difficulties which many foreigners had expressed to me. Clearly some level of analysis was missing.

China is the seat of Asian culture, and is often described as a "great cultural nation". China has a long history, a strong sense of history, and possesses a large population, amounting to perhaps a quarter of the globe's people. It has developed its own arts, philosophy, social system, medicine, and language, which are largely outside the western tradition, and yet are commonly found in the curricula of the institutes of higher learning of the west, and have been recognized as serious objects of study. The Chinese over the millennia have accumulated a wealth of experience in seemingly every type of human relations and interpersonal dealings, and in a large variety of agricultural, business, academic, literary, and other pursuits. The Chinese have made some notable inventions and discoveries which have contributed to the progress of mankind. However, what exactly all of this means to the foreigner who wishes to adapt himself to life in the China of today has rarely been mentioned in any books or newspaper articles, much less explained.

# Introduction

During my newspaper years I would frequently discuss Chinese philosophy, historical trends, ethical thought, customs, etc. with my Chinese friends, and while I found that we shared much agreement on basic notions, their feeling of what was reasonable application of these basics in practice tended to leave a westerner bewildered. The Chinese would always claim that a great deal of their thinking came from the readily available classical texts, commentaries, and compilations, and yet it appeared that there were some significant and rather basic orientations, conceptions, and related thinking which were not expounded upon adequately in any of the books. Thus a paradox was presented by noting that the Chinese could obtain a large majority of their value-system parameters from these sources, and yet the westerner, even through a thorough reading, could not. The problem of course, as I saw later, lies in not understanding the foundational basis which determines how the values are applied.

## Active Adaptation into Chinese Society

China is an important part of the modern international scene, yet it is not a modern[1] developed nation in comparison to many of the western countries. In attempting to understand, and even predict, the mental processes of present-day Chinese people, one may pause to wonder: "Where does the influence of the great Chinese traditions leave off, and where do the effects of modern third-world-country thinking begin?" That is to say, is there any sort of link between the two realities of an historically great tradition and present day third-world-country status? Does the "theory" we read about in Chinese philosophy books and the "practice" we are likely to find in everyday situations coincide in a direct or indirect fashion? Do we perhaps need to rethink a number of preconceived notions and beliefs about the Chinese, and about ourselves as well, before we can co-exist comfortably and begin to truly acculturate ourselves to China? These are important considerations for any foreigner who is visiting or living in the "Middle Kingdom".

An eager westerner once asked some of his Chinese friends for a list of important topics which he should investigate in order to understand Chinese thinking. They were happy to provide him with such a list, which was composed of the various virtues stressed in Chinese philosophy. Such an investigative approach may be of value, however it is perhaps too complex or tedious for the average foreigner who cannot devote the entirety of his waking hours, over a period of years, to such a project, and would prefer a more condensed methodology. It is also problematic in that most foreigners are easily "lead astray" in attempting this type of research, especially when dealing with an abundance of scholarly texts, and indeed may lose sight of their original investigative premise.

---

1. This is treated more thoroughly in the discussion of the historical development of China and the west in Chapter 6.

Two reasons for this are perhaps a failure to clearly define a specific study goal, and the non-optimal selection of items on one's list of to-be-investigated topics.

## A New Kind of Knowledge

After living among the Chinese people for nearly a decade, in discussions with a wide range of other China-hands, I realized that it was feasible for foreigners to systematically investigate and accumulate "acculturative knowledge" — knowledge directly relevant to adapting or acculturating ourselves to life in Chinese society. Those of us who research this type of knowledge may be called acculturologists. Much information and insight in this regard may be gleaned from the Chinese press, in addition to the multitude of Chinese philosophical texts and commentary, studies in Eastern religion, comparative management, comparative law, and important works of Oriental and Western literature. Embarking on precisely such a project, I defined my goal by formulating two major questions for my reading: 1) "How does the author's analysis help me to understand and deal more effectively with the present-day Chinese people? and 2) "What is the relevance of the author's analysis to the life of a foreigner in present-day Chinese society?" After serious contemplation, I came up with a list of ten considerations, the nature of each I felt was important for the westerner to grasp before he could begin to seriously consider other facets of the Chinese mentality.

From the Chinese point of view, we should attempt to understand the nature of
1) harmony
2) individuality
3) responsibility
4) sincerity
5) honesty
6) rationality
7) naturalism
8) goodness
9) sympathy
10) morality

Note: the ordering of the Ten Natures is not intended to be suggestive of anything more than a general progression in the search for understanding. As such, a discussion of the Chinese view of morality and all of its ramifications is greatly facilitated if one has a thorough grasp of the previous nine fundamentals.

The reader should keep these Natures in mind, and as the discussions proceed chapter by chapter I will occasionally refer to them in passing, while avoiding the temptation "to preach." The reader is well advised to consider these Ten Natures in regard to any and all situations presented in this book, and to make his own analysis of which are relevant, and how they are being construed.

## Introduction

### Back to Basics

In reading and rereading many of the classical philosophical texts, both in the original and in translation, as I searched for analysis or commentary relevant to my stated "Two Questions" and "Ten Natures" I did have a difficult time maintaining my concentration for very long. The point of the writings of these many learned authors usually appeared to be to lead the reader into the realms of theoretical discussions which were outside the scope of practical applicability, with little or no attempted analysis of any gap between "theory" and "practice" which some observers have occasionally pointed out as existing in present-day Chinese society. Many authors declare that Chinese philosophy and practical affairs have always been close in both theory and practice. However, seldom do they go on to question whether this is applicable or existent in all situations. Does this close correlation exist in the business world, the education field, in agricultural pursuits, medical treatment and research, music and the arts, etc., or is it just a correlation among the academics, those who are honorably designated in society as "scholars"? From the point of view of the foreigner who views Chinese society as a whole, is this so-called correlation actually more of a discorrelation when applied to the entire society?

In my extensive readings, I often saw that the reader is given a highly idealized rendering of many Chinese concepts, with no clear explanation of where and in what ways they are at a disparity with western thought, and how the average westerner could deal with the difficulties thereby generated. Most of the analysis in such works is also notable in that it tends to be historical in nature, and how, (or if), it applies to the Chinese in the present era is something rarely mentioned.

I was able to add to my research from a variety of first-hand sources, primarily interviews, correspondence, and discussions with the many Chinese and foreigners I came across in my lecture tours, TV appearances, newspaper editorial meetings, and in my position as manager of a local organization.

As various aspects of Chinese thinking became clear, I was continually surprised that despite all the work done over the centuries by westerners researching Chinese culture, and the vast number of books, treatises, scholarly reports, dictionaries, language textbooks, and other published works which have appeared in the marketplace or in the high school and college classrooms, or which have circulated in various scholarly circles, the image of Chinese as "inscrutable" remains, and reports regularly coming in from tourists, visiting dignitaries, journalists, and a wide range of academics, recounting their tales among the Chinese continually serve to bolster this image. In reality, the behavior of the Chinese follows definite patterns, although they are not western ones. It is, I believe, our failure to recognize the patterns, and to recognize the thinking processes behind them, which prove without-a-doubt the lack of our "acculturative knowledge". Books or other materials which contain such knowledge are seemingly not widely available to the western student or other interested individual, or else do not exist in an appropriately organized fashion to make them "digestible" to the average man's reading tastes. The availability of other cultural material, especially historical treatises, is contrastingly quite abundant.

## Shared Values

Among human beings, we often find that the acceptance and use of common norms are the great bonds that tie different people together. These norms include a shared cultural and linguistic background, and a common sense of history, as well as commonly perceived cultural and national goals, and generally shared definitions of what is acceptable and proper in terms of personal conduct, ambitions, and personal desires. Thus the Christians have many ideas, feelings, and expressions of emotions which the Buddhists would consider alien, and vice versa.

The Chinese have been influenced strongly by Buddhism, Taoism, Confucianism, and other schools of thought over their long history, as well as being subject to the dictates of the Emperor, to whom absolute obedience was required. Many foreigners researching Chinese studies in the west are often unable to come to grips with the practical aspects of these philosophical or religious doctrines, and even tend to lose sight of this common thread of authoritarianism and any or all of its ramifications. I recall the story of a Caucasian professor who had a lengthy background of Chinese studies both in the U.S. and China, and who was teaching in an Ivy League University. She had taught Chinese language courses for a number of years and was well respected by the student body. One June, a number of her graduating students were making plans to continue their studies in China in the very near future. They were anxious to go and get a feel of the rich cultural heritage of the great nation, to appreciate its art, language, and philosophy. One of the students asked her about what kind of diversity would be found among the populace. The teacher was very surprised at this remark, and she replied straightforwardly: "If you are looking for diversity, stay in the United States."

In talks with hundreds of westerners who have come to live in China for varying and lengthy periods, and who have more than casual or superficial impressions of the people and the society, I have found a large degree of acceptance of the relevance of this teacher's remark. While I would not be so simplistic to claim that all Chinese are all stamped out of the same mold, nevertheless I do note that there are pronounced tendencies away from "developing individualism" within the educational system, philosophical outlook, family organization, and social structure in general. Far larger emphasis is placed on recognition and acceptance of one's role in the group, and acquiescence to its goals and concerns, as well as obedience to one's superiors without discussion or debate.

## Introduction

### Acculturation & Language

There has always been a widely held assumption that the quickest route to acculturation in a foreign land is to study the local language with diligence. Such study may of course begin well before actual arrival in the country, and many high school and college bookstores offer a mutitude of language texts designed for the express purpose of instructing anyone who desires communicative skills in any particular language. Certainly the foreigner who has successfully adapted to life overseas will have done in-depth research into the study of the local language, not only in terms of speaking, but also in terms of reading and writing. However, just because a foreigner has done in-depth research into the local language, and attained a high level of language skills, does not necessarily mean that he has adapted to the local culture in a maximally beneficial fashion, or that he has no "communication problems."

Many foreigners have done in depth research into Chinese literature, language, philosophy, and sociology, and yet still express puzzlement at many of the goings-on which they witness in the society during their stays of residence. In addition to having a different cultural background, at the root of their difficulties is the fact that the words which are used to translate or correspond to various Chinese philosophical concepts, however carefully these words are chosen, still do not carry the same senses of meaning in English that the original Chinese characters do in Chinese. For example, any of the "Ten Natures" listed above could be translated directly into Chinese, and a comparison of the range of meaning, between English and Chinese, could be represented by one of these three diagrams, which represent the intersection of the Chinese and western view of, for example, "naturalism".

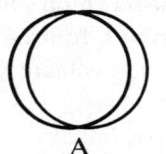

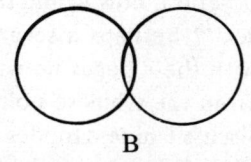

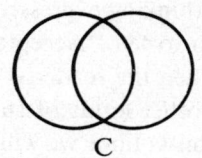

A　　　　　　　　B　　　　　　　　C

Many people might assume that the relation between concepts in the two cultures are represented by (A), and no doubt not represented by (B). However, what we usually find is (C).

A foreigner who has approached the obtaining of "acculturative knowledge" strictly through the study of the local language, may have done very little work in recognizing and categorizing the different conceptions, points of view, patterns of reasoning, or other parameters which underlie his own language and the foreign language. In this situation, even with advanced language skills, his strivings to adapt or acculturate himself, rather than being facilitated, may become blocked in many areas, although unconsciously.

His cerebrum may then continually come back to the basic assumption, since he lacks any workable or concrete knowledge to the contrary, that words in different languages have a direct one-to-one translatable correspondence. Indeed, this may seem a reasonable supposition in light of the training he has received in other western languages, especially in regard to the vocabulary covered in the first one or two years of study. However this assumption is clearly far wide of the mark when comparing Eastern and Western languages.

As an example of this, we may consider the word *jen* 仁 , which some scholars have called "the cornerstone of Confucianism". In different dictionaries and scholarly treatises, we find such various renderings into English as "human heartedness", "virtue", "perfect virtue", "moral life", "true manhood", "charity", "man-to-manness", "magnanimity", "benevolence", "moral character", "compassion", "kindness", "benignancy", "humanity", "humanistic intuition", "human-ness", "mercy", etc. It appears that there is no one term in the English language that corresponds exactly to this fundamental Confucian concept. If the true meaning of this word is to be grasped, then we must assume that many examples of various situations in which *jen* comes into play will have to be given, observed, or otherwise assembled from various sources, and the course of action which the Chinese take in such situations must then be examined. The collection of suitable examples is a time-consuming affair, but it is worthwhile from the point of view of understanding the local people, and a necessary adjunct to the study of language, while being quite more important to the individual who desires to be acculturated than a theoretically thorough study of Chinese linguistics.

We will also want to look at the thinking behind various statements. George Bernard Shaw once said: "We must not stay as we are, doing always what was done the last time, or we shall stick in the mud." Most westerners agree with this. However, we need to consider what the reaction of the Chinese would be to such a statement. In terms of the thinking expressed in this quotation, how would the Chinese rate it on some kind of zero to ten "Acceptability Index"? Perhaps a seven? Or maybe a four? I believe that when the reader is finished with these pages he will be able to evaluate this and many other kinds of statements from the Chinese point of view.

In this volume we will want to discuss Chinese modes of behavior, but also to clarify in what ways many words have different meaning, weight, force, connotation, and sense in cross-cultural encounters. We will delve into the practical side of Chinese relations as opposed to the theoretical, keeping our comments relevant to the foreigner's situation, and try to offer the reader analysis and insight for dealing with various circumstances which may arise.

We will begin with eating, and follow a progressively detailed path into considerations of money management, salaried employment, freelancing, acting, hiring local people, business undertakings, consumer attitudes, language peculiarities, communication problems, politeness, logic, face, indirectness, respect & obedience, cross-cultural negotiation, Chinese psychology, sympathy, legal posturing, model building, comparative naturalism, positiveness, and other topics.

# Table of Contents

Preface     i
Introduction     ii

## Part 1 Food and the Foreigner in China

### Chapter 1 Eating, Banqueting, and Being a Guest
Eating: the People's Livelihood     1
Underlying Cultural Patterns of Eating     14
Nutrient Replenishment     22
A Pig in a Crate     23
Varying Views on Western Eating Arrangements     25
Attitudes     30
Restaurant Classification     32
Eating in a Hot Climate     33
Dieting in China     35
Cross Cultural Meal-time Complaining     38
Chinese Sanitary Habits     46
Law vs. Benevolence Questionnaire     48
Insightful Stories     49
Empty Promises in the Hotel Industry     54
Etiquette vs. Good Fortune     55
Honesty in the Environment     58
What It Is, It Is Not, or Is It?     62
Insults in the Night Market     66
Difficulties and Solutions     70

### Chapter 2 Food and Language
Categories of Confusion     77
Colors     78
Differentiations and Undifferentiations     80
Connotations and Non-Connotations     85
Combination Words     99

### Chapter 3 Purchasing, Pricing, and Value
Conflict of Interest     101
Food and Pricing     104

Old Idioms, Revisited  113
Natural Pricing  115
The Purchasing Agent  118
Different Explanations  122
Buying Vegetables  124
The Value of Merchandise  126
Paradoxes  128

*Part 2 Enlightened Money Management*

**Chapter 4 Opportunities and Obstacles**
Money  131
Private and Public Concerns  132
TV Work and Studio Organization  140
Reward/Effort Relationships  141
Employing the Locals  143
New Business Investment  149
A Backyard Investment  152
Banking Relations and Credit  153
Unfair Descriptions  156
The Sunglasses Incident  158
Smog Problems with New Yarn  163
"Growth" and Its Significance  165
A Questionable Consulting Contract  168
Teaching Language to the Locals  171
Translating Poetry for Fun and Profit  174
Foreign Language Schools in China  177
Law, Ethics, and Business Philosophy  180
Something For Nothing  186
Different Ideas  189
TV Shooting In France  191
Freelancing in China  194
Lessons From the Chinese Laundry  196
Enrollment in Chinese Elementary School  199
Law vs. Benevolence Questionnaire  204
The Western Hotel Consultant  205
Raising Money with the Hui  210
Ten, Seven, Three, Four  213
On the Homefront  214

*Table of Contents*

### Chapter 5 Justice and Jeopardy
Failure in Understanding   216
Clarifications of Injury   217
Clarifications of Liability   226
Discussion of Liability   235
Debate Topics   237
The Visit   238
An Insurance Settlement   238

## Part 3 Explorations of Cultural Differences

### Chapter 6 Awareness
Building Awareness of Cultural Differences   240
Pre-Industrialism and Post-Industrialism   245
Organization of Language   252

### Chapter 7 Comparative Ideals of Obedience
A Relaxing Day in the Countryside   254
Reading at Home   255
Taxi Troubles   257
Ancestors and Ancestor Worship   259
Why do you ask "Why?   261
Proposed Revisions of Historical Documents   264
Grandparents, Parents, and Obedience   266
Ethical Reasoning   272
The Chens and the Wus   276
Basic Ethical Doctrines   284
Objectivity   290
Broad Overviews   291
Ethics in the Schools   295
Sharp Teeth   296
Filial Piety and the Westerner in China   297

### Chapter 8 Face Saving as a Way of Life
Here Comes the Judge   305
A Professional Girlfriend   306
Utopian Questions   308
Western Face   309
Freedom and Face   313
Preliminary Investigations   318

Face: A Four Letter Word    319
International Conferences    339
Perceived Favoritism in the Workplace    340
Facial Omissions    344
Face for Everybody    348
Living with Face    352
Immigration Problems    356
The Answer is a "Yes, maybe"    357
The Rise of Face    359
Direct and Indirect Remarks    363
Indirect Words and Action    371
Justice, Righteousness, etc.    376

## Chapter 9 Language, Communication, and Non-Communication
Detailed Contents    377
English Language Difficulties    378
English and the Asian Student    380
Dealing with the Language    383
Contrasting Emotive Content    393
Integration of Concepts    409
Rationale Weight Indexing    413
Unknown and Unadopted    417
Alligators, Crocodiles, and Other Topics    419
Chinese Proofreading Marks    428
Grammatical Bias and Related Issues    432
Communication    438
Total Fluency    441
Artistic Impressions    443
The World of Translation    445
Language Guessing Games: A Comparison    458
Researching the Mental Flow    465
Word Games and Paradoxes    467
Chinese Language and the Westerner    479

## Part 4 Bases for Action and Non-Action

### Chapter 10 Opposing Explanations and Varying Worldviews
The Five Relationships Model    494
Sympathy: A Primer    503
Sympathy and Legality Test    529

*Table of Contents* xiii

    Harmony as a Social Basis   532
    Basic Organization of Chinese-style Continental Law System   533
    Conflicting Views of Naturalism   535
    The Implications of Positiveness   544
    Rejection vs. Acceptance of Orthodoxy   549
    Logic and its Ramifications   556
    Syllogisms and Illogic   577
    Psychological Peculiarities   581

## Part 5 Coping with Non-Western Behavior

### Chapter 11 Strategies and Responses
Introduction to Chinese Negotiation   587
The Sunglasses Incident (continued)   595
Task Completion   599
Proper Replies and Responses   607
Behavioral Modification Exercise   608
Steps in Project Management   609
Go Roman Strategy   611
A Short Course in Human Relations   613
Let the Police Handle It   616
Zip the Lip   618
Building-Up Company Culture   619
Trademark Imitation Headaches   621
Simple and Successful Negotiation   625
Indirect Stalling and Refusal Techniques for Persistent Salesmen   627
True Intentions   631
Differing Management Orientations   634
Managing Your Way Through the Chinese Holidays   635
Positive vs. Negative Financial Reinforcement   637
Uninvited Guests   638
Telephone vs. Letter   639

### Chapter 12 Cross-Cultural Model Building
Making a 3-D Model   640
Yes You May, No You May Not   641
Taking Responsibility   653
Differing Harmony Models   654
Problem Solving   661
Implementation vs. Excuses   661

Spectra Charts    666

**Appendix**
Confusing Terms    674
Caution with Terminology    677
Types of Definitions    683
New Chinese Idioms    683
Acculturology and Other Sciences    685
Author    686
Acknowledgements    688
Notes and Analysis    689
Bibliography    696
Index    699

# PART 1 Food and the Foreigner in China

## Chapter 1 Eating, Banqueting, and Being A Guest

### Eating: the People's Livelihood

Perhaps no other activity offers us a better insight into the basic attitudes and mentalities of a culture than a full examination of the way in which eating is accomplished, from the selection, purchase, and preparation of food to its actual consumption. "Eating habits" in the widest sense, covering the range of topics from what is suitable fare, in what way it should be cooked, what constitutes good table manners, how guests are treated, the entire range of behavior involved with dining in restaurants or sidewalk stalls, taking meals with co-workers and associates, all the way to considerations of nutrition, sanitation, politeness, generosity, fairness, reasonableness, etc., all serve as a foundation for the natives' general thinking processes. Perceptions and procedures inculcated in the child from the earliest days of awareness, sitting at the meal table with the family members, will often become a permanent part of its mental makeup. This is noted in an East European proverb which says "The way one eats is the way one works." Thus a complete overview of the various aspects of the issue of food consumption, and all related side-issues, as well as some commentary on the various ramifications thereof, will serve the foreigner as an excellent introduction to the more difficult topics involved in acculturating himself to the value system of the local inhabitants.

"The Problem of the People's Livelihood", while containing a wide sphere of general issues in the mind of the westerner, such as employment opportunities, income distribution, wage levels, welfare programs, retirement policies, etc., yet to the Chinese is synonymous with one and only one topic: Eating. It is no accident that the most common form of Chinese greeting is "Have you eaten your fill?", whereas a westerner is more comfortable with a simple "Hi", "How have you been?", or "How is it going?", all of which strike the Chinese as ignoring the main issue. That Eating holds this central role in the common Chinese person's perceptions is indeed highly significant, and is illustrative of a number of historical trends. As such it also holds many far-reaching implications for our understanding of Chinese society as a whole. The impact of this will be found throughout our discussion.

### Differing Mentalities

Asked to cite one issue which separates the Chinese and westerners more significantly than any other, one acculturologist of my acquaintance was quick to reply: "The Group Mentality". Without an understanding of this, he said, one cannot hope to have any real understanding of the Chinese people. While not being overly difficult to present as a concept, "The Group Mentality" is, he admitted, often extremely difficult for the westerner to rationalize or put into practice over the long term. Significantly, "The Group Mentality" is not gained by the westerner from a thorough reading of any of the great books written by Confucius, Mencius, Lao-tze, Chuang-tse, or even Han Fei-tse, whether in translation or in the original. It is rather a basic ingrained feature of the Chinese social system, an internal orientation, an ingrained subconscious philosophy below the level of articulated conscious philosophical concerns, and far below the perceptual influences due to the peculiarities of the Chinese language. We may compare it to the circuit boards of a computer's hardware which represent a level of structure below the operating system, and far below any applications programs written in a language such as BASIC, COBOL, or dBASE.

Psychologists and sociologists will tell us that the growing child is pulled between two competing human longings, or needs, as he matures. The first is the need to be included, and the second is the need to be independent. Although the final percentage composition, or balance, of these needs in the adult will vary, some have suggested a 30% need for "being included", 70% need for "being independent", or a 30/70 ratio in the westerner. To the Chinese however, the ratio is closer to 70/30, meaning a 70% need for "being included" (which means being part of the group), and a 30% need for "being independent". This is especially true as regards attachment to or dependence on the family, since Chinese of all age groups are seen to take great delight in being together with family members and enjoying the communal family atmosphere. By comparison the Japanese, who are also Orientals, on their vacations or holidays tend to go on trips with co-workers or friends, but the Chinese almost universally go home to be with relatives. While many westerners might consider "homesickness" a childish emotion, yet the Chinese promote "homesickness" as a normal part of the adult's emotional makeup, along with respect for ancestors. Idioms such as "Fallen leaves return to the roots" and verses such as Tang Dynasty Poet Li Pai's poem "Night Thoughts" — "The bright moon shone before my bed, I wondered was it frost upon the ground? I raised my head to gaze at the clear moon, and bowed my head remembering my old home" — all serve to indelibly impress the longing for one's home, and the communality of neighborhood, relatives, and family members on the consciousness. Thus while the westerner perceives "independence" as the natural order of things, long exposure to Chinese society enables him to see that the need for independence is as much a culturally acquired trait as a preference for a breakfast of pancakes and maple syrup, or the desire for a large slice of hot apple pie after dinner.

The Group Mentality finds some of its most forceful and yet innocuous foundations in the way in which the Chinese have traditionally engaged in, and up to the present day continue to engage in eating their meals. The Chinese like to eat, and any reason or excuse is adequate enough to hold a banquet. The example of the man who won $500 (US$ equivalent) in the local lottery, and treated his friends and relatives to a banquet, the final price for which added up to $600, for a loss of $100, is quite common. It is felt that by treating all these people, he will certainly bring good fortune to himself and his business/personal affairs, and no doubt open up many additional avenues for making more money. It is not an exaggeration to state that the Chinese idea of happiness and well being is probably more closely related to "a large group of relatives and friends eating a sumptuous meal" than anything else. Such a large group provides the host with an opportunity to spread his fame and influence, to show off the width and breath of his social contacts, and prevents any loneliness or self doubt from arising. A complete eight or twelve course banquet will commonly accompany a wedding, a funeral, acquirement of a new job, a promotion, or retirement, the first month of life of a new child, or the successful signing of a business contract. Likewise a large banquet to celebrate a wedding anniversary, a company founding anniversary, a move to a new house, the winning of any significant prize, the acquirement of royalty payment, the "resignation" of an employee after he was shown proof of his embezzlement of company funds, etc. is not at all unusual. Illustrative is the case of one westerner who attended a banquet celebrating the 70th birthday of a co-worker's mother, and was surprised when they had eaten five courses and the mother had still not made an appearance. Upon inquiry with his host about this he was told that since she, the guest of honor, had had to participate in the wedding banquet of a cousin's daughter that same evening, so she was unable to attend. As far as the foreigner could detect, her absence seemed to have no dampening effect on the merriment whatsoever.

Chinese-style business organization deals heavily in assistance from relatives and help from friends, and such arrangements are best discussed over the dinner table. Indeed, to the Chinese, no reason for organizing a banquet is considered too exceptional, no rationale too tenuous, no oversight in planning is particularly important, and any lack of elegance in the decorations or cleanliness in the environment is not considered worthy of criticism, as long as everyone eats their fill. For all these reasons, social eating among the Chinese is highly developed, and the Chinese not only eat in restaurants often, but also frequently invite people as guests into their homes. The pleasure which the Chinese get from the communal atmosphere around the meal table exceeds the pleasure obtained from hobbies, whether collecting stamps, butterflies, rare books, foreign coins, or whatever other pursuits one engages in by way of a hobby; exceeds the pleasure obtained from reading, board games, watching or participating in sports, movie or TV viewing, travel, touring, manual labor, inventing, repairing, quiet contemplation, or philosophical debate.

Eating to the Chinese is a major past-time, and the attentions which the Chinese attach to eating of course profoundly affect the foreigners who live in Chinese society, since they are immediately given the impression of the Chinese as a warm, hospitable, and generous people. Contrasts with the western way of eating reveal many dissimilarities between the two cultures.

The westerner, especially one in his 20's or 30's would probably rather be at the disco with his friends, reading some books of his own selection, or otherwise pursuing his own interests, than sitting around the communal table enjoying the polite conversation of relatives or the parents' co-workers and other acquaintances. This is in opposition to the prevailing Chinese attitude for eating: the more the merrier. Westerners have developed the snack food culture and fast food culture, which give rise to the whole tendency to "eat when you are hungry", and the legacy left by the Earl of Sandwich, as well as an appreciation of the convenience his invention represents, underline this tendency. The individual orientation which this accents is in direct contrast to the Chinese preference for group dining and the atmosphere of togetherness thereby engendered.

During the cold winter months, the Chinese preference is often for eating "firepot", where all the meat and vegetables are placed in a pot and cooked in the center of the table. That everyone consumes from the common pot is most indicative of the fact that the individual attains his sustenance from the group. In a similar fashion, the standard day-to-day Chinese table arrangements where all the dishes are all placed in the center of the table and each person helps himself from the common fare, are equally illustrative of the group orientation. In Chinese-style family eating around the dinner table at home and in restaurants, children are generally not given a "portion" of various foods, although they may be given bite sized amounts from time to time by elders, using chopsticks to place the food in the child's bowl. They are ordinarily left to choose from the common dishes, in imitation of their older brothers, sisters, and parents. Family eating in this fashion in this and other ways tends to be much less structured than in typical middle class or even-upper middle class western meals. The child is not given an individual portion which is meant to be his and his alone, but rather eats from the common selection available to all. Even the main course of rice or noodles is made in such a quantity that each takes his helping from the common pot.

From this it is clear that in the Chinese style of eating arrangements, the individual makes his choices from those available to the group. Furthermore, we see that in times of scarcity the food on the table tends to be allocated not equally but in a preferential manner to particular subgroups: namely first the elderly, then the very young, and only later the other family members. Thus it is evident that the group indicates which choices are available to the individual, even to the point of excluding him from any choices at all.

Flexibility

The less structured atmosphere, or as we should say the more flexible arrangements for people consuming their meals around the table are reflected in the way the dishes are placed in the center of the table, offering an apparently random choice to the people in attendance. There are also many other ways in which the increased flexibility of the Chinese mealtime arrangements are apparent. For example in the west, if someone is invited to dinner, and they come with a friend, or with two friends, this is something of a real dilemma for the chef or housewife involved with preparing the meal. The way that the westerners eat, in terms of a main course which is usually meat or some meat-related dish, and the preparation of the other courses, is usually made in exact proportion, or within close limits, to the number of people coming to the meal. This is particularly apparent in terms of eating such things as steak, pork chops, pot pies, and even items such as casseroles, and especially apparent in terms of TV dinners, and other pre-packaged frozen foods, where each person gets a set menu portion, or the box specifies "Serves six". Cooking of the main course is most often done in anticipation of precisely how many people are coming to the meal, and whatever the other dishes are, they are typically all prepared first and placed on the table prior to the commencement of the meal. (The dessert is the general exception.) Spagetti, lasagna, ravioli, macaroni, and other dishes of this style are perhaps much more flexible in this matter, which indicates that in eating habits the Italians are closer to the Chinese than to the Americans. The Americans often do set a sumptuous table at Thanksgiving, Christmas, and Easter, with the careful arrangement of the family's best china on the dinner table, but it is still questionable whether the host would be delighted at, or at best "have no objection to", several more people showing up for the meal than were originally planned for or invited.

In China a different set of social rules apply. If one person is invited to dinner, and he brings a friend, or two, or three, this rarely causes any dilemma at all, and the flexibility of the Chinese eating arrangements quickly becomes apparent. There are several reasons for this. First of all, the main Chinese dish is rice, or noodles, and since the other dishes are all placed in the center of the table for selection by the group members, the number of dishes is very easily adjusted in variety and quantity. As some dishes are consumed, more steaming hot ones from the kitchen are added, and this additional placement of new dishes on the table throughout the meal is quite standard procedure. Although more guests require more dishes, the meal procedure is essentially unchanged. Chinese cooking is often done in a wok, over a large gas burner, using oil to stirfry vegetables, meat strips, seafood, and other items, and preparation of a dish in this manner sometimes takes less than three minutes. It is a fairly simple matter to come up with a few more dishes of steaming hot, delectable food. Moreover, soups and many meat dishes are often prepared in abundance, especially such items as sliced chicken, sausage, meat stewed in soybean sauce, Chinese ham, etc. so that it is seemingly impossible to finish all of it. Adding more guests thus presents minimal problems.

In western homes it is the custom to place all the dishes on the table first, and complete the meal in this straightforward manner. The traditional Chinese custom of men, elders, and children eating first, while the wives of the married son(s) do the cooking and preparation, these wives then eating after everyone else is done, can still be seen in varying degrees in Chinese eating arrangements, whereas the western wife is more likely to prepare everything first, and feel that it is her right to eat with the family members and enjoy the mealtime environment. Thus we note in China the wife is generally willing to retire to the kitchen to do further preparation of food, thus assuming the role of staff, when more guests come, because that is seen as the wife's place. Moreover, guests are most important.

All of these are significant considerations of which the foreigner should be aware, so that he can understand some elemental ways in which Chinese thinking patterns are different from his own. Many of these differences find their foundations in, and are a direct reflection of differences in the way Chinese and westerners deal with the whole subject of "mealtime". Certainly the flexibility and informality of Chinese meal arrangements is one important part of this.

Mealtimes and Invitations

A French lady and her Chinese fiance were preparing for their wedding banquet (a ten course meal) to be held in China in a large local restaurant. She inquired with a number of her local and foreign friends if the engraved invitations should include some indication of "R.S.V.P.", or if a separate reply card should be included for this purpose. Everyone agreed that that was not the normal procedure nor the custom in China. She considered this for some time and then said: "But how can I possibly inform the restaurant of how many people are coming, and how can I possibly make the seating arrangements if I do not get a 'oui' or 'non' from each of my invited guests?" The Chinese, in accompaniment with the fiance's family, considered this for a while and first determined how many invitations they were planning to send out. After various calculations, the figure of 200 invitations was established. The Chinese then did some quick mental arithmetic, and said: "Tell the restaurant to prepare 15 tables, with 2 tables on standby. We can sit 10 to 12 people at each table." The westerner should be aware that there is nothing at all unusual in this type of formulation, even though it is so far away from the western norm as to be almost unbelievable.

The newly arrived foreigner, or even one with lengthy in-country residence experience, is often disappointed when inviting some thirty or so local Chinese co-workers, associates, students, etc. to an evening dinner party, and even after telephone confirmation of the exact number of people who are coming, still perhaps only twenty or so show up, or on the other extreme, more than forty make an appearance. But while the foreigner may be a bit baffled by such behavior, there is nothing particularly unusual about it from the Chinese point of view. One basic cause for this, especially in the former instance, is that unless one's friendship is quite close and has developed over some period of time, the Chinese one invites are liable to respond to invitations in an "indirect" manner (according to their semantic analysis), meaning that their standard of politeness tends to avoid giving the questioner a direct refusal. Therefore their answer of "Yes,

I will come" may very well mean "Yes, I will try to come", which translates into, "I will come if I remember it and if nothing comes up of an urgent nature" which in the end is equivalent to a good solid definite "maybe".

Some years ago I knew a Chinese man and American woman who had both had wide experience in the United States, England, France with western table etiquette, and often gave lectures, in accompaniment with an evening meal, on Western table etiquette in the large Chinese city where they lived. They were frequently faced with the problem of making reservations for 52, and having only 40 or so people show up. Or, another situation that was equally as troubling, people would be calling up the morning or afternoon of the lecture, saying that they were cancelling because some unexpected event or family problem had arisen. While difficulties of this nature are certainly solvable from an organizational or management perspective, nevertheless the point is well taken that the Chinese assume a degree of flexibilty in their meal arrangements that is unknown in the west (outside of Chinese restaurants). We might want to make some initial suppositions about Chinese tendencies to do (or not to do) future planning or forecasting in other fields of endeavor, such as manufacturing, marketing, educational research, management organization, etc. based on even these preliminary observations.

Obviously the flexibility in eating arrangements is nothing for the foreigner to get upset about, he should however pause beforehand, and make provisions to adjust his party-treating to a buffet style, with wide latitude for the number of people who may be served. A sit-down dinner Chinese style would be suitable too, but obviously Western eating arrangements are very difficult to deal with, unless one can exactly determine the number of guests, the calculation of which requires some careful guesswork based on more than average in-country experience. This means that eating western style may often only be practical if dining with another couple, or perhaps a small family. "When inviting Chinese guests, eat Chinese style" seems to be the best rule of thumb to follow, and a buffet seems to fit the bill nicely.

Of course the "western style buffet" is not what is meant here. I recall one American couple who invited their Chinese friends to a Saturday afternoon buffet around the pool, and they provided hors d'oeuvres, soft drinks, potato chips, cheeses, and related snack items, tossed salad, pies and cakes, and the tour de force: "all the shrimp you can eat". Even the more westernized Chinese were shocked at the lack of some very important items, namely vegetables, which Chinese prefer fresh and quickly cooked. The more traditional Chinese were further shocked by the lack of a "main course", which to the Chinese is either rice or noodles. Of course all of the Chinese were too polite to say anything. Many Chinese do not eat raw vegetables, since they consider them "primarily suitable for rabbits", and so were uninterested in the salad. At the same time the cakes and pies were much too sweet for the Chinese taste buds. The lesson is clear that in planning a menu selection one should confer with some local housewives, and certainly everyone would consider it proper to do so. Of special note is that the western ideas of "what is good" or "what is suitable" for a buffet party and what the Chinese would consider proper or suitable, in terms of variety, nutritional balance, or taste satisfaction, are often very dissimilar in many respects.

Seating Arrangements

In regard to the seating around the table itself, the Chinese generally sit at a round table. However when sitting at a square or rectangular table, they do not particularly seem to feel that any one of the corner positions is in any way off limits, unlucky, or awkward. The joy of eating is all the more if there are more people, so if you can squeeze in, you are welcome. In the home environment, if absolutely no other people can fit in, the children or younger members will move to another location in the living room or terrace, and as their seats become available the problem is quickly solved.

The entire seating arrangement is much less structured than in western situations. In the first place, the Chinese have far less of an assigned seat idea, as in the west a child might say "That is father's chair, that is mother's chair", etc. However the Chinese parents at most might sit near one particular position of the round table, and most likely neither parent (nor grandparent) has a specific or assigned chair. All positions are quickly amended, changed, or reorganized when more people arrive. In banquet situations, the westerner at a formal Chinese banquet, wedding dinner, celebratory dinner, etc. may be asked to sit in one seat by the host or personnel in charge, and later asked to move, and even perhaps asked to move again for the convenience of whatever situation has arisen: late coming guests who want to sit together, the failure of an adequate number of people at this table to "open" it, (therefore the people here being asked to move to another more well-occupied table), the restaurant's desire to move this particular table to another room, etc. This tells us that the Chinese are much more "changeable" in seating arrangements in general, and we see this observation borne out in tour buses, auditoriums, and all types of official and unofficial functions, that having initially been given a seat, one is then asked to move, (and the convenience of elders or anyone older than you is often brought into play here), though that may put you in an unwelcome or inconvenient seating arrangement. If we mention that the foreigner might (or does) take objection to this, the Chinese are quite surprised.

Actually the foreigner, often being in something of an esteemed position, is perhaps asked to move for what the Chinese feel will be to his benefit. Naturally some allowance should be given to such feelings, nevertheless the westerner often is given the impression that there is a lack of advance planning, and that the Chinese like to make up the rules as they go along. It is not particularly important if initially the foreigner specifically asked "Where is the best place for me to sit?", since this still leaves him as fair game to the "Would you like to sit over there?' line of polite questioning a few minutes later. The fact that one may like this particular seat because of its view, or due to the fact that the chair is particularly comfortable, or because you have already begun to drink some beverages or eat some other snack items, and so have "dirtied" some plates or glasses, is all seen as unimportant. Although one may be asked in a polite manner, even in terms of a question, to which you appear to have the choice of a yes or no answer, but in reality the "Would you like to sit over there?" is an indication you are being told to "Move". In tours organized by a wide variety of Chinese staffed companies, language institutes, the YMCA, and other organizations, there may often be a seating problem or rearrangement on a bus, or in an auditorium, and the Chinese expect to handle it in this way. The Chinese are not looking for a discussion on this, but perhaps by playing innocent and stalling, one may sometimes be able to keep his original seat in a banquet situation.

In an auditorium, before the curtain goes up on a lecture, speech contest, etc. occasionally someone will go up to the mike and say that rows one through three are reserved for such and such people or participants, and will everyone there please move. The foreigner is advised to carry around some cotton to stuff in his ears on such occasions. Otherwise, if it comes down to a dialogue, one might first specify that the stipulation to vacate rows one to three could be said to equivalent to having everyone move three rows back, hence if I am in row two, I will perhaps be willing to move to row five, although I am not willing to move to the back of the auditorium. The correct response in this case becomes "Tell the people in row five to move first," said in a smiling and friendly manner.

Togetherness and Sharing

The Chinese eat together and foster the idea of mutually dependent relationships. While the foreigner may go out and buy a sandwich or other food, and come back and consume it in the office, even at the lunch or dinner time break, and eat his entire portion himself, a Chinese would rarely do this without first 1) asking a large number of his/her co-workers or associates if they had eaten or were hungry, 2) arranging to buy items for them by-the-way, and often wholly at his/her own expense, 3) sharing his food with them when he/she got back, even to the point of cutting a hamburger into pieces, or whatever, "so that everyone can have some". This was brought home to me most vividly once when a foreign friend of mine, who had a strong attraction for one Chinese girl in his office, brought her a box of candy on Valentine's Day, February 14th. Although the Chinese Valentine's Day is the 7th day of the 7th lunar month, (the idea of giving candy is a western one, and this holds for cards as well, even though the Chinese invented paper) nevertheless the people in the office were familiar enough with western ways to know that the westerners gave gifts to people they liked on this day. However, this girl was so eager to pass out the candy to her co-workers and other office staff first, everyone from the broom boy to the office manager, that by the time the box came back to her there was no candy left! Everyone thanked the foreigner for his candy, but he felt rather strange, and was heard to comment: "I didn't buy the candy for them, I bought it for you!"

Eating in Restaurants

When speaking of attention paid to food, the westerner immediately thinks of the French, who have a highly developed "eating culture". By way of brief comparison, both the Chinese and the French like to entertain in restaurants. It is noted that the French would complain to the waiter or even ask that the chef be called out if they felt a particular dish was not palatable, but for the Chinese to do this would be highly unusual; they would generally keep their comments to themselves, or limit discussion to the people at the table. If it was brought to the waiter's attention, remedial measures would generally not be forthcoming, rather the reply of "Everyone says that it is very good" is more likely to be heard. The French linger more over their dinners, and prefer a restaurant with some atmosphere, the Chinese eat and go, and prefer a restaurant that is brightly lit, while interior decorations are only noted in passing. The French often have lively discussions, even debates, over dinner, the Chinese consider that differences of opinion are best downplayed.

In terms of preparation methods, the French are said to employ every technique known to the Chinese but one, which is stir-frying. (The Chinese recognize three types of frying, the other two being simply frying on a grill or in a flat pan, and deep-frying.) For dessert, the French have one dish which is made by cooking rice in milk, and adding sugar and cinnamon. The Chinese are not known to partake of rice in this manner.

In a banquet in a Chinese restaurant, one must be aware of the number of other group members, and mentally adjust the amount that one takes, so that all can share equally. This seems to be common sense, so that if there are twelve pieces of chicken on the plate and twelve people at the table, everyone should take one piece. However I have come across some foreigners who seem unaware of this, and will take more than an appropriate portion as the plate is passed, usually adding the disclaimer that "This is my favorite dish." If that is truly the case, one is well advised to wait for all to have a chance on taking their portion first, and then perhaps wait for the possibility that someone else may pass up the option on their share, thus leaving it to the lot of the first person who is quick with their chopsticks.

In the western restaurant, whether it be an elaborate establishment or a hamburger joint, one is almost always served one's portions individually, per person, and the only thing which one shares with others is perhaps the steak sauce, condiments, or other spices. The more elaborate restaurant does separate the meal into courses, and one eats these in sequence as they arrive. However except for salad, each course is removed before the next one is brought on, which means that one is still more regimented than in the Chinese fashion where dishes are brought out almost continuously, and none are removed unless they have been completely eaten, or the table becomes too full to place anything else, in which case either the remainder of some dishes are combined to other, more empty plates, or simply taken away by the waiter/waitress when no one expresses any more desire in eating that particular delicacy.In the Chinese restaurant it is certainly no imposition to add more dishes of vegetables, meats, or other fare, and a further call to look at the menu once more, or repeatedly, does not bring even the slightest irritation from the waiter. This facilitates the adding in of more people to the meal situation when they show up unexpectedly, and is another important indication that the orientation of Chinese eating is toward the group.

When an extra person shows up and joins your group in a western restaurant, he must still order his own fare, and as the others continue with their meal, he is waiting for his to come, since he did arrive late. He is therefore still treated as outside the group, and extremely rarely would anyone say "Here have a bite of my meat and potatoes while you are waiting for your order to come." In China however, as soon as the person arrives he is immediately brought into the group, and can commence eating at once. The main course of rice or noodles is generally always available in large quantity. Having advanced this far, we may stipulate an Important Rule for our reference:

**THE FIRST RULE OF CHINESE EATING**
**When there is food, everyone eats.**

In the west when people arrive unannounced at meal time in someone's home, they are often as not asked to wait in the living room while the people who are engaged in eating finish their meal. Clearly the unexpected newcomers are being left outside the group. If they are Chinese, they are almost always insulted by such a gesture or course of events, even though the westerner means no harm by it. Indeed, this is the treatment which a westerner would normally expect if he happened to show up at someone else's home unannounced at mealtime.

If we can delve into the minds of both parties at this instant in time, taking out their thoughts for examination, it will be quickly realized that the Golden Rule of "Do unto others as you would have them do unto you" has broken down as an unfailing guide to correct behavior, since the attitude and conduct which one party feels appropriate and acceptable, the other party does not. In cross-cultural dealings this type of difficulty often develops.

Calculation of the Bill

In western restaurants, regardless of who is picking up the tab, if four, five or more people are dining together, the tendency is for each person to be charged for his meal based on what he/she ate, and the total for the table is the total of all the separate meals. This is also done in China, however it is even more common to eat "by-the-table", thus each person is spared the trouble of ordering individually. Using this by-the-table method, a certain number of dishes are given for a fixed price, and it makes no difference if the people seated around the table number six or twelve, the price is the same.

By way of contrast, Japan tends to use a combination of the individual and by-the-table methods, because the portions are figured carefully, and the Japanese restaurant has more of an idea that they are selling not only food, but "seating space" as well. Many observers have noted that in China, to order a complete banquet and leave most of the dishes only half-eaten is acceptable, whereas in Japan this is frowned upon. This is a major underlying reason why restaurant consultants remark that in Japan the "portions" are calculated much more exactly, and in China considerably less so. To look at an example, if seven people come to eat and are seated at a table, a price may be agreed upon for a multiple-course banquet. If, after eating two courses, two more people show up, and after eating another course another person shows up, we would expect that in China the price, figured on this by-the-table basis, would remain as originally stated. However in Japan some adjustment upward would be made, since the serving staff is now "adding in more portions", and more people are seated around the table. Needless to say this causes much confusion and disagreement between Chinese customers and Japanese restaurant personnel when the former are touring the land of the rising sun.

Discussion Over the Meal Table

While a definitive list of the topics the Chinese prefer to talk about over meals is hard to compile, nevertheless the food on the table, as well as food in general, the employment, or prospective employment of those seated, as well as who is getting married, all seem to be popular topics, whereby it is felt warm feelings can be promoted. The Chinese tendency is then to stress common interests over the course of dinner table discussion, as opposed to the western tendency to often take sides on an issue and begin weighing the merits of each point of view. The Chinese would not throw down a challenge at the dinner table, nor would they engage in sarcastic verbal sparring.

Tracing the course of the talk around any one particular table, one can soon see that the Chinese interact not so much individually but with a distinct sense of being a representative for their entire family and clan. I witnessed the discussion around one table which seemed to center on one gentleman, Mr. Chen, who had introduced himself as an employee of the Chinese Post Office. Another gentleman, Mr. Wong, stated that he was dealing in international trade, and shipped a lot of merchandise both into and out of the country, generally by means of a private freight carrier. He inquired as to the latest regulations concerning the maximum size of parcels, the Post Offices's packing services and facilities, and the postage rates, and Mr. Chen filled him in on the majority of these details, while the other ten people seated around the table listened attentively. A Mr. Chang spoke up and inquired about the procedures for sending registered parcels, and the various aspects of insuring some valuable merchandise which he wanted to send. Another man, Mr. Ding, mentioned that he raised various kinds of rare flowers, and that the export markets for flowers had been picking up recently. Several of the ladies at the table were interested in flowers and the discussion took off in this direction. Mr. Chen noted that his wife was home most of the day, and that they had a large empty roof on the top of their apartment building, so perhaps his wife could go into the flower raising business. Mr. Ding promised to keep in touch with him. One of the ladies mentioned that she had a niece who was very much interested in flowers, and was majoring in botany in college. Mr. Chang mentioned that he had a brother-in-law who was employed in one of the Government's horticultural research stations, and perhaps there might be a vacancy there for someone of that niece's particular talents. This seemed promising. Another lady mentioned that her husband was looking for a larger floor space in a particular part of the city in order to expand his electrical appliance business, and several people mentioned knowing people who had property in that part of town which might be suitable.

The idea of a "mutual interest society" formed clearly in my mind. Here were a group of Chinese brought together by some common event, many of whom did not know each other, and all engaged in discussion of mutual concern, trying to determine what common interests they had, or in what ways they could cooperate together for a smoother tomorrow. Everyone was eager to exchange information and carry on with a wide variety of possible projects.

However to the foreigner, after he has settled down into the routine of local life, there often occurs the problem of establishing a purpose for going to the large number of dinners to which he may be invited, after the initial novelty has worn off. We may compare his situation to that of a foreigner, Mr. Freeni, living in Washington, D.C., who is 5,000 miles away from his home, family members, and relatives. Employed as a salaryman for a small company doing no government or diplomatic business, and having no plans to do any, this foreigner nevertheless finds himself on the social circuit, going along with friends to a wide range of diplomatic banquets, where all sorts of proposals, arrangements, and other information are swapped and discussed by the various officials, officials' aides, and other personnel, who represent a wide variety of vested interests. Hereupon we add the stipulation that since these people enjoy holding such banquets, the more people the merrier, so Mr. Freeni is often invited on his own right. The question becomes "What is the point of Mr. Freeni attending all these functions?" If he enjoys the talk, even though it has nothing to do with him, his position, or his social circumstances, then he may take enjoyment in his participation for its own sake. If he feels that all the matters discussed are of no relevance to him, that he has no favors to swap, no connections to play off, and no contracts to pursue, then he may decide that in regard to such social eating functions, he would rather "stay at home".

We might feel that Mr. Freeni would be better off if he had the background necessary to socialize with these people on their own level, or at least the desire to do so, and that he might thereby be able to raise his own social position. This is exactly the situation in which the foreigner in China often finds himself. Generally lacking the family background, business connections, and social contacts, in the local environment anyway, and when employed as a salaryman in an administrative position, having no particular project to push, or connection to play up, he is at something of a disadvantage in discussing proposals of mutual interest or advantage, although of course he usually receives a number of offers to become employed as an English teacher.

The situation is further complicated by the fact that the types of arrangements which are discussed and agreed upon over the dinner table do not always come about in the way in which they were originally stipulated, and more will be said on this later.

## Underlying Cultural Patterns of Eating

The whole range of table manners, table settings, and use of plates, bowls, and eating utensils allow us to see that the Chinese style of eating differs from the western one, and helps us to gain an insight into what constitute the Chinese Cultural Patterns of Eating. However, as with Chinese philosophy, there are some basic underlying orientational assumptions to the way the Chinese eat. The most important of these we may term "Festival Eating", and by this we mean that the Chinese view the whole issue of eating like a sort of festival and celebration. Having spent a great deal of my youth in the Tennessee countryside, such an orientation comes naturally to me, although it does come as a surprise to some other westerners. For those without my Southern U.S. rural background, I can make a comparison by stating that the Chinese idea of a good meal resembles Memorial Day weekend, a celebration for the local patron saint, birthday of Andrew Jackson (Congressman and Senator from Tennessee, and later 7th President of the USA), and a family reunion picnic all rolled into one. In Tennessee, not only does the call to "Come and get it!" on such an occasion go out to all the relatives near and far, but also all the neighbors and their kin, everybody at the old age home, all the girls at the shirt factory, the postmaster, everyone down at the fishing hole, and all of their friends. The abundance of food offered up assures that no one leaves the table(s) without first having to unloosen their belt, or unbutton their shirt.

Although the Chinese banquet has far fewer baked goods than would be normal fare at a western banquet of this type, since the Chinese rarely use ovens in their cooking, it is nevertheless remarkable what they can do with all their vegetables, meats, and seafood by chopping, slicing, boiling, stir frying, deep frying, steaming, stewing, broiling, etc. Of course they have a substantial headstart in research in this area, since they have been cooking for 5000 years, and "Tennessee cooking" per se did not get started until about 1760 when the early settlers were trying to figure out the best way to barbecue bear meat over an open fire. (As a separate consideration, we should not overlook the fact that most of these early United States settlers were Europeans, and had brought much in the way of cooking techniques and other cultural knowledge with them from the old country.)

For we Tennesseeans such a big meal is an event that only happens a few times a year, if that, no doubt due to our relatively short history. However the Chinese have been celebrating all sorts of Buddhist, Taoist, and Confucianist holidays and other events for many thousand years, so such eating is already a standard part of their history, culture, and consciousness. They consider such festival/celebratory type eating synonymous with good fortune, happiness, and blessedness. This type of eating orientation naturally serves as an important adjunct to the Group Mentality.

Another important eating orientation is "Nutrient Replenishment". By this is meant the Chinese assume that by eating certain kinds of foods, especially on certain occasions, the body can be replenished of necessary nutrients and good health can thus be assured. Probably the most important of these is the food cooked for a mother who has recently given birth, which we are told includes a lot of chicken, and the food eaten at the coming of winter, to build up the body and ward off the winter chill, so to speak. We have the same beliefs in Tennessee, and many of the old-timers who roam the hills recommend various dishes of groundhog with mushroom gravy, baked wild turkey with cranberries, and stewed squirrel with crabapple sauce, as the best thing to keep a person in the prime of health. Furthermore in Tennessee we have certain kinds of privately concocted and privately sold medicinal spirits, commonly called "white lightning", which have a sterling word of mouth reputation passed down from our ancestors, and which will not only keep the body in the peak of health, but indeed "cure anything that ails you." In our state we also have a "Medicinal Herbs" orientation, although far less advanced than that of the descendants of the Yellow Emperor. Like the Chinese, we Tennessee noblemen are unconcerned with the fact that doctors state that there is no medical evidence whatsoever to support the claims of exceedingly healthful benefits to be derived from our home state's choicest wild game, cooked with our special condiments and secret recipes.

The medical authorities, unfortunately shortsighted, make the same disclaimer for our spirits, however, as one Tennessee old-timer told me, after a long draw on his bottle and several minutes of deep contemplation, "The powers of this brew are far beyond what medical researchers will understand for at least another century." In China, the same claim seems appropriately true for the varying and many tonics and herbal medicines sold in the friendly corner Chinese herbalist shop or drugstore.

## Modern Chinese Food Science

This was all the more impressed upon my mind once when I met a group of Chinese college students who were studying Food Science and Nutrition in a local Chinese University. In the Food Science Department, all students first study Chemistry, then pursue separate areas of research in Fermentation, Meat, Poultry, Oil, or Vegetable studies. In the Nutrition Department, there are three main branches, namely Restaurant, Hospital, and Mass Production. All of the students were able to give me a complete breakdown of the four food groups, and the necessity of regulating the diet so as to obtain foods from each group every day. As I got out my notebook, I asked them if this type of food grouping was a Chinese concept. They replied: "No, that is a western concept." I stated that in the west we felt that a balanced diet was essential, and that minimum daily requirements for all the vitamins and minerals were a recognized part of this. I then inquired about the Chinese concept of proper components in a nutritious daily diet, and none of them knew.

A wide variety of reportage in the Chinese newspapers and magazines concerned with eating tends to deal with the "Nutrient Replenishment" orientation, and "Medicinal Herbs" orientation, describing the so-called healthful benefits to be obtained from various herbs used in cooking, and special kinds of fruits, meats, and vegetables prepared in various special ways. I asked these students what the status of these preparations was from the point of view of a Chinese university course in Food Science and Nutrition. None of them knew.

Moving on, I posed a question: What is the relationship between traditional Chinese medicine and the modern study of Food Science and Nutrition in China? None of them was aware of any relation. I recalled reading somewhere that a healthy diet in the Chinese conception involves a balancing of certain *yin* and *yang* elements, and I asked the students about this. None of them was aware of the specific details of this formulation. I asked if they could inquire with their professor, and give me a more detailed answer for my reference. This they agreed to do.

Some ten days later I met with these students again over lunch. They said that they had asked several professors my questions. Professor Chang and Professor Lee both attended Graduate School in the United States, and the textbooks they had studied had not dealt with such concerns. They did not know the answers to any of the issues I had raised. They assumed that such research was being done somewhere, but they were unaware of where, or by whom. No such Chinese eating-culture oriented research was being done at any Chinese universities that they knew of. Professor Min had completed his Graduate School education in China, and since he had used all American textbooks, he was unable to provide any answers to my questions either.

The issue of textbooks intrigued me, and I asked if these students were using some English language textbooks. They had brought their textbooks along, so I was able to look at them. They were of two types: English language textbooks, and translations of English language textbooks. "Certainly there must be original Chinese language textbooks on Food Science and Nutrition?" I asked. They said that yes there were some textbooks which were compilations of translated articles from foreign magazines and journals.I said that what I meant was "original Chinese language textbooks on Food Science and Nutrition, based on Chinese language sources and studies, and upon other native Chinese research into Chinese Food Science and Nutrition using Chinese methods." There were four seniors in the group, but none of them or any of the others were aware of any such books being available. They thought that I was perhaps confused: "Food Science and Nutrition" was, after all, a western science. Upon reflection I saw that I had incorrectly assumed that it was an international science, of concern to all. Obviously I was off the mark.

At this point we turned the discussion to Chinese poetry, art, literature, and history. I found that all of these students were well versed in these areas, and we had a delightful mealtime conversation. On the way to the bus stop we passed by a shop selling snake meat, fried squid, seahorses, many types of locally grown mushrooms, roots, dried berries and seeds, various kinds of sliced or powdered horn, and other interesting medicines. The students gave me the Chinese name for each item I pointed to, however since they were unaware of any of the nutritional values, I decided it was better not to press the point. The store manager assured me that all of these items were of healthful benefit, and that if I would eat them for a period of time I would certainly become convinced of their value. The students eagerly agreed.

## Nutrition and Medicine

I had some further discussions on related topics with representatives of several major American and European pharmaceutical companies in China. They told me that in many old societies throughout the world, including Southeast Asia, India, Africa, South America, and other localities, there are a wide variety of local concoctions which have a claimed nutritional or medicinal value. However, from the pharmaceutical point of view, several significant problems exist in dealing with these concoctions. First, it must be recognized that to test and eventually market one of these substances as a remedy for whatever it is supposed to cure, the active ingredient must be isolated and synthesized in the laboratory. Nature is very inconsistent in the concentration of various chemicals it puts in roots, herbs, or other botanical items. In order to control the dosage, the relevant ingredients must be found, and the concentration must be standardized.

Second, there is the entire issue of secondary reaction, side effects, which must be investigated in detail, as well as the complications with the simultaneous administration of other drugs and substances, or the necessary precautions required for use by people with various types of ailments or allergies. Few of these traditional societies, with their non-research oriented citizenry, have taken any efforts to systematically address these concerns over the ages. The possibility that certain of these substances provide beneficial effects precisely due to coming into contact with other items in the native diet has rarely been examined, nor has the reverse consideration been explored, i.e. that by coming in contact with certain non-native elements in a foreign diet, some adverse reactions could develop.

The comment that "we have been using this for centuries and feel it is very good", along with sworn testimonials from hundreds of non-professionally trained, non-medically expert members of the populace, plus newspaper clippings and other related data is not very useful when going up against a screening committee in the headquarters office (of a western pharmaceutical company), and asking for US$5 million so that some "preliminary testing" can be done. It is of even less use in going up before the stringent requirements of the FDA, or the corresponding agency in other western countries. In fact, most of the pharmaceutical products which will be introduced into the markets in the next ten years are already in the laboratories today, and many experts stress that with the skyrocketing costs of liability insurance in the pharmaceutical industry, "you do not go on the market unless you are very sure indeed of what you are dealing with." Before submission to the relevant agency for approval, a top laboratory might take eight to ten years to develop clinical data, and five to seven years to develop toxicology data.

I talked to one representative in a car on the way to the airport, since he was hurrying back to Germany to participate in the inauguration of his firm's new US 350 million dollar expansion of their existing research facility in that country. He echoed the comments of Harold Geneen, former Head of ITT, when he said that in the pharmaceutical business, no one is interested in apparent facts, assumed facts, reported facts, or hoped-for facts. Their only interest is in "unshakable facts", and the discipline of adhering to factual objectivity in dealing with the realities of research and problem solving.

As we stood at the gate of the Entry Lounge, I posed a question. "Isn't it true that many of these Oriental medicines of the more established medicine houses have been capsulized or pelletized and are presently sold in the west?"

"Some," he said, "but even those are most commonly available only in Chinatown. Also, you will find that they rarely have the legal status of 'medicines', but rather are sold as food supplements, vitamin and mineral supplements, digestive aids, nutritional aids, herbal tonics, etc. As such, their supposed curative powers have yet to be formally established, and until they are established, they cannot be advertised as being medicines in the west. In ads that I have seen, such products are claimed to contribute to general revitalization, regeneration, and stimulation, or to promote and strengthen metabolic, organic, and nerve functions, as well as to improve as the body's own defensive power."

In reply, I offered some weighty comments based on the large number of Chinese books and other essays I had collected on nutrient replenishment and medicinal herbs. I suggested that it would be most proper if the western pharmaceutical companies began researching these medicines.

He replied calmly "In order to recoup our investment, there must be the possibility of obtaining a patent on the product, so that it may be sold in the marketplace on an exclusive basis for a certain number of years, not subject to other companies' competition. However, only original compounds made or synthesized in the laboratory are patentable, not generic ones which exist naturally. Most of these 'Chinese medicines' are exactly that – generic."

"Perhaps you should read the abstracts of all the data presented to the Chinese Health Authorities when these products were approved and licensed for sale in China," I suggested. "Then you will be convinced of their efficacy."

"The Chinese government, unlike the the government in any western country, uses a double standard for approving the license applications for medicines. One standard is used for western pharmaceutical products, and another standard for Chinese medicines.

Hence I doubt that those abstracts would be of much reference value to the western medical community."

"But the local libraries here are filled with books on Chinese medicinal techniques and formulations." I said, "Certainly there much be much valuable information in all those texts."

He paused for a moment, then reached in his pocket and took out an old Chinese coin. "This" he said, placing it in my palm, "is payment in advance for translated abstracts of all important data and unshakable facts contained in those volumes. Please send them to me care of our local office address."

I examined the coin and noted that it was one of the type my mother used to use for curtain weights. "But this coin has a hole in it," I remarked quizzically.

"Yes," he replied, "you'll want to think about that." When I looked up again, he was gone.

### Medicine and Health

I once heard a similar discussion between a Chinese, Mr. Chinn, and a westerner, Mr. West, on the topic of Chinese medicine. The Chinese recounted any number of stories where people had spent much time and money visiting western trained doctors, and yet no cure for their maladies was obtained. After visiting the Chinese herbalists and other practitioners a few times, they were completely cured. This Chinese even mentioned that he had met other foreigners who had some experience in the field, and who told stories of any number of startling remedies which have been produced by Chinese medicine in the present era and previous eras, many of them dealing with diseases "for which western medicine has no cure."

Mr. West agreed to that, but noted "In order to promote these methods globally, you are going to have to produce some scientific evidence."

Mr. Chinn said "If you would be willing to try it, you would immediately recognize its value."

Mr. West shook his head. "But that is not going to happen, because outside of the group of your immediate family, relatives, and friends, other people are not inclined to 'try it' unless it is recommended by people in positions of medical authority and expertise."

Mr. Chinn said "This scientific evidence which you require is a western concept, from our point of view, several thousand years of successful use among the populace are already more than enough proof."

Mr. West smiled "If that is the case, why don't you have a prestigious Chinese Academy of Science or other organization to recommend and guarantee these medicines?"

Mr. Chinn shook his head. "Unfortunately, there is no such kind of organization which has this kind of expertise and qualifications and that is recognized throughout

Asia and the world. You would be best to examine the medical records of the patients involved."

"But I doubt if these 'medical records', maintained by traditional Chinese doctors, would meet the recognized medical standards for scientific reporting. However, in any case, I am not competent to really judge. You must have a recognized medical authority look over the evidence."

Mr. Chinn resignedly stated that the recognized medical authorities were all "western doctors", and were not inclined to accept traditional Chinese medical evidence, however well presented.

Mr. West added a question at this point. "An anthropologist friend of mine recently visited some tribes in a remote area of South America. They have a number of herbal medicines which they prepare and eat for a variety of maladies, in accompaniment with various rites which involve the placing of very hot stones on various parts of the body, and forming the twigs of a certain type of thorned tree as clamps which are applied to the hands and feet. If you were sick, would you consent to being treated by one of their doctors?"

"I sincerely doubt that any benefit could be obtained from such uncivilized methods. All of it sounds like a bunch of superstition to me. I cannot imagine that any reputable medical authorities would approve of such practices, but of course if they did that would be another story . . ." Mr. Chinn frowned in a displeased fashion.

"But they have been using these methods successfully for thousands of years," Mr. West countered.

"That is not especially significant. After all these tribes have a very low level of culture, indeed many of them are barely out of the hunting and gathering stage." Mr. Chinn went on to say that there were many problems using this type of unproven methodology, and he thought it unwise to go into this irrelevant digression any further. He suggested that they return to the original subject.

Mr. West thought he remembered a quote from the Analects. Confucius had received some medicines from another man, and he was very respectful, but he pointed out "Since I do not know about these, so I am afraid to use them." (X, 10)[1] . However, this juncture seemed an inappropriate time to mention this quote, so he kept it to himself.

And so the controversy continued on, and does indeed continue on to this day. How are we to prove the value of Chinese medicine and medical techniques and have their greatness recognized in the world community?

Certainly the Chinese herbalists, acupuncturists, bone doctors, foot massagers, diviners and others would not collectively or individually claim to be able to cure the entire list of diseases for which western medicine has not as yet found a remedy. However, there certainly seem to be enough first-hand accounts to suggest that there are a great number

---

1. Quotes from Confucius' *Analects* will occasionally appear in the text. The chapter and verse number(s) are given for reference.

of diseases and injuries which the Chinese doctors can cure and yet the western doctors cannot, or where the Chinese cure is relatively simple, and is accomplished without a scalpel, and yet the western cure involves complicated surgery. I know of many people who would be happy to see the Chinese publish a list of "The Top 40 Notable Diseases, Maladies, and Other Injuries for which Chinese Medicine has a Better Cure". Such a list would ideally be updated and published at least once a year by the appropriate Chinese medical organization, and particulars offered as to where the sufferers of these problems could go for treatment. Some details of the treatment would be outlined, and statistical comparison of cures achieved from Chinese and western techniques, as well as other related data, would be discussed.

However, in talking to many of my Chinese friends, including many doctors, I feel that the possibility that such a list will be made available in the near future is next to nil. (Naturally I hope I am wrong about this.) One of the major problems is that there is no central agency or academic organization which is collecting all of this "Chinese medical data" in China. Some books are available which list which herbs are good for which maladies, but as has been stated before, nature is very inconsistent in the concentration of "active ingredients"; additionally, present efforts at quality control in the marketplace do not appear very thorough or energetic.

In fact, even a basic listing of all the Chinese doctors who deal in any particular medical specialty is largely unavailable, and this often confuses the foreigner, who asks: "Who is the best Chinese doctor for treating ankle injuries?", "Who is reputable for treating paralysis?", "Where is a clinic that treats gallstones?" or other such questions. The Chinese populace accept it as a matter of course that there is no medical authority or organization which can offer this information, and it is thus left to the patients, or their relatives, to inquire with other friends and kin as to who might be a good doctor to see for any particular type of injury. This, we suppose, reflects the general Chinese preference to deal with most issues on a person-to-person level.

As a related concern, there also seems to be no centralized agency dealing with the standardization, testing, or inspection of the various herbs sold in Chinese medicine shops, so many times the consumer is not aware if he is getting the real herbs, some substitute, or some adulterated combination. "Let the customer beware" seems to be the accepted byword.

It must be noted that many of the "miraculous cures" recounted in a great number of stories have been obtained from Chinese doctors (unlicensed and unregistered in many cases) who use secret techniques and medicinal recipes passed down over the ages in their family, and unknown to even the general Chinese medical community, or to the doctors teaching Chinese medicine in the colleges. Many of these healers of course would not be inclined to give away their knowledge, and a great many of them would not even consider "selling it," since they are not materialistically oriented. Western medical research, for all its failings, does have a tendency to keep expanding, and to keep building on the work of predecessors, and seems directed outward for the benefit of humanity.

Chinese medical research appears poorly-funded and poorly-coordinated even in China. Many Chinese doctors appear uninterested in passing on their knowledge for the benefit of humanity, and are more properly described as directed inward: wanting to keep their knowledge closely guarded, although happy to treat relatives, friends, and acquaintances. Certainly it would be unfair to totally blame the doctors, their attitudes have arisen while living in Chinese society, and must be reflective of a generally poor environment for widespread research and/or promulgation of knowledge/techniques in the nation as a whole.

On a more fundamental philosophical level, in order to come up with such a Top 40 list, and to actively promote Chinese medical knowledge and methods, a necessary precondition would be that the Chinese were self confident of the correctness and beneficiality of this Chinese medicine, and willing to support it in scholarly debates, produce evidence of its efficacy to non-believers, etc. Unfortunately, self-confidence in one's own abilities seems to be very closely associated with "arrogance" in the Chinese mind, and this is in direct opposition to the presumed virtue of modesty, so the possibility that such a self confident stance could be taken seems unlikely. Indeed many observers have noted that the Chinese lack the crusade mentality [1] , and its psychological basis "the overwhelming desire to want to prove something". Admittedly, in terms of promoting harmony in many types of circumstances this lack may actually be of great benefit, nevertheless in terms of doing promotional work for the use of new and better methods in any and all types of situations, it is highly detrimental.

## Nutrient Replenishment

Although largely unknown to the Chinese, certain aspects of nutrient replenishment in Korea are illustrative of the communality of Oriental thinking on the subject. In the Korean countryside, it happens that some elderly people occasionally take to bed with a variety of illnesses, and news of their infirmity quickly spreads throughout the community.

Periodically an itinerant goat seller, or goat-man, arrives in the village with a collection of goats for sale. The family in need arranges to purchase a healthy black goat, and the price paid includes all cooking and preparation. The cooking method is simple although lengthy. The goat is placed live in a large container, and vegetables, herbs, spices, water, and other necessary ingredients are added. The container is sealed and a roaring wood-fire is built underneath it. The goat-man keeps this fire going for several

---

1. When we say that the Chinese "do not have a crusade mentality" we are not generally speaking of political movements, such as revolutions, since the fanaticism associated with such upheavals represents the exception rather than the rule. We are speaking of a "crusade" in the more general sense of a long term, vigorous, and concerted action for some cause or idea, or against some abuse or injustice.

days, as the goat, including horns, hooves, hair, head, brains, eyes, intestines, tail, bones, blood, and even the spirit of the animal, in other words the entire works, simmers. The result of this is a goat-broth of a very thick consistency.

The person who is ailing and confined to bed is fed this broth, spoonful by spoonful, three times or more per day, and indeed he is fed nothing else. Within the space of less than a week, many miraculous cures are reported. After a complete recovery, the affected individual goes back to his work, as good as new.

A western doctor commenting on this train of events said "The diet of many people in the Korean countryside does not tend to be very well-balanced. They eat too much rice and related grains, often with little else except pickled vegetables, and there is a large lack of animal proteins. This often leads to varying degrees of vitamin deficiency.Obviously, stewing up a goat in this manner provides an infusion of protein and vitamins into the ailing person's system. Of course a side-of-beef would work equally well, as would a deer, a kangaroo, or a baboon."

A Korean doctor who had studied in the United States for many years was incredulous at this remark. "No," he said, "you must have a goat, and it must be black."

Other Korean specialists were consulted, and they concurred with this statement. Many members of the public were interviewed, and they declared emphatically that there was no possible room for contention. "It must be a black goat."

Many westerners asked "What are the special characteristics of a black goat that a side-of-beef would not satisfy?" No one knew the answer to that question.

"Then why does it have to be a black goat?" the westerners repeated.

The Koreans succinctly replied "Because it has always been a black goat."

## A Pig in a Crate

A large group of foreigners were attending a lecture on Chinese customs and traditions. At one point it was described how in many provinces a common practice after an engagement was to butcher a pig, and present half of the pig, packed in a large wooden box or crate, to the bride-to-be's family. Members of the audience were asked to comment on this type of gift.

A New Yorker thought for a long moment, and concluded that this could possibly be a polite and subtle way of indicating to the family that their daughter was not very attractive, and the groom-to-be wanted out of the marriage, which he felt would be too confining.

A Canadian felt that inclusion of the head and tail of the half-pig was suggestive of some underlying insult, although he could not put his finger on it. He recommended that this potential for bad feelings could be avoided if the pig were properly butchered, with the different cuts of meat individually packaged.

A Middle Easterner maintained that this gift was not the least polite, and actually would be a terrific insult to the bride-to-be's family. It could only be set aright through a "holy war".

A Hawaiian doubted that any insult was intended, however he did feel that first the pig should have been cooked whole, and everyone from both families invited to the feast.

An Eskimo said that perhaps half-a-pig was not very suitable for such an occasion. He suggested seal.

The foreigners' comments in this instance are not particularly brilliant, however taken together they do indicate a healthy potential for cross-cultural misunderstanding. In the cultural setting of their own countries (or tribal areas), all of the foreigner's comments have some validity. However, in Asia, their analyses are of little value, except to note that if a large number of Asian customs could be listed, and different foreigners asked to comment on their "possible meaning", there would be a great potential for humor.

Living in many countries where the history is measured in millennia, the westerner may often forget that there is little room for "creativity" in dealing with many customs and traditions. Many customs tend to be fixed, and if they do change, they change in a way known to all members of the cultural group. A westerner in China might pause to think: "What would be nice to give Mrs. Jing on the occasion of her _____ " (anniversary, marriage, promotion, birthday, new child's birth, moving into a new home, moving to another city, acceptance to graduate school, success in the national lottery, etc.) This attempt to "think the matter through" is an interesting approach, however there is potential for misunderstanding, as in the case of a western woman who gave her Chinese friend a basket of fruit, wrapped in bright colored ribbon and accompanied with a picture of a stork, upon the arrival of her new baby. The Chinese do not associate the arrival of babies with storks, but this winged messenger does bear a remarkable similarity to the type of bird which is used in conjunction with the decorations at funerals. As would be expected, the Chinese lady fainted.

A better approach might have been to directly ask some other Chinese people: "My friend Mrs. Jing had a baby. What do you give people on such an occasion?" Even if every one of Mrs. Jing's friends gives the same thing, this need be of no concern to the westerner, since this is the custom. If some other event is stipulated by the locals as suitable for giving liquor, any Chinese will be happy to receive such a gift, even in the eventuality that neither he nor anyone else in his family drinks. If the circumstances are suitable for giving flowers, every Chinese will be happy to receive flowers, even if they are allergic to them. As to what constitutes an appropriate selection of flowers for a flowerly gift, rather than letting one's creative instincts get out of hand, better advice would be to ask another local Chinese: "What selection of flowers do you give people on such an occasion?" or to ask a friend to go ahead and make the arrangements with the florists in your name.

Although this procedure does appear a bit dead-pan, it has a decided advantage in that one need never worry about what type of gift will be appropriate in any situation. Indeed, female Chinese staff members in one's local office can be most helpful in this regard, since they are generally happy to take responsibility for the purchasing of appropriate gifts for any and all of the foreigner's social engagements. All the foreigner has to do is discuss the appropriate cost of the items to be selected, and provide the cash. If custom calls for half-a-pig in a crate, then half-a-pig it should be, or at least it should be claimed to be half-a-pig, even if it is something else entirely. This is certainly not a situation calling for any lengthy deliberation, even if the intended recipient is a vegetarian.

As a rule of thumb, many old China-hands say: "When in doubt, give money." And of course it should be given in even amounts, never odd, for this is the custom. If this proves prohibitively expensive, second best advice is: "Play dumb and send a card." Being a westerner, you will of course be forgiven.

## Varying Views on Western Eating Arrangements

Over the past several years I have been able to persuade several of my American friends to share some of their correspondence from home with me, and this bulk of material has included letters from their mothers, fathers, and relatives. I have often noted some peculiarities, in regard to comments on "eating", which I believe are worthy of comment. These can serve as an excellent introduction to cross-cultural differences in eating habits and customs.

Some Reflections on Eating in the West

a. The parents of George, a friend from North Carolina, wrote once in early November that Thanksgiving was rapidly approaching, but since they had retired a few years earlier, and were both a bit overweight, they were aware of the value of cutting down on their food intake. Their cooking preparations for Thanksgiving dinner were therefore being greatly simplified, and they were planning to go for a long stroll in the countryside that day if the weather was permitting. They commented: "Your sister Mary and her husband's family were planning to drive over from Missouri, but I am over 70 as you know, and quite frankly tired of cooking, especially as regards the cleaning up afterward. We are both watching our diets, so I discussed it with your father, and we told them it really was not convenient. They will make other plans I guess. I am really not in the mood for being a maid for three or four days while the six (or more) of them are here, and your father does not like the little grandchildren running around all over the house and turning everything upside down."

b. Roger's mother wrote from Minnesota that: "Your Dad's brother has been coming over a lot more frequently on Sundays since his divorce, and generally eating lunch and dinner before going back Sunday night. At this point I don't think the two of them have much to talk about, having worn out all the war stories, and reminiscences from their youth, long ago. Your Dad would prefer to spend Sunday afternoons more quietly without listening to him jaw whatever topic he is off on at the moment. It gets me too that he never leaves any money in the 'cookie jar', as if to say that we owe him free meals whenever he feels like coming over. Your father and I may go for some long rides on Sunday afternoons in the future if something does not change. If he comes and we are 'not home', well that is not our problem . . ."

c. Albert's parents from San Antonio, Texas, commented that: "Our old friends Bill and Alice were down from Arkansas last week and dropped in unexpectedly Thursday evening while we were having dinner. They were watching TV in the living room while we finished our meal, and Bill saw a report of a bridge repair being done on the interstate, so they decided they had better spend a few more days in San Antonio, rather than heading on to Dallas the next day, lest they be caught in a big traffic jam. We weren't prepared for such sudden guests but did manage to make some calls and get them a room in a local motel down near the fairgrounds. We met for lunch on Friday in a new restaurant that opened up here recently. Bill is still a big eater, and Alice can pack it away too. Your father and I eat rather sparingly. Their check was considerably higher than ours, but with Bill's salary, I guess he doesn't mind."

d. Carol's parents wrote from Oregon that: "We asked Ginger and Philip to come over for dinner and cards, but when they hadn't showed up by 6:30, (the invitation was for 6:00) we decided to go ahead and eat first. We were watching TV at 7:15 when they finally arrived. It seems that Philip was tied up at the office with a report that just had to be completed, so he was a bit late. It didn't matter really. I warmed up a few things and they ate, and we got down to our bridge game by about 8:00. It was a good night for your father and I, we won four games, and I suppose if we were in Las Vegas that would amount to something, but we don't play for money here, just for amusement."

Asked to comment on these goings on, my American friends said that there was nothing particularly unusual about them. Numerous Chinese friends however expressed the feeling that they were more than slightly "odd". We will want to examine why.

In example a), George's parents seem to have taken exception to an orientation which equates happiness with "a large group of relatives and friends eating a sumptuous meal together," furthermore they appear unwilling to go out of their way for relatives, however relatives are seen as most important to the Chinese.

In example b), the parents have given the impression that they are not willing to make a show of their generosity by treating the uncle to free meals indefinitely, rather they expect him to pay his own way. The Chinese consider generosity an important character trait, and the lack of it a character flaw.

In example c), Albert's parents express the idea that they are not willing to go out of their way for guests, since Bill and Alice were not invited to stay in their home, but the Chinese feel "Guests should be considered first." When meeting for lunch, they failed to pay the entire check, thus ignoring the chance to make a display of generosity.

In example d), the parents ate before the guests arrived, thus denying the guests any sort of esteemed position. The western idea that at home the breadwinner may regard himself as "king of the castle," and can do as he pleases is alien to the Chinese, and often comes in conflict with their view of guests being of premier importance.

As a general overview of these four situations, the (western) parents can be seen to have all effectively denied the Group Orientation, since they have considered themselves (and their own convenience) first, as opposed to considering others, or the larger group, first. Upon reflection we are not surprised at this, since westerners have a pronounced individual orientation. However, to the Chinese this often appears "odd", and we may formulate another rule for our reference.

THE SECOND RULE OF CHINESE EATING
Guests should be considered first.

We may consider some further situations below.

Some Reflections on Eating in China
* Frank, one of my foreign friends in China, had an earache one day, and visited the local western style hospital. They advised him that he needed an operation, and noted that a hospital stay of several days would be required. After talking to the doctors in attendance, and consulting some other area doctors, he decided to go ahead with the procedure. While he was recovering in the hospital, his friend Douglas, and Douglas's mother who was on vacation from the USA, came to visit him one afternoon. Douglas and his mother were in the middle of packing for a move to Japan, and so were rather hurried. They ate the box lunches they had brought along, and discussed various topics with Frank, in addition to promising to write when they had arrived and were settled in Tokyo.

Analysis: From the Chinese point of view, Douglas and his mother were very impolite by eating in front of Frank and not offering him any food. In fact, it would have been best for them to bring an extra portion for him to eat.

The fact that Frank is in the hospital and is having all of his meals provided by the hospital staff, and/or may be on a restricted diet, is essentially irrelevant, since by bringing an extra portion of food Douglas and his mother still will be credited with appearing generous. If indeed Frank cannot eat the items offered, they could then present them to someone else nearby, thus further demonstrating their generosity, and their group orientation.

* William, who was leaving for Singapore, invited his western and local friends out to dinner in the private room of a big restaurant for a small going-away party. William does not drink, and after his vacation in Singapore he will be entering the Ph.D. program

at the University of Washington in the Fall, so it was BYOB, and Dutch treat. Over twenty people attended, and there was a lot of joking and good times. After the check was divided up, each guest's share came to about $600 in local currency. Everyone agreed that Chinese food is delicious and you can eat a lot for a little.

Analysis: The Chinese thing to do would be for William to pay for the meal himself. The act of dividing up the bill exactly insults the Chinese sense of generosity. Although the Chinese will bring a gift of money to a wedding banquet, or a feast in honor of the arrival of a new child, or even a funeral, however this is seen as giving good blessings to the family involved, and certainly does not represent payment for an exact proportion of the cost of the food consumed at the accompanying banquet.

* Carl goes out drinking with the local expatriate gang about three or four times a week, and it usually comprises a group of five or six regulars, and a few others. John took his girlfriend out for dinner the other night in a small western pub, and ran into Carl and the gang. They had a lively discussion, and exchanged a lot of news. When John and his date were ready to leave, they estimated up what they had drunk and eaten, and dropped some bills in the center of the table. Carl offered a parting toast, and said that if he quit his job and went into movie-script writing full time, he would be coming over to hit John for some plot suggestions. John promised to make some notes if he thought of anything interesting.

Analysis: According to Chinese thinking, someone should have made the show of proving they were the more generous. When John dropped the bills on the table, Carl could have refused to accept them thus giving a clear indication of his munificence. To avoid this, and get the upper hand in a display of magnanimity, John could have gone to the cashier and payed the entire bill discreetly, then informed Carl after the fact.

* Katherine finally decided to splurge and buy some banana bread the other day. Most of the Chinese bakeries do not sell it, but there is one that does, and she happened to be nearby last Tuesday, so she bought three slices, as she said: "One for my midmorning snack, one for after lunch, and one for after dinner." Later in the morning she visited her Chinese friend Ma-ling in her office, and was introduced to many of the other Chinese co-workers. While she was waiting in the outer office when Ma-ling dealt with a client, she had her mid-morning snack of one slice. "It certainly was tasty," she commented, "and maybe if I eat banana bread more regularly I can put on some weight."

Analysis: Katherine made no attempt to share her food with the others in the office. She has denied the Group Orientation and the first rule of Chinese eating. She may feel that she has only purchased enough for herself, however this is clearly an outgrowth of her individualistic orientation. The Group Orientation is not "sharing when it is convenient," but is rather sharing at any and all times, even to the point of oneself doing without. We now clearly see the existence of another rule.

## THE THIRD RULE OF CHINESE EATING
Seize the opportunity to show your generosity.

A Swedish writer, Jan Myrdal, who lived in a village in Northern Shanshi Province for several years commented:

> We lived considerably better than the villagers. This way of treating strangers and guests is no specific Chinese trait; you meet it in every village in all the peasant societies. In the evenings, when we had finished the day's work, the peasants came with gifts from their private plots, melons, corn-cobs, fruit, nuts. It was kind of them; they gave out of their poverty. But it was also pride. I have stayed with peasants in villages in Afghanistan and India and Europe and it has always been the same, the pride of the household, the pride of the village demands that the guest is given the best there is.

That many westerners much less commonly make displays of generosity in this fashion is a direct outgrowth of their middle class, as opposed to peasant class, thinking. This "middle class value orientation" has arisen for a number of historical reasons, and these will be discussed more thoroughly in our essays outlining the comparative significance of "The Industrial Revolution" in the West and in China.

* Rob, Joyce, Candy, Joseph, and Martin are all westerners and all work in a large Chinese organization. Joseph is the newest arrival among the group, and Candy is the old-timer. For lunch Rob usually brings a sandwich, Joyce eats dumplings and soup, Candy eats noodles, Joseph still prefers to go to the restaurant in the hotel downtown, and Martin often eats steamed buns or noodles from the local corner stall. If they are all back in the office before work starts in the afternoon they sometimes exchange a few comments, or often as not read a magazine or newspaper on their own during the remaining lunch hour time.

Analysis: These westerners' behavior appears unusual to many Chinese because they did not eat in a group with each other, or with other employees. Eating individually denies the ideal of happiness being "a large group of relatives and friends eating a sumptuous meal together," and this is central to Chinese thinking.

Chinese Hospitality and the Foreigner

Upon their initial arrival in the country, many foreigners are enthralled by the hospitality shown to them by their new Chinese acquaintances. Referring to the three rules of Chinese Eating which we have formulated in this Chapter, it is not hard to see how the existence of these "rules" or "orientations" among the natives will result in a very "advantageous situation" for new foreign arrivals. This is especially true when we consider that these orientations are carried over into other areas besides eating as well, such as gift giving, living arrangements, and the local people's allocation of their time and effort.

The foreigner's situation is further enhanced because the Chinese all share a belief in *yuan fen*, which we may translate as "fate in personal relationships." This seems to assure that the foreigner is not left out of the sharing, partying, or banqueting, because the view is that to some extent "Our relationship is predestined," hence the Chinese feel "You are my guest." Added to this, the Chinese view relationships as a two way street or "mutually beneficial", so it is expected (although unstated) that an expression of largess now will come back double or triple in the future, either directly or indirectly. This is closely related to the attitude which Chinese take toward personal and business relations, or toward human relations in general, and we will delve into this more thoroughly in the initial Chapter on Money Management.

## Attitudes

Barry Klinedorf went with some Chinese friends out for a walk. On the way home they happened to pass a small bakery shop, and as Barry was feeling like a little snack, he decided to step inside. As soon as he got in the door he noticed that the shop was extremely dirty and unkempt. The plastic tile floor had holes and was curling up in many places. He noticed a collection of ants in one corner, and some cockroaches crawling on the wall in another place. A number of the canned goods on a lower side shelf had appearances of rust. There were cardboard packing cartons in various states of disarray piled around the interior of the shop, as well as a large and varied collection of empty bottles. One of the glass doors on the refrigerator unit which held cold drinks was cracked. There were cobwebs in evidence in the upper corners of the walls where they met the ceiling, and the flourescent lighting fixture which illuminated the entire scene was hanging crooked from a long chain, with the middle bulb burnt out.

In the midst of all this, on some dusty wooden shelving in the center of the shop were piled several large baking trays, and Barry noted that the usual type of Chinese baked goods that he had seen in hundreds of other bakeries around the country were in evidence. In front of all the baking trays was a carefully lettered sign in Chinese which said "Chocolate Cake, special today, $20". Barry was familiar with Chinese ideas of cleanliness, and so he tried not to let the general state of the shop bother him. The landlady came out, and asked in Chinese: "What do you want?" (This is more or less the standard Chinese expression from a shop owner or shop employee to a customer. The Chinese do not use the term "May I help you?", which most westerners consider much more polite.) Barry explained that he wanted a piece of chocolate cake, and proceeded to take out $20 of the local currency. The landlady said: "We do not have chocolate cake today."

Barry was surprised at this remark, and pointed to the sign. The landlady looked at the sign and repeated: "Not today." She then tried to interest Barry into buying some of the other baked goods she had for sale. Barry was not interested. Considering the general condition of the shop, he decided not to discuss matters any further or press the point, and left with his friends.

A few weeks later Barry was with the same group of friends having some soft drinks in the coffee shop of a five-star hotel. The shop was newly decorated in a very pleasing manner, sparkling clean, and the tables, chairs, etc. were fashionable and comfortable. Barry was feeling a little hungry and decided to order something. He asked the waiter for a menu. The waiter was spotlessly dressed, and appeared promptly with the desired menu, handing it over to Barry courteously. Barry ordered a club sandwich, and continued his discussion with his friends.

A minute later, the waiter came back and said: "I am sorry sir, we do not have club sandwiches today." Barry asked why, and was told, "Because that is what the headwaiter said." Barry asked to see the headwaiter.

The headwaiter came and Barry said he wanted to eat a club sandwich, could the headwaiter please speed up that order for him. The headwaiter said "I am sorry sir, we do not have club sandwiches today." Barry picked up the menu and said: "Show me where it says you do not have club sandwiches today." The headwaiter smiled and said: "The menu does not say anything about that." Barry smiled, "Then you do have club sandwiches today. Good. I would like one." The headwaiter replied with the original line about not having them today. When Barry asked why, he said: "Because that is what the chef said." Barry asked to see the chef.

After a few minutes delay, the chef appeared. He asked what the problem was. Barry held up the menu and asked if this was indeed the menu for the coffee shop in which he was sitting? Or perhaps it was the menu for another restaurant in the same hotel? Or that of another restaurant in another city? The chef said it was indeed the coffee shop's menu. Barry then opened to the page of the club sandwich, and said: "I would like to order one of these." The chef replied, as Barry was learning to expect by now, "I am sorry sir, we do not have club sandwiches today." Barry again asked to be shown where on the menu or in the restaurant there was any notice to that effect. The chef said there was none. "Then why don't you have club sandwiches today?" Barry inquired. The chef replied: "Because that is what the coffee shop manager said." Barry asked to see the coffee shop manager.

After going over the same general train of discussion a fourth time with the coffee shop manager, Barry was back to the point where he stated: "Then why don't you have club sandwiches today?" The coffee shop manager replied: "Because we were not delivered enough bread." At this point Barry looked out of the window. Across the street, a few shops down, he could clearly see a western style bakery that was open. He suggested to the manager: "Why don't you go to that bakery and buy some?" The manager thought about this for a moment, bowed, and made his exit. Ten minutes later, Barry had his club sandwich.

His Chinese friends' reaction to this series of events was general incredulousness.

However, as he found out from talking to them, their amazement arose not from the fact that you get something when you make the demand for it, and not accept excuses as answers, since they were unable to consider taking this kind of approach in their daily affairs. They were amazed rather at Barry's discourtesy toward the waiter, headwaiter, chef, and coffee shop manager, and his generally argumentative attitude. They expressed the feeling that that was certainly not the way to promote harmonious relations in society, or among individuals. Barry thought back to the time that they had all visited the bakery together, and he had tried unsuccessfully to buy some chocolate cake. All of the Chinese agreed: "Yes, you handled yourself much better that evening. You would certainly find it easier to get along with people if you conducted yourself that way in the future."

Barry tried to analyze the way that he had conducted himself in the bakery. The major idea that he came up with was that "he had not pressed the point." Yet in Barry's mind there was something very dissimilar in the two experiences. One took place in a run-down shop, and one took place in a five-star hotel. We would expect the standards of service to be different in these types of establishments, and we would feel that "what the customers could expect" in these different types of establishments would be different. This time it was the Chinese friends who asked: "Why?"

Of course bread does not play an important role in menu considerations among the Chinese, so one might expect that they would not be terribly bothered by the fact that their bread delivery for the day had not come, thus failing to make any adjustments for such a "minor" menu item. Nevertheless one would suspect that this indicates a lack of planning, or even worse, the lack of acceptance of responsibility for such planning. This would of course have to be examined in other types of incidents before solid conclusions could be advanced.

## Restaurant Classification

When we speak of Chinese restaurants, hotels, etc. our terminology may often cause some confusion. Let us consider the following primary types of restaurants as a model:

Possible definitions of "Chinese Restaurant":

| In China | *our abbreviation* |
|---|---|
| A. a restaurant run by Chinese and serving Chinese food | CCC |
| B. a restaurant run by Chinese and serving western food | CCW |
| C. a restaurant run by westerners serving Chinese food | CWC |

In North America & Europe
D. a restaurant run by Chinese                    WCC
   and serving Chinese food
E. a restaurant run by Chinese                    WCW
   and serving western food
F. a restaurant run by westerners                 WWC
   serving Chinese food

When necessary in the following discussion we will point out exactly which type of establishment we are speaking of, in order to avoid unclarity. Our abbreviations use "C" to denote China or Chinese, "W" to denote western. The first letter indicates the locality; the second letter, the management; the third letter, the type of food served. Some people would no doubt consider the CCW and WCW types as "western restaurants."

## Eating In A Hot Climate

It was a hot summer day and several Chinese staff members of a trading company were taking a foreign client out to lunch. No sooner had they walked out of their air-conditioned offices into the street, than the heat of the early afternoon met them like the billowing waves radiating from some giant steel furnace. The foreigner began to prespire freely, and reached up to loosen his tie. At this point there was a protracted discussion among the Chinese about which restaurant would be best, and they debated the merits of Hunanese, Chechiangese, Szechuanese, and other provincial cuisines for several minutes. Mongolian barbecue seemed a bit much for lunch, however perhaps that new noodle shop across the street would be good, or that simple cafeteria in the back alley? Even though the seating in either of these places was not too fancy, but the food was really tasty.

They finally settled on a small restaurant which served excellent Chinese dumplings, and in addition to a large quantity of these, they also ordered some side dishes of meat and vegetables, and some egg-drop soup as well. It was a good meal, but with the heat of kitchen drifting out into the dining area, and only a few ceiling fans to provide air circulation, still a bit too "steamy" for the westerner. Added to this was the fact that there was no place to hang his coat, and when the serving boy folded it and placed it on a counter nearby, he was left with a wrinkled appearance for the remainder of the afternoon.

After one has gained some experience dining in Chinese restaurants (CCC) with the Chinese, it soon becomes apparent that they are connoisseurs in regard to the many different provincial varieties of food, and that they have quite discriminating taste buds. However, in the mind of the newly arrived foreigner, such "gourmet" considerations are generally secondary to the standard of comfortableness provided by the restaurant's interior decorations and facilities. Many traditional Chinese restaurants offer excellent fare, however their backless stools, wobbly tables, poorly maintained lavatories (or the total absence of a lavatory at all), and lack of adequate air conditioning on summer days make them less than desirable eating places in the eyes of the foreigner with relatively little appreciation of the finer points of Chinese cuisine. His first consideration is a cool comfortable place to sit down and relax.

The western method of deciding on menu choices also often leaves the Chinese puzzled. When a choice of fish is made, and the westerner is asked for his approval, he may state "If there are a lot of small bones I don't want it, otherwise I will go along with your suggestion." Many types of saltwater and freshwater fish do have an abundance of small bones, however Chinese generally regard this as irrelevant when making menu selections: taste is the primary consideration. That the foreigner would regard the degree of boniness to be of primary importance is curious in their viewpoint. In order to cover for this, the foreigner may be advised to offer an excuse such as "I do not use chopsticks very well yet" or "The little bones seem to always get stuck in my throat," and to more properly phrase his objection as "If there are a lot of small bones that is inconvenient for me, otherwise I will go along with your suggestion."

Many Chinese restaurants which are primarily geared to serving Chinese clientele also tend to be a bit more noisy than restaurants with primarily western patrons, (other than in western bars, pubs, and other drinking establishments). Often as not, the serving staff will speak in loud voices among themselves, or when calling orders to the kitchen. The general clamor of many people dining at the same time is also significant, being comprised of not only the many simultaneous conversations being carried on, but also the click and clack of glasses, plates, bowls, chopsticks, and serving spoons, and the not-just-occasional diner who takes great gusto in slurping his soup. The relatively close spacing between tables in a typical Chinese restaurant seems to amplify even some of the more minor noises associated with dining, thus making them all the more apparent to the westerner seated nearby. It is not uncommon that the patrons at some tables may even begin some hand guessing games, and the idea that this might disrupt other people's dining privacy, or otherwise strain the peacefulness of the surroundings is not a consideration that apparently enters into their consciousness. In reaction to any and all of these factors the westerner may feel some discomfort, and unfortunately it may indeed outweigh the pleasure which he gets from the excellent taste of the meal itself, thus resulting in a disappointing dining experience.

Certain other aspects of Chinese dining in China often call for some real social and physical adjustment by the foreigners. For example, many westerners assume that Chinese serve tea during their meals, and in some of the higher class restaurants this is true. However in many ordinary restaurants, no beverage is served with the meal whatsoever. Among the westerners present, this tends to lead to increasingly pronounced levels of an irritation in the esophagus which can only be called the "dry itch." Although all the laryngologists I have spoken to in my many years of residence in the Orient have confirmed that there is no difference in Chinese and western throats, it is puzzling to me that the Chinese do not get thirsty during the course of a meal, and are thus unaffected by the dry itch ailment. They are content to serve the soup as the last and crowning dish of any repast.

Despite all the differences in Chinese and western eating habits, of course we can not deny that many westerners are often seen making the rounds of the food stalls in the night markets, and enjoying the simple local cuisine offered therein, in the typical Chinese environment. Trips to such establishments are certainly facilitated if one is of the disposition to "go local" for an afternoon or evening, and dressed in a casual fashion, without a briefcase, sample-case, or other paraphernalia in tow. The foreigner who visits such stalls or other small shops of his own volition has no doubt made some note of their cleanliness standards, and perhaps has a working scenario of what action he will take when and if stomach problems develop. The ability to regard this type of environment as acceptably clean may come quickly for some foreigners, and more slowly, or not at all, for others.

Not surprisingly, in talking to many foreigners in China, we find that oftentimes they retain a preference for eating western food on a regular basis, not because western food tastes better, (often as not it tastes worse), but because the "style of eating" is more in line with their general life style or mood at the moment. A typical comment of one American is: "When I am in a hurry to make an appointment, I cannot very well eat a rice-box meal in a taxi. If I grab a sandwich or hamburger there is no problem eating on the go." Obviously this American has not totally discarded his western eating style orientation, even after long residence in China. A newly arrived European stated: "I do not care one way or the other whether I eat Chinese or western style, but I would enjoy some appetizers, an aperitif or two, some cheese, and some nice pastries after the meal." This type of comment, while seemingly non-biased, actually expresses a preference that is typically only available in western restaurants (CCW).

Other remarks which reflect the desire for breads, wines, cocktails, hors d'oeuvres, cakes, pies, or other western menu items with the meal, certainly fall into the realm of western style eating. Also included as part of this partiality would be the desire for lower levels of lighting, less crowding at the table, or between tables, comfortable chairs with backs, adequate ventilation, more adequate or more uniform air conditioning, etc.

## Dieting In China

Sales of Chinese cookbooks continue at a brisk pace year after year in the west, and of course a wide variety of cookbooks are available for sale domestically in China as well, and in a variety of languages. Something that is often missing however is the Dieter's Guide to Chinese Cooking.

In fact, the importance to which the Chinese attach to eating often makes it difficult going for westerners who are on a diet. This is because the Chinese expect people to eat, drink, and be merry together.[1] If one person abstains from the eating, much of the pleasure of the meal seems to be decreased. Indeed the host may feel that you do not like him.

With the Chinese preference for eating in a group, even a simple meal often tends to take on the appearance of a small banquet. It is almost inconceivable that the Chinese host would assent to just order or prepare "a few dishes" or "something simple" because the foreigner (who might be the main guest) is on a diet. The Chinese take great pride in showing their generosity, and the standard way to do this is to order more food than the people at the table can eat. Indeed, if dishes are being ordered individually (as opposed to ordering at a fixed price "per table"), and the guests eat all the food on the table, the host will invariably order more dishes, until the point is reached where there is sufficient food left over. This is the way of Chinese hospitality.

Moreover, the expected behavior of a good Chinese host is to continually encourage his guests to "Eat some more", and this phrase tends to be often chanted and rechanted. Experience has revealed that it is extremely rare that the foreigner will be spared this type of repeated ritualistic urging and imploring, and certainly not just because he informed the host beforehand "I am on a diet."

To reply to the Chinese greeting of "Have you eaten your fill?" with a statement like "I do not want to eat my fill, I am on a diet" strikes most Chinese as puzzling. It would be better to redefine your definition of "full" to correspond to your present desired food intake, and then reply directly "Yes, I am full."

All factors considered, the best advice we can offer to the dieter in group dining situations is to employ various stalling tactics. For example it may be possible to lift vegetables, meat, seafood, etc. to the mouth with your chopsticks, and pretend to take a small bite, while actually only rubbing this item against your teeth. You may then place the "leftover portion" back in your bowl, and lay your chopsticks back on the table while you "chew slowly". This may be repeated several times. When you finally do take a bite, it should be very tiny, and masticated thoroughly before swallowing.

Diet Cookbooks

There is news of some westerners who have begun to assemble diet recipes for cooking Chinese food, and of course we hope that these cookbooks will be published in the near future. Advice on how to lower one's cholesterol intake in China, (certainly relevant for all people over age 20) whether cooking for oneself, or eating with others, is also an important issue which these cookbooks will want to address. The following food items, commonly found in many Chinese dishes, have a very high cholesterol content:

A. Egg Yolks from any type of fowl, especially chicken, duck, quail, goose, etc.

---

1. Although the Chinese attach much importance to eating, in no way do we equate this with gluttony. The consuming of food is more of a catalyst for social relations and promoting harmony in the group.

B. Fatty meat

C. Animal skin, whether of fish or fowl

D. Internal organs of all animals, especially the liver, brain, stomach, kidneys, thymus, heart, intestines, gizzards, etc. Brain is by far the highest in cholesterol content.

E. Shellfish such as clams, shrimp, crabs, etc.

F. Other aquatic life such as cuttlefish, ribbonfish, octopus and squid of all types, eels, oysters, abalone, fish eggs, etc.

Elimination or severe restriction of these items from one's diet is advisable if cholesterol is a concern. Milk and dairy products of the low fat variety are low in cholesterol and more highly recommended than the "full fat" varieties.

Various types of meat broths are used as a base for many Chinese dishes. An easy technique for removing fat (and cholesterol) from beef broth, pork broth, chicken broth, etc. is to prepare it one day early, and then leave in a refrigerator overnight. The fat will chill and float on the top of the broth where it may easily be removed with a spoon the next day.

White Boiled Cooking

Some foreigners on diets have experimented with modified Chinese cooking techniques in recent years. One of the most successful of these is "White Boiled Cooking", + in which a collection of vegetables, meat, etc. is cut up and placed into a pot, and then boiled for a suitable length of time in clear water. While the nutritional content of this is reasonably good, the taste is, as one would expect, rather bland. However, for the overweight people in the crowd, this is good news, since they are always disinclined to take a second helping.

The Chinese, rather than seeing this as a technique as the culmination of serious reflection on the meaning of life, and the proper road to health and happiness, feel that it is equivalent to "not knowing how to cook". It is highly uncommon that they will approve of it, even though the fat person's intention (i.e., to lose weight) is admirable. For those westerners who live with Chinese, it may be possible to disguise this technique by adding several slivers of ginger to the water, and/or several drops of soy sauce, so that it is aromatically more appealing.

As a further note, many foreigners have suggested that for people who are allergic to MSG and living in China, cooking at home may be the only feasible long-term solution.

---

a.白煮

## Cross Cultural Meal-time Complaining

CHINESE COMPLAINTS

Eating Implements

Over the years I have collected a number of complaints from Chinese about westerners' eating habits and customs. The most common one of course is that the use of a knife (since knife, fork, and spoon are the typical western table setting) is barbaric, and that the use of chopsticks is much more civilized.

Many westerners have no response for this, but some have suggested that while chopsticks can be fashioned easily from sticks, reeds, small tree branches, etc., nevertheless the widespread use of steel furnaces which are required to supply table knives to a large population represents a higher level of industrial and cultural development.

Where the truth may lie in this dispute I have no idea.

The Nose Knows

Another complaint, or misunderstanding, of a more serious nature occurs when westerners, especially those accustomed to French eating habits, use their fork or spoon to lift their food to their nose before eating, and give it a hefty smell. Rather than seeing this as denoting appreciation and enjoyment, the Chinese are more likely to interpret such gestures as indicating a suspicion that the "food has gone bad" or is otherwise unsuitable for human consumption.

In a similar fashion, western sanitary standards occasionally strike the Chinese as insulting. For example, a Chinese visiting a fast-food outlet in the United States with an acquaintance was seated eating her meal. She asked her American friend if it would be alright to take back her packaged piece of cherry pie, and exchange it for an apple pie. The American said that would probably be no problem. When the Chinese gave this request to the counter girl, she was happy to make the switch, and then in clear view of this Chinese customer, she threw the returned cherry pie into the trash can.

The Chinese customer took this as an insult, as if to suggest that she was unclean, or had some communicable disease. One suspects that an even worse reasction could easily have been obtained if the cashier had enhanced the situation by first asking the customer "What nationality are you?", and upon receiving the answer, then frowned in a pained manner, and dropped the cherry pie into the can as one would drop a stinky baby diaper into a bucket of disinfectant solution. Nevertheless, as innocent and unembellished as this actual situation was, it took quite a bit of explanation to clarify that it was just standard business practice, in light of company policy, and that there had been no intent to imply anything.

Preparation of Eggs

Much discord has been created in East-West relations in regard to the subject of soft-boiled eggs. It appears that in a large number Chinese-run hotels or restaurants, even those which serve western food and are reasonably well equipped for doing so, some sort of contraption for soft-boiling eggs to the customer's requested 2.5 or 3 minutes is almost universally lacking. Added to this is the absence of a specific person on the kitchen staff being assigned to "soft boil eggs", since Chinese do not usually prepare eggs in this fashion for domestic consumption. Many Chinese hotel managers have remarked to me that in a large number of cases when soft boiled eggs are ordered, a complaint is almost always forthcoming, because the patron will maintain it is "overdone", or more rarely, "underdone". To add insult to injury, often times the western patron will refuse to pay for the egg(s), even after having eaten them entirely, because, he maintains, "They were not the way I ordered them." Claims for financial reimbursement due to emotional or psychological damage are also occasionally filed, since the western customer says: "You ruined my day."

According to our research, the "soft boiling" of an egg will certainly depend on 1) whether the water was boiling when you put the egg in, or whether it had not yet come to a boil, and could vary due to 2) the size of the vessel, 3) the number of eggs put in at one time. In addition there is a difference between so-called "soft" and "hard" water, and other related factors, which could come into play when dealing with the preparation of soft eggs in widely differing geographic localities. This being the case, many westerners would perhaps be best advised to either ask that their eggs be prepared some other way when in China, or at the least to be public-spirited enough to pay for what they have ordered and eaten. As I have come to recognize it over the years, the most common way for Chinese to prepare eggs at breakfast is fried on both sides, the so called *he bao dan*.[a]

In regard to hotel arrangements in general, there is of course always the regular crowd of western tourists who will make various complaints about their accomodations in a hotel, and upon checking out ask that the price be adjusted downward. Such complaints, when they are of the nitpicking variety, of course have the effect of giving Chinese a bad impression of all westerners.

Lighting

Another complaint often heard from Chinese who go to the West and have opportunity to eat in a large number of restaurants is: "Why do you westerners always eat in the dark?" Casual comparison of the lighting arrangements in a typical Chinese restaurant in China (CCC), and the average restaurant in the North America or Europe (WWW) will indeed reveal that the Chinese restaurants (CCC) tend to be brightly lit, whereas in the above average western restaurants, the lighting tends to be considerably

---

a. 荷包蛋

subdued. Some foreigners have commented on this by noting that with the Chinese preference to eat in a group, and the desire for bright lighting when eating, the idea of a "romantic dinner for two" in a Chinese restaurant (CCC) is almost a contradiction in terms. Thus in China we frequently see that a romantic dinner for two is more properly held in another style restaurant (CCW).

No doubt many Chinese restaurants in the west have adjusted their lighting and seating arrangements to accomodate this type of romantic dinner, however we should realize that this is a western affectation, and not the normal Chinese arrangement.

Dutch Treat

Another behavioral inclination which irritates the Chinese is that, when eating in a group, the western concept of fairness often seems to be that "each pay his own share". The Chinese consider it particularly ludicrous when someone even takes out a calculator to figure up the exact amount that each person owes. To the Chinese this is the epitome of stinginess, although to the westerner no doubt "this has nothing to do with stinginess". The Chinese preference would be for one person to pay for the meal, and thereby demonstrate his generosity.

Of course this type of Chinese arrangement works well if it is likely that these people will be frequently eating together in the future. In that case it is probable that by rotating in paying the bill, everyone will have a chance to pay his share. However, in China it often happens that in practice only a few people in the group rotate between paying each time the group goes out, and therefore some people do not ever pay their share. Since westerners are generally "treated" more than they have a chance "to treat" in most Asian countries, so sometimes the effect of this policy, or the unequal distribution of payment responsibilities, is not apparent to them over the short term.

The story is told of two westerners, Robert and Joseph, who were walking down a Chinese street, and wondering what they would have for dinner, since it was two days before the end of the month (payday), and neither of them had any ready cash. Seeing a Chinese friend coming out of a small shop, Robert called out to him, and when they were close enough to exchange greetings, Robert said: "Let me take you to dinner. It is my treat." Joseph was surprised at this, knowing as he did that Robert had no money. However, Robert had made the assumption that his Chinese friend would at least try to pay the bill first, and indeed when the meal concluded this was exactly what happened.

While we do not approve of foreigners developing a "freeloading" mentality when dining with the Chinese, we do note that the Chinese value system tends to promote this result, especially over the short term.

Peking Duck

A problem frequently develops involving the eating of Peking Duck. Although such ducks come in various sizes, it seems common that there is some kind of understanding in Chinese hotels and restaurants that their Peking Ducks "serve eight" or "serve twelve", although admittedly this is often not marked on the menu. The unsuspecting foreign tourist, eating with a few travel companions, often finds that there is a vast quantity of Peking duck left over after everyone has eaten their fill, and then often tends to accuse the hotel staff of "trying to pull a fast one" by bringing far too large a portion, thus forcing the diners to pay for much more than they can eat. The westerner states: "You saw that there were only four of us. You brought far too large a portion." Again, this problem goes back to the difference in eating habits. The westerners tend to eat in individual portions, and the Chinese tend to eat in group portions. If we relate this at all to the American Thanksgiving dinner, of course the westerner would not hesitate to go to a restaurant with a friend and order a turkey dinner, and few would expect that the "turkey" only comes in the form of a cooked whole bird. The concept of "individual portions" is still applicable. However, this does not seem to be the standard way of serving Peking Duck.

If three or four Chinese went out for a meal, it is unlikely that they would order Peking Duck, since they know that that requires a larger number of people to handle adequately. The Chinese do not consider it impolite that leftovers be wrapped for taking home, however some tourists may feel this impractical in some situations. Clearly the best advice is to try to determine how many people such large dishes feed, before ordering them casually.

Raw Vegetables and Undercooked Meat

Many Chinese consider raw vegetables "appropriate food for rabbits", and not for people. This seems especially true of the older Chinese generation. Thus a tossed salad of lettuce, tomatoes, cucumbers, carrots, onions, etc. is considered much more delectable to many Chinese if it can be taken back to the kitchen and boiled or stir-fried.

On a similar consideration, many Chinese do not eat what westerners refer to as rare meat ("saignant" in French), since they consider eating inadequately cooked meat to be uncivilized. A Chinese official who was touring a ranch in Texas was given a large cut of rare beef for dinner one evening, and was shocked that this was food considered worthy of his palate. Since this was his first trip to the west, he was totally at a loss as to how to eat the offered beef, since the Chinese always chop or slice their meat before cooking, to facilitate the use of chopsticks, and are not accustomed to using a knife and fork at the table.

Many Chinese parents also complain that it is difficult for little children to eat western style. I have observed many young Chinese children in western restaurants, with their knife held in the right hand and their fork in the left, trying to cut into a piece of meat. This does appear to be a great problem, since they are unpracticed at it. Hence most Chinese feel it makes more sense to eat Chinese style, slicing everything up before cooking, and putting all the dishes in the center of the table, so that old and young alike can help themselves easily. For children it does appear that meat is best prepared in bite sized portions.

As a final complaint, many Chinese object to the practice, or sometimes the necessity, of giving tips in restaurants. Indeed it is only the highest class Chinese restaurants in China that engage in this activity, and they have adopted it from the west, no doubt because they deal with much western clientele. In most of the average Chinese restaurants, tipping is unknown, and many Chinese object to the introduction of it into their society.

## FOREIGN COMPLAINTS
### Politeness

Foreigners are of course not without their complaints toward Chinese eating habits either. Some westerners have remarked that while the Chinese consider themselves a polite race, nevertheless they cannot define what "politeness" means in terms of specific action during their main activity — eating. An example of this is "spitting bones on the table." Many foreigners ask their Chinese friends: "Is this polite?" None of the Chinese seem to know, and occasionally when one does venture an opinion, it is noticeable that he/she is unable to put it into practice (by pointing it out to other Chinese). Hence, there is little agreement with the western phrase "If you are not part of the solution, then you are part of the problem." In this regard the Chinese are more disposed toward the doctrine passed down from Lao-tse: "Non-action is action."

Another no-no in the west is placing your glass on the table upside-down to indicate that you do not want anymore to drink, although the Chinese feel free to engage in this practice, and none can offer the definitive statement as to whether or not this is "polite". In addition, the Chinese may take out their handkerchief to wipe their hands or face, even when napkins are provided, while in most restaurants of any caliber in the west, this is considered crude. Again, it is extremely difficult to find any Chinese who can make a determination if these kinds of actions are polite or not. The modern book of Chinese etiquette, or the authority on Chinese etiquette, is nowhere to be found, apparently, or his/her opinion carries no weight. In ancient China the society was divided into many classes, and people generally ate with members of their own class. The rule of "Follow the superior in your group" seems to have served everyone well as a doctrine of table etiquette in those times.

The story is told of the Chinese girl who moved with her parents to the United States and began going to the local 3rd grade. During lunches she would frequently place her mouth to her food tray and shovel the food into her mouth with her spoon. American teachers who noted this would frequently go out of their way to point out to the child that it was proper to sit up straight at the table, and not to eat in this fashion. Thereafter the child was seen to pick up her tray, and shovel the food into her mouth while sitting up straight. Again this brought correction from the teachers.

At home, when the child would eat with her Chinese family, they would castigate her: "Why do you leave your bowl and plate on the table? Why don't you pick them up so you can eat?" The child replied that the teachers in school had told her "That is not polite". Her Chinese parents balked at this, saying "That is the way we eat. It is polite." The daughter replied, "My friends say that pigs put their noses in the trough, but people are not supposed to."

Indeed the entire issue of cross-cultural etiquette seems to be one still wide open for analysis. I felt that one foreigner made an insightful remark when he said that: "Most people in the civilized world eat three times a day, and if you cannot put people together without some common table manner etiquette so that they are not revolted by each other's eating habits, I think your goals of world peace or world harmony are quite far off." Whether this is a serious topic worthy of consideration is something upon which there is not a whole lot of general agreement. The Chinese tend to avoid the issue, while at the same time being convinced "We are polite." A more detailed discussion of Chinese etiquette and its relationship to other aspects of Chinese thought is given later in this Chapter.

Pricing

Due to the Chinese curiosity about foreigners, another type of potentially impolite situation has been known to arise. Many times when a foreigner attempts to make purchases in the traditional marketplaces, he may be unaware of the prices for certain unmarked merchandise. When he inquires about a particular item, it is not unusual that the Chinese salesperson will glance him over from head to foot slowly before quoting a figure. This unfortunately gives the "foreign guest" the impression that his race, clothing, jewelry, etc. are all being taken into account in the determination of the "price." Some resentment is easily caused, although no doubt the motive for the sales person's glance was nothing more than simple curiosity.

Baking

A foreign lady newly married to a Chinese gentleman moved into a new apartment building. Surveying her needs over and above the wedding gifts received, she quickly decided to purchase a gas oven and a large freezer. When the relatives made their first visit, she was happy to present them with several dishes of food which had been baked. The reaction was: "This meat and vegetables would have been better stir-fried." To this the foreign wife replied: "But we have stir-fried food at your homes all the time, so I thought we were due for a change." In whispered tones she remarked to her husband: "Stir frying is good, but everything comes out being so oily, I really would prefer to cook some other way."

Asked by an aunt if the vegetables were fresh, she replied: "Of course they are, I just defrosted them this morning." Several types of bread and rolls were served with the meal, in addition to baked potatoes. The relatives queried: "Where is the rice?" The wife replied: "When you have potatoes, you do not have rice. Here, have some fresh-baked bread."

For dessert the wife had prepared a large dish of a yellow concoction which she had baked to a golden brown. All of the relatives enjoyed it, and asked what it was. She was a bit surprised by this, and said: "You mean that you never had rice pudding before?" Several of the ladies present asked for the recipe, and seriously discussed the possibility of making rice pudding in a wok.

Observation: In this type of simple example, some basic differences between Chinese and western taste buds, concepts of meal planning, menu selection, etc. quickly become apparent. Many westerners assume that since refrigeration was traditionally not developed in China, so the Chinese tendency to purchase fresh meat and vegetables on a daily basis was, or is, more in the way of a habit grown out of necessity than a preference. In this modern day and age, many westerners are happy to go to the supermarket once a week, and they assume that many modern Chinese would feel the same way. However, the Chinese preference for fresh vegetables is rarely changed by advances in refrigeration, and many more traditional Chinese frown on the thought of eating frozen foods, while many westerners may frown on the inconvenience of going to buy fresh foods daily.

It is not due to the lack of other cooking options being available that the Chinese prepare many types of dishes quickly with the stir fry method. They feel that this retains the crispness of many vegetables, and rather than "putting up with" the oily taste, they actually enjoy it. After some period of time foreigners often get tired of the oiliness inherent with this cooking style, and either express a desire to "drain the grease" before serving, or to come up with other cooking strategies. Naturally, no comments of this kind are considered worthy of serious discussion in the Chinese viewpoint.

The western comment that Chinese food tends to be oily is supported by reference to most Chinese cookbooks. In a cookbook of 110 recipes (excluding soups) the following "top four" preparation methods were noted, and their percentages calculated.

1) Fried: 60 recipes, or 55% of the total. This was broken down into three subdivisions: 26% for stir-fried; 20% for deep-fried, and 9% for fried on both sides.
2) Steamed: 16%
3) Boiled: 14%
4) Roast: 15%

Although stir-fried is the largest single percentage category here, in reality this type of statistical analysis is more valid for considering the range of menu items in a Chinese restaurant. Stir-fried could be expected to tabulate to an even larger percentage in terms of frequency of use in the daily home environment. "Baking" of any sort is a notable absence from the list, and indeed the kitchens in most Chinese homes do not have ovens.

The wife in our example was surprised by the relatives' response to her dessert. However, some reflection should bring to mind that puddings and custards are primarily European inventions, therefore it should not be strange to us that the Chinese are unfamiliar with rice pudding.

Some westerners have been taught in their Home Economics classes that potatoes and rice are mutually exclusive when devising dinner menus, however no such "rule" exists in the Chinese concept of meal planning. That someone would prefer rice over fresh baked bread strikes many westerners as unusual, but the history of Chinese eating habits, where rice was traditionally not a side dish, but indeed the main dish, is still carried on in China today with some force. Rice is then in somewhat of an exalted position, and not subject to exclusion due to the presence of other dishes, whether potatoes, sweet potatoes, taro, breadfruit, yams, etc.

Looking from the point of view of even 100 years ago, we see that the main course on most Chinese tables was rice (or noodles in the northern provinces), while the main course on Western tables was meat or some meat related dish. Thus while some people make the generalization "The Chinese eat rice, the westerners eat bread", bread in the western menu does not play the role of rice in the Chinese menu. Indeed, some foreigners find it useful to categorize the people of the world on the basis of their stomach's "filler preference", thus we have most Chinese either belonging to the Primary Rice Group or Primary Noodle Group. With the movement toward vegetarianism gaining increased acceptance in the west, we hesitate to say that the westerners belong to the Primary Meat Group, however there is a tendency in this direction among many. We are more confident in saying that the westerners belong to a Secondary Bread Group.

We Eat Everything, or Do We?

Chinese commonly make the statement that "We eat everything", and many citizens are proud of this fact, feeling that a wider range of culinary appreciation than known in most western countries is somehow evidence of inherent cultural superiority. Asked to be truthful and come up with a list of some items that the Chinese do not eat, one government spokesman said "Of those things with four legs, we Chinese eat everything except tables and chairs. Of those things with two legs, we eat everything except other humans." This seemed a humorous reply under the circumstances.

Further research would suggest other items however. One of my friends from the Philippines stated that the ethnic Chinese, the Han Chinese, appear to have an aversion to bat meat, which is considered a delicacy in some localities in the Philippines and Thailand. Africans have pointed out that the Chinese do not eat fresh cow's blood, which is a common staple of some African diets. Japanese have noted that the Chinese have a repugnance to raw beef liver, raw horse meat, and raw chicken meat, all of which are served in some areas of Japan. Various kinds of fermented stinky beans, another Japanese taste treat, are also absent from Chinese menu lists. French people are surprised that Orientals turn up their noses at many kinds of naturally cured and rather odorous cheeses, of which many Europeans are fond; "Brie bien fait" comes to mind as one particular example. The famous "embryo eggs" (left under the mother duck or hen up until a day or so before hatching, then taken out and hard-boiled) also appear objectionable to many Chinese palates, although they are well favored in Vietnam and many other Southeast Asian countries. As such, the Chinese claim that "We eat everything" would appear to contain some degree of idle boasting.

## Sanitary Storage Conditions

Concepts of sanitation have come to China primarily from the West. Many traditional markets in China still allow the flies and bugs to hop, skip, and jump all over the meat and vegetables, and the idea that this is "unsanitary" seems strange to the managers of the various stalls. I recall reading an article in the Chinese press one time which was commenting on the reaction of a tour group from Belgium which had come to China, and had the opportunity to visit many historical sites, museums, palaces, temples, and also a number of traditional markets. Upon returning to Brussels, one member of the group had written an article for the French language press criticizing the unsanitary conditions in selling meat and other products in the Chinese open-air markets.

News of this article made its way back to China fairly quickly, and the city government issued a statement that the various vendors in the market should be much more careful in the future to keep their stalls clean and neat, in order to avoid criticism of this kind. Foreigners in China were quick to point out that even sweeping or rinsing out the stalls 100 times per day would have no effect on giving any visiting westerners a better impression of "sanitary conditions" in the open-air market, because the Chinese had failed to grasp the force and meaning of the word "sanitary" as perceived by the Belgians and other Europeans.

Many Chinese believe that since they chop their meat before cooking, and fry or stew it thoroughly, never serving it rare or even medium, so any footprints or other residue left behind by various species of insects are completely sterilized and eliminated. I am still waiting for medical corroboration of this rationalization, but I assume it will be forthcoming in the relevant Chinese medical journal any day now.

In fact the entire issue of sanitary conditions is worthy of treatment at greater length.

## Chinese Sanitary Habits

Not too long ago an important American buyer of sporting goods came to the Far East to order some merchandise for his chain of sporting goods stores. He made the usual rounds of the Trading Companies and Buyers Information Services, and even visited a number of factories in various localities. After one tour of a large factory complex in China, the Manager invited him out for dinner at a well known local Chinese restaurant.

This restaurant was in fact so well known that all the government officials who passed through the area would invariably stop and eat there, not to mention other Chinese businessmen, radio and newspaper people, teachers, vacationers, etc. Everyone agreed that the food was wonderfully fresh and deliciously prepared.

Nevertheless, the foreigner had scarcely entered the restaurant with his hosts when he began to notice the bones, grease, and vegetable scraps on the floor. After a moment's deliberation, he informed his Chinese host that he would prefer to eat in a another establishment, whereupon the party moved on to a fancy western restaurant in the nearby downtown area. After they were settled into their meal, one of the Chinese politely inquired as to the cause of the foreigner's displeasure with the previous establishment, and was told about the bones, grease, and vegetable scraps. He considered this for a few moments and then informed his guest: "I am afraid you have misunderstood, in a Chinese restaurant we do not eat off the floor."

This story may not be exceptionally humorous, but it does begin to illustrate the differences in the Chinese and western conceptions of what is right and proper in terms of cleanliness in the eating environment. In a related example, a tour of a Chinese kitchen reveals that the personnel do not typically wash the outsides of their woks, pans, and pots. By using a line of reasoning similar to that presented above it is not hard to understand their rationale: "We do not cook the food on the outside of our woks."

However this does not perhaps explain why the typical Chinese fruit juice stand or fruit juice shop merely rinses out the customers glasses in cold or lukewarm water before serving them up to the next patron, since such rinsing at best would rearrange any germs on the glass, but not kill them. And yes, what of this Chinese habit of boiling water to sterilize it before drinking? Is it fair to say that turning off the heat as soon as the water reaches boil is adequate sterilization? Or how about when I complain about the bug in my bowl of soybean milk, and the waiter kindly takes away the bowl, ladels out the bug, and sits the bowl back in front of me? Is this in keeping with local ideals of what is sanitary?

Well, it is if you go along with the Chinese line of reasoning, "we eat it and do not get sick, [a] so that means it must be adequately clean and sanitary." And indeed this is the way that Chinese approach many of their traditional customs as regard eating, the use of eating utensils, and the condition of the nearby environment. (Don't check hepatitis rates in the local hospitals, they are high.)

The average foreigner quickly notes that many of his Chinese friends are in the habit of using the same chopsticks to help themselves to more vegetables from the main serving plate, as they use in eating directly out of their own bowls. Likewise, each individual soup spoon is seen as eminently suitable for ladeling more soup out of the large soup bowl in the middle of the table. If my saliva and your saliva get mixed together in the process, it is overlooked, or perhaps seen as a sign of true comradeship.

Upon going to pay the bill in a small restaurant, occasionally there is no handy counter to put one's money upon, but after clearing our throats several times to get the manager's attention, we are surprised when he indicates that we may toss our coins and paper money directly down on the cutting board, where he prepares the meat, fruit, and vegetable dishes.

---

a. 不乾不淨吃了沒病

It is an understatement to say that the westerners will need some adjustment period to accomodate themselves to these new concepts of what is sanitary, or at least what is adequately sanitary. For the sake of east-west relations it is very worthwhile however, lest you embarrass your Chinese friends by casting some questioning glances or making some pointed comments as to the propriety of the conditions you observe.

But our discussion is not over yet, because we still haven't discussed what is "unsanitary", and indeed some surprises await us here as well. As a guest in a Chinese home, or when visiting an office for example, you might be inclined to pick up a glass off the table or shelf and help yourself to some drinking water which was in a nearby pitcher, kettle, or thermos, and ostensibly provided for this purpose. Be forwarned, it is most likely each glass belongs to one specific member of the family, or one specific employee, and although they may have been washed, for you to drink out of someone else's glass is seen as "unsanitary", and hence highly improper.

And some advice for the western man who has just had a hot spicy dinner with lots of garlic in the accompaniment of his Chinese girlfriend, and is now in a quiet little place where he would like to have a quick, or not so quick, kiss. Well, chewing on raw tea leaves may get rid of garlic breath, but that will not solve all your problems. You see once every few years the Chinese newspapers run a series of articles to the effect that kissing is essentially unsanitary. So if your girlfriend shys away from your amorous advances, try not to take it personally.

Moving away from mere talk about eating and drinking, let's progress on to the final result of all these activities: a trip to the bathroom. You open the cubicle door in varying degrees of expectation, and what do you find? 1) no toilet paper, and 2) a wet floor with a carefully designed ceramic hole in its middle. Which way is forward, which way is back? Your guess is as good as mine. The reason why this is the local substitute for the lavatory? Simple enough: the western toilet is "unsanitary" by Asian standards. Many local people consider the contact between the toilet seat and one's derriere to be very unclean. So, hold your breath and away you go.

## Law vs. Benevolence Questionnaire

Directions: (1) Consider the situation which is given. (2) Write down your answers to the five questions at the end. (3) Present the situation to a Chinese person whom you consider to be non-westernized, and record their answers. (4) Compare the two sets of answers. (5) Review the Conclusion Questions.

Suppose you were going to buy some canned fruits or vegetables for your own personal consumption. Two countries supply these items.

| Country A | Country Z |
|---|---|
| All sanitary regulations in canning factories are strictly enforced. Factories which are found upon inspection to have inadequate sanitary conditions are shut down by the authorities immediately, and not allowed to resume operations until they bring their sanitary conditions up to required standards.<br><br>There is an adequate number of personnel in the Health Dept. to complete inspections of canning factories on a regular basis. | Sanitary regulations for canning factories have been established, but they are loosely and haphazardly enforced. Factory owners who are close friends or blood relatives with inspectors or other high officials in the Health Dept. are often allowed to ignore the regulations. Factories which are found in violation are given a warning and a small fine, however they may continue production. Drastic measures such as closing down the factory and putting people out of work are avoided, and many extra-legal extensions for compliance are granted.<br><br>The Health Dept. is vastly understaffed. |

Questions:
1. From which country would you buy your canned vegetables or fruits?
2. Which country operates on a legal basis?
3. Which country operates on the basis of benevolence and sympathy?
4. Which is more important, law or benevolence?
5. If people in the world community are fully informed on the way sanitary regulations are enforced in the two countries, which country will be more respected and have the higher international standing?

*Conclusion Questions:*
*1. Are any contradictions present in either of the sets of answers you have received?*
*2. Can you consider the question "Is the western value system valid for westerners?"*
*3. Can you consider the question "Is the Chinese value system valid for Chinese?"*

## Insightful Stories

### The Freelancer

My American friend Jim wrote some articles for a local magazine in China. When they were published, the magazine sent him a check in the mail. When the Chinese co-workers in the office where he worked heard of this, they congratulated him and said: "Jim, you should treat us!"

Jim thought to himself: "I did the research and collected all the data to write these articles, and I worked hard on putting them together. I did this all in my spare time, and it had nothing to do with any of you. Having now received payment for my effort, how is it that I am supposed to treat you fellow co-workers to a meal? In what way have you determined that 'I owe you' something?" Jim turned these comments over in his mind, however, he made no remark at the time.

A few days later, Jim met his old Chinese friend Mr. Rwan over dinner. Mr. Rwan was working in a large government agency which was part of the Chinese Defense Department, and frequently went to the United States on business. Jim mentioned his feelings of the previous day, saying "After my Chinese co-workers learned that I had been paid for the magazine articles, they then immediately felt it fitting and proper that I should spend this money on treating them to something to eat. I don't understand where they get off."

Mr. Rwan thought the seriousness of Jim's tone of voice indicated he was attaching far more importance to the co-workers' remarks than was necessary. He smiled broadly, and explained: "This is our custom to speak in this manner. But if it bothers you, you may just reply 'Yes, of course I will treat all of you.'"

"But I don't see why I have to treat them, or why it is polite for them to make such a statement or request." Jim replied.

"Well, it is not worth worrying about. You can just say that you will treat them, agree to what they suggest, and then later if you do not, it will not matter."

Jim thought for a moment. "I cannot do that," he said.

"Why not?"

"That would not be honest."

Mr. Rwan smiled again. "Actually this has nothing to do with honesty. This is just politeness."

## The Artist

Calvin, a watercolor artist from Idaho, went to Mr. Sammy Ling's house one afternoon to chat. He noticed an engraved invitation on Mr. Ling's desk, referring to a dinner that very evening in honor of the 20th anniversary of the founding of a magazine.

A telephone call came, and Sammy answered it. From the tone of the conversation, it seemed to be in reference to that very invitation. Calvin heard some bits and pieces of Sammy's conversation.

Sammy said: "Yes, I received it. Congratulations to your magazine on this anniversary."

"What time will you start?"

"Well, I will do my best to make it."

"Of course, I know. Yes. Certainly. Bye-bye." He hung up.

They went to the botanical gardens for a walk, and Sammy introduced Calvin to several beautiful types of Chinese flowers. Sammy ran into his friend Mr. Lai, who invited him to dinner at 7:00 the same evening.

"I have another appointment," Sammy said.

"Oh, but you must come, several of my friends have been wanting to meet you," Mr. Lai urged.

"I would like to come, but I might not be able to make it."

"If you want to come, come! You can arrange your schedule," Mr. Lai stated.

"Alright, that will be good." Sammy said.

Later, Calvin and Sammy Ling returned to the Ling's house. The wife, Mrs. Ling, was visiting her relatives in another city, and Mr. Ling said that he had some business to discuss with his brother-in-law, who had invited him over to his house for dinner the same evening. "Maybe he can help you sell some of your paintings too," he remarked.

"What time is your banquet with the magazine?" Calvin asked.

"Oh, I probably won't be able to go to that," Sammy replied.

"Don't you have an appointment with Mr. Lai for dinner?" Calvin asked.

"No, I told him I was busy."

"I believe he thinks you are coming," Calvin remarked.

"Why do you say that?" Mr. Ling asked quizzically.

Observation: These types of stories are frequently repeated by foreigners in China. The incidents are not particularly important, however what the analysis shows for the differing points of view is significant. The Chinese have two types of talk which are important to be aware of: *ying chou hua* [a] and *ke tao hua* [b]. The best translation we have for these into English is "Empty Talk". To give an affirmative reply to some request which you have no intention of fulfilling is "Empty Talk", and is a form of Politeness. It is therefore seen as outside of the Honesty/Dishonesty Spectrum.

To most westerners, an agreement to do something implies an obligation. Rarely does the westerner feel that "Empty Talk" which is trying to be polite is more important than the overall demands of honesty. (Speaking to someone on their deathbed might be a good example of an exception). Therefore, few westerners would accept a starting point for social relations the axiom "It is alright to make an empty promise to do something which you have no intention of doing." Some allowance and adjustment for the Chinese mode of thinking (and speaking) in this respect must be made if the foreigner is to have a successful and non-frustrating stay in China.

What comes into focus here is the entire topic of "saying what you mean". Any foreigner with a wide range of Chinese acquaintances may recognize various non-western patterns of expression in this regard. Upon investigation, we find that the Orientals have generally been taught from childhood to reply in the following manner —
If asked: "Are you hungry?"

---

a. 應酬話
b. 客套話

If you are not hungry, reply "No, I am not hungry."
If you *are* hungry, reply "No, I am not hungry."
If asked: "Are you thirsty?"
If you are not thirsty, reply "No, I am not thirsty."
If you *are* thirsty, reply "No, I am not thirsty."
If asked: "Can you come over early on Saturday and help me cook for the Party?"
If you are available, reply "Yes, I can."
If you are unavailable, reply "Yes, I will try my best."
If you have a possible conflict, reply "Yes, I will try my best."

It is therefore worthy of consideration that many times the Chinese idea of politeness will conflict with the western precept of "Say what you mean" or "Speak straightforwardly." The issue of politeness is also of concern when discussing the force of any statement which could possibly appear to imply "obligation". Some more specific characterization of Chinese obligation may be made after considering the following story.

## Leave It Up To Me

One morning, Mr. Chang saw a person of his acquaintance, named Ming-fen, going out. "Where are you going, Ming-fen?" he inquired.

Ming-fen politely replied: "I am going out to buy some meat, fish, and vegetables."

Mr. Chang thought for a moment, and said: "I want to go fishing today, and you know that I am a pretty good fisherman. If you are going out, I think it best that you just buy meat and vegetables. Leave the fish up to me, and I will give you several when I come back."

Ming-fen thought that this would be a fine arrangement, and replied in a spirit of comradeship: "Thank you Brother Chang. Thank you very much."

Mr. Chang began to prepare his fishing equipment, and called up his friend Mr. Lee to suggest the idea of a fishing outing for the day. Mr. Lee agreed to this and said he would prepare some bait.

Waiting at the arranged meeting-place on the outskirts of town, it was some time before Mr. Lee arrived. He explained: "Some neighbors came over to borrow some tools, and my brother-in-law stopped by for a chat. Also I had to run an errand for my wife, so I am a bit late. Very sorry. Very sorry." Mr. Chang did not mind this, as he had passed the time talking to some men who were playing checkers under a tree.

On the way to the river, Mr. Chang and Mr. Lee came across a baseball game being played in the park. They decided to watch an inning or two, but the game was quite good and went extra innings, and they watched it until the final pitch was thrown. After the game, some of the players were instructing some children in the proper technique for holding the bat, and while watching this instruction, Mr. Chang noticed some of his old friends nearby, so he called them over to discuss old times. As it was already late in the afternoon, one of them said: "Let us all go out to a sumptuous dinner." This seemed an excellent idea. Another one suggested a restaurant which served delicious Szechwan cuisine, but due to the fact that it was quite far away, it took them some time to get there by public transportation.

When they were done with dinner and their drinking games, it was already dark. The manager of the restaurant was also very interested in fishing, and he said: "I know of an excellent fishing spot off the beaten track where we can go. If you can wait a few days, I may have some free time, and we can all go together." This pleased Mr. Chang, and he and Mr. Lee continued talking with the manager for some time about the best use of different types of bait.

Another customer joined the conversation, and mentioned that he and his son were going fishing the next day. He said: "If we catch a lot of big fish, I will be sure and give you some." A fresh round of beers was ordered to celebrate this announcement.

A while later everyone went home, very happy with the day's events, and the new friends they had made. Arriving back at his house, Mr. Chang put away his fishing equipment for the day, and helped his children get ready for bed.

Meanwhile, that afternoon Ming-fen had visited a neighbor's house (the Jwang's), and was given some of the fresh clams which the Jwang's relatives had just brought in that morning. Returning home, he had seen some steamed buns on sale, and purchased several. The family's evening meal of meat, clams, steamed buns, and several kinds of vegetables was more than adequate. He read in the evening paper that a large shark had been brought in by some boats in a neighboring town's harbor. He thought to himself: "Perhaps I will be able to buy some shark meat in the market tomorrow or the next day."

Observation: We see here that Mr. Chang's Perception of Obligation has not caused any problems for his friend Ming-fen. From Ming-fen's later arrangements for dinner we see that he has not been inconvenienced in the slightest by Mr. Chang's failure to provide fish, as per "the original promise." Even if Mr. Chang were to give a full accounting of his actions, Ming-fen would not be inclined to view them as having any content of dishonesty, since Mr. Chang has followed a natural approach to his daily activities, and allowed his actions to "Go With the Flow." [1] (GWF). It is most likely that both parties share a GWF Perception of Obligation.

By way of contrast, the average westerner more likely has a PSA Perception of Obligation, denoting "Planned Specific Action". If an unknowing westerner is placed in Ming-fen's position, he may end up being disappointed, angry, or otherwise flustered. He might have refused the neighbor's offer of clams, or skipped the opportunity to buy steamed buns or other items, rationalizing to himself: "I am having fish for dinner. Mr. Chang promised to bring me some."

---

1. Although the English terminology is primarily derived from 聽其自然 and 細水長流, this certainly bears overtones of 隨波逐流.

The offer to bring fish could have just as easily been an offer of employment, or an offer to loan some books, to go to the movies, play chess, take a vacation together, purchase some materials, make an introduction to some influential party, or almost anything else.

Clearly the westerner is being overly naive if he takes such "statements" as those of Mr. Chang as equivalent to "promises".

## Empty Promises in the Hotel Industry

How many hotel managers do you know? Have you had the opportunity to watch any of them "in action", when dealing with guests' complaints? That kind of observation is often excellent training in human relations. I remember one hotel manager of a large international hotel with a constant traffic of western guests in China told me "We tell all of our employees not to believe anything the foreigners tell them." When I asked why this was so, she replied "Because the foreigners will make a lot of empty promises." She gave examples of this by noting some comments that many westerners will make, along with their "failure rate" in terms of later performance.

Westerners will tell Chinese acquaintances: "If you need an invitation letter or guarantee letter in order to come to my country for a visit, just drop me a line. That will be no problem." Failure to meet this promise when the Chinese person later did actually send them such a request: 90%. Fulfillment rate: 10%.

Westerners will tell Chinese acquaintances: "I have quite a bit of money, and if you get a chance to come to my country be sure and look me up, because I can take you out to see all the sights, have some nice meals, and go touring, etc. Don't worry about it." Failure to meet this promise when the Chinese person later does actually show up at their house: 65%. Fulfillment rate: 35%.

Westerners will tell Chinese hotel staff: "I will be out of town sightseeing for a few days. But when I return I will want to stay in your hotel for another night or two. So could I please trouble you to keep my luggage here until I come back . . . " Failure to stay in the hotel for at least one more night when coming back to pick up their luggage: 40%. Fulfillment rate: 60%.

Westerners will tell Chinese hotel staff: "I often come to this city, and I have many friends who do business and frequently travel through this area. I would be happy to introduce them to come here. So why don't you give me a discount on the price?" Failure to introduce more customers when a break on the price is actually given: 98%. Fulfillment rate: 2%.

Running a hotel is a business, but a certain amount of hospitality is generally given to the guests, sometimes to the extent that they develop warmly personalized feelings toward some staff members. Promises given in such a situation sometimes appear to border on the non-business type, falling into the area of social or new acquaintance

## Etiquette vs. Good Fortune

Westerners often look for guidelines of Chinese etiquette, but what they more commonly find are dictates on what type of behavior is considered unlucky, and should be avoided, and which are considered lucky, and should be practiced, as opposed to strict rules of etiquette. This is especially true for the foreigner eating at the meal table. After continuous exposure to many of these remarks dealing with fortune and misfortune, some westerners would be inclined to say that in reality these are the bulk of Chinese etiquette. Whether or not this statement is true is a fact which each person may judge for himself, based on his own observations and research.

Some common rules which we do find consistently are in regard to the eating of fish. The Chinese prepare fish with head and tail intact, and the meat is picked off the body with the chopsticks. After the upper side is eaten, some arrangement must be made to enable the diners to eat the remaining side, since there is generally a large spinal bone. On land, we may turn the whole fish over with our chopsticks, however when dining with sailors, or on a boat, the fish must not be turned over, lest the boat turn over as well. In this case we must remove the central bones with our chopsticks, and place these off to the side.

Since in Mandarin the word expressing "surplus" ("bounty", "excess") and the word for "fish" are pronounced the same, many Chinese believe that fish cooked and placed on the table on New Year's Eve should not be eaten, but rather left whole, and this will ensure "surplus" in the coming year. The expression *nien nien yeou yu* [a], roughly translatable as "May you have bounty every year!" (hence equal to "May you have fish every year!") may be seen written on red paper and pasted over the doorway or hearth. The foreigner is advised not to help himself to the fish on a New Year's Eve table unless the Chinese do so first. If the fish is eaten, it should not be consumed entirely, some portion must be left on the plate. This then becomes the "excess" or "bounty" which is carried over into the New Year.

On many occasions such as birthdays, New Year's, festival days, or other appropriate times, long noodles will be served in soup or broth. The foreigner is tempted to cut or slice these for ease of eating, however this is considered very inauspicious. The long noodles are associated with a wish that everyone will lead long lives, and so they must be eaten "as is", no matter how clumsy this proves to be.

A wonderful expression which is a part of Chinese etiquette is *sui sui ping an* [b], which

---

a. 年年有餘 equals 年年有魚.    b. 歲歲平安 equals 碎碎平安.

we may translate as "May there be peace every year!" and which conveniently rhymes with "May there be peace among breakage!" If we drop something at the table, in the kitchen, or in any other locality, and it breaks, we have only to say *sui sui ping an* and the bad luck associated with the incident is quickly dispelled.

Many times children will make casual remarks or statements expressing natural curiosity that, upon closer analysis, seem very unlucky, or perhaps even degrading to the adults present. If this occurs, we have only to say *tung yan wu ji* [a], which we may roughly translate as "Do not care about children's talk", and the entire affair is quickly forgotten about.

The Chinese will often take fruit, canned foods, or other food items to people of their acquaintance who are sick in the hospital. Since "goodbye" in Mandarin, *zai jian* [b], literally means "see (you) again", one must not use this phrase when departing the hospital, since that would be unlucky. See additional comments on this in the **Contrasting Emotive Content** essay in Chapter 9.

In any situation where gifts, presents, or other items are given, it is considered proper etiquette for the giver to use two hands. The receiver should do likewise of course. This appears to indicate an undivided heart, and is associated with sincerity.

Other rules refer to chopsticks. Often in the middle of a Chinese meal it is necessary to leave the table to go to the restroom or make a phone call. A problem arises when the westerner looks for a place to put his chopsticks. In fancier restaurants, there are little fixtures called "chopstick pillows" upon which he may prop them up, however in more simple dining arrangements, these are seldom in use. Not desiring to soil the table, and having no other convenient place to put them, he often simply sticks the chopsticks upright into the rice in his ricebowl. This is considered very unlucky however, since the act of sticking the chopsticks upright in the rice bowl resembles the funeral ritual of sticking incense sticks in the incense bowl to make an offering to the dead.

Another no-no is use of the chopsticks to practice a drumroll on the table. This is often tempting, both to the drummers and non-drummers in the crowd, especially when there is nothing else to do while waiting for the dishes to come. Chopsticks do look quite a bit like drumsticks anyway, and with some practice one may be able to tap out a pretty nice rhythm. However, the westerner will quickly become aware of the unacceptability of this procedure from the stares he is getting.

An interesting example of trying to determine a specific rule of Chinese etiquette is the question of whether picking your teeth, with a toothpick or other implement, is acceptable at the meal table. The reply of "no" because it does not look very attractive is more the result of western influence. In fact we are unable to find authoritative commentary on the entire issue in any traditional Chinese sources. Since there is nothing particularly "unlucky" about this act, we feel confident in saying that covering the mouth with a napkin or handkerchief while engaging in it is more than adequate observance

---

a. 童言無忌    b. 再見

of the dictates of propriety. It is certainly not necessary to leave the table. Most westerners of course realize that chopsticks should not be used to pick the teeth, but may wonder whether one chopstick may be used as a substitute for toothpick or fork to spear pieces of fruit or vegetables. We believe that it is not nice to regard a chopstick as a spear, since this would imply that we are actively using "weapons" at the table, hence someone might be injured. That would be unlucky and so this should be avoided.

Among some who eat Shan-Tong style steamed bread (or rolls) there is a statement that bite-sized pieces of the bread should be taken in the fingers and then placed in the mouth, as opposed to biting into the entire piece of bread. The correct process, or rule of manners, for eating this bread then appears to be: tear off a bite-sized piece, and place it in the mouth, eating the bread piece by piece. However, this rule is often forgotten, and indeed when confronted with steamed meat buns or spring rolls, or western type sandwiches, it is often discarded altogether, since the multiple layered contents of these items are far more suitable for biting than for tearing.

Another rule which is often discarded is the statement by some Chinese that the host in a Chinese banquet sits across from the door (or facing the wall in which the door is located), and that the guest of honor sits across from him.

To the westerner who has browsed the pages of Amy Vanderbilt, Emily Post, or Miss Manners from time to time, many of the etiquette rules which he runs across in Chinese society will probaby appear not to have much to do with etiquette at all, more likely they are observed out of superstition. Even more frustrating, they are often paradoxical, or lack a true objective standard. For example, is it polite to sit hunched over at the meal table, or must we sit up straight? If we pick up our soupbowl to drink our soup, or pick up our ricebowl to eat our rice, should the bowl be lifted to the mouth, or the mouth be brought down to the bowl? Or should we meet halfway? Of course the Chinese rarely discuss such topics, however when they do their reasoning tends to be typically Oriental: if a young person eats in a fashion which his elders consider impolite, the youth is wrong. If the elders eat in a way which the youth considers impolite, the youth is wrong again. It is, apparently by definition, wrong to tell someone older than you are what etiquette consists of in any and all occasions, especially when your stipulations are not in accordance with their actions.

With this in mind, we may conveniently downplay consideration of whether or not it is polite to make a slurping noise when drinking soup. Most Chinese [1] seem to feel this indicates that you really enjoy the soup, and we are happy to take that as the last word on the subject.

---

1. Japanese and Koreans slurp their soup with even more gusto than the Chinese do.

## Honesty in the Environment

My friend Joseph was raised in Wisconsin in a devout Catholic family, and I was raised in a Lutheran one in another state, so we both share a common Christian background, although we do have our differences in regard to accepted standards of Church organization. Not long ago, upon visiting a private academy to inquire the exact location of their various branches around the city, Joseph and I met some Chinese girls, Joyce and Alice, who had been raised in Chinese Christian households, and were devoted Christians. Joseph was newly arrived in China, and enjoyed practicing his Mandarin, although it was heavily interspersed with English. I was satisfied to sit by the side drinking a glass of tea on this pleasant Sunday afternoon, while the three of them discussed their views on life.

The conversation ranged over a number of Biblical topics and concepts, although it seemed to me that Joyce and Alice were unaware of a great deal of Middle Eastern history that occurred during the writing of the Old and New Testaments, as well as the general philosophical development of the different chapters, and thus were perhaps failing to see some of the broad premises which underlie much of the Biblical writings, and upon which those writings should be interpreted. This impression was deepened as I listened to the course of their remarks.

At one point the conversation reached the subject of "honesty", and Joseph mentioned that he felt this was a topic which was strongly stressed in the Bible. Joyce and Alice agreed. Joseph said he had recently been to a friend's home for dinner. Some other relatives of the host family happened to drop by, and they were warmly welcomed. The host asked them "Have you eaten?", and Joseph noted that their little boy said: "No, we haven't eaten" but this was quickly denied by the parents, who claimed that indeed they had already eaten, and were not hungry. After much urging they did assent to sit down at the table and "eat a little", although Joseph noted that they ate quite a lot.

Later, Joseph had a chance to talk to the newly arrived gentleman privately, since it happened that they were both interested in stamp collecting. In response to Joseph's question of how much dinner they had eaten before coming, the man remarked in a low tone of voice that they had actually not eaten anything first. "It would be better for this man to speak more honestly in the future," Joseph commented to the girls.

"Yes, everyone should speak honestly," Alice said smiling.

"It was wrong of him to speak dishonestly to our host," Joseph said.

Joyce and Alice looked at each other. "What did he say dishonestly to your host?" Joyce inquired.

"He said that he, his wife, and child had eaten," Joseph said calmly, "and that was not true."

A smile flashed across Joyce's face, and she appeared as if she were going to laugh. "That was just being polite!"

"Polite?" Joseph asked quizzically, "What does that have to do with politeness?"

"That is our custom," Alice added, also beginning to laugh. "Why would you think it is dishonest?"

Joseph looked at me, and I stood up, taking my cup of tea over to the hot water bottle in the corner of the office where we were seated. As I added some more water to my glass, and in order to change the subject, I mentioned that Alice's brother-in-law was one of the managers in the "Clam House Restaurant" where I had taken Joseph to dinner a few nights ago. Alice was happy to hear this, and asked if Joseph had enjoyed the food, especially the clams.

"They said they were sold out of clams the day we went," Joseph said. "I was very disappointed, since many of my friends have said that they cook clams excellently. I will be leaving in two weeks, and may not have another chance to go back there."

"Yes, I have heard that there has been a shortage of clams recently," Alice nodded.

"I pointed to the menu, the signboard, and to the electric display, all of which advertised clams for sale, but the waitress said they had not had any clams for two days, and asked us to order something else." Joseph added, "She seemed very interested in having us eat crabs, although I saw that they were much more expensive."

"Crabs are very delicious," Alice assented.

"That is not quite my meaning," Joseph replied. He then turned to me and asked: "How do you say 'bait-and-switch' in Chinese?"

I shook my head, then leaned over to speak in his ear: "The words exist, however the concept does not. I would not bother to mention it."

Joseph paused for a moment to consider this. He asked Alice: "Why didn't they put up a sign or something?"

"Maybe they were too busy," Alice said.

"Maybe they had sent someone to the fish market and had expected to have clams later in the day," Joyce commented.

"But it seems to me that advertising or displaying something which you do not have for sale is not good business policy." Joseph paused for a moment. "Maybe you could speak to your brother-in-law about that," he looked at Alice.

Alice looked at Joyce. "You could order something else," they said almost in unison. "There are a lot of other excellent dishes served in that restaurant," Joyce added.

Joseph was puzzled at this reply, since the meaning of his remarks seemed to have been missed. I broke in with a comment of my own at this point, saying: "Joseph likes to eat Chinese pork chops. He found a small shop that serves very tasty pork chop and rice dinners."

Joseph seemed to brighten up at this remark, but then he assumed a rather thoughtful expression. "You know, another restaurant opened up near our office the other day, and I went over with some of the Chinese people in our office. They had stuffed leaflets in the mailboxes of all the homes and offices in the vicinity, and of course I took one of those with me. We all ordered pork chops and rice, which I thought was an excellent buy at $7 a plate, as advertised on their leaflet. When it was time to pay, one of the other co-workers, Frank Chang, was nice enough to treat. But I noticed that he was paying a lot of money, so I went over to investigate. The manager claimed that the price printed on the leaflet should have had another zero, and Frank agreed that that was a more 'reasonable' price for such a large plate of rice with a big pork chop and some other vegetables, although he had assumed from their leaflet that there was some sort of introductory offer or something.''

Alice nodded her head, ''$70 for a large plate like that is about right.'' Joyce agreed that this was a fair price.

''But they advertised at $7 per bowl, and I had the leaflet with me.'' Joseph said. ''The manager's attitude seemed rather . . . ''

''You should pay the fair price,'' Alice broke in. ''The manager is not responsible for the printer's mistakes.''

''He explained the situation clearly, and noted that it was due to a printing error,'' Joyce said.

''I failed to follow his reasoning,'' Joseph continued. ''In the restaurant I asked Frank to step aside, and I showed the manager a copy of the leaflet. I explained that we were only required to pay $7 per plate, but he refused to accept my analysis.''

''That settles it,'' Joyce said, ''The polite thing to do would be to go along with his determination. And anyway, he is older than you are.''

Rather than let everyone's verbal exchanges go any further in this manner, I routed the conversation onto a discussion of the Psalms. I related that a friend of mine had rewritten one of the Biblical verses to comment on the tour guides he had known during his many trips to Asia. It was entitled ''The Traveller's Psalm''. Although I could not remember the beginning, the ending went something like this: ''Thou preparest a cafe table before me in the presence of my kaopectate; thou anointest my mouth with costly wine; my budget runneth over. Surely good bargains and thy customs inspector shall follow me all the days of my trip; and I will dwell in the house of the poor forever.''

Joseph laughed heartily at this, although the two girls did not recognize the play on words that it represented, and so only smiled politely.

As it was nearly 7:00, and we had been talking since about 5:30, Joseph wanted to go and get some dinner. The girls said they hoped that Joseph would come and participate in some of their church activities during his two weeks left in the country, and they gave him their names, addresses, and telephone numbers. Joseph asked if perhaps they were hungry and would like to go out to dinner together, but they declined, saying ''No, we already ate.''

Later on the street, Joseph asked me what had happened to our discussion of ''honesty''. He felt it had derailed somewhere, but he was not exactly sure where. ''In regard to many situations, other Chinese have told me 'that is the way we do things here', and I recognize that type of reasoning. However, in regard to the three incidents I brought up, and considering that our topic was 'honesty', I had thought that Joyce and Alice would be able to clear up some of my confusion."

"Are you cleared up now?" I asked.

"No, I am much more confused than when I began."

I sensed the nature of Joseph's confusion, since I was also a westerner, and had dealt with many of the same feelings a decade or more before. "It would be unfair to say that the girls are not sincere in their religious convictions," I said, "although of course they have a completely different cultural background than we do. I am reminded of the Chinese idiom which refers to the young monks who beat on the 'wooden fish'[a] to accompany their chanting. It might add some light to the issues here."

"What is that one?"

"The idiom is 'With a mouth and no heart.'[b] I believe it refers to the fact that while the youthful new monk voices all the Buddhist scriptural tenets, he does not really have a true grasp of what they mean, or how to put them into practice."

"I do not quite follow you."

"Well, it was only a thought. Perhaps it is not really relevant. Certainly much more relevant is the whole issue of the indirectness of Chinese communication. For example, in practice, I would say that few Orientals would seriously agree with the statement 'Honesty is the best policy.' Certainly, from talking to them and posing various situations for their analysis, you quickly see that modesty, politeness, and some other considerations are regarded more imporant than some abstract ideal of honesty."[1]

Joseph thought for a long while. "That might not be totally unreasonable," he said. "But first I would want to hear their exact definitions of 'modesty' and 'politeness', as well as the rights and obligations associated with each."

I shook my head. "China is not the land of exact definitions . . . so I imagine you will have to gain any and all insight into these matters from experience." After walking for another block, we were accosted by a man selling steamed meat dumplings. I remained silent, although Joseph spoke a few words of Mandarin to let the man know we were not interested. The man's eyes lit up, and he took out a steaming rack of dumplings for our inspection, letting the delicious aroma drift in our direction. He said that Joseph should sit down and have some dinner, pointing to his menu and describing all the types of soup he had available as well. He was very insistent.

Joseph had wanted to go have pork chops and rice, but the man had already pushed him into a chair, and passed him a small dish and a bottle of soy sauce. Joseph paused for a long moment, looked at the man and said: "I already ate." At this point the man stepped back, bowed politely, and Joseph and I went on our way.

---

a. 木魚    b. 有口無心

1. Scholars consider Chinese ethical thought as "situational ethics", i.e. very pragmatic, very concrete, and generally lacking the ability to deal with concepts in the abstract.

As we moved away from the dumpling salesman I turned to Joseph and said: "You are learning." He shook his head and seemed lost in thought. I offered some more comments. "Consider this. You normally eat three meals a day, and around mealtime you generally find that you are hungry. That is why you eat. Now suppose that you are seated at a table in some impoverished African nation at noontime, and that what you consider your normal food intake is put on a plate at your place. As hundreds of starving natives move in around the table with outstretched hands, you gaze at the food in front of you, and a voice says: 'Do you need that?' If you reply 'Yes', is that an honest statement?"

"Living in those regions in Africa is often a difficult proposition," Joseph replied, "and there is no easy answer to that kind of question."

'That's the point," I said. "Define 'honesty' in a cross-culturally relevant fashion."

Joseph suddenly seemed to become very tense, and quickly darted toward the street, pulling me out of the way of a motorcyclist who was roaring down the sidewalk. Joseph walked forward briskly without speaking, and I looked at him just as he walked into the shadow of a large building, so I could not see the expression on his visage.

The rain began to fall down in large drops, and we pulled our jackets over our heads and ran the last two blocks home.

## What It Is, It Is Not, or Is It?

Quenton is a friend of mine from New York. He has been in China for several years. He was discussing some peculiar aspects of cross-cultural humor with me the other day, although I suppose you would have to be an East Coast person to really appreciate Quenton's "sense of humor".

Although I am not a psychiatrist, I did ask Quenton a few questions about his attitude toward life and human relations at the outset of our discussion. I found out that he, like many other Americans, has a strong feeling that "it is not necessary to state the obvious." From experience I recognized that this could easily become a source of irritation in his dealings with Oriental people, and as he related his tale, my worst doubts were confirmed.

Quenton said that he had met some girls some time back who were interested in arranging a private class to study English, and had been teaching them in the evenings two or three times a week for the past several months. After class he generally walked home, which took about thirty minutes. On the way he would always pass a street hawker who was selling meat buns, and Quenton would usually buy two or three.

Arriving home, he would eat these in the small dining room of the place where he lived. As the landlord's home was right across the hall in the apartment building, and they shared a common living room, he would of course often run into the landlord. Initially, on noting that Quenton was eating, the landlord had remarked "You are eating meat buns." Quenton had nodded and said "Yes."

However, after nearly two weeks of this kind of questioning, Quenton began to feel very strange. He came home one night after a class, and sat down to eat. The landlord looked up from his magazine and said "You are eating meat buns." Quenton looked at his meat buns, and looked at the landlord, thought for a second, and replied "No, I am eating an ice-cream sundae."

The landlord cocked his head off at a peculiar angle, looked at the meat buns on the table, paused for a few moments, then went back to reading his magazine.

Several days later, the landlord was also in the living room when Quenton arrived home. When Quenton took out his meat buns and began eating, the landlord said "You are eating meat buns." Quenton finished chewing the bite he had just taken, and without looking up, said "No, I am eating shark's fin soup."

Quenton asked me "Why does he keep giving me the third degree?"

I sighed. "You would do well to reread the Chinese classics," I said.

"I read them," Quenton replied, "but they did not say anything about eating meat buns."

"As with many other foreigners, in attempting to note specific data, or to locate the answers to specific problems as you read the classics, you have failed to perceive the broad underlying premises."

"Are you talking about the 'unstated premises'?"

"Certainly, there are many of those, however the situation we are dealing with in your case is more concerned with a major stated premise."

"Which is what?"

"The importance of 'ritual' in our daily life," I said.

"Doesn't that refer more to religious practices?"

"No, no, the application of ritual in Oriental society is much wider than that," I corrected. "And the kind of discourse you have had with your landlord here is a good example of it. In each case, your most appropriate reply would have been 'Yes', just as in the first instance."

Quenton thought about my analysis for a moment. "But why does he ask me every time?"

I tried to smile. With Quenton's western educational background, and long exposure to the western media, it was very difficult for him to accept a mentality which approved of any sort of day-in and day-out deadpan routine in one's conversational encounters. He therefore had a hard time recognizing the need or desirability for "ritual" in such situations.

He went on to relate the case of his American friend who had lived in a small Japanese hotel on the outskirts of Tokyo for many months. His daily routine was to wash, shave, and dress every morning, which is a bit odd to the Orientals, since they tend to wash in the evening, and not in the morning. However, this occasioned no comment from the hotel staff. Every morning when the American went downstairs at 7:45 he was dressed in his business suit, with a tie, and well-polished shoes, carrying a briefcase and oftentimes an overcoat. After eating his breakfast in the small hotel restaurant he came out into the lobby at 8:20. Invariably, the house keeper would be mopping the floors, and would say to him: "Are you going to work?"

Initially, this caused no problems, and he would reply "Yes". After a few weeks however, his patience was beginning to wear. One morning when the snow had begun to fall, and the wind was blowing, he came out into the lobby in his usual attire at 8:20. The housekeeper looked up from her mopping and said "Are you going to work?" He thought for a moment, and then replied "No, I am going to the beach." The housekeeper looked out the window, turned back to him and said "It is not a good day for the beach I think." She then went back to her mopping chores.

I had heard of similar incidents from my friends who lived in Korea. Examining these experiences, I believe there is more to them than can be explained by noting that many westerners have a general sarcastic bent, or that they hold to the notion that "it is not necessary to state the obvious." Actually to many westerners, after a period of time such remarks begin to rub on their "sense of creativity". Rather than be so "totally uncreative" in engaging in this type of discourse day after day, they would prefer a simple "Good morning", "Good evening", or "Good afternoon", and leave it at that, if there is nothing more substantive which can be said at the moment.

Quenton was confused as to their real purpose in asking such questions repeatedly, although he admitted that oftentimes the foreigners' replies in many situations probably left the Orientals confused as well. To illustrate this he mentioned an incident which he had seen when walking down the street one day. A number of foreigners who lived in a nearby house were all dressed up in neat clothing, wearing sunvisors, holding minature Chinese flags, and on their way out. A Chinese neighbor nodded in their direction and asked "Are you going to the parade?"

The foreigners looked at each other and said "Is the Pope Catholic?"

The Chinese man pondered this reply for a moment. His wife came out of their house. Seeing the foreigners going down the street she said "I think they are going to the parade."

Her husband said "No, I think they are going to church. They mentioned something about the Pope. But I did not know that he was in town."

Since Quenton had read that Chinese philosophy has strong undercurrents of naturalism, he asked me if, rather than referring to a western religious figure like the Pope, a more natural reference, such as "Do fish swim in the sea?" would have been appropriate.

"No, certainly not," I shook my head.

Quenton then passed me the following list which he had made while observing another foreigner in a restaurant asking to have his teacup refilled. The waiter and waitress all spoke English. Each request was separated from the previous one by a minute or more, as the waitress made her rounds.

| | |
|---|---|
| Round 1 | |
| 1st statement to waitress | May I have some more tea please? |
| Round 2 | |
| 2nd statement to waitress | May I have some more tea please? |
| Round 3 | |
| 3rd statement to waitress | Do you have any more tea? Could I have some? |
| Round 4 | |
| 4th statement to waitress | Excuse me, where is the teapot? I would like to get some more tea. |
| Round 5 | |
| 5th statement to waitress | Do you have ears? I have been asking for tea, where is it? |
| Round 6 | |
| 6th statement to waitress | Waitress! Tea! Here! Now! |

"Perhaps my friends and I should improve our Chinese language skills, so that we can more easily communicate with the local people," Quenton said.

"No," I said, "your problem is not language, your problem is thinking. The Orientals do not think in this fashion. You are always better with a straight 'Yes' or 'No' answer, or an expression of your wishes in a plain unruffled manner."

"That westerner's patience was really wearing thin. He wanted more tea."

"I would guess that not only was the Chinese waitress surprised by the customer's remarks by 'Round 6', but the other people eating at his table, or at other tables, were surprised too.[1] He would have been better to retain the initial 'May I have some more tea please?' throughout. 'Endurance' or 'Patience' is an Oriental virtue, and it is rarely if ever subject to 'wearing thin'," I clarified.

"I suppose that advice applies to dealing with a wide range of Chinese organizations."

"Yes, of course. When requesting information in a company or agency, or making other inquiries, we are well advised to be patient, and to 'go with the flow' of whatever happens. Indeed patience should be maintained even in confrontation with inefficiency, incompetence, or other types of exasperating situations in general."

"That is a tough order sometimes."

"True, indeed. You may find it helpful to consider that your relationships with any and all parties in other Chinese companies, organizations, bureaus, shops, etc. are not that they are serving or dealing with you as a 'duty', but more in the way of a 'personal decision' or 'personal favor'. You might also want to consider that they have probably had a very trying day. The necessity for patience, politeness, and a pleasant demeanor

---

1. The (Han) Chinese are a very homogeneous race. In a situation such as that presented here, the host and other Chinese at the table will tend to side with the waiter and waitress, and this of course reflects the Group Mentality. As a group the Chinese would then regard the westerner's impatient and overbearing remarks to be an insult to all the Chinese present.

is much more apparent when using this orientation."

"And I should deal in a simple, almost ritualistic manner with restatements of the obvious?"

"Obviously."

## Insults in the Night Market

For foreigners of any length of experience in China, there will have been many occasions to visit the night market and make purchases of food and other items. It is often the case that the local people will strike up a conversation with the foreigner, asking him what he thinks of the food, or whether this type of delicacy is available in his home country. For the beginning language student, this is an excellent opportunity to try expressing himself in Chinese, and see if his meaning can be understood. For the person without the requisite language skills, it may be a bit frustrating however, since he can only smile and nod his head.

However, I believe foreigners are well advised not to underestimate the value of "smiling and nodding", since it constitutes a useful technique in various situations in the night market and on the street in general. Indeed, in many types of daily situations even the serious language student may often find himself confronted by many linguistic problems which are best handled in this manner. This is because China, in addition to having Mandarin as the official language, also has many regional dialects, which for all intents and purposes are mutually unintelligible. Thus the foreigner who speaks Mandarin or any other dialect will frequently be queried on a few basic sentences of other dialects by people who are native to those regions.

Some embarrassment or bad feelings may be generated when, finding that the foreigner is linguistically incompetent to some degree, the Chinese continue to make a few quick remarks among themselves and then begin laughing uproariously. Many foreigners quickly assume they are being ridiculed, insulted, called names, or otherwise characterized as fools. It is therefore important to consider the nature of the "uproarious laughter" that the Chinese engage in on such occasions.

Long observation indicates that the Chinese sense of satire, especially as used in daily conversation, is much less developed than in the West. Consider the example of a fruit shop, where one employee could not get the fruit blender to work, and asked another employee (of the same age group) for help. If the second employee noted that the plug had fallen out, a westerner might say "In order to use the blender you have to plug it in first," thus casting doubt on the first employee's intelligence through the tone of his remarks. The Chinese rarely make this kind of comment or engage in this type of "humor". A Chinese would most likely simply say: "You did not plug it in."

Likewise, where the witty American might reply to a question of "Should I include some sliced pork in the Vegetarian Platter?" by saying: "Do elephants walk on two legs?" or "Do fish grow on trees?", this type or style of comeback is almost totally unknown in Chinese conversation.

A friend of mine once studied the dialect of Fukienese, and he noted that among people native of that region, the common appellation for foreigners tends to be "big nose", as in "Hey, look at the big nose over there." With this in mind, we gathered a group of westerners familiar with this dialect together, and asked them what sort of remarks a Chinese who spoke Mandarin and his local dialect of Fukienese might make to a foreigner in the night market, or in a food stall, etc., which would evoke much laughter from the other Chinese in attendance.

I suggested one phrase for starters: "Hey, Mr. Big nose, I bet the size of your brain is inversely proportional to the size of your nose." All the experienced westerners in attendance agreed: "That is western humor, the Chinese would never say that."

"Never?" I queried.

"To put a number on it, I would say there is less than a 5% chance that a Chinese would make that remark, or any related remark which reflects that type of humor," one of them clarified.

"Considerably less than 5%, I would say," another member of the group commented.

Considering Chinese in general, and not any dialectial group in particular, I tried to offer another possibility: "I bet he drops his food everytime he tries to use chopsticks."

Everyone shook their heads, noting: "The Chinese do not talk like that."

As an even more extreme example I suggested that, when buying bananas, someone might make the disparaging remark: "Oh, he wants to eat bananas, just like a monkey."

"The Chinese eat bananas too, so they would never make that kind of comparison," several members of the group quickly stated.

I though it important to come up with some sort of categorical label, and we decided to call this type of remark "Belittling Humor", meaning that it is speaking slightingly of, or deprecating other people, or casting doubt on their intelligence. The consensus was "The Chinese do not engage in Belittling Humor."

Upon further reflection, we concluded that one major reason for this is that the Chinese consciousness is much more heavily influenced by the precepts of "humility" and "modesty". Additionally, the Chinese are group oriented, and not individually oriented. Thus they far less inclined to make a show of personal superiority by trying to "cut down" another person. [1]

What then are the type of remarks that would cause laughter among the Chinese, in referring to a foreigner? After more than an hour of discussion, we came up with the following possibilities:

1. "If I was that tall, I would bump my head everytime I got on the bus."
2. "If my waist was that big I do not know where I would buy a belt."
3. "If he were to speak English to me, I would not know what to say in reply."

---

[1]. In a similar fashion, the idea of "Well, we will see who gets the last laugh . . . ", as used in making practical jokes, appears essentially non-existent in the Chinese mentality.

4. "If he orders bread, I do not know what we will do, this shop only sells rice and noodles."

5. "If he wants a fork, I do not know what we will do, we only have chopsticks here."

No doubt most of these examples would not generate even a chuckle from the average westerner, however they serve as useful reference for us in understanding what types of comments will elicit laughter among Chinese in a marketplace or food shop situation.

While noting that the Chinese do not tend to engage in Belittling Humor, we must add the consideration that the Chinese are often very frank in their comments, thus reflecting a degree of naturalism in their speaking. However, such remarks do not carry the negative emotive content that they do in the west. Thus, the Chinese will often say that a foreigner is "fat", or "has a big nose", or "has big feet", etc. The intelligent foreigner will recognize these remarks are essentially neutral in their connotations. They are merely statements of fact: Compared to the average Chinese, "You are fat". Compared to the average Chinese, "Your nose is bigger", etc. The worse remark that the foreigner will hear in this category is "You have hair on your body just like a gorilla." Again, this reflects the reality that the Chinese have far less body hair than westerners. It is properly regarded as merely a statement of fact, bearing the same emotional overtones as the statement "You put sugar on your pineapple." (The Chinese sweet tooth tends to be far less developed than that of the westerners, thus they tend to have far fewer cavities. Most Chinese put salt on their pineapple.) Even though many Chinese will laugh, no ridicule is intended, and no rejoinder is necessary.

An interesting additional point in this regard is that it would make no difference if any foreigner could produce medical evidence that the average nose size of all westerners is not to any degree larger than that of the entire race of Chinese, including all ethnic Chinese subgroups. "Big nose" in this sense is not a scientific term, but only a handy catch-phrase, referring to something which other Chinese understand. In a similar fashion, many Chinese will look at a brown-haired, grey-eyed westerner and say that he is blonde-haired and blue-eyed, since this is their standard idiomatic description of westerners.

To return to the original premise of this section, the foreigners are well advised to frequently employ the combined technique of "smiling and nodding", since it is an ideal way of reacting to many situations that can be characterized as essentially innocent encounters.

Politeness Taken To Extremes

Another technique that many westerners fail to employ to its full advantage is the "Excessive Politeness Approach". Recognizing that the Chinese consider themselves a polite race, a useful technique in many encounters in the marketplace, or even on the street in potentially troublesome situations, is to try to be more polite than the Chinese are. This tends to make the Chinese feel uncomfortable, and so they will quickly try to improve their behavior, if only temporarily.

In this regard, the foreigner is well-advised to redefine his thinking of the meaning of the expression *dui bu chi* [a], which is generally translated as "I'm sorry" or "Excuse me". Unfortunately, the force of "I'm sorry" in English is that "I did something wrong", therefore I say "I'm sorry". This is not the force of the term *dui bu chi*, which has an essentially neutral connotation, and does not indicate that I am at fault. Indeed, the issue of who is at fault is not relevant to the use of this term. Hence, a better translation would perhaps be something closer to "Oh, my!" or "Pardon everybody!"

When bumping into people while entering or leaving a restaurant, when buying food in a crowded shop, stumbling over a child who has darted into your path, noticing that the elevator door has closed on someone accidently, when the other party has shown up late for a dinner appointment, or other similar situations, it is an excellent phrase to use.

Unconsciously Eliciting Negative Reaction from the Chinese

Many foreigners are worried that in some types of mealtime or other eating situations, some innocent gesture or remark may elicit a negative reaction from the Chinese, when of course this was not the intention. Some may ask: "If I speak a few words of Chinese, would it be possible that my host or the other Chinese guests might think I am patronizing them? After all, I do not speak more than a few sentences."

In the English dictionary we see that "patronizing" has several meanings, one of which is **to show favor or kindness in a condescending manner**. Again we may refer to our discussion of Belittling Humor above, and we realize that since the Chinese consciousness does not tend to generate remarks of this kind, so of course it does not tend to attach this type of adjectival description to another's remarks when they are heard. Of course we are well advised to avoid speaking in a patronizing manner, however at the same time it is unlikely that any of our comments will be interpreted in this way unintentionally.

Another foreigner mentioned that he had once visited a Chinese home before the New Year Holidays, and noticed that there was a strip of characters on the wall of the kitchen, read *sz ming zao jwun*. [b] On a table in front of this was a small dish with some candies. Upon inquiring about the significance of these items, his host said that the calligraphy and candy were part of a ritual observance and offering to the kitchen god, who traditionally went to report to the Jade Emperor (in the sky) on the 24th of the twelfth lunar month, and returned on the fourth day of the lunar New Year. The candy was to insure that his mouth would be sweetened, and only report good things about the goings on in the family during the year, so that the Emperor would be pleased with the report. "Doesn't that mean that the candy is something like a bribe?" the westerner said without thinking.

His host seemed puzzled at this remark, and after some thought he dismissed the entire matter by saying something to the effect "I am not sure of the exact purport, but anyway this is our custom."

---

a. 對不起　　b. 司命灶君

This and certain other incidents often catch the eyes of the foreigners as perhaps having more significance than the Chinese normally realize. As to whether certain acts are actually equivalent to giving bribes, we can only say that there seems to be no consensus on this among the Chinese populace, so until some more definite determination can be made, it is perhaps better to downplay such analysis, lest offense be taken.

Other areas where foreigners may wish to take care in order to avoid potential "negative reaction" over the mealtable, or in the kitchen, are discussed below.

## Difficulties and Solutions

Difficulty: Before deciding on which restaurant to go to, my host has asked me if I want to eat Chinese or Western food. Will offense be taken if I do not reply "Chinese food"? I am, after all, in China.

Solution: The Chinese take no offense if the westerner wants to go to a western restaurant. Since the guest is generally considered most important, his preference will usually be honored.

In deciding on which kind of restaurant to patronize, you might be wise to consider what kind of food you want to eat, and justify your choice on that basis. For steak, a western restaurant would be preferable, but for seafood a Chinese, or a Japanese restaurant would probably be better. If you are accustomed to drinking cocktails before your meal, ordering wines and other western liquors with your meal, or having cake, pie, or other similar dessert after the meal, you should realize that these will probably not be available in a Chinese restaurant. Chinese have their own brands of alcoholic beverages which may be ordered however. For dessert the Chinese generally have fruit, and occasionally some sweet rice concoction, or sweet buns.

D: I do not like being forced to toast every drink with my Chinese friends, since I am usually moderate my intake of liquor. How can I avoid giving offense?

S: Unfortunately, the Chinese custom is to toast every drink. With traditional Chinese, there seems to be no middle road here, in that the Chinese will generally not agree to you setting a limit on your own intake of liquor, unless it is a very formal occasion and the manners in use are more "westernized". The rule seems to be "If you start drinking, you have to continue drinking," until the group decides to stop. You may gauge the possibility of getting into such a situation by noting the westernization, and level of western language skills, among the people with which you are associating. If they are essentially non westernized, you can expect that your pleas for moderation will go unheard. You might be best advised to not start drinking, perhaps by complaining of a liver ailment, intestinal inflammation, or other malady, and citing "doctor's orders". You may ask for tea, orange juice, or some other fruit juice. If you have begun drinking and wish to stop, it is admissible to turn over your glass when it is empty, or to hide it.

D: Often when I order carbonated drinks, beer, or other beverages and specify that they should be cold, they are not. When I point this out to the waiter he sometimes maintains that the drinks are indeed cold. What is the best way to handle this?

S: The Chinese are not accustomed to arguing over issues of fact. It would be best to ask for the waiter to "exchange" another colder bottle, and if that is still not satisfactory, to ask for ice cubes.

D: I am not adequately practiced at the art of using chopsticks. What should I do to avoid embarrassing myself or my host?

S: In most of the larger and fancier Chinese restaurants, forks and spoons are available. Chinese do not generally consider it laughable or unusual for a foreigner to ask for these in such an establishment. In regard to chopsticks, you should ask your host to show you the proper grip, and might want to practice when you get back to your room.

D: What should I do if I drop a chopstick on the floor?

S: Ask for a new pair.

D: Is there any proscription against holding chopsticks in my left hand? I am left handed.

S: The Chinese consider this unusual, but they rarely frown on it.

D: My hands do occasionally get greasy in a Chinese restaurant, and often I am not provided with any napkin. Will I be considered uncivilized if I point this out to my host?

S: In a Chinese restaurant it is permissible to get out your handkerchief when you have not been given a napkin or wet towel. Chinese are generally taught from childhood to carry toilet-paper with them wherever they go, and the tourist or other foreign resident is advised to do the same. It is also permissible to ask your host for a napkin, and he/she will most certainly figure out some way to supply it. No offense will be taken.

In high-class restaurants in the west, if it is necessary to leave one's seat, placing the napkin on the seat indicates "I am coming back", whereas placing the napkin on the table means "I have to leave now and will not come back". Napkins have been introduced into China from the west, and we do not find that there is any established "napkin etiquette" of this sort.

D: I do not regard the Chinese practice of holding the rice bowl up to their lips and shovelling the rice into their mouths to be very attractive. I am unsure if there is another acceptable way for me to eat.

S: If you prefer to leave the bowl on the table, the rice may be eaten with a Chinese ceramic spoon, or metal spoon. The spoon may be held in the left or right hand. When holding the chopsticks in the right hand, it would be customary to hold the spoon in the left, and to push the spoon into the rice, helping the rice onto the spoon by use of the chopsticks. The Chinese can accept the sight of a foreigner eating this way, although it is unlikely they will follow suit.

D: When having soup, is there any rule as to which way I should move the spoon? In the west, moving the spoon away from oneself is considered most polite, and some hosts consider it rude not to do so.

S: The main point of the "move the soup spoon away from you" idea in the west is for the diner to present more of his countenance to those seated across the table, since conversation is encouraged. The Chinese however have no established etiquette on the "proper" movement of the soup spoon.

D: I have gone into a restaurant where my friends and I were the only customers. Is there any custom as to where I should sit in a situation like this?

S: There is no real established custom in this regard. You should pick a table big enough for all members of your party, or two adjoining-tables if you have more than can sit at one table.

D: And what about the other eventuality, where the restaurant is very crowded? Must I wait, or can I leave politely?

S: After entering the restaurant, if you feel it is too crowded, you may leave. Take note that in many parts of Asia, if several people are seated around a large table, and there are enough empty seats at the table for your group, it is alright for you to "share the table."

D: I have invited my foreign friends out to a Chinese restaurant for a meal, but I am really not an expert at making menu selections. What is the best procedure in this case so that I can order food without displaying my ignorance to the restaurant staff?

S: In any Chinese restaurant where you are ordering dishes, it is quite acceptable to ask the waiter/waitress or manager to make recommendations. If the food is on display in the live form (very common in seafood restaurants), you may make your selections of the food right there, and have the waiter suggest ways of cooking. If the kitchen is "open style", and within your field of vision, you may even walk over and look over the facilities.

D: Are their any particular fruits or other light desserts to be recommended after the meal? What sort of fruits do the Chinese prefer?

S: The Chinese enjoy a wide variety of fruits, many of which are relatively unknown in the west, such as the carambola, persimmon, wax apple, durian, longan, etc. In China, tomatoes are considered fruits, as they were in North America until the early 1900's [1]. You may order a large plate of mixed fruit after your dining, and feel free to specify any types which you do not care to be included. It would be pointless to ask for fortune cookies after a meal, since native Chinese have no idea what these are. Of all the melon varieties available, bitter melon would not be served after a meal, since it must be cooked (with fish or pork preferably).

D: Are there any precautions to be taken when eating steamed buns, dumplings, and cakes?

S: There are some types of steamed glutinous-rice dumplings, containing some sweet paste which has been heated to a high temperature, which give off no steam whatsoever. To avoid any possibility of injury to the mouth or throat, all steamed dumplings should be cut open before consumption, so that the interior may be inspected. In general, anything placed in the mouth which produces an unpleasant sensation should be spit

---

1. Tomatoes are believed to have originated in the highlands of South America near the equator. They were introduced to Europe in the mid-1500's.

out quickly onto one's plate or into one's spoon, and examined further. This is not considered impolite.

D: The Chinese do not debone their fish, chicken, and other meats before cooking. When eating Chinese food I am often left with bones in my mouth. What is the proper way to get rid of these?

S: The Chinese tend to spit bones, pieces of shell, seeds, etc. from their mouth directly onto the table(cloth). In fancier restaurants, they may spit them onto a separate small plate which is not being used for anything else at the moment. If you feel uncomfortable doing this, you may delicately spit them into a spoon, and dump the contents of the spoon in an appropriate dish, ashtray, potted plant, etc.

D: I am often asked by my Chinese host to take some items that I do not eat, such as "Here would you like to have this chicken head?" How can I avoid this problem and not insult or embarrass my host?

S: You should reply: "Thank you, but I would prefer a wing." (or leg, breast, etc.)

D: May chicken's feet or duck's feet be eaten with the fingers?

S: We feel confident in stating that if you feel comfortable eating these with your fingers, it is highly unlikely the Chinese will object. After all, that is the way they eat them.

D: My husband has been a very finicky eater since his childhood. Although not a vegetarian, he does not eat chicken, duck, seafood, liver, kidneys, etc. We have been invited to attend a formal banquet at a Chinese seafood restaurant. What is the best procedure in this situation in order to avoid insulting our host?

S: We suggest that your husband eat first before going to the banquet. After you are seated and the dishes have begun coming you may inform your host and the other guests at the table that your husband recently had an operation for a gastric ulcer and is on a very restricted diet. You might add "He is not permitted to eat anything after 5:30 pm", or make some other excuse. Your husband is then free to participate in the mealtime environment, drink some tea, etc. No offense will be taken.

D: The Chinese, especially in offices, often serve tea in a clear glass with loose tealeaves. What is the technique for drinking this so that one's mouth does not get full of tealeaves?

S: Sorry, we have never been able to figure this one out, although we have been experimenting for over a decade. We do however feel that whatever tealeaves do get in the mouth may be spit in an appropriate receptacle, such as a clean ashtray, or other small dish. Enjoy your tea and try to make light of these minor inconveniences.

D: What is the custom as regards refills of coffee or tea in a restaurant?

S: The Chinese have traditionally imbibed tea, and coffee is only slowly coming into vogue. If your teapot is empty, a refill of hot water is generally free. Coffee is however calculated by the unit (cup, pitcher, etc.) and you pay for every unit, there are no free refills.

D: Our host has suggested ordering a dish called "The Ants Climb the Tree." I feel too embarrassed to mention I may not be able to stomach this.

S: Although this dish has a strange name, it contains no ants or tree branches. Actually the main component is thin clear noodles made from a type of green beans. In general, if you are embarrassed or hesitant in eating any dishes, you should tell your host that you would like to try them next time, and would prefer ordering something else this time.

D: In a seafood restaurant our Chinese hosts ordered a plate of small fried shrimps in the shell, all under one inch in length. How does one deal with these shrimps before placing them in the mouth?

S: With such small shrimp, the Chinese tend to eat head, shell, body and all. You may want to limit your intake to a dozen or so, to see how your stomach reacts. These may be eaten individually with the chopsticks, your spoon, or, as a last resort, with your fingers.

D: People at another table are making a lot of noise and it is disturbing my fellow diners and me.

S: Tell your host of your feelings, and ask him to inform the manager. If you have no host, inform the manager directly but discreetly. Avoid any confrontation with the people causing the disturbance. If none of these tactics yield a remedy, ask the server/waitress/waiter that your remaining food be bagged, and leave the premises.

D: I have enjoyed the meal and the discussion we have had with our Chinese friends. However I am now tired and wish to go back to my hotel room. Will I offend my host by making an early exit?

S: We think not. A simple excuse like "I did not sleep well last night and am rather tired, so I want to get back early." is usually acceptable, or you may change it to say that you were raised in the countryside and keep farmer's hours, in bed by 9:00 and up by 5:00. China being a predominately agricultural nation, this is quickly comprehended. Claiming that you have to get up early the next morning to work on your paperwork or other notes is also an excellent excuse, even if you plan to go to a disco later.

General Discussion and Free Talking with Newly Acquainted Chinese Friends

D: I am unaware of what jokes may be appropriately played on April 1st. For example, if I send out engraved invitations to a banquet to be held at 6:30 pm in the "Mirage Room" of a leading hotel in the city, would this be considered good clean fun?

S: Although there is occasionally some reportage of various shenanigans which go on in western countries on April Fools' Day, this holiday is essentially unknown in China. We suggest saving your humor for your western friends and associates.

D: The Chinese often tend to ask personal questions like "How much is your salary every month?" What is the best way to reply to this and not cause problems?

S: In the west this sort of question is not considered polite, however the Chinese do not see anything wrong with it. You might try making a roundabout reply such as: "I make more than some people but less than others," or "I make just enough for my family's needs." Any other similar statement would be equally acceptable. In response to "How much did you pay for your suit?", you might say "It was a gift." If the Chinese then ask you to contact the friend who gave this item to you, in order to ask about the price, you might say "He moved to Brazil and I do not have his new address." (Refer to comments on indirect communication later in this volume.)

D: When talking about parents, are there any special considerations?

S: The Chinese consider it immoral to disobey parents, and such statements as "I decided to do it this way, even though my parents objected" are usually best avoided when talking about one's actions. It would be more proper to say "I decided to do it this way" and leave off any mention of your parents' feelings. If you were to be asked specifically in this instance, you could reply: "My parents let me decide it for myself." The traditional Chinese conception is that parents belong with their children in sickness and in health. It would therefore be preferable to say "My parents are retired" rather than to say "My parents are in a nursing home."

D: Are there any special considerations when talking about marriage?

S: The Chinese will often ask if you are married. If you are married this presents no problems, and a simple yes answer is adequate. You might also want to add some details about your spouse, children, etc.

If you are not married, the Chinese will generally ask if you have a girlfriend/boyfriend. In this case it is better to say "Yes" or "Yes, I have one" rather than giving the specific number. The traditional Chinese moral conception seemingly does not approve of "playing the field" before marriage, and a statement like "I date four boys regularly" or "I have three girlfriends" is frowned upon by many.

D: A Chinese girl was pointed out to me, and I was asked to judge whether she was pretty or not. Are there any taboos here?

S: The Chinese are rarely interested in your analysis of something like beauty, efficiency, cleanliness, etc. In this case it would generally be pointless to analyze the girl's face, figure, legs, and specify your views on each. A simple statement like: "Yes, I think she is pretty" will suffice.

D: What should I be aware of when the discussion turns to political issues?

S: It is best to state your views in a neutral fashion. Avoid criticizing the government, until you can gauge from your friends remarks whether *they* are prone to take a critical stance on any issues. Oftentimes many Chinese will be quite uncomfortable about hearing any criticism of their government. It may also be true that criticism made by a Chinese person would be felt to be acceptable and proper, but the same criticism spoken by a westerner would be considered improper.

D: What are the limits on telling jokes with sexual overtones?

S: In general, and in mixed company, even jokes which are suitable for telling in the west are rarely suitable for telling in China. Such jokes fall into many categories, two of the main ones are (1) plays on words, double entendres, (2) funny situations and comparisons.

Of the former type is the story of a Mrs. Wong who decided to take a trip to the U.S.A.Mr. Wong told her to have a good time and be sure to hurry home. He was quite surprised when she had not returned after nearly a year, and went to the United States to find her. When he finally located her, she was living in a suburb of a large city, and nursing her newly born caucasian-appearing child that had brown hair and blue eyes. Mr. Wong was startled at this, and tried to explain in his broken English: "Two Wongs don't make a white!" To which his wife replied: "Purely occidental." Since the Chinese would have to have an absolutely top-notch command of colloquial English to understand such double meanings as these, this kind of joke is essentially useless. Additionally, the connotation of sexual promiscuity is unacceptable and immoral in their eyes.

We recall another joke whose punch line was "Your son resembles the mailman much more than he does your father!" The connotation here is also unmentionable in proper Chinese social relations.

A third joke went something like this: "The rooster at the bird farm had been sick for several weeks, and had just returned to his flock of hens. When he set out for a stroll after doing his cock-a-doodle-do at sunrise, he little realized that in fact his first day back was Easter morning. Seeing an abundance of colored eggs scattered around the yard, and even inside and outside the hen house, he quickly sized up the stituation, took a gun, went out and shot the peacock." Some knowledge of western customs as regards the observance of Easter is necessary to understand this type of witticism, however since it talks of animals in a rather innocent fashion it does appear more acceptable than the average run of the mill off-color joke. Whether or not it gets a laugh will depend on the audience.

We should remember that even in terms of such a basic thing as "what is natural", there is disagreement between the Chinese and the Westerners, because the Chinese cannot accept that nakedness of the human body is natural. Jokes about nudist colonies are therefore inadvisable in mixed company.

# Chapter 2  Food and Language

Whether or not the foreigner retains a western eating style preference is something that each individual will have to decide for himself. In any event it is most unlikely that the westerners will be able to immediately change their language and speech habits upon arrival in China, and so they should be aware of potential difficulties that await them in written and oral communication at the meal table, in the kitchen, when purchasing foods and beverages, or when alluding to various related items in their speech.

### Language and Expressions Referring to Food Items
### Categories of Confusion

In terms of eating, there are many idiomatic phrases which are used by the foreigners which will not commonly be understood by Chinese speaking people. For example, among westerners who like to raise their own vegetables, or other types of plants, there is often talk of some person having "a green thumb". The Chinese have words for "green" and "thumb", yet the expression "a green thumb" does not exist in the Chinese language. If translated word-for-word, it would not be understood by the average Chinese person, and in fact even many Chinese with quite a good command of conversational English are unaware of its true meaning.

The number of such assumedly "conceptually simple" idioms or expressions which we use in English, and which would not readily be understood by the Chinese citizenry is quite large. From the Asian point of view, idioms such as "Changing the soup but not changing the medicine" [a], "With the head of a tiger but the tail of a snake" [b], "A cupful of water, a cartful of firewood" [c], etc. are regarded as conceptually simple, yet they are not readily recognized by the westerner. A listing and analysis of such

---

a. 換湯不換藥　　b. 虎頭蛇尾　　c. 杯水車薪

"mutually unintelligible" idioms is an excellent research topic for the serious language student, although being rather beyond the scope of this text. However, it will still be of benefit for us to consider a few interesting idioms or phrases that are common sources of confusion. Some of these are not understood, while others are problematic in that they are misunderstood, thus resulting in unclear or mixed-up interpretation.

The following will be of concern to any westerner who is involved in cross cultural communication and dealing with foods, beverages, and related terms, whether in written or oral form. When speaking to Chinese who have above average English language abilities, some confusion may be generated in any of these areas where differences, unknowns, undifferentiations, non-connotations, and other problems are noted. If one's remarks are to be formulated for translation into Chinese, special attention should be given any and all forms of speech or idiom.

## COLORS

As a starting point we may consider the entire issue of colors in relation to food, beverages, table settings, eating expressions, and related concerns. The following similarities and differences are noteworthy —

**White:** Sugar, flour, egg white, and salt are all considered to be white. "Egg white" is used as the word for protein. "White vegetable" is cabbage.

"White wine" is a western conception, although in some places in China these types of wines, either imported products or Chinese versions, are gaining popularity. Some provinces have so-called "white liquor" that could easily be confused with this, and this liquor does in fact correspond to what some westerners call "white lightning". (The Chinese lack this latter appellation however.)

Many Chinese are not aware of what is meant when the foreigner orders chicken and specifies a preference for "white meat" or "dark meat". The term "breast meat" may be used as a substitute for white meat in this situation.

The Chinese may use "white" as a substitute for transparent. Thus, "white boiled water" is clear boiled water, and "white vinegar" is plain vinegar. More inexactly, some Chinese may describe something silver, such as silverware, as white. Both the words for "transparent" and "silver" do exist in Chinese however.

**Brown:** Brownies are American snack items, and there is no equivalent in Chinese cooking.

The Chinese refer to brown rice as being rough or unpolished, and rarely as being "brown". Brown rice [a] is not available in 98% of Chinese restaurants, mainly because the Chinese have a decided taste preference for white rice.

The Chinese use both "tea color" and "coffee color" as synonyms for brown, although the former may be a lighter shade. "Rice color" is generally used to mean tan or very light brown color, and not white as the foreigner might expect.

---

a. 糙米

There is some crossover in English and Chinese between brown and black: what the westerners refer to as brown bread the Chinese call black bread. Although there is a difference between the quality and consistency of brown sugar in China and the USA, nevertheless the Chinese tend to refer to it as "black sugar".

**Green:** The reference to unripe fruit as being "green" is not widely made in Mandarin, although it does exist in some dialects.

The Chinese call a greenhouse a "warm room".

No Chinese mythology has ever been uncovered which suggested that the moon or any of the planets in our solar system were made of "green cheese".

The reference to an inexperienced person, beginner, or novice as being a "greenhorn" is not a Chinese idea.

**Red:** There are several types of edible red beans in China.

Red pepper is widely available, but the Chinese in some provinces use more of it in their cooking than others.

"Red wine", as known in the west, is recognized by those Chinese with some experience in foreign wining and dining. Some local Chinese products may also be commonly referred to as "red wine" in some provinces, and may or may not be made from grapes.

There is some crossover in English and Chinese between red and black: what the westerners call black tea the Chinese call red tea. Of course most of the tea shops which deal with foreigners are aware of this.

In English the term "red herring" may figuratively refer to something used to confuse, or to divert attention from something else. This is a truly unknown expression in China, although the concept (i.e., a diversionary tactic) is not at all unknown.

To refer to someone who is 1) embarrassed, or 2) getting drunk, as "red in the face" [a] is well understood in Chinese.

**Black:** Black beer is generally imported from Germany.

Also see "Black Sheep" below.

**Silver:** The westerners tend to use "silverware" as synonymous with "knife, fork, and spoon", even when these items are made of stainless steel. The Chinese have a more literal idea of silverware, and view it as referring to ornaments, decorations, or other objects actually made of silver. "Silver Building" in the Chinese conception is a jewelry store.

Westerners use the expression "born with a silver spoon in his mouth" to indicate someone who was born into a very wealthy household. Silver eating implements suggest something different to the Chinese mind however. Silver chopsticks may be used to taste-test food for its safety—if the food contains poison, the chopsticks will change color.

**Yellow:** The Chinese refer to soybeans as "yellow beans".

---

a. 臉紅

Cucumber has several appellations, one of which is "yellow melon".

The term "yellow cow" may refer to a common type of Chinese cow, or its beef, but also often refers to "scalper", the person who sells tickets to movies, sporting games, or other events at inflated prices.

DIFFERENTIATIONS AND UNDIFFERENTIATIONS

I. Everyday Food Items

There are a number of food items which are differentiated in English, but are not differentiated in Chinese, or are otherwise commonly confused. For example, many people consider goat's meat and sheep's meat (mutton) as referring to different things, however in Chinese the words for these are the same [a]. Similarly, the expressions for goat's milk and sheep's milk are the same [b]. Thus if a westerner wanted to refer to one of these as opposed to the other, he would want to double-check that his translated remarks were being adequately explained, or accompanying pictures drawn, to exactly get across his meaning.[1]

Such mix-ups may occur with other items or products as well. Thus, in order to promote harmony in our dealings, if we requested that a Chinese get one thing for us, and the person came back with something else, before getting overly frustrated we might want to first examine the possibility that the distinction between these two items is not a clear one in the Chinese language.

The food items below may cause difficulties for us in two different ways: 1) they tend to be undifferentiated when translated into Chinese, thus extra explanation or illustration is most likely required, and 2) Chinese individuals speaking English will commonly confuse these items. The reader may ask his Chinese friends for further explanation as the need arises.

\* Cookies and Crackers. The Chinese terminology for these is the same. In actual use, the adjectives "sweet" and "salty" tend to be added to this expression to differentiate the former from the latter. This rather limited ability to distinguish these two types of items often results in poor communication. The phrase "a real smart cookie", indicating a person who is very clever, does not exist in Chinese.

\* Snacks and Desserts. The essential generality of these terms may lead to confusion when dealing with a populace whose eating habits are highly non-westernized. It is true that even in the western idea, the range of meaning covered by these two terms may overlap to some extent, nevertheless we would rarely consider potato chips, popcorn, or pretzels to be dessert items. An additional complication is that in many Chinese provinces there are a wide variety of local snack/dessert items available, such as various types of dried fruits and seeds, and many of these may be unknown in western countries.

---

a. 羊肉    b. 羊奶

1. The words for sheep 綿羊 and goat 山羊 are (arguably) different, but both are commonly called 羊 .

* Turnip, Radish, and Carrot. These are commonly called by the same name in Mandarin, and are all considered carrots. A westerner might suspect that by adding a color designation, some differentiation could be obtained: white carrot, red carrot, orange carrot. Some problems arise with these appellations however. The Chinese have several types of white carrots which may not exactly be equivalent to turnips. Red carrot is simply a synonym for carrot, and the term "orange carrot" does not exist. Some Chinese refer to beets as "purple carrots", or sometimes as "sweet vegetable". (Sugar is made from beets.)

* Dates and Prunes. The distinction in Chinese is essentially unclear.

* Buffalo, Bison, and Wild Cow. The buffalo is native to North America. Its meat is now seldom served in restaurants even there, however it is interesting to note that there is no word in Chinese for buffalo. The inexact term "wild cow" tends to be used instead, and this can lead to confusion. Water buffalo is rendered as "water cow".

* Nuts. Chinese has no commonly understood general term for "nuts", although there are names for many specific nuts. The expression "You are nuts", translated word-for-word, is unknown.

* Raisins and dried grapes. The Chinese language only refers to these as dried grapes, there is no separate and distinct term for "raisins".

* Candy and Sugar. Although arguably existing as different words in Chinese, these are often mixed up.

* Butter and Cheese. These items are not part of a typical Chinese diet. Outside of those with long experience in eating western menu items, many Chinese do not understand the difference, and may confuse one for the other. Due to this confusion, an idiom such as "like a hot knife slicing through butter" may not be readily understood. Margarine is also a little known item outside of food shops selling western products. Cream and butter may also be difficult to distinguish in some usages, such as between "fresh cream cake", "fresh butter cake", etc. Cottage cheese is a western dairy item for which we find no equivalent in the Chinese diet, (although the Mongolians do consume some similar items), and indeed most Chinese find it unpalatable.

* Wine and liquor. Wine is the fermented juice of grapes or some types of fruit, whereas liquor is more commonly made from grain, sugarcane, etc., and through a distilling process. However the Chinese tend to use these words interchangeably.[1] The term "liqueur" is unknown to many.

* Beans. The Chinese have many kinds of green, red, black, and other beans, many of which are uncommon in the west, and do not correspond to the beans commonly called by these names in the westerners' home environment. Many Chinese will carry their color appellations over into English, as when they call soybeans "yellow beans", and some confusion may be thus generated.

---

1. Both are called 酒.

* Lemon and Lime. The small greenish-yellow fruit called lime is unknown in many Chinese provinces. A handy substitute is an unripe (green) lemon.

* Lemon juice and Lemonade. These are not equivalent in English, since lemonade has been sweetened and is considerably less sour. In Chinese, both may be referred to as lemon juice, although sometimes the former is noted as "original lemon juice" to distinguish it from the latter.

* Juice vs. drink. Technically speaking, pineapple juice should be primarily pure juice with very little else (especially water) added. Pineapple drink may contain a large portion of water. Guava juice, orange juice, mango juice, etc., ideally should be nearly pure juice, and if water is added to cut the percentage of juice, the resulting product should be labelled "drink". The Chinese language tends to call pure juice "original juice", while drink (i.e., with water added) is just called "juice". This usage is frequently carried over into English by Chinese restaurant personnel and on translated menus.

|  | English nomenclature | Chinese nomenclature |
|---|---|---|
|  | lemon juice | (original) lemon juice |
|  | lemonade | lemon juice |
| in general: | juice | (original) juice, or (pure) juice |
|  | drink | juice |

II. Grammatical Bias

A western nutritionist had a copy of his lecture translated into Mandarin. In it he referred to the fact that we should "Eat three times a day", and discussed the four food groups, paying special care to outline the vitamin and mineral requirements of growing children. Upon returning to the United States, he showed the translated copy of his lecture to an overseas Chinese. The Chinese said: "I can see that you were profoundly influenced by your stay in China. Now, even you agree that we should 'Eat rice three times a day.' " The nutritionist was surprised that his remarks had been "translated" in this way, but at that point there was little he could do about it.

In referring to "Eating" and "Cooking", the Chinese language has a grammatical bias, in that these terms tend to be translated into Chinese as "Eating Rice" and "Cooking Rice". In the same manner, breakfast, lunch, and dinner may be commonly translated as "Morning Rice", "Noon Rice", and "Evening Rice". (In some provinces, the local food staple, such as "noodles", may be the preferred term.) If this is not the meaning intended, special care should be taken, and the words "food" or "meal" subsitituted for "rice" as necessary. Many Chinese Christians frequently mention that Jesus recommended rice in our daily diets; for justification they point to the New Testament verse which says "Man shall not live by bread alone."

Further on this topic, we know that in everyday encounters, a typical Chinese greeting in the Chinese language tends to be "Have you eaten your fill?" or "Have you eaten?"

Many Chinese will even greet each other by saying "Have you eaten rice?" This brings to mind the story of two foreigners who had just begun their Chinese studies. Upon hearing this question for the first time, one replied: "No, I had noodles." The other person said: "No, I had hamburgers."

These types of replies struck the Chinese as very strange, although the foreigners assumed that they were adhering to the dictates of correctness, in keeping with the facts. Obviously, they were unaware of the Chinese grammatical bias, which results in the Chinese using some common food and beverage terms in very unspecific ways. Hence "tea" primarily refers to "tea", but may refer to "water", and vice-versa. "Rice" primarily refers to "rice", but may refer to "noodles", or to "steamed rolls", and even perhaps to "hamburgers", or anything else with which one may fill his stomach. This is especially true in the greeting "Have you eaten rice?", in which rice is being used in a very unspecific sense. In the sentence, "Do you want to eat rice or noodles?" it is being used much more exactly. In any case, the foreigner may find it desirable in many situations to adhere more closely to his own way of expression, and avoid vague usages of the word "rice" in his own speaking, or in his translated remarks.

In terms of referring to the grain itself, the Chinese language differentiates very clearly, and separate expressions for "rice" are used depending on whether it is on the stalk, off the stalk, hulled, unhulled, uncooked, cooked. Obviously, some of these are edible, some are not yet edible. In addition, the Chinese commonly distinguish between different varieties of rice. Thus, to the Chinese mind, the individual word "rice" as used in English is vague and unclear.

We note that the term "Peanut Rice" [a] rarely refers to a combination of peanuts and rice; most commonly it is a synonym for shelled peanuts. "Rice barrel" [b] does not refer to someone who has a preference for having rice with every meal, but rather to someone who is stupid, lazy, etc. "Rice paper" may arguably be divided into two kinds: What the westerners call "rice paper" (used in art) is more commonly made from the pith of certain plants, the bark of trees, or various leaf fibers, and not necessarily from straw of the rice grass, thus it is largely unrelated to rice in the Chinese conception. Another kind of "rice paper" which is pressed from glutinous rice may be used to wrap some Chinese pastries, and is edible. "Rice milk" [c] may refer to a white liquid obtained by boiling rice; "Peanut rice milk" [d] may refer to this beverage with peanut paste or other flavoring added.

III. Eating vs. Drinking

Commenting further on the word "eat", in Chinese the range of meaning is quite broad, and tends to include the idea of "drink", (although not vice-versa). In a fruit juice shop, a Chinese may ask a westerner: "Which kind do you want to eat?" Addi-

---

a. 花生米　　b. 飯桶　　c. 米漿　　d. 花生米漿

tionally, "eat" often includes the idea of "chew" as in "Do you want to eat some gum?" In some Chinese dialects, "eat" is indistinguished from "smoke", and the local people may ask "Do you want to eat a cigarette?" The Chinese use the verb "eat" in speaking of "medicine", as when someone asks "Did you eat your medicine yet?" This sounds rather strange in English, and "take" is generally substituted. In a similar fashion, "drink" is used in speaking of "soup", as "Do you want to drink your soup now?" English is perhaps more comfortable with "have".

In a restaurant or bar, the idea of free drinks being "on the house" is not directly translatable, more easily understood would be "the boss treats", or "it is free".

The difference between "soft water" and "hard water" is recognized by many Chinese, however "soft drinks" are not considered soft.

The Chinese do have the expression "to eat one's words" [a], however the meaning is **1) to break one's agreement, 2) not to fulfill one's promise**. Some examples would be:

1. He promised to meet me for dinner at 6:30 but he ate his words.
2. She agreed to bring that cookbook over for me to look at today but she ate her words.
3. You often eat your words, so I do not want to be your friend.
4. What about everything you said before, have you eaten all those words?

This is generally different from the English usage of "to eat one's words" denoting **1) to retract something said earlier, 2) to admit being wrong in something said previously**. An example: Albert said that the world's record for eating bananas was 38 in two minutes, but when we got out the Guinness book he had to eat his words. This kind of usage does not correspond to the Chinese use of the expression, and a substitute such as "to admit he made a mistake", "to retract his statement", etc. is perhaps more suitable for clarity in cross-cultural communication.

IV. Units of Measurement

In regard to food and beverages, many units of measurement or volume which are clear and distinct entities in English tend to be much less clearly separated in Chinese. Even when separate words exist, in actual use the Chinese may confuse them. An example of this is when someone asks for a bottle of beer and is given a can, even though the shop, or bar, has both bottles and cans of beer for sale.

No doubt one reason for this type of confusion is the influence of many regional dialects, in which these units are not commonly differentiated. Many Chinese who speak these dialects carry this rather haphazard usage over into Mandarin. The following listing includes most of the terms which might cause confusion: (D) indicates the terms actually exist as different words in Mandarin, although still commonly confused, (S) indicates the words are the same in Mandarin, and thus probably always confused, (A) indicates

---

a. 食言

a great deal of ambiguity between the two terms.
* Bottle, Can (D)
* Bottle, Carton (D) (carton of milk, carton of juice, etc.)
* Bottle, Jar (A)
* Bottle, Jug (S)
* Carton, Can (D)
* Pitcher, Teapot, Kettle (A)
* Glass, Mug (S)
* Glass, Cup (A)
* Barrel, Keg, Vat (A)
* Bag, Sack, Packet (S)
* Pail, Bucket (S)
* Ball, Spoon (in terms of ice-cream, one of these terms must be used. Chinese has no separate word for "scoop".) The expression for "cone" [a] does exist in a geometrical sense, but this is rarely used in speaking of ice-cream, hence indicating a certain bias away from preciseness.

When dealing with measurements in recipes, the Chinese do not talk of "tablespoons" or "Teaspoons", but rather in terms of a Chinese "soup-spoon" and a Chinese "bowl" (referring to a ricebowl).

We note that "bottleneck" 瓶頸 in both the literal and figurative senses does exist in the Chinese language.

## CONNOTATIONS AND NON-CONNOTATIONS

Many expressions containing food words have extra connotations in English which do not exist in Chinese, hence we say they are "unknown" in the Chinese language. This means that: 1) if translated word-for-word into Chinese they would not be understandable, 2) spoken or written in English their meaning is quite frequently lost even on many Chinese people who possess above average English language skills, 3) the imagery which they call to mind means little or nothing in the Chinese conception, 4) the experienced translator will have to convert these to more simple wording, or use an equivalent definition when translating into Chinese, and much of the symbolism, metaphor, or flavor may be lost, 5) when the meaning of any one of these phrases is explained to Chinese people, they will usually forget it over a period of a few days or weeks; rarely will it stay and form a permanent part of their mental processes.

Many possible entries into a listing of this type would be considered by the intelligent foreigner as "highly unlikely" to exist in Chinese due to the differing diets of westerners. Since bacon is a western food item, and Chinese style pig-butchering does not make allowance for any portion to be set aside and later cured into bacon, we would not expect the expression "to bring home the bacon" to be readily understandable. Bread is not a staple of the Chinaman's diet, so we would not expect any idiomatic usages

a. 圓錐

of this, such as "to know on which side one's bread is buttered" to be understood. Recalling that Chinese has no commonly used word for nuts, we would no† expect the expressions "in a nutshell" or "a hard nut to crack" to exist in Chinese. Likewise, other references to western food items, eating habits, table settings, or highly colloquial metaphors, similes, etc. related to these would similarly fall into this category of being "unknown". (A more exact explanation of of these differences is given in the **Unknown and Unadopted** essay in Chapter 9.)

Idiomatic adjectival descriptions are often difficult to translate. Consider the following, all except for two of which are unknown in Chinese in a word-for-word translation:

| selected vocabulary | English language expression or figurative usage |
|---|---|
| cool | cool as a cucumber |
| hot | a real "hot potato" |
| slow | slow as molasses in January |
|  | slow as a snail |
| fast | fast as lightning |
| pretty | a peaches and cream complexion |
| ugly | so ugly I wanted to throw up |
| grouchy, bad-tempered | a crab, crabby |
| happy | happy as a meadowlark |
| short & thin | "a shrimp" |
| tall & thin | a string bean |
| fat | fat as a pig |
| easy | easy as pie |
|  | a piece of cake |
|  | like shooting fish in a barrel |
|  | easy as falling off a log |
| difficult | like finding a needle in a haystack |
|  | like pulling teeth |

Our choices for the two idioms above which would be easily understood by the Chinese are "fast as lightning" and "slow as a snail". A third choice would be "fat as a pig", however China has historically known times of shortage and famine, so one would be best to check the condition of the local pigs before carelessly using this one. The expression "a hot potato" [a] seems to be coming into the Chinese language, or is quickly understood after simple explanation. Regarding the other expressions on our list, these are mostly idiomatic or slang usage, and for maximum clarity we would often be well advised to avoid them, or find appropriate substitutes in order to facilitate communication. Otherwise, we must explain our choice of words carefully. (Note: We have not included the expression "big as an elephant", because even though it is readily understood, in the modern age it is often not an adequate comparison for things that are big.)

Some westerners have asked: "Are there related or equivalent expressions in Chinese to any of the above items on the right?" We could reply to this by noting that for "easy" the Chinese might say "As easy as turning over the palm of the hand." [b] For "difficult", they might say "like finding a needle on the bottom of the ocean." [c] For the other items, the related Chinese phraseology is more complex, or has a different range of applicability, and is comparatively difficult to render directly into English.

*English phraseology:* further examples are outlined below. Where word-for-word equivalencies exist in Chinese they are clearly stated and footnoted. Where they do not, we have abbreviated "unknown" as (U), and offer the reader some explanation, or alternate terminology for reference as appropriate.

*Chinese phraseology:* items of broad applicability which the foreigner may want to use are marked as [%]. Where alternate renderings of certain terms in this translation are possible, they are given in brackets, [mussel = clam], etc.

### FRUITS

**Lemon.** That new _____ I bought is a real lemon. (U).

**Apple of one's eye.** Used in regard to a relationship between 1) teacher and student, 2) boy and girl friends, 3) parents and children, there appears to be no handy Chinese equivalent, hence we regard this as (U).

**Upset the applecart.** (U).

**In apple pie order.** (Very orderly) (U).

**The bad apple spoils the barrel.** (U). This phrase appears to be a conspicious absence in the Chinese language, although "One smelly fish makes a pan of soup fishy" [d] may often be used as a close equivalent. [smelly = stinky, pan = pot] See additional comments under "Black Sheep" below.

---

a.棘手的問題:燙馬鈴薯」、「燙山芋」　b.易如反掌　c.如海底撈針

d.一條臭魚弄腥一鍋湯

**Bananas.** When he heard the news he went bananas. (U). He is the top banana around here. (U).

**Banana skins** (are slippery). Although there is no standard idiomatic phrase in Chinese to express this conception, some Chinese people appear aware of it, others not. Western movies, TV shows, and cartoons frequently use this ploy, and so many local people have been exposed to it during their viewing of foreign productions. To those to whom it is unfamiliar, there seems little need to question it, any more than they would question someone slipping on a mango peel, tomato peel, papaya peel, etc. If it happens, it happens.

**Banana.** (as a synonym for a certain part of the male anatomy) This appears widely understood. If bananas are purchased, it is perhaps inadvisable for a man to refer to them (or it) in front of others as "my banana".

[%] **Throw a peach, return a plum.** [a] This calls to mind the returning of a favor with a favor, or the exchange of gifts between friends.

[%] **A peach orchard beyond this world.** [b] A very peaceful, lovely place, without conflict, crime, etc.

[%] **Peach flower luck.** [c] Refers to a time when a man had good luck with the ladies, or was popular with them.

**Cherry.** (as a synonym for a certain part of the female anatomy) (U).

**Fruitcake.** Referring to the cake itself, "fruitcake" in Chinese is a much more general term, and refers to any type of cake with fruit in it, or on it. To say someone is a "fruitcake" in English seems to imply that they are mixed-up, or nuts, however in the Orient this expression carries no such overtones: fruitcake in this essentially slang usage is (U).

**Heard it through the grapevine.** (U).

**Cara piña.** (Spanish term, literally translated as "pineapple face", which refers to someone who has a rough, uneven, or pockmarked complexion) (U).

**Sour grapes.** [d] This is used in Chinese in the sense of **the grapes which one is not able to eat are regarded as sour, i.e. 1) something which cannot be had and is therefore scorned, or 2) something which was not gotten is therefore claimed to be of little or no value.** It is clearly related to jealousy. Some westerners use the expression "sour grapes" in other senses, however this usage does correspond to that found in Aesop's fables. Sentence examples:

1. I think Robert's new house is beautiful, but when I asked Laverne she said it was nothing great. I think she has the sour grapes mentality.

2. Annie got a scholarship to college, but the other people who applied and were turned down were heard to say: "Oh, that is a lousy college anyway." They are sour grapes.

3. Ronald built his company up from nothing, and now it is very big. Other people in the industry were heard to comment: "His company is very shaky", "His company may collapse at any time", "He uses dishonest methods in many of his business dealings", etc. I believe they are all sour grapes.

---

a.投桃報李　　b.世外桃源　　c.桃花運
d.酸葡萄

4. Peggy wanted to marry John, but later John got married to Susan. Peggy was heard to comment: "Actually, I think John would be a terrible husband and a lousy father." I think she has the sour grapes psychology.

In Chinese to say that someone is "eating vinegar"[a] also means that they are jealous. Carrying this usage over into English, many foreigners in China use the chemical terms "acetify" or "acetification" to denote when anyone becomes jealous — saying that he/she has acetified a particular situation. For example, a) a western girl goes out with a Chinese gentleman a few times. One night she goes with some girlfriends to a party and meets a western man whom she dances with and has an interesting discussion. A few days later when she mentions this to her Chinese gentleman friend, he becomes very irritated, and says that she should not have been with another man at a party. They quarrel. b) A resident of one community fixes up the exterior of his house so that it is the most beautiful house in the neighborhood. Other families see this and feel that he is trying to show off, so they cut off relations with him, and make some bad remarks about his character. c) A teacher in a local college is selected by the Ministry of Education for a special teaching award. When word of this gets out to other teachers in that department, they become very upset, and say that the award should have gone to someone else. In each of these instances, certain parties have acetified an otherwise inoccent situation.

**Acetify: 1) to change into vinegar. 2) to regard something as a cause, or source, of jealousy. 3) to become jealous.**

## POULTRY & EGGS

**Chicken.** Are you going to _____, or are you chicken? Chicken as a synonym for coward or cowardice is unknown in Chinese. Yellow as a synonym for coward is also unknown.

She is no **spring chicken.** (U).

Running around like **a chicken with its head cut off.** (U). The Chinese seldom kill chickens in this manner, so they are generally unaware of how chickens behave when decapitated.

**Chicken pox.** More commonly referred to in Chinese as "water pox".[b] [pox = smallpox]

**Henpecked.** (U). Generally rendered into Chinese as "afraid of his wife"[c], although this loses much of the true flavor of the expression.

[%] **Would rather be a chicken's mouth than a cow's behind.**[d] Said of the desire to hold an independent position where you are your own boss, rather than a high position in some organization where you are under the control of others, and have to follow their orders. [behind = rear end] This mentality is quite common in China. To use more colloquial English phrasing, this appears close to saying "would rather be a big frog in a little pond, than a little frog in a big pond."

[%] **A crane standing among chickens.**[e] Indicates someone who far surpasses everyone else in excellence; standing head and shoulders over others.

---

a.吃醋        b.水痘        c.怕老婆的or妻管嚴
d.寧爲雞口不爲牛後        e.鶴立雞群

**A wild goose chase.** (U). This is only said of actually physically chasing wild geese, and is not used in any wider sense.

**Your goose is cooked.** (U). The Chinese have several ways of cooking geese, however this expression has no wider range of applicability outside the kitchen.

[%] **Chicken feathers and garlic skins.** [a] Unimportant matters; trivialities; petty or trifling things.

She got **goose pimples** when she heard the noise. This is more commonly known as "chicken pimples" [b] in China.

[%] **Iron rooster.** [c] This refers to a fighting cock that is always ready for a battle, and can become infuriated easily. More broadly, it is used to describe a very argumentative, grouchy, touchy person who is hard to get along with.

He got a **goose-egg** on the test. The Chinese use the expression "duck-egg" [d] to refer to zero, not goose-egg.

**Putting all your eggs in one basket.** This would be interpreted literally, and is not given any wider, figurative applicability. However it is arguably equivalent to the Chinese expression "To bet all on a single throw" [e] in some circumstances.

You are a **bad egg**. This expression is known in Chinese, 坏蛋. However the meaning is stronger than in English, and probably closer to S.O.B. It is unsuitable for polite society.

You are a real **egg-head.** (U).

He really **laid an egg.** (indicating complete failure in a performance, speech, etc.) (U).

It's **hot enough to fry an egg on the sidewalk.** (U).

[%] **Selecting bones in a chicken egg.** [f] This is used to describe a person who is too picky, demanding, strict, etc. [selecting = picking out]

**Go suck eggs.** (U).

**A nest egg.** (referring to savings of money for use after retirement, or in an emergency) (U).

**Kill the goose that lays the golden eggs.** The story from which this expression has emerged appears widely known in China, since it is frequently included in translated collections of children's literature. The Chinese idiom "Kill the hen to get eggs" [g] also corresponds to it very closely, indicating a foolish act, or lack of farsightedness.

**A sitting duck.** (U). Chinese enjoy eating duck meat, and normally either raise their own ducks or buy them in the marketplace; duck-hunting (from which this expression has arisen) is not a widespread outdoor sport. In any event, this only refers to ducks that are actually sitting down, and has no wider applicability, such as indicating that one is "an easy mark", etc.

**Get all your ducks lined up in a row.** (U). Before going to court, many western lawyers involved in trademark infringement or other cases follow the classic admonition which

---

a.雞毛蒜皮　　b.雞皮疙瘩　　c.鐵公雞　　d.鴨蛋　　e.孤注一擲　　f.雞蛋裡挑骨頭
g.殺雞取卵

says "Get all your ducks lined up in a row." This is good advice, but difficult to translate literally.

**Like water off a duck's back.** (meaning without producing any effect) This is an idiom that is difficult to understand when spoken in Chinese, and many locals are unaware of the meaning even when they see it written down as *shuei gwo ya bei* [a], hence we regard it as (U).

**Good weather for ducks.** (A rainy day) (U).

I have **heard ducks fart underwater before.** (spoken of someone who makes idle boasts about his future plans or prospects) (U).

[%] **The well-cooked duck has flown away.** [b] This refers to an opportunity or other beneficial arrangement, often involving financial gain, which was felt to be nearly on the table, or in the bag, (prepared for our imminent "consumption"), and that now has been lost.

**Lame duck.** (U). Rarely used in anything but the strict literal sense.

[%] **Ducks listening to thunder.** [c] Used to describe people who cannot understand what is being said to them in a class, speech, public performance, etc. Such incomprehension is of course often due to the language barrier. This is stronger than the English "went over their heads".

[%] **Stuffing ducks style.** [d] This refers to a way of raising ducks, and is used in a broader sense to refer to educational methods which are "stuffing the students with whatever they need to pass examinations", hence relying more on memorization than analysis. Chinese educational methods certainly fall into this category, and the populace recognizes this. In contrast, western educational methods are perceived as "Prompting Mental-Development Style". [e]   [also rendered: Like stuffing ducks]

**Swan song.** (referring to the last of something) (U).

[%] **Thinking of eating swan's meat.** [f] Dreaming of obtaining impossible pleasures, or wanting to obtain something far beyond one's station in life.

He is **birdbrained.** (U).

**For the birds.** (indicating uselessness or lack of value) (U).

**Birds of a feather flock together.** Equal to the Chinese "Things of the same kind get together." [g]

**To kill two birds with one stone.** Directly translated this appears quite comprehensible, [h] and it is also very close to the Chinese "One arrow, two big birds." [i]

**A bird in the hand is worth two in the bush.** Although often quickly understood when explained [j], Chinese appears to have no close idiomatic equivalent.

[%] **A place where birds lay no eggs.** [k] A very desolate, remote, cheerless, uninhabited, lifeless region or area.

---

a.水過鴨背　　　　　b.煮熟的鴨子飛了　　c.鴨子聽雷
d.填鴨式　　　　　　e.啓發式　　　　　　f.想吃天鵝肉
g.物以類聚　　　　　h.一石兩鳥　　　　　i.一箭雙鵰
j.兩鳥在林，不如一鳥在手　　k.鳥不生蛋的地方

**In the catbird seat.** (in a position of power) (U).

I did it **for a lark.** (U).

**Turkey.** The slang use of "turkey" to refer to someone or something who is stupid or foolish is unknown in Chinese. Likewise, the statement that someone quit smoking or quit drugs "cold turkey" is unknown.

### SHEEP & GOATS

**Sheepish.** (Shy, awkward, embarrassed, timid, etc.) (U).

**Black sheep of the family.** The Chinese place a premium on good family relations, so this expression does not exist. "A horse that troubles the whole herd" [a] is a related Chinese phrase, albeit used in yet a broader and more extensive sense.

**A scapegoat.** This terminology is found in Chinese, 代罪羔羊, and hence is quickly understood.

[%] **A lamb going into the tiger's mouth.** [b] Going into a very dangerous situation unknowingly.

**Get someone's goat** (disturb someone, make them angry) (U).

[%] **Lead away the sheep in passing.** [c] This refers to an unpremediated theft. [sheep = goat]

[%] **To repair the pen after the sheep have escaped.** [d] This indicates that the action taken was too late to prevent the initial accident or loss. Future incidents of this type of problem will no doubt be avoided now that the necessary structural adjustments have been made, however the fact that the initial loss could have been prevented is something worthy of serious reflection.

**In like a lion, out like a lamb.** (U). The Chinese preference is to say "In like a dragon, out like a bug", [e] and this phrase is by no means limited to a discussion of the weather.

**That old goat.** (U). Reference to old people as "goats" is not understood in Chinese; reference to children as "kids" is also unknown.

### CATTLE

[%] **Playing the lute in front of an ox.** [f] To expose someone to a performance, exhibition, etc. or to speak to someone about something which he cannot appreciate. [lute = harp, ox = cow] (The focus of this idiom is *cannot appreciate*. Confer "Ducks listening to thunder", in which the focus is *cannot understand*.)

There seem to be many **sacred cows** around here. (U) Most sacred cows in China are not recognized as such by the populace, and we suspect that this is largely due to the fact that there is no colloquial expression or equivalency for this "sacred cow" idea in the Chinese language. Upon hearing this expression, most Chinese assume it is related to the specific Hindu notion that cows are sacred.

---

a.害群之馬　　　b.羊入虎口　　　　　　c.順手牽羊
d.亡羊補牢　　　e.進來像條龍，出去像條蟲　f.對牛談琴

[%] **Panting like a cow.** [a] This simply refers to being "out of breath", such as after running down the street, or up the stairs. In China cows traditionally worked very hard.

We are just sitting around **chewing the fat.** (U).

That is **a bunch of bull.** (U).

We have **a bull session in my house every night.** (U). Why don't you come over some time and **shoot the bull**? (U).

**A bull in a china shop.** (U).

**Take the bull by the horns.** (U).

**Bull's-eye** (of a target). (U). The Chinese more commonly refer to this as the "heart" [b] of the target, or simply the "center".

**Bull-headed.** Approximately equal to the Chinese "having a bull's temper." [c]

[%] **The newly born calf does not fear the tiger.** [d] Refers to inexperienced young people who are not afraid of dangers because they do not know how serious the dangers really are.

## OTHER MEATS

**Rabbit's foot.** (As a symbol of good luck) (U).

[%] **A cunning rabbit has three exits.** [e] Said of someone who makes elaborate precautions for self-protection, or is hard to capture, or pin down, because they are cunning, crafty, shrewd, etc. This expression has a negative emotive content. [exits = burrows]

[%] **Standing by the stump awaiting a rabbit.** [f] The person in this old story originally was able to capture a rabbit when the animal accidently ran into the stump and knocked itself unconsious. However, to continue to stand-by in this manner is to trust to dumb-luck repeatedly, to be stupid and unimaginative.

You are **full of baloney.** (U). To refer to someone who is acting up in front of a camera as "a ham" is also unknown.

[%] **Throwing meat buns at a dog.** [g] The implication of this phrase is "they go but they do not come back", and it is often used when speaking of lending money, to indicate that there appears little hope of repayment. If a Mr. Smith is asked if he approves of a loan to a particular person, and he does not, he need merely reply "It is like throwing meat buns at a dog."

The usage is not limited to money however, and indeed may refer to the loaning of any foods, liquids, etc. consumable items of value to another person, where there is essentially no hope of repayment. In a wider sense, it may refer to any input (e.g. investment of money or effort) which does not match with output (e.g. results).

**Stubborn as a mule.** The Chinese preference is to say "stubborn as a donkey." [h] It carries the additional implication of being stupid.

---

a. 氣喘如牛　　　　　b. 心or中心or靶心　　　　　c. 牛脾氣
d. 初生之犢不畏虎　　e. 狡兔三窟　　　　　　　　f. 守株待兔
g. 肉包子打狗　　　　h. 固執的像一頭驢or和驢一樣固執的

Stop the **horseplay.** (U). (Literally translated into Chinese, "horse play" *ma hsi*[a] is the term for "circus".)

Stop **horsing around.** (U).

**A horse of a different color.** (U).

[%] **The horse's hoof is exposed.**[b] To reveal one's true form, character; to leave gaps, loopholes, or inconsistencies in one's story. [hoof = foot, exposed = revealed]

I could **eat a horse.** (U). The Chinese might reply to this by saying "Oh, we did not cook that."

**Straight from the horse's mouth.** (U).

[%] **Patting the horse's bottom.**[c] Flattery. Another related phrase in Chinese is *Giving someone a high hat to wear,* which means "giving flattery". The person who has received this flattering, compliments, etc. and feels very good about it is said to be *wearing a high hat.*[d]

**Prince on a white horse.** This appears widely understood: 白馬王子 . However girls seem more attracted to the entire idea than boys.

To **eat like a horse.** (U).

**Stud.** (indicating a man who has amorous relations with many women) (U).

[%] **Neither a donkey nor a horse.**[e] A strange or grotesque thing, unlike anything one has seen before. This is often said in the realm of clothing styles, clothing design, art, or art objects, and also of any imitation or imitating done unsuccessfully or unrealistically. It clearly carries a negative connotation.

**Hold your horses!** (U). Only used in the strict literal sense.

[%] **Horse horse, tiger tiger.**[f] So-so; average or a bit better; nothing worth getting excited about. (The origin of this expression is unclear, but it is widely used in speaking of achievement, performance, quality, ability, and other concerns.)

**Get on your high horse.** (U). **Get down off your high horse.** (U).

**Look a gift horse in the mouth.** (U).

[%] **The head of an ox does not match the mouth of a horse.**[g] Said of anything irrelevant, not to the point, unconnected, incongruous. [ox = cow]

**Put the cart before the horse.** (U). With thousands of years of an agricultural society tradition, it is somewhat surprising that this idiom does not exist in Chinese. However the closest we can come is "the first and the last turn around."[h]

[%] **When the journey is long one knows the strength of the horse.**[i] A person (or organization's) true ability is only known by evaluating their performance over a significant period of time.

**A dark horse.** Generally equivalent to the Chinese "a black horse": 一匹黑馬 . This is frequently used in referring to people who win various contests, much to the surprise

---

a. 馬戲 or 馬戲團　　b. 露出馬脚　　c. 拍馬屁
d. 戴高帽子　　　　　e. 非驢非馬　　f. 馬馬虎虎
g. 牛頭不對馬嘴　　　h. 本末倒置　　i. 路遙知馬力

of others.

**Horse sense.** Although not directly translatable, the Chinese idiom "An old horse knows the way" [a] appears closely related to this, and describes someone who is experienced and capable of leading others wisely in a particular field.

[%] **Riding a horse, looking at the flowers.** [b] This indicates examination of a thing hurriedly, taking a fast look, doing a once over lightly. It may indicate that one has gained a superficial understanding as the result of cursory observation.

[%] **Pointing to a deer and calling it a horse.** [c] Stubbornly saying that black is white, or that one thing is something else.

**Beating a dead horse.** (U).

**Paper tiger.** This is widely understood: 紙老虎 .

[%] **Tiger's head, snake's tail.** [d] To the Chinese mind this suggests starting something with vigor but failing to see it through; a fine start and a poor finish.

[%] **Talking to a tiger about its skin.** [e] The man in this old story made a remark to the tiger to the effect "Your skin would make a nice warm rug." The tiger did not agree however, and became very angry. Hence this idiom suggests entering into a discussion with someone (or some organization) much more powerful than yourself, with the suggestion that they do something, or take some course of action, which will cause them harm (whether physical, financial, etc.)

[%] **Unsuccessfully drawing a tiger, looks like a dog.** [f] Trying to do something notable or worthwhile, but achieving a very bad result, perhaps resulting in a worse situation than existed originally.

[%] **To draw a snake and add feet.** [g] This indicates something done redundantly, or done with unnecessary embellishment, excess, or superfluousity.

**Kangaroo court.** (U).

**That old buzzard.** (U). Related to this, although weaker in force, is the Chinese "that old antique" *lau gu dong* [h] , indicating someone highly conservative.

## FISH AND SEAFOOD

**A big fish story.** (referring to exaggerated statements) (U). The Chinese are essentially modest, so the remarks they make or stories they tell rarely involve real boasting, unless the figure involved is some famous person in Chinese history or mythology. (Sometimes Chinese will state the facts in an overly favorable light, but we believe this is not real boasting, just indirectness.)

**Fishy. Smells fishy.** (speaking of something strange or suspicious) (U). This is only used in the strict literal sense of "having the smell of fish".

I have **other fish to fry.** (referring to other more important things to do) (U). Nor do the Chinese have any similar expressions such as "I have other rice to cook."

a.老馬識途　　b.走馬看花　　c.指鹿爲馬
d.虎頭蛇尾　　e.與虎謀皮　　f.畫虎不成反類犬
g.畫蛇添足　　h.老古董

**A school of fish.** (U). The Chinese merely speak of fish, dolphins, seals, etc. as travelling in a "group" [a] ; the use of "school" in this sense is unknown.

**A pretty kettle of fish.** (U).

**Like a fish out of water.** (suggesting **being unadapted, out of one's element, in unfamiliar surroundings**) Interestingly enough, in colloquial Chinese this expression is not used, (in literary Chinese there is a close equivalent [b] , although carrying stronger connotations of being in a difficult or dangerous situation, as opposed to merely being ill at ease.) Much more common is the reverse "like a fish getting into water" [c] : in one's element, in familiar surroundings, happy and contented.

**He drinks like a fish.** (U). The Chinese would say "He drinks like a cow." [d]

[%] **To fish by emptying the water of a pond.** [e] Suggests making a thorough but unwise exploitation; a foolish act, lacking farsightedness. [pond = lake]

**The fish that got away.** (indicating something which was captured or in-hand, and then escaped) (U). Slightly different is the Chinese "The fish that escaped the net" [f] , indicating a fish which was never in the net to begin with, but which we had wanted to capture.

**Like shooting fish in a barrel.** (very easy) (U).

**Fishing in troubled waters.** [g] General use of this expression in the west seems to be at some variance with the Chinese *huwn shwei mwo yu* [h] "Fishing in Muddy Waters": in Chinese this primarily indicates **being opportunistic, taking advantage of a situation, etc., during times of confusion.** Examples:

1. He wanted to fish in muddy waters, so he went in the burning building to help move people's belongings out, and seized the opportunity to steal many things.

2. Albert waited until there was a big crowd of people outside the theater between shows, some entering and some leaving, everybody pushing in every direction, and he was able to slip in without buying a ticket. He can really fish in muddy waters.

3. She spilled her shopping bags in front of that large display of imported merchandise, and when she picked everything up again she was able to take several items off the shelf without being noticed. She is an expert at fishing in muddy waters.

4. When the manager went out of the office Mary put away her papers and took out a comic book to read. She really likes to fish in muddy waters. (In this instance, the secondary meaning of "Fishing in Muddy Waters" is used, meaning **to be lazy, to kill time in unproductive activities, etc.**)

Note: Many dictionaries mistakenly equate "Fishing in troubled waters" with the Chinese "Fishing in muddy waters", and the reader should be aware that they are different.

---

a.群　　　　　　　b.涸轍之鮒　　　　c.如魚得水
d.牛飲　　　　　　e.竭澤而漁　　　　f.漏網之魚
g.觸犯敏感問題　　h.混水摸魚

[%] **Climbing a tree to seek fish.** [a] Refers to the attempt to get something by impossible means, or make a futile attempt.

[%] **A frog in a well.** [b] A person of very limited outlook or experience.

Will he **clam up**? (stop talking or refuse to make further comment) (U).

**Clams.** (as a synonym for money) (U).

[%] **A fight between the snipe and the mussel, the fisherman gets the benefit.** [c] An ancient story in China describes a snipe which saw a mussel sunning itself on the beach. When the snipe went to take a peck at this delicacy, the mussel closed its shell on the snipe's beak. At this point neither could move away. A little while later a fisherman came by and took both of them home to put in the pot for dinner. Hence this phrase refers to an argument that benefits a third party.  [mussel = clam]

[%] **Fishing for three days and taking two days to dry the nets.** [d] Being negligent in one's work. (Good fishermen spend most of their time fishing, and some time untangling their nets, but actively overseeing the regular drying of the nets every few days is essentially pointless.)

**Electric eel.** (U). Many Chinese are unfamiliar with the fact that some 500 species of fishes have electric organs, formed from muscle fibers that have lost their power of contraction but have retained the capacity to produce electric potentials. Electric eels are most commonly found in the rivers of Brazil, Colombia, Venezuela, and Peru, and readings of up to 650 volts, at 1 ampere, have been recorded.

**Hermit Crab.** (U). In Chinese marine-biology circles these are regarded as parasite crabs.

## BREAD, GRAINS, & PASTRIES

**Bread** or **Dough** (as a synonym for money) (U). Nor do the Chinese refer to rice, noodles, steamed buns or rolls as synonyms for money. However, among some Chinese youth there is the expression "Do you want love or bread?". This is some sort of westernism, and refers to making the choice of marriage partners between someone whom you love (who is perhaps only of modest means), or someone who has a sound financial base.

Reference to the head of a western household as the "bread winner" is easily understood if explained.

**Going crackers.** (going crazy) (U).

**A tart.** (a woman who likes to flirt with many men, and to be noticed by all men) (U).

[%] **To try to satisfy hunger by drawing cakes.** [e] This is empty solace, or a false solution. [cakes = biscuits = pancakes]

**To separate the wheat from the chaff.** (U). Nor do the Chinese talk of separating

---

a.緣木求魚         b.井底之蛙         c.鷸蚌相爭漁翁得利
d.三天打魚兩天曬網    e.畫餅充飢

the rice from the chaff (or husk) in any but the most literal sense.
**Sow wild oats.** (U).
**Eat humble pie.** (U).

### CONDIMENTS, SPICES, & BUTTER
He/She is a real **butterfingers.** (U).
Don't try to **butter me up.** (to flatter me) (U).
You should **take his remarks with a grain of salt.** (U). Nor do the Chinese have any related expressions, such as "You should take his remarks with a drop of soysauce."

### LIQUIDS
**That does not hold water.** (U). This is only said of buckets or other containers, and is not used in the wider sense of referring to statements, propositions, explanations, etc.
**A drop in the bucket.** Generally considered equal to the Chinese "One hair from nine oxen." [a]
[%] **To change the soup but not the medicine.** [b] This suggests a change in name only, a superficial alteration. (The original reference is to Chinese herbal medicine which is often placed in a pot with water and cooked over a low fire for a lengthy period. If drinking the resulting potion does not cure the disease in question, it is unlikely that merely changing the soup, or broth, and recooking, will be effective in rectifying the situation. New medicine is needed.)
**To get into hot water.** This may be used in English in many types of ordinary situations, such as in minor types of misbehavior, failure to obey rules and instructions, etc. We fail to find a close equivalent in Chinese, and hence regard it as (U). The Chinese "water deep and fire hot" [c] refers to the citizenry being under many hardships, and leading very difficult lives; "to go through hot water and walk on fire" [d] indicates going through much danger.[walk = tread]
**Makes my mouth water.** "Saliva" in Chinese is commonly rendered as *kou shwei* [e], which translates as mouth water. Hence saying that something makes one's mouth water is quickly understood in Chinese: 流口水 .
That's really his **cup of tea.** (referring to a favorite thing, or activity) (U). Further research on this idiom reveals that it is also unknown and unadopted in Japanese and Korean.
[%] **Half a bottle of vinegar.** [f] Refers to someone who tries to show off his/her wisdom but in fact has only partial or incomplete knowledge of the subject at hand. In some situations this could be a serious insult.
It is **no use crying over spilt milk.** Equivalent to the Chinese "Spilt water is difficult to recollect." [g]
**Break the ice.** (in a situation or conversation) (U). This is only understood in the

a.九牛一毛　　b.換湯不換藥　　c.水深火熱
d.赴湯蹈火　　e.口水　　f.半瓶醋
g.覆水難收

literal sense of physically breaking ice.

**Rocks.** (as a synonym for ice cubes) (U).

[%] **A cupful of water, a cartful of firewood.** a In this old story the cartful of firewood was on fire, and someone brought a cupful of water to put it out. Hence this indicates inadequate measures, or an inadequate response to a serious problem.

OTHER ITEMS & EXPRESSIONS

It's **peanuts.** (indicating that the amount of money involved is very low) (U).

We do not need any **comments from the peanut gallery.** (U).

[%] **Like bamboo shoots after a rain.** b Numerous, everywhere to be seen.

**To have a bone to pick** <with someone>. (U).

That is **a difficult explanation** (statement, story, etc.) for me **to swallow.** (U). "Difficult to swallow" is only said of food, beverages, medicine, etc. and other digestible items; others are merely considered difficult to accept.

[%] **To refuse to eat for fear of choking.** c This is widely used, and indicates a refusal to make a few changes for fear of some minor trouble which may be caused, or the refusal to try a new approach for fear of the minor difficulties which are expected. Hence this idiom is essentially equivalent to "having ungrounded fears", and may be used in many types of situations.

[%] **Mistaking the shadow of a bow in a glass as a snake.** d This indicates unfounded fears, a false alarm, etc.

You are **full of beans.** (U). She does not **know** <a hill of> **beans about this.** (U). He **spilled the beans** (He told everything) (U).

**In a pickle.** (U). **A pretty pickle.** (U). (referring to a predicament or plight)

Use **the old bean.** (U). Use your **noodle.** (U). (referring to the brain)

**You reap what you sow.** Equivalent to the Chinese "When you plant melons, you get melons" e or "When you plant beans, you get beans." f

Summary: As may be seen from the above listing, many phrases containing food or beverage items which are viewed as conceptually simple in English will not be understood when translated word-for-word into Chinese. A translator who comes across these expressions will have to convey their meaning by using much simpler terminology, and/or translating their dictionary definition for the benefit of the local audience.

COMBINATION WORDS

The names of some plants and fruits in English are combinations of other shorter words, with which they bear a very tenuous relation. Thus pineapple may be said to equal *pine* plus *apple,* however no such relationship or conceptualization exists in Chinese. Likewise in English, eggplant may be said to equal *egg* plus *plant,* and milkweed to equal

---

a.杯水車薪        b.雨後春筍        c.因噎廢食
d.杯弓蛇影        e.種瓜得瓜        f.種豆得豆

*milk* plus *weed*. Clearly, this type of analysis is not translatable, and plays on words which deal with this type of formulation would have little cross-cultural relevance or value. Likewise, "catfish"[1] are not viewed as related to cats, and "butterflies" are not considered related to butter. "Horse radish"[2] is not related to horses, and "jellyfish" certainly bear no relation to jelly. Guinea pigs and ground hogs[3] are not considered members of the swine family. Peanuts are not generally considered close cousins to peas, except by Chinese botanists. "Watermelon" in Chinese is called western melon. The student of Chinese may check his dictionary for further clarifications.

Some combination words that do exist in Chinese when translated directly, and that refer to things conceivably found in a market, are as follows:

| | |
|---|---|
| goldfish | (Of course these are rarely eaten) |
| bull frog | (Frog-legs may be cooked using a variety of methods) |
| breadfruit | (This fruit is however unknown in many parts of China) |
| hotdog | (This is a western food item which has been introduced in some localities) |
| blackmarket | (No explanation necessary) |
| cocktail [liquor] | (Chinese liquors are not widely used in mixing these, and foreign liquors are generally preferred) |

As a final note, the Chinese use a lot of ginger in their cooking, yet we seldom find they have any acquaintance with "gingerbread" or "ginger jars".

---

1. Often translated as 鯰魚 although it is unknown in some regions of China.
2. Generally rendered as 芥末 although this term may refer to other mustard-type items as well. Certainly very close to the Japanese *wasabi*.
3. Ground Hog Day is unknown in the Orient.

Note for frog lovers: another name for this animal in Chinese is 田雞 "field chicken".

# Chapter 3  Purchasing, Pricing, and Value

### Conflict of Interest

A group of American students came to China for a ten-day study tour, during which they each had a two day "home-stay": each student placed with a local family, living, eating, and otherwise participating in the Chinese communal family life. At the end of the tour, and before their return to the United States, there was a roundtable discussion of what they had learned during their stay in China, and some of the conclusions they had reached. Many of the students felt that they had done their share to promote peace in the world, living harmoniously with the Chinese for ten days, and showing to them the sincere good-will of Americans. They felt that if everyone could experience the warmth and generosity of the Chinese people as they had, and communicate their feelings and impressions with each other, there would be no real reason for any sort of inter-cultural conflict or unpleasantness. The students cited numerous examples of their association with Chinese in daily situations, where everyone was able to deal together in a pleasant manner, and even make some real inroads at mutual understanding, "despite the language barrier".

Such sentiments are certainly praiseworthy, however they do tend to overlook an important precept of acculturology: "Where there exists no conflict of interest situation, there is an extremely low potential for disagreement or unpleasantness."

Conflict of interest situation: **A situation where the selection of a course of action involves a loss to one party and a gain to another party; where one party has a vested interest in seeing a disagreement resolved in one manner, and the other party has a vested interest in seeing the disagreement resolved in another manner; an injury/benefit relationship.**[a] **The loss or gain may be real or perceived, literal or figurative.**

Having experienced no conflicts of interest with the local populace in their pre-arrranged, pre-planned ten-day stay in the country, these westerners were able to have

---

a.利害關係

an enjoyable study tour. Surprisingly, they were unable to even fathom that such difficulties could arise. Nor were they able to realize that incidents or friction produced by differences in thinking between people of variant cultural backgrounds, which might be insignificant over the short term, could very well reach a "critical mass" of explosive potentiality if left to build up over the long term.

Regarding food, and all the situations related to eating, we may see some differences in the way Chinese and Westerners perceive their place in and relation to their world through some conflict of interest examples. These may serve to illustrate some of the types of thinking which characterize people of different cultures.

Point-of-Sale

In my observations of and discussions with hundreds of Chinese college students, parents, and businessmen, it is apparent that there is room for dialogue in regard to an aspect of commercial relations called "Point-of-Sale Freedom of Acceptance/Refusal". One situation may be presented as follows: A customer enters a seafood restaurant and orders a large lobster, some vegetables, and rice. During the ordering, the manager feels that the customer uses a disrespectful tone of voice, furthermore he does not like the way he is dressed, or the way that he has combed his hair. In order not to be bothered with this customer any further, he informs him that "I am sorry, we have no lobsters today." The customer feels this is unreasonable and protests, and an argument ensues, further angering the manager and staff. The question necessarily posed at this juncture is: "Does the manager have the right to refuse service to customers he does not like?", and the overwhelming Chinese consensus is "Yes, of course." The Chinese feel this answer is in line with the manager's freedom to run the business the way he pleases. He therefore has the liberty to make a Point-of-Sale Acceptance or Refusal.

In the west such a freedom is not taken for granted, nor would it be supported by the citizenry. The different attitude of the modern Chinese in this regard appears to exist as a by-product of the essentially homogeneous nature of the populace itself: China has no significant history of "racial conflict." To this can be added many other considerations. One important one is that Chinese commercial enterprises, restaurants, food shops, etc. tend to be small family-run operations, without the regard to public relations, particularly in terms of long term and consistent attention to service, reliability, and quality, which many large firms cultivate. Thus to most Chinese, a shop's "refusal to sell" is not a particularly sensitive issue, as it would be to many Americans.

Consequently, the true facts behind a statement such as "Sorry, we are sold out", or the attempts to determine the truth, are seen as relatively unimportant, and the manager is free to use this statement on any and all merchandise, including merchandise advertised in the newspaper, on the billboard or marquee, on a wall poster, or in the menu. The Chinese rarely see that this state of affairs violates any basic principles of business relations.

I recall an incident my mother described to me which happened when she was working as merchandise manager of a big midwestern-U.S.A. department store in the early 1940's. A large selection of winter coats had been brought in from New York, and they were priced at US$150.00 each. A full-page ad was placed in the local newspaper announcing the arrival of these excellent coats. As the managers of the store and the heads of the newspaper later reconstructed the course of events leading up to the sale day, they all agreed that the final layout of the ad-copy had been checked-over by all relevant personnel at both ends. Nevertheless, somewhere from the time the ad left their hands to its completed run through the presses, a decimal point got moved, and the coats were advertised for sale at $15.00 each.

When the store opened in the morning, a large crowd had already gathered. The managers of the store went to the coat department, where the salespeople were trying to explain to the customers that the advertisement in the newspaper had been a mistake. A very small minority of the customers were amenable to this statement, more typical was the remark of one man who said: "I am taking a coat to the cashier, I am paying her $15.00 plus tax, and if you try to stop me I will call the police." Seeing that the crowd was becoming impatient, the store lawyers immediately contacted the newspaper, and an agreement was quickly hammered out: in addition to running a corrected version of the department store's advertisement the next day at their own expense, the newspaper agreed to reimburse the department store $135 on each coat sold that day. The final bill to the newspaper, at that time in the early 1940's, was something over $50,000.

While not directly related to eating, the same result would have been obtained if the store had advertised boxed selections of imported food delicacies at $150 each, with the newspaper moving the decimal to become $15 each. It is significant to note that at that time in the United States there was no pronounced "consumer movement". Today not only countries in the developed world, but also many third world countries have announced programs for protecting consumer rights. Yet everytime I relate this department store example, or a similar one, to the Chinese, their reaction is invariably unfavorable. Even within the social and political structure of "rule by law", they feel that this is not the way to settle the dispute.[1]

Naturally the same considerations as in the above example apply to the person who wants to buy a kilogram of ground beef, a selection of steamed buns, two pounds of almonds, or an ice cream sundae in China. Upon being told that the price is other than that marked or advertised, the resolution of any conflict between sales people and consumers is not handled in the way westerners might consider typical. The foreigner who desires to acculturate himself to Chinese society must learn to deal with the subject of conflict resolution when disputes arise, so that he may gauge when to press the point,

---

1. See comments on "natural pricing" later in this chapter.

when not to, when to advance, when to retreat, and how otherwise to gain a feel for the basics of Chinese negotiation.

Let us consider some actual examples of the types of conflicts of interest which may arise between foreigners and Chinese. We will temporarily limit our discussion to the selection and purchase of food items.

## Food and Pricing

We may now look at a practical example in the present era concerned with pricing. A customer eats a certain food item, with a marked price $P1, however upon going to pay the bill, the customer is told by the relevant personnel that the item was mistakenly marked, and the correct price is $P2.[1]

### Bi-directional Price Readjustment Possibilities

If the second price is less than the first, it is unlikely the customer will object. If the second price is greater than the first, and the customer is only willing to pay the first price, a conflict of interest has arisen.

From the store, shop, or restaurant's point of view, such a situation might come about in a number of ways: (1) There was an error in advertising, in menu printing, in billboard or wall-poster lettering/numeration. (2) The newly updated menus, wall-posters, billboards, etc. have been ordered, but have not yet arrived. (3) An employee put the "wrong" price label on the merchandise in question. (4) New prices were posted, but the posters/labels have fallen off and are nowhere in sight. (5) The manager has decided to institute a price revision, and store employees have had no time to change the prices of the marked merchandise, or to put up any other notice of the price change.(6) Since the store was sold out of the exact merchandise/product the customer ordered, rather than disappoint the customer, it substituted another very similar item, which just happened to be of a higher price. (7) Due to various forces in the international monetary markets, the value of the local currency has gone down, and purchases of some imported ingredients, or components, have gone up. Of course, other scenarios are possible.

### The Fried Rice Example

Let us consider a specific example where the customer has eaten a fixed dinner or lunch selection, for example a plate of some style of fried rice, with a marked price, as per the menu, of $85 local currency. Upon going to pay his bill, the "store" (as represented by the cashier, manager, or other personnel) says that the correct price is $95. The customer states that he is only willing to pay the original price of $85.

---

1. $P1 is dollar-price #1, $P2 is dollar-price #2.

In terms of discussing the value of the plate of fried rice, the majority of westerners tend to hold an "As Offered Orientation". Regarding the value of the merchandise in question, in relation to the marked price, this may be described as an As Offered Perception of Value. In this situation many westerners would be inclined to say that the customer's attitude is FAIR.

Many philosophers, social scientists, and religious leaders have noted that Chinese thought contains a great deal of naturalism. Therefore, from a traditional point of view, many Chinese could continue to hold to a natural value orientation, meaning that the value is inherent in the merchandise, and the price, if "incorrect", may be adjusted to reflect this at the point-of-sale. Regarding the value of the merchandise in question, in relation to the marked price, this may be described as a Retroactively Readjustable Perception of Value. The Chinese could easily take the view the that customer's attitude is UNFAIR.

Such an outlook is not without its philosophical foundation. In the most likely event, the shop feels that since its component costs have changed, this is a natural fact which should be recognized by the buyers. The marked price is of secondary importance.

Minimum Pricing

Further comments regarding the Chinese and Western views of how "Pricing" is determined are necessary at this point, especially as regards the idea of "minimum pricing".

In the west, one feature of the industrial age, which is highly unknown in traditional agricultural societies, is the legitimate, planned sale of merchandise at a price which is below the production cost. This is made possible in many ways. The bankruptcy of one merchandiser could easily result in his goods-in-stock being quickly sold off to the highest bidder in order to raise cash, despite the fact that the highest bid could easily represent a value "below manufacturing cost". The buyer then could decide to sell this merchandise through his own outlets at a below cost price. In the clothing industry, the need to move wearing apparel out of the warehouse to make room for next season's fashions often results in below cost sales. Modern marketing strategy also uses the "below cost" sale of merchandise in order to achieve market penetration, drive out the competition, launch new products, etc. Many manufacturers of soaps, tissues, and other toiletry items spend millions of dollars in giving away samples of their products every year, and in other related types of below cost promotional activity, and view it all to be a part of their overall advertising budget. Manufacturers of some types of fruit juices, soft drinks, and snack foods also regularly give away samples of their products or sell them at a heavy discount.

The marketing concept of "the loss leader" is also fairly well established in the west. In this technique, a merchandiser advertises a popular item at a price well below cost, and the large number of consumers who are drawn into the store to get this good-buy also purchase other products as well. Everyone views this kind of transaction as a normal part of modern business activity.

Although many people will say "The overall merchandising benefits achieved by such strategies as these outweigh the 'losses' involved", this type of thinking is most properly seen as an outgrowth of the western big-business mentality, in which businesses are, or operate from the point of view of being, large and well-capitalized concerns, oriented toward the long-term view.

The prices of many vegetables, types of seafood, etc. often vary widely from season to season, yet in restaurants in North America and Europe, "year-round stable pricing" is in effect, and the customer pays the same price in fall, winter, spring, or summer. Certainly this is quite the norm in many fast-food restaurant chains. The customer is not subject to a point-of-sale readjustment of the price just because the staff says: "Our costs have gone up on these items since the menus were printed (or since the signboard was painted)". In a related consideration, the majority of restaurants in the west are never "sold out" of something. Certainly many people go to fast food restaurants all their lives and are never confronted with the statement that items printed on the menu or signboard are "unavailable". If such an eventuality does occur, a sign is clearly posted for customers' reference.

Most of these marketing concepts are not entirely unknown in China, however the Chinese are still decades away from accepting a view that: 1) you can sell products for whatever price you want to, and hence 2) the marked price represents a price to which the consumer (or buyer) is always entitled. Rather, if and when a disagreement over pricing arises, especially when the seller takes exception to, or begins to have reservations about what appears to be his originally offered price, the Chinese feel it is appropriate to enter into a discussion on what constitutes "the fair price" of the goods, based on a natural value "formulation".

Chinese businesses in general tend to be small or medium sized, family run, and inadequately capitalized. Such a lack of capitalization severely affects overall policy and thinking, resulting in, among other things, a tendency toward the "short term view" in profit-taking. Therefore, where the western concept of minimum pricing is related to "market strategy", the Chinese concept of minimum pricing reflects the so-called natural value orientation, and is much more related to "component cost". (Component here refers to all factors of the production process, including materials, labor, and other allowances for variable and fixed costs.)

Some westerners have pointed out this scenario: It is possible that due to efficiencies of scale, and the varying degrees of use (or non-use) of advanced machinery, four different factories producing the same product could have four very different pricing structures. Thus, if Mr. Cheng is a very good cook and wants to offer his services to the public, he may combine with some friends to open a new restaurant. He will want to inquire about buying chairs. Even after some serious price bargaining, essentially the same chair could be quoted as $12.66, $11.70, $6.54, and $2.59 by four different factories, due not only to differing degrees of experience in producing this item, but also to differing production runs, which might vary from a low of 200 to a high of 2,000,000.

If a selection of ten chairs is taken from each production run, mixed together, and verified to be essentially the same, upon picking up one chair and examining it, how would one attempt to determine an answer to: "What is the fair price of this chair?" Up against the four dissimilar claims of the factory managers, the westerner might tend to think that the "fair price" is indeed a rather nebulous concept. Westerners are much more prepared to talk about the "offered" or "quoted" price, since this deals with an objective type of fact.

To further complicate the issue, what if, through some clerical error, the first factory made a sales offer of $2.66 each for a quantity of its chairs. Would this represent an "unfair price"? Is the buyer in no way entitled to this price, despite the written quotation? The reader may form his own opinion on this matter.[1]

If asked to determine the fair price of a chair, especially "the minimum fair price", similar to the situation above, the Chinese would then tend to say that here there are four different definitions of "fair", depending on which factory one is dealing with. To the westerner, this renders the concept of "fair" in this type of situation to be meaningless.

Diagram 3-1
PREVALENT MODES OF THINKING AND VALUE ORIENTATION IN TWO SOCIETIES

| Dates | Society 1 | Value of Goods and Services | Society 2 | Value of Goods and Services |
|---|---|---|---|---|
| pre 1785 | Pre Industrial Revolution Mode of Thinking | Natural Value Orientation | Pre Industrial Revolution Mode of Thinking | Natural Value Orientation |
| llate 1780's to late 1850's | Transitional Period Mode of Thinking — changes in various types of traditional ways of habitation, commerce, transportation, education, social structure, etc. | ↓ | Pre Industrial Revolution Mode of Thinking | ↓ |
| late 1850's to present | Post Industrial Revolution Mode of Thinking | As Offered Orientation | Pre Industrial Revolution Mode of Thinking | Natural Value Orientation |
| | | As Offered Perception of Value | | Retroactively Readjustable Perception of Value |

---

1. One old Chinese expression gives us good insight into answering these questions. The idiom says: "There are people willing to engage in killing others, but there are no people willing to do a business where you lose money." Hence, the Chinese would tend to support the point of view that the seller is not required to sell at a loss, despite the written quotation and offer of sale, because that would be "unfair". This is in direct correspondence to their view of Pricing, which is primarily related to Component Cost, as stated above.

殺頭生意有人幹，賠本生意没人做

In this simple diagram, some difference in mental process are outlined.

Society 1: The people in Society 1 gradually modified and developed their thinking as they went through the long-term changes brought about by the Industrial Revolution. Most of the citizenry's thinking has developed into a pronounced post Industrial Revolution mode.

Society 2: The people in Society 2 did not go through the Industrial Revolution, but rather found themselves faced with the results of this Revolution as a fait accompli. The increased geographic mobility of people in the world has caused many of the ramifications of this Revolution to exert influence on their society in one degree or another. Most of this influence has been materialistic as opposed to psychological, and may be described as short-termed and superficial. Much of the citizenry's thinking remains in the pre Industrial Revolution mode, even though in many respects it may be said that they live in a "post Industrial Revolution world".

**Perceptions of Value:** From the point of view of the person with a post Industrial Revolution "As Offered Orientation", the Perception of Value of various merchandise is "As Offered". To this person, since the natural value orientation allows a bi-directionally adjustable price at the point-of-sale (if the seller determines that he wishes to make such an adjustment), it corresponds to a Retroactively Readjustable Perception of Value, although of course the citizenry of any country who held to the doctrine of [pre-Industrial Revolution] naturalism would not see it as such.

In the present era we will want to be aware of an As Offered Perception of Value and Retroactively Readjustable Perception of Value, in order to clarify the thinking of different people in different societies.

If problems arise in a buying/selling transaction in terms of pricing, we may desire to compare the attitudes of the two different parties, depending on whether they hold the AO or RR Perception of Value. The following diagram will be useful for outlining all possibilities.

Diagram 3-2

| (seller) party 1 | (buyer) party 2 | of goods or services |
|---|---|---|
| | | *Result* |
| RR | RR | no problem |
| RR | AO | possible conflict of interest |
| AO | RR | possible conflict of interest |
| AO | AO | no problem |

Complications in Buying and Selling

Some further examples will illustrate how differing Perceptions of Value may complicate dealings between Chinese and westerners. The comments in parentheses at the end of each situation outline the possible rationale of the seller, who maintains a more traditional naturalist stance.

1. A customer enters a coffee shop, is shown to a seat and given a menu. He notices one listing for "Orange Juice", and decides that this is what he wants to order. The price is marked as $65.

Upon going to pay the bill, he is asked to pay $98. The shop personnel's reasoning is that the "Orange Juice" on the menu refers to canned orange juice, but because the shop has run out of canned orange juice today, so the customer was given fresh orange juice, and that is more expensive. The correct price is therefore $98. The customer pauses to think about this.

(The coffee shop personnel feel they are being fair.)

2. In some Chinese provinces, several differing units of weight are used. The two most common are the metric kilo (2.2 lbs or 1000 grams), and the provincial kilo (generally 0.6 of a metric kilo, hence 600 grams or 1.32 lbs.), both commonly abbreviated as "kilo" (Chinese: jin 斤), in an undistinguished fashion. This leads to some confusion among some consumers, especially when buying meats, beans, candies, and all other sorts of items that the store purchases in bulk, and then sells to the customer in the portion he requests. In order to unify the measurements in the marketplace, and due to government prompting, several large food stores decide to use the metric kilo exclusively, and post a sign to this effect in their front entrance: All references to "kilo" in this store's price labeling refer to the metric kilo.

A customer goes to the meat department and orders a kilo of ground beef, which is packaged by the head of the meat department. The posted price for ground beef is $170 per kilo. His package is marked, as per the posted price, of $170. Upon receiving the package, the customer feels it is a bit too light, and asks that it be placed on the scale. It weighs 600 grams. The customer says that by ordering a kilo, he wanted 1000 grams. The store personnel repackage the meat, adding the 400 grams requested, and adjusting the price to a total of $283. The customer remarks that the policy statement sign in the front of the store had lead him to expect that the correct price should be $170, reflecting the 1000 grams/metric kilo measurement. The head of the meat department, after conferring with the store manager, says that he is sorry but he has not had time to adjust his price labelling yet to reflect the new policy, and therefore the correct price is $283. The customer stops to consider this for a moment.

(The people in the meat department feel that they are being fair.)

3. Ronald and his friends go to dinner in a large restaurant. They select a number of dishes off the menu, as well as ordering rice, and soup, and have an enjoyable meal. At the end of their repast, a fresh pot of tea is brought, along with fresh finger-bowls and a large plate of fruit.

Upon going to pay the bill, Ronald finds that he is being charged $200 for the fruit. He tells the cashier: "I have been in many restaurants in your community, and whenever I was given a plate of fruit at the end of the meal it was always complimentary." The cashier says that she is unaware of this, their restaurant policy is to charge for fruit.

Ronald further notes: "But I did not order the fruit, why are you asking me to pay for it?" To this the cashier replies: "But you ate it, didn't you? So you should pay for it. We are sorry for the misunderstanding." Ronald pauses to consider this turn of events.

(The restaurant personnel feel they are being fair. Note: Although normally in the restaurants in the community fruit is given free at the end of each meal, the restaurant here has readjusted the value of the fruit with no notice to the customer. By offering a token apology, they feel they add weight to the reasonableness of their position. This is an interesting ramification of the RR Perception of Value, since it holds that merchandise which the customer did not order, but which was served to him and he consumed, should be paid for by the customer, at the price stated by the larger party or "group".)

Questions

Several questions posed by westerners about these pricing examples are given below. The answers are given from a traditional naturalist point of view, which reflects a great deal of Chinese thinking.

In the fried rice example, $85 vs. $95 —

Q: The store has a right to mark the goods at the price it pleases. The customer has the obligation to pay the marked price. Likewise, the customer has the right to buy at the marked price, the store has the obligation to sell. There is a balance of rights and obligations. If you say that I have the obligation to pay the $95 which the store says is the real price, where is my corresponding right?

A: A balance of rights and obligations is not the issue here. The store has made a clear explanation of its case, noting that the situation has changed. This would be accepted by a person aware of current price trends in the market, which is to say by a person who was reasonable. The store has the right to be properly reimbursed for its costs in producing this item, and to deny this is to deny a right as well.

Q: If I have read my Chinese classics correctly, the ancient Chinese philosophers, Confucius in particular, were concerned with establishing order in society. How does the store's reasoning and action here establish order in society? What if every store was allowed to do this? They could just as easily say the real price is $195, and by their reasoning, that would be just as valid. This to my way of thinking sets a bad precedent. I recommend placing the responsibility for correct price-marking where it belongs, with the store, and I would think that the demands of being a *chwun tze* (gentleman, or exemplary person), as per Confucius's teachings, would require that the party who "incorrectly marked" the merchandise accept responsibility for its own mistakes. That being the case, the customer should be entitled to pay the marked price and no more.

A: Your analysis attempts to take into account the long term view, as indicated by your feeling that this sets a "bad precedent". However, the long term view is not the issue here, the Chinese are only looking at this particular case: $85 vs. $95. In this sense, the difference of $10 in local currency is not particulary significant, and certainly not worth arguing about. The difference between $85 and $195 is more significant, however that is another case altogether, bearing little or no relation to the present discussion. In regard to Confucius's teaching, its cornerstone is "human-ness" and "benevolence", while "propriety" is a major tenet. These dictates would require that the customer take a benevolent attitude to the store's present situation as the personnel have expressed it, and in this way he may approach the ideal of becoming a *chwun tze*.

In the orange juice example, $65 vs. $98 —

Q: There is an important concept involved in this difference of opinion, and it says that the consumer is entitled to purchase the merchandise offered for sale at the price marked, plus whatever taxes may apply and subject to other quantity restrictions which the seller may announce. To add the stipulation that the seller may adjust the price after the fact, with no announcement or indication to the consumer, throws considerable confusion into the otherwise orderly price structure of the marketplace, and opens up limitless possibilities for fraud. To assume across-the-board that the store's motives and intentions in this and related types of encounters are honest, while an admirable assumption, is still without proof. The same result, i.e. the demand that the customer pay $98, would be obtained if the store were acting dishonestly. Therefore the store's honesty, being indeterminate, is in serious question. The customer however consumed an item marked $65, and is willing to pay $65 for it. His honesty is all apparent. Therefore, from the point of view of honesty, I believe the customer is in the right.

A: The customer having consumed something which the seller, larger party, or group has determined to have a value of $98, should be willing to pay $98 for it. By paying this price, he suffers no loss, since he received an equivalent value of merchandise. To refuse to pay this amount is to be acting unfairly and dishonestly.

Q: The point is made that the "correct" price as stated by the store personnel is $98. This I believe is invalid. The only possible definition for "correct price" is marked price, moreover this is supported by the reality that the marked price is a fact: a fact that everyone agrees upon.[1] The statement that the marked price is incorrect, or that it refers to "another similar product" is a supposition, for which we have seen offered no tangible proof. Such proof would have to be displayed on the menu or some other prominent place. In the balance, fact must rationally take precedence over supposition.

A: Local custom has established that the price for canned orange juice and fresh orange juice are different. This is a natural fact of the marketplace and certainly known to most local citizens. Few would question or argue about it; in truth most citizens would be happy to have fresh orange juice as opposed to canned, and would gladly pay the price difference for the increased health benefit. Clearly this would be the course of action for an upstanding individual to take, and this is the "fact" of the matter.

---

1. This view stresses 憑事實作判斷 .

In the ground beef example, $170 vs. $283 —

Q: There seems to be some internal communication problem among the store personnel, as revealed by the incident here. The personnel who have the most up-to-date information on the store's policy as regards units of measurement and are in charge of placing promotional or advertising posters in the front of the store, and the personnel who were in charge of marking, or changing, the prices in accordance with these specifications have, according to the store's statement, gotten their signals mixed up, or communication has otherwise broken down. Nevertheless, as with any other issue concerned with promotion or advertising for which there is a claimed "mistake", I fail to see how this is the customer's problem. This is clearly the store's problem, and they may sort it out, internally, as best they see fit. The customer in my view is not obligated to make up for, or suffer financial loss due to, the store's internal management mistakes or lack of communication.

A: Reference to current prices in the other stores would confirm that the store's final determination of $283 is indeed a valid price for this quantity of ground beef. The attempt to make the store sell at a reduced price is a selfish rationalization of the consumer, who is unwilling to pay a fair price, and desires to gain the difference (400 grams) for nothing.

Summary

In situations of this kind, where a conflict of interest has arisen, one may gain some broad insight into Chinese thinking not available through other approaches. We note the following tendencies:

1. The Chinese relationship model is hierarchical and authoritarian, therefore, by definition, duties and rights are not balanced.[1] They would only be so in relationships based on equality. "Equality" is in many ways a typically western idea, which has come about due to the growing strength and influence of the middle class. The growth of a middle class in China is a fairly recent phenomenon, and as a class it is comparatively less influential.

2. The Chinese historical tradition has tended to view right and wrong in terms of the dictates of those in power. The idea of weighing the evidence objectively and attempting to arrive at a conclusion thereby, is a western concept. The functioning of Chinese civil law courts, originally established in the early 1900's, largely follows western reasoning and evidence methods. Among the general Chinese population there is little history of this type of activity however. Furthermore, the search for truth, and the debate between different points of view by which it is reached (or approached), while being central concerns of Aristotle's teachings, are outside of the Chinese tradition. Therefore in every-day practical terms, in dealing with the general Chinese populace, a statement

---

1. This imbalance runs through most of the philosophy of the Confucian school, and is an issue of serious concern to any Chinese interested in democratic reform in the present era.

that "fact must rationally take precedence over supposition" must often be discounted.

3. In urging that the seller take responsibility for its own actions, rather than *everyone sharing in the consequences,* is an individualistic stance, and denies the Group Mentality. Harmony is achieved if the individual (the smaller party) acquiesces to the demands of the larger group. The larger group thus dictates its view. Any suggestions of equality among parties in the negotiations, or assessment of responsibility which singles out one party over the other, are criticized as equivalent to selfishness. This was also a common view in the west before the late 1770's.

## Conclusion

A few months ago, I had the opportunity to speak to several North Americans who had spent considerable time living in several countries of Central and South America, where the annual rate of inflation regularly topped 250%. In regard to a discussion of the issue of pricing, a Canadian in the group commented: "Down there it is not at all uncommon that posters or signs put up in the morning are completely outdated by mid-afternoon, and new prices have already taken effect." One Virginian in the group noted: "It is quite conceivable that the price of your lunch or dinner selection could change *while you were eating your meal.*" Whether or not this represented "naturalism" they were unprepared to say, however they did agree that it seemed to represent economic reality. With this background, of course they were not overly bothered by any of the issues raised in this section, and tended to downplay the significance of many of the remarks herein. The reader may want to consider their comments as representing a commiserative point of view in dealing with conflicts of interest of this kind.

It may also be true that for the foreigners who do not make the effort to read a lot of the signs (and prices) posted in many Chinese restaurants and shops, most of these pricing considerations will be outside their line of sight.

## Notes on Prices

1) What we are speaking of here are goods offered for sale in the free market. Some types of goods have been established as "fixed price" by government edict, (wine, cigarettes, alcoholic beverages, etc.) and therefore represent a controlled market. These goods, even if marked at a lower price, are still subject to payment at the government established price.

2) An important point in international law says: a valid offer and acceptance of sale is predicated on the fact that neither party is in distress. Thus, the sale of a loaf of bread to a starving man for a marked price of 10 ounces of gold is legally invalid.

## Old Idioms, Revisited

### *You Get What You Pay For*

"You get what you pay for" to the westerner and Chinese tends to imply different things—the Chinese take this expression much more literally. To the westerner, the purchase of a certain type of appliance or machine for $X comes with the guarantee that it will work for a certain number of years, despite the price paid, and whether or not it was purchased in an exclusive boutique in New York or a nationwide discount chain. There is then some idea of "minimum standards of acceptability." The Oriental manufacturer may however hold to the view that in order to meet the target price of the foreign customer (importer), it is permissable to make substitution of various specified components, use inferior materials, leave out parts, by-pass various manufacturing processes: QC, testing, rust-proofing, etc., and therefore there are no so-called "minimum standards of acceptability", but literally "You get what you pay for." This Chinese idea is much closer to the Chinese idiom "One part money, one part goods", [a] meaning that you must pay what the goods are worth, and if you do not pay what the goods are worth, (their Component Cost, as per my factory's calculation), then of course you will get something else.

Later when the foreign buyer complains because his specified quality standards were not met, the Orientals incredibly reply: "You are a fool. How could anyone believe that we could make that product up to your quality standards for the price you paid?" The result is that the foreigner thinks the Chinese are being unfair and unprincipled, and the Chinese think the foreigner is being not only unfair but also very naive.

A foreigner would say: "Why didn't you explain that to me at the time?"

The Chinese would say: "I think it is your job to know, after all you have been buying in our country for a number of years."

*You Don't Get Something For Nothing*
The Chinese concept of buyer-seller relations tends to look at this expression in a very short-term, concrete perspective, whereas the westerner might commonly take a more long-term, or even abstract, view, noting that the seller is gaining future benefits, perhaps intangible ones (goodwill, reputation in the marketplace, building up customer trust, etc.), by a "below cost" sale now. We note that selling at-a-loss or giving samples away might be reasonable in the long-term marketing view, while being unreasonable in the short term view, thus the Chinese and westerners could easily disagree as to "when" or "in what types of situations" this expression was relevant, and in what types it was not. To the westerner with his primarily legal orientation, payment of the marked price represents payment of a "valid price", not subject to readjustment due to the charge "You are not entitled to that price because it would represent getting something for nothing." The consumer in the Chinese economy however appears subject to this stipulation, since the thinking of the citizenry is more oriented toward paying an assumed "fair price", subject to subjective determination (and retroactive readjustment) by the seller at the point of sale.

---

a. 一份錢一份貨

## Natural Pricing

With regard to food, one area where we may find some divergent opinions between westerners and Chinese is in terms of what constitutes fair pricing policy. In order to understand the issues involved with this topic more completely, let us first examine the pricing for agricultural and other food items in a Pre-Industrial Revolution Agricultural Society. Several basic assumptions may first be clarified.

PRE-INDUSTRIAL REVOLUTION AGRICULTURAL SOCIETY MARKET ECONOMY

In any given region:

A) The variety of goods in the marketplace is essentially unchanged year after year. Of course some fruits, vegetables, and other items are available in some seasons and not in others, however in terms of any given season over a period of years, the variety of goods available is generally constant.

B) The quality of merchandise among different sellers is largely the same.

C) Prices in the economy are generally stable year after year.

D) Both buyers and sellers are aware of the average price level, and are quite well informed as to the approximate prices for most goods, and even the specific prices for many goods.

E) Buyers and sellers live in the same community, and are aware of all factors that affect the local harvest.

In this type of market economy, of course there are very few "marked prices" or "posted prices", for the simple reason that there is very little need for them. Most of the buyers are engaged in agricultural pursuits themselves, and are aware of the costs involved for growing carrots, melons, cabbage, and other produce. Since the prices do not change much year by year (except in times of war, disaster, etc.) they have through experience become familiar with the prices for all agricultural produce, various types of fish and other aquatic products, as well as any and all animals, whether hunted or raised. As a slight variant of this, they are also aware of common seasonal variations in these prices, or other natural factors (such as typhoons) which affect the price level.

Let us advance a few hypothetical situations which might arise and see how the buyers and sellers in this type of market economy might react. For ease of discussion we will refer to one piece of brass cash as being one dollar.

1. Although there is seemingly no need to do so, one proprietor, Mr. Chi, places a notice up in the center of town outlining the variety of food items he is offering, and the prices for each. On this notice the price for sugarcane is given at $10.00 per 7 foot stalk, and the price for pears is given at $2.00 each.

A customer sees this notice and goes to Mr. Chi's stall. He wants to buy two seven foot stalks of sugarcane. He mentions to the proprietor: "Oh, by the way, your notice is wrong, everyone knows the price for sugarcane is $8.00 not $10.00." The proprietor agrees to this, since that is indeed the common price, and says he is sorry about the mistake. The customer gives him $16.00, smiles, and leaves.

Another customer goes to the proprietors' stall and wants to buy six pears. He gives Mr. Chi $12.00. The proprietor says: "Oh, I am sorry, the notice is wrong, the price for pears is $3.50 each, not $2.00." The customer thinks for a second and realizes this is the case, and gives the proprietor $21.00 for the six pears, smiles, and leaves.

2. A customer goes to Mrs. Cheng's fruitstand and asks the price for 10 beets. A girl in the stall says the beets are $1 each. The customer says he will come back in the afternoon when he is done with his other shopping. When he comes back, Mrs. Cheng says she is sorry, the beets are four for $7.00, or $1.75 each, the girl quoted the wrong price. This customer is new in the community, but asks several other people standing nearby. They all confirm that $1.75 is the standard price. The customer agrees to buy twelve beets if a slight discount can be allowed, and the price of $20.00 (a savings of $1.00) is quickly agreed upon.

A lady goes to the same fruitstand and is sold eight small onions by the girl for $4.00. Mrs. Cheng comes back from an errand, finds out that her helper sold the onions for $4.00, but the correct price should have been $3.00. The girl points out the lady in the market the next day, and Mrs. Cheng refunds her $1.00. The lady remarks: "I thought that that $4.00 price was higher than usual, and I was going to mention it to you the next time I bought onions. Thank you."

3. A customer goes to Mr. Jung's vegetable stand and wants to know if a certain kind of melon will be available the following week. Mr. Jung says it should be available on the following Thursday at $4.00 each for the standard size. The customer comes back the following Friday. Mr. Jung informs him that due to flooding, the price of melons has gone up. The customer asks for a discount but is told that it is not possible. He buys four at the new price of $6.00 each and takes them home to his family.

Another customer comes to Mr. Jung's to buy some beans. He says that he believes the price is $5.00 for ten handfulls. Mr. Jung laughs and says: "You must be a newcomer in this area. Everyone knows that the standard price is $3.00 for ten handfulls." The customer selects his beans, pays $3.00, smiles, and leaves.

Asked to describe the goings on in these examples, some social scholars would say that the dealings in this marketplace are typified by harmony and honesty. In addition to those two factors, we may also pause to consider the buyers and sellers' views of the value of the merchandise they are dealing with. We quickly see that the the buyers and sellers both tend to have a "Natural Value Orientation". Over time, the price has already settled at its present level in a natural sort of way, and is well known to everyone of experience in the community. At the most basic level this Natural Value reflects the component costs in raising these items and getting them to market, plus a small profit margin. The price of any item is, as noted above, generally stable throughout the region, and over time, and is well known to both the buyers and the sellers.

Additionally we see that price quotations are of secondary importance, or often irrelevant. In terms of a "quoted price", the actual price at point of sale is bi-directionally adjustable to reflect the natural price, or real price. The buyer and seller regard each others oral statements at the point of sale as being true and honest, almost by definition, despite any written "prices" or other stated data to the contrary. Bargaining tends to be within fixed, known limits. There is little or no sense of "contractual obligation". In fact, if confronted with a buyer who insists on paying less than the natural price, the seller may refuse to sell, and that is the end of the matter.

Let us now turn the situation around to reflect a different type of market economy.

## POST-INDUSTRIAL REVOLUTION COMPETITIVE MARKET ECONOMY

In any given region:

A) The variety of goods in the marketplace changes from year to year.

B) The quality of merchandise among different sellers is different, and changes over time.

C) Prices in the economy change from year to year, reflecting changes in quality and availability.

D) Both buyers and the sellers are aware of the average price level, but are only well informed of the approximate prices for the goods they buy frequently from any one particular outlet. They are often unaware of the specific prices for many goods, especially new goods in the marketplace, or goods from outlets with which they have not dealt with before.

E) Buyers and sellers may live in widely separated regions, or even on different continents, and are often unaware of all factors that affect local production in any given region.

Among other considerations, technology and geographical mobility are two important elements that have been introduced into the marketplace in the Post Industrial Revolution economy. Another major difference in our Post-Industrial Revolution model is that **change** has been introduced into the marketplace. It is no longer true that prices of products and their quality are virtually the same year after year. Both the amount and the cost of the factors of production (land, labor, capital, and entrepreneurial ability) vary over time. Technological knowledge is no longer constant. Since geographical mobility has been introduced as a relevant consideration, the market knowledge shared by producers and consumers is often quite limited.

The result of this is that buyers and sellers are no longer mutually aware of anything which could be called a "Natural Value". Their transactions are based on the quoted or marked price.

Asked to describe the goings on in a model of this type, some social scientists would say that the dealings in this marketplace are based on rights and obligations. In regard to the value of any particular merchandise, the the buyers and sellers both tend to have an "As Offered Orientation". ("Offer" here used in the sense of **to present for approval** or acceptance, to proffer, to tender.)

Hence, we realize that price quotations are of primary importance. In terms of a "quoted price", the actual price at point of sale is uni-directionally adjustable (i.e., downward) to reflect any relevant discounts to which the buyer may be entitled, including those available due to friendly bargaining. The buyer and seller regard each others oral statements as being secondary to factual evidence. There is a pronounced sense of "contractual obligation". In fact, if confronted with a seller who insists on charging more than the marked or quoted price, the buyer may sue, and the court would yield a judgment in his favor.

Due to the increased geographical mobility of the populace in the Post-Industrial Revolution age, society has become more and more varied, and non-homogeneous. A "refusal to sell" is looked upon as ethnic or racial discrimination, and is not allowed.

In summary, we may say that depending on whether we are dealing with a Pre- or Post-Industrial Revolution style of thinking, it is possible to delineate the following :

How the Value (of Goods and Services) is viewed, and Pricing is Determined –
1. Natural Value Orientation
   To be more specific in our terminology, and in light of the analysis given above, we can see that this orientation corresponds to a "Retroactively Readjustable Perception of Value".
2. As Offered Orientation
   This orientation is fairly straightforward, and corresponds to what may be simply called an "As Offered Perception of Value".

Clearly there is some disparity between the two Perceptions.

## The Purchasing Agent

Other Perceptions of Value also come into play in some situations. The example of the Purchasing Agent is useful in illustrating another set:

While working for a company, (denoted Ai-Deh Associates), an employee named Eric is placed in charge of purchasing box meals, i.e. lunches and dinners, totalling 48, or more, per day. The budget for each meal is placed at $65 apiece in local currency, to be paid for by the company. After some trial period in which box lunches were ordered from various food shops or restaurants, Eric is still undecided as to which food shop has the most attractive terms in regard to quality and selection, although delivery terms are essentially identical. The employees eating the lunches all feel that good value has been gotten for the money spent. In consultation with various owners of the restaurants, Warren, the proprietor of one establishment, (denoted Win Tin's), who shares some mutual friends and classmates with Eric, in addition to the fact that their fathers were neighbors during their youth, etc., etc., says that in light of their special relationship, he is therefore willing to offer the following terms: if he is granted the agreement/contract to provide the box meals, he will make available a $10 discount on each meal, to be paid to Eric, while billing the company normally. Eric finds this arrangement agreeable and Ai-Deh Associates is thereafter daily provided by box meals by Win Tin's. Mutual understanding: Due to Eric's special relationship with Warren, he has been able to purchase goods with a value of $65 for a lower price ($65 minus $10), unavailable to others.

Conclusion and Summary: In regard to each box lunch, Ai-Deh Associates receives $65 value of merchandise for $65, Eric receives special consideration owing to the nature of his special relationship with Warren, and Warren completes the sale of his merchandise according to a pricing structure which he chose of his own free volition. Everyone is happy.

In order to deal with this explanation and rationale it will be necessary to define additional differences in Perception of Value, in regard to the worth of various items, and how commissions are dealt with.

Organizational Privateer Perception of Value: Under this Perception, the organization pays one price for the merchandise (goods, services, etc.), and receives what is seen as an identical corresponding value. The person working for the organization, and in charge of purchasing or negotiating, feels entitled to take private commissions, because of special personal relationships or connections which he alone enjoys. In terms of the organization, he therefore obtains a right for which there is no corresponding duty. Abbreviated "OP" it has the connotation of opportunism, which is exactly what it suggests to the western mind.

Organizational Middleman Perception of Value: Under this Perception, a goal is set for each employee to have a balance of rights and duties within the organization. Any special personal relationships or connections which he alone enjoys, or special negotiating skills which he possesses, should be suitably brought to bear in the performance of his job, as a middleman between his organization and outside parties, and with the ideal of furthering the overall interests of the organization. All commissions negotiated rightfully belong to the organization, of which he is a part. If individual commissions or profits are allowed, it is with full knowledge of all the heads of the organization and/or stockholders. Abbreviated "OM", it has the connotation of omega, the last letter of the Greek alphabet, and suggests that the organization is entitled to the final result or determination.

Note: Some discount may be available to any and all comers in making many types of purchases, however this is not the issue here, and this is not "bargaining in the public market" as usually understood. Rather it is a special agreement which has only come about due to the existence of a special relationship between the two negotiating parties: for example, between the seller and the buyer's representative. It is a special price discount available to this representative only, and allegedly not available to others.

The following figure illustrates a similar situation.

A Box Meal

Figure 3-1

price (on billing): $550

seller offers special discount of $50 to buyer's representative

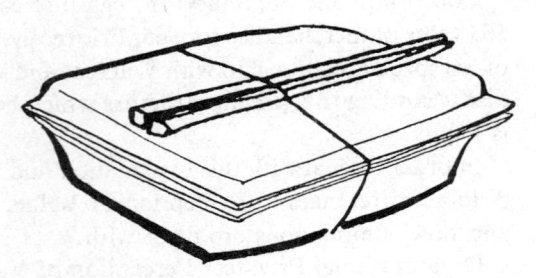

OM Perception of Value: $500
$50 difference is property of company which makes purchase

OP Perception of Value: $550
$50 difference goes in representative's own pocket

The determination of what constitutes ethical behavior will depend on which Perception of Value is being used.

Due to the sentimentalistic orientation of Chinese, and their emphasis on family and ancestral ties, preference for harmonious relationships between classmates, neighbors, etc., stress placed on "human-ness", kindness, and benevolence, their view of social and business relations as falling within the "Five Relationships" model,[1] and other traditional ideals and rationale, the OP Perception of Value in commercial dealings is quite widespread. The Chinese would refer to the above example by saying that Eric has received a "red envelope" from Warren, the proprietor of Win Tin's. The issue of whether this is compatible with honesty (or more broadly speaking, morality) depends on how one views the value of the merchandise obtained. As in the above diagram, for something costing $550, the value of the merchandise received (by the organization) in one Perception is $500, but in another Perception is $550.

Although Warren's payments to Eric are secret, let us suppose that someone else in Ai-Deh Associates, a Mr. Fao, finds out about the arrangement. There would be little to gain if he exposed the situation for all to see, indeed this would cause discord inside and outside the organization. For example, if Eric got a tongue lashing or was fired, he and his friends would certainly want to find out who had exposed him, and it would be expected that they would take pains to "get even", thus resulting in much disharmony for Mr. Fao. Most likely, if Mr. Fao finds out about the arrangement, he will

---

1. The Five Relationships are fully discussed in Chapter 10.

keep quiet, or if he feels he is in a solid and powerful enough position, he will ask for a cut of the action.

Ramifications

There are a number of ramifications to the OP Perception of Value. The first of these is that for any seller, operating in an environment where the OP Perception of Value is prevalent, may find that personal relations with the buying agent, representative, or negotiator are far more important than the fact of any provable superior quality (over the competition) of the merchandise being sold. Widespread use of this Perception would result in "quality" not being a determinant factor in sales of products between organizations. For the seller to defeat the effects of a widespread OP Perception of Value, it would seem necessary to not only have a significantly superior quality of products, but also abundantly available financial resources to maintain operations until this superior quality has become fully recognized in the marketplace, and actual sales may begin.

The OP Perception of Value may be institutionalized in some organizations, even to the extent that the agent or representative never becomes very involved in the negotiations. Foreigners in China must be concerned with living arrangements, so one example from this area may be relevant: People working as main desk manager, receptionist, building maintenance, etc. in some large apartment/office buildings may have a narrowly defined scope of duties, such as sorting mail which comes into the building, making rounds of the hallways, dealing with routine inquiries by visitors, and related duties. However, there may be no central office for handling inquiries about renting/buying apartments that become vacant, and the desk managers may commonly feel entitled to private commissions of a few percentage points for bringing together any particular "renter" and "rentee" or "seller" and "purchaser" merely due to the fact of handling a routine inquiry at the front desk. Such type of arrangements are a kind of unwritten rule in the operation of the building, and arise from an OP Perception of Value. Thus in selling a condominium for $365,000, when the buying party was "introduced", even in the most indirect fashion, by the front desk personnel, these personnel might well feel entitled to a red envelope of $20,000, or more. The holder of an OM Perception of Value does not deny that some commission may be due in cases of this type, however he feels that it rightly belongs to the organization (the building management company for example) which the desk personnel represent, not to the desk personnel themselves. In that light, if such commissions are due, they are certainly spelled out in the building regulations, and if they are not so spelled out, they cannot be considered due.

In such a case where no established procedures exist, if the desk managers or related personnel do not expect such a red envelope, there is no problem. If they do, a diagram may be drawn as follows:

| the buyer (new tenant) | the seller (old tenant) | the desk managers | Who pays the red envelope? (result) |
|---|---|---|---|
| OM | OM | OP | Maximum potential for conflict |
| OM | OP | OP | Seller pays |
| OP | OM | OP | Buyer pays |
| OP | OP | OP | Seller pays, or buyer pays, or perhaps they split it |

In a society where the OP Perception of Value flourishes, if the desk managers use harrassment, neglect, or other means to make the new tenant's life uncomfortable, in order to enforce the demand for a commission, the society would not consider this behavior out of proportion with the "wrong" which the desk managers have suffered. If anyone's behavior were to be considered unjust, it would be the the new tenant's, since he has not paid the rightful commission which is due, as per custom & tradition, (however not according to law). From a practical standpoint, this serves as an excellent example of how unwritten rules in some societies can have very much influence over determining what is proper or improper, moral or immoral, reasonable or unreasonable behavior.

### Different Explanations

Some comparisons of different patterns of reasoning are useful reference for the commentary in this chapter, and will also be important later in the text when we discuss differing views of liability.

Whither-To Reasoning: **In any conflict of interest situation, this type of reasoning attempts to clear up the issue by considering the present circumstances as a starting point, and examining "Where do we go from here?" in order to arrive at a solution. Hence, consideration is only made of what actions can *now* be undertaken by the parties involved to deal with resolution of the controversy at hand.** Discussion of either party's preceding actions is avoided. Combined with the Group Mentality, it attempts to spread the blame among many.

This is opposite to Where-From Reasoning.

Where-From Reasoning: **In any conflict of interest situation, this type of reasoning attempts to resolve the issue by considering "How did we get here?" and assigning responsibility for resolution of the conflict based on the seen accountability of those who caused the present predicament.** Combined with the Individual(istic) Mentality, it attempts to assign blame to individuals for their actions.

This is opposite to Whither-To Reasoning.

With the recognition of these two different types of reasoning, we may now offer more formal definitions of the initial two Perceptions of Value discussed in this chapter. These Perceptions clarify different ways that the value of goods and services may be viewed.

Ready Readjustment Perception of Value: **Under this perception, the seller has final determination of the price at the point of sale, and may readjust the marked or quoted price to more properly reflect his "component cost", according to his own subjective determination. In this way he can bring the price of the goods in question more properly in line with their (assumed) natural value.** Hence, seemingly unintentional mistakes or oversights in regard to price, quantity, unit of measure, and other types of marking, labelling, displaying, quoting, advertising, etc. made by the selling party are not his responsibility, but rather their consequences are shared by "all", meaning "the group" in the largest sense. **The seller can refuse to sell, and the buyer is only entitled to buy at a price which the seller has determined to be correct.**

This Perception of Value arises directly from the Group Mentality and its stated concerns of Maintenance of Harmony, Whither-To Reasoning, and Primary Sympathetic Orientation, [1] and as such it assumes that the parties involved in any dealing are primarily inclined to be mutually helpful and mutually forgiving.

In a larger sense, the RR Perception of Value can refer to retroactively readjusting the "value" of any items, concrete or abstract, at the point of use, implementation, or final disposition.

As Offered Perception of Value: **Under this perception, all mistakes, whether intentional or otherwise, of one party are the direct responsibility of that same party. Employers are directly responsible for the mistakes or oversights of their employees, representatives, agents, etc., whether due to lack of training and supervision, or just plain incompetence. Any price marked represents a "valid price", and the consumer/buyer has the right to buy at the price offered. At the same time, the seller cannot refuse to sell.**

This Perception of Value arises directly from the Individualistic Mentality and its stated concerns of individuals being responsible for themselves. It stresses facts and reality taking precedence over supposition, Where-From Reasoning, and a Primary Legal Orientation. As such it assumes a contractual arrangement, stated or implied, between the parties, with buyers and sellers being assumed to have an equivalence of rights and obligations.

In a larger sense, the AO Perception of Value can refer to maintenance of the original terms and conditions of any situations, agreements, stipulations, or other circumstances.

Determinations of what constitutes fairness, honesty, and reasonableness will differ

---

1. See the beginning comments in Chapter 5.

depending on which Perception of Value is used as a starting point. The idea of what constitutes "principle", and to what extent "principle" is inviolate, will also depend on which Perception of Value is employed.

## Buying Vegetables

With improved living standards, more modern shops and markets are being built in China, and some of these, especially in the major cities, have standards of cleanliness which are quite high. The foreigner thus often has the option of purchasing his needed food items in such locations, or if such shops are not available in his immediate vicinity, he may take his chances on purchasing foods in the more traditional open-air markets. If stomach problems develop, any of the local herbal doctors may be consulted for a modest fee.

Walking through the open-air markets, one sees many interesting items on display. In the stalls that deal in eels, octupus, frogs, fish, squid, and related aquatic life, many times everything is held in tanks or aquariums, and are sold "still swimming" or "still jumping", so the buyer is assured of freshness. Various types of pork, beef, chicken, duck, goose, and other meat have to be butchered before sale, at least when each customer is buying relatively small quantities, thus the question of freshness and cleanliness is something which is best determined by bringing along a Chinese friend and asking their opinion. With the introduction of defeathering machines into many shops and stalls, if one is buying a whole bird, it is now increasingly possible to choose a healthy live one and have it "cleaned" while you wait. This also is a good way to ensure freshness, quality, and excellent flavor.

In regard to vegetables, many Chinese agree that vegetables with bug holes, and other evidence of insect damage, are generally the most safe for human consumption, even though they do not look so nice. Picking up the perfect and unblemished vegetables for comparison, we realize that if the bugs did not bite into them, it is most likely they have been treated by insecticides and pesticides in vast quantities, or excessive concentrations, since there is little effective regulation of such practices. Some portion of these chemicals is likely to remain even after the most thorough scrubbing, soaking in salt water, or blasting with a high-pressure water hose.

If we could ascertain that the vegetables we were purchasing had been raised in a greenhouse, such considerations might not apply however.

### Individual vs. Unit

Fred, a new arrival in China, went to buy some fruit with his friend Jeffrey, who was a long term resident. When gazing at a number of melons, Fred noticed a small sign with $35 written in large letters. He said: "These are $35 each."

Jeffrey was examining some apples. He shook his head: "That is unlikely."

"Well, how much are they apiece?" Fred questioned.

"The real price? How would I know?" Jeffrey replied.

"You mean to say that they will try to change the price on me when I get ready to buy?"

"Oh, I doubt that. They do not do that deliberately. Why don't you pick out a melon and ask the manager what the price is?"

"But the sign says $35 apiece," Fred countered.

"No," Jeff clarified, "the sign says '$35', and there is a big difference."

Fred picked out a melon and the manager weighed it. He said in halting English: "Sixty-eight dollars please." Fred looked at Jeff: "He wants $68."

"Offer him $60," Jeff countered.

Observation: Another aspect of pricing in many Asian markets is that when melons, cabbages, lettuce, carrots, other vegetables or other items are packaged or displayed individually, with a price clearly marked on the signboard, the price indicated often does not refer to the individual item price, but rather to the "unit price". The unit referred to could be the kilogram, the provincial kilo, or perhaps some other unit of measure, such as 100 grams. This is especially true in regard to vegetables or related items which come in various sizes and weights, such as watermelons. Apples or oranges are naturally more standardized in size, and thus would have some greater possibility of being sold individually.

Chinese Notation

The Chinese characters *je* 折 and *chi* 起 are important in the reading of signs. Essentially, *je* means discount, but is used in the opposite way from English: 8 *je* is 80%, in English we would say "20% off"; 6.5 *je* is 65%, in English we would say "35% off"; etc. The character *chi* has many meanings, however in reading signs it may be translated as "starting at." Hence, $ 100 *chi* means "starting at $ 100", which is to say that the lowest price of any of the offered goods (sold either individually or by unit) is $100, and other goods are more expensive.

These two characters may be combined, as in a sign which says 9 *je chi,* "starting at 90%," which means "starting at 10% off." Some buyers may wonder "10% off of what?" That is certainly a good question, however we have no answer, and indeed the Chinese consumer appears unconcerned with this.

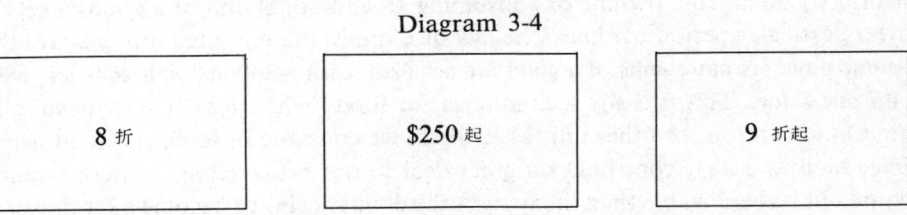

Diagram 3-4

| 8 折 | $250 起 | 9 折起 |

Another peculiar type of price marking is found as follows:

Diagram 3-5

| 5 × $25 = $100 | 3 × 80 = 200 元 |

It is by no means true that the seller is poor in arithmetic. What is meant by the first sign is that the items are $25 each, or five for $100. The second sign indicates that the items are $80 each, or three for $200. The Chinese character yuan 元 means "dollar", and will be frequently encountered.

### The Value of Merchandise

To round out our discussion of value, we will consider how it relates to other economic concepts, especially the labor theory of value.

The economist Stanley Jevons (1835–1882) was the first to show that consumers would increase purchases of a good until the marginal utility gained from a small additional quantity would be equal to the marginal utility of its money price. Karl Menger (1840–1921) also devised a similar formulation. This marginal-utility-based explanation of pricing conflicts with Marx's labor theory of value, which claims that the price is the value of the labor "embodied" in a good. Followers of Marx believe that a good is valuable only because labor is used to make it. Observations of purchaser's behavior in the marketplace are at odds with this interpretation, and Jevons explained this by proving that a good is valuable only if it provides utility; then labor becomes valuable when it is used to produce the good. Labor is not the only valuable factor of production, and when the four elements of land, labor, capital, and entrepreneurial ability are taken into account there is no unjust appropriation of a "surplus value" (over and above labor cost), therefore workers are not exploited, as Marx's writings maintain.

Utility is a measure of the satisfaction obtained from a purchase. Marginal utility is the utility gained from owning or consuming an additional unit of a good or service during a particular period of time. The law of diminishing marginal utility states that after some point, as more units of a good are acquired, each additional unit adds less utility than the one before. This is easily seen in terms of food items. If we like soybean milk, the first bowl, carton, or other unit of it which we consume in some specified period of time, such as a day, contributes a great deal to our satisfaction. A second unit is still good but less enjoyable than the first. A third unit begins to become a bit tiresome.

If pressed, we can get a fourth unit down, but we wish we were eating or drinking something else. Many pleasures tend to diminish in this fashion, the more we indulge in them. The same analysis would apply if we were purchasing the soybean milk to give as gifts to other people: the more gifts given, the less our additional pleasure received from the expressions of thankfulness of each succeeding recipient. People's purchases of goods and services vary according to the marginal utility that goods and services provide.

For discussion purposes, marginal utility is generally measured in the imaginary unit of utils. Although the unit of measurement is imaginary, the satisfaction derived from consumption is not imaginary.

Money can also be said to have marginal utility. People do not like to spend all of their available funds; they prefer to have some cash on hand, to put some money into a bank account, to put some funds into certificates of deposit, etc. The marginal utility of money is greater for some people than for others: we would expect that people with a relatively low income would recognize the last dollar available for spending as having a greater marginal utility, because it would be more precious; whereas people of a relatively high income would view the last dollar available for spending as having a lesser marginal utility, because it would be less precious.

Let us consider S, which is a product or service. From the consumer's point of view, the marginal utility of each additional unit consumed (MU), divided by the Price of each unit (P), yields the marginal utility per dollar (MU/P). As the consumer begins to spend his income, the marginal utility of each additional unit of money used (MU\$) may then be considered, and a relation established.

It will be seen that as the consumer or other buyer begins his purchases of a particular item, the marginal utility attained by each dollar of purchase exceeds the marginal utility of retaining the money, hence $MU/P > MU\$$. According to the law of diminishing marginal utility, eventually the point is reached where the marginal utility of each dollar spent equals the marginal utility of keeping the money, hence $MU/P = MU\$$. The consumer will not purchase beyond this point, for to do so would yield less marginal utility than that achieved by simply holding on to the money, which would be expressed as $MU/P < MU\$$.

Hence, at the limit, the consumer's purchases of this item will reveal a relationship expressed by $MU/P = MU\$$, and this is the simplest formulation of Jevon's analysis. By equating MU/P with MU\$ at differing price levels of the products or services in question, an economist can plot the consumer's demand curve. Jevon's work in utility theory has been carried on by later economists, especially Alfred Marshall (1842–1924), as an explanation of the various factors operating in the marketplace.

A Better Life for Labor

The socialist and communist writers claim that their societies better promote the workers' interests, are more favorable to the workers' livelihood, place labor in an exalted position, etc. Such claims are quickly disproved from an economic standpoint by referring to comparative wage earnings and retail prices in various regions. If we check statistical bulletins and assemble data on earnings of employees in the manufacturing industries in various Chinese provinces, as well as data on the local prices of food, clothing, electric apparatuses, appliances, etc. some insight can quickly be gained. It is no accident that the Taiwan worker can buy more goods with every day of wage income: Taiwan is the one Chinese province which has most successfully instituted the capitalistic economic system. That communism leads to a much more inefficient and non worker-beneficent allocation of resources and production is seen by the vastly decreased purchasing power of the workers in the communist controlled provinces (as revealed by a comparison of local income levels and local price levels). Analysis of data for workers in other industries, (mining, construction, transport, business services, etc.) reveal similar trends: clearly the workers' efforts have greater "value" in a capitalist system than in a communist one. All of these factors are important illustrations of the flaws of Marx's theories.

## Paradoxes

### Praise

My American friend went to a Chinese fruit shop one day and ordered some sliced pineapple. Upon going to pay the bill, he found that he had not brought enough change. After expressing his regret to the store personnel, he was surprised to hear them say: "Oh well, it doesn't matter. Don't worry about it." His natural reaction was that "The Chinese are very generous, warm hearted, and hospitable people. They will help you out if you need it."

### Criticism

Another western friend of mine went to a fruit shop one day and ordered some mango juice. Upon going to pay the bill, the store personnel told him that the prices had recently been changed, although the wall posters and menus had not yet been amended to reflect this. They stated that the correct price was several dollars higher than the marked price. After debating this state of affairs with the manager for several minutes, his natural reaction was "The Chinese people are most unreasonable, and will try to switch prices on you if you are not careful, all the while maintaining that their new price is 'the correct price.' I feel sorry for the Chinese public who are continually gouged by these dishonest shop owners."

Actually, what the first foreigner is praising here, and what the second is criticizing are one in the same thing. In the first case, the Chinese shop owner did not make a fuss about the shortage of a few coins. In the second case the average Chinese consumer would not have argued about the additional amount which the "new price" represented.Stated simply, this idea could be put as "The Chinese tend not to quibble over small amounts of money, especially in regard to common daily expenses." This is our first example of a Praise-Criticism Paradox.

**Praise-Criticism Paradox: Differing conclusions or inferences, from the view of foreigners, in regard to two different experiences, one of which is felt to be praiseworthy, and the other of which is felt deserving of criticism, but which merely reflect differing facets of an identical underlying mentality, belief, or orientational preference in the natives of the Entry Culture.**

In discussing the dealings between Chinese and westerners, we will run across the Praise-Criticism Paradox frequently if we only care to be on the lookout for it. A foreigner living in China need only catalog the "praise" and "criticism" he hears from other expatriates over a period of weeks or months, and he will see that many "match up" as forming a complete PC Paradox. It is thus a truism to note that many of the pleasures and irritants of living in China are inseparable: they are two sides of the same coin, due to the way the Chinese value system is organized.

Of note is that: 1) generally the "praise" and the "criticism" are being expressed by different foreigners, and 2) although the two elements of the Paradox are "two sides of the same coin" in the Chinese thinking processes, psychological makeup, or way of doing things, they may not exist as such in a more westernized mentality. Some may see PC Paradoxes as being the result of a double standard, however we believe this is a vast oversimplification of the cross-cultural considerations involved.

Here is another example of a PC Paradox in the realm of eating:

Mr. Chang, my architect friend, bumped into Mary and John on the street one day, and invited them to go together with him to a local hotel, where he and his Chinese associates were having a big dinner. Mary and John were free at the time and went along. They were very impressed by the hospitality shown them, and all the food they were offered. It was certainly a very delightful meal, and left them feeling very pleasant.

Joan and Ronnie were newly arrived in China, and held a big dinner party at their house for all the Chinese co-workers in their company's local branch office. Having planned for 35 people to come, they were dismayed when 46 showed up, and there were not enough seats at the tables, nor enough food to serve everyone. This situation left them rather exasperated.

Again we see here that what is being praised as being "pleasant", and what is criticized as leaving us "exasperated" are one and the same thing. The thinking which ties these two situations together, which we will call the "thread", may be stated simply as: Due to traditional eating habits, the Chinese are not bothered when more people show up for a meal than were invited, and they cannot imagine that anyone else would be either. To the non-natives living in China, this has both its good and bad points.

In reviewing the experiences of other foreigners who have come before us, if we can recognize the "threads" and become aware of PC Paradoxes, it will then be possible to formulate better strategies for our own dealings, in order to maximize our chances to be involved in situations which we will want to praise, and minimize our chances to be involved in situations which we will want to criticize.

# PART 2 Enlightened Money Management

## Chapter 4 Opportunities and Obstacles

### Money

The financial considerations in which a foreigner must involve himself are primarily in terms of his economic livelihood, which at the most basic level is the income and outflow of money. Thus a discussion of Foreigner's Finances and Money Management must include not only considerations of being an employee, being a boss, or otherwise earning money, but also borrowing, or in other fashions accumulating money, as well as investing, spending, loaning, and otherwise making use of money to fulfill various obligations, needs, or desires in the foreign country. Some extraordinary expenditures such as social expenses, liability for accidents, and other items must also be considered as well.

In this chapter we have chosen some representative examples to illustrate various facets of these different financial issues which are important when dealing with the Chinese. Several new and important perceptual tools are introduced so that we may analyze and come to grips with Chinese behavior which to the untrained foreigner may appear contradictory, enigmatic, or without logical basis. A number of liberal digressions have been taken where it was felt that an important point of Chinese thinking could be clarified in the process.

$ Income: In terms of employment in the Chinese community, we have chosen to go into the various considerations involved in doing Movie and TV acting work, which leads us into a discussion of the differing views of "the relationship between reward and effort". We see how this affects the negotiation for rental of a meeting room, and the hiring of a secretary. A Chinese investment proposal is outlined, and its characteristic features are examined. A promising backyard investment is also mentioned, and its essential unworkability is brought to light. Banking and Credit are overviewed. Since many foreigners deal or hope to deal in international trading, some unusual aspects of this are pointed out. A business consultant's methods for dealing with construction problems in a new foreign-invested hotel are discussed. Many types of freelancing activities are covered, and common pitfalls are listed. Some consideration is made of how to choose joint venture partners. Normal ways in which local Chinese raise money outside of banking circles are outlined in detail, both as they relate to financial income and outflow.

$ Outflow: Further on the outflow side, some peculiarities of the Chinese thinking about liability are discussed, since the foreigner who is unaware of these could find himself caught off guard and in serious trouble. Western concepts of liability are reviewed. Methods of comparing the Western and Chinese views of liability, injury, and damage are examined in several illustrative examples. Attitudinal adjustments necessary for dealing with incidental expenses in laundry, housing, employment, international trading, and other activities are considered.

A multitude of other topics which deal with unusual aspects of income and expense are also examined.

## Private and Public Concerns

Due to the generally sympathetic[1] nature of the Chinese people, which they apparently regard as a highly moral, and almost noble, trait, and their general lack of demanding or pushy behavior, we often find that many times the private citizen will come forth and be willing to expend of his time, money, and effort in order to rectify essentially public ills, i.e. those arising from outdated, unrealistic, or irresponsible policies of organizations, departments, corporations, and the bureaucracy in general, or any bureaucracy in particular.

"Private" then as used here refers to the private individual, or a group of private individuals. "Public" is used to include both government and business, since in Chinese the two character word for public, 公共 (government, party-in-power, etc.) and the two character word for corporate 公司 (business, company, etc.) begin with the same character and are often lumped together under this general category in the Chinese thinking.

Thus we frequently see the case of broken promises of an organization to an individual are "set aright" through the private actions of one or a more of its employees. The expression "I will take you out to dinner" is often heard.

Examples are numerous. A foreigner, or a Chinese who studied abroad, receives a request from an organization for some course of action to be taken, or some job to be done. The day has arrived to do the work, and the individual hired for the job shows up, only to be informed of a sudden change in plans, or a delay to a later date. This person replies: "You have a right to change your plans, but I also have a right to the salary which I was promised for today's work. Please pay me my money."

---

1. See the *Sympathy* essay in Chapter 10.

The organization however has no procedures for paying for work requested but "not done" in a real physical sense, so some unpleasantness ensues between the representatives (employees, etc.) of the organization, and the individual involved. The native Chinese are always surprised when such arguments erupt, since they do not see why everyone does not agree to the concept of maintaining harmonious social relations, which would solve all problems.

In the end, since no payment is forthcoming, one or more of the employees agree to take the aggrieved party out to dinner (or some other similar arrangements are made), as a way of compensating him for his "loss", which "loss" of course the organization neither recognizes nor feels responsible for. The employees pay for this dinner out of their own pockets.

Thus rather than encouraging organizational responsibility, we often see total avoidance of the issue altogether. Regarding outside personnel and consultants, no procedures are set up or meetings held to discuss how to avoid similar difficulties in the future, or how to assess responsibility within the organization when such difficulties occur. As one might expect, similar situations are repeated every few months. The suggested advice to the foreigner who gets involved or is getting ready to get involved in cases like this can be simple or complex. The simple advice would be: "Roll with the tide, play the cards as they fall, take your chances." Better advice would be to ask to talk to someone who had done similar work for the organization before, and find out their feelings and impressions on the way the organization handled itself, especially in the area of keeping promises. Sometimes, admittedly, this option is not available.

If one had an adequate reputation or professional skills, payment of part or all of the fee involved could be requested in advance. This option is also often not available to the average individual. However, questions could be asked about who is in charge of the actual payment, when payment will be made, and how far in advance cancellation notice has to be given if the organization decides on different or postponed arrangements. Hopefully, agreement could then be reached between the party being hired and the organization involved that after the deadline, no cancellations would be acceptable, (except in the case of a natural disaster such as flooding, earthquake, typhoon warning severe enough for all government offices and schools to be closed, or an act of war), but certainly not in the case of a secretarial oversight or mistake, a last minute change of plans by the head of the organization, mechanical failure of equipment, or the failure of gear and other apparatus to arrive or be prepared in time, etc. The money would fall due after the cancellation deadline had been passed. Admittedly, this type of discussion and haggling does not endear one to the Chinese, since they see this sort of attitude as evidence of a lack of sympathy for their position should plans change. They are often unable to conceive of the western idea that the irresponsibility of the organization in not following up on the promises of its employees, given in the line of duty, is not acceptable.

One of the most important questions for the foreigner to ask, and receive an answer to in work for which he is being hired on a part time, temporary, or short term basis is: "What am I being paid for?" Due to the demands of the new technology in the world today, the best illustration we can give of the importance of receiving an answer to this question is in the field of doing TV work in China.

## The Acting Profession

The foreigner is often hired to do small walk-on parts in a variety of TV shows, some requiring spoken Chinese ability, and some not. Introductions to such work are generally haphazard and unorganized, since there is no central casting office or registration office for small part players, foreigners, extras, etc. Notices of such opportunities to act are, however, occasionally found in the classified advertisement section of the local English newspaper(s), or on the bulletin boards of the Language Schools, Youth Hostels, etc. The typical notice states that the foreigners are wanted from perhaps 7:00 am to 5:00 pm for all day shooting, or other hours if the shooting is only half day, or at night, or whatever. The pay is noted as perhaps "X" number of dollars, which usually works out to a bit less than what the foreigner would get if he spent the same amount of time teaching English at some academy. However, since it is a new and potentially exciting situation, the foreigner thinks it would be fun to try.

After contacting the producer and arranging the details of where to meet and what to wear, the foreigner generally makes the assumption that he is being hired for the hours stated, at the price quoted. And based on this assumption, he makes other relevant plans such as cancelling or postponing other classes, engagements, appointments, etc.

However, if he would care to inquire a little deeper, he would ask: "Now wait a second, let me get this clear, I am being hired from 7:00 to 5:00 for $X, is that correct?"

The producer replies, "Yes, that is correct."

He reaffirms, "I can leave at 5:00 no matter what."

"You can leave at 5:00 if we are done."

Here we see a new stipulation has been added. The foreigner says, "But I have made an appointment for 6:00, and since it will take me some time to get there, it is necessary that I leave at 5:00. If I do leave at 5:00 will I get my money?"

"We can pay you if we are done, but not if we are not done."

The foreigner quickly thinks of the possibilities of camera trouble, late arrivals by the leading actors, late arrival by the director, etc. and asks if there is a possibility of any of these events occuring.

The producer says, "Yes, that might happen."

"In which case we might not get done by 5:00."

The producer says, "Yes, that might be the case."

"And then I would not get my money?" the foreigner asks.

The producer restates his revised position: "We will pay you when we get done shooting."

Hence we see that what the foreigner thinks he is being hired for, and what the Chinese thinks he is hiring the foreigner for are two different things. Thus the foreigner must weigh this commitment against his other engagement(s) in terms of importance, and make a decision as to which one is more important should a conflict arise. Ideally, no other plans will be made for the rest of the day or the evening.

However, this still does not cover the possibility of last minute cancellations, in which case the foreigner finds himself with no income for the day at all. If he had arranged for someone else to cover his other teaching or work commitments, he may even suffer a loss for the day. Therefore it is almost imperative that some agreement be reached on cancellation policy for TV and Movie work, yet, when dealing with the Chinese, it is difficult to establish any such agreement which they will stick to when problems arise, and they generally are repelled by the thought of putting contractual arrangements for walk-on or bit players down on paper.

In the TV line, many directors who shoot outdoors are famous for saying: "The weather is lousy today, let's postpone everything until tomorrow," after the camera crew and actors are all assembled bright and early at 7:30 am. While the actors and camera crew are conceivably on a salary, and can take such rescheduling in stride, bit players are generally not. They are surprised when they are sent home with nothing more than an "I am sorry." If protest is made, several dinner offers are generally forthcoming.

Therefore it is all-important to thrash out beforehand exactly: "What am I being paid for?" since Chinese and western concepts of what is fair or reasonable in such instances vary so widely.

It is also important to establish the line of authority responsible for making actual payment of money. In many cases where the Producer or other person in charge does not speak enough English to communicate with foreigners, someone else with better language skills may act as go-between. Often this go-between has only a very tenuous relationship with the production company. If the foreigner is on his toes he will ask: "Are you guaranteeing me payment of the acting fee if any misunderstandings arise with the production company?" Typically the go-between will reply: "I am only helping to translate." Obviously this is not the person with whom you want to reach agreement. You should make an effort to talk to the person who is actually in charge of making disbursement of the funds, and then try to assess his position in the power structure of the organization as well.

Further Complexities

In summary, we see that the Chinese TV people tend to view a job in terms of whether it is done or not, and not according to the originally agreed upon time limits, which they assume everyone knows to be vastly adjustable depending on any circumstances which come up. However, there are many more twists. During a filming of *Alive in the Bitter Sea*, in which there were over a dozen foreign part-time actors selected out of the local foreign community, the payment was not given on the spot, since every foreigner had many days of studio shooting and outdoor work, but rather was calculated by the accounting department of the T.V. station, who then notified them to come pick it up.Upon going to get their acting money, two girls noted that according to their records of days shot, their payment was short by one day. The accounting department of course could only verify the accuracy of the documents they had been given by the people in the program department, and were unaware of any discrepancies. The lady in charge said she would make inquiries. The girls left, and later called up the assistant producer about this problem. He explained that they were not actually short one day's payment. They compared notes on the days shot, and verified that they *were indeed short* one day's payment. "No, I am sorry, you misunderstood," he said, "the T.V. station had too much footage and so could not edit the recording we did on the 11th into the final tape. Since it was not broadcast, so of course no payment can be made."

The girls protested that when they were hired for the job, they were told they would be paid for shooting. Nothing was said about payment depending on actual broadcasting.

The assistant director said that that was the procedure of the T.V. station in such cases. The girls refused his offer of dinner.

Thus we see that a failure to understand clearly "What am I being paid for?" is a major source of misunderstanding in a wide variety of similar circumstances. Admittedly in the dealings such as the one above, when fees are being calculated by the T.V. station for payment at a later date, another possible source of problems is the discrepancy between the station's records and the actor's, with the resulting burden of somehow proving that you actually worked the days you said you did, or that you have been paid for W number of days, and still have Y number of days outstanding, while according to the station's records you have already been paid for R number of days, and only have S number of days outstanding. Needless to say you are not being paid for the time it takes you to get everything straightened out.

But even when there are no discrepancies, problems can still arise, as the following example illustrates. A foreigner named Cindy was found to work in a series being produced jointly by a Hong Kong film company and a local company. She had done some T.V. work before in Asia and believed she understood how these companies operated. Since the part would have her in and out of the studio part-time for a number of weeks, she was asked if she wanted to be paid by the day (which would mean being paid a fixed sum for any and all hours worked in a day's shooting schedule), or the script (scripts are numbered, with one script for each broadcast day). She said she wanted to be paid by the script. To give an example of this, if the amount of money offered per performance was $50, and today you shot two scripts, if paid by the script you would be entitled to $100, if paid by the day, then only $50. However if today you are shooting script #14 and you are shooting some more scenes from script #14 next Tuesday, then if paid by the script you would receive $50 for the two days, but if paid by the day you would receive $100.

The arrangement was to pick up her payment in the accounting office an unspecified number of days after the shooting of each episode. As the situation came to develop, Cindy could generally expect that if the producer called and said she could go pick up her money for three shootings the next day, if she waited three days and then went across town to the studio and down into the basement in the accounting department she could generally get one payment, and the girl in accounting would say that the others "had not come down yet." Keeping track of the payments and going to get them was a major source of confusion and discomfort. After the shooting was finished, Cindy calculated that she was still owed for five shootings. She called the contact man in the T.V. station who had arranged for her to appear originally and discussed this with him. He agreed to her calculation.

However, no further news was forthcoming. Cindy called him up the next week, and he said she could come and get her money. She went over the next day. The girl in accounting said no further payments had come down. The contact man was not in. The producer and his assistants were in a large room on the second floor going over scripts. Cindy went to talk to them. They went over the records of her acting, however, they could not find copies of some days of the shooting schedule. Estimating as best they could, they determined that Cindy was owed nothing, since the five shootings she felt she was still owed were actually shots in other scenes in scripts which she had previously begun. According to their records she had agreed to be paid by script, and not by the day. Cindy had never run into the situation before that T.V. scenes shot so many days apart were part of the same script, but she admitted that this could have been true, and the records which she kept in her looseleaf notebook were too undetailed to prove otherwise, so she went along with the T.V. station's decision. She never could understand why the contact man had told her to come and get her money however.

To summarize the situation of the T.V. work, one must always understand what one is being paid for. The stated hours? Or getting the shooting done? Will overtime be paid if we go past the stated hours? What is the policy as regards cancellations, and how much advance notice will be given? Will I be paid at the close of the day's shooting? Or will I have to come back at some later date for my money? If I have to come back for my money, am I being paid for shooting or for broadcasting? Am I being paid for the script or the day? Ideally, if you are given this latter option you should ask for both: the script(s) or the day(s), whichever is greater. And yes, you can comfort yourself with the thought that Charlton Heston never had these problems.

Advanced Negotiation with Producers and Directors

As the T.V./Movie Producers and Directors in China expand their foreign contacts, and begin to treat more international material, there is more and more opportunity for foreigners, even sometimes some "big name" foreigners, to participate in Chinese filming. I have run into my share of western talent (both locally and non-locally hired) in making the rounds of Chinese studios, and have had the opportunity to discuss contractual relations with many of them. There is of course much "upcoming talent" in Europe, North America, Australia, etc., for example people who are already established models, or have had supporting roles in big box-office successes, who have won beauty contests, or muscle-contests, and others who may have a chance to be hired by the Chinese. To all of these people, some comments on advanced Chinese negotiating tactics are perhaps useful.

A typical case occurred when a former Miss Spain was approached by a Chinese movie company with an offer to star as the female lead in one of their upcoming productions. As negotiations between the two parties developed, it appeared that the Chinese company was offering considerably less than what Miss Spain thought she was worth, in light of her status. The Chinese movie company countered with this statement: "We appreciate your point of view, and we think it is valid. However, there is something more important to be considered, and that is the working relation between you and our film company. Let consider the facts: we are not familiar with you, and you are not familiar with us. Our customs and traditions are different. We do not even know if we can work together successfully on this movie—it is 'an experiment' of sorts. But we can tell you this, if the word gets out in China that you can cooperate successfully with the Chinese way of doing things, there are going to be a lot of other film companies getting in touch with you. After all, they are unfamiliar with most actors in the west, and would prefer to deal with people who are recommended by other Chinese. When that time comes, we can give you a strong recommendation, you can probably name your price, and they will be happy to pay it. So, we think that going along with our offer now will actually be most advantageous to you in the long run."

She accepted their offer.

Essentially the same approach has even been used successfully on overseas Chinese, 1) the Chinese gentleman who won an Oscar for his role in *The Killing Fields,* 2) the Chinese youth who co-starred in *The Temple of Doom*. Other examples are numerous. The offers were all accepted.

While not wanting to question the sincerity of the Chinese negotiators' statements, we would like to present the reader with a more "realistic" view of how actor's fees are "calculated". In China, with no actors' union or guild of any real bargaining power, these fees are primarily dictated by the studios, and tend to be essentially "fixed" in very narrow ranges. This is the standard fee, although more often it is referred to by the term "transportation fee". The primary consideration in selecting name-talent is "box-office pull", and closely following this is "investor or advertiser support and interest". These factors will generally determine what level of payment is feasible, over and above what the Chinese view as the standard fee, and in addition to transportation and lodging for those who do not live in the local community.

Among the Orientals, it is known that while most Chinese actors do not earn much, nevertheless some Chinese actors are very highly paid indeed. The highly paid Chinese actors tend to fall into a few categories: 1) top lead stars with a proven "track record" in Chinese movies, with tremendous box-office pull in China, 2) stars of above average box office pull who invest in their own productions and thus share directly in a portion of the profits when such productions are successful, 3) TV people who handle all the advertising for the shows in which they star, and thus receive large advertising commissions, 4) actors who convince others to invest in their productions, and hence receive some commissions from the production company for their efforts in locating capital.

Even among the stars of category one, standard practice is to stipulate the payment of the acting fee for a movie in one lump amount. Due to the vagaries of Chinese accounting practices, stipulations of A) additional payment of some percentage of the gross, over and above the acting fee agreed upon, or B) further payment in the event of a "re-release", etc. are rarely made, and generally unenforceable anyway. One possible point of negotiation involves "foreign release rights" however, and if it were felt that the movie had potential in the west and these rights could be resold at a profit, these rights might want to be pursued.

For a person of Mr. Universe status, someone with a Hollywood background, or other big-name talent, what often happens is that after working for a relatively low fee in one movie, the next Chinese production company, if there is another offer, will expect to be granted the same treatment. Since there are few secrets about money matters among the Chinese, it is most likely that any companies which inquire will have an easy time determining the exact amount of money which the actor received in the first film job. During the negotiations for future movies, the first production company may even stick in their two cents worth and ask the actor to accept these same terms (the second time) "as a personal favor".

A similar situation exists with Chinese TV production which is contracted out to foreign companies. Since the budgeting allowed is usually inadequate by foreign standards, there is often the sweet-sounding stipulation added by the Chinese parties to the effect "Why don't you do one season, and show us what kind of quality you can produce? Then we will be able to go to our higher-ups and get much more money for the next season." A lot of the foreign production companies fall for this, and when no higher budget is forthcoming for the following season, the foreigners go packing. Before long another foreign production company comes on the scene, and the entire "show" is "acted out" again.

In summation, we can see that for the foreigner, acting in Chinese movies or TV is best viewed as an interesting sideline, or supplement, to one's other activities, but not as a potential career, and the same is probably true of producing as well. It is a wonderful chance to meet some of the people, and learn about a different way of life, but one is best advised not to entertain any hopes of striking it rich.

## TV Work and Studio Organization

The westerner may gain some further insight into the nature of TV work in China by considering several types of organizational structure which affect the delineation of responsibility among TV personnel. Basically speaking, two areas of responsibility must be determined: 1) Production, which includes payment for all personnel including cameramen, producers, directors, actors, scriptwriters, etc., and for rental of studio, cameras, sound equipment, purchase of scenery, props, film, arrangement of vehicles and transportation, and all related items. 2) Advertising, which includes finding advertisers and arranging all the details for their support of the program. If a one hour show which is on the air once a week is considered to have a season of 13 weeks, obviously it is advisable to have advertiser support for the first several weeks (or more) already firmly lined up before the first show is even aired.

If production is handled by the TV station, it is considered "internal" or in-house; if it is handled by an outside production company, it is considered "external", and we may call this ex-house. If advertising is handled by the TV station, it is considered "internal" or in-house; if it is handled by an outside advertising agency, it is considered "external", or ex-house. Hence, four possibilities are available:

1) In-house production, In-house advertising
2) In-house production, Ex-house advertising
3) Ex-house production, In-house advertising
4) Ex-house production, Ex-house advertising

For the foreign actor who is invited to participate in a filming, it could be expected that discussion of acting fees and other terms of employment could contain a bit more room for negotiation and flexibility if the production is ex-house, whereas an in-house production probably has its payment structure firmly fixed by the TV station. The possibility of receiving commissions for advertising which is firmly lined up would be most feasible if the advertising is ex-house. It is not true that all TV shows filmed inside the TV station are in-house production, they could be ex-house, with the outside production company renting the use of the studio.

Sometimes a foreign production company may contract to shoot a program or series for showing on Chinese TV, with the station responsible for obtaining advertising support. In the view of the Chinese TV station this would clearly fall under variation 3. Any actors or other personnel hired to participate in the filming would negotiate their fees directly with the foreign production company.

Many Chinese TV stations regard their relations with, or rights to relations with, overseas TV stations with some jealousy. Some stories have been heard of westerners (who were employed in other fields of endeavor) being asked by TV station personnel to locate certain types of foreign TV films, film-clips, documentaries, or other special programs for use by Chinese TV. When the unwary foreigner did locate these, and attempted to sell the rights for their broadcast to the local station, it was found that no such sale was possible, since the TV stations do not allow casual outsiders to act as middlemen in the purchase of such rights. What the foreigner had done was merely to save the TV personnel a lot of footwork, and of course a warm thank you and several offers of dinner were received.

Whether the situation would be any different if the foreigner was a registered and accredited production company (in his home country) is hard to say, we suspect this would depend on the solidity of his contacts in the Chinese mass media.

## Reward/Effort Relationships

One factor which is important in our discussion of Perception of Value, and which has not yet been covered, is the relationship of reward to effort, in which we must attempt to deal with the issue of "What constitutes reward without effort?",[1] and the opposite "What constitutes reward with effort?" In another phrasing, "When should effort not be rewarded?" and "When should effort be rewarded?" This distinction will play an important role in our discussion of situations where conflict of interest arises in relation to earning or paying money, or what types of work or leisure are entitled to be remunerated financially.

Agricultural Society Reward/Effort Relationship: **In this relationship, reward to which a person is entitled corresponds to physical effort he has expended in getting the work done. Where no work has actually been done, no reward is due, thus time is not money if one is not physically working. Likewise, remuneration is not due if, in doing activity X, certain portions of the expense relevant to this activity were already covered by activity Y, and one has essentially not incurred any additional expense in doing activity X, since this is considered "by the way". Moreover, remuneration is not due in regard to work which is seen as a trading of favors.** Abbreviated: AS Reward/Effort Relationship.

Industrial Society Reward/Effort Relationship: **In this relationship, reward to which a person is due is seen in regard to the stated or implied contractual relationship between parties. When contractual arrangements have been completed, reward is due. Work is recognized as having both physical and mental dimensions, and it may be concrete or abstract, tangible or intangible. Time is money, and the allocation of time, capital, or other resources to any particular project represents effort which is worthy of reward. Although no additional expense may be involved in doing some activity, it is seen as a "specific project", and reward is due. Information, knowledge, expertise, and intellectual property also represent effort spent, and are therefore worthy of reward. Trading of favors is very limited in scope.** Abbreviated: IS Reward/Effort Relationship.

---

1. This essay attempts to illustrate and clarify some views of what 不勞而獲 consists of, in the Chinese idea.

(Note: Gambling is one significant field of activity which the local populace may regard as outside any consideration of a Reward/Effort Relationship.)

The determination of what represents honesty, fairness, reasonableness, or ethical conduct will depend on what type of Reward/Effort Relationship is held by the different parties.

We may consider a few examples to clarify these Relationships.

Renting a Room

Mr. Chang works for a Chinese company, and is assigned to organize the holding of a one day seminar for a number of business people to discuss some new management techniques and other knowledge. He is presently unable to find a suitable location. Through a friend, Mr. Wong, he is introduced to a foreign manager, Mr. Smith, of a large company. Mr. Chang explains his situation, and Mr. Smith notes that his office has a large meeting room suitable for such a meeting, and that it will be vacant on Sunday, the proposed day of the meeting. Remuneration for use of the room for one day is discussed, and Mr. Chang states that "talking about money is harmful to personal relations", however he will discuss the matter further with their mutual friend, Mr. Wong, and see what he feels is a reasonable figure.

Later Mr. Wong calls Mr. Smith. After some polite preliminaries, he offers this analysis of the situation: since the room in question is not being used that day, as Mr. Smith has announced, and Mr. Chang will provide all of his own personnel, refreshments, as well as cleaning-up afterward, Mr. Smith will actually incur no additional expense (over and above normal payments for rent, upkeep, custodial fees, etc.) and so it is fair to let Mr. Chang use the room for free. (Water and electricity expenses for the day are estimated as minimal.) As if this were not enough, Mr. Wong hopes that Mr. Smith will consider making use of the room available as a "personal favor". Mr. Smith pauses to consider this proposal.

Here we see that Mr. Chang and Mr. Wong ascribe to an Agricultural Society Reward/Effort Relationship. Mr. Smith, being a westerner, more likely ascribes to an Industrial Society Reward/Effort Relationship. Effective discussion or communication between the two sides is therefore hampered. Serious conflict of interest has not yet arisen however. Such conflict of interest could occur if the seminar were held first, and a discussion of what constitutes "fair payment" held afterward.

People ascribing to different Reward/Effort Relationships may find their attempts to communicate are disjointed at the conceptual level. Examples are numerous and will be brought out frequently in our text.

We note that further inquiry by Mr. Smith revealed that Mr. Chang's company was a profit-making concern (as opposed to a charitable one) and that participants in the one-day seminar would be paying a fee for attendance. Yet this seemed to have no effect on the reasoning of the Chinese parties, and in fact the consideration of "personal favor" was brought up. This is an important aspect of the discussion, in that it gives us insight into an "Integration of Concepts", which is important to clarify.

Integration of Concepts: **to bring concepts, as represented by words or terminology, together into a whole, and regard them as unified. Such integration may be spoken of as "high" indicating that the terms are seen as truly united, or "low", meaning that the terms are seen as essentiallly separate.**

In our example here, regarding the concepts of "Business Relations" and "Personal Relations," the Chinese parties appear to assume a high degree of integration, meaning that there is no separation between the concepts. We may designate this as: Business Relations = Personal Relations. The westerner would probably be more inclined to assume a low degree of integration, meaning that he would consider them as separate concepts. We may designate this as: Business Relations ≠ Personal Relations. The suggestion that the use of the room be made available as a "personal favor" is perhaps inappropriate by the westerner's standards, since he sees this as a purely business concern.

People from different cultural and philosophical backgrounds often have assigned different degrees of integration to various key concepts, thus resulting in different ideas of what is fair, reasonable, or proper.

## Employing the Locals

There is the story of the European manufacturer who set up a small manufacturing facility on a South Pacific Island. With the help of the local government officials he was able to hire a workforce of over thirty people. After a few days of training, production began, and at the end of the month salaries were paid. The next day the manager waited from dawn to dusk, but no one showed up for work.

Upon checking with the local officials it was quickly verified that all the employees had taken their salaries and gone on big shopping sprees, and since they had not yet spent all of their money, they were too busy to show up for duty. The officials assured the manager that all the employees would come back to work "when they were broke", and suggested that in the future, instead of paying salary once a month, it would be best to pay on a daily basis. Most employees would then spend their money shopping or partying in the evening, and would be "sure bets" to blow it all. This would guarantee that they showed up the next day for work.

I have talked to many foreign managers in charge of overseeing production in various factories in China, and they have assured me that this kind of situation is unknown. It is more typically found in a populace where the educational standards are quite low. In China, much value is placed upon education, and thus educational standards tend to be high. The Chinese worker is intelligent, conscientious, and diligent, and often wins much praise from foreign supervisors.

Nevertheless, there may be employment situations where conflicts of interest arise. Over the years we have collected a few representative examples along these lines, and present them here for reference.

## Apparent Contradictory Reasoning

By employing various perceptual tools, we will be able to rationalize, or attempt to rationalize apparently contradictory types of reasoning. The following case is one example.

A survey was taken of 25 upper-middle class Chinese. They were given a situation. Part A: "An employer desires to hire a girl for his office with duties including receptionist, organizing documents, some accounting, filing, etc. Due to some problems he has had before with people who did not work out, he states that if this new employee does not complete a minimum of one full month of service, no salary will be paid. Is this fair?" Twenty-two of the Chinese said "Yes, this is fair."

Next they were given Part B: "A girl is chosen for this position from a group of applicants. After a while her grandmother falls ill and moves into the hospital, in addition one of her cousin's is involved in an industrial accident and requires an operation, and her brother is accepted to college and must begin assembling the necessary tuition monies. Furthermore, she learns from a former classmate that there is an opening in another company which may come available shortly and which pays a higher salary than this job does. One day, three weeks into this new job, when her father comes by to meet her after work, she informs him of her decision to quit this job, primarily so that she can stay with her grandmother in the hospital. The girl and her father then jointly inform the manager of this decision, and ask to be paid for the three weeks already worked. Is the girl's request to be paid for this three week's work fair?" Nineteen of the Chinese said "Yes, it is fair."

Twenty five westerners were given this situation. Twenty-five said the stipulations in Part A were fair, twenty-four said the girl's request in Part B was not fair.

A story was recounted at this point. A medium sized service and sales company of a particular type of product hired a number of local Chinese employees for instructional and promotional work. Over 80% of these people were recent college graduates. After an initial month or two of service, the employees were given the option of working for a 20% higher than normal hourly salary, if they would sign a contract guaranteeing a minimum of one year of service. It was specified that if they did sign a contract, and did complete one full year of service, they would be given one month's pay bonus as well. The majority of the employees did sign the contract, and there seemed to be minimal problems with this arrangement. Working hours were primarily afternoons and evenings, and employees were stationed at different offices throughout the city.

And then there was Celia. Hired in January, she signed a contract in late February. She worked in an energetic and responsible manner. However in early September, complaining of her father's ill health, she said that her parents had requested that she move back to their hometown (some two hours away by train) and find a job in the nearby community. Indeed this would also facilitate being near her father and taking care of him during his illness. She was therefore forced to resign. Since her family needed money, she politely asked if she could have the stipulated bonus for full completion of her contracted service. The Manager of the company had lived and studied in Japan and Europe for many years, and she felt unable to grant this request.

On Sept. 10th, at 10:30 a.m., a meeting for all personnel was held in the Main Office to discuss administrative details and new plans for the Fall season. Although having been notified of this meeting twice in the previous ten days, and returning a signed slip saying that they would attend, only three of the twenty-two contracted employees showed up. All reported for work at their regular duties that day and thereafter however. Several foreigners were informed of this situation and asked to venture a guess as to why the contracted employees had not shown up for the meeting. Various answers such as "I guess they forgot", "Perhaps they overslept", etc. were offered. Several Chinese workers in the company were asked to venture a guess as to why the contracted employees had not shown up for the meeting. They said "I suppose they did this as an indirect way of protesting to the harsh manner in which Celia was treated." Further inquiries revealed that this was indeed the truth of the matter.

A number of the contracted employees were later asked to consider a hypothetical situation. Part A: "Employees in a certain company are given the option of working for a 20% higher than normal hourly salary, if they will sign a contract guaranteeing a minimum of one year of service. If they do sign a contract, and do complete one full year of service, they will be given one month's pay bonus as well. Is this fair?"

The employees said "Yes, that is fair."

Now they were given Part B: "An employee works seven months and then resigns. They ask to be paid the one year bonus. Is that fair?"

The employees said "No, that is not fair."

This seemed corresponding more closely to the western conception. It was then asked "What about the circumstances with Celia? Do you agree that the Manager's decision in Celia's case was fair?"

"No, that was not fair, because Celia's family needed the money. The Manager's decision put her in a bad way with her family. How could she help pay for her father's medical bills?" This then appeared to be the final determination of Celia's case.

We may compare the viewpoints in each situation in Part B as

Office girl's request to be paid for three weeks work
   Western majority viewpoint: UNFAIR
   Chinese majority viewpoint: FAIR

Celia's request to be paid a month's bonus
   Western majority viewpoint: UNFAIR
   Chinese majority viewpoint: FAIR

Notes:
1) The situations presented here are closely related in that they both involve contractual relation, and do not entail physical damage or injury to the contracting party as a result of job-related activities.
2) The westerner in China may occasionally have the opportunity to talk with his Chinese friends about situations such as these in a general fashion. In fact, the conclusions or determinations of many Chinese people will often correspond to those of westerners in hypothetical models, nevertheless the Chinese will often reverse their stance in real-world actual situations, and this is the focus of our discussion here.
3) Further insight into the Chinese point of view will be gained by reading the Sympathy essay in Chapter 10.

Without any conceptual tools to examine this flow of reasoning as regards what is "fair", it does appear strange or puzzling to the westerner. There are a number of ways we can arrive at the "Chinese viewpoint" however. An advanced analysis would see that it merely represents another application of the RR Perception of Value, which by its very nature stresses the changeability of terms and conditions. More simply, reasoning from the standpoint of an Agricultural Society Reward/Effort Relationship, we can also justify the secretary's demands for wages, noting that after physically doing three weeks work, she is entitled to three weeks pay. This added to her present circumstances would cause the refusal to pay her to be regarded as bordering on "immorality". In either situation, another possible analysis is that the Chinese may feel the manager should justify this payment on a "personal" level—thus again denoting a high integration between business and personal relations. A rather broad application of the AP Perception of Liability (to be introduced in the next chapter) also yields the Chinese viewpoint.

It is interesting to note that while many Chinese recognize that the western verdict of "fair" in each instance represents the legal reality of the situation, yet, having a Primary Sympathetic Orientation they tend to feel that the strict legal interpretation is not the most suitable one to use. These are further examples of the ramifications of what we are calling the legal/moral gap, which in general refers to any activity where the legal solution is not considered by the Chinese as being moral. Some westerners have attempted to paraphrase the Chinese idea, to wit: "If it is convenient for the employee to keep the terms of the contract, fine. If it is not convenient for the employee to keep the terms of the contract, then that is the manager's problem."

Some international linguists have objected to the complexity of the above analysis however, pointing out that the Chinese viewpoint may be obtained in a much simpler fashion. The Chinese language lacks verb tenses, and in situations similar to those cited here, the stipulations of initial hiring clearly demand the use of the future perfect tense, to wit: "When you shall have done your work, you will receive your money." To the Chinese this becomes "Do work, get money", and the financial overtones embed themselves most solidly in the Chinese consciousness, while the inherent time relation is totally lacking.

## Head Hunters and Employment Agencies

Perhaps it is too strict to require that a secretary or office girl work a minimum amount of time, such as a month or 60 days, before any salary payment will be paid. Perhaps it is advisable to pay bonuses after six months of service, rather than one year, since many Chinese prefer to work with more of a short-term orientation. However, it is possible that for some very highy paid and highly specialized positions, the foreign company does assume the burden of extensive training, and as a result there may commonly be a minimum amount of service specified, or desired, before the employee may resign. If the employee were to leave before this time period had elapsed, for any reason (except a fatal accident), all salary monies paid out to-date would be expected to be returned, in addition to any other penalties specified at the time of hiring.

We may consider the case where a nine month minimum period of service is required by the European firm MKM International Co. In light of the legal/moral gap, when hiring a Chinese employee through an employment agency (even through the local branch of an established international agency) in China, it would seem necessary that MKM (the hiring firm) have a contract with the employment agency for the "supply" of the required personnel for the minimum specified time-period, and then that the employment agency have a contract with the personnel in question specifying minimum length-of-service requirements, penalties for non-fulfillment, etc.In this situation, the employment agency would be responsible to MKM if the employee left before his minimum time period was up, and this would include the liability for the reimbursement of salary paid out to-date and other training expenses. The employment agency would then be able to get these monies back from the non-performing personnel in any way they chose.

The reason why MKM would want to do this are simply explained, by the foreign manager, to the Chinese head of the employment agency as follows: "We do not understand the thinking of the local people, especially as regards their concept of contractual relation. We want to hire you as our middleman to deal with these wonderful people and sort out these problems as best you see fit."

Of the established employment agencies and "head hunters" in China with which I have come in contact, none uses this arrangement however. They have largely adopted the western mode, hence 1) they introduce qualified personnel to the hiring company, 2) the company hires the one(s) it wants, and 3) some fee (such as 20% of the first six months salary) is paid to the employment agency for this introduction service. No guarantees of any kind are given, not even to the extent of guaranteeing that the hired employee(s) will complete a minimum six-month term of service. The employment agency says: "You may establish a contract with your new employee(s) according to your own terms and conditions." In reality, if problems do occur, the "contract" may very well not be worth the paper it is written on, because many foreign firms do not have the time to institute formal legal proceedings in matters of this sort, and if they do much bad publicity is likely to be generated, with the public seeing the foreign firm's lack of sympathy as being essentially "immoral".

If we consider a western company as primarily holding to an IS Reward/Effort Relationship model, and the local society as primarily holding to an AS Reward/Effort Relationship model, a company representative who attempts to negotiate with a member of the local society (an employee) when problems have already arisen will often find that the thinking of the two sides is disjointed at the conceptual level. It is best not to put oneself in such a "middle" position unless one possesses many years experience in cross-cultural negotiations.

Non-Performance of Duties

Where some changed personal or family interests come to conflict with the demands of the workplace, and where a minimum length of employment has been specified, many country Z employees will choose to arrive everyday for work and do nothing except read the newspaper, hopefully leading to their being fired, thus removing any need for them to make reparations for failure to serve out the required time limit, (since the decision to leave was not theirs). This will not be a bad reflection on their credit record, since they have no credit record. As those familiar with Chinese banks often notice, banks keep records of bounced checks, loan repayment dealings, etc., but seemingly no agency collects other related "credit" information which is available to the general public or general business community.

Previous Employment History

Due to a lack of credit information, many prospective employees' previous employment history is often hard to determine. The higher and more responsible the position being filled is, the more serious a problem this becomes. Interestingly, 95% of country Z managers, if asked to produce a letter of reference about a former employee, will mention only the good points, and not the bad ones, fearing that this would unfairly prejudice the employee's chances of starting over somewhere else. To discover the real picture, it would be necessary for the prospective hirer to develop a personal relation with this former employer (a time consuming procedure), before he could be expected to "open up". Otherwise it would be necessary to make discreet inquiries through friends or friends of friends. The final option is just to take the prospective employee's word for it.

Company Manuals and Other Data

Further reflection on the ramifications of the Agricultural Society Reward/Effort Relationship can enable us to understand why many local employees, upon leaving (quitting or being laid off from) their places of work in the trading, manufacturing, or sales sectors, will endeavor to take, or make copies of, all company manuals, mailing lists, customer data records, etc., for their own use in the future. This they believe is "fair". Since they have physically used, and in many cases often helped to compile, these materials, they naturally feel that the materials, or the knowledge and methodology contained therein, are theirs, or at the least they are entitled to some large portion of them, and that the company boss should recognize this. A direct comparison goes back to the feudal landlord who gave a portion of his harvest to those who helped him work in the fields during the year. Application of the the Agricultural Society Perception of Injury, which will be introduced later, also confirms that taking these materials is "fair".

## New Business Investment

A new investment proposal was recently offered to my friend Mr. Hu, in Taiwan, and he asked me for some advice upon it. I believe the entire proposal can serve to illustrate a number of trends in Chinese thinking in regard to investment in new enterprises. The plant to be set up requires an investment of $10,800,000 in local currency, or an equivalent of nearly US$ 375,000.

This factory will use red-mud, an unwanted by-product (i.e. waste) of the manufacture of aluminum, to manufacture "red-mud plastic" which is a combination of red-mud and plastic, and has a wide range of applications as insulation material, roofing, and paneling, with none of the environmental or medical drawbacks of asbestos. The knowledge, skills, and related technology to manufacture this type of product have been developed locally, but are largely unknown out of a few select individuals who have worked in government research organizations. Mr. Su possesses such knowledge, and desires to set up a factory to manufacture this item with the help of his friend Mr. Hsiao, who presently operates a small local plastics firm, as well as engaging in several types of whole plant exports. The necessary funds will be accumulated in the following way: Out of a total of 100 shares in the enterprise, Mr. Su will be given 25 shares for his contribution of knowledge and expertise. The remaining 75 shares will contribute the actual capital, therefore each share is $375,000/75, or approx. US$5000. Mr. Hsiao will subscribe to 55 shares, and the other 20 shares are being made available to Mr. Hu and his associates.

This enterprise is projected to break even within a year, and at the end of the second year of operation, profits will be divided as follows: 10% into company capital fund, 2% for executive/staff bonuses, 3% for worker bonuses, and 85% to be distributed among investors. A conservative estimate says that each share can obtain $140,000 (US$ 4900) in profits at this point. More profits will be available in succeeding years.

One production line will be set up initially, using one machine costing $2,750,000 (US $95,000), and another production line will be set up with the purchase of another machine six months later. Three workers will be needed on the production line, plus four other office personnel and a security guard.

Mr. Hu feels that this proposal looks very promising, since Mr. Hsiao has assured him that there is an abundant demand for this type of product on the market, and promises of orders from several big firms have already been obtained. For each stock share he purchases now for $5000, he will receive $4900 in profits two years later, and more profits later on.

Looking over the financial documents, income and expenditure projections, and technical specifications relevant to this venture, I felt that a serious problem was the lack of independent expert evaluation of the suitability of red-mud plastic to be employed in the many construction related uses which Mr. Su and Mr. Hsiao had outlined. The number of competing firms now in the marketplace was also a factor to be considered. I was therefore unable to advise Mr. Hu of the soundness of this investment proposal without further information and study. Private enquiries which I made in the industry suggested that red-mud plastic is quite brittle, and breakage in storage and shipment tends to be a problem. As a roofing material, it tends to absorb heat, which is undesirable in warm climates, especially in the summer months. Another related product, White Mud Plastic, is now being marketed by some companies, and in addition to being highly resistant to acid, alkali, and aging, with a life span of perhaps five times of traditional RMP products, it is reflective of light and tends to keep rooms cooler, and does not break easily.

In any event, several aspects of this proposal are typical of Chinese small or medium-sized business strategy and are useful to us in our discussion of a Foreigner's Money Management, since any foreigner might become involved in a similar undertaking. 1st) there is no mention of any banking relations which the new firm will have, including the establishment of savings and checking accounts, and the credit terms felt necessary, both long and short term. 2nd) all capital is being raised privately, primarily through friends and relatives. 3rd) allowances for taxes, registration, and other legal matters are unaccounted for. 4th) if, for the sake of example, we estimate an average annual income in the late 1980's of US$ 6,500 (equivalent in Chinese currency) per Chinese household in Taiwan,[1] and compare this to an average American income of US$ 26,000, the investment of US$ 375,000 in a new enterprise is a very significant sum. From this we may gain an indication that the Chinese pattern in regard to expenditures and investments is not by any means "a 1/4 scaled down version" of the American pattern. This realization will be very important as we consider the uses of money in Chinese society in general.

Note: Dollar figures on the following pages are all US$ or US$ equivalents, except where specifically noted as otherwise.

---

1. Taiwan is regarded as the most economically prosperous Chinese province.

## Shares in An Enterprise

Some discussion of the distribution of shares in a new Chinese enterprise may be informative for the foreigner who is directly or indirectly involved in such projects, whether in the position of organizer, invited participant, or sidelines observer. Four types of shares are commonly recognized, with a distinction in terms of the nature of the "investment" they represent:

1) Monetary-invested Shares

Shares given for an actual monetary investment in the new enterprise. As such, they represent the entire capital amount.

2) Labor-invested Shares

Shares given for work done in the new enterprise, usually in lieu of whole or partial salary payment, especially during the early years of the enterprise.

3) Technical-Knowledge invested Shares

Shares given for contribution of technical knowledge into the new enterprise.

4) Public Relations invested Shares

Shares given for contribution of social and other related wheeling-and-dealing, and promotion of good *guanxi* which enable the enterprise to get started, and/or continue operating in a successful manner. An example would be where a large site of land was to be purchased for the founding of a new factory, but the local owners were not inclined to sell, or other objections were raised by important people in the community. If another local person, Mr. Y, is found to smooth out these problems, his reward for such meritorious service could then be discharged by awarding him PR shares in the new enterprise, as opposed to some one-time settlement with cash or gifts. The awarding of PR Shares would generally only be done with the belief that Mr. Y could put forth even more efforts in the future to contribute to the continuing "good health" of the enterprise.

In terms of distribution of profits, all shares share equally. If the new enterprise is organized on the basis of 1000 shares, each share receives 1/1000 of the profit, and an owner of 13 shares receives 13/1000 of the profits, etc. In the examples we are considering, "investments" are from friends, colleagues, and relatives, but the shares are not being offered to the general public, nor sold through the stockmarket.

Noteworthy is that each type of Shares may, if desired, be further divided into two categories: a) "named", with the investor's name known to all concerned, and b) "anonymous", with the investor's name only known to a top few people in the company.

PR Shares are equivalent to complimentary shares. It may often be desirable to give Anonymous Complimentary Shares to certain private or public individuals, and further consideration of this will appear later in the text.

## A Backyard Investment

My friend Clifford, who has a Chinese wife, decided to go into the bull-frog business some years ago when he was living in China. This was undertaken to supplement his regular salary as an employee of a large local import concern, and was done at the urging of his wife's uncle, who had made over US$25,000 equivalent in the previous eight months raising bull-frogs. At the time when Clifford began his bull-frog business, a pair of adult bull-frogs were selling for nearly US$30 and were in great demand by a wide range of local restaurants. He invested a little over US$100 for the construction of a series of troughs to raise the bull-frogs, and researched that their diet consisted of snails and fish innards, as well as flies and other insects. The snails were abundantly available in local fields and parks, and fish innards could be had for a pittance from the local fish markets. Flies and insects seemed easy to catch with a butterfly net.

Since the uncle was already in the business, he was kind enough to give Clifford and his wife 500 tadpoles for free -- thus representing a savings of over $20 and promising to be a very auspicious start to their new business. Some algae and other aquatic plants were collected, and after the troughs were prepared by several days of rinsing and water changing, the tadpoles were put in.

Week by week the tadpoles grew, first gradually losing their tails, and then becoming small frogs. Clifford and his wife calculated that at $11 or $12 apiece, 500 bull-frogs would represent a substantial profit for them over and above their initial investment and minimal labor and upkeep costs, a profit of at least US $5500. Clifford and his wife were in good spirits planning how they would spend all this money when it came in.

Approximately one year into their bull-frog venture, some problems began to develop. First, the local fields and parks had been almost completely depleted of snails, and foraging trips to collect these needed to be conducted farther and farther afield. This was a very time consuming procedure. Secondly, it was becoming apparent that bull-frogs are very cannibalistic in nature, and "only the strong survive". Despite repeated attempts to separate the bull-frogs into different troughs according to size, this process of "natural selection" continued unabated, with the result that as they reached the mature adult size, only some 100 bull-frogs remained.

Added to this was the problem that the market price of adult bull-frogs had been fluctuating in recent months, similar to the fluctuations in the US stock market in 1929. This was due partly to the large number of raisers, and also to the fact that the "fad" of eating bull-frogs in local restaurants had for the most part passed. Clifford, his wife, and some other relatives had a meeting, and they decided the best course of action was to sell the bull-frogs immediately, and at least try to recover some of their investment. Several days of inquiry failed to produce any interested buyers however.

The best course of action at this point appeared to let the bull-frogs fend for themselves, and not waste any more time or money feeding them. As a result, on a typical summer evening, several bull-frogs would jump out of the troughs, bound through the garden, leap the bamboo fence, and Clifford would watch their escape serenely, totally unmoved. As he sat nearby in an easy chair drinking a glass of lemonade, not only did he refuse to lift a finger to catch them and bring them back, he would happily raise his glass and offer them a toast, wishing them the best of luck in their new found freedom.

One day his wife's brother came for a visit, and when he understood their situation in regard to raising the bull-frogs, he made a useful suggestion: "Why don't we have frog legs for dinner?" Upon hearing this brilliant remark, Clifford put down his lemonade and jumped up, and the three of them spent nearly two hours collecting bull-frogs from the backyard, garden, and neighboring community. Meeting a number of neighbors and other friends during their search, they invited them all over to join in the big meal.

Clifford's wife is an excellent cook, but even her skills were not up to the task of turning this $5500 worth of bull-frogs into enough food for the dozen or so people who showed up, and Cliff had to go out for additional quantities of squid, clams, and oysters to round out the meal. Along with abundant vegetables and plenty of beer, a good time was had by all.

Reviewing this investment we see that it was straightforward and comparatively small-scale, but it still serves to illustrate the failing of many foreigners to thoroughly research a proposed investment project before it is undertaken. In dealing with various types of plants, animals, etc., in another country, it would certainly be desirable to assemble all relevant information on their growth cycles, climatic requirements, resistance to disease, predatory habits, and all other related information before making an investment of this type, unless one's only desire was for one very tasty meal, similar to the final result achieved in this example.

## Banking Relations and Credit

Once while travelling through San Francisco in 1985 I decided it would be nice to set up banking relations with a local bank. I therefore looked through the yellow pages of the phone directory, picked out the name and address of a large bank in Embarcadero Center, the Financial District, and presented myself there in person later that same morning. Unfortunately, two types of identification were required, and the only document I could present to establish my identity was a US Passport, having misplaced my Tennessee driver's license during my lengthy residence in China.

The bank was kind enough to allow me to complete the paperwork however, which they promised to hold pending receipt of further identification, and a letter from another bank attesting to my good credit record and upstanding character. Being unable to deposit the funds I had brought with me in cash, I purchased some travellers checks and made my departure for lunch at Fisherman's Wharf.

After leaving San Francisco a few days later, I first flew to St. Louis to visit some relatives and then on to Nashville, where an additional three hour bus trip brought me to my parents' home. During my stay in Tennessee I was able to renew my driver's license, and I sent a xeroxed copy of it to the bank in San Francisco. Additionally, I was able to have the local bank in Livingston, Tennessee, where I have maintained a small savings account for many years, send out a letter attesting the necessary good credit record and upstanding character. I left $475 in Tennessee with my parents, to be transferred to San Francisco if the need arose.

Arriving back in China some weeks later, I quickly received confirmation from San Francisco by mail that my checking and savings accounts had been opened. I therefore notified Tennessee to mail out the funds. Before long I received further word from San Francisco that they were in receipt of the funds, and informing me of the details of my accounts: My checking account has an automatic overdraft feature, and if there is not enough money to cover a check, the procedure is to first transfer funds from the savings account automatically, or if that is not adequate, to loan out the funds to me at a prescribed rate of 18% per year. Because I did not apply for a higher limit, the initial limit on such lended funds was set at $500. Furthermore, I am entitled to apply for several types of consumer loans, and several thousand dollars appear to be available to me through this loan arrangement. In addition I am entitled to apply for a Master Card or Visa Card, or both, through the bank, and several thousand more dollars in credit are available to me through those channels. I will call this the A-country model of credit arrangements.

All this was done without my being in possession of a job, of any kind whatsoever, in the San Francisco area. Nor was I able to produce any evidence that I had paid state or federal taxes in the previous year. Furthermore, I had no local San Francisco mailing address, and I requested that my checks be printed with my address in China, and that all monthly statements be sent to China. I provided the bank with my parents' address in Tennessee "for reference only". Interestingly, I had had no previous dealings with this bank of any kind, but had merely "walked in off the street".

Let us now consider the situation of Mr. Rwan, a citizen of country Z, who has grown up and attended school in an average community in this country. He has had a savings account with a local bank for seven years, the average balance in which has been well over US $1000 equivalent. He has also maintained a checking account, and he has no record of any bounced checks. He is employed locally in a firm which is registered with the government and pays taxes, and has been steadily employed there for several years. He is presently renting an apartment with his wife and two children. Since he is planning some major household purchases in the next month, he has made inquiries with his bank and asked what credit terms are available, and what amount of money he would be able to borrow.

Until a few years ago, the answer he would have received was a smile, or perhaps a frown if the loan officer had had a trying day. A person in Mr. Rwan's position was regarded as having no credit standing, because there was no credit standing to be had. Country Z's banks operated on the pawnshop principle: money was loaned out strictly in regard to what collateral (generally "local collateral") could be produced. Often as not there has been an additional stipulation that two or more other people, who also must produce equivalent collateral to the full amount of the borrowing, co-sign the loan agreement. (The situation would be better for Mr. Rwan if he were purchasing an entire house, or some other similar object, since the house itself could serve as collateral. With a down-payment of 20% or more of the purchase price, and some co-signers, it is possible that he could obtain such a loan.)

In this society, it might be true that to apply for anything as "simple" as a checking account, a substantial time deposit might be required for six-months or more, in order to demonstrate one's good financial standing. Such a deposit could be nearly US $20,000 equivalent. Concurrently, due to the widespread lack of any sort of credit arrangements being available to the average man or woman of Z nationality, for any purpose for which they need or desire to borrow money, a very strong undercurrent of "private loaning and borrowing" will probably exist in Z society, technically known as "a thriving underground curb market". Since banks and other related institutions are not keeping track of this kind of credit information, in order to evaluate people's creditworthiness, there may also be a great lack of credit type information available in general, including work employment history, banking relations, bad debt history, failure-in-business history, etc.

Chinese credit arrangements have traditionally tended to resemble the Z-country model, and this is only slowly changing in the present day, with some small types of consumer loans now gradually becoming available to members of the populace who are well known to a bank, and who can produce co-signers. Corporate loans for new investment and for working capital (not secured by collateral) are often still difficult for Chinese companies to obtain, although the larger companies can to some extent get around this problem by setting up an employee savings plan and paying 1% more interest than the banks, thereby attracting the idle funds of employees, relatives, and friends.

For the foreigner who comes to this society and deals with people therein, it must be remembered that all of these factors are influencing their lives, and may over the long run influence the foreigner's own economic affairs in a direct manner.

For example, the foreigner may personally find it quite difficult to build up any credit with local financial institutions over the long term, and will have to pay cash even for major purchases, unless local collateral can be produced. To the many Chinese who find themselves in this position essentially all their lives, the importance of harmony in the group, obedience to parents, mutually helpful relations with neighbors, etc. are paramount, for without parents, relatives, and friends to act as guarantors, they cannot build up a financial base.[1] If we compare this to the situation which the author confronted in San Francisco, and from other dealings which are common in American banking circles, it appears that many USA banks are willing to recognize a person as an independent financial entity, without relation to his parents' or relatives' status.

That the insurance industry is far more developed in the west than in China is another reason why western banks are better able to deal with a wide variety of business risks, whereas the Chinese banks prefer a much more conservative approach. Reflecting a traditional attitude, one Chinese banking official was overheard to comment "After all, nobody was ever fired for not granting a loan."

## Unfair Descriptions

Many Chinese of course will deny that the credit situation in the west is any different than it is in China. Despite many statements to the contrary (by Americans for example), Chinese will still reply "No, I had some friends who lived there for many years, and they told me a lot of stories. Actually the banks in the USA operate just as conservatively as the Chinese banks. Credit is largely unavailable to the common man."

I have even read these types of statements in the Chinese press from time to time, often as part of lengthy accounts of Chinese people living and working in the west. One such series of articles was particularly "interesting" in that the Chinese writers, a husband and wife team, in addition to their comments on banking and credit, had concluded in regard to many of their dealings with people in the USA that "Americans actively discriminate against Oriental people." The examples they gave, such as 1) being shunned when they asked for directions in a suburb of Chicago, or 2) being treated rudely in New York's Central Park when asking to borrow some change to make a phone call, or 3) being told "No, you cannot just park your car in this restricted area for two minutes while you pick up a package" in Cleveland, etc., all seemed rather strange. Native Americans living in China remarked that these situations did not even have a remote connection to "racial discrimination", since they were quick to point out "If I had done the same thing, I would have gotten the same treatment."

Of course, not many westerners read the Chinese press on a regular basis, and hence can only comment on such reporting when it is translated by a friend and brought to their attention. Few letters of protest are likely to be written to the Chinese editors, since the westerners are inadequately skilled in the Chinese language, and their Chinese friends, who may be asked to help, often reply: "Writing that kind of letter wouldn't be nice."

I chose to do some further research on the story which this husband and wife team

---

1. Mencius' natural law philosophy states that it is according to reason that a ruler should care for his people in a 王道 "kingly way", and that a truly benevolent ruler will concern himself for the economic welfare of his people. The antiquated banking system in China appears to stand in direct oppositon to this doctrine.

had presented. By way of correspondence and through the help of a Caucasian friend who worked as an electrical engineer in a nearby community, an informal interview was arranged one Saturday afternoon in the suburb of a northeastern American city. It was even possible to take along a fellow who worked in a local bank there and who was interested in cross-cultural dealings. The following facts were discovered:

They had lived in the United States for eight years. The husband had originally been in the employ of a large US firm, but was later laid off during a recession. He and his wife had been running a small restaurant for the past five years. At the time of their encounters with the "US banking community" over five years previously, when they were selecting a location and assembling funds to begin their restaurant, they had been in the United States for not quite three years, and had already obtained Permanent Residence status. At that time 1) they had no savings account or checking account in any US bank, nor had they ever tried to open one, since they "had not felt the need to do so", 2) they had no credit cards, for although they had purchased much furniture, clothing, appliances, and a car during their time in the US, they always paid in cash, because "we felt that was more convenient", 3) in addition to having no credit cards, they had never bought anything on any sort of installment plan, to facilitate establishing a record of prompt repayments.

The engineer and his banker friend said "Of course you could not get a loan at a bank in the USA, clearly at that time you had no 'credit'."

They replied, "Why not?"

After a lengthy discussion on this topic, the Americans added: "If you do not mind us asking, what did you do with all the money you earned in those first few years in the USA?"

The Chinese said that they had lived very frugally, and were able to save a good amount of the husband's salary every month. They kept some of their savings hidden in their home, put some of them in a safety deposit box, and remitted most of the rest of them back to China to their parents and relatives.

Later the four of them all went out for a nice Chinese dinner in their restaurant, and the Americans were able to give them some more suggestions on the selection of a suitable location for opening a second restaurant, even though of course neither of them had ever been involved with such a selection process before. The Chinese were undecided as to whether to purchase one large establishment which was up for sale and seemed an excellent location. The husband said, "Some of the facilities are very old, but the owner said that he has good connections with the inspectors in the Health Department, and could make sure that that is not a problem for us. He also said he could get us a break on taxes with some of the officials he knows."

"How long did you say you have been living in the USA?" the Americans queried.

"Eight years."

"Do you have many American friends? Where do you get all your information on 'American rules, regulations, and business practices'?"

The husband remarked that of course they talked to many of their Chinese friends in the community, and often even placed overseas telephone calls back to their relatives for advice.

The foursome spent a long evening in discussion, and over the next few weeks the Americans were even able to help them locate a more suitable location for their expansion. One day the Chinese couple said that they had some friends who were planning to invest in real estate in the U.S., and wondered if there was any special information or advice in that regard which they should pass along. Another Chinese gentleman had introduced a large parcel of land in Delaware which seemed very promising.

"No, I can't think of anything special," the banker said, "will your friends be living here in the USA or staying in China?"

"They are just making this investment for the future," the wife clarified, "so they will be staying in China for the time being."

"What arrangements are they making to pay taxes?"

"Taxes? Are there taxes? The man who introduced the land to them said that since they were foreigners and living outside of the country, it would not be necessary to pay any US taxes."

The engineer was surprised at this remark. "You would certainly be subject to the provisions under the Foreign Investment in Real Property Tax Act, the so-called FIRPTA. No doubt other taxes would apply as well."

"Yes," the banker added, "Investments in US real estate by foreign nationals are also subject to state and local taxes, state and city property taxes on sale of assets, and estate taxes after death. If your friends were running a business, some branch profits taxes might be applicable too." He gave the couple the names and addresses of several tax lawyers, and suggested that their friends investigate the matter more thoroughly before making any final decision.

In writing back to me, the engineer and the lawyer were most grateful that I had given them this opportunity to do the initial informal interview, because they were now granted free meals in the new establishment on a regular basis.

Even though this situation reached a successful conclusion, nevertheless we suspect that in the future still more stories will be seen in the Chinese press similar to those that this couple initially wrote. This is certainly not the kind of article that the Chinese editors would feel compelled to censor.

## The Sunglasses Incident

Many foreigners living overseas hope to become involved in doing some international trading. Ronald was no exception, and so he found a job working part-time for a local trading company, SSS Trading Company, in order to gain relevant experience. This company was managed by an American, and employed over twenty local (native) merchandisers, and several secretaries. One day in late February, a large US buyer with whom SSS did substantial yearly business telexed a request for a price quotation on 50,000 pairs of sunglasses, each in a pouch. This buyer had purchased sunglasses from the Trading Company several times before as well. A merchandiser was allocated to handle this inquiry and began locating domestic sources by telephoning a number of factories with whom SSS had been doing business for several years. After determining which price quote was the most favorable, in light of all relevant factors, the merchandiser made his recommendation to the American manager that Factory G, managed by a Mr. Lin, located in Taichung, with a price of US$5.00 each, and delivery terms in 60 days, was the best. The trading company's 5% commission on this type of item was already included directly in this price quote, as is the usual practice, and is understood by the buyer.

SSS Trading Company then telexed the buyer with this price and an ETD (estimated time of departure) of April 24th. The buyer accepted this offer promptly by telex, and immediately FAXed a Purchase Order to SSS Trading Co. as well as opening an irrevocable Letter of Credit (LC) through its USA based bank, Citibank.

Two days later the factory called up and said: "Oh, by the way, the price we quoted you the other day was just for the sunglasses, it did not include the pouch. Each pouch is US$0.20 extra."

The merchandiser involved with this case, Mr. Chang, a graduate from a Chinese college who had majored in accounting, made a note of this and proceeded to draft a telex explaining this situation to the US buyer. When Ronald came to work February 26th, Mr. Chang asked him to look over the telex, which was quite lengthy, and see if there were any English grammar mistakes, or other unclear terminology. Ronald read over the telex and said "Your grammar is fine, it is what you are trying to say that does not make sense."

Ronald went on to explain that when SSS Trading Company quoted a price of US$ 5.00 each for "sunglasses with pouch", the American buyer certainly took this to mean that the price for one pair of sunglasses, enclosed in a pouch, was US$ 5.00. What this draft of a proposed telex was now attempting to tell the buyer was that the price should have been US$5.20. By what rationale could this be said to be a 'true' statement? If this telex were to be sent, the American buyer would be most certain to telex back "We want the US$ 5.00 price."

Ronald queried if the factory had originally been asked to quote on "sunglasses with pouch" or just "sunglasses". Mr. Chang remarked that it was the former, "sunglasses with pouch". Nevertheless, Mr. Chang, a college graduate, now felt that since the factory had this very day clearly stated that the price for sunglasses was $5.00 each, and the pouch was $0.20 extra, the American buyer should be able to understand this. As a merchandiser he was puzzled how Ronald could know what the American buyer would reply to this telex before it was even sent. Ronald said: "Well, I suppose that you could say I have mental telepathy."

The manager of SSS Trading Company, Mr. Jones, was consulted, and he agreed with Ronald's analysis of the issue. The proposed telex was scrapped, and Mr. Chang was rather mystified at why this "simple solution to the problem" was not even tried. Mr. Jones wanted to consider another range of options, which he felt more realistic. He outlined SSS's possible moves as follows:

1. Accept the order, deduct the 0.20 from our profit. Since a 5% profit on each $5.00 of merchandise only amounts to 0.25, this deduction would be substantial.
2. Accept the order, ask the factory to deduct the 0.20 from their profit.
3. Accept the order, split the loss of 0.20 on each item with the factory.
4. Accept the order, make up for the 0.20 by cutting corners on the quality of the sunglasses and/or pouch, possibly by switching suppliers.
5. Refuse the order, let the LC expire. Mr. Jones felt this would undoubtedly anger the US buyer, and reflect poorly on SSS's reputation, with the resulting possibly of decreased orders from this important buyer in the future.

He summarized the situation by saying that the real difficulty confronting them now was "who is going to swallow the $ 0.20", and then ranked the various options in order of his personal preference 2, 3, 1. He eliminated 4 and 5 as being too dangerous. Mr. Chang, the merchandiser, was told to put option two into action. After a long talk with the manager, at which Ronald was not present, Mr. Chang left on the train for Taichung the next morning. It will be clear to the reader at this point that Mr. Chang stands in the middle of a conflict of interest involving an AO Perception of Value and an RR Perception of Value. This is not an enviable position in which to be.

Obviously there is more to operating a trading company in China than just being a middleman between buyers and sellers, taking orders and waiting for the commissions to pile up every month. An international businessman of long experience in the Far East once confided to me that in terms of setting up a buying office in an Oriental country to purchase a large variety of local products, there was a rule of thumb which said that for staffing requirements in China, there would be one staff member for every US $1 million of purchases in a well established office. In Japan, the ratio is closer to one staff member for every US $10 million of purchases. Thus a foreign company's buying office which does $50 million worth of business would normally be staffed by five people if located in Japan, and fifty if located in the R.O.C. We stress again this is in terms of a company that deals with a large variety of local products, not just one or two items.

The additional staffing requirements in China are made necessary by the fact that the buying office must have technical personnel and engineers to help factories with production, since the great majority of Chinese manufacturers are not research-oriented and do not have designers or researchers to develop their own products or technology. In addition, quality control inspectors are needed, preferably in two or three teams, to inspect the merchandise at all stages during production, as well as during boxing and packing into the containers, lest poor quality items be included or the quantity be short. Furthermore, many merchandisers are needed to deal with locating product sources and dealing with factory problems such as the one described above. Most companies in the land of the rising sun take care of all these kinds of issues by themselves, and in an efficient manner, so staffing requirements are less in Japan. Of course all of these considerations must be balanced against the considerably higher salary payments and office rentals which must be paid in a large Japanese city, as compared to the lower ones paid in China. By way of comparison, Korea seems to be close to the Chinese model.

The Sunglasses Incident, Questions and Commentary by other westerners, with answers by the author:

Q: I believe the initial problem could have been avoided if SSS had waited for written confirmation of the price-quote from the factory, instead of just relying on an oral statement over the phone.

A: In response to your comment, my expatriate friends based in China, with long experience in international trading, told me "It would not have made any difference." In other words, the factory would have seen the situation in the same light, whether the price-quote was oral or written. In fact, a factory will commonly mail or FAX a written price-quote confirmation out to the trading company the same day.

Q: If I recall my Chinese proverbs correctly, there are two well known ones which would be relevant here – "A promise is worth a thousand taels of gold", [a] and "When the words are spoken the action must be carried out." [b,1] Also of relevance is the concept of *hsin* [c] "faithfulness" or "trust". Mr. Lin must certainly be aware of these concepts. Frankly, I am surprised that he did not honor his Factory's original promise when it was pointed out to him.

A: Traditionally, Chinese society was divided into three classes: 1) officials, 2) commoners, and 3) the "mean" people. Among the commoners, four divisions were generally made: 2a) the scholars, 2b) the farmers 2c) the artisans, 2d) the merchants. [2] In this schema the factory would fall into the "merchant" class. Another Chinese proverb "There is no honest businessman" [d] gives recognition to the low standards of conduct which members of the merchant class were often found to possess. [3] Hence, there is little effort given to putting the proverbs you mentioned into practice for the merchant class. The assumption is that if the merchants wanted to raise their moral standards, they would devote themselves to scholarly pursuits, thus giving up their merchant ways and becoming scholars, or more ideally, sages. Notably, while the western mind tends to see all Chinese as "Chinese", and all the same, due to our presumed notion of equality, the Chinese see themselves as divided into classes in the traditional way. Thus the statement that the "merchants" have low moral standards would come as no surprise to

---

1. Also worthy of discussion would be"Words once spoken, four horses cannot recall" : 駟馬難追 .
2. The three classes are ①士大夫　　　②一般人或平民：士農工商　　　③賤民
3. Even though many merchants in Chinese society have entered the middle class during the last 50 years, however the influence of this maxim is still felt both in the attitudes of the Chinese populace toward the merchants and in the attitudes of the merchants toward themselves.

a. 一諾千金　　b. 言出必行　　c. 信　　d. 無商不奸

your Chinese teacher, who considers himself in the scholar class. There is little attempt to have one morality applicable for all classes, and by the same token there is little attempt to bring "theory" and "practice" together in the real world. Here, and in later essays, we will need some terminology to deal with this type of phenomenon.

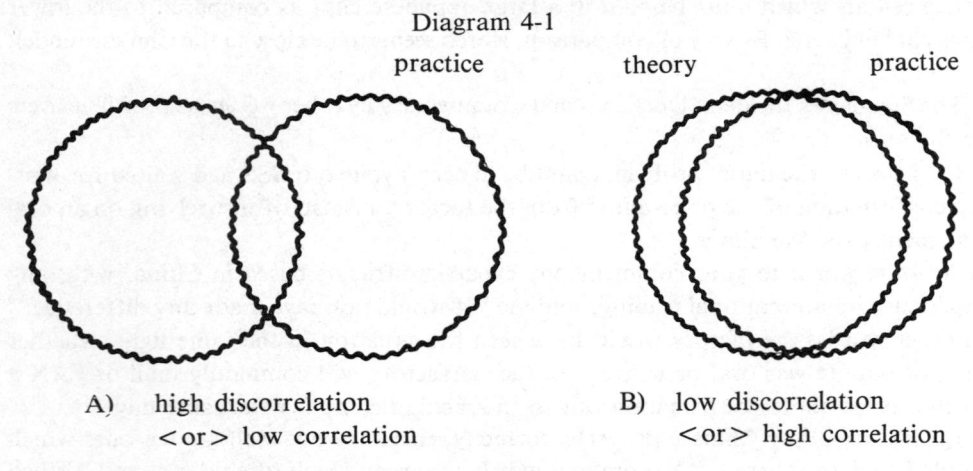

Diagram 4-1

A) high discorrelation
   < or > low correlation

B) low discorrelation
   < or > high correlation

In diagram 4-1A) the theory and practice have "a high discorrelation", or to use the alternate terminology "a low correlation".

In diagram 4-1B) the theory and practice have "a low discorrelation", or to use the alternate terminology "a high correlation".

In the discussion just concluded, the two Chinese proverbs represent the "theory", and the actions of the sunglasses factory represent the "practice". A comparison indicates that this corresponds to to the diagram on the left, with a high discorrelation between theory and practice.

Agricultural Ideas

The Chinese, despite their increasing educational standards in recent years, still maintain an essentially subsistence agricultural mentality of inexactness. My businessman friend illustrated this by saying that "the kind of mentality which is suitable for fixing a farm wagon — 'Well it wobbles and shakes a bit but it seems to run alright . . . ', 'Oh, this should hold for a few more days . . . ', 'Maybe if we shoved one of these things in here backwards it would solve the problem . . . ', etc. — are not suitable for dealing with the exacting requirements of a sophisticated piece of electrical machinery on the production line."

Another problem reflecting the subsistence agricultural background is the lack of adequate capital to engage in production, with the result that many Chinese businessmen are trying to do $100 worth of business with $10 worth of capital. Under these conditions, a lot of corners get cut.

## Striking Out in New Directions

Yet a further problem is the Chinese reticence to do what has not been done before. This was amply illustrated in the case of an American buyer of various types of metal parts, who said that his company required that each piece be given twenty coats of paint, in order to deal with any and all possible climatic changes in any location in the world. Through a local trading company a large number of local manufacturers were contacted. All stated that the standard procedure for manufacturing such parts was to give them four coats of paint. The buyer then had individual meetings with several established producers, re-explaining his company's requirements, and noting that "We are prepared to pay for twenty coats of paint." One producer finally agreed to this procedure.

Production samples were submitted to the buyer ten days later. Upon inspection, they were found to have only four coats of paint. The manager of the factory was called, and he explained over and over "I am telling you that no one manufactures these metal parts with twenty coats of paint! Why can't you understand this?"

## Smog Problems with New Yarn

There is one case which comes to mind in the textile industry which can serve as an excellent reminder of the issues involved when foreign companies deal with Asian manufacturers. No one likes to have difficulties with the production run, with the result that contract stipulations cannot be met, however some problems are due to largely uncontrollable factors, and hence are unpredictable. They are not due to any initial lack of sincerity of the overseas buyer or the local manufacturer in wanting to make a successful business dealing.

An American textile firm once contacted a number of Chinese factories to spin a new type of yarn, containing an unusual combination of special fibers, which was to be made into sweaters. Due to the unusual combination involved, with which the factories were not accustomed to working, none could be found who were interested in the order. However, with the help of a Chinese trading company acting as intermediary, the American firm finally located a small factory which agreed to spin the yarn according to the specified combination of fibers. A contract was signed for a quantity which would keep the factory busy for several weeks. The yarn was booked to be shipped to Hong Kong on June 7th, to be knit into sweaters.

The production run did not go smoothly however. With the special combination of fibers it happened that much fiber particle debris, so called "loose staple", continually kept coming out of the machinery, almost like smog. This was found to be due to the flaking of some polyester threads, and the breakage of some other threads which had to be continually retied. In order to alleviate these problems, the spinning machines were run at a slower rate of speed. However some "smog" was still generated and thus the workers had to wear mouth and nose-covering masks to prevent the inhalation of these nasty little particles, in addition to thoroughly brushing their clothes during every change of shift. This caused many worker complaints.

Due to the slower running speed of the spinning machines, the production rate of 1500 lbs. per day was cut down to 750 lbs. per day, and hence the manufacturer was losing a production (and profit) of "half-a-day per day". As the factory struggled on to produce the requested amount of yarn, the deadline for shipping neared. The owner of the factory was agonized: obviously he would have to delay the shipping date, because with his present maximum rate of production his workers could not possibly meet the deadline. After some quick mental calculations he figured out that the proper amount of yarn would be ready for shipment approximately 20 days late. On June 5th he explained the situation to the Chinese trading company, and they immediately telexed the American buyer to request an extension.

"No extension," came back the reply.

The Chinese trading company then telexed to ask that partial shipment be allowed on June 7th, with the rest to follow later. The buyer replied that this would be acceptable, but added the stipulation that if the final knitting of sweaters could not be completed in Hong Kong on time, and meet the scheduled departure date from Hong Kong for shipment to New York, whatever portion of sweaters missed the boat would have to be sent air-freight, with the Chinese factory responsible for the charges.

When the trading company tried to explain this to the Chinese spinning factory, the manager became very upset. "I am effectively wasting half of my production capacity every day by spinning this special yarn for you," he said, "and in addition to the lost profit this represents, I have also caused much discord among my workers, who do not like to deal with these fibers. Now you are asking me to pay air-freight charges on some portion of the sweaters after they are knitted in Hong Kong? It is quite unreasonable."

In this situation, we can see that both the foreign buyer and the Chinese factory have valid points of view, and each looks at the other's position with a skeptical eye. No matter how the dispute is resolved, someone will feel they have been treated unfairly.

Certainly some of the potential sources of problems in a case such as this one could have been overcome if the buyer, in conjunction with the trading company, had been visiting the spinning factory and checking up on the production day-by-day, instead of assuming that all was well. Thus, we see that good communications between the factory, the trading company, and the buyer are imperative at all stages of production. Here we notice that the spinning factory, retaining an optimistic attitude until the end, was unable to confront the full seriousness of its plight until two days before the shipment deadline, and only then did it inform the trading company of its problems. At that point it was really too late for the three parties involved to do anything but argue.

In general, if the foreign buyer is coming into the market with a new yarn, and four or five factories refuse to spin it, the advisable course of action would be to ask the spinners to come up with what they feel is a close substitute which they "are comfortable working with", and which is suitable for their production processes. This may then be sent back to the designers or other relevant decision-makers in the home office for their approval.

If this is acceptable, then many initial problems have been solved. If not, and the originally requested combination of fibers is still insisted upon, then it must be specified that there be some flexibility on shipment and delivery dates in case problems develop. When the spinning is undertaken, a production sample should be thoroughly inspected, and "on line" inspection of the production should be done on a daily, if not hourly, basis.

It is easy to see how a similar analysis could apply to the manufacture of new toys, hardware items, sport shoes, electric appliances, and a wide variety of other merchandise. The buyer is best advised to be on his toes, to do his homework, and to do his inspections, rather than jumping in with both feet and praying for the best.

## "Growth" and Its Significance

My friend John Henson from Iowa is a statistics major who has been living in China for several years, employed by a European engineering firm. He is on good terms with a local Chinese girl, Eva Eu, and they get together for dinner frequently. Recently Eva said that she was planning to quit her job, which is with a local computer keyboard manufacturer, and perhaps go to the United States to do advanced study.

"Have you decided on your future career plans?" John asked. "I think that is important in determining what course of study to take, and whether to go for just a Masters, or a Ph.D."

"Well, I would like to teach in a University in China," Eva explained, "so I will need to get a Ph.D. If possible I would like to go to a school on the West Coast."

"What will you major in?" John queried.

"Japanese," Eva replied confidently, "I have always been interested in Japan and the Japanese language since I was in high school."

John was puzzled by this choice of major, and said: "Did I hear you correctly? You are going to the United States to study Japanese? I know this will probably sound strange, but why don't you go to Japan?"

"That would not be practicable," Eva said, "because the Ph.D. program in Japanese in any Japanese University would take at least seven or eight years to complete. In the United States, I can get a Ph.D. in Japanese in three or four years."

John decided that this discussion was a bit out of his depth, so he moved on to the question of Eva's present job: "I thought you were happy in your present position, why do you want to quit?"

"My language skills are not very good, and I hope that by going to the USA to study I can improve my English as well as my Japanese."

"But your language skills are excellent," John countered, "I have read some of the correspondence you write in the office and send out to your foreign customers, and there are very few grammatical mistakes."

"There must be many mistakes," Eva sighed, "because no one ever replies to my letters."

"No one replies?" John questioned. "As I recall your desk is usually covered with mail, and your company does a lot of business in computer keyboards."

"Oh yes, we have a lot of inquiries and a lot of orders, and in the few years I have been there we have grown at the rate of 70% or more per year. But what I mean is no one ever replies to my second letters."

"Your second letters?" John was puzzled. "What exactly does that mean?"

As the story unfolded, Eva said that she had begun to see a pattern developing in the company's computer hardware business. Initially, in dealing with new customers, they were able to get orders based on low prices and "solid references". These references were simply the documentation of other orders they had previously received from a number of big name computer manufacturers in the west. However, Eva said that in the last four years, despite impressive growth rates, their company had never had a repeat order from any buyer in the United States or Europe. "And when I write them another letter, they don't reply," Eva complained.

John had some other contacts in the local computer industry, and arranged to borrow some testing equipment one afternoon, whereupon he and Eva went to the factory to do an inspection. In three hours of testing, he found that 50% of the keyboards he tested were faulty, and yet they were all being wrapped and boxed for shipment. John inquired around for the Quality Control personnel, but was told: "There aren't any." Originally there had been a few girls doing Quality Control work, but with the large growth in orders month after month, year after year, they had been moved to the production line long ago, and no one had been assigned to take their place.

Not only was there no Quality Control on output, but there was none on input either. The factory was of course primarily an assembly operation, and bought most of its simpler components and sub-assemblies locally, while importing the more sophisticated ones from Japan. According to what John had heard from confidential Japanese industry sources, Japanese production is separated into three grades: A, B, and C. The A grade is 100% defect free and is sold to the USA market. The B grade has a few percentage points of defects and is sold in the domestic Japanese market, but due to strict input Q.C. in the average Japanese factory it is easily culled out. The C grade has a much greater percentage of defects and is sold to other countries, primarily in the third world. Hence to be in Asia and not do Q.C. inspections on incoming shipments of components from Japan is asking for trouble. No one in the factory was aware of this, but it was apparent they were not too concerned with the whole issue since they were not doing incoming Q.C. checks on locally purchased components either.

John suggested that Eva should tell her boss about their discoveries during the afternoon inspection tour, and a few days later when the boss came back from Dallas and Los Angeles she did tell him. He was unable to understand much of what she said however, since he reasoned: "If there was any trouble with our production, why would our sales keep growing so dramatically year by year?" He rather jokingly compared her views to those of the man from the State of Chi, in Chinese mythology, who was worried about the sky falling.[a] He smiled and said, "Your fears are totally without foundation. Our best advice is to let nature take its course."

Eva stopped working at the end of the month, and began procedures to apply to several US universities, as well as begin studying for the GRE and TOEFL tests. John said he hoped that she would have the chance to study for some period of time in Japan before attaining her Ph.D., and perhaps even be able to get some feel for the way the Japanese do business. Eva thought for a moment, but then said: "But I think the way the Japanese do things is too slow, we Chinese are more practically oriented and like to get off to a fast start."

"I don't see quite what you mean," John said, "unless you are talking about the start-up time for something like the camera industry, or the computer industry. I know the Japanese did spend over ten years cooperating with the Germans to learn how to grind optical lenses, and I suppose they spent the same amount of time, or longer, learning how to make silicon chips, ICs, power supply cables, and the other basic components of computers."

"The Chinese computer industry got going in a much shorter period of time," Eva said, "and we have had very impressive rates of growth."

"Well, that is true, of course," John said, reflecting on his knowledge of statistics, "but Japan now has the entire computer infrastructure from A to Z on which they may improve and innovate, whereas it seems your countrymen only have W, X, and Y."

"We will catch up with Japan in another fifteen years," Eva said confidently, "and probably even surpass them. History does, after all, run in cycles."

"Well, that will take a very thorough approach, but I certainly wish you the best of luck." John replied. "If you are successful I am sure you will make many and better keyboards in the future."

Many considerations which the foreign buyer will want to make in terms of where to place his purchase orders in Southeast Asia are also relevant to the foreign firm which is looking for a joint venture partner in the area. Local companies which have strong growth records will naturally appear to be excellent prospects for mutually-profitable endeavors in all respects. However it is sometimes necessary to look behind the "growth", and to see if it has any deeper significance, positive or negative.

In considering a factory's production, it is necessary to look at the actual production run.If the products are electrical appliances, electrical components, computer keyboards, or other such items, a selection may be made from the assembly line, and they can be "plugged in" and run to get some idea of their performance. For textiles, the size specifications, yarn weight, or other details should be gotten, and the items produced

---

a. 杞人憂天

compared to the items specified in the order. If it is possible to get one's own size, it would be useful to try it on and note any problems. In-house Q.C. inspection procedures should also be carefully noted for efficiency and thoroughness.

The foreign buyer in Asia is well advised not to "jump around", for it is far better to "move in stages". If it appears that a price break may be had on some items in one market, then one is best to proceed with a sample order, and gradually build up orders with this new firm, while obtaining experience in dealing with different factors of the differing countries' business styles. Since manufacturers are eager to show references of other firms they have sold to, the buyer may want to make a note of these, and when the products reach the home market in his country, to spend some time analyzing their quality.In this way it is possible to let the "competitors" do a portion of one's investigative work in dealing with new factories, to find out if they really produce top-quality merchandise.

## A Questionable Consulting Contract

Fred Lakenstrutt, a friend of mine from Wyoming, was increasingly famous for his local teaching seminars. He was asked by some private Chinese academies to do consultant work, and to help them expand their English language training programs. Fred has a Masters Degree in Teaching English as a Foreign Language, and has even done some further research in the field in preparation for perhaps one day pursuing a doctorate. The terms he was offered appeared quite generous: he was to be paid over US$ 1000 per month for locating and introducing suitable teachers for these four academies, as well as visiting their premises in person once a month. He would also need to recommend suitable teaching materials to the academies, as well as lend his name and photograph for their advertising. They wanted to sign a one year contract. Fred thought that this arrangement might be the start to similar arrangements with other institutes, and could easily lead to the establishment of his own book import concern, in order to provide suitable textbooks for everyone's use. Later on it was possible he could expand into editing and publishing.

He had asked his local Chinese friends for advice in considering whether he should sign this contract or not. His friends thought that it would be a wonderful arrangement, because he would be free to carry on most of the activities of his present schedule,

*Teaching English as a Foreign Language (TEFL) is English teaching activity undertaken in a non-English speaking country, such as China or the Soviet Union. Teaching English as a Second Language (TESL) is English teaching activity undertaken in an English speaking country, such as the United States or England, to residents who have inadequate English language skills, and who speak another language as their mother tongue.*

while helping the academies out with these minor duties and receiving a sizeable pay-envelope every month. I heard of his situation through the foreign grapevine, and after some discussion over the telephone we decided to gather a group of foreigners and Chinese around a table one Saturday afternoon to "kick the proposal around for a while." We thought that perhaps by analyzing the proposed contract from various angles, its good and bad points could be more fully brought to light.

At our roundtable meeting, we first tried to think of any possible things which could go wrong with this arrangement, and then translated our comments into Chinese, and posed it to our Chinese participants. After some discussion, one of the foreigners raised our first real question: "What if you arrange for teachers to go to the classes, and then one day one of them gets sick and cannot come in? Who covers in that situation?"

Various answers to this situation were posed. It was determined that if the school had the necessary qualified personnel to teach English, and one of them could step in to substitute on a second's notice, then of course Fred's situation was much more solid. If they did not have those personnel on their staff, then, according to the Chinese, of course the academy in question "will call you up on the spur of the moment and ask you to substitute."

"No, there is nothing in my contract about having to substitute teach when other people get sick or anything," Fred objected. "My duties are entirely in the way of consultant, and not as 'teacher' per se."

The Chinese shook their heads at this. Their feeling was "It is understood. You are responsible for introducing these personnel, so of course if they do not show up, you will have to go in their place." It was also mentioned that in the case where Fred had not yet arranged suitable teachers, and students were registered and ready to begin classes, Fred would certainly be called upon to teach.

In any event, these were additional points that Fred's contract had not clarified, and which everyone agreed would need further explanation before he could consider signing it. In his estimation, the English language skills of the majority of people in these academies were inadequate for doing any substitute teaching.

Another foreigner mentioned the entire issue of teaching program development. "Who is going to develop your teaching outlines and testing materials? Who is going to explain it to the students, or introduce the program to the students' parents when they come?"

Fred said that he understood that the school was taking full charge of these administrative matters, and he was only in charge of introducing teachers, and recommending suitable textbooks.

The other foreigners were quick to rebut this by noting "You just mentioned that the academies in question do not at the present time have adequately trained English speaking staff. It is impossible that they will take charge of these duties, and even if they do their explanations will not be very convincing."

"At the least you will have to train their staff members how to talk to parents and students about your program," the Chinese agreed.

Fred admitted that this was another point that he had failed to consider.

Another issue was raised: "Who is going to handle the basic communication between staff members and foreign teachers if neither can speak the others' language, especially not well enough to discuss specifics?"

Fred said that his understanding was that he was just being hired to recommend teachers, and textbooks, and that the other matters would be handled by the staff of the academies.

The foreigners said: "They cannot handle them if they do not even have the requisite language skills to talk to foreigners on the telephone, or discuss teaching methods face to face."

One Chinese gentleman stated: "Of course they will frequently call you in on the spur of the moment to deal with these matters." The other Chinese nodded their heads.

"But my contract says that I have to be given 48 hours notice if a special appearance is to be scheduled."

"But they will say that this is a crisis, and want you to come right away," another Chinese pointed out.

Fred admitted that this was a point he had not considered, and jotted it down as requiring further clarification.

This issue of Fred's "lending his photograph and name for advertising" was brought up. "What if," one American suggested, "at the end of your contractual period you decide not to continue in the arrangement. What will happen to all the advertising leaflets, posters, notebooks, etc. that they have printed with your name and/or picture?"

"Of course, if there were any left over at that time, they would have to discontinue their use. Probably they would destroy them," Fred commented matter of factly.

The Chinese balked at this. "A warehouse full of perfectly good printed materials, and they are supposed to destroy them? That is not fair. That is a significant economic loss to a school such as this."

"Morally speaking," Fred began to speak in a serious tone, "at the end of our contractual relation they would have no further rights to use my name and picture. The use of all materials printed in that fashion would have to be stopped immediately."

The Chinese had trouble understanding Fred's sense of morality. "Morally speaking," they countered, "it would be wrong for you to force them to suffer the economic loss which this would represent. Such action hardly seems in keeping with the dictates of humanity."

Fred was troubled by the entire direction the roundtable meeting had taken, and decided to call it quits for the day. After we had thanked the other people and they had left, Fred and I began walking back in the direction of his apartment. We went into a western style coffee shop and ordered some tea. The shop was elaborately decorated, with attractive wall murals and a beautiful serving counter. The name used, and the design of the shop logo was also very clever, I thought. I mentioned my observations to Fred.

"Yes," he said looking around, "this is an exact copy of a famous coffee shop chain operation in France. When I studied in France during the summer before my senior year in high school I used to visit those shops frequently. When I came to China, I was happy to find one."

"Well, it is nice to know the French have established cultural links with China, and have expanded their chain-store operations here."

"No, no," Fred corrected, "this is just a copy. Chinese owned and operated. I believe the French parent company instituted a law-suit in the Chinese courts to have them put out of business, but nothing ever came of it."

"The tea is excellent," I commented, taking a sip.

"And the prices much more reasonable than in France," Fred added. "But that is irrelevant to our present discussion. Do you think I should sign the contract or not?"

"You will have to be the final judge of that. It does seem to be quite more complicated than either of us had originally envisioned."

A few months later I ran into Fred at a party, and he was with an attractive Chinese woman. I shook his hand warmly. In an attempt to retain a typical Chinese greeting, even though speaking in English, I said: "Have you eaten rice?"

He laughed, "If that is the equivalent of 'What is new?' I will tell you. I have organized some private English and French lessons for local secretaries in my spare time, and it has been working out well."

"What about your consulting work?"

"I am waiting for a more promising opportunity to come along," he replied, "and if you need any advice, I would suggest you do the same."

The last I heard in the continuing saga of Fred Lakenstrutt, he was several years older and wiser, and planning to invest in the opening of a local restaurant as a cooperative venture with some of his students.

## Teaching Language to the Locals

After discussing T.V. and Movie work, it is easy to see how many of the considerations involved could apply to photographic modelling, tape recording projects, etc. However interesting such assignments may be, the number of foreigners involved in them is still small, and it is therefore desirable that we specifically relate our comments to the far more popular endeavor of "language teaching". Throughout the world it is common for foreigners to teach English in various academies, institutes, schools, colleges, companies, and other organizations, because English is becoming more and more of an international language with each passing day. The Chinese high schools and universities make increased use of English language textbooks every year, and the business community does substantial dealings in the international community, so English language skills are very important to many sectors of the population.

Much advice on teaching methods and general administrative matters can be obtained from other foreigners with whom one comes in contact, and so we feel it appropriate that our comments here be brief and to the point. The issues discussed below are often raised by newcomers, and are of particular interest to all.

## Private Class Arrangements

Inquiry: What are the important considerations to take into account when arranging to teach students privately, in their homes or offices, without dealing through an institute?

Observations: The exact address of the meeting place should be specified.

Most experienced teachers recommend getting at least two weeks tuition payment in advance. Specific arrangement for cancellation of classes should be made, and most westerners feel 48 hours advance notice is a bare minimum. It may be specified that for cancellation made over 48 hours in advance, no charge is made. For cancellations made within 48 hours, 50% of the tuition payment will be charged. For A) cancellation within twelve hours, or B) no notification and where the student does not show up, the teacher is entitled to the full tuition payment. Cancellations may be due to personal reasons, sickness, special appointments, etc.

Two hours is generally considered the most suitable length of class. A ten minute break may be taken in the middle. Most teachers recommend that no classes be held on any Chinese National Holidays, since some more exciting activity will generally come up on those dates.

For group classes taught privately, a class representative should be appointed. He/She is responsible for communication of all class scheduling details between teacher and students. If the teacher desires to cancel any class for any reason, one call to the class rep will then do the job.

It should be specified that if the class at any time goes to a coffee shop, restaurant, or other similar establishment, the student(s) pay the bill for the teacher, unless other arrangements were specifically discussed before entering the door.

The teacher may introduce books for the class members to use, but their cost is extra and must be borne by the students.

For private students who live far away, the teacher should consider negotiating a transportation fee in addition to hourly salary. The actual trip may be timed, and negotiations begun from this point.

Many private students have further questions which they would like help with after class, such as correction of business letters, translation of instructional booklets, and other matters. The Chinese will frequently offer to invite the teacher to dinner in exchange for such "favors", and the teacher may negotiate this to his best advantage. One established teacher of our acquaintance, with a long list of privately-arranged individual and group classes, had another technique however. He was in the habit of arranging every Tuesday night 8:00 to 10:00 in his apartment as "open-house night". Any of his students who had additional English questions, or wanted additional conversational practice, were invited to "Come over Tuesday night".

Such an open-house night arrangement has many advantages, not the least of which is concentrating all the loose odds-and-ends of student questions, difficulties, requests for assistance, etc. (which have been left over after class) into one weekly time slot, and leaving the remainder of one's time open for other projects, including rest and relaxation. Of course it is true that sometimes no one will show up, but in that case the teacher is free to attend to his other paperwork or listen to the radio.

Students, especially businessmen, frequently have urgent problems which come up after class, and it may happen that the foreigner receives a late night phone-call for assistance in composing a reply to an important overseas inquiry which the student's company has received. That the teacher would expect payment for such consultative discussion (which might run over an hour in some instances) strikes the Chinese as "overly practical", and hence it is generally desirable to achieve some understanding with one's students on how "telephone consultations" will be handled, as well as setting limits on how late in the evening, or how early in the morning, such calls may be made.

## Promises

My friend Wayne has been studying and teaching in China for over half a year now. He went from teaching 35 hours a week to teaching zero hours per week recently. Wayne is a very good teacher, and of course the schools at which he had been teaching had not fired him—it had been his own decision to quit. He was getting along very well with the Chinese staff at these places, as well as the students, so of course he had not wanted to quit, he had wanted to keep working. On the third day of his new-found unemployment, May 18th, he came to visit me, and to ask for a loan, since the drop in income which his new status represented was a real shock to him.

As the story unfolded, Wayne had met the head of another company who offered him fewer hours and more money, with a teaching schedule beginning mid-May. "I would have been a fool not to accept it," he said, analyzing his motives.

"Undoubtedly true," I replied, having not really given the matter any serious consideration.

"He even had me over to dinner and to visit his wife and family, so I figured he had really taken a liking to me, especially when he said that he thought my English was more understandable than some other foreign applicants he had interviewed."

"The Chinese are quite hospitable," I agreed.

"He said he wanted me to have enough time to take over a full schedule of correcting English correspondence and teaching at his company by mid-May, and I arranged to be free of all other work commitments by then."

"Oh."

"My old boss said they would be happy to have me back to teach whenever I had time."

"Might be something you could fall back on."

"So, can you loan me a few thousand in local currency?"

"What about your full schedule of work with this new company? You should have more than enough to meet your needs: food, clothing, tuition, some girlfriends."

"He called the night before I was supposed to go to work and said there were some problems. He wants me to wait a week or two. I do not really think it is fair, but I am not working there yet."

"So why don't you go back to your old job?"

"They found another teacher."

Wayne's situation is not at all atypical. We may summarize his circumstances at the outset by posing an inquiry in this fashion —

Inquiry: I was offered twenty-four hours a week at one Institute beginning the middle of next month, and for a better than average hourly rate. The manager wants me to be sure that I have enough time to take on this schedule, so I am quitting all my present teaching jobs. Will this work out for me?

Observations: We certainly hope that it does, but at the same time we urge caution. The important question for you to ask is: "Are the students registered?" If so, you are on much firmer ground. If not, you are dealing with the Manager's "hopes" and not anything which could be construed as "promises". Perhaps you should consider asking for a month's salary in advance, before you quit all your present jobs. That may or may not be acceptable to your new manager.

In the case where the students are not registered, and in order to cover yourself, you may decide to keep all your present jobs, until the new position really comes through, and then make a final decision to take it or not at the last minute, which corresponds to the way the Chinese do things in many similar circumstances. At that time if you feel that it is not more ideal than your present arrangement, you may then attempt to renegotiate the terms the manager has offered. Lay your cards on the table, saying: "Look, here are the terms I have at X School and Y School, and with my private students Mr. P, Miss Q, and Mrs. S. If you can better the terms, I will be happy to come to work for you. I am just trying to support myself."

In summary, the foreigner is best advised against putting all his eggs in one basket.

## Translating Poetry for Fun and Profit

Since the Chinese language is rich in rhyme, possesses an excellent sense of balance, has vast possibilities for parallel structure and subtle allusion, it is a beautiful language for writing poetry. As would be expected, there have been countless people over the ages who have been engaged in the writing of Chinese poetry and verse, and much of their work has been passed down over the ages. Many foreigners may even have the opportunity to meet some modern poets during their stay in the country. Of course it is highly rare that a westerner would ever devote himself seriously to original composition in this field, yet it is possible that the diligent language student may be called upon to undertake the translation of existent works, both ancient and modern, into a western language.

Obviously, to those with a love for the arts, and with a love for poetry in particular, the opportunity to translate such works is reward enough in itself, and monetary payment is a minor consideration. With this type of attitude, it is easy to endear oneself to the Chinese poets or scholars involved. However, with the thought that there may be a few members of the western reading audience who are more inclined to look at such projects in terms of "a job", and would expect to receive a reasonable rate of pay for their efforts, some discussion of how payment for poetry might be calculated is in order.

The problem involved in translating poetry, as opposed to translating other more general types of essays, reports, or catalog descriptions, is that for this latter type of work it is seemingly reasonable to calculate a payment based on the number of words in the final translated document. Thus, if a charge of $X per thousand words is agreed upon, and a rough check of our typed final copy (translated into the target foreign language, such as English) gives an approximate word count of 250 words per page, then the translation of an article which results in nine and one-half typed pages, amounting to nearly 2375 words (no one ever counts exactly), is precisely 2.375 times $X.

For translating poetry, this hardly seems a workable arrangement, since there may be lengthy deliberation over the choice of certain words, and much time and effort spent in trying to achieve a certain balance and smoothness of expression. Thus the final "word count" of the translated piece is often a very poor measure as to how much work the translator has actually done.

If one is being hired by an organization which is providing a desk, typewriter, dictionaries, reference books, a Chinese research assistant, and office space, it may be feasible to be "paid by the hour", and come in for work so many hours per day until the entire translation is done. The hiring organization would then be able to verify that the work is indeed progressing, and the translator could continually keep them informed of what difficulties have arisen, or seem to be arising. Frankly speaking, this type of arrangement is often not feasible.

Much more common is that the foreigner is asked to take the work back to his place of residence and complete it on his own time. In this event it is unlikely that the hiring individual or organization will accept his claim that "I spent six hours on these eighteen lines", or "I spent two hours on the choice of this word". An additional difficulty is that certain lines of poetry will most probably require more than just reference to the dictionary. A true understanding of their meaning may necessitate the help of a Chinese assistant, who can fully clarify for the the translator the historical background of the times in which they were written. Some modern poetry may need the explanation of the author (or other individual close to the author) in order that their full significance may be grasped.

With all of these factors in mind, we see that there are many stipulations upon which both parties will want to reach agreement before translation work is begun. If the entire project is looked upon as an exercise in improving one's Chinese ability, or perhaps as the subject of a Ph.D. dissertation, then monetary payment may be unimportant. In the event that this is not the case however, the following listing may serve as a good starting point for discussions between the foreigner who is undertaking the translation and the Chinese party who is desirous of hiring him. In this way it is hoped that future generations of translators may avoid the complaint of one American from a mid-west state who said: "When I calculated up all of the time I had invested in the project, and the payment I received, it worked out to something like US$ 0.20 per hour."

Suggestions:
* Several poems may be selected as representative samples, and work begun on these first. The amount of time required to translate these may then be extrapolated to the entire body of work, and some estimate for the time necessary for its completion may thus be gauged. This may then serve as the basis for a discussion of what an appropriate hourly fee, or charge-per-line, should be.
* If the foreigner's knowledge of history, geography, or other peculiar details surrounding the works, or of the author's life (or authors' lives), etc., is inadequate for undertaking the translation independently, some arrangement should be made for the hiring of a Chinese research assistant, and agreement reached as to how his payment will be handled. In the case where the hiring party feels it necessary to go into lengthy explanations of the meaning of the poetry, in preparation for the actual translation work, (quite a common situation in dealing with modern poetry, where the author or his apointee desires to explain the meaning line by line), some understanding should be reached as to whether the translator is being paid for taking notes and otherwise accumulating the information presented in these sessions, or if this is considered "on the translator's own time".
* Some payment schedule should be agreed upon so that the work is paid for as it is done. For example, the total price for the undertaking may be divided into five units, with one unit payable upon finishing each quarter of the translation. Upon successful completion of the entire project, the fifth unit is paid, and serves as a kind of "bonus" for total completion.
* Conditions of partial payment should be stated, with the understanding that in the case of sickness, family emergency, or other unforseen eventuality, the translator may resign from the project, while still remaining entitled to partial payment for that por-

tion of the work already completed.

\* In the event where the translated work will be published, when it is desired that the translator proofread the preliminary and/or final typesetting, some hourly fee should be negotiated.

> All poetry is difficult to read,
> — the sense of it is, anyhow.
> ——— *Robert Browning*

## Foreign Language Schools in China

Many European, American, and Japanese language schools are increasingly interested in extending branches into China. In a previous essay many considerations necessary for a teacher who is arranging a teaching schedule in China were outlined. Now we will turn our attention to some matters relevant to the actual opening and establishment of branch schools. Since the foreigners (and their Chinese partners) investing in these are in the private sector, these are commonly called private schools, private academies, or private institutes. Such institutes may be organized to teach "general self improvement" or "specific goal attainment" courses.

### General Self Improvement Courses

In China, most of the students who come to language schools are adults, of high school age and above, and the main languages in which they are interested are English and Japanese, since these are most valuable for travelling, doing international business, or making plans for overseas study. European languages such as French, Spanish, and German, and the Middle Eastern language of Arabic, are secondary choices, and usually only appealing to those students who have specific business or travel interests in those areas. In northern China, of course there is quite a bit of interest in Russian, and to some extent Korean.

There has also been a growing interest in recent years in English classes for Chinese children, and this is a rapidly growing sector of the language instruction market.

In Japan, North America, and Europe there are many language schools which organize long programs in which the tuition is paid by the year, perhaps in conjunction with a financing package through a bank or credit agency, and the student is bound by a contractual relation. However, in China these types of arrangements are quite rare. This is primarily due to the undeveloped consumer credit system. Thus, most private academies in China organize their semesters on a two month, three month, or six month basis. Classes meet two or three times per week, for two or three hours. Most students in these institutes work or go to school during the day, so class hours are primarily concentrated in the evenings, although there are classes during other hours of the day as well, since different people have different schedules.

### Specific Goal Attainment Courses

There are many locally run (i.e., wholly Chinese owned and operated) institutes which do organize programs on a yearly basis, and these tend to fall in the "specific goal attainment" category. For example, since the Chinese must take rigorous national examinations to get into high school, and more examinations to get into college, or commercial school, there are many local institutes which offer full-year training for those who have failed the national test and wish to take it again. The students may often raise the money necessary for going to such an institute for an entire year from friends and relatives, in the typical Chinese fashion. Classes may meet eight hours or more per day, five or six days per week. Some institutes of this type even have their own dormitories.

Other types of schools which are available to the goal-oriented student are those which are geared toward preparing for the GRE, TOEFL, and other related examinations in preparation for study overseas, although many of these do offer shorter programs of study such as three months, or six months.

Many schools' programs which fall into the specific goal attainment category often add the stipulation that, upon completion of the program, all tuition monies will be refunded if the student does not pass the test in question, and this is especially true for institutes that prepare students to retake the national examinations for Chinese high school or college entrance. This amounts to free instruction, but only for those who fail the test. Nevertheless, it is an interesting promotional gimmick.

Related to this is the story of a private institute (of 100% Chinese ownership) which made the direct offer in its advertising for "free English language lessons". Although free language lessons (of the "general self improvement" category) are occasionally given by some government affiliated organization, it is of course unusual that such lessons would be offered by schools in the private sector. For the students who were interested enough to make inquiries, the conditions of these free lessons were as follows: 1) Classes were to meet three times a week for two hours each time. 2) The student had to purchase the textbooks and other related materials, although it was true that these did not cost much. 3) A deposit for the amount of the tuition, approximately in line with what other similar institutes were charging, had to be given in advance. 4) If, at the end of the semester, all homework assignments had been done, no days of class had been missed, and the student was unsatisfied with the program, his money would be refunded, and he would have received his "free" language lessons.

I happened to meet the Director of that institute in a social gathering one time, and asked him what percentage of tuition monies were actually refunded. He replied "Considerably less than 5%. Something always seems to come up, and the students will miss a class or fail to hand in a homework assignment."

"What do the teachers say to the students when that happens?" I asked.

"Of course, they say nothing," the Director pointed out, "except for some vague comment like 'Yes, I understand you were busy. That is alright.' Then they make a mark on their class scheduling sheets and inform the office."

This appeared to me to be a good way of promoting harmony in the classroom environment, and not "putting the student on the spot". It is a strategy that recognizes and effectively deals with the complexity of Chinese social relations, family problems, and "go with the flow" type of scheduling preference. The institute staff says "We understand your difficulties." The employee in charge of accounting notes on his books "Your deposit is forfeited."

Levels of Study

Recent research has shown a big turnover in the student bodies of institutes where the students are studying for self improvement. Most language school managers note that as the level of difficulty gets higher, the number of students rapidly decreases. Obviously, the entire issue of how to mitigate this trend is one of the major challenges facing most language institutes. For adults enrolled in a twelve level program, from P1 to P12, with each level comprising three months, often more than 80% of an institute's business comes from P1, P2, P3, and P4 levels. By the time the students are ready for higher levels, they may have lost interest, or become involved in other activities, which could include other courses of study such as flower arranging, Chinese knotting, karate, judo, yoga, Chinese cooking, or various types of music lessons.

Teacher - Student Relationships

A possible conflict of interest quickly arises in the case where a class was originally arranged by the institute as a one-on-one, (i.e. one student with one teacher, in an essentially "private" class). While a student will continue in these arrangements for a semester, most often that will be the end of it, and there will be no more desire for further lessons, or at least that is what they will tell the institute. In reality, since they have become good friends with the teacher over the semester, and have probably taken the teacher out to dinner several times, and built up a good personal relationship, so they will often feel it more convenient to invite the teacher to their home or office, and continue the lessons in that manner, thus eliminating the middleman commissions which the institute would normally earn. Obviously, the same situation could come about in any class where the student count fell below five or six, in that they could make arrangements to hire the teacher "directly" and to use another meeting place. Reference to the AS Reward/Effort Relationship and the AS Perception of Injury show us that these developments would not be viewed as improper.

If the teachers which the institute has hired are essentially part-time employees, it may be difficult to make effective counter measures to this state of events. If the teachers are full time, of course it is more feasible to sign a detailed contract, and provisions against this type of eventuality may be specified.

### Employee - Teacher Relationships

It may also often happen that Chinese employees of the institute will be asked by their friends or relatives to introduce "teachers" to them for language classes to be held at some outside locality. The employees may then introduce teachers of their acquaintance from the school to these outside jobs. If this kind of situation is not desired, Employee Rules should include specific mention of the fact.

### Size of Classes

The meaning of "large class" is different in China than in the west, due of course to China's vast population. In junior high school or high school for example, a class of fifty or sixty might be considered average, even in an English language course. A considerable number of students in excess of this amount might be considered a "large class". In many private institutes teaching language courses, classes of thirty might be average, and classes of twenty might be considered small. A class of less than ten would probably be considered very small, or mini. Attitudes on what constitutes appropriate class size are changing however.

## Law, Ethics, and Business Philosophy

The traditional view that many Chinese have of law is that such crimes as murder, arson, disobeying the emperor's instructions, assisting the enemy, etc., are highly serious, but most other matters can be left up to the subjective handling of the citizens and officials involved, since they do not really amount to a threat to society. No doubt many westerners, who stress the implementation of objective standards, would disagree with this view.

Leaving the issue of these highly serious crimes alone for the moment, some businessmen and old China hands have often lamented that the Chinese view of the remaining law tends to be peculiar in many respects. First, there is a lack of the sense of "uniformity" or "continuity" as generally taken for granted in the west. Just as an "Environment Week" is a movement sponsored by some public organization with the hope that everyone will pay more attention to the environment, so the Chinese government and relevant agencies tend to enforce laws as "movements", with no necessary consistency from week to week, or month to month. One week illegally parked cars are towed at all hours. Two weeks later all illegally built buildings (or extensions to buildings) are served with notices that they must be torn down. The following week health inspections are held of all hotels, restaurants, taverns, and nightclubs. A short time thereafter illegal signs on the sides of buildings are removed by wrecking crews, although illegally parked cars are ignored. The next month drivers making illegal right turns are caught and fined, and blockage in alleyways is torn down and hauled away, for the first time in five years. Fire safety inspections of large shops and department stores are done two weeks later, and then no more is heard of the fire inspectors for a lengthy period. So on and so forth. The result of this erratic enforcement is of course the general lack of respect for law among the Chinese populace, and the general feeling that one is "unlucky" if he is caught, or it is "unfair" to be caught. One Chinese expression even parodies this situation: "This week they are grabbing the street vendors, lets all go rob houses."[1]

Intellectual Property Rights

In dealing with counterfeit merchandise, copyright infringement, patent infringement, etc. the "sequential movement" nature of Chinese law enforcement is often all too apparent. Yet to the visiting foreign dignitaries and press, it is pointed out that "several new laws have been passed recently", since the foreigners tend to be naive enough to think that passing the law and enforcement (or an even more gullible belief of "consistent enforcement") go hand in hand. In this regard it is certainly important for the foreigner to inquire what sort of laws are being passed. Is possession of counterfeit merchandise over a certain quantity or value seen as intention to deal and therefore a crime? Are the laws of evidence excessively stringent, for example requiring a signed receipt of the purchase of counterfeit merchandise noting the "brand name", quantity, price, etc. details before prosecution can be obtained? Can testimony be provided by affidavit, and are there provisions for protection of witnesses? What is the consistency of decisions handed down by judges in cases which concern counterfeit merchandise? Do you have wide disparities in the sentences which were handed out in similar cases? Do the judges tend to view repeated prosecution by the same foreign manufacturer against local companies as "harassment", therefore tending to render more lenient decisions over time? Is enforcement consistent? When the statistics indicate that increased numbers of sentences are handed down every year, is it nevertheless true that a vast majority of these are suspended or commuted to monetary fines, which tend to be totally out of proportion to the damage the foreign manufacturer has sustained? Are customs inspectors granted the same status as health and fire inspectors, so that they may enter any factory or office any time to check for violations, or are complicated procedures necessary in filing for search warrants? Is it true that judges and prosecutors are overworked and are in fact not fully up-to-date on all provisions of the Chinese law in regard to dealing with intellectual property rights violations? These are all questions which might be considered.

The Populace Speaks

Another peculiarity in the Chinese legal notion is the idea that everyone should follow the law, "but I am the exception". The Chinese believe that in trying to be overly ob-

---

1. This is a fairly common attitude among self-employed workers in many food service industries or street stall retail sales of borderline legality, although its conclusion is not, thankfully, always "implemented" in a strict literal fashion. 這個禮拜抓攤販，我們都去作小偷

jective, the law loses touch with the individual circumstances of people in society, which are essentially subjective in nature. Therefore they feel it is far better to use sentiment and sympathy in deciding how to deal with disputes. This was dramatically illustrated one July when a weekly Chinese magazine did a survey of 500 unlicensed street vendors who were operating in a large Chinese city, primarily in the major shopping and market areas. Among the items sold included clothing, purses, belts, handbags, all varieties of foods, and many other items. The comment of one 28 year old vendor was typical. In response to the question: "Do you think that unlicensed street vendors should be arrested and prosecuted?" He replied: "Yes, I think they should be. But as for myself, I am only doing this part-time, to cover my mother's medical bills due to her recent illness. Actually I have another job which keeps me busy most of the day. I won't be selling on the street anymore after I take care of these unexpected expenses, probably in another two months or so. Of course, it would be unfair to punish me, but as for the other illegal street vendors, yes, I believe they should be taken in."

Another man said he was temporarily out of work, and with three generations living in the same household, he needed the income that such selling provided, at least until he could find another stable job. A woman said that her brother's textile factory had gone under after several post-dated checks it had received from local retailers bounced, and she was helping to sell off their garments so that necessary cash should be raised to support their families. Many other stories reflected similar situations. The themes of "only doing this temporarily", "it would be unfair to punish me", and "the other illegal operators should be taken in" were echoed in the great majority of the vendors' remarks. A law major in a local Chinese university who was selling toys replied: "We university students are only doing this to earn our tuition, and we certainly will not be selling any more after the school semester starts in September. Most of these other vendors are real rascals, and something should be done about them. It is unfair to the established retailers who are paying taxes and complying with other government relations to allow these illegal vendors to continue in business."

Dealing With Legal Complications

In a related consideration, most Chinese agree to the acceptability of knowing (or locating) someone who can intercede in such disputes, so that the "problem" may be more amicably settled, or may perhaps just evaporate. Thus the use of "pull" to avoid many legal hassles is a long-standing tradition. To the extent that one has friends in places of importance in the local or national government hierarchy, it may be possible to convince the authorities to leave the disposition of one's case in permanent limbo.

Although many of the articles appearing in locally based English language news publications are translations of articles from the Chinese press, the stories of goings-on such as those above are rarely translated, for some unexplained reason. Not long ago a major Chinese newspaper ran a series of articles on several large supermarkets which had begun to operate in the basements of many local department stores. According to the local building regulations, since these areas were to be retained primarily for the parking of vehicles, and no other use was authorized, all such supermarkets were illegal.

The manager of one supermarket frankly revealed his strategy for dealing with this problem to the press as follows: Locating a run-down open-air market in a poor section of the city where many unemployed persons gathered, he picked a likely old fellow, and invited him back to the supermarket for discussions. The manager offered to rent this man's I.D. card for a specified amount of money, and this was quickly agreed upon, since the gentleman in question had no other source of income, and was wondering where his next meal was coming from. This I.D. was taken to the local tax authorities and presented as the "owner" of the supermarket, which we will call the Tong Tong Supermarket, and a "tax number" was obtained. Business had already begun the previous month.

When the government authorities received more and more complaints that illegal supermarkets were operating around the city, a full scale investigation was launched. Tong Tong was visited, and the store was presented with a hefty fine in the name of the owner. If the fine was not paid by a certain date, the owner would have to go to jail. The manager felt this fine was very high, and used some of his connections in the local government to negotiate to have it reduced, or cancelled. Before these negotiations could come to a successful conclusion however, the expiry date ran out, and the "owner" was located and taken to jail. Asked how this problem was handled, the manager admitted that this did cause him to have a moral obligation to the now inconvenienced "owner", and in fact he had sent representatives to visit the man in jail several times, and to assure him that a daily allowance was being put aside for him during the time of his incarceration. This was in line with the "standard fee" given for similar arrangements in other industries, and was to be paid in a lump sum upon the man's release. Word from the man in the slammer was generally favorable, since he now had three meals a day, and was accumulating a retirement pension of sorts, both of which represented an improvement over his previous position. He did not feel that his prison record would have any adverse effect on his credit rating.

The manager of Tong Tong moved all the merchandise out of his store in order to pass government inspection. After this technicality was completed, all the merchandise was moved back in during the space of one night, and the store was back to business as usual. A new "owner" was located, and the appropriate procedures completed to have the store's tax number re-registered to his name.

Many westerners will note one curious feature of the above story is that the store may make arrangements to pay taxes without having an operating license. Many times it is heard that the reverse procedure is workable as well, and an equal number of businesses open without either a tax registration or an operating license. I talked over this situation with the manager of a large open-air beer garden on the outskirts of a large Chinese city. "Is application for an operating license exceedingly difficult or time-consuming?" I inquired.

"I would not know," he said.

"What about your own license?" I asked.

"These types of beer garden restaurants are illegal," he said, "so it would be pointless to apply for a license."

"Surely you must be joking," I said as I glanced up and down the avenue on which his establishment was located. "There are at least a dozen other beer-gardens in the vicinity, and some of them are quite large. I believe it is impossible that all of them are operating without the necessary licenses."

"Some of them have licenses," he agreed, "and they are operating illegally too."

I could not quite follow the manager's explanation, but after we had a few more toasts he began to speak more simply. There were, he said, numerous regulations regarding fire safety procedures, lighting requirements, health checkups for employees, sanitary conditions for the kitchens, maximum charges for foods, beverages, and other services, as well as a ban on any accompanying entertainment, etc., which none of the restaurants complied with. Citing one example, he said that the local health department did not cooperate with the legal requirement that restaurant employees had to be inspected periodically. The last time he had taken a group of employees in for a health check, they had had to wait a long time, and the medical personnel did a very perfunctory job. One of the doctors remarked: "None of the other restaurants bother us by bringing in their employees, why do you have to make all this trouble for us?" When the nurse checked the cook's eyes, he read every line on the eye chart as E, E, E, E, E. It was only later that the cook discovered that while every letter on the chart was indeed E, nevertheless he should have indicated if the E was pointing in the right, left, up, or down position. Actually it did not matter, he had been given a passing mark anyway.

In another situation, there was a stipulation that fire inspections must be done periodically. However, when the officials had not paid a visit in the required period of time, the restaurant had made a few phone calls, and were promised that someone would come out. No one ever showed up however. A few months later an inspector from another government department came to inspect the kitchens. He asked to see certification of periodic fire safety inspection, and when they could not produce it they were given a fine. They were also told that their new ultraviolet high-pressure dishwashing machine imported from Germany, and installed by German engineers, was not up to the required sanitary standards. Although they were able to negotiate the cancellation of the fine in that case, there were certain other fees that had to be collected separately. The manager shrugged his shoulders. "You have to take things one day at a time. We do the best we can."

When I asked if it would be alright to speak to the owner of the establishment, the real owner, he said that was not possible, because the owner was out socializing almost all the time, in order to develop CPR (Close Personal Relations) with various people of influence. I mentioned to him that several recent books published in the United States on successful management practices had stated that "Excellent companies succeed by superior service and superior quality." I asked him for his philosophy of business.

"Make your service and quality good enough to get by," he said flatly, "in order to satisfy most of your customers. Most importantly, develop your connections."

The Standard of Rule

A strong undercurrent in the department store and beer-garden examples above, immediately recognized by the Chinese, is that the enforcement of all relevant regulations in the society reflects "Rule by Man", rather than "Rule by Law." The meaning of the former expression may not be immediately clear to the westerner, however the force of it is to state that the "personalities involved" are very important in the disposition of any and all conflicts, disputes, or "illegalities", and that various regulations may be bent if the person in charge feels like bending them, in order to help his friends, relatives, or other people who may somehow "make it worth his while". The latter term, "Rule by Law", suggests more of a fixed standard, objectively applied.

I talked to the Manager of a large international hotel (Chinese owned and operated) about these considerations, and he confirmed for me that since the days of the Chinese emperors, "Rule by Man" has been the established way of government in China. Although things are changing, the traditional notions still have strong influence. When asked if he had any problems in this regard in running his business, he mentioned many of the same topics that I had heard in my discussion with the Manager of the beer-garden. Particularly troublesome to him however, were the myriad small hotels which had sprung up in buildings throughout the city. Being unlicensed and unregistered, they paid very little in the way of government fees or taxes, and hence could charge far lower rates than his own hotel could. Since most of the operators of these places had sufficient pull to deal with any official inspectors who came around, so their daily operations were minimally affected by their illegal status. The Chinese practice of "going into business first, obtaining necessary licensing later" also gave them a great deal of leeway in dealing with a wide variety of legal requirements, since they could always state "We are in the process of applying."

This intrigued me, and I asked if he thought that allowing these small unlicensed hotels to operate was fair to those hotels that were complying with all relevant government regulations.

"From a legal standpoint, it is not fair to the hotels that are properly registered," he said, "but from a moral standpoint, since the operators of these hotels are supporting their parents and children, in addition to providing salaries to the many employees they have hired, who are in turn supporting their families, it would be immoral to demand that they cease operations."

I saw that in the final analysis, he felt that morality was more important than any notions of legal fairness, and he agreed that the officials in power certainly recognized this. I recalled hearing similar comments from the Secretary-General of Central Police College when I had toured their campus several months before. Clearly, this concern with morality was one major reason why such illegal establishments were not unequivocally put out of business. However, there was also another much more practical reason, as the hotel manager went on to state.

"Since all the power in a typical Chinese organization tends to be concentrated at the top, so the officials at lower levels are often left with shuffling a lot of paperwork, and only rarely given any real decision making responsibility. In cases like the operation of unlicensed hotels or restaurants, the normal procedure requires coordination of literally dozens of inspectors in various departments whose paperwork must be completed before final disposition of their case may be made. If a snag develops anywhere along the line, or if some special arrangements can be worked out, then of course the case could sit in limbo indefinitely."

Since I had agreed to help one of my American friends gather information on the improving health and sanitation conditions in the Chinese hotel and restaurant industry, in connection with a writing asignment which he had received from a professional Hotel Magazine published in Denver, Colorado, I had hoped to turn our discussion onto this track. However, the manager said that he had several important meetings that afternoon, and had to be going. He did mention however that his hotel's Health and Sanitation rating had improved dramatically over the years, and suggested that I could easily verify that with a check of official government statistics. "Our kitchens facilities were imported from Switzerland fifteen years ago, and installed by a team of Swiss engineers," he said. "During the first few years of operations we rarely passed a Health and Sanitation Inspection, but after a few years our Chairman's contacts in the relevant bureaus improved considerably, and now we have one of the highest ratings in the Province."

"That must reflect the fact that you are doing something right," I said.

"Yes, our hotel owner told me that he had finally realized a need for the granting of Anonymous Complimentary Shares to certain individuals."

Due to the time restriction, I was unable to press for more details, however I did ask him for a statement of his business philosophy. Pausing to think for only a few moments, he stated in a whispered tone: "Keep your customers happy. Make your service and quality good enough to get by, and develop your connections."

## Something For Nothing

When talking about business dealings, some level of trust must be shared between 1) business partners, 2) consumers and shop-keepers, 3) mass media (newspapers, magazines, TV stations, radio stations, etc.) and the listening or reading audience, 4) buyers and sellers of any and all other goods and services. A good starting point for discussing issue of trust is to look at the idea of getting something for nothing.

There once was a local Chinese businessman, new in the furniture business. After a not very successful first week of selling furniture, he decided to sell everything at a price of 10% off, and put up a sign to that effect. Another unsuccessful week of business followed. With a strong belief that he could open up the market for his products, he took an additional 10% off the original price every week until the sales price eventually reached 90% off. At this point there was still not much business in his shop, so he decided to put up a sign saying that everything in the store was for free. Interestingly enough, there was not much reaction from the public.

A middle-aged lady walked into the store and asked one of the salespersons whether or not it was true that everything was free.

Attempting to avoid the issue, the salesperson said "No, but these items are," and pointed to some small second-hand tables stacked in a corner. "We also have some other free furniture in the back room which I could show you," he continued.

The lady looked around for a short while, asked the price of some other items, and was quoted an average price (similar to that offered in other stores) by the sales person. She looked over several types of chairs, and then walked out.

This type of reaction shows that the Chinese consumer is not very pushy, and tends not to press the point. The idea of an "absolute statement" or "absolute standard" is largely absent, i.e. "Everything is free" is not taken at surface value to mean 100% everything, but rather is interpreted as "Everything is free, but there are also many things that are not free" and the latter things may include 99% of those on display. The consumer, a middle-aged housewife in this instance, accepts this, and rarely attempts to argue about it. On the other hand, had the same sign been put up in a store in New York, the store would have been empty by the time the lady came in.

It is easy to see how such an story relates to the whole idea of trust. Seeing a sign in the window "Everything is free!" the foreigner may be surprised by the relative lack of reaction from the populace. Obviously, the local people are not regarding the advertisement literally or absolutely, and the westerner should recognize this as a typical "normal" consumer attitude. Of course, we may say that the average consumer has considered other angles of the problem: Perhaps the furniture is free, but you must pay for delivery, and that is very expensive. Perhaps all the "free" furniture has already been given out already, and they have not had a chance to take down the sign yet, etc.

Hence, advertising or promotional strategy which attempts to attract customers by this sort of "free" ploy is often not regarded seriously by the Chinese public. In order to get around this natural hesitation, it is helpful if the product can be passed out on the street, and this would be appropriate for shampoo samples, candy samples, various stationery supplies, and other small items. Free furniture is more difficult to promote in this manner. Another more believable technique would be to offer "Buy one and get one free" or "Buy one and get two free", etc., in other words to somehow involve the purchase of something with the receipt of the free item(s).

There once was a large sale at a local Chinese supermarket on a variety of goods, canned products, snack foods, and beverages, stating that the consumers who purchased over a specified amount of any one product would be eligible to participate in a special drawing. They were asked to fill out their name and address on a prize entry form, and the name of the product they had purchased was stamped thereon. First prize was a week's paid vacation in a resort area. After the drawings, the results were printed in a newspaper which co-sponsored the event. The winner was one of the suppliers of canned tuna for the promotion. At this point the consumers realized that the drawing was for the suppliers, and not for the consumers. The announcement in the newspaper added that all prize entry forms had been forwarded to the relevant suppliers, and they would keep in touch with the consumers in the future with their mail advertising. At this point most of the consumers said: "If I had known that the drawing was for the suppliers, I would not have wasted my time filling out the cards."

A local Chinese resident saw an advertisement for a new magazine in a well-respected daily newspaper, and was interested in the free calendar, notebook, and pencil set that was offered in conjunction with a two-year subscription. He made postal remittance of the required funds, and received the free items. A short time later the first issue of his subscription arrived, and he enjoyed reading it. He received a copy every month for five months, and then no more copies came. When he wrote a letter to the magazine offices requesting clarification, his letter was returned, indicated by the Post Office as "Moved, no forwarding address". He was able to dig up a copy of the newspaper advertisement which he had originally seen, and took it into the newspaper offices to see what responsibility they would take for the apparent loss of his remaining subscription monies. The newspaper's reply was "That is your problem, you may handle it however you see fit."

A related difficulty occurs when certain merchandise is offered with the stipulation that "It may be returned if not satisfactory and your money will be refunded." With this type of wording, the issue of "satisfactory to whom?" is still unresolved, (the seller could conceivably claim that the "satisfaction" referred to is his, and not the consumer's), but beyond this there are often many sellers who refuse to honor this stipulation, by the specification of other technicalities. They may easily claim that "If you want your money back you have to return the merchandise to the factory", and in fact the factory is located in some distant community. It would indeed appear that there is nothing in such wording that specifies that the refunding of the purchase price is to be done by the shop that sold the merchandise, and the determination of whether or not this meaning is "implied" is a subjective issue.

Having been "disappointed" in these and other related dealings in society, it is easy to see why the average Chinese adult is reticent in believing the wide variety of advertising and promotion with which he is daily confronted. Foreigners are well advised to adopt a similar attitude.

Of course there may also be many types of local products which are claimed to have certain properties or benefits for which no proof is actually available. Such advertising is more than misleading, it is outright false. Unfortunately, due the lack of international regulation, many foreign concerns also engage in similar practices in China. For example, many pharmaceutical products which are outlawed in Europe or North America (due to serious side effects among users) may still be on sale in Asian markets, and other products may be advertised in a much more favorable light than they are in their home countries of manufacture. Various medicines which are classified as "By prescription only" in the west, are sold over the counter in Chinese drug stores without prescription, and it is possible some individuals could suffer adverse reaction to some western drugs purchased casually by their non-medically trained Chinese friends. If buying locally, following the ancient Roman dictate of "Let the buyer beware" appears highly advisable.

## Different Ideas

**An electrical appliance repair.** A consumer takes a malfunctioning electric appliance into a shop. The repairman only spends a few minutes adjusting some wires inside, and then hands back the appliance in full functioning condition.

We can ask this visitor a question: "Do you expect to be charged for this service?"

Interviewed on the spot, most westerners will reply "Yes, I expect so." After paying the fee, they will leave with their appliance.

Most Chinese will reply "No, I expect not." After thanking the repairman warmly, they will leave with their appliance.

**A visit to the doctor.** A person goes to a private medical clinic, complaining of a discomfort in some bodily area. A brief examination by the doctor reveals that nothing is wrong, and there is no need for a blood test, x-rays, pills, or a shot.

We can ask this person a question: "Do you expect to be charged for this checkup?"

Interviewed on the spot, most westerners will reply "Yes, I expect so." After paying the fee, or arranging for the bill to be sent, they will leave promptly.

Most Chinese will reply "No, I expect not." After thanking the doctor warmly, they will leave the premises.

Explanations

If we ask the Chinese to explain these differences in attitudes, many will say: "Westerners are overly practical, but we Chinese are very hospitable. We are happy to help others." This explanation seems to satisfy the Chinese.

A more accurate analysis is given by noting that the westerners do tend to allow for, and accept the existence of, intangible expenses, [1] whereas the Chinese do not. Hence, when we speak of what constitutes "appropriate" remuneration or reward for any work, we may commonly find different views among westerners and Chinese.

In one view, when we consider the issue of what costs are valid, the tangible com-

---

1. The reader should note that intangible expenses are abstract items, and not concrete ones. Social scientists have advanced the premise that "the Chinese have difficulty dealing with abstractions", and the reader may look for further evidence to support this premise throughout this volume.

ponents for materials, supplies, and physical labor needed in the work are recognized, however most or all of the intangible components of the work are not. There is the feeling that "since no additional physical expenses have been generated, so no additional reward is due" for the intangibles. At best the the allowed charge for the intangible items is very low. This sums up a great deal of the thinking behind the AS Reward/Effort Relationship.

In another view, work is viewed as having both tangible and intangible components. This is the thinking inherent in the IS Reward/Effort Relationship.

What are intangible components of work or effort? Some are categorized below:
* expertise in any area, and time spent in the application of that expertise
* design, structure, process, formula, pattern, patent, invention, or other knowledge
* literary, musical, photographic, etc. artistic creation or composition, or the reproduction or use of same
* trademark, trade name, or brand name use
* franchise, license, or contract formulation, explanation, translation, etc.
* collection or compilation of any type of information
* locating or introducing personnel to do any sort of job
* the right to use various physical, tangible property arising from the status of being the rentee, leasee, or owner
* time spent in a stand-by condition on the job site, in a state of readiness to begin work immediately
* lost-opportunity costs
* planning or outlining any method, program, system, procedure, campaign, survey, study, forecast, estimate, customer list or technical data, or the translation of same
* any similar activity

Some observers have commented that the drab and unexciting nature of much present-day Chinese apartment, commercial building, school, etc. construction is directly due to the fact that the authorities-in-charge were (and perhaps still are) adverse to spending much money on design and architectural fees, regarding the intellectual effort which these represent as "invalid" costs, because they are essentially intangible. To the extent that this kind of attitude is changing, present day architecture in Chinese cities is becoming more aesthetically appealing.

Further ramifications of the failure to recognize the validity of intangible expenses are evident in the following story.

## TV Shooting In France

Some time ago, I talked to a French student, Oliver, who had come back to China for a visit. As with many French people who have travelled and lived extensively abroad, he speaks excellent English. Having studied Chinese in France before spending three years in China, his Chinese is also above average.

Oliver described an interesting series of events which had occurred in Paris the previous year. One day he received an overseas call from some Chinese friends who were planning a trip to France with their associates. Since they planned to do some exploration and filming of the country, they wondered if he could serve as their guide and consultant? Since Oliver's schedule was fairly flexible, he agreed to do this, thinking it would be a good way to pick up some money as well as refresh his Chinese language skills.

The Chinese group arrived some weeks later and Oliver met them at their hotel. They were involved in shooting scenes for a new T.V. serial to be aired in China, and which involved a number of overseas scenes to be shot specifically in France. They were anxious to begin their filming schedule, since their budget was small, and the time that they could stay in the country was limited as well, due to their visa status. They outlined their needs to Oliver: they would need to shoot for several days in and around Orly Airport, in the Paris subways, and in various museums and parks. They would need to hire approximately fifteen to twenty local extras to use in filming. They also needed the use of a chateau to shoot some indoor scenes. Could Oliver communicate their needs to the local authorities and arrange the details? He promised to get to work on it right away.

After checking with the relevant Ministries and Departments, Oliver assembled the collections of forms and documents which would have to be completed before application for such permission could be obtained. When he went to see his Chinese friends, he began to go over the necessary procedures, but soon became aware of the fact that they had very little in the way of documentation in French from their own private or government agencies to support the propriety of the project in which they were engaged, and in fact they had very little documentation in Chinese either. Oliver suggested that perhaps they could wire home for the appropriate documents.

The Chinese had another idea: Did Oliver know anyone in a local translation agency or government office who could fix it up for them? Perhaps they could all get together over dinner to discuss it. Oliver said in fact that he did know some local officials, and translators, but they all operated strictly by the book. The Chinese considered this for a few moments and then asked how long it would take before they got the permission if the necessary documentation were obtained. Oliver said it might take weeks. They said: "That is far too long, we want to begin shooting tomorrow."

Moving on to the topic of extras, they asked what arrangements Oliver had made for hiring a suitable number of people. Oliver said that some modelling and personnel agencies had been contacted, and again there was some amount of paperwork to be completed, including forms for the appropriate withdrawl of taxes from the actors' fees, the specification of the days to be worked, the salaries to be paid, the agency fees, and their various registration numbers and documentation as employers.

The Chinese suggested that it would be best to have the extra actors come to work for one day first, to see how much actual shooting could be done. In that way it was hoped a better estimate of the number of days necessary for actual shooting could be arranged.

Oliver was able to convince one modelling agency of the special nature of the circumstances, and he was able to get nearly ten actors to come to the first day of unauthorized shooting in a location near the Airport. Whenever the police came near, the cameras and other equipment were quickly covered up or taken out of sight, and it proved to be an exasperating day, with not much being accomplished. At the end of the day, Oliver was asked to explain to the extra actors that since not much was accomplished, and everyone was still getting used to their shooting schedule, they thought that the best thing to do was to "write off" the day, and start over again early the next morning. Oliver said he was not sure if he could get the modelling agency to circumvent regulations again, and allow another day of shooting, since none of the procedural paperwork had been done, or other standard arrangements made with the official agencies. The Chinese said that if the modelling agency could not sympathize with their position, they could understand it, since they had heard that foreigners were overly pragmatic. However, that did not matter at this point they said, since they now had all the names, addresses, and telephone numbers of these actors, "and no longer had any use for that modelling agency."

The actors were understandably upset by the statement that the film crew decided not to pay for this day's work, despite the fact that little was accomplished, and the Chinese were appalled at the lack of sympathy which the French showed to their position. Nevertheless they were able to smooth out relations with the locals by noting that if the shooting in the next few days went well they would quite possibly be in a good position to offer everyone bonuses. They further offered to treat everyone to a large dinner that evening and discuss future shooting plans.

Oliver went along to the dinner, and met a number of other resident Chinese who were being treated by the film crew. Oliver was asked to explain to the French that due to the limited budget constraints of the Chinese crew's finances, they hoped that the French would agree to work for them privately, thus bypassing the modelling agencies commissions. Most of the French were surprised at this idea, and said that that would seriously jeopardize their future dealings with the agency if it was discovered. The Chinese made a joke of the fact that "even if we walked by the agency some afternoon and discussed our arrangements in broad daylight, they would never realize what we were talking about" (referring to the fact that the French obviously could not understand spoken Chinese), and a round of toasts was offered.

The French found it hard to accept this explanation however, and gave their excuses for not being able to go along with it. The Chinese were very hard put to understand why the French were unsympathetic to their position, but later thanked them for their help. The French took Oliver aside and asked what arrangements were being made to pay for the day's work, and Oliver said he thought that had been discussed, the evening dinner was payment in full. Oliver was lucky in being able to slip out a side door of the restaurant, thereby avoiding further confrontation with his countrymen. Later that evening when calling at the hotel suites of the Chinese crew he found that they were making plans to go to southern France to shoot for a few days with some of their other long time France-residing Chinese friends, and they would make their own arrangements to hire local extras there. They thanked Oliver for his help, and gave him some money to cover his "transportation expenses" incurred during his runnings-around for them, although Oliver noted that in terms of an hourly basis, it was considerably less than he earned as a part time French teacher.

Oliver related some of his experiences to Chinese friends with whom he occasionally corresponded, and some months later he received from one of his friends some copies of a series of articles which one of the crew members had written upon his return to China, recounting their crew's French misadventures in rather humorous detail, and noting at length the constant run-ins with police, the fact that some of them were expelled from the country and had to exchange identities with other Chinese in Paris for periods of time in order to smooth out the difficulties, the absurdity of the documentation required for this crew which was "essentially engaged in a mission to promote increased cultural understanding among the French and the Chinese", and making sad note of the lack of response of the French people to many of the Chinese problems "in a strange and foreign land where we were unaware of their foreign customs, and therefore should have been offered sympathy."

The true impact of Oliver's story did not hit me until several months later, when I happened to be discussing it with the mother of a Chinese friend. Mrs. Chou was helping me with a news article out of the Chinese newspaper which I was attempting to read. I had just gotten to the part where the author lamented the generally low level of morality among modern people in society. Looking up from the newspaper, I could not help but sigh, nodding in agreement at the writer's statement, and I briefly recounted Oliver's adventures with Chinese people in France.

Mrs. Chou listened attentively, and I was careful not to raise my voice or become irritated during my description of events. After I was through I asked for her impression, and she agreed with me that this was indeed a story of Chinese and French people interacting in France. However she pointed out that nothing I had said had anything much to do with the subject of "morality" per se.

This is explained by noting that if the members of this film crew wanted to raise their moral standards, they would devote themselves to scholarly pursuits, and she suggested that I turn back to the Chinese classics to see the high moral standards that many people in ancient society had maintained.

From my own perspective, I later recognized that further reflections on the implications of AS Reward/Effort Relationship and the Primary Sympathetic Orientation show that these crew members had done nothing out of the ordinary.

## Freelancing In China

Often the foreigner may find many freelancing opportunities available in China — some of which he looks for, and others which just seem to fall into his lap. In addition, there are many types of work which border on freelancing, for example, work that is done first for approval, and then paid for after completion if it is found acceptable. Work which falls into this latter category might include many types of art, design, photography, design of computer programs, etc. In any such type of freelancing work, the most important thing for the foreigner to determine before the expenditure of any and all effort is "What am I being paid for?", and a failure to clearly define this will often result in various psychological disorders.

The following story illustrates such a case:

Julie, an American girl, recently arrived in China on a one year work assignment with an American company. She made many friends and met many people through attending various gatherings and at informal dinner parties at her friends' houses. At one of the parties, she met Mr. Chang, the editor of a popular women's magazine.

Although Julie could only speak a few words of Chinese, Mr. Chang praised her fluency. "How long have you been in China?" he asked.

"Oh, I have only been here for two months. I was going to come here earlier, but my best friend got married, and I stayed to attend the wedding. It was quite a lovely wedding too!"

Mr. Chang smiled: "Say, you know, that is very interesting. I edit the 'Modern Women's World' magazine, and we are planning to do a feature article on weddings. When you mentioned your friend's wedding a thought came to my mind: we are really in need of information on Western weddings. Do you suppose you could help us get some material on that?"

"Well," Julie thought for a moment, "that is possible, I do have some photos from my friend's wedding."

"That is very good! Maybe you can write something as part of the coverage."

Julie was happily surprised, and saw this as a chance to make some money as well as to undertake an interesting research project. After all, there is always a certain magical aura encompassing weddings which leaves girls fascinated. "Alright," she said, "but when do you need the information?"

"Shall we say within a month?"

"That seems workable . . . I believe I can do a good job in that period of time."

Julie was in bright spirits for the rest of the evening. After coming back to her apartment she immediately sat down to write to her friends and relatives for information and photographs, and the next day she began to compose a long essay of what she already knew. There was going to be quite a bit of research required, she thought. But perhaps with the information her friends would xerox out of the library, and what she could collect locally in the English language section of the local library, things would begin to come together in a good fashion. Later that evening she even placed a few overseas phone calls to get things rolling.

Within a short space of time, thanks to her friends and relatives, much information was sent over from the USA, and she was able to complete her essay which covered all the main points of engagement and wedding procedure in the west. When she took all the information to Mr. Chang's office, he was very pleased, and insisted on taking her out to dinner that same evening, although due to another engagement she was forced to leave the invitation open to some other unspecified date.

Julie frequented the magazine stands for the next several weeks, and she was thrilled when she finally saw the issue come out with the feature article on weddings. Opening the magazine she noticed that two of her photos had been used, however she was not able to see how much of her article had been excerpted, since of course everything was written in Chinese.

She called Mr. Chang to talk about the article, and he was happy that she had seen it. "Yes, Julie," he said, "I am very happy about the wedding article in this issue. Our staff really enjoyed working on it. Come to the office in a week or so and get your pay."

When Julie went to pick up her money she was surprised and dismayed. They had only used two of her photos, and were allowing only the equivalent of US $1.75 each as a copy or reproduction fee. Since they had only used a few sentences of her article in their final manuscript, so they were unable to allow any payment for that. Thus the entire remuneration for Julie's effort was equivalent to about US $3.50. Julie went to a teashop and sat for a long time. She was shocked, speechless, and did not know what to do. In her estimation she had easily spent ten times that amount on postage alone.

The general flow of this story represents a situation which the foreigner may encounter in varying forms. During the research for this book, we presented this train of events to a number of Chinese businessmen, businesswomen, academics, and even some average citizens. The question we posed was "What should the foreigner do when he/she is asked to help in assembling data, information, photographs, etc. in this manner?" After some thought, over 90% of our respondents replied: "It would be best to do nothing."

Upon consideration we quickly see that an informal dinner party would of course not be the appropriate place to haggle out the exact terms and conditions of an offer such as the one illustrated here. Clearly this should be done at another time and place. If the foreigner was truly interested in the editor's offer, he/she might be well advised to ask a Chinese friend to serve as an intermediary to contact the editor and find out more details. Certainly, questions which the foreigner needs to clarify include: "Will I be paid for all the data I submit, or just the portion which is actually printed?", "Will I be paid for locating, xeroxing, and assembling materials, or only for wordage that

I actually write, or photos that I actually take?", "Will I be given an allowance for postage and telephone expenses?", etc.

Actually, the budgeting of many of the Chinese editors in these types of situations tends to be in terms of an AS Reward/Effort Relationship, so that it is assumed that collection of the relevant materials will be done on a "by the way" basis, (i.e., in conjunction with the fulfillment of other tasks, other duties, assignments, etc.) The westerners, who more subscribe to an IS Reward/Effort Relationship, tend to view the necessary budgeting requirements for such an undertaking on a "specific project" basis. There is a significant difference between the two viewpoints.

If Julie had presented an article and accompanying photographs on weddings to a magazine on her own initiative, as a budding writer would do, then of course she would have been more psychologically prepared if and when her efforts were rejected. To anyone with hopes of becoming a writer, and dedicated to pursue this line of work, it will of course be necessary to determine what sort of materials the editors are looking for, and then try to write something suitable. Monetary payment would then have to be regarded as a minor consideration, since the real aim would be to accumulate "experience". Julie assumed that the material requested by the editor, or other authorized staff member, would "be paid for" no matter what, however this is often not the case in Asian publishing houses.

Some of the same advice applies to requests from government offices for short term consultations or other projects which are of the nature of freelancing. Problems can develop when the department that is authorized to request the work has no authority to authorize the payment for it. It is therefore often desirable in many circumstances to obtain an official letter which specifies the work requested and the terms of payment, especially if the work to be undertaken is complicated, or involves various costs which would properly be handled by an expense allowance. The letter then serves to prove that the request is being made by someone in authority, (since approval for the issuance of such a letter generally has to make the rounds of all the relevant departments), and that the terms of payment are as specified.

## Lessons From the Chinese Laundry

With the importation of huge quantities of textile machinery in the last few decades, the textile industry in China has really taken off. Large quantities of wearing apparel are exported to the west, and of course a substantial amount is consumed locally. Foreigners in China certainly do their part to support the local mills, by selecting local brands in many of their clothing purchases. Sometimes such purchases are not totally pre-planned however, as my friend Benjamin from Rhode Island pointed out. Benjamin, being busy with his work and studies, does not have much free time to devote to laundry chores, and so has a contract with a local Chinese laundry to do all of his dirty clothes, in fact they even provide pick-up and delivery service all for one set monthly fee.

On first analysis, the price Benjamin pays is less than what these services would cost in any city in the western hemisphere, however Benjamin is quick to note that there are additional expenses involved with this type of arrangement, namely "replacement of lost or missing clothes". Underwear is one thing in particular of which Ben purchases locally-made goods in some quantity, because he says: "Over every period of three or four months I regularly seem to come up short in T-shirts and undershorts. My number is 169, but I never seem to get back all I send in."

Obviously one way to solve this problem is to maintain an exact list of what items were collected and when, but Ben says: "I really do not have time for the hassle." Such a listing arangement would be more suitable if one were taking one's laundry in to be washed, and charged on the piece-by-piece basis, as opposed to having it picked up. However, many laundries also wash by the kilo, and so individual listing is still not always feasible. Another method which often works is to have one's Chinese name embroidered on the insides of one's shirt collars, the inside pocket of one's sportcoats, and some other appropriate place in pants and other garments. With the large demand by Chinese students for such embroidering on school uniforms, shops that do this kind of work are very numerous. Ben may have some new clothes made before Christmas, and he is planning to have the tailor mark them in this fashion.

On the other hand, some foreigners report no problems with the local laundries whatsoever. Kirk is one example. He says that he has sent his laundry out regularly for nearly a year, and as far as he is aware, he has never lost a shirt, pants, or any underwear. In considering Kirk's testimonial I have often felt that the fact that he weighs 320 lbs. puts his clothing in a rather "unique" category in the eyes of the laundry service, and somehow makes it easier to keep track of. Kirk has no comment on this.

Benjamin is not unhappy with his laundry arrangement. Actually he expresses an "understanding" and yet unconcerned disposition in regard to purchasing new replacement items as the need arises every few months. His rather debonaire attitude serves as a good example of a foreigner who has incorporated some idea of "bad debt allowance" or "goodwill allowance" into his everyday thinking in dealing with the local Chinese citizenry. In fact Benjamin is allowing for 10% to 15% of his common laundry to fall by the wayside, or otherwise come up unaccounted for, and thus require periodic replacement purchases. "It helps to stimulate the economy," he says.

In terms of more valuable items such as sportcoats, dress pants, or his wife's evening dresses, Ben takes these in separately to be dry-cleaned, and retains a receipt for each. In this way misplacement problems are largely avoided, and if something does come up missing he has a receipt and a specific item description on which to base a claim.

Ben goes to his office by taxi quite frequently. Generally it is $62 in local currency, but occasionally it is $68. "I don't worry about it too much if it is in that range," he comments. Once it was $138, and Ben says: "I thought maybe something sneaky was going on but I didn't have any proof. I told the cabdriver my aunt had died recently and I had been laid off from my job. I offered him $75, and he took it."

Thus we see that Ben is not only easy-going in money matters, but also knows how to tap a sympathetic note in order to get out of potentially argumentative, troublesome situations. On the other end of the scale from Ben's attitude are the foreigners who will dispute assuming the cost of a small basket which the laundry service might feel suitable for placing in one's home, so there is a convenient place to put the clean laundry upon delivery. In the business world, there are the foreigners who will argue about responsibility for the cost of the Postal Money Order when the manager says that a portion of their commissions will be remitted from some distant branch office, or those who will argue over footing the bill to pay the cost of an occasional box-lunch in the office. When it is decided that all the employees should have a company shirt or jacket, some westerners are inclined to say: "Fine, but only if someone else pays for it." Reflecting on this type of attitude, we are reminded of the man of whom it was said "could squeeze a quarter until drops of water came out." Asked to comment on the meaning of this phenomenon, his friends replied: "He is so tight he makes the eagle cry."

Additionally worthy of discussion here are incidental expenses associated with rental costs for housing. For example, it may often be the case that water, electricity, trash collection, and some other expenses are not included in the price of housing rental in some areas, but the local understanding is that these are paid by the house-, apartment-, or room-occupant on a separate basis, (unless there is a specific understanding to the contrary at the time of renting.) Also along this line is the expense of purchasing plastic garbage bags to bundle up one's trash before it is put out, since many Chinese apartments do not have trash cans or dumpsters. For the foreigner to deny these charges when they fall due is certainly questionable, even though he rightfully maintains "I was never told about this." A better approach would be to regard them as "an investment in goodwill", or part of the general "overhead" of living in China.

## Generosity and Business

Contrasted to anything which could be called "an essentially stingy approach" is the behavior of the Chinese businessmen, many of whom give presents to their friends and customers on each of the three big holidays: Chinese New Year, the Dragon Boat Festival, and the Mid-Autumn Festival. Such generosity is usually contagious in China, since many people will reciprocate in kind, and serves to build up good customer and supplier relations, as well as establishing good neighborly relations. In a company, a more generous attitude on the part of foreign employees will greatly facilitate working with the Chinese staff. This may result in a better chance of being assigned more duties, thus earning more income, or even of being promoted, since Chinese managers will almost always take into account the feelings of the Chinese staff in making placement of foreign personnel.

Thus a willingness to assume a slight loss in covering various incidental expenses in many cases will actually be more advantageous to the foreigner in the long run. Even in the case of the laundry, it may be that the "new" appearance which Benjamin, and others like him, continually present will earn them respect in many circles, and the good impressions and friendships thereby generated will more than make up for any displeasure associated with this "potentially irritating" situation. Certainly the best recommendation is "Keep smiling."

This is especially good advice when we consider that the basic nature of the Chinese is sympathetic, and that they are generally displeased with expressions of anger. Hence if one expresses anger over the outcome of these lost or missing clothes, it is possible that the Chinese parties will be alienated immediately, and this is not conducive to further negotiation on the issue.

In another situation, one may have some Chinese friends who are rather careless with their belongings, and the foreigner is well-advised to adjust his basic daily thinking to cover for this. When these belongings do indeed turn up missing one day, it is inadvisable to castigate the other parties for their carelessness, (in light of previous warnings on the subject), or to make the suggestion "I hope you learned a lesson from this." [1] Actually, some kind words of sympathy and understanding are usually much more well received. The next time their belongings turn up missing, the same reaction may be employed.In this way the entire issue is regarded as a psychological exercise in "loss management." An example of this would be girls in the office, factory, etc. who leave their purses and other valuables lying around carelessly when they go to the restroom, run an errand, or visit someone in another department. Many times the suggestion that they should lock-up or otherwise securely safeguard their belongings will get some reaction like "That is not our custom", "It probably won't happen again", "We never had such a crime problem in Confucius' era", or other philosophical maxims. It is certainly bad form to question the appropriateness of the attitude this type of rationalization represents, and the foreigner may circumvent the entire issue by appearing patiently concerned, while avoiding the temptation to offer any constructive criticism.

## Enrollment in Chinese Elementary School

Many foreigners living in China, including overseas Chinese, know that sending their children to an English-speaking school is a lot more expensive than sending them to

---

1. The typical western reaction here is not a lack of sympathy (in the western view), but merely attempts to establish a rational base-line for the application of sympathy.

In an incident of lost money: "If the affected party followed ordinary precautions, guidelines, and common sense safety measures", the westerner is inclined to be sympathetic. "If the affected party did not follow ordinary precautions, guidelines, and common sense safety measures", the westerner is much less inclined to be sympathetic, especially when the loss occurs repeatedly.

a local Chinese school, and therefore would consider enrolling them in the latter. Of course, there are advantages and disadvantages that must be taken into account, analyzed, and correlated carefully in the process of making such a decision. In the end every family must weigh the various factors and come up with their own determination. The lessened financial considerations involved may count heavily in the decision making of some foreign families, and relatively lightly in others.

My friend Ken, a native Malaysian brought up by a Chinese family in Penang, was talking to me recently about the advantages of a Chinese elementary school education. He said that Chinese education provides a sound foundation in the basics, the Chinese students are noted for their neat handwriting and competence in math, they have good manners, are taught to respect their teachers and elders, have a serious attitude toward studying, and have to put up with extremely high standards of academic excellence. To top that off, they have a good sense of self-discipline. Ken has a six year old daughter, and felt it beneficial to enroll her in the local Chinese school. His present job is in the Malaysian banking sector, and he is stationed in China with the goal of establishing a local branch of his Kuala Lumpur based bank. After listening to his various comments on the Chinese educational system, I wished him good luck, and he in turn invited me to come to his home for dinner the following Saturday night.

When I arrived at his residence, I smelled many tempting aromas coming from the kitchen. After introducing me to his Malaysian wife and little daughter, we began our meal. Ken asked for my advice as to what the procedures were for enrolling his child in the local English-speaking school. I was surprised at this question, and said: "Weren't you planning to send your daughter to the local Chinese public elementary school?"

"That does not seem to be possible," he replied, "they said that they were not responsible for educating my child." The expression on his face suggested that there was something more to it. I was going to repeat his earlier remarks about the advantages of a Chinese elementary school education when he commented: "I really cannot understand their reasoning."

"What do you mean?" I inquired, trying to appear concerned.

"You know what? I was born in Malaysia, but my parents died in an accident when I was very young, so I was adopted by a Chinese family and raised with their three other children. They made sure that we knew we were Chinese. They taught me the Chinese scriptures, Confucius, Lao-tse, etc. and stressed the importance of self-discipline, respect for the self and for the family. They also made sure that along with my "foreign" education, I was also enriched by the Chinese cultural heritage, the martial arts, and Chinese brush painting. In brief, they wanted me to be a well-rounded Chinese person, and I would like the same for my daughter. But when I mentioned this to the principal, he just stared at me."

"What did you say to him?" I asked, somewhat curious.

"Well, after hearing the school's position that they were not responsible for educating my child, I was suddenly struck by two tenets of Chinese philosophy – "All people should be educated equally without discrimination, and without separation into kinds', and all people should strive for 'Universal Brotherhood'." Ken took a sip of tea, pointed to his daughter, and continued: "I have a Malaysian passport, and am considered a different 'kind', so they will not let her go to public school. Why is this?"

I tried to avoid the issue. Of course the quotes Ken had brought up were irrelevant in this situation. I said: "Why not send her to a private Chinese elementary school?"

"I considered that, but the nearest one is quite far from our house, and anyway I think that there is not enough benefit in the first few years to merit the extra expense." Ken sighed, ". . . and you know, the child of our neighbor Tsai Ying-mei (Mary Tsai), he was not accepted either."

"Is her child too young to meet the age requirement?"

"No, he is the right age, but, well, among common friends we say that she is divorced, but actually the child was illegitimate, and Mary was never married. Without a father the boy cannot obtain a household registration record, and without that he cannot register for school. Mary also mentioned that Confucius stressed 'Education for all without separation into kinds',[1] but the principal said that was irrelevant."

"Essentially true," I agreed. "You and Mary have both forgotten to take into account the basic underlying premise of the 'Group Mentality', and have made the error of thinking of your children as if they were individuals. From the point of view of the group, the Malaysians should be with the Malaysians, and likewise, the Chinese with the Chinese. Your daughter is after all Malaysian."

"The principal did not use those exact words, but he did suggest that the education of my daughter is the responsibility of the Malaysian schools," Ken nodded.

"Of course," I continued, "and in Mary's case, since Chinese kinship is patrilineal, until her son's father can be determined, or some other male member of the community can agree to assume fathership, the boy is without any place in the kinship structure, and therefore without a 'group' in the most basic sense—a family."

Our discussion moved on to Ken's banking business. "I imagine I will be here for several years," Ken commented, "we want to build up our local contacts in the community, and establish a good business base."

"Things are progressing smoothly then I presume?"

"I was very surprised," Ken replied. "There are a lot of restrictions on foreign banks that do not apply to local Chinese banks.[2] I know that Chinese are discriminated against in my country, because the Malays resent the economic grip the Chinese have historically

---

1. In terms of higher education, it is commonly heard that students with physical disabilities, Chinese or foreign, are not allowed to register in the Teacher's Colleges or Normal Universities for programs which would lead to degrees qualifying them to teach in Chinese elementary or junior high schools. This clearly appears to be another separation of the student body "into kinds", in violation of Confucius' teachings. (Reference: *Analects* XV, 39: 有教無類 )

2. Contrastingly, the United States, U.K., and most other western countries offer "national treatment" to any banks which set up operations within their borders.

had on Malaysia, but in China I had thought that the doctrine of 'All men in the four seas are brothers' would imply equal treatment for all. Didn't Confucius say: 'Is it not a pleasure to have friends come from afar?' ... but the officials at the banking regulatory board said that those maxims were not applicable in any way."

We lapsed into momentary silence to take a bite. I thought about what type of explanation could be used in order to more properly clarify the situation. "Ken," I began, "with all due respect to your adopted parents, I think that your approach to Chinese philosophy is a bit off the mark, you are trying to read something into it, and it is confusing you. It is important to know the broad underlying ideas on how the values are applied in certain situations, and from the tone of your remarks it appears that you have even forgotten about the Pre-Industrial Revolution Subsistence Agriculture orientation."

"What relevance does that have here?" Ken asked.

"There are many ways to look at things. Although friends come from afar, not too many do in a Pre-Industrial Revolution age, and in any case they also go back; we expect that their primary focus is on their own group."

Ken finished the rest of the meal in comparative silence, although his wife was kind enough to inform me of the correct technique for baking several of the delicacies she had prepared for the evening. Of course it is not every day that I come across someone of Ken's mental orientation (or disorientation), but with the possibility that there may be others equally confused among the reading public, a brief rundown of the high points of our discussion has been presented above.

In reviewing these initial problems, one suspects they could be largely solved by enrolling one's child in a private Chinese school (which may be considerably more expensive), or cultivating some influential friends in the Chinese Legislature, who could then plead one's case with the public school officials. It is also worthy of consideration that the school may simply be full, and application at another school may prove more satisfactory.

In any event, we believe it is also advisable for the foreign parents to make thorough inquiries with other Chinese families as to the exact fee structure in a Chinese school, before making any final budgeting estimates. Although many schools in the United States are fairly straightforward in the collection of yearly fees for any and all causes or expenses, the Chinese schools tend to have many "extra fees" which are continually coming up. Examples of these are charges for supplemental textbooks (used for reviewing course material) over and above the cost of the regular textbooks. The Chinese parents inform me that such fees are always announced and collected separately, because official Ministry of Education policy is not to allow the students to use such texts, and therefore they must be purchased surreptitiously.

Additionally, often times children in the 3rd grade or beyond will stay after school several times per week (on an entire class basis) and receive additional instruction from the teacher, in order to do better in their lessons and on tests. Each child must of course pay the teacher a monthly fee for this extra instruction, since this is not part of the teacher's salaried duties. Again, the Chinese parents inform me that such payments are always announced and collected separately by the teacher, since official Ministry of Education policy is to forbid this practice, and it must be done clandestinely.

It is also often the case that a Chinese teacher in the elementary, junior high, or high school will introduce students to "supplementary academies" where they go for instruction after school, on weekends, etc. several times a week. Many teachers strongly recommend that students enroll at one particular academy, sometimes even to the point of "registering the students first, and informing them of their registration later", or using other such coercive tactics. Of course each student must come across with the funds specified, even if they have schedule conflicts and are unable to attend. Once more, the Chinese parents inform me that such payments must be made discreetly, since the Ministry of Education recognizes that teachers engaging in this practice are receiving substantial commissions from the academies in question, and hence official policy is to forbid the practice.

Of course occasionally there will be a student of the school whose parent was seriously (or perhaps fatally) injured in an accident of some sort, and since the Chinese do not tend to carry insurance, so this may cause his family to become hard pressed. In any event the student body will certainly take up a collection for the concerned child's family, and a small contribution to such a cause would not look nice, especially from the foreign child who is seen as being perhaps in a superior economic position. The rule in such situations is best described as "From each according to his ability, and to each according to his need", and of course such monies are collected separately.

The interested foreign parents may make further inquiries with their Chinese neighbors and friends for more details as the need arises.

## Law vs. Benevolence Questionnaire

Directions: (1) Consider the situation which is given. (2) Write down your answers to the five questions at the end. (3) Present the situation to a Chinese person whom you consider to be non-westernized, and record their answers. (4) Compare the two sets of answers. (5) Review the Conclusion Questions.

Suppose that you want to travel on a commercial ferry-boat across a large, deep river. Since this river runs through two countries, two services are available.

### Country A

All safety regulations in boat construction and maintenance are strictly enforced. Boats which upon inspection are found failing to meet safety regulations are put out of commission immediately, and not allowed to resume operations until they bring their safety equipment and procedures up to the required standards.

An adequate number of government inspectors has been assigned to handle routine inspections of all commercial passenger craft on a regular basis.

### Country Z

Safety regulations for all types of boats have been established, but are loosely and selectively enforced. Boat owners who are close friends or blood relatives with inspectors are often allowed to ignore the regulations. Boats which are found in violation are given a warning and a small fine, however they may continue operations. Drastic measures such as drydocking a boat and hence putting crew members and other staff members out of work, inconveniencing passengers, etc. are avoided, and many extra-legal extensions for compliance are granted.

The number of government inspectors assigned to handle routine inspections of all commercial passenger craft is inadequate to complete its duties on a regular basis.

Questions:
1. Which country's ferry-boat would you take across the river?
2. Which country operates on a legal basis?
3. Which country operates on the basis of benevolence and sympathy?
4. Which is more important, law or benevolence?
5. If people in the world community are fully informed on the way safety regulations are enforced in the two countries, which country will be more respected and have the higher international standing?

*Conclusion Questions:*
 *1. Are any contradictions present in either of the sets of answers you have received?*
 *2. Can you consider the question "Is the western value system valid for westerners?"*
 *3. Can you consider the question "Is the Chinese value system valid for Chinese?"*

## The Western Hotel Consultant

I once met a western business consultant who had been brought in to oversee various details of the final stages of construction, inspection, and new opening of a large Philippine-invested hotel in China. The total investment was approximately US $150 million. This consultant, whom I will call George Hamrock, was interested in the fact that I had lived in the country for a lengthy period, and asked me some questions about the language and getting along with the people. We went out to a pub one evening for a chat.

"Actually," I said, "you must know a lot more than I do about dealing successfully with the people if you are a famous business consultant. I imagine that I should be learning from you."

"Well, I do know a few tricks and strategies for getting along in the Southeast Asian market," George replied, "but nothing very fancy."

As our discussion continued, I described to George my friend Benjamin's method of dealing with the local laundries. "Writing it off as a 'goodwill expense', yes, that is an excellent technique, and I use it frequently," George nodded in approval. He mentioned that some of his Chinese friends were planning to bring their children back to China to attend school, and we discussed the local school situation briefly. I mentioned that many fees and charges were collected from the students separately. George smiled knowingly, "Separate collection of fees, yes, that is common in this part of the world, I am well aware of it, and always work it into my overall planning."

Asked to discuss his work as consultant in the new hotel, George shrugged his shoulders and said: "It is nothing too complicated really. There were a number of problems regarding construction work that was done, and I was brought in to help straighten things out. I have developed a strategy, I call it the P.I. Strategy, in dealing with such problems, and of course it works quite well." George excused himself to place a phone call back to his secretary, he said that he was required to leave notice of his whereabouts 24 hours a day.

When he came back I offered a toast, and then tried to get the conversation back on track. "Could you tell me some more about the P.I. Strategy? Is it a difficult strategy to put into action?"

"It does require a readjustment of one's mental orientation," George said, "but other than that it is not difficult. The first step is to get a full grasp of the issues involved."

"What are the construction problems that came to light?" I asked.

"Oh, it is rarely an issue of construction problems, it is generally more in the way of budget problems. The investors failed to budget correctly, so of course various difficulties arose regarding the final inspection procedures on the construction."

I was not quite able to follow what George was talking about, but after we had a few more drinks he began to speak more plainly. The hotel had been completely designed by a cooperative of Chinese, Filipino, and American architects. All local specifications, ordinances, and regulations were strictly complied with. "For the electrical wiring the hotel imported the best products available from the USA, and maintained rotating teams of Q.C. inspectors on the site to be sure that it was installed correctly." George said, "It was a top quality job from start to finish."

"Well, at least that means there will be no problem from the local government inspectors in regard to your electrical wiring," I summarized.

"Oh no, not at all," George replied, "that is where the bulk of the problems were when I was called in, although now I have them pretty well straightened out."

"I thought your wiring was perfect," I said, "Why would there be any problems?"

"The hotel thought so too, so they called in a large electrical consulting firm from Japan to check over the work. Everything was found to be in perfect shape."

"Well, that settles it."

"No, when the government inspectors came in and did a thorough inspection over a period of two days, they found that the wiring did not meet local regulations in a number of areas, and gave us a lengthy report. They stated that the hotel would have to be completely rewired."

"Completely rewired!" I gasped, "that would involve a tremendous expense! Maybe everyone needs to meet and compare notes, there must be a misunderstanding somewhere."

"Well, we had several meetings to discuss things. The Chinese officials stated that the Japanese electrical consultants were not recognized by the Chinese government as qualified to do this type of inspection, hence it was impossible to determine if the Japanese report was true or false."

"Isn't that Japanese firm recognized internationally?"

"Oh yes, of course, top credentials, but being 'recognized internationally' has no real meaning in China. We made some further inquiries, through indirect channels of course, and we found that there were a number of difficulties in our entire design, due to the existence of several unwritten regulations regarding electrical wiring and a number of other considerations which the inspectors considered particularly relevant to our situation. I had dinner with several of the inspectors myself, and they were quite hospitable. However they said that if we still desired to run the hotel, it would have to be completely rewired, or else various other work would have to be done to bring it up to the required standards."

"How much would that other work cost?"

"After considering the various factors involved, the chief inspector came up with a rough estimate of less than $20,000 for that work, as opposed our own estimate of nearly $725,000 to have all the wiring redone."

"What was your advice to the board of directors at this point in the negotiations?" I asked.

"Of course, I recommended the P.I. Strategy."

"What does that mean?"

Before George could answer he was called to the phone by the manager of the establishment. I took the opportunity to go to the restroom. When I came out, I overheard George talking. He was saying: "From your description it does seem that the boy was not responsible for the breakage, but if they do not accept the testimony of witnesses, there is nothing much you can do about it. What are the costs by their estimation? . . . Well, I think there is not much you can do at this point. My recommendation is: Pay It!... No, I don't think there is any advantage to be gained . . . . . . "

Since I could not understand what George was conversing about, I walked back to our table and sat down. He came back several minutes later.

"Was it an important problem?"

"No, nothing really, the son of one of our overseas employees was involved in some sort of accident in a China shop, and there was quite a bit of breakage. They wanted my advice on how to settle it."

"We were discussing the P.I. Strategy for settling disputes."

"Yes, that was the strategy we adopted."

"What exactly does it mean?"

"Well, that is something we do not discuss openly. We did however go ahead with the required modifications."

"And who did you hire to do that?"

"Well, the chief inspector said that he knew a contractor who was well versed in the required type of work, so of course we took his advice and allowed that man to take care of all the details."

"And that was included in the total cost of the government's inspection work?"

"Oh, no, those fees were collected separately."

"So, you had to make a revised electrical wiring budget to allow for that."

"No, it was not really formally considered as part of the electrical budget, because we did not really sign a contract, or get a receipt or anything. We just wrote it off as a 'goodwill expense'."

"The members of the board were happy with this arrangement?"

"I was called in during the negotiation for the price of the extra work. It seemed that several members of the board had misgivings . . . they mentioned that they knew in the Philippines with Marcos it was necessary to make various special arrangements on such projects, but they had thought that coming back to China would be . . . "

"Would be what?" I asked.

"I have no idea," George said. "My hearing is not what it used to be, and I missed the last part of their comments."

"Well, at least you solved all of the difficulties with the hotel."

"Oh, not at all." George shook his head, "Similar problems developed with the final inspection for the water system, elevators, fire safety facilities, and gas piping."

"And you had to hire local firms to bring the work up to standards?"

"Well, we did not exactly 'hire' them, but they were recommended to us, and their fees were collected separately."

"So how do these fees show up on the income statement and balance sheet?"

"I am really not qualified as a CPA, however I assume they are all included under the heading of 'goodwill expense'."

"And justified by explaining the necessity of adopting the 'P.I. Strategy.'"

"Precisely."

Several days later I mentally went over the course of George's remarks, but I was still unable to interpret their true meaning. Some readers will undoubtedly have more insight into such matters than I do, and they are free to come to their own conclusions.

### "The Mark-up"

Much more understandable to me was the case of Ronald Appleby, who runs a local trading company, employing over fifty Chinese staff members. Ronald called the other day and wanted to go out for a drink, or preferably an entire bottle.

Ronald has built up his trading business bit by bit over time, and now does over $30 million worth of export orders every year. Recently, the international markets in many of the lines in which he deals have been very competitive, with many companies engaging in price cutting in order to get orders. A number of his large American buyers asked if he could come down a few percentage points on his price, so that they could alleviate the pressures they were getting from their bosses to "switch suppliers". Ronald of course agreed to check into this and get back to them.

Over a period of several days, Ronald visited a number of factories with whom he had been doing business for many years. After engaging in some small talk, he got around to the subject of whether they could come down a bit on their prices. The factory managers were generally receptive to Ronald's comments, since they desired to continue the mutually beneficial relations which had been going on in the past. One manager, Mr. Wen, was a typical example. He agreed to come down 2% on the prices of a number of the items he was manufacturing, and 3% on some others. He also suggested to Ronald: "You should come down a bit on your mark-up too. That will be even better."

"I would certainly like to," Ronald replied, "but the mark-up of 7% which you add into your price quotes for us is pretty much standard. We need that much to provide staff salaries, office rental, water & electricity, and some small measure of profit."

As in dealing with most other trading companies, this factory included the trading company's mark-up, (7% in Ronald's case, as per his previous specification) directly in its price quotations, therefore simplifying much of the paperwork between the trading company and the overseas buyers, especially the discussion of prices.

"Oh no," the manager said, his eyes taking on a rather surprised look, "we always include a 12% mark-up in all quotes we give to your firm."

"Twelve percent?" Ronald shook his head, "Surely there must be some mistake, I believe that the figure we previously discussed was seven."

"Yes, but your office manager changed that. He said it was on your directions. Really, I think that twelve percent is rather high, and if you would cut your own mark-up a few points, your customers would no doubt be more happy."

Ronald was confused at the direction their conversation had taken, but he promised Mr. Wen to fully consider the issues he had so kindly raised. Later, visiting several other factories, he heard much the same story when it came to a discussion of his own firm's "mark-up".

Ronald thought for several days about the confusion which had somehow come into his factory relations, but he was busy with other work and had no time to formally discuss the matter with his staff. One afternoon a man from the shoe department, Mr. Ting, came in for a chat. He asked if Ronald could intercede for him with the office manager and other staff members.

"Intercede? In what? Has some sort of personality conflict arisen? Or is it that you want to change desks or something?" Ronald asked politely.

"No, nothing like that," Mr. Ting said, "it is actually in regard to the sales in our department. As you know, shoe sales have not been very good the last few months, but the problem is not with our department, the problem is with import quotas in the USA and European markets."

"I am aware of that."

"So, we believe that we should not be penalized because of this, and that there should be a more equal distribution of the monthly bonus."

"What monthly bonus?" Ronald inquired.

"The monthly bonus we have every month of course," Mr. Ting said, "it is calculated on the sales in our department divided by total company sales, times 2%, and we distribute that among the people in our department. There is some additional allowance for the secretaries."

"Times two percent?" Ronald asked. "You mean five."

"Oh, no," Mr. Ting said, "the other 3% goes to the office manager."

"Two plus three equals five," Ronald summarized.

"What?" Mr. Ting said, as Ronald ushered him out of the office politely.

We were seated in a quiet lounge in a large international hotel, as Ronald recounted all of these events to me. He was already on his fourth gin-and-tonic. "What is my next move?" he asked, trying to maintain calm.

"I don't know that there is a need for any next move," I said.

"What?"

"Look at it this way," I explained, "I have recently been reading some books on business management, and they all stress the importance of profit-sharing. What you have encountered here is simply 'profit-sharing' on the most basic level, which is to say that the profits are shared before their existence is even known to the upper management."

"I own the company."

"Precisely," I said, "and that makes you the upper management."

"I always wondered how my secretary could afford to buy a new BMW on her salary," Ronald gazed at one of his empty glasses, deep in thought.

"Furthermore," I continued, "if you consider the F.O.B. price here in China, and multiply that by three, then add 30%, that gives you a rough estimate of the average retail price of merchandise sold in retail outlets in the west."

"That is a rough approximation."

"So their profit-sharing does not amount to much, and in essence it is all transferred to the buyer and the final consumer anyway," I stated.

"Somehow I feel bad for not having known all along," Ronald said.

"Drink up."

## Raising Money with the Hui

A large amount of money may be raised fairly quickly through the use of the Chinese *hui* system.[1] In this method, a leader is first chosen, and generally this is the person who organizes the *hui*. An amount of money is then specified, and a number of people, perhaps twenty or more, are asked to participate. During the existence of the *hui*, each person in the *hui* is entitled to bid for funds once. Bidding is held on the to-be-assembled funds every month, and the highest bidder wins.

Let us take a practical example of a *hui* organized by Mr. Chow with the figure of $25,000 in Chinese currency as the amount. (Acting the part of organizer or banker in such dealings, Mr. Chow is said to *zuo jwang*.[a] ) Mr. Chow has found 27 people among his friends, relatives, and co-workers who have agreed to participate. The first month, everyone gives Mr. Chow $25,000. The second month bidding begins. Mr. Jeng finds himself in need of funds for his business, so he bids $2200, which is the highest bid received that month. Mr. Chow collects $22,800 (representing 25,000 minus the $2200 bid) in cash from all the participants, and he passes on these funds to Mr. Jeng, along with his own contribution for the month of $25,000. Thus Mr. Jeng has received the use of $595,000, ($22,800 times 25, plus 1 times $25,000), and the other members of the *hui* have received a monthly rate of 8.8% interest on their "investment" of 25,000. Everyone is happy.

The third month someone else wins use of the funds by making the highest bid. The fourth month another person wins the funds. This continues on until each person has had his use of the funds for one month, which in this case would be 27 months. (If

---

1. Some foreigners call this a "cooperative loan system". 標會

a. 作莊

the *hui* was run on a twice monthly basis, it would run for 13 1/2 months in this example.)

The basic formulation of the *hui* in this example is thus: 27 people in the group, willing to invest $25,000 per month in this scheme. Each person represents an income stream of 25,000 per month for 27 months. By pooling their funds together, a person who needs the funds at this moment may take his 27-month income stream now. His price for this privilege is the interest he bids.

Let us assume that the *hui* has run its course. We may consider the members of the *hui* in the order in which they made use of the funds. Mr. Chow was Member 1, Mr. Jeng was Member 2, etc. For the purpose of discussion let us say that the bids for the months 2 through 6 were $2200, $2400, $2750, $3100, $2600. Other months would have had varying bids. You are only entitled to deduct the interest bid from your monthly contribution if you have not yet used the accumulated funds one time.

Financial Contribution per month by *hui* members

|  | month 1 | month 2 | month 3 | month 4 | month 5 | month 6 | etc. |
|---|---|---|---|---|---|---|---|
| member 1 | ---- | $25,000 | $25,000 | $25,000 | $25,000 | $25,000 | ...... |
| member 2 | $25,000 | ---- | $25,000 | $25,000 | $25,000 | $25,000 | ...... |
| member 3 | $25,000 | $22,800 | ---- | $25,000 | $25,000 | $25,000 | ...... |
| member 4 | $25,000 | $22,800 | $22,600 | ---- | $25,000 | $25,000 | ...... |
| ,, | ,, | ,, | ,, | ,, | | | |
| ,, | ,, | ,, | ,, | ,, | | | |
| ,, | ,, | ,, | ,, | ,, | | | |
| ,, | ,, | ,, | ,, | ,, | | | |
| ,, | ,, | ,, | ,, | ,, | | | |
| member 26 | $25,000 | $22,800 | $22,600 | $22,250 | $21,900 | $22,400 | ...... |
| member 27 | $25,000 | $22,800 | $22,600 | $22,250 | $21,900 | $22,400 | ...... |

Instead of keeping to himself and dealing with the $25,000 he is able to generate every month, any member may bid on the entire pooled funds available in any one month, just by offering to pay more interest than anyone else. For the person who does not really need the pooled funds in any particular month, and can wait until the *hui* is nearly concluded, he may then bid a very low amount of interest. For example, for the member who had no special emergencies and waited until the last month in this example, he could collect the full amount of $25,000 from each other member, thus yielding $650,000 ($25,000 times 26) of income. If his average payout for the previous 26 months was $22,790 per month, that is a total of $592,540. The difference of $57,460 is profit, nearly 10%. When the average monthly bidding is higher, of course the interest earned is higher.

Deficiencies of the Hui

The example of the *hui* may be too involved for some readers. I know of no other scheme of this degree of complexity which is in common use among the average men and women in the west. In this regard we do see that the Chinese have some elaborate ways of assembling funds outside of normal banking circles.

Nevertheless, what we should be concerned with are any possible drawbacks of the *hui* system, and how these may influence the personal finances of the members of the *hui,* or, through the ripple effect, how these drawbacks may influence the members' friends, relatives, and co-workers.

In terms of a general overview, we may say that the *hui* is a reasonably efficient method for pooling funds. However, the true determination of its role in society can only be considered when we look at it in terms of the way in which the Chinese engage in it. Being non-contractually oriented, the Chinese tend to organize a *hui* in a very informal fashion. No agreement of any sort is signed between the *hui* members. Generally everyone pays in cash, and it is rare that any sort of receipt is given. In one case that I was informed of, the head of a *hui* was killed in a car accident after collecting the funds for the month. Since it hardly seemed the time to bring up the matter during his family's time of mourning, and some discreet inquiry through a close friend of the family indicated that there was no knowledge among family members of this person being involved in a *hui* (and there was no reason why there would have been), so everyone considered that month's contributions as going to his funeral expenses, and were content to forget about their loss, or write it off to "fate". They continued on the next month from where they were, although short one monthly contribution.

With no written agreement between parties, there are of course no stipulations, stated or implied, in the event that 1) the head of the *hui* dies, as in the above example, 2) a dispute arises between the head of the *hui* and some participating parties, with the head claiming that he has not received their payment for the month, and they claiming that they already paid it, 3) the head of the *hui,* or some other whom he has entrusted with safekeeping of the funds, loses some portion of the monthly monies, or the entire amount, 4) the funds are stolen or otherwise turn up missing, 5) some members become financially disabled and cannot keep up their monthly payments, etc., etc.

The *hui* will often run into problems when an event of this type occurs, since, as in the formal banking sector, business is hard to do when you have lost your credibility. At whatever point this comes about, the people who have already taken one month's use of the funds (the fund-takers) are in a fairly good position, since they have gotten far more money out of the arrangement than they have put in to date. The people who have not yet made use of the funds for a month (the upcoming fund-takers) are in a very bad position, since they have paid in a good deal of cash, but have received no money yet, and their "profits" (interest deducted from their share each month) are all on paper only. Some upcoming fund-takers, having lost confidence in this scheme due to any of the above reasons, precipitate a full scale collapse when they refuse to pay in the following month's contributions, thus causing that month's pooled funds to fail to accumulate. As word of this situation spreads, the other upcoming fund takers turn to the head of the *hui* and demand that he refund all of the monies which they have paid in so far, since they no longer wish to participate. This he is unable to do, since he is not insured, and has minimal cash on hand, having no doubt already used up all of the pooled funds he obtained in the first month. The upcoming fund-takers are then forced to conclude that they have been taken. If the *hui* collapsed in the 6th month, over twenty people would lose over $100,000 each in this example.

It will not be hard for the reader to overview the entire *hui* arrangement at this juncture and see that, in this type of framework, the opportunities for unscrupulous dealings present themselves at every turn. It is possible for a devious person to participate in several *huis* at the same time, make a high bid to take all the funds in one particular month, and then "disappear". Incidents of this type where the culprits skip the country on forged foreign passports are frequently recorded in the Chinese newspapers.

It may be true that 80% of the *huis* which are organized in the Chinese community run to full term without any problems. However, the difficulty for the foreigner who takes part in such an arrangement is that if problems do develop, the Chinese approach to problem-solving and his own approach may be some distance apart.

## Ten, Seven, Three, Four

Many people with abundant experience in third-world business dealings know that it is often easier, and more profitable, for a businessman who is in financial trouble to go bankrupt than to continue carrying on his company operations normally.

For those suppliers, dealers, and others caught in this kind of "trap", the experience can be painful, since they may lose all but a small portion of the value of their merchandise.

Example: Let us consider the case of wholesaler W who sells a quantity of goods to Businessman B at a price of $10.

Normally, Businessman B might sell these at $12, for a profit of $2. In a "deliberate bankruptcy"[a] situation, Businessman B sells these for $7, and declares bankruptcy. In a settlement with the creditors involved, he repays only $3 (on every $10 of merchandise purchased). This results in a profit of $4, and may be called the "10, 7, 3, 4 formula".

Such situations are all the more common in countries in which 1) the local businessmen are in the habit of paying for merchandise with post-dated checks, or other oral promises of future payment, 2) many businesses are quasi-legal, due to the loose government regulatory structure, 3) credit bureaus and credit information services are poorly developed and do not receive government cooperation or encouragement with their work, 4) local banks only make loans based on what collateral the applicant can produce, and many businessmen thus are unable to qualify for new plant and equipment loans, or

---

[a]. 惡性倒閉

working capital loans, 5) the insurance industry is very underdeveloped and the "risk" on most types of business dealings must be borne by the parties involved, etc.

The "dollar units" in this example may be anything reasonable: $10,000 or $10,000,000 or any other multiple of $10. The analysis remains the same. The Chinese conception is to view "10 parts" as equalling the whole, so this figure was chosen for purposes of illustration.

It is not always true that a third-world businessman finds himself in trouble due to poor sales of his products or services in the marketplace. It may often happen that a co-investor has a relative who needs money for some business dealing or family emergency. Since the Chinese view "benevolence" as the most important trait (and indeed the characteristic trait) of man [1] , it would be expected that this co-investor might divert a portion of the company's treasury monies to this relative for "temporary use". When this relative is still unable to repay the funds later, the company immediately falls into serious financial trouble. Seeing this situation, the investors might have a meeting and conclude that all of these circumstances were dictated by fate. In order to bolster their financial position, they could order $10,000,000 of merchandise from suppliers, agreeing to pay in 30 days, and put the Ten Seven Three Four formula into action.

Naturally, it would be expected that after this company had gone bankrupt, the suppliers would not press for payment too hard, for that would be failing to show a benevolent attitude to the company's plight.

## On the Homefront

Money management in the Chinese household is often relegated to the wife. This of course will result in a very harmonious marriage situation if the husband and wife are of similar orientation in regard to how their money should be spent, invested, or loaned. If they are of a differing orientation, some unpleasantness and disharmony will be created.

Oftentimes it will be seen in many companies in China that when men receive a year-end bonus, they will ask that it be separated into two envelopes, each of which is clearly marked with the amount. Hence, a man who was to receive a bonus of $100,000 in local currency might ask that it be placed into two envelopes, perhaps one marked $80,000 and the other marked $20,000. Casual reflection will allow us to immediately see why such a request would be made. In this manner the man can give the $80,000 intact to

---

1. In direct opposition to this, many western philosophers have discussed a Ladder of the Soul concept: from the human soul, the immaterial component of human nature, comes the ability to reason, to will, to feel.

According to Thomas Aquinas in *Summa Theologica*, the soul has three levels or types: 1) the soul of grass and trees that produces life and growth, 2) the soul of insects and animals that enables them to be conscious of the environment about them, 3) the human soul that, in addition to the soul-like qualities found in plant and animal life, enables human beings to reason, thus giving them the ability to use logic, and to make the distinction between truth and error. Hence, **the ability to reason** is seen as the characteristic trait of man.

his wife, and retain the remaining portion for his own personal use.

Further inquiry into this type of situation reveals that many a Chinese wife exercises a very vigilant and most jealous control over her husband's salary, commissions, and other income. "House rules" often require that monthly salary is brought home and presented in toto to the wife. After she makes a full accounting, she may then allocate some small allowance to the husband for any and all expected monthly expenses. Final say over any questionable items is retained by the wife, who effectively wears the pants in the family.

One story is told of a Chinese man who received $2000, (approximately US $65 equivalent), for writing an article for a local scholarly journal, unknown to his spouse. He folded these bills up and put them in the bottom of his sock for safekeeping. One evening when the family members were lounging in the living room of their home, the wife leaned over to pick up something off the floor, and happened to bump into the bottom of the husband's foot, as he was relaxing on the couch. She had a distinct impression that the sock seemed "hard" on the bottom, and questioned him about this.

When the full story came out, the wife was very upset, and they argued for some time. The conclusion was that the husband had to give his wife the $2000 with a lengthy apology, and promise never to act in such an insincere or surreptitious manner ever again.

See additional comments in any large reference dictionary under "Henpecked".

# Chapter 5 Justice and Jeopardy

## Failure in Understanding

A major failure of westerners in understanding the Chinese lies in adopting one of the typical approaches to study via the routes of history, philosophy, literature, etc., and ignoring all concerns of a differing Chinese foundational basis.

In order to look at this foundational basis, and its ramifications, in any depth, we must derive a focal point upon which to build our structure. One qualification, I think, for this focal point is that it be one which the Chinese accept and agree to. Many theories (by westerners) which attempt to explain a large amount of Chinese thinking and behavior have a major flaw in that the Chinese do not accept them. This seems a serious drawback for a "starting point". Some theories I have heard advanced by my associates concerning various Chinese religious practices fall into this category. The Chinese will agree that they engage in these types of practices, however they fail to assign any broad significance to these observances, and hence question the foreigners' attempts to explain all of Chinese thinking by reference to them: including such points as why the quality in the factories is not always up to par, why the children have too much homework, why the policemen are often lax in enforcing traffic laws, etc. Foreigners often claim that all of these considerations can be traced back to certain Chinese religious practices.

In searching for some starting point to get a grip on Chinese thinking, we have chosen the *ching, li, fa,*[a] which is a three-tiered concept of which every Chinese is aware, and to which the vast majority agrees as being valid. The name which we have chosen for this concept in English is Primary Sympathetic Orientation. A major current in our explanatory remarks in the following pages will be to explain what this means, in all of its various ramifications. From this point of view, then, we will be much better able to see how the Chinese are thinking and behaving. We are quick to point out that Chinese Sympathy and Western Sympathy are different in a number of areas, and these dif-

---

[a.] 情理法

ferences will be thoroughly discussed.[1] The fact remains that the Chinese view themselves as essentially sympathetic, and this will be thoroughly delved into.

How to go about showing the operation of the Primary Sympathetic Orientation? It is a truism to say that when Chinese and westerners are together, and everyone is happy, and having a good time, and there are no problems, then there is relatively little to be said about conflicting cultural differences. However when problems develop, such as a disagreement, or argument, we may be able to analyze the point of view of the Chinese side, and gain a clearer understanding of the true nature of Chinese thinking, as it differs from the western style. If the thinking does not conflict in a serious manner, then harmony is easily achieved. If the thinking does conflict, harmony is achieved only after overcoming certain obstacles. If these obstacles cannot be overcome, then the westerner is of course best advised to route his way around them.

In the course of our research, we have collected a large number of problems suitable for our scrutiny. Through examination of these problems, we have been able to analyze some significant differences in thinking between Chinese and westerners. To the extent that this type of examination gives us insight into the practical application of the Primary Sympathetic Orientation, it is possible for the westerner to gain a broad understanding of how Chinese think, and how they tend to react to a wide variety of situations.

## Clarifications of Injury

Two types of Injury Perception are relevant to our discussion here.

Agricultural Society Perception of Injury: **Injury of this type is largely seen in terms that a pre-industrial society's agrarian oriented citizenry would understand, with their relatively simple concepts of commercial dealings. Primarily it consists of real physical injury, or injury that can be measured in terms of today, and in a very concrete manner.**

Industrial Society Perception of Injury: **Injury of this type may be seen in the concrete or abstract terms that a developed industrial society's citizenry would understand, and thus recognizes comparatively up-to-date concepts in psychology, economics, finance, and many other fields, both as they relate to present and future activity, with short term and long term ramifications.**

These definitions are not legal, but acculturological. Please refer to further comments in Chapter 6. The determination of what conduct is reasonable, fair, honest, proper or ethical will depend on one's Perception of Injury and Perception of Liability.

Our friend Freddie Foo fell in a manhole and broke a leg, which is injury in concrete terms, something recognizable in an agrarian society, thus falling within the Agricultural Society Perception of Injury. Our associate Jonathan Rogers came across a stockpile

---

1. The reader will find a more formalized analysis of this in the discussion of "The Iceberg Model" in Chapter 10.

of imitation patent attache cases equipped with shortwave radio transmitters, but the unlicensed invasion of intellectual property rights which this represents is injury in abstract terms, essentially only recognizable to people who are familiar with advanced industrial society. It falls within the Industrial Society Perception of Injury but most likely would not be included within the Agricultural Society Perception of Injury. It was not surprising then that when Jonathan tried to get a court order to seize this merchandise, the producer's initial reaction was to ask him to reimburse them for their raw material and production costs.

In many types of similar incidents, there may be a multiple damage compensation provision (such as "500 times the actual retail unit price of the infringed merchandise") in the Chinese law, but the courts may hold that strict application of this provision allows the patent (trademark, copyright, etc.) owner to be "unjustly enriched", hence resulting in the Chinese infringer being "excessively" punished. This rationalization may arise from the more traditional Perception of Injury held by the judges.

Diagram 5-1

| item | included in the Perception of Injury | |
|---|---|---|
| | Agricultural Society | Industrial Society |
| breaking a bone | yes | yes |
| pain and suffering | probably not | yes |
| patent infringement | no | yes |
| copyright infringement | no | yes |
| unauthorized use of company trade secrets | no | yes |
| loss of companionship of spouse | probably not | yes |
| loss of interest on money loaned to relatives | probably not | yes |
| loss of interest on money paid ten days past due-date | probably not | yes |

When people have different Perceptions of Injury, there may be disagreement over what is "fair", "reasonable", "moral", etc. in regard to many types of issues.

## Check Borrowing

In a society where banking and credit are undeveloped, it may be common for many people to conduct a wide range of business dealings and pay for them through the writing of post-dated checks. However, since some people who want to do business do not have the necessary qualifications (in the view of the local banks) to open a checking account in their own name, or in the name of their business, they may want to "borrow checks" from friends or relatives. Let us examine the case of the businesswoman Amelia Chang who, on April 5th, expresses the desire to borrow a check from her friend Mary Chen. The amount of money requested is approximately US $25,000 (equivalent), not a very large sum in business dealings.Mary asks for details of this proposed arrangement, and Amelia explains: "You write the check for $25,000, payable to me (Amelia Chang), dated July 5th. I will endorse the check on the back, and put the appropriate "pay to the order of . . . " notice thereon, indicating the name of the party to which I owe money. I will have some funds coming in in late June, and so I will be able to deposit these in your (Mary's) checking account by June 30th at the latest."

Mary says: "Well, I don't know. What if your funds don't come in in late June? That could be a problem."

Amelia: "Oh, you don't have to worry about that. That is a shipment of goods to an established customer of mine. We never have any problems."

Mary: "My husband and I were going to make a downpayment on a house with that money, but we have not found a suitable one yet."

Amelia: "Oh, really? I have some relatives in the construction business, and I can introduce some new houses to you at a discount."

Mary: "That would be nice, but I don't know whether I should or not. We were hoping to invest that money for a few months anyway, and earn some interest."

Amelia: "Believe me, the amount of money I can save you on a house with my connections is more than you can earn in interest for these few months. Anyway, your money is not earning you anything sitting in your checking account now, so you won't be losing anything by letting me borrow it for a few months. In the future you may need money some time, believe me you just give me a call, and I will take care of it. I have some deals in the works now that are going to bring in some excellent profits."

Mary: "Well, you certainly seem sincere. Ok, I will write out the check for you. Here you are. Be sure to call me in June when you have deposited the funds in my account."

Amelia: "That will be no problem. Let's keep in touch. We should go out to lunch more often."

In late June, the shipments that Amelia makes are rejected by her buyers due to a production flaw, the funds do not appear, and Mary's check bounces on July 5th. Amelia, found some days later in a drunken stupor in her house, says she is very very very sorry for the way things turned out. Legal proceedings are instituted against Mary, and she must borrow funds from her friends and relatives to make up for this bad debt. She and her husband's plans to buy a new house are postponed indefinitely.

Underlying Assumptions

We may analyze some assumptions inherent in Amelia's thinking below. Mary obviously shares these assumptions, since she has agreed to go along with Amelia's proposed arrangement.

1. The relationship between people in society, especially friends and relatives, is bas-

ed on the doctrines of "mutual helpfulness" and "mutual dependence". A Chinese adage says: "When at home depend on your parents, when away depend on your friends." [a] Amelia, in her comments, has amply demonstrated that she is willing to be helpful to Mary in the future, in return for the favor she is asking now. Mary has accepted these remarks at surface value as an indication of Amelia's good faith.

2. There is a strongly implied sense of "Please be sympathetic to my situation" in Amelia's remarks, because both sides can see that Mary, by granting Amelia's request, will be able to help her out of the situation in which she now finds herself, i.e., the lack of funds for an important and imminent business dealing.

3. The rationale that Mary will not be losing anything by loaning Amelia the money for three months is given. This is arrived at by noting: that a) the business deal in late June is sure to go through, b) Mary does indeed have the funds and is not using them at present, c) Mary is not earning any interest on the funds right now by having them in her checking account. Mary accepts this analysis.

4. Neither Amelia nor Mary seem to feel that there is any need for a formal contractual relationship in this type of dealing. Any loan company, bank, or other financial institution would require such a contract if it were to make this kind of loan. Mary is acting as a lender in this case, but she is willing to dispense with such formalities.

5. Point 2 above illustrates an appeal to sympathy, Point 3 clarifies that a reason can be given for this proposed course of action, and Point 4 shows the lack of a legal concept. Amelia and Mary's dealings show the existence of a "Primary Sympathetic Orientation", which is typical of Chinese society in general.

6. As a further clarification, we may see that Amelia and Mary's dealings are highly indicative of an Agricultural Society Perception of Injury. Besides the assumption of a high degree of "mutual dependence" which is characteristic of a traditional, pre-industrial revolution agricultural society, and the lack of a legal, contractual mentality, neither party is able to conceptualize or deal with a) the risk which Mary takes in loaning the funds to Amelia, and how she should be compensated for this risk, b) the "lost opportunity cost" which Mary may suffer if more promising, or more important, uses for these funds turn up in the coming three months, and c) the necessity of establishing a specific delineation of each party's rights and responsibilities in this arrangement, so that no misunderstandings will occur in the future. A number of possible eventualities could be easily listed at the outset of the discussions.

As it stands now, Amelia has seen Mary and offered her apologies, however Mary's next move in resolving these difficulties is unclear. Many Chinese would claim that the entire flow of events was predestined by "fate", and tell Mary to smile and accept her lot in life, while strongly urging that she forgive Amelia (give Amelia sympathy) for this unfortunate turn of events. This outlook reflects the basic Chinese assumptions

---

**a.** 在家靠父母，出外靠朋友

that "Nature controls man" [a] and "Events control man". The westerners, who for the most part do not have this essentially "passive" outlook, would tend to assume almost exactly the opposite, i.e. "Man controls nature" and "Man controls events", especially in regard to a "starting point" for discussing the default-loan problem which has developed here, or the possible ways of dealing with similar situations in the future.

What we do see developing in this instance is a vicious cycle, where the results of Amelia's default spread like ripples through the society, as Mary's friends and relatives scrape up money to "bail out" Mary, thus putting them in financial straits, other people must scrape up money to "bail them out", etc., etc., and this effect stabs deep into the social structure.

## Temporary Working Capital Loans

After receiving some purchase orders, factories must buy various raw materials so that production can be undertaken. Since the overseas buyer commonly only pays after the manufactured goods have completed export procedures, and many domestic buyers pay with post-dated checks, there is clearly a time lag between the factory's purchase of raw materials and receipt of payment for production. Every factory and many other small shops and businesses must have a certain level of "working capital" to deal with this type of problem. In Chinese the term for this is *jou jwan*, [b] as in "Can I *jou jwan* $50,000?" We may see *jou jwan* as meaning "make a loan for temporary working capital" from (or to) someone else. (Note: *jou jwan* is used in a similar fashion to *jie*, [c] in that it can carry the sense of "borrow" or "loan" depending on the arrangement of words in the sentence.)

The Chinese tend to have well developed family structures, and many people are engaged in business, so relatives tend to *jou jwan* frequently. Often friends and neighbors engage in the practice, and it is even possible that a new acquaintance will ask to *jou jwan*, saying that he, or his close relative, is in temporary financial straits. To not come across with the funds, especially when one has it in the bank or under the mattress, is seen as unreasonable. Thus if you are the person being asked to produce the money, and you do not agree to do so, when word of your refusal gets around to the larger relative group, other neighbors, associates, etc., they can easily conclude that you are acting selfishly. At that point they might take various measures to ostracize you from the group, or use group pressure to force your compliance. Of course the six assumptions outlined in our "Check Borrowing" example would come into play in a similar fashion in any and all *jou jwan* arrangements.

Sometimes of course the person asked is only too willing to comply, and a story from the USA illustrates this, as well as illustrating how such loans can come to have dif-

a. 聽天由命　　　b. 週轉　　　c. 借

ferent connotations when viewed "from another angle". A certain American manufacturer of motorcyles was in serious trouble from Japanese competition, and asked an influential Congressman for help in passing a stiff trade bill which would place a heavy import tax on similar Japanese models. The Congressman agreed to help out as best he could. Several days later this Congressman, in speaking to the Director of the company, asked if the firm could make a private loan to his brother who was in the metal castings business, as well as perhaps routing some of their spare parts orders to that concern. This was quickly agreed to by the Director, who had every desire "to make the Congressman happy".

More "temporary working capital loans" were paid out over the next several months, and eventually some legislation quite favorable to the motorcycle company's interests was passed in the US Congress. The loans were never repaid, however the Director felt that he had gotten his "money's worth". In Asia such "mutually helpful" dealings as these seem to be quite common when various members of the business community need the assistance of some influential legislators in solving problems regarding business licenses, operating procedures, regulatory requirements, tax statements, reduced assessment (or outright cancellation) of fines, and other matters.

### Loan Guaranteeing

Another interesting situation often develops among friends and relatives in relation to "loan guaranteeing". To model a description of this after the "Check Loaning" case previously described: Mary owns property and Amelia does not. Amelia is running a business and wants to borrow money from a bank, and they have agreed to loan it to her if she can produce two people (perhaps three) to use their property to guarantee the loan.

Amelia asks Mary to do this favor, using her property to guarantee Amelia's loan, to enable her to obtain financing to do her business, or make other financial dealings. Amelia stresses that her dealings are sound, the money will be repaid with no problem in such and such a period of time, there is no loss to Mary because this does not affect

---

Notes: 1) To use accounting terminology, we may say that in considering whether a loan should be granted, the Chinese banks tend to look closely at one's "Balance Sheet", whereas western banks tend to look more carefully at the "Income Statement". In addition to examining these documents, most wise bankers also make a physical check of all plant and equipment, investigate real estate documents, and make other verifications.

2) Where property is used as collateral, it is commonly required that each guarantor's property must have a value exceeding the total value of the loan. Generally only "local" property is acceptable, not property in some other towns or areas. This is often stipulated because of the existence of many "title disputes" in land holdings which have been passed down over several generations in a society where wills are not commonly written. The banks are thus generally only able to assess the ownership of local land holdings as collateral for loans.

her present situation – it is just a technical matter, etc. The agreement is concluded orally, and no contract of any kind is signed. When and if Amelia's business dealings go sour, Mary is left out in the street, as her house is auctioned off to make up for the bad loan. Amelia says she is sorry, and Mary's friends and relatives conclude "That's fate". Originally only Amelia was poor, now Amelia and Mary are both poor.

Urgency of the Need

Oftentimes, the urgency with which the request (for funds, guarantees, etc.) is made will be a determining factor in the other party's decision to grant the request, even if normally they would not have done so. Thus when a businessman pleads to his relative: "If you do not loan me $X by tomorrow, my company will collapse" he adds a very real note of urgency to his plight, and puts himself in the same position as a drowning swimmer calling for help. To not grant this type of request is viewed as "seeing someone dying, and not rescuing him"[a] – and considered essentially immoral.

This is further complicated by the fact that the Chinese place a high value on relationships between family and among friends. Many westerners for example may remark: "If our relationship is going to sour because I refuse to loan you money, then that is just fine, because I no longer desire to have any dealings with you. I do not want a relationship based on money." Some social commentators have estimated that over 90% of westerners could make this statement to friends, or even relatives with whom they have blood ties. However, from the Asian point of view this is incredible, and we estimate that over 90% of the Chinese could not make this statement to their friends, much less to their relatives. In their view, maintenance of mutual relationships is all important, and if one has to sacrifice some of his own financial stability to do so, then so be it. This of course completely reflects the outlook of the Group Mentality, and the Primary Sympathetic Orientation.

## PRE-IRAS Thinking

Due to their cultural background, Mary and Amelia's thinking has remained in the style of PRE-IRAS: Pre-Industrial Revolution Agricultural Society. The economic theory of those times was an outgrowth of feudalism, where the serf (or peasants) and landlords shared bonds of allegiance, righteousness, loyalty, etc. in good times and bad. As economic conditions improved over the centuries and cities began to grow, people began to believe that although land represents wealth, the source of true value of merchandise is labor,[1] since it is human effort that transforms raw material into marketable pro-

---

1. "Labor" is generally defined as **the purposeful work of human beings**. In a simple Pre Industrial Revolution Agricultural Society market economy, generally only "physical labor" is regarded as true labor. The reader may contrast this with our discussion of "Intangible Work" in the Different Ideas essay in Chapter 4.

a. 見死不救

duce. This came to be known as "the labor theory of value", and certainly it has much validity in explaining the prices of goods in very simple non-industrialized economies.[1] However, economists considering this and many other classical economic conceptions, in relation to much more complex market economies, had firmly determined by the late 1800's that there are four factors of production: land, labor, capital, and entrepreneurial ability, all of which are entitled to "return on investment".

Amelia is doing the work (in engaging in the organization of materials for production and in conducting her business dealings), so of course she feels she is entitled to whatever benefits accrue therefrom. The borrowing of capital and the use of another's land, in a real or abstract sense, are seen as incidental and unimportant, or certainly far less important than the mutual bonds of loyalty, comradeship, and righteousness between the two parties. Such bonds, whether stated or implied, also stand above the need for any written contract.

We may consider some questions and comments raised by westerners on these check-loaning, loan guaranteeing, etc. types of dealings. Answers are provided as a compilation of the Chinese point of view.

Q: Since these types of dealings are potentially detrimental to one's economic and financial health, I say "Do not engage in them." You take care of your financial affairs and I will take care of mine.

A: What happened to the axiom "It is better to give than to receive?" and the basic tenet that "We should help those in need?" The blatant selfishness of your stance is only surpassed by your own greedy materialism, which is blind to the plight of others and considers its own comfort and convenience first and foremost.

Q: I am willing to loan money or to offer my property as collateral to guarantee my friend's bank loan. However, I consider it only fair that we both draw up a contract, and that I be paid a respectable rate of interest.

A: The insincerity in your attitude is apparent from the overly practical and money-grubbing approach you take to the entire issue. The drawing up of a contract in such affairs, despite casting doubt on my honest intentions, also is a time-consuming matter, not to mention the additional cost that it incurs and which will therefore serve to reduce the overall amount of capital available. The nature of the business which I am conducting does not allow wide profit margins, and by asking for interest, what you are doing is pushing me into a corner, without any way to financially provide for my family, my aged parents, or my employees. I had not expected a person of your standing, coming as you do from a so-called "advanced" western nation, to be so totally lacking in human sympathy.

---

1. And in simple economies where there is widespread bartering, 以物易物.

Q: I have previously been heavily invested in a number of venture capital organizations, and I am now setting out on my own. I do not charge interest, but I want a piece of the action. Give me the details of the kind of business you are dealing in, let me look over the operations, and if it looks good to me I'll make a sizeable investment, in return for a percentage cut of the profits now and in the future.

A: Your proposal is not worthy of a serious reply, since your excessive concern with your own personal profit and total lack of human-heartedness are evident in every word. What you outline might be proper for dealings between total strangers, but certainly not between friends, or relatives. I would have thought that the western notion of "brotherly love" and recognition of the fact that "blood is thicker than water" would be evident in your thinking, but I now see your true nature, and see the arrogance which has grown out of that little bit of culture your young nation happens to possess. All in all I would have to say that you are more like an animal than a human being, because your attitude toward human relations is totally without any sense of the need for mutual assistance or mutual forgiveness. You are unable to consider anything over and above the gratification of your own materialistic desires.

Refusals

If any person in the community is refused in his request for check borrowing, a temporary working capital loan, loan guaranteeing, etc. he may complain to others and they (the group) may bring pressure on the person in question to grant the request. This would be in line with a "Group Mentality" orientation, not an individualistic or independent one. Clearly the assumption is that the individual is subservient to Group interests, and Group interests tend to be mutually-sympathetic in nature.

Of course it is not true that all such dealings end up in disaster, and as a matter of fact many businesses have been successfully built up through the use of the *hui,* check loaning, temporary working capital loans, and loan guaranteeing. However, I believe that there is a Chinese proverb which says "For every successful General, there are several thousand soldier's skeletons buried somewhere."[a] In a similar line of thinking, one might suspect that for every successful business which has been organized in this way, there is a long line of people who have burned in similar undertakings.

Many economic planners have stated that in order to compete effectively internationally, companies need to be large and/or well capitalized. Chinese companies tend to be small, undercapitalized, and of the family-run type, and many observers have pointed out that the inability to obtain financing is one major restriction to their growth. The westerner would be quick to clarify that any of these informal approaches to accumulating money could be brought into a structured framework if all parties involved would agree to the necessity of a contractual relation, with penalities specified for non-

---

a. 將成名萬骨枯

performance. This approach effectively denies the "Primary Sympathetic Orientation", and thus is difficult to put into practice.

For many foreigners who are low on funds themselves, the considerations presented here may rarely fall within their eyesight. Having no sizeable amount of money to lend, no property to put up for collateral, etc., they may have no opportunity to become involved in dealings of these kinds, at least initially. If their residence in China is lengthy, or they marry a Chinese, or otherwise become intimately involved in local dealings, it could be expected that over time, as their financial base becomes established, these situations will begin to appear. Of course they were there all the time, but the foreigner was unaware of their presence.

## Clarifications of Liability

Another factor that we must have in mind when we consider Money Management and Personal Finances is in the case where we, or our friends, cause damage to another party, and a claim for restitution is made. Such claims could put a serious dent in anyone's budget, and cause a ripple effect through society, due to the need for private borrowings to make up for the demands of this real or perceived Liability. This is illustrated by the following typical example, which we will call Accident 1.

Accident 1: A boy in his early 20's is riding his bicycle, which has no headlight, down the street in a Chinese city at night. He turns on to a one-way main thoroughfare, going the wrong way, and rides on. A car in excellent mechanical condition, travelling at a legal rate of speed, driven by a properly licensed driver in full command of his faculties, turns into this street. The driver sees the boy at the last minute and is unable to stop in time to avoid hitting the youth. An ambulance is called, but the boy dies on the way to the hospital.

We may ask: "Who is responsible for the boy's death?"

The Chinese will of course conclude: "The driver of the car is responsible, and should make restitution to the boy's family."

Some westerners are surprised at this conclusion. Certainly it is necessary to examine it closely, and to see how it has been formulated. However, it will be of benefit to us to take a slight digression first, and consider why this conclusion is "unexpected".

### Problems in Understanding the Chinese

At the root of our difficulties in understanding or predicting Chinese thinking is the fact that the words which we use for dealing with various Chinese philosophical concepts do not carry the same range of meaning in English that they do in Chinese. Thinking in English, we are therefore unable to "weigh" them, and decide which is more important in any given situation. Terms which need to be weighed in this instance include: "kindness", "propriety", "fairness", "justice", "duty", etc. Even if we speak Chinese fluently, our reasoning remains in the western mode, and we deal with such items as these, or the more difficult axioms, epithets, and philosophical dictates by categorizing them under some general heading, or more specifically, regarding them as aliases for concepts in our own language, or combination of concepts. Rarely does this ever hit the mark exactly.

China has an old and well-developed philosophy, however most acculturologists of my acquaintance have concluded that the average foreigner of above-average intelligence who wishes to collect data which will help him to deal with various conflicts of interest in daily dealings in China will not find much of it in philosophy books, unless his primary interest is purely academic.

Some would take exception to this view, noting that if read in the proper manner, these texts could be of much value. I recall my friend Glenn from Cleveland who, reviewing the status of both parties in a car accident similar to the one described above, felt that the bicycle rider (and/or his family) should accept full responsibility for his actions and their consequences, since such actions were illegal. Glenn submitted several quotes from Confucius to support his "the illegally-acting party should take the responsibility" theory:

The faults of a gentleman are like eclipses of the sun and moon. When they occur, all men see them: but, when he rectifies his mistakes, all men look up to him as before. — XIX, 21.

When you have faults, do not hesitate to correct them. — IX, 24.

In your public life in the state as well as in your private life in your family, give no one a just cause for complaint against you. — XII, 2.

Act upon what is right. In that way you will do honour to virtue. — XII, 10.

Advance the upright and set aside the unjust. — XII, 22.

Discussing the question of responsibility in light of this type of traffic accident, Glenn offered these quotes to a number of Chinese people for their evaluation and comments. He later talked to me about the entire issue.

"It seems to me that these quotes are largely irrelevant to the situation at hand," I said after a moment's thought.

"That is exactly what the Chinese told me," Glenn sighed.

"Well, I imagine you see the real situation now."

"But doesn't this amount to saying that party that acted in full accordance with the law is at fault?" Glenn queried.

"Since when is it legal to kill people?" I asked.

"It was an accident, and after all the bicycle rider was going the wrong way on a one-way street."

I shook my head sadly. Even though Glenn and other scholarly-oriented westerners like him have read a large number of Chinese philosophy texts, and dealt with the Chinese in daily encounters for many years, however they have not yet clarified anything which approaches a Chinese view of "Perception of Liability".

I posed this situation to Glenn: "Number 1). In a Pre-Industrial Revolution Agricultural Society, if I hit and ran over someone with my wagon, causing their death, would I be held responsible?"

Glenn said yes, most likely.

"Number 2). Is the idea of 'a one-way street', or 'a person going the wrong way on a one-way street' one that would be firmly recognized in such a society?"

Glenn said no, probably not.

"Number 3). To rephrase question 1), substituting 'vehicle' in place of 'wagon', leaving out the first part of the wording, since it is understood, and adjusting the verb tense: If I hit and run over someone with my vehicle, causing their death, will I be held responsible?"

Glenn said: "Well, if you put it that way, yes."

Over a period of several months I collected other examples relevant to a discussion of cross-cultural concepts of liability, and presented them to Glenn and his friends for their edification. A summary of these remarks is given below.

Explanations of Cultural Differences

Although not the optimal analysis, it is worthy of consideration to say that "in practical everyday dealings, many of the differences between people of different cultures arise from different economic backgrounds", since the average level of wealth in different cultures, compared on whatever basis, is often not the same. We may call this the **Differing-Economic Background Explanation of Cultural Differences**. This nomenclature is intended to suggest to us that many commonly-perceived "cultural" differences may be essentially "economic" in numerous respects. Having received my Bachelor of Science degree in Economics, I find this formulation more than slightly appealing. The corollary of it would say that people of similar economic circumstances tend to react the same way to various situations, regardless of their cultural background. We may call this the **Similar Economic-Background Explanation of Cultural Similarities.**

Certainly this theory has a major flaw in that it does not account for the existence of various and differing religious beliefs, or the lack thereof. Undoubtedly, some other major and minor flaws could be listed. However, if we do not deny its worth outright just because it lacks advanced refinement, we may find that it has some degree of perceptual utility, just as using 3 for an approximation of $\pi$ is better than having no approximation at all. Thus many international hotel managers will tell us that the kind of Chinese guest who lives in the Executive Suite whenever he comes to town has an outlook on life that in many ways has considerably more in common with North Americans living in Executive Suites in other first class hotels in the city, and considerably less in common with those of his fellow countrymen living in the same city in 3rd rate hotels for 1/10 the price.

It has been my own experience that in dealing with Chinese multi-millionaries (calculated in US$), many of their thought processes in regard to Money Management dovetailed very closely with the thought processes of people of advanced economic standing in the west. At the opposite end of the scale, I have met different families of Chinese residing in small homes in extended-family type living arrangements in the countryside, where the head of each household has many children and very little income to support them with, and the family has no car, no bank accounts, and no credit. I found that many of the thought processes of these people with regard to Personal Finances dovetail very nicely with those of some of the poorer American families who are living in Appalachia.

Historically China has not had a strong middle class, such as that in the west after the advent of the Industrial Revolution, and this is only slowly changing. The traditional Chinese economy was based on subsistence agriculture for thousands of years, and this economic reality seems to have firmly molded the thought processes of the common people, with the result that it is "everywhere in evidence" even today. Foreigners who attempt to analyze the differing responsibilities of the two parties in a traffic accident example such as this, rather than turning to Confucius for insight, would be better advised to consider some basic Pre-Industrial Revolution Agricultural Society conceptualizations, similar to the ones I outlined for Glenn originally. This yields "the Chinese viewpoint" in a relatively quick fashion.

### Injury and Damage

Our conclusions and comparisons may be still more formally clarified with the introduction of appropriate terminology. In regard to a discussion of restitution for injuries or damages which we have caused another party, it will be helpful for us to define two differing "Perceptions of Liability" as follows—

Legal Duty Perception of Liability: **Where there is injury, there should be restitution in accordance to the laws and relevant contracts. In complex cases, the courts or an independent arbitrator may be called upon to interpret the laws and other facts. When a legal determination states that the perpetrator did not act intentionally or negligently, or in violation of a contract, restitution may be withheld.** Abbreviated as: LD Perception of Liability.

Ability-to-Pay Perception of Liability: **Where there is injury, there should be restitution by the party who can better afford to pay—as determined by superior economic position.** Abbreviated as: AP Perception of Liability.

### Sources of Liability Perception

Let us consider the case of a child who has just learned to walk, and who steps from behind a packing box into the path of a man who is carrying a computer video monitor.

A collision follows, with the result that the child's hand is stepped on and requires medical attention, and the video monitor is dropped and broken. At this point few people would hold the child responsible for the breakage of its own hand, or of the video monitor. Medical costs for the child's hand and repair costs for the monitor would most likely all be paid for by the man. This would appear to be the demands of benevolence. It also closely approaches the Ability-to-Pay Perception of Liability.

In the western world, the basic concept of liability is based on negligence. The Ability-to-Pay Perception is not unknown however, and in addition to examples such as the one above, its use is most common in five major types of legal action: 1) determination of "appropriate" alimony payments in divorce settlements, or palimony payments in separation settlements, 2) determination of "appropriate" child support payments, 3) claims regarding difficult-to-evaluate terms such as "pain and suffering", 4) civil fines, especially where the law does not specify a specific amount, but rather gives a low to high range of dollar figures, 5) bankruptcy settlements, where it must be determined what percentage the bankrupt party will pay on each dollar of debts.

The AP Perception of Liability is often widespread in societies in Africa, Asia, South America and other areas, whose traditional economic structure has been based on subsistence agriculture. It is allowed to exist within the government's announced policy of "rule by law", and is another reflection of the legal/moral gap. After the police or the courts have determined that the driver is not at fault in this type of traffic accident, the bicyclist's family and relatives would still demand monetary restitution. If the driver objected to this, they would say: "Legally you are right, but morally you are wrong," and continue to press their demands with increased vigor.[1,2,3]

## "Ability-To-Pay" vs. "Moral Obligation" Terminology

I have had some serious discussions with some highly paid New York lawyers about my choice of terminology here, especially as regards the "Ability-to-Pay Perception of Liability". Many of them feel that a better choice of terms would be the "Moral Obligation Perception of Liability". The Chinese would also tend to label their own Perception of Liability in this way. However, over the course of many discussions with foreigners

---

1. Clearly the Chinese view considers 人道 "humanity" as being above the law.
2. This could easily lead to harassment and (threats of or actual) violence against the party which refused to "pay up".
3. Even though the Chinese law does not recognize these claims, the Chinese populace for the most part does. If the populace pressed its demands with vigor, and the government officials, police, or courts refused to take active measures to stop such developments, many foreigners might describe the situation as 無法無天, which we may translate as "lawless and godless" or "without law and without government".

The precise translation of 無法無天 is difficult. 法 may be viewed as 王法 and 天 as 天子. However in the present era there is no 天子, so we must render this as 政府. Hence "without law and without government". Viewing 法 as 法律 and 天 as 上天, we have "without law and without god". The reader may make his own determination.

in China, I have found that to the westerners uninitiated in all the ramifications of current Chinese thought, it is not clear that by breaking no law in accidently hitting someone going the wrong way on a one-way street, the driver has incurred any moral obligation to make a settlement with the bicyclist's family.

In this regard, some Chinese have suggested to me that the westerners' sense of morality is incomplete. Considering this I see that perhaps the western sense of right and wrong has mutated into some Post-Industrial Revolution mode, making various distinctions about the rights and obligations of parties using powerful types of machinery, and with specific clarification in relation to deliberate and non-deliberate action. These kinds of distinctions would rarely be made in a Pre-Industrial Revolution Agricultural Society. No doubt some people would maintain that such a Pre-Industrial Revolution Agricultural Society is more pure and natural.

The question of liability is obviously a very complex topic. We many consider the case of a patron in a restaurant who becomes drunk, crashes into a door, cuts himself up severely, and dies on the way to the hospital. Who is liable? In the United States, the thinking on this varies from state to state. Some states have laws which stipulate that the tavern owner is responsible for the actions of drunken patrons, some do not. In the states where these kinds of statutes are on the books, the tavern owner has the right, and indeed the duty, to refuse service to any patrons who appear drunk.

In another situation, a customer slips in a grocery store and breaks his leg. Who is liable? In the USA, this depends on the circumstances. If the floor had been freshly mopped, and no notice was posted to that effect, the store could easily be held liable. If another customer had just dropped a bottle of ketchup on the the floor ten seconds before, and this was the cause of this accident, the store would probably be relieved of the majority of liability.

No matter how the law makes a determination, in either of these two cases the store or shop is "morally responsible" in the viewpoint of the Chinese populace, and restitution should be forthcoming. "He cut himself up in your shop", or "He slipped and broke his leg in your store" are reason enough, since the Chinese inclination is to side with the more disadvantaged, or more potentially disadvantaged, party.

Contrary to many articles published in the international news magazines about the difficulty of buying liability insurance in the United States in the present era, tavern owners, grocery store owners, restaurant owners, and the like are generally able to purchase such insurance at affordable rates. If it were necessary to make financial restitution in the USA in the two types of accidents described here, it would generally all be paid by the insurance company. In China most shops of this variety would (or do) carry no insurance. The real difficulty of purchasing liability insurance in the west is in regard to products or services that are physically dangerous by their very nature. Examples would be the manufacture of power mowers, chain saws, or various drugs, the operation of railroads, underwater demolition equipment, organization of skydiving exhibitions, etc.

A further reason why I have not chosen the "Moral Obligation Perception of Liability" terminology is that I am unaware of any Chinese or international insurance companies that offer liability insurance on this type of eventuality (i.e., that the family of the injured or deceased party is demanding restitution from the other party, even withstanding a court determination that the latter was not at fault).[1] Certainly this must be because the sense of "Moral Obligation" it expresses is not recognized by law, even when the case is appealed. In many conversations, I have found that a multitude of westerners fail to see why a modern society should have one set of moral values, and another set of legal ones, and they feel that it is up to someone (they could not specify whom) to either change the law, or redefine the morality, thus bringing them into closer harmony.[2] To the Chinese this appears to be rather nonsensical, since by rereading the ancient Chinese philosophers we see that social organization would ideally be maintained completely without laws, and rely exclusively on "morality".[3]

Often reported in the Chinese press, in various versions, is an additionally illustrative type of case which may clarify our discussion here of what constitutes appropriate terminology. This occurs when a person of above-average financial standing and notable social position in government, business, or academic circles has loaned his/her car to a friend. This friend unfortunately is subsequently involved in a traffic accident which was not his fault, but in which the other party dies, or is severely injured. This should be the end of the matter, however of course it is not. An interesting outcome is attained when this friend, who is of moderate means, or even downright poor, claims that he is "unable" to meet his "obligation" to the injured party's family and relatives, and so the family turns to the car-owner, who is of notable social position and above average financial standing, and demands that he make restitution for this "wrong", reasoning that since his friend cannot pay, he should: after all it was his car. Clearly the "moral obligation" should rest with this friend, but surprisingly enough he is still able to pass the buck, so to speak. This appears to be a classic example regarding "Perception of Liability", and renders its true nature, in practice, as being dependent upon "Ability to Pay".

---

1. Operating from the viewpoint of "the faster you settle, the less you pay", many large, well-established, and internationally experienced insurance companies will try to settle liability claims out of court, and some monetary compensation will customarily be offered to the party which suffered injury/damage, even when a strict legal determination shows them to be the party that acted wrongly. In many isolated individual cases, large insurance companies can write off such payments as "goodwill expense."

This type of stance would appear to satisfy the injured party in China who holds an AP Perception of Liability, however in fact it may anger them, since many times they view such compensation as too "impersonal", "unfriendly", and "insincere", and will state "We do not want your insurance company to pay, we want *you* to pay."

2. Many Chinese lawyers have privately stated that generally speaking the Chinese sense of "the demands of humanity" would be very difficult to incorporate into the Chinese law. From a legal standpoint it is often unfair, unjust, and unreasonable, as well as setting very bad precedents when considered from a long term view of the proper goal of social development. Concurrently, it lacks any objective sense of right and wrong.

3. Many Chinese citizens assume that the same situations exists in the west, and that "morality" (or the so-called "demands of humanity") is largely outside of, or above, any discussions of law.

In the last one hundred years, the Chinese legal system has absorbed much foreign influence, but as several examples in this section have tried to show, below the surface of Chinese society there is some basic disequilibrium, in that law is not accepted as the final or optimal resolution in many difficulties. It is perhaps insightful to say that the discourses of Washington, Adams, Jefferson, and later US Presidents on the role of government and social organization are for the most part predicated on the fact that society functions for the benefit of the individual (the Individual Mentality), whereas the Chinese expect the individual to function for the benefit of society (the Group Mentality). The differences between these two types of thinking are often quite pronounced.

## Liability in Society

In dealing with products, merchandise, and various services, it is worth noting that "you get what you pay for", and this (i.e., what you get) often includes a Perception of Liability. One relevant example comes to mind, concerning a hotel guest (a businessman) who notified the front desk to give him a wake-up call at 7:00 am the following morning. The desk personnel made an entry in their records to this effect, however the next morning the staff on duty missed this guest's call, which resulted in his being late to the airport. When he arrived at the airport, his flight to Johannesburg (of which there was only one per week) had already departed. Upon returning to the hotel, he informed the hotel manager of his problem, and asked how the issue of liability would be handled.

In a large international hotel, where rates are high, and there is much concern about customer service, maintenance of good customer relations, and the entire issue of the hotel's reputation, it is likely that the customer's request that the hotel pay for his room and board for a week, until he can catch the following week's flight, will be looked on favorably. In a small, local, family-run hotel, where the rates are low, customer relations are not particularly cultivated, and the hotel's reputation is a minor issue, it is likely that the customer's request of this nature will be looked on as nonsense.For the westerner to feel that the employees of a small, local, family-run hotel in Asia have a different set of value system parameters than his own countrymen do, appears to overlook the fact that the differences are probably more economic than cultural, at least in this type of case.

### The Violinist

As an additional example we may look at the case of a Symphony violinist who, returning from breakfast, sends his tuxedo to be cleaned in the hotel laundry, specifying that it must be returned by 5:45 pm or preferably earlier.These conditions are accepted by the laundry department, and "rush service" charges, if any are applicable, are agreed to by both parties.When the tuxedo has not been returned by 6:20, the violinist is forced to go to a nearby tailor and rent a tuxedo for his command performance that evening. When he arrives back at his hotel and his cleaned tuxedo is finally brought in, not only does he refuse to pay the cleaning charges, he requests that the hotel reimburse him for the cost of the tuxedo he had to rent.

We may diagram differing levels of opulence in different Asian establishments by picking appropriate-sounding, although fictitious, names for each hotel involved:

Diagram 5-2

| in Asia | room charge per night |
|---|---|
| A. in a large luxurious top-class hotel THE CIN-MIN COURT | US $500 |
| B. in a medium class hotel THE MING HOTEL | US $225 |
| C. in a 3rd class hotel THE GE CHUNG LOU | US $ 40 |

In any of these three types of hotels, the possible reaction to this guest's demands could be 1) the guest is right, or 2) the guest is crazy. We would suspect that there is a much greater chance of the A-type hotel agreeing to the guest's demands, and a comparatively remote chance that the C-type hotel will agree. A westerner may feel that acceptance of the violinist's view of the situation would be considered "normal" in North America or Europe. This merely reflects the reality that the A-type hotel is of a level of economic affluence which corresponds more closely to that of the western society in general. The C-type hotel is not.

Diagram 5-3

| | Businessman's or Violinist's Claim | |
|---|---|---|
| | possibility of accepting | possibility of rejecting |
| A. THE CIN-MIN COURT | 80% or more chance | 20% or less |
| B. THE MING HOTEL | 60% chance | 40% chance |
| C. THE GE CHUNG LOU | 10% or below chance | 90% or higher chance |

When we put some percentage numbers on the possibility of accepting or rejecting the businessman's or violinist's claims, we see that it is also feasible in 20% (or less) of all cases that an A-type hotel in Asia could deny the responsibility for such liability. This could be explained by noting that even though the hotel gives the outward physical appearance of being very advanced and up-to-date, nevertheless it operates in many respects from the point of view of the relatively non-affluent society in which it is located.

In the event the hotel management refuses to accept responsibility, it may try to push the blame off on the staff-member in charge, saying that the fault was theirs. Comparing the economic prosperity of the staff-member and the complaining westerner, clearly it is the latter who is in the superior economic position. Hence, we would expect that many local people would feel that the complaining party should bear the burden of his "loss" or "inconvenience". Such a determination is in line with the AP Perception of Liability.

In summary, we see that if the westerner visiting Asia is really of high standards, he should be living in a large luxurious hotel, and willing to accept paying large hotel bills. If he is an established musician, or other entertainer, he should either have more than one tuxedo, or a local coordinator who will handle minor misunderstandings with the hotel laundry staff for him, so that he may retain both composure and concentration for the demands of his concert engagements.

## Discussion of Liability

Accident 2: The law stipulates that no pedestrian or motorcycle traffic is allowed on the superhighways. A jogger, who is running alongside a limited access superhighway, is hit by a motorist travelling at a legal rate of speed, and sustains serious injuries. The jogger dies the next day. The different Perceptions of Liability may be diagrammed as follows, with some comment on the perceptual result obtained in each situation.

Diagram 5-4

| case | Party A jogger's family | Party B motorist | perceptual result |
|---|---|---|---|
| 2-1. | LD | LD | no problem |
| 2-2. | LD | AP | reparations will be offered to jogger's family |
| 2-3. | AP | LD | a Problem |
| 2-4. | AP | AP | no problem |

We could state that in general, the following would be typical examples of these four cases.
2-1: An American motorist hits an American jogger. There is no problem in determining liability.
2-2: A Chinese motorist hits an American jogger. When reparations are offered to the jogger's family, they are moved to sing the praises of the human-heartedness of the Chinese people.
2-3: An American motorist hits a Chinese jogger. When reparations are demanded from the American motorist, he becomes extremely irritated and says some nasty things.
2-4: A Chinese motorist hits a Chinese jogger. Both sides agree on a settlement.

Observations and Questions:
A) This is another illustration of a PC Paradox. In essence, the quality to which the Americans are singing praises in case 2-2, and the quality which is serving as a source of irritation in case 2-3 are one and the same: an AP Perception of Liability. It is quite hypocritical for the Americans to accept reparations in case 2-2 when, if the situation were reversed, they would be unwilling to offer them.
B) The LD Perception of Liability causes no (or minimal) problems for the people who adhere to it, as per case 2-1. The AP Perception of Liability causes no (or minimal) problems for the people who hold to it, as in case 2-4.

C) Case 2-3 could be said to be a "worst case" situation. Consider the outcome of a discussion between the two parties in this eventuality.

D) If the AP Perception of Liability is held by a large percentage of the populace, and is supported by most sectors of society, including the press, educators, government employees, etc., what would be the advantages and detriments to social order over the long term? Would any citizen be able to make the charge "I obey the law, but I am not protected by the law"? If so, would this undermine "respect for law" in the society?

E) Discuss how the AP Perception of Liability may be directly derived from a "1st) Sympathy, 2nd) Reason, 3rd) Law" orientation, and how this Perception corresponds to the demands of compassion, kindness, and humanity, which some people say are the most important social values.

Accident 3: A small car, making an illegal U-turn in the middle of the street, is hit by a large car. The small car is totalled and its driver seriously injured. Our diagram of four possible cases is as follows.

Diagram 5-5

| case | Party A small car owner's family | Party B large car owner | perceptual result |
|---|---|---|---|
| 3-1. | LD | LD | no problem |
| 3-2. | LD | AP | reparations will be offered to small car owner's family |
| 3-3. | AP | LD | a Problem |
| 3-4. | AP | AP | no problem |

In a case 2-3 or 3-3 situation: a) Discuss the outcome of a talk between the two parties. b) If Party A decided to use harassment, violence, or threats of violence to persuade Party B of the latter's liability, discuss how the propriety or morality of such a new development would be seen by the differing parties.

Overview:

I. Consider again the event of a case three situation such as those described above (2-3 or 3-3). Clarify the possible change in the outcome of the discussions which could occur if it became known that Party A was an extremely wealthy family, and therefore by its own rationale was better able to cover financial loss than Party B. Is it possible that some token financial settlement by Party B in this situation would be seen as adequate, or even that Party B could pay nothing, without overly angering Party A?

II. Consider a case four situation (2-4 or 3-4) where Party A was an extremely wealthy family.

III. Some have described the Ability-to-Pay Perception of Liability as: (1) "Big vehicle hits little vehicle, big vehicle pays." (2) "One vehicle hits pedestrian, this vehicle pays."[1] In the first sentence, the actions of the little vehicle were not clarified. In the second sentence, the actions of the pedestrian were not brought into the discussion. Does the AP Perception of Liability used in this fashion represent an attempt to be objective?[2]

IV. Lu-Ding is a man with an LD Perception of Liability, and is described by his friends as "a man of strong principles".

Ai-Ping is a man with an AP Perception of Liability, and is described by his friends as "a man of strong principles".

In a conflict of interest situation which involved liability, would Lu-Ding consider Ai-Ping "a man of strong principles"? Would Ai-Ping consider Lu-Ding "a man of strong principles"? What would be their view towards each other's sense of fairness and reasonableness?

V. The local customs in Country Z are, among other things, that people eat rice with every meal, that they use the abacus to add up their sums, and that they wear cotton-quilted coats in the wintertime.

Must the foreigner residing in this country follow the local customs?

The local laws in Country Z are, among other things, that all people who live and earn income there must pay taxes, that no private possession of firearms is allowed within its borders, and that people who ride on the train must first purchase a ticket.

Must the foreigner residing in this country obey the local laws?

In cases of accidental injury and damage, in which a legal determination shows that the foreigner has violated no law, must the foreigner make monetary compensation?

Generally speaking, do local customs have the force of law? Must they be followed? Is there a "dividing line" as to which customs must be upheld, and which are optional? Does everyone in the society, natives and foreigners, agree where this "dividing line" is? Or is it necessary to specifically establish in law what types of behavior are forbidden, and what types are required, in order to eliminate any possible confusion?

## Debate Topics

Recent observation indicates that more and more attention is being paid to training in public speaking in the Chinese high schools, colleges, and universities, and that debate clubs are being organized. Topics are chosen, and students are assigned sides, some to advance the reasons for, and some to advance the reasons against any particular course of action or rationale. (This is of course regardless of their personal opinion on the subject under consideration.) In connection

---

1. In the event of an actual collision, the Chinese handling of the situation is generally 小吃大 "little eats big", due to the influence of traditional sympathetic, moral, and benevolent notions.
大車撞小車大車賠，小車撞行人小車賠
If there was no actual collision, the "biggest" generally assumes the upper-hand in an argument between two drivers, or between a driver (and members of the vehicle) and pedestrian(s). This is called 大吃小 "big eats little."

2. A legal sense of fairness, right and wrong, justice, etc. appears missing from either of these formulations.

with our discussion of Liability in Chapter 5, and Sympathy in Chapter 10, we propose a debate on the following topic(s), (each of which deals with the issues from a slightly different angle), and hope that the results of such debates will be fully covered by the news media.

1. Resolved, China has a long and glorious philosophical tradition, and this should be reflected in the modern Chinese legal code. **We must change the law to reflect a more proper view of "the demands of humanity".** In a traffic accident, the party which suffers the most serious physical damage or injury is entitled to compensation, regardless of whether or not he/she violated any laws or other regulations.

2. Resolved, law is one thing, and morality is something else, there is no real need for the two to be in close agreement. The present-day Chinese laws regarding injury and compensation are quite adequate, and indeed this is recognized by the world community. Nevertheless, **all people in society should recognize that it is fully acceptable for the party which suffers the greatest physical loss in a traffic accident to demand off-the-record "private compensation" from the party causing the damage,** regardless of whether the injured person(s) acted in violation of any laws.

## The Visit

In Chinese society, in situations which have resulted in injury or death to another party, it is customary that the involved individual quickly seeks out the injured party, and/or the family, and offers condolences. The issue of liability and/or restitution may be put off for discussion at a later date, perhaps by saying "I am in too much of a state of shock (grief, sadness, etc.) to talk about that now."

The foreigner who accidently injures another Chinese party is well-advised to follow along in making this customary oral expression of sympathy, although this must be done with caution so that one is not putting oneself in a "hostile" situation/environment, or literally "entering the lion's den". When in doubt, consult your Chinese friends, or send an intermediary.

## An Insurance Settlement

Several reports of underhanded dealings in insurance companies in third world countries have been uncovered. In order to close out our discussion of liability handling, we will give a typical example of of such tactics.

A Mr. Lin had insured his warehouse and the merchandise therein for US$350,000 equivalent. One evening the warehouse burned down. The insurance company quickly got word of this and sent an inspector to the scene. After surveying the damage, he said to Mr. Lin "This is an unfortunate accident. Our company knows that you will need some funds now to help in your current cash-flow problems, so we are granting you $5000 immediately until a figure for a full settlement can be calculated." Mr. Lin thought this was very generous and signed the receipt.

No more was heard from the insurance company, and when Mr. Lin called them several weeks later for some further word on his settlement claim, the administrative officer in charge said "I thought you understood that the $5000 was in full settlement."

Mr. Lin said "No, your inspector said that was in partial settlement."

The administrative officer said "You must have misunderstood his explanation, but anyway we have your signature on the document. I will send you a xerox copy for your reference. We are sorry about the mix-up."

The next day Mr. Lin received a copy of the form he had signed when the inspector visited his warehouse after the fire. Upon close inspection he saw that it was an agreement to release the insurance company from any and all further liability for the fire damage in question, and to accept a full one-time payment of $5000.

Total loss to Mr. Lin: well over $300,000.

**Moral:** Write your own receipt, or do not sign anything when you are in a state of shock.

Other problems can come up however, even when negotiations are carefully conducted between the two parties. The insurance company may ask for copies of receipts for relevant construction work or purchases done years or decades previously. Examples of these would be receipts for payment of fees covering the original plant or warehouse construction, interior decorations, purchase of machinery, equipment, appliances, other facilities, etc. When the insured party is unable to produce these receipts, the claims adjuster may hold that the value of all these items is considerably less than the insured amount ($350,000 in Mr. Lin's case), and insist on beginning the negotiations from that point, with further deductions for depreciation, etc.

**Moral:** Do not assume that the "insured amount" will be the starting point for negotiations in a damage claim settlement. Discuss specific details of this procedure with a company representative before problems occur, and make sure everything they say is backed up in writing.

Another technique is for the claims adjuster to come with a tape measure, and physically measure the portions of buildings, equipment, facilities, etc. which were destroyed, and to limit the discussion of the insurance settlement to this portion of the damaged items (or of this portion of the depreciated value of the damaged items).

**Moral:** Do not assume that the insurance company is responsible for paying the charges necessary for a qualified contracting firm to restore all equipment, facilities, interior decorations, etc. "to their original condition before the fire (explosion, flooding, etc.)" if that is not what it says in the contract. Discuss specific details of the entire damage evaluation process with a company representative before problems occur, and make sure everything they say is backed up in writing.

A Chinese businessman with much experience in the practical side of insurance matters summed it up well when he stated: "The people who sell accident and liability insurance and the people who handle claims settlements are two very different types of people."

# PART 3 Explorations of Cultural Differences

## Chapter 6 Awareness

Having completed our chapters on Eating and Money Management, we have recognized a significant number of areas where Chinese and western thinking are at a variance. It is appropriate at this point that we return briefly to the entire subject of "acculturative knowledge" which was raised initially in the Introduction.

### Building Awareness of Cultural Differences

Upon encountering differences in the local culture, the foreigner is forced into doing some accomodation and adjustment. One foreigner newly arrived overseas compared his situation, and the situation of others like himself, to playing a pinball game in an amusement arcade.

In this comparison, the foreigner (represented by the ball), is launched into the entry society largely unaware of what awaits him. As he is bounced around the board (which represents the country in which he is now residing), he becomes more and more aware of cultural differences, and accumulates points of "cultural understanding". As his point total builds up, his increased understanding leads to increased degrees of acceptance of the foreign environment in all respects. As long as he remains in the foreign society, he continues to be on the playing board.

This comparison typifies a general assumption among many newcomers, especially those who intend to work hard at making a new home for themselves in this different land, that acculturation proceeds from gradually increasing levels of awareness (of cultural differences), crossing over to the beginnings of understanding, further on as understanding increases in degree, acceptance of the new social patterns follows. Full adjustment and accomodation to the newly adopted culture are then directly dependent on the amount of time and effort one makes in getting to know it, including its sociology, economics, government, history, literature, and language.

However, I believe this common type of assumption has a pitfall in that it would seem to indicate that the foreigner's final goal in adjustment and accomodation is to become 100% native-like, or nativist. At the least, it does not specifically exclude this notion. Nor does it exclude the related notion that the foreigner should view going totally native as an ideal and then work toward it, as economists set up the ideal of a perfectly competitive market, and base their analysis of the correctness of any policy actions on whether the result brings them nearer this envisioned perfect model. The dictionary definition of "acculturation" is **1. the process of conditioning a child to the cultural patterns. 2. the process of becoming adapted to new cultural patterns.** The second definition is most relevant to our discussion here, however it is also not clear on what the final goal of such adaptation is or may be.

It is probably an extreme example, but we may consider the case of a foreigner who goes to live with a tribe of "reformed" headhunters in the interior of New Guinea. He soon discovers that during special festivals, the natives still need to "go hunting", and that the meat on the table must include specialties over and above the typical fare out of the forest. Other rites which the natives practice in respect to honoring their gods, promoting fertility in their fields and among their populace, engaging in coming-of-age ceremonies, etc. all strike the foreigner as quite bizarre to say the least. For reasons which need not be specified, he desires to continue living with this tribe, and they are willing to accept his presence. His recognition of what constitutes "acculturation" into this society is then not becoming 100% native,[1] but rather — **becoming adapted to the new cultural patterns, with the goal of living in the society with a minimum of friction, and achieving his own personal, business, scholarly or other goals.**

Acculturation then properly stresses accomodation, adjustment, and awareness, but not capitulation, assimilation, or across-the-board acceptance, and states that the foreigner is and will always remain a foreigner, for in the eyes of the local people that is almost certainly true. Acculturation recognizes however that there are various behavioral and attitudinal adjustments which the foreigner who seeks to acculturate himself into the society will want to make. It realizes that there may be various local perceptions which the foreigner may never fully be able to rationalize or understand, yet he may learn to deal with or "work around" them, so that they cause him the least difficulty, and cause the least difficulty to the natives with whom he comes in contact.

The acculturated foreigner living in an alien society thus stands somewhere between, although not exactly in the middle, of the isolationist and the nativist. The isolationist, although living in an alien environment, has minimal contact with the local people, and makes limited efforts to understand their language, behavior, etiquette, or ways of thinking. He lives primarily within the confines of an enclave, and deals mainly with other foreigners. The nativist is the opposite extreme, since in trying to go 100% native he makes every attempt to minimize contact with his own countrymen or other non-natives, and attempts to adopt all the local customs and beliefs.

---

1. So-called "indigenization."

The isolationist, in varying degrees, is quite common in foreign societies, the nativist is comparatively rare, but a very large group of foreigners fall into the category of "preparatory nativists", because they fully believe they are gradually adapting themselves to adopt all the native ways at some time in the future, when they can reach the point of full understanding and acceptance. The person who attempts to acculturate himself takes neither the isolationist or nativist stance, but arranges his pattern of life to enjoy the best elements that both the local society and the resident foreign community have to offer.

The correct route to acculturation in this sense is then most aptly taken through research into the field of cross-cultural acculturology. Certainly with the decrease in travel times made possible by the many advances in transportation in the last 100 years, and the increased interaction among different peoples which this has brought about, this field is a very important one if global understanding and peaceful cooperation among citizens of different countries are to be achieved. Thus it is most fitting that when discussing the acculturative processes of mankind, this "cross-cultural" aspect be seen as being of premier significance.

Let us define our terms as follows.

Acculturology: **The study of the process and rationale whereby one may become adapted or adjusted to new cultural patterns; primarily, the study and accumulation of knowledge relevant to living in another country, as a foreigner, and maintaining peaceful, productive relations with the local inhabitants.** (pronunciation: ac·cul·tur·OL·o·gy)

As such, acculturology stretches across a wide range of disciplines including sociology, psychology, history, philosophy, ethics, language, anthropology, etiquette, aesthetics, management, human relations, etc.

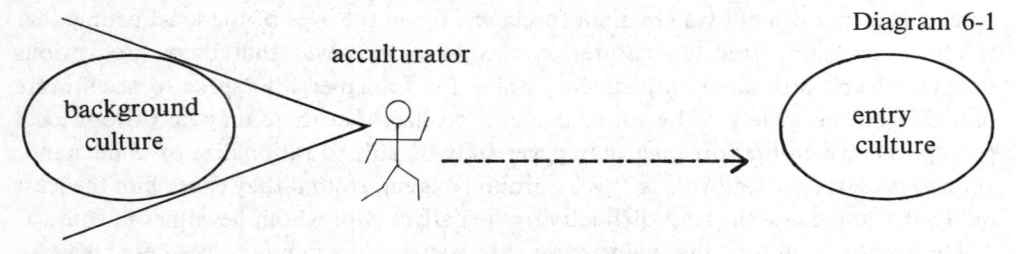

Diagram 6-1

In this drawing we can see that the person proceeding along the path to acculturation, the acculturator, has a background of behavioral patterns and thought processes which reflect the culture to which he is native, which we may call his *background culture*. The culture into which he enters may be called the *entry culture,* target culture, or new culture. To avoid confusion, we will want to be consistent with the use of some terms: by "natives" we are referring to members of the entry culture; by "foreigner" we are referring to the acculturator; by "a person who is native to another culture" we are referring to non entry culture natives, i.e. foreigners (who may or may not be proceeding along the path to acculturating themselves).

Diagram 6-2

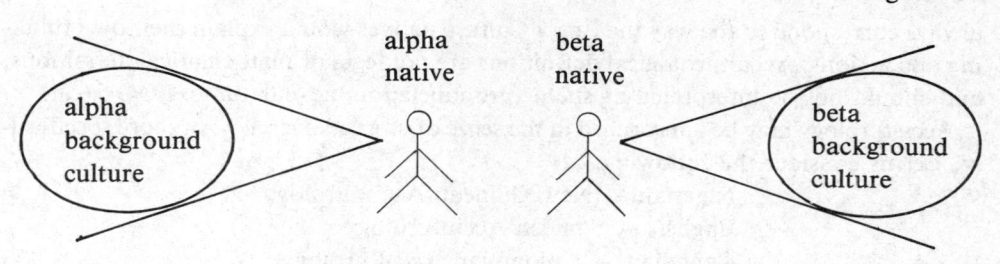

```
    alpha         beta
    native        native
┌─────────┐                    ┌─────────┐
│  alpha  │    O      O        │  beta   │
│background│    ╱╲    ╱╲       │background│
│ culture │                    │ culture │
└─────────┘                    └─────────┘
```

We often speak of persons as having "different cultural backgrounds", and this is illustrated in our second drawing. These two people may meet in country alpha, or in country beta, and our definition of who is the "acculturator", which is the "background culture", and which is the "entry culture" would be different in each case. If they met in some third country, we would want to look at the individual situation for each, and this would take us back to our first drawing. (For further discussion of terminology, see the Appendix.)

Culture may be defined in many ways, however we will use it in the following sense. Culture: **a pattern of thinking and doing which reflects the deposit of knowledge, experiences, beliefs, values, attitudes, meanings, hierarchies, religion, timing, roles, spatial relations, concepts of the universe, and material objects and possessions acquired by a large group of people in the course of generations through individual and group striving.**

Note: Culture is used in a number of other ways in the English language as well, and these include, **1) the training and refining of the mind, emotions, manners, taste, etc. 2) the result of this; refinement of thoughts, emotion, manners, taste, etc. 3) the raising, improvement, or development of some plant, animal, or product, and/or the attention given to such undertakings.** Hence we often say that the Chinese have "tea" culture, Americans do not; however, the Americans have "vitamin" culture, and the Chinese lack this to a large degree. Additionally, Americans have "silverware" culture, the Chinese have "chopsticks" culture.

By subculture we will mean: **a racial, ethnic, regional, economic, or social community exhibiting characteristic patterns of behavior sufficient to distinguish it from others within an embracing culture or society.** In China, in addition to Islamic Chinese, Jewish Chinese, and other religious subcultures, the people in some areas seem different enough to warrant classification as a separate subculture, such as the Cantonese, Hakkanese, Shanghainese, etc. Many western reporters, consultants, and businessmen refer to the "culture" of a particular company or large organization, and we recognize this usage, although academically speaking it is probably more appropriate to call this a "subculture" as well.

We will speak of an "acculturological definition" as being: **a statement or explanation of what a word or phrase means, and serving to clarify a point of view held by particular cultural groups, especially as seen by members of other unrelated cultural groups.** This means that we will endeavor to explain Entry Culture phenomenon using terminology, phraseology, and methodology that the foreigner can understand, yet which may, of necessity, not always correspond to the way the Entry Culture natives would explain their own thinking and actions. Acculturological definitions are not legal or mathematical definitions, and should not be interpreted as such. (pronunciation: ac•cul•tur•o•LOG•i•cal)

Acculturology may be approached in the sense of a broad overview, or more specifically. Let us consider the following.

> Nigerian → New Guinean Acculturology
> English → Spanish Acculturology
> Canadian → Colombian Acculturology
> French → Japanese Acculturology
> American → Chinese Acculturology

The country on the left represents the Background Culture, and the country on the right represents the Entry Culture. As such, it will be seen that German → Pakistani Acculturology is quite different from Pakistani → German Acculturology.

Less specific in terms of countries, some people may wish to examine European → Asian Acculturology, South American → South Sea Island Acculturology, Scandinavian → Middle Eastern Acculturology, etc.

## Going Astray on the Route to Acculturation

For the serious language student, studying the typical language texts designed for foreigners, it is easy to become lost on the route to acculturation and proceed along the presumedly blissful path to nativization. This is often the case even among scholars and researchers, as they attempt to "pin down" the meanings of various Entry Culture terminology in terms of their Background Culture language. Many of the scholars tend to feel that by coming up with an even better translation of the Entry Culture terminology (such as the discussion of *jen* in our Introduction), their readers, who may have widely varying degrees of knowledge of the Entry Culture language, will be able to get a much firmer grasp of what the term means. This sort of reasoning I believe still falls within the "preparatory nativist" camp. The person who really desires to become acculturated however assumes that any term which is difficult to draw a simple picture of, or which is beyond the communicative power of simple sign language that a twelve year old could understand, quite likely does not exist in any one-on-one translatable relationship to another term in the Background Culture language. Even when it does appear to have a close one-to-one translatable relationship, it may in fact hold different connotations and emotive content.

Collecting the various definitions which the scholars, researchers, and lexicographers have assembled, the acculturator proceeds to assemble data on real life present-day happenings, and notes how the local people react to various situations which call for, he feels, applications of the quality which this term seems to express. Next, it is necessary to formulate and clarify the perceptual basis upon which the natives are acting, in terms that he and others of his background culture can understand. In this way the first glimmerings of acculturative knowledge may be obtained.

### China Through the Looking Glass

In the western news media, we often read accounts of increased demands among the Mainland Chinese population for modernization, democratic reforms, and even input of some capitalist economic practice. The Republic of China on Taiwan has been instituting exactly these types of policies for several decades, and therefore offers a valuable insight into the direction Mainland China will most likely head. In these pages it may be seen that, in a number of respects, significant perceptual differences exist between the modern day westerners and citizens of the R.O.C. If we were to make a very conservative estimate that the living standards of the Mainland Chinese are twenty-five years behind the R.O.C., one would expect that even greater degrees of perceptual difference would be found between westerners and the Mainland Chinese.

The Republic of China then offers an excellent starting point for the study of American — Chinese Acculturology, or to use a somewhat broader terminology: Acculturological Sinology.[1] The R.O.C. is especially valuable because it offers us a chance to glimpse the workings of a Chinese society that is developing without Communist ideology—an ideology which is at odds with democracy, freedom of speech, freedom of the press, etc., as well as serving to stifle a great degree of individual initiative. In this way we can gain a view of a more pure and natural nature of modern Chinese people. We may then turn back to focus our attention on the Mainland and see the goings-on there with a clearer eye.

Students, scholars, and even businessmen have often favored the treatment which they receive in dealing with the Republic of China, and have commented that long term residence for the foreigner in the R.O.C., although there is no Permanent Resident (PR) status as known in many western countries, is nevertheless much more feasible than in Mainland China. It is exactly during such a term of residence that the foreigner may devote himself to beginning, intermediate, and advanced levels of acculturological studies.

## Pre-Industrialism and Post-Industrialism

It is often said that agriculture is the first stage of economic development, and industrialism is the second. However we commonly find much confusion in dealing with the expression "The Industrial Revolution." According to the notions of some people, this indicates the time when mankind "began to use machines" or "began to mechanize

---

1. The person who studies and researches this field is an acculturological sinologist.

human effort." Actually, such a definition is inaccurate. The first strivings to mechanize human effort would most properly be called the "The Origins of Mechanical Engineering." When exactly these origins occurred is lost in history, although according to informed scholars, a certain type of water-raising instrument, affirmed to have been in utilized in the Sumerian civilization in 3000+ B.C., is still widely used in the present era in some Middle Eastern regions. Many types of mechanical, hydraulic, and pneumatic devices are known to have been highly developed by the 1st century A.D. Gears, pulleys, cylinders, pistons, valves and many other elements of modern machines were present in the machines of the Greeks and the Romans. Properly speaking, these items all fall in the realm of Mechanical Engineering. In contrast, the Industrial Revolution specifically refers to an event which first happened in Britain in the late 1780's, and later "spread" to certain other countries.

How did this "Revolution" come about? In fact, few intellectual refinements were necessary to establish the early factories, other than those that had been around for well over one hundred years. James Watt's rotary steam-engine, introduced in 1784, is an excellent example of something which could have been invented earlier, in other countries, by persons with sufficient motivation and a modicum of imagination. Indeed, the knowledge of physics required was not very advanced by the standards of the time, and continued to use the basic formulation based on boiling water, a technique known to all cultures. Earlier steam driven devices and apparati are described in literature throughout the ages, with the earliest references in the *Pneumatica* of Hero of Alexandria, written in the 1st century A.D.

Hence, many people ask: "Why Britain?" Since the greater part of the eighteenth century was a period of prosperity and economic expansion for most of Europe, many social commentators have argued that sooner or later this expansion would have pushed some country across the threshold from a pre-industrial to industrial economy. However, this analysis misses the key-point. Most of the eighteenth century expansion was leading to an increase in output by use of old methods, which might have eventually resulted in some sort of limited collective-cottage, collective-artisan, or more organized domestic/craft movement.But this is not equivalent to industrial revolution, which would include a division of labor, the training of relatively unskilled people for individual tasks, and the entire creation of a mechanized "factory system". It is only with such a system that production is made in such vast quantities, and at such rapidly diminishing cost-per-unit, that it is no longer dependent on existing demand, but rather serves to create its own market. This is the true nature of the revolution which occurred in the cotton industry (textiles) in Britain. As a result, the demand derived from cotton for more building construction and more infrastructure, for new industrial areas, for machines, for chemical improvements, for industrial lighting, for roads, for shipping, and many other technical advances also served to stimulate the entire economy. As the factory owners reinvested their earnings in bigger and better plants, the industrial growth of the economy was stimulated even further.

Factories require people, and in agricultural societies most people are working on the farms. Numerous developments in agriculture in Britain were extremely important as a precursor to industrialization, and admittedly more consequential than any particular mechanical expertise on the part of British workers. The conditions prevailing in the British agricultural sector in the mid to late 1700's showed significant advances over previous eras, and much of this was due to the discarding of traditional ideas. The agricultural production was already predominately for the market, as opposed to merely subsistence agriculture. Both production and productivity in the agricultural sector were rising due to the use of crop rotation techniques, and additional crops enabled more cattle to be raised as well. This abundant food supply enabled the nation to feed a rapidly rising non-agricultural population. Marshes were drained, and areas of sandy soil were improved through the addition of clay and other substances. The Enclosure Acts passed by Parliament permitted larger landowners to consolidate and fence their property, resulting in more efficient farms, better management, and hence larger yields.Social infrastructure was also rapidly being developed, notably the building of new ships, port facilities, and the improvement of roads, waterways, and communications.

Speaking on the psychological conditions necessary for a successful Industrial Revolution, one finds in the literature of the times references to the need to "get rid of that dronish, sleepy, and stupid indifference, that lazy negligence, which enchains men in the exact paths of their forefathers, without enquiry, without thought, and without ambition."

Asian Influence

Yet this Revolution's influence on the common man in Asia was not apparent in even a superficial fashion for another fifty years. Actually, since the dawn of time, Europe had always imported more from the East than she had sold there. This was because there was little the Orient required from the West in return for the spices, silks, art, jewels, tea, and other items which it provided. The Industrial Revolution's mass produced textiles reversed this situation for the first time, however the Chinese still refused to buy what the West, or Western-controlled economies, offered, until between 1815 and 1842 it was found that there was a market for Indian opium in China. After the Opium War of 1839 - 1842, the Treaty of Nanking (and supplementary treaties) established foreign trading posts in China, and established the beginnings of foreign relations, which had effectively been cut off for centuries.

Industrial Revolution Era Thinking

That the Industrial Revolution strongly affected the minds of Englishmen and other Europeans after the 1780's is supported by the data on increases in non-agricultural population year by year. As the populace cast off agricultural lifestyles, they took on new habits and new ways of thinking, and rethought much traditional methodology and customs. Statistics show that by the early 1850's, the industrially employed population in Britain outnumbered the agriculturally employed for the first time, and in the present era the agricultural workforce is less than 5%. Looking at the situation for China, we see that from the earliest days of industrial development in the late 1800's,[1] and the completion of the first eight km. railway line (out of Shanghai) in 1876, up to today, the industrially employed population has grown to a percentage of approximately 20% to 30% of the workforce in the present era. Clearly, the majority of the Chinese population, nearly 70%, still remains primarily involved with agriculture, even if we make some allowance for employment in the service industries.

If we consider the meaning of the statement "Country X went through the Industrial Revolution" to be that Country X eventually reached the point where the percentage of industrially employed (and related service-industry) workers exceeded that of agriculturally employed ones, with the resultant changes in thinking that this reorganization of society brought about, we will recall that this happened in Britain in the early 1850's. Taking 30 years as a generation, it can be said that the west has raised nearly five generations of citizens since this occurred, and we may call this our "generation count". Examining the statistics, we see that China has yet to undergo the full force of the Industrial Revolution.

China's situation is further complicated by a factor which we may call the "historical overhang" of traditions, customs, philosophy, and religion. Looking at England, some would date the beginning of English history in 1066, however we can be more liberal and go back to the seven early Anglo-Saxon kingdoms in 600 A.D. For the sake of discussion we may take 1850 minus 600, which gives an historical overhang of 1250 years preceding the full realization of the force of the Industrial Revolution. Many of the attitudes of the present day westerners, especially in regard to the "Ten Natures" mentioned in the Introduction, may be said to be the result of the combination of these factors: 1) 1250 years of pre-existing customs, traditions, etc. before the 2) realization of the full force of the Industrial Revolution, and 3) nearly five generations of citizens raised since that realization.

Looking at comparative data for China, if we eliminate the early legends, we may date the beginnings of Chinese history with the Yellow Emperor in 2697 B.C. Calculated from 2000 A.D., 1) we have 4697 years of historical overhang, nearly 2.5 times the English figure, 2) we have yet to realize the full force of the Industrial Revolution, and 3) we have zero generations of citizens raised since that realization. (Granted, if we consider the situation for some individual Chinese provinces separately, the discrepancy may seem less extreme.)[2]

---

1. Empress Tsz Hsi 慈禧太后 (a dominant figure in Chinese political life and the power behind the throne 1860–1908) actively opposed industrialization.

2. Taiwan is the most prosperous Chinese province: the portion of its total workforce engaged in agriculture dropped below 50% for the first time in 1961.

The point of these computations and comparisons is to clarify this: Analysis of many aspects of the westerner's behavior, norms, ideals, thought patterns, moral reasoning, etc. will reveal that they are characteristic of advanced "Post Industrial Revolution thinking". Many times we will also see that they are at a variance with typical Chinese thinking. At this juncture in our analysis, it is overly simplistic to offer the rationale for this discrepancy the oft heard statements "The Chinese are different" or "The Chinese have their own ways of doing things". Perhaps slightly better is the claim "The Chinese retain many vestiges of feudalism," however a much more reasonable rationale would be "China never went through the Industrial Revolution." As we have established, this happened in the west nearly five generations ago.

Statistical Comparisons

The percentages of agricultural populations of some countries may be useful for reference:

| | | | |
|---|---|---|---|
| Canada | 5% | West Germany | 7% |
| Austrailia | 7% | India | 70% |
| China | 70% | Italy | 10% |
| Egypt | 50% | Japan | 9% |
| France | 9% | South Korea | 30% |
| Netherlands | 6% | Great Britain | 3% |

United States less than 4%

Although the percentages of agricultural population for some Asian countries have fallen below 50%, we must still consider the problem of historical overhang and a low generation count. Due to these factors, the thinking of most South Koreans is more similar to Chinese norms than it is different.

## Pre Industrial Revolution Subsistence Agricultural Society[1]
## Modes of Thinking and Behavior

Even though many sectors of Chinese society in the present era incorporate various machines and other products of an advanced Post Industrial Revolution age, innumerable facets of Pre Industrial Revolution thinking and behavior may be seen among the populace. Many western tourists, businessmen, and other observers have noted the general lack of maintenance and upkeep of equipment, facilities, housing, etc. in China, and the specific lack of preventative maintenance in using a wide variety of machinery and apparatuses. Numerous westerners have stated that this is hard to understand, however we believe this is easily correlated to a society whose members "skipped" the

---

1. "Pre Industrial Revolution" is one adjective, "Subsistence Agricultural" is another adjective. Both are used here to modify the noun "Society". We may say Pre Industrial Revolution Society or Subsistence Agricultural Society. For emphasis, we are saying: Pre Industrial Revolution Subsistence Agricultural Society.

Industrial Revolution. A westerner takes it for granted that the additional expense and effort required in maintaining equipment is more economical in the long run, since the equipment may be used for a lengthier period, and will continue to function in a correct fashion. The long term planning inherent in these notions is typical of Post Industrial Revolution thinking. Such ideas are rarely found in a society of Subsistence Agriculture. When we speak of the Chinese views of planning, we see that their concepts are often more indicative of a pre industrial age, and we may call this Pre Industrial Revolution Planning. It contains much go-with-the-flow reasoning and is typified by a "crisis intervention" style of management: crises are dealt with when and if they occur, otherwise developments are left to proceed on their "natural course" in a laissez-faire fashion.

In the Chinese schools, much emphasis is placed on the fact that the Chinese are a polite [a] and moral race. We have no quarrel with this, but it does merit some qualification. When we see the chaotic traffic conditions in the Chinese cities, where bigger size is the accepted standard for determining who has right of way, where anyone who ventures into the crosswalk does so at considerable risk of injury to life and limb, where people frequently drive motorcycles on the sidewalk, honking their horns, narrowly missing pedestrians, etc., we wonder: how does this qualify as politeness? Yet we are told "The Chinese did not invent motor vehicles. Motor vehicles have nothing to do with Chinese politeness." Certainly the same rationale can be offered when discussing the pushing and shoving often seen accompanying the people's efforts to get on a public bus. Clearly the failure to relate men's actions with motorized vehicles, the products of industrialization, and inability to integrate such actions into the Chinese mental framework is indicative of some peculiar aspects. This we may call Pre Industrial Revolution Politeness.

The incapacity to accept the right and wrong dictated by traffic regulations, whereby the Oriental people still consider the driver of a vehicle who has broken no law "guilty", "at fault", and "responsible" when he hits someone who has violated the regulations, clearly seems reflective of Pre Industrial Revolution Morality, and we will see still further aspects of this style of thinking in later chapters.

The "stars" of the Industrial Revolution were not the inherited wealthy or royal families, but the people of enterprise and initiative who participated in supply, manufacture, and distribution. These people became a strong middle class, and Post-Industrial Revolution society took on middle class values. The maintenance of aristocratic thought in the present era may then be said to be largely a holdover from an earlier age. We will see in later chapters that the Chinese people do in fact have many aristocratic ideas. In a related aspect, they also have many ideas which are common to the peasant class. Both of these considerations are reflective of Pre Industrial Revolution society. In China there is little or no tradition of middle class values.

---

a. 禮儀之邦

The assumption of very limited geographic mobility is typical of a traditional subsistence agricultural age. Since sellers and buyers in the marketplace are assumed to be fairly well known to each other, and aware of all factors affecting local production and distribution, there is little need for marked prices, nor little discussion necessary if one member of the seller's family quotes one price for a particular product, and another member quotes another price. That the consumer would think this was dishonest is "unreasonable," we are told, and he is apparently only entitled to take it or leave it at whatever price the seller finally determines is "correct".The preference of businessmen for personal and family relationships in making a wide variety of dealings in the marketplace, and frequent choice of buying from close friends and relatives, while regarding quality as a secondary or even minor consideration, no doubt was valid business policy at some time in history, since in a subsistence agricultural era, quality never varied very much. The willingness of employees in different organizations to consort together for their own personal gain, and place the interests, financial and otherwise, of their organizations off to one side, perhaps does promote brotherly love and mutual dependence on the most basic level. In a larger sense, all of these factors appear indicative of Pre Industrial Revolution Honesty, Pre Industrial Revolution Commercial Organization, Pre Industrial Revolution Work & Living Patterns, etc.

The selection of various types of nutritionally poor foods for feeding infants (rice soup and pickled vegetables are two examples), as opposed to more wholesome ones now available in the marketplace, and the tendency to ignore the availability of these items, maintaining dietary preferences in a rather similar fashion to a society of subsistence agriculture, seems indicative of Pre Industrial Revolution Nutrition.

The situations of sanitation and safety in our Law vs. Benevolence Questionnaires would only come about in a Post Industrial Revolution world, where the maintenance of machines and equipment was involved. The retention of a sympathetic or benevolent attitude by the enforcement agencies, similar to that found in old China in the agriculturally based society before such machines were introduced, appears indicative of a Pre Industrial Revolution style of Human Relations.

The Industrial Revolution stimulated scientific research for better machines, chemicals, processes, etc., and contributed greatly to the specialization of sciences. We have seen in the preceding five chapters that Chinese thinking contains many elements of "non scientific", "non factual evidence" bias. More examples of this bias will be found in later chapters as well. Clearly the existence of this kind of mentality in many areas, exemplified by the oft seen willingness to ignore scientific evidence and the results obtained thereby, maintaining "We have our own methods", is a holdover from a Pre Industrial Revolution age.In that pre-specialization-of-science era, scientific research was not a major focus of attention in society.

The feeling that it is better to speak indirectly or roundaboutly, often taking seven sentences to say something that could be expressed directly in two, seems to indicate that time and efficiency are relatively unimportant. This to some extent is attributable to the retention of Pre Industrial Revolution Speech Habits.

There is probably no complete list of such considerations. Certainly the westerner who cares to research the issue will find many more indications of Pre Industrial Revolution thinking as he examines other aspects of Chinese thought and rationale. All of these exist as undercurrents in present Chinese society which may show up in a variety of manifestations in a number of different areas.

## Organization of Language

The Chinese language is organized in a way much different from English, and in many ways reflecting the mentality of the Chinese people themselves. It represents a mainstream of culture outside of the western tradition, and in its own ways it is highly developed, highly polished, highly sensitive. Chinese is a fascinating language, with a far greater component of "art" than English, it also has far greater sense of poetry. Of the world's major languages, it would not be extravagant to say: "Poetry, thy name is Chinese." Consider the poetic sections in *Journey to the West*, and *Dream of the Red Chamber, All Men Are Brothers,* and other works, in addition to the collections of the poems from different dynasties. These are simply remarkable. Just the other day I saw on the television that a famous 90 year old Chinese calligrapher was displaying a selection of one hundred of his recent works, and offering them to the public at the equivalent of over US$ 1500 each, with the funds raised to be given to local health care facilities. They were sold out in the space of one morning. I doubt that there are not several times in the lives of all foreign students of Chinese that they sigh at their lack of fortune in not being born and raised in China, so they could truly immerse themselves in all of this art, poetry, calligraphy, literature, etc.

Being such an ideal language for poetry, Chinese can generally mold any sort of English expression and turn it into a rhyming set of Chinese characters, especially if one works at the project hard enough. Once, some days before a cocktail party reception, one western liquor exporter asked the translators how his proposed toast might be best translated. The wording was: "Here's to the happiest days of my life, spent in the arms of another man's wife—my mother." Although this seemed a bit "too subtle" for the Chinese sense of humor, and appeared bordering on the risque, nevertheless we were able to come up with a rhymed translation in one evening of brainstorming.[a]

The depth of the Chinese language is astounding in the amount of written material which is there, and even more astounding if one considers the amount of written material

---

**a.** 記取生平何時最愉快，莫過於擁抱別人的太太──我的母親

which is not there, because it has been lost or destroyed over the ages. It is easy to find among the records of the court historians in past dynasties a large number of references to books and manuscripts that no one in the modern era has been able to locate. Nevertheless, with the texts available, if the curriculum in the Chinese schools were changed today to include nothing but Chinese, (i.e. language, literature, and poetry), a year by year syllabus could be quickly drawn up by the relevant Ministry, and it would be quite possible for the native Chinese student to spend 10 hours per day studying only Chinese (his native language), from kindergarten through 12th grade, or even for many more years after that. No doubt many Chinese would be happy to participate in this type of program too.[1]

The Chinese language's rich hertiage in art, poetry, phonology, humor, historical allusion, as well as the classical treatises on medicine, warfare, kungfu, philosophy, metaphysics, astrology, and other numerous topics are all waiting there for the westerner who is "super-fluent". Unfortunately, we have to work to support ourselves, so the amount of time even the most diligent student can devote to his Chinese studies is limited. This is true whether he is a native Chinese or a foreigner. One could become a hermit or a monk, but this alternative appears outside the realm of practical reality for the great majority of the population.

Like many westerners who have spent much time in the Orient, I like the Chinese language. It is extremely interesting. It has ways of expression that do not exist in English, most notably in parallel constructions and rhyming schemes. It has triple entendres and many other types of plays on words. Nearly every character has a long involved explanation behind it, although I must admit that upon reflection and attempt at unified analysis this has proved more confusing to me than otherwise beneficial, notwithstanding the fact that I have spent many pleasant hours over the years listening to such "character stories". In addition to this, there are hundreds of calligraphic styles for writing the characters, and no two calligraphers produce works that are exactly alike. Certainly no one doubts that the Chinese are in love with their language, and it is easy to lead them into a long discussion on the topic on nearly any occasion.

Unfortunately, most of the Chinese are unaware of the potential for confusion and misunderstanding when foreigners use the Chinese language for communication, conceptualization, and daily activity organization. We will delve into these problems more thoroughly in the following chapters.

---

1. In a related consideration, a newly opened Chinese publishing house can assemble, edit, print, and publish a 100 or 200 volume collection of classic literary works and historical treatises without violating any copyright laws or paying a cent in royalty fees. The authors of these texts, having been dead for thousands of years, are unlikely to voice any objection.

# Chapter 7 Comparative Ideals of Obedience

## A Relaxing Day in the Countryside

Grandfather Liu's house was situated in the countryside some 90 minutes drive from town. His son Theodore Liu, who was in the ceramics business, had invited us to go out for a visit. After leaving the city, we had a long drive through green rolling hills and finally entered a valley where Theodore pointed to his family's small curving driveway off to the right. We pulled up to a large cement fishpond with a dragon-shaped water-fountain in the center, which was spewing water over the surface of the pond. Parking the car in the shade of a nearby tree, we walked over to a building which resembled a small temple. High on the wall to the right of the door were the characters *jin shr*,[a] and on the left *wen kwei*,[b] all in large flowing calligraphy and engraved in marble. Many additional smaller characters were engraved vertically on the sides. Theodore explained that over 250 years ago these plaques were given by the Ching Dynasty Emperor to one of the Liu family's ancestors who had qualified in the Imperial Examinations. Since the wooden plaques themselves had not withstood the ravages of time, they had been skillfully recopied and engraved in marble several decades ago through the employ of some local artisans.

Inside the temple we were shown the Liu family's ancestral tablet which went back over 300 years, to the time when their ancestors had moved to this Province. The walls were covered with various plaques and inscriptions, and in addition to the Buddhist and Taoist ones, there were a number of which had been given to his great-grandfather, grandfather, and father for their service in the local government and other demonstrations of public spirit. One large piece of velvet-like material was covered with various medallions which the men of the family had obtained in military service, for scholarly awards, and in other positions, and many of these dated back to the middle of the Ching Dynasty. One particularly interesting collection was of photographs of all the family

---

[a]. 進士　[b]. 文魁

members who had obtained college degrees, and the oldest of these appeared to have been taken about 1890, while the most recent was that of Theodore's brother's daughter, signed and dated the previous year. Some incense was burning in a vessel in the center of the room, and several statues were displayed in a glass case, appearing to be connected to some sort of idol worship. Grandfather Liu came out as we were looking over the photos and he pointed out to us several of his relatives who had graduated with advanced degrees from universities in the United States and Europe.

We walked into another room off the south side of this display area where Grandmother Liu had prepared some tea, and made ourselves comfortable on some large rattan furniture. Grandfather Liu told us some more about his family, and invited us to take a walk around the fruit orchards and rice paddies, and visit their many fish ponds. During the course of the discussion, he mentioned that he was regularly sending money to two of his grandchildren who were currently pursuing advanced studies in the United States. Theodore added some comments at this point, noting that his father had always strongly believed in education, and had worked hard during his younger years so that all of the children could go to the best schools. Sometimes the tuition money for the better Chinese schools had been expensive, but Grandfather Liu had always managed to work things out. Now that the children had grown and had children of their own, Grandfather encouraged them to get the best education that they could, and was eager to help with tuition monies whenever necessary, even if it meant going without, or putting off, various purchases which he felt necessary for the maintenance of the farm.

The discussion went on to mention the accomplishments of some of the more famous Liu ancestors. One could not help but be impressed by the attention which this family, like so many Chinese families, placed on education. This appeared to be a strong family unit, and it was evident that the brothers, sisters, uncles, aunts, cousins and other relatives were in frequent contact, sharing the common desire to build a stronger clan, and willing to mutually contribute money, time, and other resources for the benefit of the next Liu generation. Even though the grown sons had now moved to the city, they came back regularly to visit their aged parents, and were still involved in some activities here in the locality of their birth.

Before we left, Grandfather Liu showed us several letters he had received from his grandchildren abroad, and the pictures they had sent. I could see that he was very proud of their accomplishments.

## Reading at Home

Returning to my residence I picked up a copy of a new Chinese magazine which one of my coworkers had passed on to me. The magazine was primarily concerned with analysis of various economic trends in the country, but also offered advice on consumer purchases, employment, and family finances. One article particularly interested me. It discussed how one Chinese family had begun a modest savings plan when their children were still toddlers, and over the years had saved up enough money to put the son and daughter through the National University (similar to a State University in the USA, and different from a private university). In addition, the savings plan had included a substantial "nest egg" to be given to each child at the time of their marriage, to get them off to a good start.

The savings plan had been brought to a successful conclusion, and now the son was graduating from college, and preparing to be engaged to a classmate. His younger sister would be beginning college in the fall. The family of four was pictured outside the gates of the college, with the son dressed in his graduation gown.

Discussing this husband and wife's financial planning for their children's education and marriage, most of my Chinese friends and coworkers expressed the feeling that this sort of arrangement was highly typical of Chinese families. Of course among the poorer families it might not be possible to prepare a fully adequate amount of money, but they would certainly try their best.

Picking up another copy of an English language international news magazine, I saw an article on "Asian American Whiz Kids". In case after case, describing the academic achievements of the Asian immigrants in the US schools, the entire family's involvement was stressed. Two Asian girls were studying music at a prestigious New York school, and the news report stated "The girls' parents have built their lives around their daughters' musical educations." To help pay the bills, the mother, father, older brothers, and other relatives all contributed.[1] When the children were asked to comment on this, they stated "We feel that we have to do well because our parents are devoting their whole lives to us." They were typical of the Asian-ancestry high achievers in the US schools, as the entire eight page article went on to show.

---

1. In recent years much attention has been given in the United States and even the international news media to the increasing influx of Oriental children into United States schools, particularly into a large number of very prestigious institutes of higher learning, including private colleges and universities. That many of these students have achieved outstanding academic records has often been a main highlight of the press coverage. Less attention has however been paid to how many of these Oriental children, especially those from lower class or lower middle class economic backgrounds, have managed to afford the tuition, room & board, and other expenses involved in attending these first rate institutions. Why is it that at same time many upper middle class families in the USA look at the price-tag of such an education for their own children and shudder? One of the main contributing factors to the Oriental's ability to pay such tuition costs, besides the traditional emphasis which Oriental societies have placed on education, lies in the way that money is used and allocated among members of the family group or clan. The particular usage patterns which the Chinese have developed are in actuality a direct outgrowth of the Group Mentality.

## Taxi Troubles

A few days later a Chinese friend of mind recounted an interesting story she had heard from a taxi driver which dealt with the same general themes of the importance of children, and the dedication of parents. It was late one rainy night when she had gotten a cab on the east side of town, and the cabbie was a middle-aged Chinese man in his late forties, sullen in his look, and unusually blunt in his speech. After the usual "Where To?" and, after her directions were received, the usual reply Hau, hau [a] (meaning "good" or "alright"), the driver continued to have a melancholy expression on his face. When asked what was the matter, he simply replied: "My son passed away." My Chinese friend of course quickly responded with some sympathetic remarks.

As if his emotions had been bottled up by some invisible cap for quite some time, the cabbie now began to pour out his story, recreating his son's whole life-drama with a sad and bitter tone. My friend suspected that she was not the first customer to hear his story:

"My son was a treasure to me and my wife—a very obedient boy. He was very smart too, and learned things at an extraordinarily fast rate. We decided to hire tutors to give him extra lessons in math, piano, violin, English, art, Chinese composition, Chinese brush-painting, etc. beginning when he was in second and third grades. It was a real delight for us to have such a talented son."

My friend listened very closely, giving him an understanding nod whenever he glanced in her direction.

"He was in the top five students in his class when he graduated from elementary school, and graduated number three overall from Junior High School. After High School he successfully passed the college entrance examination and got into a very good local college, majoring in engineering. Things were really going well for him, and all the grandparents and relatives were very proud. He studied so hard, until the late hours every night, and my wife would often take a mid-night snack of some rice-gruel and vegetables up to his room. My long laborious hours working at the factory did not seem to be much of a burden to me, since I was making the money for his tuition. We planned for him to continue his studies and pursue an advanced engineering degree in the USA."

The cabbie cleared his throat as he stepped on the accelerator to rush through an intersection on the tail-end of a yellow light. "Then one day we got a telephone call. The school said he had been involved in an accident. My wife and I rushed to the hospital, wondering what could have happened to our third-year college boy. We were hoping for the best, but when the doctor came out of the operation he looked very grim. 'Our son . . . ?' we accosted him, but he just shook his head slowly. Then he looked at us and said: 'We will do our best to save him.' When we were allowed into the emergency room he was already in a coma."

---

a. 好，好

His eyes showed increased sadness as he continued on. "I kept on praying to Kuanyin, and my wife and relatives all went to the Buddhist temple to burn incense and make offerings. But two days later he passed away in his sleep . . . our little boy . . . " Shaking his head, he managed to break the solemn atmosphere with a doeful smile, then went on: "It happens so quickly doesn't it? I have lost my son. Now what is an old man going to do without his highest hope? Now there is no meaning in my work anymore. I just drag on day after day . . . no future grandchildren to keep me happy, and no son to comfort me in my old age."

My friend adopted a polite tone and asked if he had any other children. The cabbie stopped to think about this, and said: "Only two older girls, but they only went as far as high school. Now they are married and living down south." He swerved around the corner narrowly missing a small boy on an unlighted bicycle travelling the wrong way on the shoulder of the road. "We are here," he announced.

After giving her regrets my friend paid the fare and left.

Of course it would be possible to write an entire book relating stories similiar to those presented above. The major undercurrents of family solidarity, parental devotion to children, stress on education,[1] children's diligence in educational pursuits, sacrifice of other interests to meet educational expenses, etc., are present throughout. It is our feeling that these types of stories serve as an important backdrop to a consideration of the entire doctrine of filial piety, which we will briefly outline and illustrate in this chapter. (pronounced: FIL i al  PI e ty) 孝順、孝道

**filial: 1) of, suitable to, or due from a son or daughter, as filial attachment**
**piety: 1) loyalty, dedication, and devotion to parents, family, etc.**

We speak of behavior as filial or unfilial. We speak of an action as showing filial piety or filial impiety.

The bonds between Chinese parents and children are mutual, and assumed to be of bi-directional responsibility. Other relationships in Chinese society are viewed in the light of "mutual helpfulness" as well, however the parent-child bond is the most important one which the child will have throughout his/her existence. The idea that the parent-child bond is to be actively maintained through the children's entire lives, including into adulthood and after marriage, that the children owe obedience to the parents' dictates and wishes, that the children have responsibility to provide for the aged parents,

---

1. Although the Chinese place a great stress on education and on tradition, nevertheless the formal establishment of institutes of higher learning has lagged far behind the west. Some institutions, their locations, and dates of founding are useful for reference: Sorbonne College, France, 1253. Cambridge University, England, 1318. University of Edinburgh, Scotland, 1583. Harvard College, USA, 1636. University of Halle, Germany, 1694.

Similar data for China is: Peking University, 1898. Fu Dan University, 1905. Wuhan University, 1913. Central University, 1915.

etc. is often more pronounced than similar parent-child relationships in the west.

Some historical factors in relation to the doctrine of filial piety, including its development and promulgation, are significant to our understanding, and will be touched upon as well. Because of the importance of filial piety in Chinese culture over the ages, all of these considerations will be important to the foreigner's understanding of a major undercurrent in Chinese thinking, and the establishment of a basis upon which Chinese view the happenings in the world around them.

## Ancestors and Ancestor Worship

After a significant thaw in East-West relations, an East German government official was invited to attend some important talks in West Berlin, the first such talks in forty years. One morning he took the opportunity to visit the old family gravesite in the small community in West Berlin where he had been born and attended primary school. During his visit he placed wreaths on several of the graves.

When this scene was shown on the evening news in China, the audience throughout the nation nodded their heads in an approving manner. Wondering why this particular news report had received such favorable reaction, a westerner who lived with a local family asked the head of the household, as well as many neighbors, shop keepers, teachers, and other Chinese citizens: "What was the East German official doing?"

The confident reply given in each case was "He was worshipping his ancestors."

Carrying on with his research, this westerner contacted some local German trade officials and cultural representatives, and asked what significance they attached to this official's visit to his family gravesite and the placing of wreaths thereon. The representatives said that they attached very little significance to it at all. This visit was "paying his respects", nothing more, nothing less. Would they equate that with "worship"? Well, they said, "You must remember that we are in China . . . so, speaking for the western press, we should clarify that Germans do not worship their ancestors, however, if we stretch things a bit, in order to satisfy the predilection of the Chinese media, we might say that 'Germans respect their ancestors', and no doubt the Chinese would much more prefer to hear that."

Returning to his Chinese friends, this investigator found that this was indeed what they liked to hear. Moreover, in regard to the ancestors, "respect" seemed naturally to lead to "worship" in the Chinese conception, and there was very little attempt to separate the force of the two words, as a westerner would be inclined to do.

Many people have stated at various times throughout history that there is nothing wrong with respecting one's ancestors, and then of course there have been others who disagreed with this statement.However, the lengths to which the Chinese go, even in the modern era, to conform with this doctrine, and to subtly elevate it to a form of "worship", often strike the westerner as highly unusual.

## Funeral Arrangements

To be thoroughgoing about the funeral rites for parents and the worship of ancestors is considered a primary moral consideration in Chinese society. Funeral arrangements may often be held in temporary structures outdoors near the person's residence, and then often become an essentially community affair.

There is generally much chanting, drum beating, gong sounding, and assorted noise from other Chinese instruments associated with Chinese funerals,[1] in marked contrast to the quietness of western ones. It is inconceivable to the Chinese that any person of the community would object to such noise, classify it as a "disturbance of the peace", or regard it an invasion of other individuals' right to privacy, right to quiet, etc.[2]

For the westerner who is disturbed by such clamor, ear-plugs are generally the only answer, short of moving into a hotel a few blocks (or a few kilometers) away for the duration. One is therefore always advised to keep note of interesting and low priced hotels in one's not too distant vicinity, where a room can be rented upon need.

## Medical Bills

The Chinese feel it moral to consider their ancestors, and their opinions, when making decisions. We recall the case of a 78 year old Mr. Jao. His sons and daughters occasionally would remark in passing to their closest acquaintances that their father was worth a great deal of money, since he owned much land. One day he was taken into the hospital for chest pains, and the doctor determined that he would need an operation on his heart. When news of this reached the family members, the sons and daughters began to scurry around to raise enough funds for the operation, since their father had been a farmer all his life and had no medical insurance whatsoever, nor was he participant in any government medical plan. They were quite worried because it appeared that they would not be able to raise sufficient money. A foreign friend remarked to one of the daughters: "Didn't you say that your father was very wealthy, because he owned a lot of land? If you are having trouble raising the money, why don't you sell some of the land?"

The daughter was shocked at this proposal. "Our relatives would not approve of selling that land," she said.

"I thought you said the land belonged to your father," the foreigner replied.

"Yes, it is in his name, but our relatives would not approve of selling it."

"Why not?"

"Because our ancestors would want to keep it in the family."

Before the foreigner could ask if they had recently had a family meeting in which

---

1. Thus providing an environment which is 熱鬧 "bustling, noisy, thronged", which is the Chinese preference.
2. Making no objection to the noise and racket associated with such ceremonies (which may continue for days) is clearly related to the ideal of 敦親睦鄰 "promoting and strengthening the relations among kinsfolk and neighbors."

the ancestors came forth and made such a statement, the daughter had left to contact the neighbors about "borrowing money for this emergency", so he decided to drop the subject.

## Why do you ask "Why?"

A Chinese man worked as an account executive in an export publications house, an organization with Chinese ownership, but all of whose publications were published in English and distributed overseas. Over a period of years he built up a large clientele, comprising many large Chinese manufacturers and trading companies. Although he had had no experience working with foreigners before entering this job, and his actual job duties contacting his clients for advertisements in the various publications also involved very limited exposure to foreign companies and/or foreign personnel, he was nevertheless in contact with the Americans in the Editorial Department, and even had some chances to get together with them after hours for relaxed talk sessions. When asked to sum up some major points of different thinking between his Chinese and western friends, he stated: "I think that western education must teach the students to want to know the 'Why?' about everything, because the westerners are always asking 'Why?'. Chinese education is different."

Aurelius J. Furrow became aware of the difference in Chinese and western thinking in this regard during his many years of teaching adult English classes in China, and attendance at many social gatherings of the local people, in which the discussions ranged widely into many different areas of fact and opinion. Aurey, as his friends call him, recalls one class with fifteen reasonably advanced students. The youngest in the class was a college junior, and the oldest had been out of college and working for a few years, so we could say the age range was from the early to mid 20's. This class enjoyed allotting a great deal of the English lesson time to free talking, as is common practice among many students who have more than a basic level. However, there was sometimes a lack of topics to talk about, and the teacher frequently had to come up with a topic. One day he threw out this question: "If you love someone, plan to marry them, and your parents disapprove, what would you do?"

The minority replied: "I would listen to my parents and obey them." The majority replied: "I would consider my parents' feelings first, and then consider my own feelings." When asked what the possible outcome of this consideration might be, they said: "Of course, we have to follow our parents instructions." One person in the class, a girl named Kathy, was independent in saying: "I will do what I want to do."

The teacher moved on to another question. "If your father asked you to jump off a building, would you do it?" Fourteen of the students said no. One girl named Elly said yes. When asked why they would not jump off the building, the fourteen said:

"That is not reasonable." Aurey asked why that was not reasonable. The consensus seemed to be: "I would kill myself."

Aurey tried to state this remark another way. "Do you mean to say that your parents would not feel the physical pain?" The fourteen seemed to agree with this idea. He then tried a summary: "You mean you will not do something for somebody else if you must suffer the consequences, is that what you are saying?" They agreed to this. Aurey then posed another series of questions. "If your spouse burns the food every night and you have to eat it, will your parents feel the discomfort?" They said no. "If your spouse goes out and gets drunk and comes home and beats you, will your parents feel the pain?" They said no. "If your spouse has very dirty and messy habits, does not want to help clean up around the house and treats your friends poorly when they come to visit, will your parents feel the misery?" They said no.

Aurey turned the conversation back whence it had begun. "Now let us go back to our original question", he said, "If you love someone, plan to marry them, and your parents disapprove, what would you do?" The students blinked their eyes, and then a blank look came over them. After several seconds they expressed their opinions, and the consensus was: "We have to respect our parents and obey them."

Now it was Aurey's turn to blink his eyes, and a blank look came over him. Nevertheless he recovered quickly, and moved on to another question. He asked Elly: "Why are you learning English?"

She replied: "So I can pass my examinations in college."

"Why do you want to pass the college examinations?"

"So I can graduate from college."

"Why do you want to graduate from college?"

"Because my father wants me to."

Aurey then asked: "What is your current major?"

Elly replied: "Accounting."

"Are you interested in accounting?"

"No."

"Are you interested in import-export?"

"No."

"Are you interested in English?"

"No."

"What are you interested in?"

Elly thought for several moments. Her face seemed to brighten up as she said: "I am interested in art."

"Why aren't you in a good school studying art?"

"My father does not approve."

Aurey then asked: "What is your goal in life? What are your career aspirations?"

Elly replied: "I have none. I want to get married, be a housewife, and have five children."

"As a Chinese housewife I think English would have very limited usage. Why are you studying English?"

She replied: "So I can pass my examinations in college."

Seeing a circular pattern emerging, Aurey tried to move the conversation on to other topics, and to involve other members of the class. Aurey noted that Elly never shows any interest in anything, but he has heard from Chinese girls who lived in the west for many years that they can "push her" and she will admit she is interested in some movies, art shows, some boys, etc. But she never expresses these emotions publically. Her words tend to be very different from her actions, and Aurey feels she could be characterized as "passively aggressive". She always smiles as she enters the class, sits in the back, says she is fine.

One day the teacher asked: "if you could do anything you want, what would it be?" Answers varied from "Buy a boat and sail around the world," to "Have a baby boy." Elly remarked however, "I would become a man and give my boss's wife a black eye." Her look became blank after that statement, and she refused to express any more details either at the time or upon later occasions. A westerner could easily conclude that she is boiling with anger but will not talk about it.

In summing up his experiences in dealing with a lot of young Chinese adults, Aurey drew the example of another girl he had heard of who broke up with her boyfriend and then committed suicide by jumping off a building. He said: "She did not jump off the building because they broke up, people just do not do that, even here in China. She jumped off the building because all her life she had been told what to do, and suddenly she is faced with a situation where she cannot reconcile all the demands of what she has been told she should be doing, so she goes nuts and jumps off the building."

Although the incidents Aurey has mentioned are a bit extreme, they are all from his teaching experiences in the last few years. At a basic level, they do appear indicative of the Group Mentality,[1] and as such they not in any way unbelievable.

Something which he and many other westerners have overlooked however is the mutually dependent nature of the parent-child relationship, and its bearing on the whole issue of filial piety. The majority of the young Chinese adults in his class expressed the opinion that they would follow their parents instructions and advice in marriage, if and when the parents expressed a strong opinion. Before casting a questioning glance on such blind obedience, the westerner should remember that the parents represent a great deal of financial and emotional security in the eyes of the children. Many Chinese who get married receive many important presents from the family/relatives/clan, including new furniture, clothing, household furnishings, electrical appliances, and often even a house. After marriage, the parents and other relatives frequently help the new couple with babysitting chores on a part-time or full-time basis for many years after the little

---

1. Especially as shown by the "denial of self".

ones are born. They also offer assistance to the newlyweds in times of financial problems, ill health, or other difficulties. In these and many other ways, the children are tied to the clan much more so than western children are perhaps, and as a result they feel that the wishes of their parents in an issue so important as marriage are not to be taken lightly. Given the Chinese value system, we would have to say that this is quite logical, even though it is different from western norms in many respects.

In conclusion we would state that the "problems" raised by Aurey in the recounting and analysis of his experiences are not too large. Indeed, far more serious problems await us.

## Proposed Revisions of Historical Documents

One prominent family in the United States in the past century has been the Fords. Reading the autobiography of Henry Ford, one is struck by the conflict which arose between him and his son in the late 1930's when the United Auto Workers made increasing efforts to unionize Ford's plants. In May of 1937 the United Auto Workers legally began handing out pamphlets at the Rouge River Plant. Labor leader Walter Reuther and three other men were brutally beaten by thugs hired by Harry Bennett, the head of the "Service Department"—Ford's in-house police force.

Further efforts by the UAW to unionize Ford came to a head in April 1941, when 1500 steelworkers in the Rouge River rolling mill refused to work. Henry Ford was adamant, and would not even discuss the terms the UAW offered for settlement. Edsel, President of the Company, argued that negotiations were the only way out, and his father ordered him to stay out of the problem.

In evaluating the issue up to this point, the westerner might be inclined to look at the nature of the union's demands and the benefits they hoped to achieve for the workers, and admire the foresightedness of Edsel in recommending a compromise. This solution certainly appears better able to promote harmony between labor and management. While harmony is an important consideration in Chinese ethics, it still sits on a backburner to filial piety, i.e. absolute respect to parents. Thus in the Chinese mind, the important issue now at hand in the Ford family is not to weigh the merits of unionization, for Henry has already stated his views on that. Rather, we must realize that Edsel, by disagreeing with his father, is an unfilial son, and has lost all respectability in the eyes of any moral person.

This conclusion is obvious enough to those with a full comprehension of Chinese thinking, but I must admit that in my contact with a multitude of westerners over the years there were some who were not quite able to grasp it. In speaking to them further, I found that they were unaware of some basic historical developments in China over the millennia which have had a direct bearing on the growth of Chinese ethical thought. Full coverage of this historical data is a lengthy undertaking, however I believe there is a quick shortcut which may be taken to "intuitive understanding" in this area. If the reader wishes to take this shortcut, he need only read the following brief comments, and then he may skip this entire chapter on **Comparative Ideals of Obedience.**

The Shortcut

First we must recognize that western moral thinking has, from the Chinese point of view, some serious gaps. Ritual is certainly one area where western morality is very weak, and obedience to parents, teachers, and elders is another area that is weak. The entire issue of parental respect and obedience is particularly important, and in need of immediate revitalization. In order to make up for the major historical oversight in western thought that has allowed this weakness to grow and develop, and in order to more fully grasp the significance of all the related Chinese thinking on the subject, it will be helpful if the reader mentally adjusts his cerebral processes to the Chinese norm. This can be done by "mentally rewording" various western historical documents along the lines presented herewith, and keeping their meaning in mind at all times.

### The Declaration of Independence
*originally adopted July 4, 1776 by the Second Continental Congress*
**Revision:** We hold these truths to be self-evident, that all men are created equal, that they are endowed by their Parents with certain unalienable Rights, that among these are Life, Liberty, and the pursuit of happiness—insofar as they do not go against their Parents' wishes or commands.

That to secure these rights, Governments are instituted among Men, deriving their just powers from the consent of the elders and the Ancestors.

### Declaration of the Rights of Man and the Citizen
*originally adopted August 27, 1789 by the French National Assembly*
**Revision:** Liberty consists in the ability to do whatever does not harm another, hence the exercise of the natural rights of each man has no limits, insofar as they do not go against the Parents' dictates or instructions, except those which assure to other members of society the enjoyment of the same rights. Outside of the inviolability of Parental opinions on any and all issues, these limits can only be determined by law.

No one may be disturbed for his opinions, even in religion, provided that he worships his Ancestors and obeys his Parents, or that in other matters the manifestation of his opinions does not trouble public order as established by law.

### Charter of the United Nations and Statute of the International Court of Justice
*originally signed at San Francisco June 26, 1945*
*entered into force October 24, 1945*
**We the peoples of the United Nations Determined**
to establish conditions under which justice and respect for the obligations arising from treaties

and other sources of international law can be maintained, insofar as they do not violate the wishes of our Parents or Ancestors, and to promote social progress and better standards of life in larger freedom, and for these ends to practice tolerance and live together in peace with one another as good neighbors, recognizing the wisdom of our Ancestors, and the correctness of their teachings . . . have resolved to combine our efforts to accomplish these aims.

**Article 1 Revision:** *The Purposes of the United Nations are*
To achieve international cooperation in solving international problems of an economic, social, cultural, or humanitarian character, and in promoting and encouraging respect for human rights and for fundamental freedoms for all without distinction as to race, sex, language, or religion; and to promote strict obedience to Parents and worship of Ancestors.

**Universal Declaration of Human Rights**
adopted by the United Nations General Assembly December 10, 1948
**Article 1 Revision:** All human beings are born free and equal in dignity and rights. They are endowed with reason and conscience and should act towards one another in a spirit of brotherhood, recognizing that Parents have given us everything we have and therefore filial piety is the basis of all morality.
**Article 10 Revision:** Everyone is entitled in full equality to a fair, and public hearing by an independent and impartial tribunal, in the determination of his rights and obligations and of any criminal charge against him, however the principle of seniority will be recognized, and youth may not bring charges against their elders or teachers, or violate the teachings of their Ancestors.
**Article 18 Revision:** Everyone has the right to freedom of thought, conscience, and religion; this right includes freedom to change his religion or belief, and freedom, either alone or in community with others and in public or private, to manifest his religion or belief in teaching, practice, worship and observance; the preeminence of Ancestor worship is hereby established as a precept for all religious and moral teachings.

## Grandparents, Parents, and Obedience

Looking for an incident which can serve to illustrate the nature of the relationship between the younger and elder generations in my family, I recall one particular episode which occurred at my grandparent's home in the Tennessee hills one summer. I might first clarify our situation by saying that my father's ancestors were German, and my mother's ancestors English, and both groups came to the New World well before 1776, so at the present time we have no ties with the Old World at all. There are three children in our family, and I am the second, with an older sister, and a younger brother.

My maternal grandparents were conservative, but I imagine you could say they were progressive in their own modest way, since they had lived in southwestern Ohio for a number of years, and so knew quite a bit about the ways of non-southerners, non country-folk, and non-hillbillies. Born in 1896, they had not had a lot of formal schooling, and my Grandfather often boasted that most of what he had learned of the three R's he had taught himself.

One hot summer afternoon before entering sixth grade, I went to the back porch to put on my shoes to go out and play. My Grandmother was doing some sewing at the time. I ran outside and the screen-door slammed shut behind me. My Grandmother was very upset at this, and called me to come back. When I returned she gave me a severe reprimanding, saying that she had told me countless times not to slam the screen-door when I went out, but to close it softly. My Grandfather was sitting off to one side and said nothing. I held my ground. "I did not slam the screen-door," I replied, "it slammed itself." I went on to explain that due to the fact that there was a long spring hooked to the screen-door and the door frame, so of course when anyone went outside the screen-door was bound to slam shut, and a bang of varying magnitudes would be the natural result. If it were desired to eliminate the bang, certainly the solution would be found by considering the door itself, and its spring, not me.

Grandmother insisted that the problem was due to my carelessness. I maintained that she was vastly oversimplifying the matter. My mother and father who were visiting for a few days from our home some eight-hours drive away, overheard this discussion and came out. After listening to both sides, my mother examined the screen-door, opening it once all the way to see what it would do by itself, and as I had stated, the screen-door did have a strong propensity to slam shut of its own volition, with a loud bang. Mother therefore determined that the long-term solution to the problem would be found in installing a compressed-air type door closer on the door to replace the spring. Grandmother agreed that this would work, and my father went into town the next day to purchase the required item, installing it upon his return. Grandmother and Grandfather were happy with the new arrangement, and I ran out the door whenever I pleased without worrying that I would upset somebody.

Most Chinese who hear this story are shocked. The reason is obvious: in arguing with my grandparents I was being extremely unfilial. Much disharmony was caused. Certainly the situation could have been more properly resolved if I had been strictly obedient in following my Grandmother's instructions, without any backtalk or other comments. Of course I had originally thought that the methodology I used had enabled the situation to resolve itself satisfactorily in all respects, but upon reflection I would have to admit that this could have been a special case, without any wide applicability. So for the future successful handling of a larger range of problems regarding differences of opinion between parents and children, or grandparents and grandchildren, I am willing to consider that my Chinese friends' suggestions may very well prove to be worth their weight in gold.

On the list of one hundred virtues in the Chinese consciousness, only filial piety could possibly qualify for the top position, indeed filial piety is the premier and most blessed virtue, and the virtue from which all other virtues flow. Reading through the accumulation of western philosophical thought from the ancient Greeks through all the European, English, and American philosophers over the ages, I have failed to uncover a single reference to this "filial piety is the premier virtue" conception; even in the Bible the commandment to "Honor thy father and mother" is number #4, or in some versions, #5. Not surprisingly, many westerners consistently overlook the importance of this virtue, or perhaps are totally ignorant of its premier status altogether. No wonder many Chinese have suggested to me that "an ethical education with filial piety as the cornerstone" would go a long way to curing most social ills in western societies.

This certainly warrants further investigation, and so I interviewed a number of Chinese about their daily life under the umbrella of filial piety, with the hope that the benefit of their experience could be passed on to the western reading audience.

Miss Meng's account (Chinese women may retain the use of their maiden name after marriage) was in line with similar stories I had read in a variety of western publications. She had graduated from a local college, and married a promising classmate, Mr. Shen. After the birth of their first child, Miss Meng had planned to go overseas and continue studies for an advanced degree, since she felt that in the long run this would considerably improve her employment future. Her husband encouraged this, and they had saved nearly enough money to turn this dream into a reality. Unexpectedly, her husband was killed in an automobile accident. Although her husband's father had died some years before, there was now no one to support his elderly mother, who was nearly deaf, and clearly this responsibility fell on Miss Meng's shoulders. Forgetting her plans for overseas studies, she devoted herself to taking care of the mother, and invested her savings in taking her to the best specialists for treatment of her hearing loss. Although she had been told by local doctors at the outset that this would be fruitless, she never gave up hope, and visited a wide variety of western and Chinese hospitals, clinics, and private hearing specialists, as well as several miracle-workers. In fifteen years of treatment, the mother's hearing never showed the slightest improvement. In later years, the mother developed other physical ailments, and had to be confined to her bed. Miss Meng attended to all her needs, in addition to the responsibilities involved with raising her own child, and working in the local community, and never uttered a word of complaint. Although there had been several other suitors, the mother (of her deceased husband) objected to a remarriage, and so she remained single.

This story has the typical characteristics of the youth who sacrificed his/her own plans to tend to an ailing elderly parent, and devoted considerable time, energy, and financial resources to making their remaining years pass more smoothly. The spirit of self-sacrifice is, on the most basic level, worthy of praise, although it is perhaps unlikely that a western woman would have handled this entire situation in exactly this way. Certain gaps in this story are worthy of investigation, for example the husband's family situation (brothers and sisters) was not detailed. The reader is lead to believe he was an only-child; this could be a false impression. If he indeed had some brothers and sisters, the assumption of all responsibility for care of the aged mother by his wife would perhaps strike the westerner as considerably less "ordinary" or "reasonable". However, these details are omitted and we may ignore them for the time being. In fact, if we would like to polish this story for the western audience, the mention of Miss Meng's overseas study plans may perhaps be edited out, thus deepening the sense of mother-daughter bond, and removing the hint that the daughter has other personal, and to some degree "important", concerns. This will move the western reader to feel that the entire incident is even more worthy of praise. To rephrase the Bible in line with the Chinese view of morality: Blessed are those who respect and obey their parents, for theirs is the path of righteousness.

Miss Su's recollection, or description, was also highly interesting, but I must admit that it left me rather puzzled. Perhaps the reader will be able to catch the glimmer of "blessedness" or "sacredness" in it which has escaped my untrained eye.

Miss Su's story begins in 1967 when she was 23 and married a Chinese gentleman, Mr. Ho, in Kaohsiung County. In order to take care of the paternal parents, she and her husband moved into his parents' home as is the Chinese custom. In 1971 it was discovered that Mr. Ho's mother (Old Mrs. Ho, in the friendly style of Chinese appellation) had tuberculosis. In order to show respect to the mother, in addition to doing all the regular cooking, Miss Su prepared especially nutritious dishes for her, as well as keeping the house clean and neat, and doing all the other chores. Since there were two young grandchildren in the house at this time, she mentioned to Old Mrs. Ho that she thought it most suitable to buy a separate set of chinaware and utensils for her separate and exclusive use. However Old Mrs. Ho was not accustomed to this and objected to it, saying that she wanted to use the same chinaware and utensils as everyone else. Miss Su conferred with the doctor at the hospital, and he recommended in the strongest terms that Old Mrs. Ho be given separate chinaware and utensils.

However, Old Mrs. Ho said that she would not allow it, and so Miss Su conferred with her husband. He said that of course he and his wife must follow his mother's instructions with strict obedience, in keeping with filial piety. Miss Su refused to have her children eating out of the same chinaware as Old Mrs. Ho, and so bought separate chinaware and utensils for herself and the children. This made Old Mrs. Ho extremely angry, and she accused Miss Su of being unfilial, and this was seconded by her husband and Old Mr. Ho as well. Her husband had two sisters and a brother who often came to their house to visit, and when they learned how Miss Su had gone directly against old Mrs. Ho's instructions they also accused her of being unfilial, and hence of acting immorally.

Miss Su took Old Mrs. Ho to see another specialist in a large hospital in a nearby Chinese city. He confirmed the TB diagnosis, and recommended that if everyone in the family dined together it would be best for Old Mrs. Ho to be assigned separate chinaware

## Tuberculosis

Tuberculosis is one of the world's oldest diseases, and tuberculous mummies have been found in ancient Egyptian archaeological digs. Hippocrates wrote extensively on the disease in the 5th century B.C. In the west the common lay term for this disease has traditionally been *consumption*.

Tuberculosis may affect the skin, lungs, spine, neck, heart, joints, and other areas. The contagiousness of the disease was established in the late 19th century by Jean Antoine Villemin (1827-1892), a French army surgeon. Villemin proved that the disease could be induced in humans if they swallowed or inhaled discharges from tuberculous patients. Twentieth century research on tubercle bacilli has shown them to be extremely hardy. They are able to survive when dry for over 360 days in the dark, or in moist sputum for over 45 days. Many common disinfectants are useless against them. Although boiling for two minutes is highly effective, incineration is the best means of destroying the bacilli.

There is no quick cure for tuberculosis. The length of time spent at bed rest, the use and timing of drugs or surgery, and the speed of rehabilitation therapy must be gauged from the improvement in symptoms, as indicated by an examination of X-rays, sputum, and the actual cavity closure. Many patients live for decades after being diagnosed with the disease. Robert Louis Stevenson (1850-1894) had been afflicted with tuberculosis for many years when he wrote **Dr. Jekyll and Mr. Hyde** in 1886. He later retired to live out the rest of his years in Western Samoa.

and utensils, which should be washed separately. Miss Su went to purchase a separate set of high quality chinaware and utensils for the elderly mother to use, but this made her even more upset. Since the Ho family had lived in this area for many generations, they were familiar with most of the neighboring families in the district. When word of Miss Su's disobedience to her Mother-in-law's wishes gradually reached them they became very incensed, and everyone in the community talked of the fact that she was unfilial. Her bad character was indeed the talk of the town.

Old Mr. Ho wanted to show Miss Su that there was nothing to fear from his elderly wife, and so would frequently share a drinking glass with her, to spite Miss Su. He commented that he lived, slept, and ate together with old Mrs. Ho and his health was fine, therefore there was no reason to have separate chinaware or utensils among family members. Medical checkups in 1972 and 1973 confirmed that old Mr. Ho was healthy, however he contracted tuberculosis "mysteriously" and died in 1975.

Miss Su asked her husband if now it would be best to have Old Mrs. Ho use separate chinaware, but since she was firmly against it, the son said this was not possible. Miss Su continued to have her children use separate chinaware and utensils and this was a point of constant irritation with Old Mrs. Ho. In order to combat the disease the doctor had recommended a diet high in nutrition, and Miss Su did her best to purchase and prepare the most nutritous meals she could, even to the point of borrowing money from friends.

The elderly mother was required to take regular injections to combat her disease, and Miss Su often administered the injection. In the dosage now required the doctor had noted that there would be a side-effect of several hours of numbness in the limbs, but old Mrs. Ho believed that this was caused by Miss Su's purchase of inferior medicine, or the addition of some special poisonous additive, with the intent to put her in her grave. Miss Su continued to suggest that the elderly mother be assigned her own chinaware, against the old mother's wishes. This was enough for the neighbors and her husbands' relatives to all accuse her of being unfilial in the strongest terms, and they now had the additional testimony of old Mrs. Ho that she was placing poison in the injections to add to their accusations and increase the weight of their charge that Miss Su was unfilial. Therefore they took every opportunity to heap curses upon her.

Naturally Miss Su cried herself to sleep many nights wondering how she would ever make amends to her husband's family. After long deliberation, she decided that her best recourse was to redouble her efforts to win their praise and respect, and so she went to her daily duties and household chores with renewed vigor. One day she had just returned from the junior high school where she taught, and had begun cooking dinner. She was quite tired and had not eaten anything since lunch, and had just strapped the youngest two-year-old child to her back as she went about her kitchen duties. As she took more and more dishes to the table, she became aware that her husband and his father, both of whom liked to paint, (although the elderly mother did not), were having an argument about the definition of what a true artist was. After taking in one dish which she had just prepared, she was stopped by Old Mrs. Ho. As has been mentioned, Old Mrs. Ho had never had an inclination to paint, however the elderly mother asked her: "Is your husband an artist or am I?" Miss Su said: "I don't know." Mrs. Ho replied that that answer was totally unacceptable. Miss Su then said: "Your surname is Ho, my surname is Su. I cannot make a determination on some matter in the Ho household between you and your son." She then returned to the kitchen.

Upon returning to the table, Miss Su found that her husband and his parents were all very upset at the unfilial manner in which she had replied to Old Mrs. Ho's question. The next day Old Mrs. Ho carried a large piece of charcoal into the kitchen where Miss Su was working and "accidently" dropped it on Miss Su's foot. The neighbors learned of this incident and said that this was mild punishment indeed for the unfilial behavior which this daughter-in-law in the Ho household had shown. (Presumably a public flogging would have been much more acceptable.)

For some "unexplained" reason that Miss Su did not elaborate upon, her husband moved to Japan in 1982 to devote more time to art research. Old Mrs. Ho has moved in with the second eldest son who lives in another community. Miss Su has rented an apartment in another Chinese city (some six hours by train train from their original home) and works for an advertising agency.

In summary we can see that Miss Su was the cause of much disharmony in the Ho household, all of which could have been avoided if she had upheld the premier virtue of filial piety and treated her mother-in-law with the strictest obedience and respect.

As a concluding remark, the reader may allow us to consider that Miss Meng's situa-

## How to Be a Good Lamb

A Chinese elementary school teacher told the story of a group of sheep which lived a happy life in the countryside. Every morning they were taken out to pasture by their master, and in the afternoons many of the young lambs would play on the sunny hillside. One day one of the young lambs wandered far away from the group, and was eaten by a wolf. "The moral[a] of the story is," the teacher said, "that you should stay with the flock."

One of the students raised his hand. "But teacher," he said, "if the lamb stays with the flock, he will be eaten by the man."

The teacher quickly changed the subject.

*Conclusion of the Group Mentality:* If all the members of the flock meet the same fate, it is right that you meet that fate too. Don't question it.

---

tion, or some similar such situation (which may be gleaned from the pages of magazines and newspapers), is worthy of praise, and that perhaps Miss Su's situation, or some similar situation (which no doubt will have to be collected from the mouths of the affected individuals, since the magazines and newspapers will want to avoid mentioning it) is worthy of criticism. Clearly this represents another PC Paradox. The attitude/behavior that is being praised in the former example is exactly the attitude/behavior being criticized in the latter.

## Ethical Reasoning

As a social doctrine which came to prominence in a society of subsistence agriculture, where Social Security, Medicare, retirement pensions, or other types of retirement benefits were unknown, Filial Piety has a basic level of coherent rationale in dictating that the children must provide for the economic support of elderly and/or medically infirm parents, and that consideration of the parents should come first.

Several examples from the *Filial Piety Classic*[b] will illustrate how this doctrine was applied in traditional Chinese society.

**Example A:** One young Chinese boy was visiting a friend, and was treated to eat oranges. As he was leaving, two oranges which he had stolen from the platter rolled out of his sleeve. He told his host "My mother loves oranges very much, and I wanted them for her." Pick one alternative:

The host 1) scolded the boy for his stealing and concealment, and the excuse-making which he offered to cover it up

---

a. 教訓、寓意
b. 孝經

2) commended the boy for his care and concern for his mother

3) praised the boy for his devotion to his mother, but criticized the dishonest way in which he went about getting oranges for her

Chinese answer: #2. In addition, the host gave the youth a large bag of oranges, to reward him for his filial conduct.

***Example B:*** One middle aged husband lived with his wife and his old mother. They were very poor. A baby was born but there was not food enough for it to eat. The husband and wife 1) Applied with the local government for a loan so that they could buy extra food to more properly feed the old mother

2) Decided to bury the son alive so that the food now available would be adequate to maintain his mother's food rations, with some small portion left over for him and his wife

3) Tightened their belts so the existing quantity of food would serve to feed all four

Chinese answer: #2. When the father was digging the grave, he found a pot of gold. This was heaven's reward for his filial conduct.

***Example C:*** One famous scholar loved his mother very much and was always beside her when there was a thunderstorm, in order to reassure her. His mother passed away. At this point he 1) became an itinerant preacher, to inform other old people that thunder is nothing to fear

2) Went to his mother's tomb during thunderstorms, in order to continue to reassure her

3) Began to fly kites during thunderstorms and undertake meterological investigations, predating Benjamin Franklin's experiments by 1500 years

Chinese answer: #2. His students were greatly touched by his filial devotion and applied themselves with renewed vigor to their lessons.

These types of situations may occasionally come up in the present age, and the foreigner will benefit greatly by knowing how to view them "correctly". Other situations from the present era involving monetary arrangements are also illustrative of some peculiarities of Chinese thinking.

***Example D:*** Let us consider the case of a family of nine children, where only one is a boy. We will want to look at how the responsibility for the economic support of the elderly parents should be arranged. Obviously a discussion of this issue must take into account the differing financial statuses of these nine children, however a useful point of reference is obtained by considering the question they may ask themselves: "In talking of how we shall share in the support of our parents, where is the correct starting point for our discussion?"

View 1 : For the people who see relationships as being based on equality, the reasonable starting point would most likely be: "Each child should pay 1/9th of the necessary expenses." Discussion would proceed from this preface, and some of the children (who are now perhaps adults in their own right, married and with children of their own), might try to point out that due to the particular circumstances in their present life with their own spouse and children, they are financially strapped at this moment, and are unable to contribute a full 1/9th. Each case would of course have to be considered on its own merits.

View 2: Due to the fact that many researchers now believe that women are the superior sex, and are much more capable than men in most areas, we suppose that some well-meaning individuals might say that a reasonable starting point would be: "The daughters should pay for all of the necessary expenses." The son would be entitled to act purely voluntarily, with the option of contributing some funds if and when he chose to do so, but the major responsibility would be between the daughters, who would sort it out among themselves as best they saw fit. The reasoning behind this arrangement could be that "It is the natural extension of women's liberation and recognition of women's superiority in the human race."

View 3 : Some other families might see the situation differently. They might consider a reasonable starting point to be: "The son should pay for all of the necessary expenses." When asked to explain this point of view, the other eight children could say: "Men have always been in the leading position in the typical kinship and family structure." Discussion in this situation would proceed from this premise of the son's overwhelming duty, and some substantial evidence would have to be produced to convince the other female children that they should contribute anything to their parents economic support in old age.

Thus we see that even when we are presented with the doctrine that **the children should provide for the support of elderly parents** as a given, the actual application of this doctrine is often not as straightforward as a westerner would tend to assume on first impressions. Three possible scenarios for producing the necessary funds have been outlined here, one supposes that other scenarios are possible. At first glance, we would say that View 1 would be considered reasonable by the average westerner. However the Chinese interpretation of the demands of Filial Piety often corresponds rather closely to that expressed in View 3, meaning that the male descendants bear the major burden for this support. The female descendants are seen as belonging to the family into which they marry, and the bulk of any income they can produce most properly goes to the support of their husband's family. Traditionally, daughters were generally excluded from receiving any inheritance, (the traditional rationale is "Daughters offer sacrifices for another family's ancestors"), and this further served to cut off any continuing financial relations between them and their parents after they had married. In the present era, the laws have often been changed, so that daughters may receive inheritance on an equal status with sons, however many traditional families balk at this legal stipulation, and demand that the daughter "sign away" her rights as a matter of course. Some westerners view "blood relation" more important than any of these other considerations, and feel that an equal distribution of parental financial support responsibilities is the only *fair* solution. This appears in direct opposition to the traditional Chinese view.

Considering another situation however, we can see a further clarification of Filial Piety.

**Example E:** Let us examine the case of a family of six children, where there are three boys and three girls. From the above example, one could suppose that three starting points for discussion of parental support could be outlined.

View 1 : the children all share in the support, with each paying 1/6th.

View 2: the girls share in the support, with each paying 1/3rd.

View 3: the boys share in the support, with each paying 1/3rd.

Another view could also be added

View 4: the eldest son accepts the full responsibility for support.

In this case, a westerner might say: "I vote for View 1, and I suppose that the Chinese will opt for View 3." In fact, the Chinese interpretation of the demands of Filial Piety many times is closer to View 4. Upon reflection we see that this in no way contradicts the result in Example D, but rather serves to clarify it.

What does this mean to the foreigner? Obviously, in terms of a foreign woman marrying a Chinese man, it would be helpful to have some basic grasp of these concepts, so that the income and outflow of money in family budgeting could be planned in a "realistic" manner. But other points are still of useful reference to all foreigners.

First, it is generally accepted practice in most Chinese homes that most of the money which unmarried children earn doing any sort of work in the community belongs to the parents. During the time the children are growing up, there is no gradual attempt to make a "separation of accounts" between children and the mother/father, or to establish the child's "financial independence" as is common in many western homes.

Second, when the children reach maturity (which is generally defined in terms of "getting married"), the mutual helpfulness implied in these arrangements is all the more apparent. The rule seems to be: "If you have, you should give." If the grown mature children do not have money, and the parents are well off, the parents will often give them money for many purchases that they care to make. Of course in the other situation, where the parents have no money, and the children have become successful financially, the parents expect to be given the same treatment, which means they could expect to be given any and all money just for the asking, and it is the children's duty to provide it. Perhaps we can say that there is some basic equality here.

Yet this often presents some perceptual problems for the westerner, who was raised in an environment where "financial independence" was the accepted norm. As a child, he was given many things, but as he grew up he was increasingly told: "If you want it you will have to earn it" or "You can buy whatever you can afford", but also with the additional stipulation that such purchases should be approved by the parents. In this way some sense of financial responsibility was also taught, and the child was given the message that plans for unwise expenditures could be vetoed. When the western child reached maturity, or perhaps before, he was told by the parents: "You may spend your money the way you see fit, but if you spend my money you will spend it the way I see fit."

For the westerner (man or woman) who marries into a Chinese household, if the parents are wealthy and expect no financial contribution from the children after retirement, that is one situation. If they are depending on the children for a great deal of financial support in those years, that is another situation entirely. One doubts that the Chinese child (or the foreign spouse) would be able to attach any sort of stipulations to money which was given to them. Of course, the Chinese parents' proposed usage for funds could vary from buying meat and vegetables, going to see the doctor, or selecting some new clothes, all the way to investing a substantial sum in the local lottery, going to see a fortune teller, or purchasing an expensive good-luck symbol to put over the door. All of these expenditures could be viewed as equally valid.

The story is told of a young Chinese lady, Shu-ling, who married into a family surnamed Ding. She and her husband, Ting-tong, worked in different companies, and over the years she rose to a position of authority in her firm, and earned more money than her husband. Caring only for their happy life together, she saved enough to make the downpayment on a new house, and was able to arrange some good financing terms. After it was decorated according to her preference, she, her husband, and daughter moved in. Somewhat unexpectedly, the husband's two brothers and a sister came from the countryside and moved in a month later, and began to seek work in the local community. The husband's aged parents came from the countryside to move in with everybody about two months after that. Old Mrs. Ding decided to redecorate the apartment and called in workmen to do the job, against Shu-ling's wishes. When it was finished she gave the bill to Shu-ling, and told her to pay it. Ting-tong agreed that this appeared fair, reasonable, and proper under the circumstances.

## The Chens and the Wus

Of all the more detailed stories related to the doctrine of filial piety which we have collected, the relationships between the Chens and the Wus are the most illustrative of the complexity of the doctrine in practice, and the unusual results which may be obtained by its continuing firm application generation by generation, decade by decade.

We must first briefly describe the members of three generations of each household as they stand in the mid-1980's. A "<D>" indicates that the person is deceased at the time of this writing, a "<D>s" indicates that they committed suicide.

We will use increased levels of indentation to represent different generations of family members, and adopt the shorthand of a "/f" after a name to represent "female", while "/m" represents "male". Spouses are listed together, only unmarried children are listed separately. An arrow in either direction indicates that this person "married into" the family of that person, hence the children take the surname of the party to which the arrow points. Dots in the arrow shaft indicate different generations. The arrow containing one dot is the oldest marriage on the chart. The arrows containing two dots are the marriages of this person's children, and three dots the marriages of their children, etc. Further arrows for one man may indicate polygamous marriages, or another marriage after the death of the earlier spouse. Notice that it is not always the case that the woman marries into the household of the man, even in the patrilineal Chinese society.

All children are naturally born unless otherwise noted: an "(a)" indicates a formal adoption, registered with the local authorities, a "(u)" indicates a traditional adoption, which was unregistered in any legal form. The age of the eldest living child in each generation is given in parenthesis.

The point of connection (marriage) between the two clans is indicated by "+++++", and the result of this union is at the end of section 2.

A "*" on any line followed by a dash and a number indicates the number of children, or additional children, which are not specifically listed by name. An additional dash and a number indicates further generations. Hence "*-3-7" indicates three children not listed specifically, and a total of seven grandchildren born of these three.

Where the same person appears on the same chart in different positions, a line is drawn, and a "&" is indicated.

Note on Chinese names: In conforming to the Group Mentality, the family is more important than the individual. Hence, the last name is given first, as per the Chinese custom. In the charts a comma separates the last and first names, however in the written descriptions the comma is dropped. Since Chinese women retain their maiden names after marriage, the term "Ms." has been employed frequently.

## Section 1

The Chen's clan has over 400 people living at present, (including all people who have "married in"), yet this number only includes descendants of the brothers of the great-grandfather: Chen Bing-jwang. (The descendants of all his brothers are not shown however, only Chen Bing-jwang's own line.) Relations through blood ties of ancestors previous to the great-grandfather are not now commonly in contact, nor do they consult on each other's affairs.

Diagram 7-1

**Chen, Bing-jwang/m <D>**   <--.-   **Lin, Ah-mei/f <D>**

    Chen, Ping-jing/m (78)      <--..-   Tsai. Mu-ling/f
        Chen, Ting-ju/f (58)      -...-->   Chang, Tsung-deh/m
        *-3-4
        Chen, Ting-ming/m      <--...-   Dai, Mei-yung/f
        *-4-5
    Chen, Bing-wen/m      <--..-   Jwang, Mi-tao/f
     *-2-5
    Chen, Rung-hwei/f      -..-->   Cheng, Jwang-jian/m
     *-3-8
    Chen, Hsing-tsa/m      <--..-   Liu, Hong-dong/f
        Chen, Chwan-heng/m<D>   <--...-   Wu, Shwang/f<D> +++++
          (see below)
     *-8-27
    Chen, Ping-kwei/m      <--..-   Chang, Shiou-ling/f
     *-4-6
    Chen, Ping-fu/m      <--..-   Yang, Mei-li/f
     *-3-7

Explanation of the Chen clan diagram: The first generation of our diagram is Chen Bing-jwang, who came from a large family of many brothers and sisters (not shown).

Chen Bing-jwang had six children. His fourth child had nine children; Chen Chwan-heng, and eight others. Chen Chwan-heng married Ms. Wu Shwang of the Wu family.

## Section 2

The Wu's clan has a comparatively small number of members, totalling less than 50 at present, primarily because the great-grandfather disowned his own son when the son married a woman of whom he did not approve. The son and his wife then moved away, and lost all contact with other members of the Wu clan. Their marriage only produced one child, with the following generation producing only two children.

Diagram 7-2

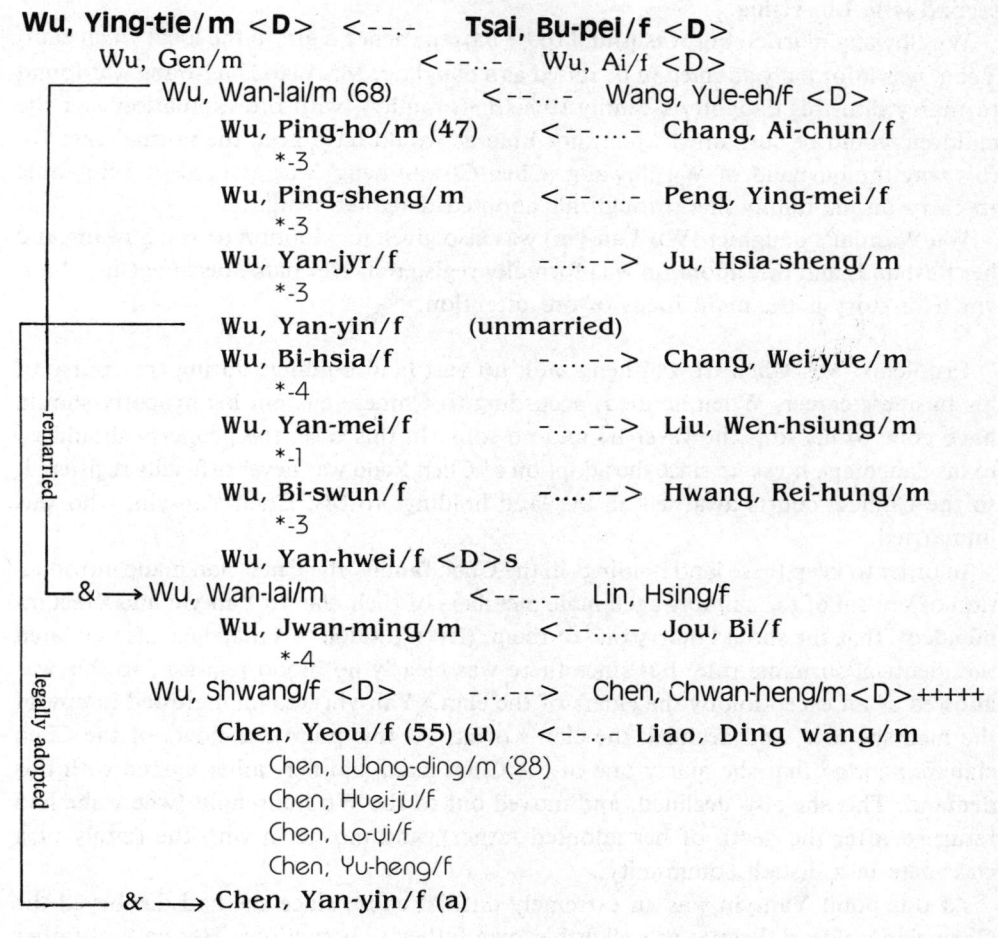

```
Wu, Ying-tie/m <D>      <--.-     Tsai, Bu-pei/f <D>
     Wu, Gen/m                 <--..-   Wu, Ai/f <D>
   ┌──── Wu, Wan-lai/m (68)       <--...-   Wang, Yue-eh/f <D>
   │          Wu, Ping-ho/m (47)    <--....-  Chang, Ai-chun/f
   │              *-3
   │          Wu, Ping-sheng/m      <--....-  Peng, Ying-mei/f
   │              *-3
   │          Wu, Yan-jyr/f         -....-->  Ju, Hsia-sheng/m
   │              *-3
   │          Wu, Yan-yin/f      (unmarried)
   │          Wu, Bi-hsia/f         -....-->  Chang, Wei-yue/m
   │              *-4
   │          Wu, Yan-mei/f         -....-->  Liu, Wen-hsiung/m
   │              *-1
   │          Wu, Bi-swun/f         -....-->  Hwang, Rei-hung/m
   │              *-3
   │          Wu, Yan-hwei/f <D>s
 ─┤&─→ Wu, Wan-lai/m             <--...-   Lin, Hsing/f
re │          Wu, Jwan-ming/m       <--....-  Jou, Bi/f
ma │              *-4
rr │          Wu, Shwang/f <D>      -...-->   Chen, Chwan-heng/m <D>+++++
ie │            Chen, Yeou/f (55) (u)  <--..-  Liao, Ding wang/m
d  │              Chen, Wang-ding/m (28)
   │              Chen, Huei-ju/f
le │              Chen, Lo-yi/f
ga │              Chen, Yu-heng/f
ll │
y  │
ad │
op │
te │
d  └─── & ─→ Chen, Yan-yin/f (a)
```

Explanation of the Wu clan diagram: Wu Ying-tie had many children, however his child Wu Gen wanted to marry another girl of the Wu family surname, traditionally forbidden by Chinese custom due to the assumed close blood relation. When Wu Ying-tie opposed this and Wu Gen insisted, the latter was disowned. He moved away and cut off all contacts with the Wu clan.

Wu Gen and his wife had two children, Wu Wan-lai and Wu Shwang.

Wu Wan-lai had eight children by his first wife Wang Yue-eh and one more by his second wife Lin Hsing.

Wu Shwang married but was found to be barren, hence a girl in the local Chen clan, Yeou, was informally adopted to be raised as a daughter. Mr. Liao Ding-wang was found to marry into this daughter's family (the Chen family), with the stipulation that the children would be surnamed Chen, not Liao as would have been the normal case. In this way the husband of Wu Shwang (Chen Chwan-heng) was assured of being able to carry on his family line through his adopted daughter's children.

Wu Wan-lai's daughter (Wu Yan-yin) was also given in adoption to Wu Shwang and her husband, and this adoption was formally registered. Her name became Chen Yan-yin. Her story is the main focus of our attention.

Problems: Mr. Chen Chwan-heng built up vast land holdings during the course of his business career. When he died, according to Chinese custom his property should have gone to his sons, however he had no sons. In this case, the property should go to his daughters, however since the adoption of Chen Yeou was never officially registered, so the Chinese courts awarded all the land holdings to Ms. Chen Yan-yin, who was unmarried.

In order to keep these land holdings in the Chen family, the Chen clan made introduction of several of the suitably aged male members of their clan to Yan-yin and "recommended" that she should marry one of them. (Even though this marriage also violated the identical surname rule, but since there was clearly no blood relation, so this was allowed as an exception by the elders of the clan.) Yan-yin was uninterested in any of the men she met, and declined the clan's offer. At this point the elders of the Chen clan *demanded* that she marry one of the Chen men, and her father agreed with this demand. This she also declined, and moved out of the Wu household (where she had returned after the death of her adopted father), and moved in with the family of a classmate in a distant community.

At this point Yan-yin was an extremely unfilial child, since she had disobeyed the Chen clan's elders' dictates as well as her own father's instructions. Her natural father Mr. Wu found out where she was living and sent some men to kidnap her, and bring her home, where she was severely beaten. She managed to escape, and through the help of some friends she left the country to study overseas.

Returning to China some five years later, Yan-yin decided to start a business. Several court notices were waiting for her, since she had not paid any taxes on any of her land holdings in five years. She retrieved her land ownership deeds from the safety deposit box where they had been stored, and began to make discreet inquiries about the status of her land and the structures thereon. As she had expected, various members of the Chen clan were living on the land and not paying taxes, although they apparently were paying water, gas, and electricity bills. When she passed word on to them through some intermediaries that they would have to pay rent, the elders of the Chen clan said that "Since the land is ours, we do not have to pay rent to anyone."

Yan-yin considered putting the land up for auction, however the members of the Chen clan made it very clear that if she did so, in direct violation of the instructions of the Chen elders and her own father, this unfilial behavior would be severly punished. In addition they said that they would send a number of people to the university where she had obtained a teaching position and cause enough disharmony in the campus and among the administrators to cast serious doubt on her suitability for teaching, and certainly result in her being fired.

She had no doubt that they were serious in their threats. An effective procedure in this situation is then to take out a loan from a bank using the land deeds as collateral, and then default on the loan, whereupon the bank auctions off the land, and the original owner can claim "circumstances beyond my control" when the clan members send people over to get even.

However, due to the large number of disputed land holdings which accumulate in Chinese society when private ownership of land is allowed, most banks are wary of this ploy, and have methods of checking out the suitability of land deeds as collateral for loans. Hence they do not accept land on which there is clear legal title but disputed private ownership.

At this point one of Yan-yin's foreign friends suggested that she go to court to have her title to the land holdings cleared once and for all. This was the most naive suggestion that she had heard in a long time, however she replied: "That is not the problem, since legally the land holdings are all mine. The problem is that the present-day Chinese law is based on western standards of fairness, since all of the early legal experts after the founding of the Republic in 1912 were educated overseas, primarily in England, America, and Europe.However there are many areas where the legal determination is at a variance with the traditional Chinese custom and moral standard, hence there are many points on which the Chinese populace does not accept the law, and they are willing to back up their non-acceptance with force. I cannot fight them all."

After further consideration, Yan-yin was able to locate one medium sized parcel of land which one family of Chen squatters expressed interest in buying, although at 1/5 the market price. Since they were already living there, she signed the deed over to them and they gave her that amount of money. Although the other clan members expressed some verbal anger at Yan-yin's "gouging" of the relatives in this manner (since the other clan members felt she had no moral right to the land holdings anyway), there were no serious repercussions.

Asked about her plans for the future, Yan-yin said that she will put the land deeds back in her safety deposit box for the time being. Eventually the Chinese courts will seize the land for failure to pay back-taxes, and offer it to the public at the official valuation of so much per hectare, with the current squatters given first option to buy. At that point her ownership deeds will be cancelled and the entire issue will be out of her hands.

Several items are of particular interest in this entire flow of events.

1) An interesting aspect of the legal/moral gap existing in Chinese society is illustrated. Further research was done with Chinese lawyers about the particular considerations raised by the discussion of the Chens and the Wus, and this question was posed: "Why didn't the early Chinese legal experts (post 1912) draft their laws in accordance with traditional Chinese thinking and customs?" The answer received was: "Because the early legal experts were educated in the west, and were taught objective standards of fairness. They brought those concepts back to China. The traditional Chinese customs . . . are inequitable in many areas, especially when viewed in modern terms."

Another question was raised: "The Chinese government actively promotes rule-by-law and filial piety. When the two concepts come in conflict, where is the citizenry supposed to go for resolution?" The only answer received to this was generally a shrug of the shoulders, however one Chinese government official remarked: "The citizenry is free to resolve the matter any way it sees fit."

2) The Chinese genealogy places extreme stress on "name lines", with the specification that the surname must be carried-on through male children. This is a very aristocratic idea, and in the west it is existent today only in the most highly placed aristocratic families. The average westerners follow a genealogy based on "blood lines", hence boys and girls are considered to have the same weight or status. In the west the stress on having male heirs often seems to more pronounced in families of advanced wealth and prominence, however this is changing, and more families are fully adopting the middle class values of equality.

However it is also true that many westerners do not pay much attention to genealogies at all. Hence they do not regard the absence of children, grandchildren, etc. as particularly serious, and the husband and wife team are free to organize their life in any way they see fit, with or without consideration of the lack of progeny.

3) The lack of male heirs in the Chinese family is generally considered disastrous. As an example, we could consider the situation where a foreign man married a Chinese woman who had no brothers. In this case it would be common for the girl's father to ask, or *demand,* that the first (or second) male child be given his (i.e., the child's grandfather's) surname. This enables the "name line" to be carried-on, a very important consideration in a land of ancestor worshippers. Mencius said: "There are three unfilial acts, the most serious of which is to be without descendants." Without a descendant, it is believed that the ancestors will become unworshipped ghosts. For the foreigner who

objects to any of this, problems may be encountered.

Although for a child to take its mother's surname is not uncommon in Sweden, this practice seems largely unknown in most western countries, outside of occasional instances in the entertainment industry.

4) In the *Analects* of Confucius it is stressed that thoroughgoingness about the funeral rites for parents and the worship of ancestors will raise and strengthen the moral fiber of the people. Various scholars have treated the lines differently: "By cultivating respect for the dead and carrying the memory back to the distant past, the moral feeling of the people will awaken and grow in depth", "If there is careful attention to burial rites, if the offerings are made to the dead, the people, I promise you, will turn fully to Excellence" are two translations of the same Chinese phrases: Chapter 1, verse 9.

In the above example, Yan-yin was adopted by Mr. Chen Chwan-heng and Ms. Wu Shwang. After her adopted father died, she was very intermittent in visiting his grave and burning incense, in addition to the more than five year period when she lived overseas and made no visits to his grave to offer periodic sacrifices, especially on the anniversaries of his death, Tomb Sweeping Day, and other important dates. This has shown her to be a most unfilial child, hence she has acted immorally.

For a foreigner who married a Chinese who was lax in his/her worship of ancestors, this could no doubt be represented on a Spectra Chart for Morality as a point in the area of an intersection of E- and Bo: the Entry Culture views this behavior as immoral, the Background Culture views this activity as unrelated to morality. In any event, it could be expected that discussions on the entire issue of morality with traditionally-minded parents of the Chinese spouse might be unpleasant. (Spectra Charts are discussed in Chapter 12.)

We note that the geographical demands of ancestor worship, such as visiting the actual grave site and offering sacrifices in front of the ancestral tablet, are greatly facilitated in a Pre-Industrial Revolution agricultural society. In such a society it is unlikely that people will venture very far from the locality of their births during their entire lives. In an age of highly-developed global transportation systems, where children may live in highly distant areas, the close geographical demands of such worship are often difficult to meet, and much disharmony is likely to be generated as a result.

5) The only brother of Ms. Wu Shwang, Mr. Wu Wan-lai, has clearly lost considerable face in the eyes of the Chen clan. His sister married into this clan, and had no male heirs. His daughter, Yan-yin, who was officially given in adoption to this sister, has proved to be a most unfilial child, since she disobeyed fatherly instructions and clan instructions many times, and caused much dismay for everyone. All of this leads to the suspicion that the Wu clan has bad-blood or is otherwise "faulty".

Confucius stressed that obedience to parents was the basis of all morality. It is not surprising that Yan-yin has many welts and scars on her body as evidence of the beatings she has received from the hands of her father. Certainly she has brought this punishment upon herself for her unfilial behavior, and her natural father should be commended for his efforts in bringing her back to the straight and narrow path, even though he has failed.

## Basic Ethical Doctrines

A large number of books and anthologies on Ethical Theory have been offered to the public in the English speaking world since the publication in 1903 of Moore's *Principia Ethica*.[1] These books have attempted to provide some account of the theoretical controversies which have developed since that time, and to reanalyze and reclarify the basic philosophical underpinnings of Ethics itself. From a the point of view of acculturation into Chinese society, to effectively study the many essays contained in these volumes does necessitate some extra effort if one is to ferret out relevant points of communality and difference between the concepts of Ethical Theory in China and the west.

Plato held that in the end the justification of every act lay in its place in the form of the good life. In this regard there remains a strong current in western ethics to search for and define an "objective good", and the consideration that there is no such thing as an objective good seems, therefore, less convincing to most western philosophers than the ancient and honorable prejudice that it does exist. (Note: The word "good" has more than one or two meanings. One dictionary we consulted distinguishes 31 different meanings). By way of comparison, a strong current of Chinese ethics has been the concept of "filial piety", which to the Chinese is the virtue from which it may be said all other virtues flow. This moral parameter may be summed up by the the Chinese expression: "Filial Piety is the most important of all virtues." Yet in in western ethical theory this concept is largely notable by its absence.

An act, to be virtuous, must, as Aristotle saw, be done willingly or with pleasure; as such it is just not done from a sense of obligation but from desire which is intrinsically good, as arising from some intrinsically good emotion. We judge a thing to be intrinsically good if it would be good even if it existed quite alone, without any accompaniments or effects whatever. Within the individual, Aristotle cited the intrinsically good moral virtues as liberality, temperance, justice, courage, friendship, magnanimity, gentleness, and truthfulness. Through these virtues and their pursuit, man arrives at the life of contemplation of truth, which is pronounced as man's highest activity.

In the end we suppose that another person cannot honestly appeal to intuitive apprehensions of *intrinsic good* where all I see is *intrinsic neutrality,* however I can accept the suggestions to consider the alternatives of my lack of action in this regard, and review the entire issue with a view to its implications and connections. We are then faced with the reality that what everyone in a particular society or culture considers an intrinsic

---

1. George Edward Moore (1873–1958), educated at Dulwich College and the University of Cambridge.

good may then perhaps somehow become one by definition.

## Filial Piety and Law

Turning our attention to China, for the purposes of our discussion of filial piety, it is necessary to make a rather broad division of Chinese law into the Dynastic law (pre-1912), and the 20th Century law (post 1912). Certainly much finer divisions can be specified, however this will suit our needs in this section. The major point of difference is that the pre-1912 law was much more a reflection of traditional Chinese customs and values, whereas the post-1912 law was revamped in more modern terms, and has been influenced a great deal by the legal codes of the west, particularly Germany.

According to the law of the Yuan, Ming, and Ching Dynasties, covering a period of years from 1260 to 1912, the rights of parents over children were much broader than they had been in even the Tang and Sung Dynasties, in the pre 1260 era. Typically in these later periods, if a disobedient child was beaten by the parents and died unexpectedly, the parents were not held guilty.

An important Chinese adage which has had influence on thousands of years of Chinese thinking is: "No parents in the world are wrong."[a] Over the ages, children accused of unfilial behavior were subject to punishment in ways which the parents saw fit, and indeed the law favored the father's authority. If a parent asked the death sentence for his offspring, the authorities generally acquiesced, and it was often unnecessary for them to give any consideration to the grounds on which the suit was brought. While the actual decision to condemn to death, to banish, or to spare the child was transferred from the father to the government authorities, the father could instigate a suit and recommend the sentencing. The government in effect merely acted as his agent in carrying out his will. In the Tang and Sung Dynasties, a parent's formal application that a child be given the death sentence since he/she had disobeyed parental instructions, disagreed with his parents on some matter, or had been impolite, was granted as a matter of course. In the Ching Dynasty (1644 to 1912) the severity of the sentencing was more commonly limited to banishment. If the parents changed their mind at some later date, the child could then be granted amnesty upon parental request with the government.

These facts indicate that the Chinese parents historically had almost complete and absolute power over their children, even though in the case of what were felt to be more serious infractions it was necessary to ask the authorities to act as agent in carrying out the punishments. Indeed an examination of Ching Dynasty records reveals that sons were often banished for trivial reasons, such as talking back to a parent, being lazy, or failing to heed advice. When parents asked to have an unfilial child prosecuted, the authorities did not need to demand any evidence, nor did they commonly raise any objections to the punishment asked. The law stated: "When a father or mother prosecutes

---

a. 天下没有不是的父母

a son, the authorities will acquiesce without question or trial."

Filial piety was the most important issue, since this was the premier virtue passed down from the time of Confucius. Right and wrong were a matter of position: I am wrong because I am my father's son. What my father says is right because he is my father. Within a family, seniors and juniors were not treated equally under the law. A child should not disagree or argue with his parents, but should obey and never show resentment.

The authorities were not required to question the adequacy of the reason given by the parents in meting out the punishment specified. For the authorities to question this would have meant that the parents might be wrong, and that the father's absolute authority was not recognized. However, as stated above, Chinese morality stressed that "No parents in the world are wrong."

Property rights of children were also controlled by parents. *The Book of Rites*[a] stipulates that children are not allowed to own any property of their own during their parents' lifetimes. This concept was incorporated into the Chinese law from antiquity, and there were provisions which nullified the sale of any family property by a child while the parents, grandparents, etc. were living, even if these elders were in a remote community, or incapacitated. This prohibition was also extended to the time interval covering the mourning period for death of the parents and/or grandparents as well, and in some localities this mourning period was commonly three years or longer.

For a son or daughter to live apart from the parents and own property of his own was also considered a serious crime, more serious than disposing of parents property while they were still living. Imprisonment and flogging were the most commonly used forms of punishment.

Dynastic law, in correspondence with traditional custom, dictated that a father's authority extended to children's marriages as well, and the choice of a marriage partner was seen as a matter of concern for the parents. The child was not consulted. The main aim of marriage was to produce offspring to carry on ancestor worship, and the goal of uniting two families was of vastly more importance than the wishes of the man and woman involved. *The Book of Rites* states that a son should divorce his wife, even when he is fond of her, if she is dislked by his parents; contrastingly he should treat her as his wife during his lifetime, even when he is not fond of her, but when his parents say, "She serves us well."

Ssu-ma Kwang, who lived in the 11th century, summed up the situation when he said: "All the inferiors and the younger ones must consult the head of the family about every event, large or small. How dare an inferior do anything without asking permission from his parents? You must ask permission from the head of the family, even though he is not your parent, before you do anything; then the orders will come from one person

---

a. 禮記

only, and the family will be in order."

## Filial Piety and Ethics

Traditional law was interested in upholding established social order and status within the family, not with the issue of right and wrong. This was made abundantly clear by scholar Tai Chen in the 18th century, (circa 1760). A quote from his commentary on Mencius is illustrative:

"The superiors reprove the inferiors with reason; elders reprove youngsters with reason; nobles reprove the humble with reason; even though they are wrong they will be considered right. If the inferiors, the younger ones, or the humble defend themselves with reasons, even though they are right they will be considered wrong."

More than one hundred years earlier, an official named Lu Kun stated: "I have seen some officials who punished the guilty party when an elder and a younger man accused each other before the court. They did not know that when a junior accuses a senior, the senior is considered as voluntarily reporting himself to the authority, while the junior should be punished for accusing the elder. When this kind of case occurs, even though the senior is absolutely wrong he should be tolerated and pardoned. Even if he speaks offensively to the official, punishment should not be meted out to him lest others think that the senior was punished because of the junior. This is the very essence of ethical principle."

## Filial Piety and Criminal Punishment

During the Tang Dynasty (618 to 907 A.D.), it frequently happened that when a parent was sentenced to death for some crime, if a child in the family came forth and asked to die with (or in place of) the parent, the sovereign would issue an edict to pardon the parent from the death sentence. The reason given was that this parent had raised a very filial child. In the Ming Dynasty such stories were quite common, and a child asking to be punished in place of a parent almost always resulted in parent's receiving a pardon for the offense committed. Sometimes the child would be imprisoned, or banished (in the parent's place), sometimes not. In many Dynasties the requests by children to offer themselves as substitutes for parent's punishment were made in accordance with a set procedure, and such arrangements were recognized as part of the parents' legal rights.

Some 900 years before this, a scholar of the Han Dynasty, Han Fei-tse,[a] writing in the third century B.C., mentioned two stories typical of his age, and reflecting the tradi-

---

a. 韓非子

tional ethical outlook, with which he had some serious reservations:

"In the state of Chu there was a man named Honest Kung. When his father stole a sheep, he reported the theft to the authorities. But the local magistrate, considering that the man was honest in the service of his sovereign but a villain to his own father, replied, Put him to death!", and the man was accordingly sentenced and executed. Thus we see that a man who is an honest subject of his sovereign may be an infamous son to his father."

"There was a man of Lu who accompanied his sovereign to war. Three times he went into battle, and three times he ran away. When Confucius asked him the reason, he replied, 'I have an aged father and if I should die there would be no one to take care of him.' Confucius, considering the man filial, recommended him and had him promoted to a post in the government. Thus we see that a man who is a filial son to his father may be a traitorous subject to his lord."

### Historical Summary

The words of the *Filial Piety Classic* say: "Among the five punishments, which amount altogether to three thousand articles, no crime is more grave than that of filial impiety." In short, there was a great emphasis on filial impiety in the ancient law, and for more than thirteen hundred years before the close of the Ching Dynasty in 1912, filial impiety was listed as one of the ten unpardonable offences in the introductory chapter of the various codes.

## Historical (Classical) vs. Modern Model

Some further insight may be gained by examining some theoretical models of filial piety. Three sets of parents are involved in each example: A, B, C.

In the **Classical Model**, three different actions are given: actions that the child desires to do. These need not be specifically outlined, since we desire to construct a theoretical model, however an example has been given for each. The parents' opinion is then given for each action, and the situation is considered where the child goes ahead with the action in question, thus completing it. The "status" in regard to filial piety is then defined for the child of each family.

## Comparative Ideals of Obedience

| Parents: | Parents A | Parents B | Parents C |
|---|---|---|---|
| Desired Action: | child desires to do action 1 | child desires to do action 2 | child desires to do action 3 |
| Example: | (child wants to go visit a friend for the day) | (child wants to help neighbors during harvest time) | (child wants to go hunting for wild tiger) |
| Parents' Opinion: | no opinion | approval | disapproval |
| Go Ahead? | yes | yes | yes |
| Status: | undefined | filial | unfilial |

Comment: In the Classical Model, three different actions are examined. In a Pre-Industrial Revolution subsistence agricultural economy, it would be assumed that society as a whole is rather static, and there is much agreement on which acts are approved and which disapproved, with only minor variation. This filial-piety-based value system then has a basic level of acceptability and presents no real problems in this analysis.

In the **Modern Model,** one action is examined. The parents' opinion is given for each child's expressed desire to do this action, and the condition of filial piety is defined for each. Two differing evaluations are offered from the standpoint of logic.

| Parents: | Parents A | Parents B | Parents C |
|---|---|---|---|
| Desired Action: | child desires to do action X | child desires to do action X | child desires to do action X |
| Example: | (child wants to move to another city to work) | (child wants to move to another city to work) | (child wants to move to another city to work) |
| Parents' Opinion: | no opinion | approval | disapproval |
| Go Ahead? | yes | yes | yes |
| Status: | undefined | filial | unfilial |

$$\text{filial} = \text{unfilial}$$
$$F = \sim F$$

Comment: In the Modern Model, one action is examined. In a Post-Industrial Revolution age, it would be assumed that society as a whole is quite dynamic, and there is a greater difference of opinion among the citizenry, and this extends to the consideration of children's acts, as to which ones are approved and which ones are disapproved. This filial-piety-based value system then may have some difficulties in application, especially among those who ask for equal treatment under the law. It appears to lack an objective standard.[1]

Considerations:

1. From the point of view of logic, to say that something is equal to its opposite violates the law of identity: F cannot equal .NOT. F    (This is always true unless empty sets are considered, and the law of identity does not deal with empty sets.) Hence to the westerner who follows Aristotle and does not regard "obedience to parents" as a given ethical tenet of human existence, this value system appears illogical.

2. However, from another point of view, people are apples and oranges and coconuts, and hence cannot be easily compared. The Modern Model claims to be dealing with one instance of filial piety, which we may denote more specifically as F1. Granted it would be illogical to say that F1 equals .NOT. F1. However some theorists would maintain that the result of Parents A's expressed opinion and their child's action is F1, while the result of Parents B's expressed opinion and their child's action is F2, and the result of Parents C's expressed opinion and their child's action is F3.

Subjectively speaking, F1, F2, and F3 are different, and cannot be said to be mutually contradictory.

In order to resolve this issue, let us examine the notion of objectivity in ethics.

## Objectivity

To many people, the language of ethics appears to be as objective as the language of science. Most western ethical thinkers, including theologians, non-theologians (secularists), intuitionists, and naturalists have agreed that ethical statements (such as: X is good, Y is bad) have a genuine claim to objective validity.

However, the Emotive Theory of Ethics, explicitly or by implication, denies this claim to objectivity, and in asserting the "subjectivity" of ethics, maintains that there is no grounds for the dispute of ethical issues. Emotivism is defined as **the theory that ethical sentences express and evoke primarily emotions or attitudes.**

Charles L. Stevenson (1908—1979) is one famous emotivist in the west, and while he and his colleagues qualify their seen "subjectivity" of ethics in various ways, in the end they have insisted that ethical statements cannot be objective in the same way that factual statements are. Various other ethicists in the west have however raised the follow-

---

1. Western thinking tends to first look at Action X (whatever it may be), and try to arrive at some objective criteria for determining whether it is good, bad, or neutral. Having arrived at a conclusion in regard to the action in question, the words and behavior of not only the son or daughter, but also of the parents, elders, etc. may be evaluated. Underlying the western reasoning is also the presumption of equality between people regardless of their relative ages, which the westerner associates with fairness, but this is essentially missing from the Chinese method of evaluating good behavior.

ing questions in regard to the emotivist view: (A) If ethical utterances are neither true nor false, why do we speak of them as such? (B) If logic is inapplicable to them, what are ethical arguments?(C) If ethical utterances are really expressions of emotion or disguised commands, why are they not formulated in the exclamatory or imperative mood?

Carl Wellman (1926–    ) has summed up twelve features of the language of ethics that would suggest that it is, or should be, an objective form of discourse. (1) Ethical utterances can be incompatible with one another. (2) We dispute about ethical issues. (3) Ethical sentences are formulated in the declarative mood. (4) We speak of them as true or false. (5) We ask ethical questions. (6) The individual may wonder if his ethical conviction is mistaken. (7) Some ethical arguments are formally valid. (8) Ethical reasoning is always possible. (9) Ethical reasoning is necessary. (10) We distinguish between relevant and irrelevant considerations in regard to any ethical conclusion. (11) Rational methods of persuasion are to be preferred to sheer propaganda, emotional rhetoric, or dogma. (12) We apply the terms "valid" and "invalid" to ethical arguments.

These various features give the ethical arguments the appearance of objectivity that seems to count heavily against Emotivism. Therefore Wellman summarizes the feelings of many philosophers when he says that ethical statements are capable of being examined as objectively true or false.

## Broad Overviews

### My Application and Autobiorgraphy

My name is Joanna W.H. Liao, I am a twenty-one-year-old girl, the seventh of parents' children. I am still studying in the University, my major is business administration. But my favorite is English. I won love of my teachers and classmates by my aminable deportment and work-harding personality.

When I graduated from First Girl's Senior High School, I decided to study English in the university. I think that everybody needs to choosing good major for living, self-fulfillment, and self-respect. But Father told me that he wanted me select business but not English. My friends say study foreign languages is best for me, but Father beleived that the future of studing BA will be better that studying langauge. My freiends no comment. To be a good daughter, I had to give up studying English.

Last Friday, I saw the poster of this job, I think it is a big task to me. I have been a English tutor for a junior high school boy for about two years. I am working under a lot of pressure because the boy will join the Joint Enterance Examiniation after two years. I'd like to be with a child than a teenager. My uncle wants me to work in his business, but but my goal is to teaching English. Someday I hope is to study childish education in Graduate School.

I really like this job better than being secretary for business and I believe I'll do my best if you gave me this chance.

A fellow we met named Albert J. Rightman gave us this letter, which he had found among the correspondence in a manager's desk at a small academy where he was teaching, since the manager had gone overseas for advanced study, and his desk had been reassigned. Albert said that several months ago he had had trouble understanding the rationale behind the last sentence in the second paragraph, but after one of his recent experiences, he had finally gotten it.

After six months of teaching in that academy he thought he was familiar with most of the typical expressions and reactions of the Chinese elementary school youth to basic English conversational dialogue. After the first day in one new class, in the Fall of 1985, he was asking the students some simple questions as they left. As is the custom with modern Chinese in private academies of this type, all the students were wearing western clothes, and had typical western hairstyles. Albert asked each student: "What is your name?", "Are you a boy or a girl?", and other simple questions, and was mildly, but not overly, surprised when one student in coat & tie, pants, horned-rimmed glasses, and medium length hair replied: "I am a girl." This was an understandable "mistake" so early in the term, so Albert corrected: "I am a boy" and indicated for the child to repeat. The child said: "I am a girl". Albert thought his meaning had not been understood, so he briefly translated the words for "boy" and "girl" into Chinese. The child nodded in seeming comprehension, and then said: "I am a girl."

Albert thought perhaps the child had become dizzy while waiting in line, and so indicated for the Chinese teaching assistant to take over, while he began questioning the next child. The story which came out of the teaching assistant's follow-up to this incident, and later checking by the Chinese personnel in the language academy was most interesting. This child was indeed a girl, although dressed entirely as a boy. The parents said that after giving birth to three girls, the paternal grandmother had wanted this child to be a boy, and during her son's wife's pregnancy had been confident that it would be a boy, announcing this fact to all friends and relatives far and wide. The child was born a girl, but rather than disappoint the husband's mother (and father too, of course), it was decided that it would be announced as a boy, and would always wear boy's clothes in front of the grandparents, although the child wore a standard girl's school uniform to Chinese public school. The parents could not conceive of doing things any other way, since that would cause much pain to the grandmother, be unfilial, and cause a loss of face.

Other parents to whom Albert mentioned this, while admitting that the situation had not come up in their families, nevertheless stated that they could sympathize with the parents' position. When asked what they would do if faced with such circumstances, they shook their heads and said: "There would not be anything you could do," expressing the idea that "morally speaking" the parents were doing what was right. They could not conceive of the fact that the child, being a human being, was entitled to any respect in this situation, or that she had any rights. As a final note to this incident, Albert pointed out that these parents were college educated, the husband was an architect, and the wife taught in a local nursing college, and indeed the majority of the parents sending their children to such academies were from the upper middle class, or even high class socio-economic levels. It would be expected that their attitudes would represent more modern and liberal type thinking among the Chinese people. Albert was of course hesitant to consider what the views of the real dyed-in-the-wool conservatives would be on such matters, but he speculated that among lower socio-economic classes, or in more rural communities, this and related types of incidents might be far from uncommon.

Another situation was related by one of Albert's friends. Having heard somewhere that it was unsafe to drink and drive, a Chinese child who was out with his parents at a party, upon preparing to return home, stated: "Father, you have had too much to drink. You should not drive the car home, it would be better for us to call a taxi." Father insisted he was sober enough to drive, even though he had trouble walking over to the car. A small argument developed. Discussion of this series of events at the time among family members and later among relatives confirmed the verdict that the child was being disrespectful, disobedient, and unfilial. The father in this case had a college degree in Business Administration.

A few weeks later it happened that one of the child's teachers in school mentioned a few basic points of traffic safety. The teacher pointed out briefly that "Drunken driving" was a major concern of most developed nations, and that when the children were old enough to drive, they should always remember the prescription "Do not drive when you have had too much to drink." One of the children asked, "What if it is someone else who has had too much to drink?"

The teacher said, "Then you should remind them that it is dangerous to drive in this condition."

"What if they refused to listen to you?" a student asked.

The teacher replied, "Then you should consider the situation and do what you consider proper and right in the circumstances."

The only values the students had ever been taught for "proper" of course were the Confucian ones of strict obedience to teachers and elders.

Rehashing and Rebashing

We have often had the opportunity to discuss many of the incidents presented in this chapter, including the TB example, the difficulties of the Chens and the Wus, and other cases, with Chinese people living in the present society (we have avoided the phrase "living in the modern era"). In answer to the question: "How can these problems be solved?", invariably we are given the reply that "In the long run, education is the answer. With a more educated and knowledgeable populace, these problems will disappear."

"But what about these specific cases? How are the people involved supposed to settle their difficulties?" we ask.

To this we have never received an answer. Many Chinese state that the Mother in the TB example is being unreasonable, the views of the Chen clan are unreasonable, the drunken father is unreasonable, etc., and that such behavior is not praiseworthy. When pressed with the inquiry "What would you do if you were living in a family and this sort of situation developed in regard to your parents and elders?" The reply we receive is: "There would not be much you could do." In connection with this it is stressed that the Chinese place much value on the tenet of *ni lai shwun shou,*[a] which may be translated as "to accept adversity philosophically", or "to accept adversity without complaint". Another popular Chinese idiom is *wei chu chiou chuan*,[b] which means that we should make great concessions in order to accomodate a situation. Certainly this is in keeping with the goal of maintaining harmony in the family environment.

We are also told that these kinds of situations represent "special cases", "highly unusual cases", etc., however our study group believes that this kind of description or classification misses two important realizations: 1) Can we agree on a method for resolving each case in a rational manner, or are we left to conclude that by definition the younger party in each case has no rights? 2) Must we not consider that any generalized doctrine is only good to the point that it produces acceptable results in specific applications? If a doctrine works in theory and not in practice, then it clearly needs further refinement, or severe limitation of its scope of use.

As regards custom and tradition, just as the writings of Copernicus in the mid 1500's overthrew the Ptolemaic (earth-centered) view of the Universe, which had been accepted as accurate and proper for many millennia, the fact that a doctrine has been viewed as correct for thousands of years does not mean that it is still correct.

Moving back to the statement that "In the long run, education is the answer", we are puzzled. Education may indeed be the answer, but the kind of education which Chinese children now receive continues to be heavily dosed with the classical texts which stress an ethical outlook geared for a Pre Industrial Revolution, Pre Specialization of Sciences, Minimally Human Rights conscious, static society of subsistence agriculture. In what way will further education along these lines serve to solve the types of difficulties outlined in this chapter, all of which have arisen in a Post Industrial Revolution, Post Specialization of Sciences, Highly Human Rights conscious, dynamic world? As the above examples show, problems among highly "educated" individuals in present day Chinese society continue to crop up: a girl is forced to dress as a boy because her grandmother wants it that way, a child is taken to task for telling his father not to drive when he has had too much to drink. What is next? A judge's father (perhaps a high official in his own right) has special interest in a particular case on the docket, and he tells his son (the judge) how it should be decided? After reviewing a host of Chinese parent-child dealings, this hardly seems outside the realm of possibility.

---

a. 逆來順受
b. 委曲求全

## Ethics in the Schools

I have a western friend who often reads books on Ethics, and who frequently enjoys getting into discussions on this topic, which includes the whole scope of moral principles and rules of conduct. A western reader attuned to the Chinese cultural differences generally sees that the index in most English-language books of Ethics and Ethical Theory is quite inadequate to locate the information which he needs in clarifying his own feelings, and contrasting those with the differing ethical conceptions of the Chinese. As with most words which relate to non-simplistic concepts, *lwun li* [a] in Chinese and "ethics" have different scopes, and whether we attempted to give each a lexical, stipulative, ostensive, intensional, or extensional definition, they would be quite different.In fact the Chinese "four ethical principles",[b] namely (1) etiquette, ceremony, (2) justice, righteousness, (3) honesty, uprightness, and (4) sense of shame are not treated thoroughly or consistently in western ethics texts, and indeed one or two of the four may rarely be mentioned at all. These concerns are perhaps often treated at greater depth and length in religious texts and the many religious oriented magazines and periodicals in the west. Often as not the access for the common man is more readily available through such popular channels, since it was always more common to find a Bible in a western home than a copy of Plato or Aristotle, or indeed any more recently written volume dealing strictly with Ethics.

This fact provides us with further insight, namely that while a strict study of "Ethics" as a separate field of inquiry is appropriate content for an "elective course" in high school or college curriculum in the west, in China such a course is more properly considered required study for children in Elementary School. Thus the Chinese populace enjoys a much broader base of attention to "Ethical concerns" than known in the west, and it is not uncommon for essays on ethical theory to appear in the daily Chinese press, popular magazines, or even student publications, to extent and depth of discussion (albeit one-sided) which is largely unknown in the west outside of scholarly circles.

Even given the different Chinese ethical framework, still further distance from western perceptions results when we consider that the primary basis for Chinese ethical considerations in the last 2000 years has not been the contentions of various schools, but rather the collected sayings of one man and his disciples, namely Confucius, and these are held "valid" essentially by definition. They have been taught for this length of time dogmatically and by rote, and if some difference can be seen in the teachings of Confucius' *Analects* and the thinking of Chinese people of today, it is one of degree and not in kind.

Anthropologists will tell us belief in a Supreme being is not characteristic of all

a. 倫理
b. 四維：禮義廉恥

religions. That Confucianism lacks such a belief therefore does not immediately disqualify it as a religion, and the debate on whether it rightfully is, or is not, has occupied many scholars over the centuries. We will leave the exact determination of this fact to interested lexicographers and relevant Church Councils. However, the mere fact that Confucianism has been seriously advanced on several occasions through the ages as an appropriate candidate (or, the only appropriate candidate) for a Chinese State religion, even as recently as the early 20th century, certainly tells us that Confucianism carries much of the force of a religion in the minds of many Chinese. As such it constitutes a basic platform of statements regarding "knowledge for life" in which the Chinese find a reflection of all the values which they hold dear, and often a succinct summary or comparison to events in the Spring and Autumn Period of their history or earlier (approx. 550 BC and before). Apart from specific words of the maxims themselves, of which many Chinese have committed a large number to memory, the philosophy that underlies them forms a basic part of the Chinese consciousness. This philosophy is thus not generally subject to going in and out of style, as is often the case with many educational theories or philosophies which circulate in the west. It is not questioned or analysized in the way that westerners have questioned Christianity, and has not broken off into the innumerable sects which Christianity has, because the Chinese, being group oriented, have seen no reason to cast doubt upon the issues which their ancestors and the majority of people in present day Chinese society consider fundamental to life. Hence while on the surface China may claim separation between church and state, and not promulgate any one religious doctrine in the schools, nevertheless its ethical philosophy with religious overtones does form the central core of much school instruction.

## Sharp Teeth

How sharper than a serpent's tooth it is
To have a thankless child!

*Shakespeare, King Lear, Act 1, Scene 2*

We recognize that there are good and bad sides to many doctrines, and some would criticize the examples we have given in this chapter as casting a rather negative light over what is in other ways an excellent "criteria for human conduct." Certainly there is much to be said for requiring children to be obedient and respectful to their parents.However, this doctrine having been formed thousands of years ago, it contains no recognition of the fact that the child does at some point reach an age where he is legally entitled to fend for himself, and make his own decisions and choices as he sees fit. In fact a notable feature of this doctrine is that it denies a wide range of legal rights to younger members of society, thus actively placing its own view of morality above the law.

It is an accepted feature of pharmaceutical technology that researchers must not only look at the positive effects of new drugs, but the negative effects, the so-called side effects, as well. A chemical formulation which relieves depression, clears the sinuses, strengthens the bones, dissolves hemmorrhoids, decomposes kidney stones, cures arthritis, prevents acne, and strengthens resistance to allergy can hardly be said to be a successful product of the laboratory if 15% of the users develop side effects ranging from cataracts and corneal ulcers in the mild cases to cerebral hemmorrhaging and cardiac arrest in the more serious ones. One might pause to wonder if this is the correct choice of drug to place in the leading position in the company catalog, and on which to rest hopes for the future establishment of a pharmaceutical empire. At best, an informed observer would suspect that if such an empire were to be developed on this cornerstone, it would have many curious features, and perhaps not a few incongruities.

When casual observation seems to indicate that the side effects are striking the user group in a completely random fashion, certainly some further research is warranted. It might be possible to bring these side effects under control by specifying who should use the product, in what manner, and under what types of conditions, and by additionally stating in exactly what types of situations its use is precluded.

Moving back from the field of pharmacology to ethics, it would seem desirable that any ethical doctrine which produces various undesirable side effects also be limited to some degree in the scope of its use. To put this in plain language, we might ask: "Where do you draw the line?" And the answer the Chinese give, of course, is: "We don't."

In order to "draw the line" one would need a legal point of view, or legal orientation. The Chinese point of view takes sympathy/sentiment as a starting point, and is therefore much less able to set bounds or limits.

A phrase out of a child's theater play says: "One need not be in the dark when there is a shining lamp to light the way." If we expand upon this kernel of wisdom and double its force, we may take Respect Your Elders and Respect Your Parents to be our two shining lamps, one for each hand. While realizing that the Chinese have a high degree of integration between the concepts of "respect" and "acceptance", we certainly see that our path is well lighted. As we stumble out upon it, we best not pause to consider a reply to the muffled cry: "Wherefore art thou going?"

## Filial Piety and the Westerner in China

Entering into a discussion of the full scope of Filial Piety as practiced by the Chinese, we do rapidly reach a point where western and Chinese thinking begin to diverge sharply. We are reminded of Herbert Hoover's words in another context: "A great social and economic experiment, noble in motive and far-reaching in purpose." Certainly these words describe a great deal of the feeling that the Chinese have for "filial piety."

What Hoover was actually speaking of was "Prohibition" – the 18th Amendment to the U.S. Constitution. Many influential thinkers supported him in this, including the illustrious ancestor Benjamin Franklin, who placed "Temperance" first on his list of the thirteen virtues. Alas, later events seem to have overtaken the ideals of all these well-intentioned men, thus considerably tarnishing any claims they have to saintliness.

"Filial Piety" is not a law, but rather an ethical doctrine. As such it cannot be repealed.

To the extent that this doctrine merely recognizes the need for a child to be thankful to his parents, certainly no one would maintain that it is right for a child to be thankless, yet the perceived demands of thankfulness will certainly vary in different cultures, geographic regions, and eras.[1] Turning to the pages of Shakespeare, in the tragedy of *King Lear*, Cordelia is the loving, loyal, and dutiful daughter, but she cannot flatter, so the aged Lear divides his kingdom among her two sisters, who provide fulsome declarations of their love, even as they plot and scheme to put the father in his grave. Edgar is the loving, loyal, and dutiful son, but he is framed by his evil brother Edmund as having patricidal intent, and their father, the Earl of Gloucester, orders that Edgar be hunted down and sentenced. As we follow Shakespeare's probing into the nature of love, we are reminded that when considering who is a thankless child, there may be some wide disparity between appearance and reality. Many in the west feel that in discussing any and all issues, such a distinction is important, however many times the Chinese do not appear to think so.

A comment and question from a concerned westerner: Filial piety has come down to us from an age when society was static and fixed, with no change from generation to generation. In that era, experience was the great teacher, and advanced age was directly equivalent to advanced experience. Therefore to say that "One should obey his parents in all respects" makes much sense in that context. I propose a middle-of-the-road approach in the world of today — let's promote filial piety, but at the same time let's put some limits on it. Let's add the stipulations that: "The children are not required to obey the parents in any matter where the parents' opinions or instructions (a) are against the law, (b) are unsafe, harmful, or physically dangerous, (c) are contrary to accepted medical practice, (d) go against the right of the son or daughter to live an active, healthy life, (e) are based on superstition, not knowledge, (f) deny the reality that the living are more important than the dead." Don't you think this would be an acceptable solution?

Answer: Your proposal is again something in the nature of a stipulation of terms and conditions, thus a type of contract. I could offer no comment on its "acceptability rating" in the hearts of the Chinese populace. I would venture a statistical analysis of its chances for promulgation by leading Chinese thinkers and policy makers, based on my research. Possibility of promulgation in the next five years: 1/11th of 1%. Possibility of promulgation in the next fifty years: 1/10th of 1%.

---

1. What society and family view as the fitting requirements of thankfulness (from children to parents) will certainly be closely related to the culturally perceived natural degree of mutual dependence (high or low) which exists as a result of the parent-child bond. Different cultures have different views of Naturalism, as discussed in Chapter 10.

## The Need for Flexibility

This westerner's question brings to mind the entire issue of "Flexibility in Ethics," and indeed this is a topic which is commonly discussed by Chinese scholars. The flexibility of Confucius's teachings is, according to these scholars, evident in a number of passages in the *Analects,* most notably in the description of his personality as being free from bias, from inflexibility, from bigotry, and from egoism. (IX, 4). The *chwuntse,* or exemplary person, is said to have no predilections nor prejudices. (IV, 10). Additionally, Confucius says that he has no course for which he is predetermined, and no course against which he is predetermined. (XVIII, 8).

We are reminded of an adage from old China which says that "there should be no physical contact between the male and female (of the human species, before marriage)." A youth once asked a question "What if a girl is drowning in the river, and the only person nearby is a boy standing on the shore? What should he do? There are perhaps no logs, tree branches, or other items in the vicinity to aid in the rescue, so he knows that he will have to attempt it solely on his own. Should he violate the proscription by trying to save her?"

An aged scholar, Professor Ying, considered this for some moments, and then remarked "Oh, in this kind of situation it would be permissible to touch the girl's body in rescuing her." The youth was quite satisfied with this remark, and the other scholars present agreed that this certainly represented a flexible application of the relevant rule.

Some years later in another distant province, another youth named Min-tao happened to find himself near a river one day, and heard shouts from a girl who was drowning. Without stopping to think, he jumped in the water, swam out and saved her. Several people in the community who did not like this fellow (because his family was better off than theirs) made a formal complaint to the district magistrate, saying that Min-tao had openly violated the dictum against touching the body of someone of the opposite sex, and thus broken the established rules of propriety. Min-tao was called in for an interrogation. He was asked if he was aware of this particular rule. "Yes, I am," he said.

"Then why did you violate it?" the magistrate asked.

"I thought that under the circumstances a more flexible application of this rule was warranted," Ming-tao replied.

"Since when are you qualified to judge on when a rule may be changed, bent, or otherwise altered in its application?" the magistrate asked.

"I am sorry, your excellency. I had heard that a statement on this was made by a famous Professor Ying in a Gwei-ji city."

Turning to his aides, the magistrate queried "Who is this Professor Ying?"

After several minutes of discussion, the magistrate turned back to the defendant, saying "In any event, I am unaware of what authority Professor Ying has to make decisions in regard to correct rules of conduct handed down to us by our glorious ancestors."

Ming-tao was found guilty, and sentenced to ten days in a labor crew, and his family charged a fine of 30 kilos of grain.

This is the crux of the problem when talking about flexibility in ethics: One person's "flexibility" is another person's "exceeding the rules" or "disobeying the dictates of propriety." Who has the authority to say when a rule of conduct may be flexibly applied? In China, presumably only the Emperor, who leads by nature of his virtuous conduct. However, what the feelings of the next Emperor will be on these same types of issues is an open question.[1]

We recall the voyage of Gulliver to the island of Lilliput, where he lived among the local people as a giant. A known rule of propriety in the Kingdom said that no one could urinate in the Palace grounds. Unfortunately, one evening the Palace caught on fire, and Gulliver was called to the rescue by several high ministers. There being no other water close at hand, he emptied his bladder on the Palace, and this seemed acceptable under the circumstances. Later however, some other ministers who resented his presence in the Kingdom brought up formalized Articles of Impeachment against him, and his punishment was imminent when he fled to the neighboring island Kingdom of Blefuscu.

"Flexibility" is a snare and an illusion unless fully established by the person or persons in authority. Of course, if the rules of "flexibility" were to be carefully set down specifically in laws, codes, or other written promulgations, passed by the relevant governing body, and amended periodically, then all possible allowed variations for application of the various precepts could be specifically outlined. Without such written guidelines, there is no objective standard. Historically, the Chinese have been oriented away from establishing rules, regulations, and legal stipulations because the prevailing moral doctrine maintains that the leader governs by means of his superior virtue, and the populace are lead to be good through following his example. Elaborate written rules are, in this view, unnecessary.

Present Day Ramifications

With this basis, and in light of the above discussion of "flexibility", the westerner might begin to suspect that the behavior of the native people in the society might be peculiar in many respects. For example, after some period of historical development, with a multitude of incidents similar to that of Ming-tao's situation described above, where differing interpretations of various moral rules, imperial decrees, and other promulgations were "discussed", we would probably see the growth of a marked tendency for the commoners in the society to develop humility, to avoid taking the initiative, and to stress a superficial harmony in social dealings. After all they could never really be sure as to how most of the generalized doctrines affecting their lives would be rendered

---

1. In a related consideration, the practice of filial piety has never been successfully construed as leading to, or developing into, a more broadly based respect for non-kinship relations, i.e. relations between strangers. The perceptual difficulty which the Chinese have in dealing with strangers is discussed more fully in Chapter 10.

in specific applications. Hence the best recourse would be to keep quiet, maintain a low profile, do what you are told but nothing more, and not cause trouble, regardless of any objective considerations of right and wrong.

In organizations, we would expect people in lower positions to avoid making decisions in any and all types of eventualities, and to consistently choose to refer everything up to the boss, or high officials, for their determination of the proper procedure in each specific case.

Many western behavioral scientists have noted that much of this descriptive analysis fits quite closely the type of behavior we find in Chinese organizations, and to a great degree, in Chinese society as well. As to what might be the reason for this attitude, or the underlying cause, these scientists were unable to say.

Western Comparisons

A philosophy major submitted the following remarks to me after living in China for over a year: "Moral philosophy, according to Kant, is an inquiry about the rational foundation of morality. The task of moral philosophers is to exhibit fundamental moral principles and show how they can be rationally justified. My question is this: in what way does Confucian ethics qualify as a moral philosophy? From the point of view of Kant's Categorical Imperative, we are told to 'Act only on that maxim through which you can at the same time will that it should become a universal law.' I cannot see that this type of framework dovetails very well with most of the Chinese ideas."

Answer: We can only say that from the Confucian view, Kant's Categorical Imperative is an unknown consideration, and Kant's philosophy is regarded as based upon an unintelligent metaphysical dogma that "empirical phenomena are causally determined." In contrast, Confucianism (being Pre-Copernican[1] and Pre-Newtonian[2]) considers the universe an organic whole, with all things happening *spontaneously* and naturally, and certainly not arising from, or moving as a result of, external forces.

To restate this, the Newtonian-influenced view of classical physics brought westerners around to the viewpoint that all causal phenomena are mechanically determined, and do not occur spontaneously. In this type of universe, Immanuel Kant (who lived from 1724 to 1804) and other western philosophers found it necessary to puzzle over the problem of the interrelationship between *causality, freedom,* and *moral responsibility,* however Confucianists do not address these issues, rather they talk of what constitutes the correct mind or correct will. Of course, to the extent that this is a logical problem, western and Chinese logic could be expected to be different.

---

1. Nicholaus Copernicus (1473—1543).
2. Issac Newton (1642—1727).

## Filial Piety in the West

Some isolated pieces of essay writing and reportage in the Chinese press concerns the lives of Chinese individuals with foreign spouses. Certainly one major undercurrent in such writing is showing how the Chinese person, upon returning to the spouse's home country (USA, England, Germany, etc.) is able to promote more harmonious relations among the kinsfolk, especially between the spouse and his/her parents. Often it is shown that the Chinese person's behavior leaves a very good impression on the foreign parents. When the Chinese individual explains that respect, obedience, gratitude, support, service, etc. to parents are considered "fundamental" in the Chinese value system, the foreign parents often remark "Well, I think you really have something there!"

The conclusion *in this context* appears that "filial piety" is an important virtue, and one which westerners quickly accept in their home environments. This is a wonderful summation, however it deserves some further clarification, especially as regards the key words "in this context". What context are we dealing with in the west? We may consider the following differing baselines, which will have an immense effect on the practice and application of filial piety in society.

### Baselines for the Practice of Filial Piety

| in China | in the West |
|---|---|
| Fostering of mutually dependent relations between parents and children, frequent interference in a child's decision making. | Fostering of mutually independent relations between parents and children, recognition of the child as capable of making his own decisions as regards college major, life work, choice of spouse, locale of residence, allocation of salary earned, etc. |
| Ancestor worship exists as a state religion. Much pressure to get married and have male heirs. Making offerings, visiting gravesites, lengthy mourning periods, etc. regarded as moral responsibilities. | Ancestor worship unknown and unpracticed. |
| Respect for tradition, the established way of doing things, what was good for our ancestors is good for us. Elders know what is best, do not argue. | Respect for change, new methodology in problem solving, progress in science, medical knowledge. Preference for a rational methodology, weighing the evidence, facts are viewed as superior to opinions or speculations. In a debate, younger and elder members have equal rights to express their views. |
| Custom and tradition are viewed to be more important than legal standards, a large legal/moral gap. | Within the family, solid recognition of the children's legal rights, a very small legal/moral gap. |
| Autocratic management, government, school, and family structure. | Democratic management, government, school, and family structure. |

Certainly one supposes that other items could be added to this listing.

No doubt the westerner would point to the right side of our chart and say: "With these underlying premises, I accept filial piety."

However, when we speak of filial piety among the Chinese, our underlying premises are more properly viewed as those on the the left. A change in any of these considerations would be most significant to the entire application of this doctrine.

Filial Piety and the Westerner: Conclusion

We have great faith in the Chinese people, nevertheless we realize that in dealing with many situations their value system is totally at odds with the western one. Therefore it would seem advisable when discussing any topics which appear to entangle Chinese moral considerations, that the westerner not get overly excited, irritated, or exasperated. He should rather adopt the cultured refinement of a Secretary of State, or member of Congress. This means that unless he has the Ace up his sleeve to force the acceptance of his analysis or decree, it is better to offer it for "reference" quietly, and then quickly leave the scene or change the subject, if unpleasantness is to be avoided.

There is an old adage that says "Defining the problem is half of the solution." Since the Chinese do not see any problems with their moral outlook, it is unlikely they will be advancing any solutions to the difficulties (as seen by the westerners) that this outlook poses. After all, we are told, filial piety is basically sound since it proceeds from the premise that "A parent would not do anything to harm a child." This is a true statement. How can it be doubted?

While we do not wish to belabor the point, reports issued by the National Center for the Prevention and Treatment of Child Abuse and Neglect at the University of Colorado School of Medicine, Denver, would cast serious doubt on this premise. Reported child abuse cases of 320 times per million population (in countries which collect data) are not uncommon. Moreover, researchers working at the School have brought forth evidence which shows that reported cases represent only a fraction of the total.

Data on child abuse in China is hard to get, and if foreigners went probing for such information they would no doubt become very unpopular very quickly. Some reports of Chinese parents drowning girl babies in rivers, lakes, etc. or throwing them off cliffs occasionally do come to light in the foreign press however.[1]

---

1. That such a practice is carried on, often in front of witnesses, and with the knowledge of neighbors, relatives, etc. seems curious. In Chapter 2 of the *Book of Mencius* is stated: "If men suddenly see a child about to fall into a well, they will without exception experience a feeling of alarm and distress. They will feel so, not as a ground on which they may gain the favor of the child's parents, nor as a ground on which they may seek the praise of their neighbors and friends, nor from a dislike of hearing such a noise. From this case we may perceive that the feeling of commiseration is essential to man . . . and the feeling of commiseration is the beginning of *jen*."

Acts of filicide in the present age are strongly condemned by the majority of the Chinese populace, yet the existence of any instances of this type of activity suggests that human nature is much more complex than Mencius recognized, and casts serious doubt on his doctrine that *jen* can be verified as "intuitive knowledge or intuitive emotion" by the so-called feeling of commiseration that Confucianists maintain every man possesses.

As a final summation, we note that the Chinese do tend to accept custom as sacrosanct by definition. Any attempts at step-by-step reasoning to point out inconsistencies, non-sequiturs, or lack of appropriateness of this moral outlook in today's world would be fraught with difficulty.

The foreigner in China is left to draw his own conclusions. In any event it is advisable to be aware of the ramifications of all the issues raised in this Chapter, especially when attempting to understand Chinese dealings with their parents, family, and clan.

# Chapter 8 Face Saving as a Way of Life

## Here Comes the Judge

It was a hot sultry morning in Hong Kong in the late 1970's. Court was in session, with an aging British judge, the honorable M.K. Stockenwosh, presiding. The Chambers had just opened for the day, and there were quite a number of cases on the docket. Three newspaper reporters were in attendance, the most senior among them James Stevenson, with two cub reporters. James showed the other two the information he had collected on who was being sentenced and for which crimes. The first case seemed relatively minor: a vehicle overparked in Kowloon. In appealing his case, the defendant had maintained that the meter was faulty, and that he still had four minutes. He and his lawyer approached the bench, and the defendant held his head in a confident manner as if expecting the best. A scowl seemed to appear on the judge's face as he looked down at the papers spread out before him. Swinging down his gavel crisply, with the hint of a faint smile on his lips, he paused only a split-second before proclaiming: "Forty years at hard labor!"

In the press gallery, the cub reporters looked at James, and he let out a barely perceptible whistle: "The judge is in a good mood this morning," he said, "It should be an interesting day."

The defendant was stunned, and seemed to collapse upon hearing this verdict, as if struck by a giant hammer. He began to stutter, as if he was trying to make some statement, but no words formed upon his lips. The lawyer furrowed his brows and gazed at the floor pensively as his client was led speechless from the room.

The next case promised to be more dramatic. According to the details the reporters had assembled, the defendant had run over four people with his truck, and then taken a knife and seriously stabbed two pedestrians. The defendant came forward. The judge was expressionless as he swung down his gavel quickly: "H.K. $200, plus costs". The defendant seemed quite surprised at this verdict, and looked back and forth from the judge to his legal counsel several times. The latter nodded, and he said a simple "Thank you, judge" before walking out of the Chambers.

At this point, the lawyer for the first defendant asked for a recess, to speak to the judge privately. The judge said that there was no need for a recess, and asked him to make a statement directly. The lawyer said: "With all due respect your honour, wasn't the sentencing in this last case extremely light, considering that this man killed six people?"

"What do you mean 'killed six people'," the judge said, "he was overparked."

"No, you are mistaken," the lawyer clarified, "that was my client, the first man."

"Certainly not," said the judge, "he ran over four people and stabbed two others."

"You have it all mixed up!" said the lawyer.

"I do not have it all mixed up!" said the judge, "and who are you to tell me that I do? I hereby bar you from practicing law in the British Crown Colony of Hong Kong for here and evermore."

Within the space of a fortnight the formal announcement was issued by the Courts, and this lawyer was never able to practice law in Hong Kong again. He resigned from his law firm and returned to Britain to an uncertain future. Of course the cause of his new-found unemployment was strikingly clear to all those aware of the proceedings on his last day in court: he had caused the judge to lose face. That was not a nice thing to do.

## A Professional Girlfriend

Sally Lortimer and Robert Reston had met when attending college in Chicago, and after graduation they had each gone their separate ways. Three years later however they found themselves employed by the same high-tech manufacturing company in South Dakota, and they began dating. Within the space of ten months they had decided to get married, and were looking around for a suitable house.

One night Robert received a call from his old classmate Joseph, who was living in a nearby town. Joseph said that he and some friends in the vicinity had come across some information which Robert might be interested in. Robert asked for details, but Joseph said it was much too sensitive to discuss over the phone. They agreed to meet in a restaurant the following Saturday night.

Robert arrived at the restaurant early, and was on his second Singapore Sling when Joseph showed up with three of his friends. As the five of them sat around making small talk, Robert asked what the big deal was. "We are good friends Joe. Whatever you wanted to tell me you could have told me over the phone."

"I don't think so," said Joe, "because it is something that concerns your girlfriend, and I was afraid she might overhear the conversation."

"At this point I do not keep any secrets from her," Robert confided, "so I hardly think that it matters."

One of Joseph's friends looked Robert hard in the eyes, "Do you think she keeps any secrets from you?"

"What is that supposed to mean?" Robert started to stand up, obviously angered by this remark.

"Cool down," Joseph put a hand on his shoulder, "it is just that we have something to show you. Something we collected a week ago when you went on that business trip." He took some black and white glossies out of a large manila envelope. "I felt the only way to explain this was in person."

The photos had been taken in a hotel room under low lighting, however they clearly showed Sally with another man and engaged in a variety of sexual activities. "This has been going on for some time," Michael, the friend seated on Robert's right, stated, "but it was only two days ago that we got these shots developed."

Robert was enraged, "My girlfriend wouldn't do this! These pictures must be phonies!"

"No, they are real enough," Michael continued, "and if you look carefully you will see a copy of a week ago Thursday's newspaper on the bedside counter. I think it was that Thursday morning that you left for St. Louis, isn't that right?"

"Where did you learn that?"

"Joseph told me."

Robert brought up his fist, swung back and landed a haymaker on Joseph's jaw. Joseph collapsed to the floor, and the other three friends jumped up to restrain Robert.

"What do you think you are doing?" the tallest one of them blurted out.

Robert sank back into his chair, "I don't know. All of this is such a shock. I thought that she loved me so."

"You should be glad that Joe tipped you off. Now you can get out of this thing before it is too late. Believe me, we have been following this case for months, but it was only last week that we got our photography people together and got these shots," as he spoke he took out his Police I.D. "We are planning to make a raid in the next couple of days."

"You mean my girlfriend is a . . . "

"That's right. That wasn't a one-time roll in the hay, she has a list of clients a mile long, and is a real high class hooker."

Robert raised his fist again and started to swing, but one of the other plainclothesmen had stepped behind him, and was able to grab his arms. "Relax pal, I know this must be a terrific blow to your pride, a real loss of face as they say, but if you disassociate yourself with this chick now, you may still be able to stay out of hot water."

"Thanks for the advice," Robert said in a barely audible tone of voice, "but I am in no mood for it. I need to get out of this city and start over." He gulped down the last of his drink and walked out the door.

For one's spouse, or prospective spouse, to be found to be regularly "stepping out" tends to result in a loss of face for a westerner, although one suspects that among some societies, such as those found in certain African and South American regions, among the Eskimo, etc., this is not the case. In a related example, many North Americans or Europeans who live in the Orient will make local friends whom they later decide to marry. When and if it is suggested (with or without corroborative evidence) that the local person is just using this relationship "as a passport out" (i.e. as a means of getting out of the country), this is regarded by many westerners as an insult, and vigorously denied. If proven, it amounts to a serious loss of face.

## Utopian Questions

During a seminar on cross-cultural religious issues, Dr. Stevens, a noted scholar and longtime resident of London, although a native of Los Angeles, had been asked to make some impromptu remarks on Thomas More's *Utopia*, published in 1516. The audience in attendance numbered over fifty, all of whom were social scientists. Dr. Stevens stated that More's *Utopia* was based on a society from which all religions were banned. Idol worship was forbidden, and belief in monotheism or polytheism had never gained much credence among the populace. Although the people had some respect for their ancestors, they did not elevate this to the level of a religion, as some neighboring nations had, because they regarded the sacrifices, and other worship practices, including the burning of paper money, the making of elaborate offerings of food (much of which was later abandoned or thrown out), the frequent visits to grave sites, the erection of monuments and plaques to the dead, the promotion of the entire ancestor ideology, etc. "as a conspiracy of those in power to keep the common people in subjection".

One member of the audience that evening, Mr. Longsmith, had recently reread More's *Utopia*, having found an old copy on sale in a secondhand bookshop not too long before. During a break in the lecture, Mr. Longsmith asked one of his friends, a teacher of English literature at an Ivy League University, if Dr. Stevens' remarks were on the right track. "That was not the impression I gained from my reading of *Utopia*," Longsmith stated frankly.

"Stevens is quite far off the mark," his friend agreed. "It is true that there is not a single predominant religion throughout the nation of Utopia,[1] but a considerable variety of doctrines is permitted. Churches are large and very beautiful, and the services are interdenominational in character. They have priests, and these are men of exceptional character and dignity. Atheists are looked down upon, and are not allowed to hold public office. There is uniformity in the belief in immortality, and the populace does not regard the approach of death in old age with much fear."

---

1. Thomas More envisioned his Utopia on a remote island. However, in reviewing the Utopian literature of Europe and the Americas from More to the present, we see that westerners generally imagine their utopia to be in the future. Contrastingly, the Chinese consider their utopia to be in the past.

"Yes, I remember most of that from my reading," Longsmith commented. "But you are more of an expert than I. Let's set Dr. Stevens right about this."

"No, that would not be the thing to do in front of so many people," his friend remarked. "It would be better to let Stevens keep his face. That is an important rule of interpersonal relations."

We do not know if the friend mentioned here was a disciple of Dale Carnegie, for in Carnegie's book *How to Win Friends and Influence People,* there is a similar incident involving a speaker at a dinner party who claims that a particular passage is from the Bible, whereas one of the guests at the party knows for a fact it is from Shakespeare. The guest is advised by a companion sitting nearby to allow the matter to drop, and let the speaker keep his face.

Many assumptions have apparently been made, consciously or unconsciously, as a basis for the adoption of this type of "face saving" method of dealing with others. Among these are the following:

1) Resolution of the difference of opinion (or contradiction) presented is not important or relevant to any of those present. Totally ignored is the possibility that a member of the audience is working on an important and related research project, or is preparing for an upcoming written or oral test covering the exact material being discussed, or otherwise in a position where it is highly desirable to determine the exact facts of the issue.

2) Spreading of false rumors about the meaning or content of various works of literature, philosophical doctrines, religious teachings, etc. is not a serious matter. The distortion, imbalance, or confusion which this brings into scholarly pursuits, or into the average man's search for knowledge, over the short or long term, is not important.

3) Reality is properly viewed in subjective terms, and the search for a more broadly-based, more objective view is not something worth pursuing. Relationships between human beings in society are facilitated if each is allowed to maintain his own prejudicial views, no matter how lacking in factual basis they may be.

## Western Face

Before going into a discussion of the concept of "face" in China, it is important for us to clarify the fact that such a concept does exist in the west, although many times we call it by other names. We will outline some types of relevant incidents here, and offer some explanation of how they compare to Chinese ideas.

\* Keeping Up With the Joneses. In the west, those who cannot keep up with the Joneses may be said to have lost face. Westerners like to engage in one-upmanship, and to compare material possessions, and regard such possessions as status symbols.

Mother : Do you want me to come and pick you up after school?
Son : If you are going to drive that beat-up old car of ours, forget it, I would rather walk home than be the laughing stock of my friends.

In some ways this concept of Keeping Up With the Joneses, (although not directly translatable) bears a relation to certain aspects of "face" in Chinese society, albeit it is by no means always directly equatable.

Different Chinese live at different economic levels, so there is often a great variety of activity, in relation to ownership of material possessions, which could be construed as having face. For the child who was brought up with no shoes, to have shoes is to have face. For the child who was brought up with hand-me-down shoes, to have his own shoes is to have face. To someone else who always wore inexpensive shoes, to have expensive shoes may be to have face. Hence, there is no answer to the question of "If a Chinese comes into possession of a pair of used shoes, does he gain face or lose face?" That depends on his economic level, real or perceived.

This is particularly noticeable in housing. A westerner may ask: "If someone has a screen door that is torn in several places, and lets in mosquitoes, do they gain face or lose face?" Looking at the situation in China, at one end of the scale, for the person who grew up in a house with no doors (not at all uncommon in some traditional types of Chinese dwellings), this may be a gain; for someone else who grew up in much more wealthy surroundings, it may be a loss. However, we suspect that often it is irrelevant: the Chinese concept of face in the home environment is much more related to putting a sumptuous meal on the table than with the physical surroundings (which may be regarded as including the cleanliness, state of repair, etc. of the actual eating environment). This reflects the reality that the Chinese have traditionally had a society based on subsistence agriculture.

In regard to clothing, since most Chinese schools require the students to wear uniforms, the different economic levels of the parents are not generally recognizable from casual observation of students' clothing, and hence the issue of gaining or losing face in relation to one's classmates is largely avoided in this area.

* Raising Successful Children.

*Martha: Did you hear about Henrietta's daughter who is running her own real estate agency in Beverly Hills?*

*Mary-Ann: Yes, my daughter mentioned it to me when she came back from her recent vacation in the Caribbean. She is investing in the construction of a new hotel down there.*

Most westerners consider it very satisfying to have raised academically, socially, and financially successful children. The Chinese are similar in this respect, and would view this as gaining face, although the exact list of considerations constituting "successful" are often different from western norms. In general, the major component of success in Chinese eyes is for the children to have graduated from college or university, and to be married. Running one's own business is regarded as having more face than working for someone else, (oftentimes irrespective of income, stability, amount of vacation time, working hours, etc.) That the child associates with, and is well regarded by important people also brings the family much face. Being wealthy is also desirable.

\* Wearing Attractive Clothing. Westerners often take the issue of clothing to extremes, and will even laugh or make fun of people whose clothing is considered of poor quality, thus causing these people to lose face.

*Father: Will you be going out with your friends to play basketball this Saturday?*

*Son : If I do not get a new pair of All-Pro brand basketball shoes, I certainly will not. The other guys will make fun of me.*

Westerners like to compare the high-priced named-brand clothes they have purchased, and to brag about their clothing expenditures. In Chinese schools, this is rather unusual, for the reasons cited above. Much locally-made modern western-style clothing in China is inexpensive, and can be affordably replaced after a relatively short period of wear. For many Chinese the purchasing of tailor-made clothes is the rule rather than the exception, since local labor costs are comparatively low. Attention to brand names is seldom a consideration to any but the most western-thinking, or western-influenced Chinese.

\* Attention to the Speaker in a Meeting. In formal meetings in the west, in auditoriums and meeting rooms, most speakers will take it as a loss of face if members of the audience are talking among themselves while the speech is being given, or if other important dignitaries seated on the platform are conversing and not paying attention to what is being said. (After-dinner speeches might be something of an exception in this regard.) In China however this type of behavior is commonly seen, and the speaker rarely takes any notice of it.

Closely related to this, all types of meetings, speech contests, plays, performances, etc. in the west are generally expected to be well planned logistically and procedurally. If props, microphones, lighting, scenery, and other equipment are to be moved around, this is usually conducted in an organized fashion, and generally with the curtain down. Otherwise, the sponsors may feel they have lost some face if uncoordinated and unplanned adjustments are continually being done on the stage by various staff employees, prop men, or other technicians. However this is rarely a consideration in China, and a wide variety of assistants, often casually dressed in normal street clothes, are frequently seen making all sorts of adjustments during all types of presentations. To a large degree we feel that this is due to the influence of Peking Opera, where such activity is commonplace, and traditionally it has been expected that this will be ignored by the audience.

\* Being drunk and boisterous in public. Normally calm and reserved people who get drunk and make fools of themselves at parties in the west are often greatly embarrassed afterwards, and feel they have lost face. However, more aggressive personalities may feel no shame. In China, the same considerations may apply, however if a situation like this had occurred, it would probably not be mentioned later by others, whereas in the west many people would make a point of bringing it up in order to "rub it in." Many Chinese women, especially young women, do not drink, and to ask that they do

## On the Radio

I recall the story of a disk jockey at a local radio station. One night when he was at the controls a record began to skip. Before he could react, the needle scraped across the entire song leaving him with "dead air" silence, a serious boo-boo, which had led to several previous D.J.s being fired. Thinking quickly, he grabbed the microphone and exclaimed over the air: "All right, I want you to make an honest confession, which one of you listeners out there just bumped your radio and made my record skip?" This seemed an appropriate face-saving ploy, and he went on to play several more songs and other pre-recorded interview material.

Upon leaving work that night the switchboard operator informed him that six people had called in to apologize.

participate in toasting (with something other than tea or soft drinks) is generally considered improper. (For those that do drink, obviously this is a minor consideration.) On the other side of the coin, for a man to fail to drink liquor with another person who has proposed a toast may be considered a loss of face by the asking party, and may lead to unpleasantness.

* Insults to one's honor, pride, etc. This seems to have gone out of vogue during the last century, hence we rarely hear someone say "You have insulted my honor!" However it may still come up occasionally. Clearly the party who was insulted has lost face if the incident is not righted. We are reminded of some Russians sailors whose trawler had capsized, and were picked up by a US Naval vessel. While eating some food in the dining hall, they were heard to make some complaints about the "dirty imperialist Americans." Of course several American crew members wanted to settle the matter on the spot, and this type of "patriotic" reaction is quite understandable to the Chinese, who would have felt the same way if they were called names.

Another story involved a Catholic bishop who went to a magic show in New York city. All of the typical big time acts were performed, including making the Statue of Liberty disappear, turning a cow into a whale, elevating a Staten Island Ferry above the Empire State Building, hypnotizing a member of the audience into memorizing the entire Manhattan telephone directory, and other stunts. After the show, an elderly man walked up to the bishop and asked him to explain how all these feats had been accomplished. The bishop replied frankly that he did not know. The man was very disappointed at this and remarked "If you do not understand magic, I do not see how in the name of tarnation it is you fellows are qualified to discuss the miracles in the Bible!" The bishop felt this was a severe blow to his pride.

* Serious Slips of the Tongue. Sometimes the innocuous remark may turn into something quite unintended, and it is possible that someone could construe this as a loss of face.

We are reminded of the story of a midwestern USA biology teacher, Mr. Duncan, who gave a particularly difficult pop-quiz one day early in the semester. Afterward, someone asked if this was typical procedure for the course, and the teacher replied, rather humorously, "No, this was just one of my quizzies." Without thinking, a student in the front row blurted out "If that was one of your quizzies, I would hate to see one of your testies!" thus resulting in an unfortunate play on words.

Another example comes to us from Germany. A German government official was asked to give a toast at an international gathering. His English was not very good, and as he formed the words "Auf die Damen" in his mind, he translated them directly, raising his glass and announcing to all the assembled guests: "Up on the Ladies!" This of course caused quite a bit of consternation. Later investigation revealed that this phrase is more suitably rendered as "(We drink) to the ladies' (health)!"

A female Chinese teacher (born and raised in China, preparing to study for her Master's Degree in the USA) was conducting an English class in California, and involved the students in a discussion of their favorite hobbies, sports, and games. Then she talked about doing these activities at home, in the schoolyard, at the park, in motor vehicles, etc. so that they could practice the vocabulary and sentence patterns. An American school official was touring the premises, and when he was shown in the room to observe the teaching method, the Chinese teacher had just gotten to the phrase: "I like to do it on the bus." The official had heard that the Chinese were conservative, and he was most surprised at this remark. Later when the staff explained to the teacher that this type of phraseology tended to have other implications, she felt she had lost much face, and nearly went into shock.

* Any of a wide variety of incidents which westerners would consider embarrassing: ripping one's pants, stumbling with a full tray of food, being declared the class dunce, being caught in an overly intimate position with one's boyfriend or girlfriend, spilling juice on one's new clothes, falling off the stage when going forward to receive an award, jumping into a pool and having one's swimming suit come off, standing in line for two hours with friends to buy tickets and then realizing you had failed to bring any money, etc. These could all be seen as loss of face.

Yet, despite these general comparisons, it is unfortunately true that the Chinese concept of face is vastly more broadly-based than the western one, and involves many more types of encounters. It is hoped the reader will have a better grasp of the entire issue after he has read the following pages.

## Freedom and Face

One of the freedoms which we enjoy in the west is the kind of "individual mentality" whereby in running our daily lives we are not worrying too much about what others think. This certainly does not mean that we are unqualified egoists, or that we do not respect the rights of others. In fact, we properly recognize that we may exercise our freedom to the extent that we do not interfere with the freedoms of others, or violate the laws. As an outgrowth of this individualism, we recognize the existence of other points of view, we have a certain tolerance for opposing outlooks, and we may "agree to disagree", or at least we do not feel it is wrong to disagree. If it is desirable to resolve our differences, we may engage in some sort of discussion, fact-finding, or public opinion survey, to collect data to support our contention, or even engage in more direct types of persuasion such as lobbying, or even picketing, etc., in order to elicit support from the silent majority.

In many societies where the emphasis is on the Group, and "Group Mentality" values are prevalent, we the people do indeed very much care about what other people think and how our peers perceive us. Is this a natural orientation? Of course, because this will have been the the way we have been brought up from childhood. Harmony within the group will be seen as an important goal, altruism will be stressed, and if certain individual desires or prerogatives have to be stifled as a result, then so be it.

Illustrative of this is that in a Chinese wedding there are no statements to the effect: "Do you take this man to be your lawfully wedded husband?" or "Do you take this woman to be your lawfully wedded wife?" For the individual to have second thoughts at the last minute is not acceptable. The families in question have, assumedly, already agreed to this match, and that is the major consideration. No further verification by the individual at the point of the ceremony is required.

In fact, to stress one's individualism in a group oriented atmosphere, even in regard to actions or options which primarily affect oneself, is generally seen as being selfish and unfair. Rather, one should be mindful of the example of the candle, just as it sacrifices of itself to brighten up the lives of others, so should each of us conduct our own life.

Undoubtedly the pure egoist or pure altruist are extreme personality types, and any one individual has some proportion of the ideology of each. For the person of an "individual mentality" who has a high altruistic bent, a quantification of his motivation might be perhaps 40% altruist. There remains a 60% egoist component, and he would clearly fall in the egoist camp.

For the person of a "Group Mentality" who has a high egoistic bent, a quantification of his motivation might be perhaps 40% egotistic. There remains a 60% altruist component, and he would clearly fall in the altruist camp.

Let us describe these two personality or motivational types as RSI (Rational Self Interest), and RGI (Rational Group Interest), and refer to them under the category of Interest Orientations.

Many of the acculturologically sensitive terms which we encounter may take on different meanings when seen by people of different Interest Orientations. What is reasonable? Does your definition depend on Group Interest or Self Interest?

> I think societal instinct much deeper than sex instinct, and societal repression much more devastating.
>
> ———D.H. Lawrence

A Rational Group Interest Orientation is taught to the Chinese child as he grows up, through interaction with members of the cultural group. The abstract concept of face appears to be an outgrowth, a bizarre outgrowth some foreigners would say, of the "Group Mentality" thereby instilled.

In speaking of the Group Mentality, we must recognize that the Chinese preference for the group does not mean any group, and they certainly are not indiscriminately gregarious. In general terms we may say that the Chinese sense of "group" centers on the five relationships, and is dominated by the family/clan.[1] The Group Mentality spoken of here is also different from a mentality of unionism, which is highly developed in many western countries. A trade union, ostensibily, exists for the benefit of the individual members, and is still an outgrowth of the RSI Orientation. Contrastingly, the Group Mentality (RGI Orientation) is predicated on the fact that one defines himself in terms of his relations to other people, i.e. in terms of his "roles", hence individual needs and desires are subservient to those of the larger group.[2] The RGI Orientation is common in many old societies, and if we research the social organization of Europe in the Middle Ages, it is quickly seen that many of the ideas of those times closely dovetail with the Chinese norms.

> I believe convention to be a collective necessity. It is a stopgap and not an ideal, either in the moral or in the religious sense, for sumbission to it always means renouncing one's wholeness and running away from the final consequences of one's own being.
>
> ——— Carl Jung

Some western scholars have made the charges that a Rational Group Interest Orientation 1) reflects a basic sense of insecurity, 2) prohibits a great deal of independent thought, 3) tends to severely downplay the concept of "self", hence, 4) serves as a major restriction on the pursuit of self-interest, and 5) stifles creativity. Overviewing present-day Chinese society, one may contemplate whether these five considerations are properly categorized as cause or effect (of this Interest Orientation); certainly this is still open to some debate among foreign observers. The Chinese however, living in a society that

---

1. By way of comparison, the Japanese sense of "group" centers more on the company or organization.
2. We have illustrated the Chinese sense of the Group Mentality with many examples throughout this volume, yet we are unable to offer a stipulative or intensional definition that is comprehensive. Several westerners who had lived in Egypt for many years before coming to China remarked that the Egyptian sense of "group" has many significant differences from the Chinese one, yet both peoples regard their orientations as "natural", "common sense", "easily understood", etc. Clearly the westerner is hard pressed to come to a full understanding of either culture's sense of groupism, and to accurately extrapolate its ramifications into guidelines for daily behavior. It would be hoped that Chinese scholars can do more research on this subject in the future.

stresses mutual helpfulness, respect & obedience, reverence of the past, etc., rarely recognize that such charges are worthy of serious discussion.

How does all of this relate to face? Essentially, you gain face by some kind of situation which is favorable to you, and which has come about, perhaps by your own doing, perhaps by someone else's doing, in front of others. You lose face through some kind of unfavorable situation which has come about, most commonly through someone else's doing, but sometimes through your own doing, in front of others. In a culture where everyone is concerned what everyone else thinks, the concept of face has fertile soil in which to grow. In a culture where everyone is primarily concerned with their own self interest, the soil is considerably more barren.

A baby does not have face. A three year old child may become angry about something, but would not consider it a loss of face. A fifth grader does, although of course in relation to his maturity, his face will not be as developed as that of a 20 year old. We might say that face begins to develop in the four to five year old child, who can occupy a separate place at the meal table, and is therefore a member of the group, as opposed to an adjunct to it, as he was in this days of infant feeding. This four to five year level of mental development allows him to participate in some degree of discussion with other members of the group, and to absorb the behavior and value systems of its adult members, often through imitation. This is done in the same way that he learns the range of what is considered "edible food", what is considered the proper etiquette for drinking beverages, or what sort of comments or jokes are only suitable for the outhouse and vicinity. By coming in contact with not only family members but also a wide range of other people in the cultural group who share in a recognition of face, it is gradually transmitted to him in small portions, as a newcomer in the tropical swamps gradually picks up yellow fever from each mosquito which greets him.

Two initial examples will be illustrative:

* Guests were invited to a Chinese home to eat. A six year old child was a member of the inviting household. The father told everyone to "eat up", and the guests reiterated this to the children, pointing to the various dishes. The children looked at one select meat dish and replied: "Oh no, we are not allowed to eat that, that is only for grandfather to eat!" In line with respect for elders, when some nutritious dishes are in short supply, the elders are entitled to them. The children are not. This was the situation generally in effect in the household, and the children had no knowledge of any change in this stance, just because guests had arrived. This innocent remark lost face for the parents, because it broke the false mask of generosity and abundance.

* A professor made the comment that an understanding of events leading up to the Boxer Rebellion in the late 1830's is extremely important if one is to grasp the significance of the Opium War which occurred some 60 years later. A student raised his hand and said: "I think you have your dates mixed up professor. The Boxer Rebellion was 1899-1900, and the Opium War was 1839-1842." This remark lost face for the professor, because it broke the false mask of expertise and competence.

## Chuang Tsu and "Self"

Dr. Wing-tsit Chan[1] in his paper "The Story of Chinese Philosophy" presented at the East-West Philosopher's Conference, Honolulu, in 1939, notes that in Chapter 7 of Chuang Tsu[a], and other chapters, it is stressed that a person should be completely vacuous, and

> When one reaches this state, one becomes a "true man" . . . "without any concern he came, and without any concern he went, that was all. He did not forget his beginning nor seek his end. He did not violate Tao with his mind, and he did not assist Nature with man . . . such being the true man, his mind is perfectly at ease . . . he is in accord with all things, and no one knows the limit thereof."

To achieve this end, we must have "no self", "have no achievement", and "have no fame". We must "let our mind be at ease in abiding with the nature of things. Cultivate our spirit by following what is necessary and inevitable." "For our external life, there is nothing better than adaptation and conformation. For our internal life, there is nothing better than peace and harmony."

Dr. Chan concludes: "Here we have primitivism, mysticism, quietism, fatalism, and pessimism in a nutshell."

This latter example is particularly important, because it shows a curious preference which has arisen due to the attention to face, namely: adherents to the face-saving mentality would rather be all wrong in a harmonious fashion than be all right in a disharmonious fashion. While the student's statement of these dates is more accurate historically, yet by causing the professor to lose face he has caused disharmony in the learning environment. This has created disrespect. How can a teacher teach without respect? Hence, it can be seen that the concept of respect is also very closely related to face: **to the extent that you can keep up an image,**[2] **even though it may be a false one, in front of a group, you have face. If you lose this image, you have lost face.** [3]

Thus any sort of remarks by a person in authority in an organization to another person in a lower position, in front of others, such as: "Didn't I tell you it was supposed to be done that way? Why did you do it this way?" are immediately seen (by the subordinate) as a loss of face.

What I must do is all that concerns me, not what the people think.

— Ralph Waldo Emerson

---

1. Dr. Chan is a former Professor of Chinese Thought at Columbia University and Dartmouth College.

2. This **image** may be the desire to appear *fair, democratic, open to suggestions, above corruption, unbiased, etc.* When evidence is brought out to show that this image is a false one, the person whose "mask" is broken loses face, and it may be expected that he/she will try to get even, perhaps by starting a smear campaign against the party which revealed this information, or framing them as having committed some despicable offense.

3. Chinese may get angry in such a situation, as reflected in the idiom 惱羞成怒 "shamed to the point of becoming angry."

a. 莊子

Do we have face in the west? Yes, we do, however as westerners we do reach a point where we do not care about the points of view of others (including co-workers, neighbors, friends, relatives, etc.) Conversely, many Chinese will live their entire lives to fall in conformity with others' points of view.

A person needs at intervals to separate himself from family and companions and go to new places. He must go without his familiars in order to be open to influences, to change.

— *Katharine Butler Hathaway*

## Preliminary Investigations

Most English language dictionaries give a wide variety of explanations for the noun "face", including uses in military science, mining, typography, architecture, athletics, etc. The basic meaning is: **1. the front of the head from the top of the forehead to the bottom of the chin, and from ear to ear; visage; countenance. 2. the expression of the countenance.** Many dictionaries include a separate entry for the Chinese idiomatic use of "face", defining it in terms of three words: **dignity; self-respect; prestige.** This latter definition is certainly part of "face", but hardly encloses the complete scope of the concept as used by the Chinese. A quick check in an English-to-Chinese dictionary reveals that none of these three words translates exactly back into 面子 *mian tse*, the concept with which we are trying to deal. Turning to our Chinese-to-English dictionary, we find the Chinese term 面子 translated into **honor;** one's face in the figurative sense. Obviously we will not find the true sense of "face" in the dictionaries.

Relevant for comparison however is the definition of the noun "mask": **1. a covering for the frontal portion of the head, or for part of the countenance, to conceal or disguise the identity. 2. a protective covering for the visage or head. 3. something serving to conceal other objects or activities from observation; a camouflage. 4. an opaque border used to cover unwanted parts of something, or to alter its shape.**

      Face may be corresponded with many other terms such as
- honor
- conscience
- dignity
- status
- conceit
- pride
- vanity
- character
- sense of personal worth
- self respect
- self esteem
- prestige

      as in the sentence "You insulted my _____ ."

However, face is a huge concept, and much larger than any of these. We may use honor for comparison, and draw some intersecting circles.

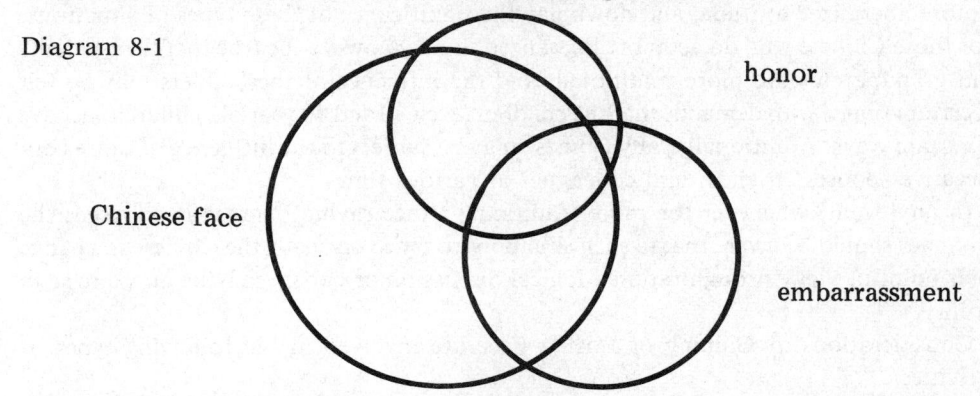

Diagram 8-1

*[Venn diagram with three intersecting circles labeled "Chinese face", "honor", and "embarrassment"]*

In relation to embarrassment, in English we say "turn red in the face" or "go red in the face". This concept of the face turning red as a result of a loss of face is also commonly used in Chinese.

Example 1: Mr. Lin bends over and rips his pants. This of course would be embarrassing in the western view, and the Chinese could quickly see that the person involved (Mr. Lin) has lost face.

Example 2: At a dinner party, someone asks me "Will you drink a toast with me?" and after offering thanks I refuse by saying that I have had too much to drink already. The westerner would have a hard time seeing how this was related to embarrassment in any way, however the Chinese could easily view this incident as a loss of face (to the asking party), since he "asked" and was "refused".

Hence we see that loss of face exists where embarrassment does not, the two are not by any means always the same.

It is thus important to recognize that face has some differences from honor, or just plain embarrassment.

Losing face is often equated with being disgraced, shamed, reproached, discredited, degraded, ridiculed, humiliated, or having one's ego bruised.

## Face: A Four Letter Word

The following comments are not designed to be the definitive analysis on face, but are rather intended to serve as a kind of guideline. The non-native who is living in China will want to make his own observations, and collect some of his own data, so that he may better deal with the entire Chinese concept of face.

Most of the reactions given herein and described as a "loss of face" are given from a fairly conservative point of view, yet all of the situations described here really did happen. The foreigner will want to note if the Chinese he meets do indeed react in these ways and regard certain types of situations as a "loss of face", or whether they adopt a more liberalized attitude, and downplay the significance of these types of situations. For those Chinese who do act more liberalized, it may however be true that their parents and grandparents are more traditional, and the influence of these elders may be felt at certain times, with demands that the children (even 30 and 40 year old children) behave in certain ways. Additionally, any Chinese may be subject to the influence of more conservative spouses, friends, and colleagues at various times.

In any event, whenever the more traditional "face saving" stance is adopted, the foreigner should be aware that in such situations to try to persuade the Chinese to change their point of view through rational logical discussion or debate may be an exercise in futility.

Considerations of Gaining or Losing Face are involved in the following types of activities:

Clothes and Wearing Apparel

Many people like to dress nicely, and hence pay much attention to wearing clean, attractive, well styled clothing. If the members of their family, their superiors, close friends, and others with whom they associate regularly, or with whom they are seen with in public, also wear attractive clothing, when they go out together with these well dressed people they gain face. If however, these people wear unattractive clothing, or dress too casually, then they lose face.

When the group feels that a particular type of clothing is suitable for a particular occasion, to not wear this clothing can cause a loss of face. For the westerner who prefers casual wear on all occasions, the failure for a male to wear a suit and tie (or for a female to wear other appropriate attire) to a Chinese friend's wedding could very well result in a loss of face for the bride and groom, their parents, and the other guests, especially those at the table with whom one is seated.

When being introduced for a new job, for one to arrive in overly casual wear, even to the extent of looking unkempt, is a serious loss of face for the person making the introduction. Hence, in regard to most types of jobs, it is good advice to ask the introducing party what appropriate clothing would be.

All of this this corresponds to many of the more conservative notions about proper clothing in the west, especially as regards going to church, going to formal banquets or dances, meeting various government officials in their offices, etc. If someone is "inappropriately dressed" it could be very embarassing to others in his party. However, the Chinese concept of face in this regard is much more broadly based, and hence any people who feel themselves well dressed and who go out with someone whom they consider "inappropriately dressed" to any sort of meeting, social function, business appointment, or even family gathering could very well feel a loss of face.

It should be noted that face in this sense is clearly a subjective matter. What one person considers nice clothing another may consider in poor taste, and the chance of this kind of difference of opinion occurring is of course multiplied when people of different cultural backgrounds come together. Being a subjective matter, it is also relational: if a country-bumpkin Mr. Ding wears old torn clothing and his wife and family members do too, it is possible than none of them consider this as a loss of face. In the context of their lifestyle, this is normal clothing.

Talking, Speech, and Actions
*A direct rebuttal of one person's statement or claim, especially in front of others, can cause loss of face.*
  Example: Mary says: "I think this piece of artwork is very nice."
           John says: "I think it is ugly."
Mary, and her friends, could interpret this as a loss of face (for Mary) because her opinion is being scorned.
  Example: Teacher says: "The French Revolution occurred in 1778. Many of the students got this wrong on the last test. Please be more conscientious in the future."
  Student says: "You are mistaken. The French Revolution occurred in 1789, and that is the answer I put on my test. I do not understand why it was marked wrong."
The teacher, and the other students in the class, could interpret this as a loss of face (for the teacher) since his/her knowledge and expertise have been questioned and/or found faulty.
  Example: Congressman says: "I have always supported legislation which will create a cleaner and healthier environment."
  Citizen says: "That is not true. Three months ago the Congress considered the case of a highly-polluting aluminum manufacturing plant some 400 miles from here, and you voted to extend the time deadline on closing the plant again, even though it has already been extended twice."
The Congressman, and the other people present when this exchange took place, could interpret this as a loss of face (for the Congressman) since his claims are being rebutted.
  Any statement to the effect that someone else is stupid or ignorant, out of touch with the times, out of touch with reality, blind to the facts, etc. is often taken as a loss of face. In situations where these statements are felt appropriate, it is often better to offer no opinion at all, if one cannot be sure that one's remarks will not be taken as losing face for the other party or parties. In a formal negotiation session, and where one does desire to make such comments, a preface to one's statement such as "I am sorry if what I want to say here causes a loss of face for (so and so), however I must point out that . . . . " although rarely effective, nevertheless does inform everyone present that you have a more than superficial understanding of Chinese culture.
  Face dictates that we respect others' opinions when we are with them, especially if they are our teachers, elders, or superiors, and not dispute the claims they make, even when they are at a variance with the facts.

Hence in China, debates between people in public, especially those with above average educational backgrounds, often tend to be seriously downplayed, since each party may try to avoid saying anything which will cast doubt on the other side's suppositions, and cause that side to "lose face". Some types of political debates appear to be exceptions to this, but the comments made therein are often not reported in the newspapers, because this would be a loss of face for the parties shown to be hypocritical, misguided, ignorant, etc.

When studying a foreign language, many Chinese feel that to speak incorrectly, whether due to pronunciation or grammar, is a loss of face. Hence, many Chinese, especially those who start studying foreign languages at a late age, have difficulty developing conversational skills, because of their fear of making mistakes and losing face.

The Peking pronunciation is standard Chinese pronunciation, and is promoted in the schools. However many teachers speak with provincial accents. For someone to point out that a certain teacher's pronunciation is "not standard", and should be corrected, is to result in a loss of face for that teacher. In some cases it is even true that the teacher's accent is so heavy that the students cannot understand what he is saying. To suggest that this teacher be retrained, or preferably replaced, is not to give face, and is therefore something not properly brought up.

A certain number of Chinese students major in Chinese language studies in college. One incident comes to mind where a group of such students asked what their employment prospects would be for teaching Chinese in western countries. An American who had studied Mandarin for several years said: "You will have to have excellent Peking pronunciation to get a job in a Chinese language department in any school in the west, and several of you speak with provincial accents." This was regarded as a loss of face by the students whom he indicated as speaking non-standard Mandarin.

The same situation can arise when dealing with Chinese who speak English, especially college graduates who majored in English. An American who was interviewing a Chinese applicant for an English teaching position in a private academy asked if the person was working at the present time.

*Applicant: No, I do not have any work now.*
*Foreigner: Do you have any teaching experience?*
*Applicant: I teach a class of four boys near my home, and I also have a small class at my sister's house on Sunday evenings.*
*Foreigner: How many students are there in that class?*
*Applicant: What class?*
*Foreigner: The Sunday evening class at your sister's.*
*Applicant: No, I have no Sunday class.*
*Foreigner: I thought you just said you had a Sunday class.*
*Applicant: That was before.*
*Foreigner: How many students did you teach before?*
*Applicant: I teach a class of four boys near my home, and I also have a small class at my sister's house*

on Sunday evenings.
*Foreigner: But your verb tenses are not correct. You should say "taught a class", "had a small class" if the action was in the past.*

The Chinese applicant was very flustered by this last remark, regarding it as a loss of face, since her ability in English had been questioned. Afterward the American changed his tactics, and would never orally mention grammatical mistakes[1] when interviewing people for teacher positions, although he did make note of them in his written evaluation to the academy's director. He thus enabled the interviewees to keep their face no matter how faulty their grammar was.

*Talking down to someone, such as an employee, hired party, etc., or scolding them, putting them on the spot, pointing out their faults, etc., especially in front of others (friends, coworkers, etc.), but also if spoken privately, is often a loss of face.*

* A Chinese employee was assigned to have a report done by a certain date. When it was not completed on time, the employee asked for a time extension. This was refused by the foreign manager, because he reasoned: "If you wanted a time extension, you should have applied for it before the original completion date, and with a full statement of your reasons."

The employee and his co-workers took this as a loss of face, because his request that sympathy be given his situation, and he be granted an extension, had been turned down.

* A Chinese secretary asked the foreign manager in her company which chops (wooden stamps) were used to complete employees' monthly income tax procedures. The manager pointed out "You have been in charge of these procedures for several months already." She agreed that that was true. "How can you expect me to keep the chops straight if you Chinese people cannot?" he asked.

The secretary interpreted this as a loss of face, because her request for assistance was being scorned. Note: A company in China could literally have dozens of these wooden stamps or chops in the office, for use in completing various types of paperwork. Since they are generally carved in highly stylistic Chinese characters, it is unlikely that the average foreigner can keep them straight, and know which one should be used where. However, it is still necessary to be patient with the Chinese employee's request for clarification, and allow her to spend the time necessary to sort the matter out, perhaps by having a discussion with other secretaries, in order to make up for her poor memory, and save her face.

Hence we see that the Chinese also tend to interpret remarks which are overly blunt and direct as "talking down" to someone, and this will often lead to hurt feelings.

*Putting someone on the spot is almost always taken as a loss of face for the party involved.*

---

1. Nor did he give them any suggestions for improvement, since these would have been regarded as coming from "a stranger". The perceptual difficulty which Chinese have in dealing with strangers is discussed more fully in Chapter 10.

* A company was expanding operations, and had rented additional space on another floor in their same office building. Some welding was being done in conjunction with the installation of the air conditioning equipment in the new office, and the foreign manager in the original office asked the head welder if he could come for five minutes a re-weld a loose metal handle on the metal door in their main office, since this was a minor job which normally he could not contact a welder to do. The head welder agreed to do it. Several days passed, and the welders finished their air conditioning work and left with all their equipment. The foreign manager asked his secretary to call and ask the welding crew why they had not welded the door handle as they had originally promised. The secretary explained that no doubt they had forgotten, but to call them up and put them on the spot, or ask that they make a special trip out to do this minor job would be a loss of face for them, and thus it was better just to drop the matter entirely.

Similar situations could occur when a Chinese service company has promised to come at a certain time to do repair work, or installation work, but does not arrive. Generally a call to the company at this point will fail to find anyone who knows anything about it, however if the manager can be located he will often have abundant excuses as to why his work crew has not yet arrived. If the caller refuses to accept these excuses, the manager and his staff can easily regard this as a loss of face.

* According to the relevant national ministry in charge of coastal area management, all the locality south of a certain costal city, including beach area and costal waters, is available for recreational purposes. However when a locally licensed passenger craft attempts to take fisherman out into these waters for recreational fishing, they are stopped on the spot by the local authorities and told that no such fishing is allowed. When they are told of the national ministry's ruling, and/or shown a copy of it, the local authorities shake their heads and say "We have not received official notification or documentation of this yet." When the people who are unable to fish complain about this, the local authorities view their remarks as a loss of face.

* A meeting is called for all licensed private academies teaching commercial type courses (typing, accounting, abacus, business letter writing, etc.) in a large Chinese city, and a number of government officials from different departments are present. New regulations which apply to the academies are announced, and various representatives of the academies raise questions. One topic mentioned is the issue of transferring a business license to a new address when an academy moves. Formerly no transfer was allowed, however nine months ago the Ministry of Education and National Tax Administration approved such a measure, and notified all other relevant departments. However the manager of one commercial school, Mr. Peng, notes that his recent application for transfer of business license was turned down by the City Department of Building Administration, and when he explained that such moves were allowed, that Department said "We have not received official notification or documentation of this yet." When Mr. Peng demands that this matter be resolved on the spot, the government officials present view this demand as causing them a loss of face, since they say

"We are sincere in telling you that we will look into it." Mr. Peng states: "That is what you said six months ago," and this is further regarded as not giving face.

*More explicitly, we see that putting someone on the spot by pointing out a difference between what they say and what they do (or did) generally results in a loss of face.*

\* A number of people have agreed to come to an important dinner meeting, and Mr. Lin is one of them. If Mr. Lin fails to show up, most Chinese would let it go at that. To call him up later for an explanation would generally be viewed as not giving face. If the host was rude enough to call, it would be expected that in order to save face, Mr. Lin would no doubt reply by saying the first thing that came to his mind, such as "I had an another important appointment", "My brother had to go have emergency surgery", "My uncle's sister-in-law's neighbor's cousin had an accident", etc.

> Examination of such remarks also gives us a valuable insight into the Chinese concept of honesty. The westerners might gravitate toward the view that "Speaking the truth is honest", and "Speaking something which is not the truth is dishonest", however in cross-cultural interchanges such a classification is not always so readily applicable. To the Chinese, when one's remarks are made without deliberate intent to cheat, defraud, or physically harm, they are essentially outside of the honesty/dishonesty spectrum. Hence we are rather hardpressed to classify Mr. Lin's remarks here as lying, and in any event they may be dismissed with the rejoinder: "Oh, that's not a question of honesty, he is just trying to save face."
>
> What we can say with certainty is that responses of this type lack straightforwardness. The Chinese would no doubt agree that such remarks are "highly indirect".

Caution is also warranted in regard to any project which one Chinese has "promised" or "agreed" to do for another person. If the project, assistance, arrangements, etc. are made on time as originally specified, all is well. If they are not, sometimes no further word is heard about the matter at all. If the affected person asks for an explanation, this may be regarded as rudeness and not giving face.

If the project is done inefficiently, vociferous complaint will also be generally taken as loss of face.

*Anything which might lead to a false impression, and be a sensitive issue (often by ultra-conservative standards) may be viewed as a loss of face.*

At a party in a Chinese family's home, the eldest girl in the family, Shu-jwan, got out a camera to take pictures of those present. At the end of her picture taking session, there were still two photos left on the roll, and she asked if any of the foreigners present would like to have their pictures taken again. Since one boy, Robert, was planning to leave shortly, it was suggested that he have his picture taken in turn with each of the the two younger sisters, Shu-ling and Shu-min. The elder sister hastily put the camera away, and no further pictures were shot.

As it was later explained to one of the foreigners who followed up on this incident, since Shu-ling's boyfriend was present, it would have been a loss of face for him for his girlfriend to have her picture taken together with the foreigner in his presence, and without him in the picture. Shu-min was also very young, an 11th grader, and for her to have a picture taken with a foreigner individually, could also perhaps suggest that something was going on between them. This would have been a loss of face for her and her parents since good girls of this age devote themselves purely to their studies.

This incident seems to have been particularly complicated by the fact that the three sister's parents were in attendance, and that Robert was essentially unacquainted with the two younger sisters. Had he been friends with this family for a longer period of time, or had taught the girls English, or had participated in some group outings with them, etc., the potential loss of face involved with this photography might not have existed.

*Anything which might lead to a very good or positive impression, especially as regards a display of power, connections, generosity, etc. is generally viewed as getting face.*

A number of photographers of my acquaintance have pointed out that among people who travel, there is quite a difference in photography habits. When Chinese on a trip take pictures, nearly every shot has people included. Westerners tend to take a lot of scenic shots. This disparity is somewhat explained by noting that the Chinese see being together with many friends and relatives as having face.

In a similar fashion, for people to have their pictures taken together with foreign dignitaries or other famous personalities is to gain face, since anyone in such distinguished company must be important. Historically, for thousands of years China was a very advanced nation which received tributes from foreign states. This confirmed China's position as the leader of civilization. Foreign leaders who visit China today invariably bring some gifts, and the Chinese dignitaries gain much face by having their pictures taken together with them and/or their "tributes".

The possession of expert scholarship amounts to gaining face, however it is not necessarily equated with being "superior in knowledge". Having been awarded a Ph.D. in Economics is to have face in an abstract sense, however for a person with this degree to argue with a layman (who might be a government official) about what constitutes "proper economic policy" would be viewed by most Chinese as rude, and to promptly destroy the layman's arguments with a superior theoretical structure and/or the presentation of more authoritative factual data would often be seen as not giving face. We must remember that the Chinese have a high integration between the the concepts of "self confidence" and "arrogance", and the announced and preferred Oriental virtue is modesty.

*Failure to follow traditional custom, especially as regards a display of wealth, generosity, superior connections, excellent ability, etc. is often directly seen as a loss of face.*

Many of the traditional customs which are associated with Chinese engagements and marriages tend to be very extravagant, especially as regards the number of people to whom "engagement cakes" must be given, the number of friends and relatives who must be invited to the wedding dinner, the amount of electrical appliances and material possessions which must be prepared for the new couple's home, and other items such as a bride price (given to the bride's family), a dowry (given by the bride's family), and additional gifts.

To not follow custom (as deemed appropriate by the elders) in this regard is frequently viewed as a serious loss of face to the family.

When a man and woman get married, it is often true that some of their brothers and sisters are still as yet unmarried. Since Chinese commonly give gifts of cash (in red envelopes) at weddings, it may occur in the future that the size of gift which the wife feels appropriate for them to give to her sister (upon the announcement of the sister's impending wedding) is objected to as being *too extravagant* by her husband. The wife may feel that if an "inadequate" amount of money is given, she will lose face. In addition to discussing the size of their own (husband and wife's combined) red envelope to give to this sister, the wife may also want to discuss the appropriate size of red envelope which the husband's parents, brothers and sisters, etc. are expected to give as well. If this is inadequate by the wife's standards, she may also feel that she will lose face.

The same problem could develop when a close relative of either spouse is getting married, and after their marriage, upon the arrival of the relative's new baby. Some sort of banquet is often held to celebrate a baby's first month of life, with friends and relatives all properly invited, and all expected to bring something more than an oral expression of well-wishes. Cash is preferred, and differing views between the husband and wife on what amount is suitable could lead one party to feel they will lose face if their opinion in the matter is not respected.

Although many scholars have noted that there is a strong undercurrent of "non-materialism" in Chinese thinking, this is not true in 100% of situations. Marriages (and related events, such as child-bearing) traditionally tend to be strongly associated with shows of wealth and possessions. If it is beyond the means of the family in question to have elaborate arrangements, then money may be borrowed from friends and relatives to pay for a suitable "display of success, wealth, and prosperity". To a certain extent, the same is true of funerals, and the amount of money spent may put the family in financial straits for a lengthy period. Much face is gained by conducting marriages and funerals in a pompous and elaborate manner.

In more traditionally minded families, an unmarried daughter above the age of 27 or 28 (approximately) may be regarded as a loss of face. This daughter "that no one wants" is a direct reflection on the family's inadequate social status and connections, and seems to imply that she was not raised properly. Due to the Chinese practice of ancestor worship, every person who is deceased is honored by a small tablet which is engraved with their name (*ling wei* [a]), and kept in the home, or paternal parent's home.

---

a. 靈位

Face as a Commodity

Two foreigners were heard discussing nutrition. One said that according to a recent scientific report he had read, eating raw fish is good for the health. His friend replied: "I don't buy that."

The use of "buy" as a synonym for **accept, adopt or agree to** (in speaking of a reason, plan, explanation, etc.), and having no direct relation to financial transactions, does not exist in Chinese, however we do find a related, though narrower, usage of "buy" in relation to "buying face".[a]

This must be considered of course within the entire framework of a "desired on-going mutually beneficial relationship". An important premise of Chinese social relations is "Don't make enemies". Under the influence of this premise, we may discuss the "buying" and "selling" of face. If there is another person with whom we desire an on-going beneficial relationship, then we will "buy" their face, which means give them preferential treatment, be especially attentive to their needs, make some sacrifices for them, not make any unnecessary trouble for them, stand up for them when they get in trouble or in a dispute, etc. (The issue of who is "right" and "wrong" in the dispute is largely irrelevant.)

In addition, we will treat their friends in a similar manner, and this amounts to further "buying" of their face. When we "buy", the other party "sells", so buying and selling are really two sides of the same coin.

One of our friends may have a problem which he needs solved by some particular agency, bureau, or other organization, however they are reticent to undertake it. If we know someone high up in the relevant organization, we may send our friend in with this a special request, and ask that he mention our name. If the person in charge then grants the request, this is clearly "buying" our face, in other words we have made a successful "sale".

This is then worshipped. A daughter is said to "offer sacrifices for another family's ancestors" – she is considered belonging to the family of her husband. A daughter who dies unmarried is forbidden from having her tablet placed in her own parent's home. (It may be rented a place in a local temple, however this is equivalent to the treatment given those without a family, and is often seen as very degrading.) Despite the lip-service given to equality between men and women in the present era, there has been no attempt to change this practice, or the underlying attitude, in the current age, and to accord women an equal place with men in the location assignment of ancestral tablets.[1]

A daughter who is divorced is also commonly looked upon as a loss of face for the family, and similar considerations to those given above for unmarried daughters apply.

For a woman to marry a rich husband is regarded as gaining face. For a man to marry a beautiful wife is to gain face.

Refusal of Aid and Assistance, Personal or Business

In terms of a wide variety of dealings, if a request for assistance is made, and a direct refusal is received, this will generally be taken as not giving face. This would happen

---

1. Clearly this entire issue is related to the state religion of ancestor worship.
a. 買面子

when someone asks for the help of a good friend, co-worker (present or former), classmate, neighbor, etc., and is refused.

* A man who served as your boss in your last place of employment calls to ask that you, (because you have a say in the hiring of people for certain positions in your company), give special consideration to his friend, Mr. Chwang, who is coming in to apply. If you hire Mr. Chwang, all is well, and your former boss has face. (If Mr. Chwang turns out to be a person of excellent ability, and is of great benefit to your company, your former boss gets much face.) If you do not hire Mr. Chwang, and do not help him to find other suitable employment, and fail to offer any appropriate explanation to your former boss, he and Mr. Chwang both lose face.

* The registration period for students in a certain school has run out. You had not realized that it was so late, and you really desire your son to go to this school. You ask a City Councilman of your acquaintance to intercede in your behalf with the school officials. If he does so, and your son is allowed to register, you have face. If he does not do so, and your son still cannot register, you have lost face.

* Mary Jones is asked by Mr. Wong to introduce some foreigners to his singing club, which is a group of people which meets twice a week to sing Chinese songs, and is now interested in forming a "foreign choir". Mary is very busy with her studies, work, and research, and knows of no one in her realm of friends who would be interested in this. In order to avoid giving a direct refusal, she says that she will try to find some suitable people, but cannot guarantee anything. At this point she is then free to go about her normal affairs, and/or forget that this conversation ever took place. If and when Mary meets Mr. Wong again, she is free to say "I am sorry, I have not been able to find anyone." This saves everyone's face.

Note: Mary's approach illustrates a "modified foreign style" of avoiding giving a direct refusal, since she uses expressions like "I will try", "I cannot guarantee anything", etc. Most Chinese would take a much more affirmative stance, (perhaps even to the point of promising to find a specific number of people), before they proceeded to 1) let their "go with the flow" lifestyle lead them to being diverted to other activities, or 2) forget the issue entirely. Some westerners would say that either of these two alternatives amount to the same thing.

In order to counter this aspect of not giving face, it may be necessary in some cases to first agree to help the other person, and then to contact them later and say that some emergency has come up, and that you are now unable to be of assistance. This is a particularly useful technique in dealing with requests for borrowing (or otherwise using your) money, checks, real estate documents, etc. Another technique is to first agree to consider the issue, and later say that a long-lost uncle or other relative has recently shown up on the scene, and needs these items for his import-export business, bank dealings, etc.

Eating and Dining

Expensive dinner parties are often associated with many types of events, such as aged parents' birthdays, friends coming back from study abroad, friends or classmates being promoted in their place of employment, birth of new children, etc. Businessmen may treat friends, relatives, and neighbors to dinner after the successful conclusion of an important business deal. Many westerners would say that these feasts could often be done without, however this attitude fails to realize that the more elaborate such arrangements are, the more face is gained by the person paying for them, even if he has to borrow money to do so. If the arrangements are too simple or modest, much face may be lost.

In restaurants in the west it is generally acceptable to send back dishes which are not prepared to one's satisfaction, including steaks, salad, vegetables, etc. However, in China this is generally regarded as a loss of face for the chef, and/or kitchen staff, and possibly for the waiters and waitresses, and even for the other people (guests) seated at the table as well. Hence, many Chinese try to avoid the issue, and will perhaps leave the dish uneaten, although paying for it anyway. If one points out to the service staff that fish or other meats are not fresh, that beancurd or other dishes have gone sour, etc. this will almost invariably be denied by them, in order to save face, and regardless of any objective consideration of the condition of the food in question. It is interesting to note that even a signed statement by a Ph.D. in Food Science that the food was indeed bad would often be denied by the Chinese staff involved, in order to save face, and this is another example of a non-evidential bias in Chinese thinking, which serves as a basis for what is considered "proper behavior".

For foreigners who are associating with Chinese (of the opposite sex) in various types of "living, loving, and learning" situations, it should be remembered that any sorts of disputes, arguments, serious differences of opinion, etc. that arise with the Chinese party's family members or relatives, over the dinner table or any other time, on any issues, could easily be viewed as a loss of face, with the result that the otherwise promising amorous relationship goes down the drain. Objective evidence which one can marshal to the defense of one's point of view will often be ignored by the Chinese family/clan.

Many businessmen and other people who wish to make a display of their generosity feel that it is a loss of face to examine the bill in a restaurant or nightclub. When they are given the bill, they pay it in a great show of carefree opulence, and do not worry about the correctness of the calculation. Many feel that much face is gained by this type of attitude and conduct.

Face in the home environment and a valuable lesson in "Chinese Style Human Relations" are illustrated by the story of Mr. and Mrs. Ching, Mr. Ching's close friend — Mr. Feng, and Mr. Ching's boss — Mr. Bin. Mr. Ching formerly invited Mr. Bin to drop by his house sometime for some imported Napoleon brandy, but no definite date was set. One afternoon the friend Mr. Feng drops by Mr. Ching's house, and they have a chat. Mr. Ching asks what he would like to drink. Mr. Feng says "Anything would be fine." Considering the situation Mr. Ching gets out some medium quality tea, and introduces it as a high-quality brand which he purchased recently. They drink tea and talk.

Unexpectedly, the boss Mr. Bin arrives. If Mr. Ching now brings out the brandy, Mr. Feng will consider this a loss of face "Oh, you had brandy all along but you didn't want to treat me!" If Mr. Ching doesn't bring out the brandy, Mr. Bin will feel that he has been slighted. The solution in this case is for Mr. Ching to loudly announce to his wife: "Where did you place that Napoleon brandy? I was looking for it all over a few minutes ago, and I couldn't find it!"

Mrs. Ching, recognizing that such remarks are a face saving gesture for the sake of Mr. Feng, will quickly say "Oh, I put it in our closet when I was cleaning the kitchen yesterday." She will then take the brandy out of its storage place in the kitchen and bring it out. Mr. Ching may then ask "Did you buy any snack items when you went to that new luxury supermarket this morning?" Mrs. Ching, who does all of her food purchasing in the alley shops and open-air markets, will reply "Yes, I have some excellent beef jerky and dried fruits," and she will bring these out. The observant westerner will see that much face has been gained for all concerned by carrying on in this manner.

* A foreign trained chemist inspected some shrimp being unloaded at the docks in a Chinese harbor, and in his chemical laboratory found that a great many of them were tainted with mercury. When word of this got out to the press, several prominent articles were written, and sales of shrimp nosedived in the next two days, finally levelling off at zero. Captains of fishing boats, wholesalers in seafood, and other economically affected parties complained to various government officials, and an official government investigation was launched. The result of this was that government employed chemists in the Chinese Health Department determined that there was no mercury contamination in the local shrimps. When the original laboratory heard of this, they demanded that samples of shrimp be taken to Japan for more authoritative testing, however this was denied. Several legislators pointed out privately that if samples of shrimp had been taken to a Japanese laboratory and found to be contaminated, this would have been a serious loss of face for the officials in the Chinese Health Department.

Educational Background and Academic Status

A person's educational achievements are directly related to his face. For a student who has graduated from high school to have successfully passed the tests to enter a prestigious university is to gain much face for himself and his family. To graduate from the university is to gain more face, and to attend a university overseas is to gain further face. If dinner parties are held to celebrate such events, to the extent that the arrangements are elaborate, much face is gotten by all concerned.

When two close relatives participate in various types of contests, academic or otherwise, for the younger person to get a higher award than the older one may often result in a loss of face for the latter. Speech contests are good examples of this. After a contest where a third grade child got third place, and her sixth grade sister got fifth place, both kept a stiff upper lip during the judging, but were seen to be in tears afterward, and a foreigner inquired "What's the problem?" The older child said "I lost face," and the younger child said "I caused her to lose face." Although the bad feelings associated with this incident may pass in a few days, for anyone to bring this up again in conversation could cause additional "discomfort".

In Confucian doctrine, teachers are highly regarded, hence to be a teacher is regarded in Chinese society as having much face. One also gains face by engaging in scholarly pursuits, and authoring books or contributing to the literary page in magazines and newspapers is an excellent way to gain face. Although many institutes of higher learning in the west have regular opinion surveys on the students' feelings toward the teachers of different courses, especially as regards the clarity of the material presented, interest generated in class, difficulty of testing, competency in subject matter, etc., it would be extremely rare for the Chinese colleges and universities to have such collected or published data. If such remarks were to be circulated, they would certainly cause a loss of face for the teachers who received low ratings. The resulting loss of respect in students' eyes would be in violation of Confucius' teachings.

Many times in the west a school will have a fair day or circus day, and teachers will even participate in various events, such as being the target for a pie throwing contest, taking their turn on the dunking stool, climbing the oiled pole, chasing the greased pig, playing tug-of-war in the mud, etc. Participation in any of these activites by a Chinese teacher clearly appears to involve a loss of face.

Although it is hard to collect objective data on the subject, inspection of the textbooks used in Chinese colleges and universities, (over and above those textbooks edited by the National Ministry of Education), reveals a preference for requiring the use of Chinese textbooks when they have actually been written by the instructor, and English language textbooks when the instructor in question has not written an appropriate text. This would appear to indicate that Chinese teachers and professors regard it as a loss of face to use Chinese textbooks written by other Chinese professors in their field. Their assumption here must be that the other teachers are more expert than they, and this lack of expertise is taken as a loss of face.[1] Some western observers have suggested that this is a good piece of evidence for examining the contention that the Chinese "heart-breast"[a] (often translated as: capacity for tolerance) is actually quite narrow.

Unequal Financial Remuneration

*The issue of salary, bonuses, and fringe benefits are often very face-sensitive, and to a degree that baffles westerners.*

---

a. 心胸

1. Certainly this is related to the Chinese idea of 文人相輕 "Men of letters tend to despise one another."

A notice was put up in a Chinese university requesting applicants for the position of teaching assistant (TA), to work part-time in the branches of a local private language institute. From among all the applicants, six were chosen and they were told that there would be no salary payment for the first three days of work, only transportation fee, since that was considered their training period. Normal salary payment at the agreed upon hourly rate would begin on the fourth day of work. At the time of hiring, all of the six were unacquainted with each other. Three were assigned to one branch location, and three to another.

At the beginning of the following month, salary payments were made. Due to an administrative error, the three TAs at one branch location were in fact given salary payment for their hours worked in the first three days of service, while the TAs at the other branch were not, as per the original stated conditions. Before this matter could be straightened out, the latter three TA's resigned because they felt that they had lost face in this unequal salary payment arrangement.

This example is particularly interesting in that it shows that the "Group Mentality" immediately came into play. These six students instantaneously formed a group, each one in contact with all others regarding all financial conditions of his/her employment. Several westerners who heard of this situation were tempted to go to the university and ask the teachers in their major departments "What are you teaching these students anyway?", but realizing that that would be a loss of face for the teachers involved, they decided to drop the matter.

A Chinese secretary who had been particularly busy during the summer months was given a bonus with her salary payment for September, equivalent to approximately 1/6 of her monthly salary. She regarded this as a loss of face, and immediately questioned her supervisor on two points: 1) How much did other people get? 2) Why did I only get this amount? If I am deserving of a bonus, surely it should be more than this?

The fact that the secretary was given a one-time bonus at a "non-bonus time" seems to have been a major cause in inciting her suspicion. Chinese employees are traditionally given a bonus at the Chinese New Year, and a bonus or other gift at the Mid-Autumn Festival and Dragon Boat Festival. Hence she regarded a bonus accompanying September's salary as perhaps indicating that the boss was trying to cover up some previous slighting of her interest or benefit.[1]

In a Book I saw once on "Games Chinese People Play" the following one was not listed, however I offer it here for reference, under the title of "Sympathetic Fence Straddling."[2] The game goes like this: first, in order to bargain for higher wages, some medium or high level administrative employees (abbreviated here as "H-employees" for ease of discussion) who feel that they are particularly valuable to the organization will convince some other employees a bit lower in the hierarchy (abbreviated here as "L-

---

1. A more in-depth treatment of bonus payments is given in Chapter 11.
2. However I find no equivalent terminology in Chinese.

employees") that the latter are underpaid, in light of their intelligence, experience, and competence. Let us assume that Teresa is the effective leader of the H-employees in this tactic. Teresa assures certain L-employees that if they express the desire to quit, and submit a letter of resignation, the boss will be sure to lure them to stay by raising their salaries. Teresa adds that when the boss calls on her to discuss the situation, she will advocate that "they are too valuable to let go", "we would have a hard time getting along without them," etc.

The observant reader will see that if some of the L-employees do submit their letters of resignation, Teresa has now effectively set herself up in a "no lose" situation. No matter what happens from this point on, she wins. In general, there are three possible outcomes.

A) If the boss does agree after some consideration to raise the L-employees' salaries in order to keep them on the job, the they will feel that this was done on Teresa's recommendation, hence will be in her debt. Concurrently, Teresa may go to the boss shortly thereafter and ask for a raise based on the fact that the other employees have already received one.

B) If the boss does not make any efforts to raise the L-employees' salaries in order to lure them to stay, Teresa can go to the boss in their support, describing them as "too valuable to lose", etc., while assuring the boss that her greatest and primary concern is of course the future prosperity of the company, since a prosperous company needs to retain good personnel. Furthermore, she can state that by not pleading with the L-employees to stay, management has caused them a terrific loss of face. If Teresa succeeds in this line of persuasion, we are back to part A. If not, we move on to part C.

C) If the employees are not retained, Teresa can tell management that: "At the final moment when everyone was contemplating quitting en-masse because of the company's lack of sympathy for their position and not giving face, I decided to stay with the company, because I am a loyal company person." In this way she should be able to further endear herself to the boss, and she can use this as a bargaining chip in future discussions over salary, bonuses, time-off, and other working conditions.

For those who think this is an unlikely scenario, consider the added eventuality that certain of the L-employees have former high school or college classmates working in other organizations and making more money, and recently hinting to these L-employees that jobs may indeed be available over there.

One Chinese manager of our acquaintance summed up the situation when he noted — If the employees clarify their real concern in the matter by saying *"It is not money, it is face,"* then it is money.

Being Financially Impoverished

*Direct or indirect references to a person as being poor are often regarded as a loss of face.*

Many more traditionally-minded Chinese husbands regard their wife going out into society and taking a job as a loss of face. The implication (from their point of view) is "I am not capable enough to earn enough money to support my wife and family. Therefore my wife has gone to get a job." Many husbands therefore desire that their wives stay home and confine themselves to the housekeeping chores only.

If a Chinese man has a girlfriend who earns more money, or is more accomplished, famous, than he is, this will generally produce various degrees of psychological imbalance in the man. Any small gestures which the woman makes in this situation, especially in terms of being attentive to his needs, can be taken by the man as a loss of face. Such gestures could include offering a cup of warm milk when the man is reading or studying late at night, or purchasing personal-care and toiletry items from the market for him, or many other seemingly innocent activities. Most couples will break up under the strain of this traditional Chinese male chauvinistic attitude. When the wife exceeds the accomplishments of the husband, this can often lead to divorce, due to the perceived loss of male face involved.

In light of these factors, it is considered rude and not giving face to introduce a man at a party, meeting, or any other gathering by saying "Let me introduce the husband of Ms. Wong, this is . . . " This type of introduction gives the impression that the woman is more accomplished, or in a superior position to the man. Regardless of the facts of the matter, attention to face requires that the man be introduced first, and his wife's status mentioned only in passing. For example: "Let me introduce Mr. X, he is involved with _____ , his wife is our Ambassador to Japan, and Nobel Laureate in Poetry, and President of the Agency for International Development, and former Dean of the local Law School."

Many more traditionally-minded Chinese parents regard their high school or college age children taking a job (in the outside community) as a loss of face. The implication (from their point of view) is "I am not capable enough to provide for my family's needs, so my child has gone to get a job." Many headmasters or principals of schools have similar feelings, and do not approve of their students taking part-time jobs doing anything which is in the realm of manual labor. (To the extent that the children are helping in a family-run business, these considerations may not apply however.)

We Do Not Need Your Charity

We recall the incident of a foreigner who frequently visited a park in the early morning hours, and met several Chinese people who were practicing shadow-boxing and martial arts. He joined in their group, although they would not accept any payment from him. After several months of practicing, the weather began to turn cold, and he noticed that none of the Chinese had gloves. From the way they were rubbing their hands together and blowing on them, he surmised that they were cold. Since he was working in a trading company that exported gloves, and had access to many free samples, he decided to give each of the Chinese a pair. The next day when he did so, they thanked him very much. However, on the following day, and future days, the Chinese did not wear their gloves, but continued to rub their hands together and blow on them.

When he asked another Chinese about this, she explained it in the following way: His fellow shadow boxers no doubt felt that to wear the gloves he had given them in front of him would be a tacit admission that "We are too poor to buy gloves", and therefore be a loss of face. The foreigner doubted that any of these people were too poor to buy gloves, and said that he certainly had never intended to imply so. However his Chinese friend explained that a traditional stance would be to view his actions in this light.

In any event, foreigners should be aware of the fact that many times when gifts of clothing, wearing apparel, or accessories are given to Chinese friends, the Chinese will not wear them in the foreigner's presence unless specifically requested to do so, and then often only after much explaining. It is also true that Chinese will often refuse gifts which are offered by foreigners, (or occasionally return them after the fact). Among most westerners, to refuse a gift would be considered extremely rude, and to return it would be an insult.

The Chinese do much gift giving, (the Japanese do more) however most of it does fall into the traditional patterns, such as in conjunction with celebrating engagements, weddings, anniversaries, new births, promotions, or other important occasions in the family/relative/clan structure, as well as on traditional Chinese holidays. It is also suitable to give gifts when meeting (especially when being introduced to) someone important for the first time, when visiting people in hospitals, when arriving at someone's home for dinner, etc. The foreigner in the above example has given a gift for no apparent reason (although he felt he was offering a token of gratitude for their instruction in shadow boxing), and this was regarded as irregular.

### Cash on the Barrelhead

Many Chinese businessmen like to pay their suppliers with post-dated checks, sometimes dated 90 days or more in the future. If the supplier asks for "cash" (which may be loosely interpreted as payment within 20 or 30 days, and could be in the form of a post-dated check redeemable in that relatively short period), many businessmen take this as a loss of face, regarding it to mean "You think I am poor and cannot pay cash?" The businessman's rationale is that of course he is financially well-off enough to pay cash, but paying by 90-day check is just his standard business practice. The supplier must then reply that he intended no loss of face by asking for cash, and certainly knows that the businessman is very reputable and creditworthy, etc.

### New Considerations in the Hippocratic Oath

Many Chinese doctors who have lived in the West make the observation that there is more transfer of patients between hospitals in North American than in China. Taking the welfare of its patients in mind, hospitals could want to transfer patients to other hospitals which have better facilities for handling their particular cases. Many Chinese hospitals however may consider the face of the hospital as more important, and be greatly hesitant to transfer a patient to another hospital, since such transfer would tend to indicate that the transferring hospital had inadequate facilities, or inadequately trained doctors, and thus would amount to a loss of face.[1] (Note: Branches of the same hospital may not be influenced by this consideration. Incurable or highly communicable diseases may also be exceptions to this "hesitant to transfer a patient" stance.) As a result of this attitude, we see that the Chinese hospitals, clinics, and private doctors' offices have a very poorly developed referral system. In the west, with a well-developed referral system, a patient could go to a small or medium sized medical facility, receive primary care, and then be referred on to a more appropriate hospital if their condition warranted it. In China, we see that increasing numbers of patients prefer to go to a large hospital for any and all maladies.

Challenges to Traditional Thinking

*A challenge to a traditional Chinese point of view, or the point of view which the Chinese want to put across at the time, is often taken by the Chinese as a loss of face.*

For example, in most Chinese history books, school textbooks, and among Chinese historians, it is generally maintained that China forced Japan to surrender in World War II, and that the dropping of atomic bombs on Nagasaki and Hiroshima was incidental. When westerners who are attending academic conferences in China offer collections of historical data which point to a different conclusion, this is regarded by the Chinese as a loss of face.

The economic growth in some Chinese provinces in the last thirty years has often been described by the international news media as nothing short of miraculous. "Yet," according to one western sinologist, "by reading the Chinese language newspapers and magazines you are given the impression that the Chinese did this all by themselves, and that it is a direct outgrowth of five millennia of history and culture." In fact, as many western economists privately point out, the basis for this growth was the billions of dollars in foreign aid pumped into these regions in the period following WWII, and the granting of a wide range of preferential trade agreements. Additionally, much of this miraculous growth has been fueled by export industries, and if the European and North American markets did not exist for these products, no such growth would have been possible. A German social historian at an academic conference in China added that "Two hundred years ago China had mass illiteracy, periodic famines in various regions, widespread epidemics, a despotic government that approved of beating and torturing suspects to extract confessions, etc. and yet in that era it would not have been an exaggeration for someone to state that 'China has five millennia of history and culture'. Therefore, according to my analysis . . . " unfortunately the microphone at his seat lost power before he could finish his remarks. He quietly packed up his papers and left the meeting hall, and indeed the Chinese were happy to see him go, since he had been

---

1. It also amounts to a loss in revenue.

so rude.

A large Opera House was built in a Chinese city, and proclaimed by the government to be "of the highest international standards". When an American consulting firm, hired to oversee certain construction problems that had developed, pointed out that the Opera House in question was barely equivalent to average European municipal standards, similar to the city Opera Houses in many localities in West Germany, but by no means equivalent to the international Houses, this was taken by the officials in the relevant Chinese government bureau as a tremendous loss of face, and local newspapers were told not to print the story. When the consulting firm added insult to injury by stating that the budgeting for the Opera House was three times what a similar structure would have cost in Germany, and that they had uncovered evidence of contractor kickbacks to high government officials, they were fired, and all copies of their report were buried in a local landfill.

Regarding the greatness of the Chinese nation and cultural heritage, many western sinologists have pointed out that "nationalism"[1] is far too weak a word to describe the feelings that are engendered in Chinese children in their home environments and throughout their schooling. For anyone to state that, historically speaking, China at her strongest could not have defeated the firepower wielded by one modern aircraft carrier, and that therefore "there is little point in revelling in the glories of the past; it is far more worthwhile to be concerned with the present and the future," etc., is invariably regarded as not giving face. With or without assembled evidence, for the foreigner to take objection to the classical Chinese notion that "the Chinese are a polite race", "the Chinese consider all men in the four seas as brothers", "the Chinese want to build a great world harmony", or any other similar classical precept, is also taken as not giving face.

Often times it happens that the pronouncements of various Chinese governing bodies in regard to a wide variety of issues are at odds with the facts, especially the facts as determined by other more authoritative international bodies. If anyone were to be so rude as to point out the discrepancy between the Chinese de jure and real-world de facto in these instances, this would certainly be a loss of face to the Chinese officials involved.

One foreigner of my acquaintance went so far as to research the entirety of Confucius, Mencius, Lao-tse, Chuang-tse, the Book of Rites, the *Yi Ching*, and a number of other classical texts, however nowhere did he find a single reference to "face". As a teacher in a local university, he had many contacts with a wide variety of Chinese people, and frequently attended many dinner parties and other social functions. Whenever it was pointed out to him that his words or actions in some particular respect had resulted in a loss of face for a Chinese person, he would say "Show me anywhere in any of your Chinese classics where it says I have to give face. Confucius did say 'Treat

---

1. Slightly better would be "nationalistic cultural elitism".

others honestly'[a] and I will use that as my rule of conduct until you can present me with a better one. Honesty is concerned with facts, not emotions, sentiments, or faces."

Naturally every Chinese to whom he made this remark was appalled by the loss of face which he caused for them by castigating them in this manner in front of others.

## International Conferences

There is much face associated with meetings and ceremonies, especially when the people involved are more concerned with back-slapping than with undertaking serious projects.

A meeting of Asian watch manufacturers was arranged in a large Chinese city, and this was already the tenth anniversary year of the founding of the Institute which organized the meetings. Many speeches were given by local government officials praising the efforts of the many shop owners, wholesalers, manufacturers, and others involved in the watchmaking industry, as well as praising the wonderful achievements of these meetings which were already in their tenth year, and had done much to improve the watch industry, under the capable leadership of the Chairman Mr. Chwing.

Several reporters approached the organizers of the conference for data, and then collected information from other sources. They found that **ten years previously** 1) the import duties on Asian watches imported into western countries were considerably less than at the present time, 2) most western countries had no quotas on watch imports, however several of them now did, 3) there were vastly fewer cases of patent infringement than reported at present, 4) the countries represented at the conference had "freer and more unrestricted" trading relations between themselves than they did at present, 5) there was much less western competition in the Asian market than at present, etc.

They therefore asked the conference organizers: "What do you see as your major achievements in conducting these ten years of conferences?"

No one could come up with anything concrete, although many mentioned that they had had some memorable meals, seen some interesting nightclub acts, and had some nice city tours. A knowledgeable westerner advanced the theory that the yearly meetings were largely an exercise in "getting face", so that the elderly members in the industry could be appointed to various ceremonial positions, and go through the motions of being important.

This statement was mitigated somewhat by noting that the travel arrangements and visa approvals in many Asian countries tend to be restricted, and by having a conference of this nature, many businessmen were able to justify a vacation overseas which ordinarily might have been inconvenient.

---

a. 以誠待人

## Perceived Favoritism in the Workplace

Although some generosity is necessary by the manager of a new company in order to instill a sense of team spirit from the start-up of operations, continued generosity toward different groups in the company may eventually lead to feelings of inequality, which will lead to charges of favoritism. The group not receiving the greatest benefit thereby may react by thinking: "Why weren't we treated that way? What is it? Don't you like us?" This reaction will lead directly to the feeling that they have lost face.

It is not uncommon for one company to have a number of offices located in different buildings, and thus the employees of any particular office constitute a group. Any one "group" may be strictly or loosely defined depending on mobility of group members between different groups.

### Comparative Group Favoritism and Loss of Face

Due to the peculiarities of scheduling, it may happen that some person of authority in the organization, most commonly the boss, visits particular offices more frequently than others, or that he generally arrives at particular offices at particular times, perhaps mealtimes. Since the employees in the office all enjoy showing off their generosity, they will buy food to share with other people in the office, and the boss will also share of their largesse. An **Inter-Group Face Conflict Cycle** thus begins: In order to reciprocate, the boss will buy food items for everyone in the office. When this becomes regularized, for example when the employees in office F come to know that the boss brings sandwiches, rolls, pastries, other snack items, etc. every Wednesday, then other groups of employees in other offices may begin to feel a loss of face because they have not been similarly treated. This will cause disharmony in the organization, although the employees, disliking direct communication on such matters, will wait until the resentment from this loss of face has reached serious proportions before mentioning it to the boss, and even when they do so it will be in an indirect manner.

As a result, when the boss finally realizes what situation has developed, he will stop buying food for the employees in office F altogether, whereupon those employees will feel that they have lost a "fringe benefit" and be angry, or at the least, unhappy. However, since the employees in the office F all enjoy showing off their generosity, they will continue to buy food to share with other people in the office, and when the boss comes he will be given a suitable portion to eat, and payment (which he may offer) will be refused. Of course it would not be reasonable for him to refuse to share in the food items passed about; for him not to take a portion would be seen as a loss of face to the offering party.

Knowing the problems which arose before, the boss will not make any real gesture at reciprocation. Before long, the employees will increasingly come to regard him as a cheapskate, or an opportunist, although nothing will be said to him directly. Eventually, when the boss learns of the employees reaction to his behavior, he will begin buying food for them, his "treating" behavior will become regularized due to the peculiarities of scheduling, and the whole Cycle will commence all over again from the beginning.

## Individual Favor Accumulation and Loss of Face

Through the use of generosity and favors, an employee, partner, preparatory-partner, or friend may try to ingratiate himself to the boss or some other figure of authority in an organization. Although the generosity is given "from the heart" so to speak, without (at the time) any spoken or felt desire for reciprocation, in the future a "repayment", in a similar or different form, may actually be called for (thus "calling in" the favor for redemption). To not accede to this "request" is to result in a loss of face for the asking party, thereby angering them and their friends/associates.

Example. An employee E1 expresses a generous nature to the boss B1 by frequently bringing in food or snack items. If B1 is regularly busy around mealtimes, and does not have time to go out for regular meals, this may be seen as very thoughtful. E1 refuses to accept payment for these items, saying that "I want to treat you", and noting that the actual amount of money is not large. Other small gifts may also be brought in from time to time. If B1 is a foreigner, and E1 is a local, the situation is further complicated in that E1 feels the duty of being a host, or "landlord",[a] in his/her own country, and therefore is especially adamant in refusing to accept payment for any of these items.

One day in the future arrives where employee E1 needs to have a request fulfilled by boss B1 which may be of a personal or business nature. If it is a personal concern, it could perhaps involve the use of company equipment without charge, or could even involve E1's relatives. Foreigners for example are often asked to help 1) do translation work, 2) fill out documents involving a large variety of international dealings, immigration proceedings, or foreign legal matters, 3) give tutorial help to people preparing for various examinations in an area of study in which the foreigner possesses competence, (most commonly: language ability), etc. The "time window" for completion of such a request may be very narrow (meaning that it must be completed within a very short time-span), and the task itself quite time-consuming. Also possible is that the request could involve the granting of some special privilege such as 4) extra leave of absence with pay, 5) the cancellation of various accumulated demerits, 6) a loan from company coffers, etc. However, in any case, to not grant the request is easily seen as not giving face.

Employee E1 feels that he/she has accumulated enough favors with B1, so that now his/her request to "call them in" is not in the least unreasonable. Furthermore the relative

---

[a]. 地主

disparity of "favors given" (food, for example) and "favors asked for" (several hours of time to sort out a mass of documents regarding my brother-in-law's new plant investment in Guam, for example) is totally irrelevant by E1's reckoning. The example could have been "I always buy lunch for you when we are together, please come and examine the machine which broke down in my second older brother's factory, because you are an electrical engineer." All E1 sees is: "I help you out, you help me out", in other words the dictates of "help" are – to each according to his need, from each according to his ability.

Here again we see recurring concepts—

A High Integration between Business Concerns and Personal Concerns. There is no borderline between the proposed swapping of personal-related favors for business-related favors or vice versa.

RR Perception of Value. Favors were given without thought or expectation of repayment, but this expectation, and indeed the entire original intention, was readjusted later. This is seen as perfectly compatible with the demands of honesty, sincerity, etc.

Questions and Commentary:

Q: The obvious solution to many of the situations you have raised here is for everyone to go Dutch treat. In terms of buying food or other items for people in the office, have each one pay for his own.

A: This is the solution that appeals most readily to the foreigner. However, it is not easy to put into practice in a society where hospitality and generosity are important behavioral patterns inculcated in the children since they were old enough to hold a piece of food in their hands. For each person to pay his own way represents the Individual Mentality, and that, by definition, is not stressed in a society which stresses Group Mentality values.

If it happens that one group goes out to dinner, it will be expected that the boss will pay, since he is leader of the group. If the boss makes the suggestion that everyone pay for their own, invariably a male member of the group will stand up and offer to pay for the group this time. He thus gains face by demonstrating his superior generosity, and the goal of an equitable distribution of expenses is not achieved.

Q: Analyzing some peculiarities of the above discussion with what I feel is a sense of rationality, I am a bit confused. In the Comparative Group Favoritism example there is some imbalance. The boss buys small food items, perhaps at the price of 1 or 2 to the dollar (US$). Even if we consider this a "fringe benefit" of employment, which it should not rightly be considered I believe, nevertheless the benefit to any one individual at at-most is $ 1.00, and perhaps once a week. However, a major loss to the employees in any particular office is the mutual treating which is going on, which might represent five or ten dollars of expense per person per month. If this mutual treating is eliminated, several dollars of expense (lost income) can be saved per month, thus resulting in effect in a larger take-home pay. The $ 1.00 to my mind then is relatively insignificant, one way or the other.

A: An important Psychological Peculiarity is at work here, in that people of the Group Mentality orientation "have a strong desire for very small gains, but are not concerned with spending small amounts of money." We may translate this into more colloquial speech by saying that they have a strong desire for freebies, but are unconcerned about small expenses. Mutual treating represents a small expense in their opinion, however when any one group does not get the freebies that another group did receive, they feel slighted, and over time this will build up to a loss of face.

Q: The impression I get from reading through all this is that everyone in the office seems hungry most of the time. Actually I worked in a company in the United States once where we had a similar situation, and we also did a lot of mutual treating of various food items during the day. The trick is to be more organized. For example, we collected a fixed amount of money, from each employee who desired to participate, at the beginning of the month. Every day, or every two days or whatever, an appointed person would go out to purchase an appropriate quantity of food or snack items. This was distributed to all participating personnel in an equitable manner. In fact, if one person only showed up once a week, (as per the boss in your example) he was also eligible to participate in our plan for that day only, and he contributed a proportionately smaller amount at the beginning of the month. At the end of the month the funds were all used up, and we started out all over again. We had very few problems with this method, and it avoided anyone feeling slighted, or resulting in the loss of face problems you described.

A: Many foreigners would offer up a plan such as the one you have suggested as a way of avoiding the problems described above. However, by stressing the equitable nature of your relationship, .i.e. equitable among individuals, you have effectively denied the Group Mentality, which would dictate that all members of the group (employees in the office) are equally entitled to share of the purchases made by any parties whether they contributed any financial support or not. In other words, to deny someone participation in the Group merely due to the fact that he cannot or did not pay his way, attempts to assign responsibility for his action to him alone, but the Group Mentality dictates that the consequences of his actions should more properly be shared among all group members.

Therefore we are sorry to say that this sort of solution is rarely workable, because the people involved want to gain face by showing their superior generosity, and they are not interested in an exact accounting of who contributed how much and therefore who is entitled to what portion. Again, the "small expense" that this represents to them is unimportant, since they have gained face.

## Facial Omissions

*My way of joking is to tell the truth. It's the funniest joke in the world.*

—— *George Bernard Shaw*

After I had spent several months assembling the above remarks on the Chinese concept of face, I showed them to a number of people of lengthy experience in China, and who possessed excellent knowledge of the language, literature, social organization, business practices, and culture in general. My conversation with Sherman, an American from Pennsylvania, was typical. "Do you think I have overdone it?" I queried.

"No," he said, "what you have outlined here is only the tip of the iceberg."

"What have I left out?" I asked.

"The considerations you have left out would fill a large set of encyclopedias. However I suspect that even much of the ground you have covered in your *exposé* will be largely incomprehensible to those without a significant length of residence in China, and extended exposure to the Chinese way of thinking and behavior. However, a few additional points will be of interest. First of all, you fail to mention the relationship between filial piety and face."

"Which is . . . ?"

"In general terms, for a child to commit suicide would be considered grossly unfilial, since he would not be able to care for his parents. However, in the case where a child had done something serious enough to lose face for the entire family, suicide is commonly considered justified."

"Yes, I believe I read something about that in the Chinese press, where some students had such poor marks in their studies, despite all their efforts to improve, that they committed suicide. In some cases it was because they could not pass the entrance examinations to college, and their parents were severely disappointed," I said.

"Of course the same thing happens in Japan, and they have a name for it: the week that national entrance examination grades are released is informally called 'Suicide Week'." Sherman took a drink of coffee, and continued. "You also failed to mention the relationship between illegality and face."

"Which is . . . ?"

"Well, many citizens do not want to get involved in reporting illegal factories or taking a strong stand in regard to forcing them to cease operations, even when noise, health, sanitation, and other environmental laws are being broken. This is because they do not want the businessmen or employees involved to lose face. They often feel that if they cause trouble then they themselves lose face as well."

"You must be kidding."

"No, the Chinese idea of conducting oneself in a proper manner is much more concerned with saving face for all those involved in a dispute than in determining each party's legal position. A Chinese friend of mine owns an apartment in a new building on the east side of town, and his ownership includes a portion of the basement, which may be used for storage purposes, or the parking of a car, although a large common area is designated as an air raid shelter. The original builder of the building, who has retained rights to over 40% of the space down there, recently rented out the entire basement area to a company which has set up a small nightclub therein, although according to the building code, this kind of establishment may not be operated in the basement. When my friend complained several times, the building manager resigned, rather than trying to sort it out with the parties involved, and thereby lose face for everyone.''

"Does that type of situation occur very often?" I questioned.

"In many different forms. My American friend Daniel smelled smoke in his apartment one day and went to investigate. It turned out that the people on the third floor were burning paper money in a large cannister in the hallway, in conjunction with some religious ritual. Daniel asked them if they could please burn it outside, since the building regulation stated that only fires used in stoves, ranges, or ovens for cooking purposes could be lit, and no barbecuing or burning of other material was permitted. They made no reply to this, and Daniel added that if they did not put it out in three minutes, he would. Daniel's Chinese wife was finally able to restrain him. She told me later that Daniel had not realized that putting out the fire would be a tremendous loss of face to the people participating in the ritual, as well as to the dead ancestors they were worshipping.''[1]

"That certainly clarifies some issues which I have been confused about," I admitted, "even though I have a hard time understanding the whole idea."

"Most westerners do," my friend sighed. "But it is an interesting subject for acculturological research. By the way, you have also failed to mention the connection between contractual relation and face."

"I assume that where face comes into play, contractual relation is out the window," I offered a guess.

"That is an oversimplification, but in its essence it is substantially correct. For one party not to sympathize with the other party's difficulties in not being able to uphold its end of the bargain, is seen as not giving face, and hence is ungentlemanly, discourteous, and the mark of an ignorant boor, or a selfish schemer."

"Well, I am glad you set me straight on that one," I nodded.

"Oh, there is far more," he said, "for example you have failed to touch upon the curious non-relation between young children and face."

"Non-relation?" I inquired.

"Yes, most curious. Young children, often even up to five or six years of age, are generally not considered responsible for their words or actions. I recall one case where a group of four, five, and six year old children were running around the tables during

---

1. The burning of paper money inside buildings (ostensibly to worship gods or ancestors), in direct violation of building regulations, is another example of the legal/moral gap.

a large Chinese wedding dinner, apparently playing tag, and none of the Chinese present paid the least attention to them. At one point the children chased their way to the front of the room, where the bride and groom were standing arm-in-arm as some important officials and other relatives made some well-wishing speeches. I was surprised to see one of the children actually lift up the bride's wedding gown and look underneath. However the other Chinese at my table had no reaction to this, and when I questioned them on it later, they dismissed the entire incident by saying 'They are only children.' He paused to consider this for a moment. "I cannot help thinking that that is not the reaction that would have occurred if this had happened in the west."

"Yes, that is putting it mildly. I remember hearing of an incident in New England where a four year girl old managed to get to the front of the church while the minister was giving his Sunday service, and before she could be stopped she proceeded to take a leak in front of God and everybody."

"What was the parents' position in the community after that?" my friend asked.

"They moved to another state, so I never did hear anything more about them."

"In the west, that would be a serious loss of face, however the Chinese are much more 'natural' in their orientation, and they regard the bodily functioning of children as quite normal. Other innocent activity of young children, such as playing hide and seek, blindman's bluff, or other games which involve running and shouting, even in restaurants, hotels, or other formal establishments, also tends to be ignored."

"I think I will write to all my friends in North America who have young children and suggest that they move to China."

"The Chinese are a most hospitable people," my friend agreed, "and they love children. Interestingly, while western children are expected to be little gentlemen and ladies, Chinese children are often left to run about freely. As they mature however, the situations change, and while western children are taught to be individuals and go their own way, Chinese children are taught to retain strong bonds of loyalty and obedience to family and relatives."

"Yes, I recall reading an article by a famous American female newspaper columnist comparing the raising of children to flying a kite, and saying that after they reach a certain stage you have to 'cut the string and let them go'."

"Totally irrational and unacceptable from the Chinese point of view," Sherman commented.

"And for the child to feel that way is no doubt a serious loss of face to the family involved," I added.

"Homesickness is a highly prized emotion, promoted in the educational system, and throughout the society in general."

"Speaking of 'home' and 'sickness', I hate to make a play on words, but it does occur to me that often times the living environment of many Chinese communities is not very clean, and there is much trash lying about. Houses often tend to go unpainted inside and out. So I am wondering if there is peeling paint on the wall and guests come, do we lose face?"

"Again this depends on the relative living conditions of the community in general, and the individual family in particular. Since the Chinese scholar-ethic, formulated in a Pre Industrial Revolution age, tends to look down on manual labor, you often find that Chinese men or boys lack a 'handyman' orientation, as is common in western households. In general, eating is most important, and what is on the table is of more relevance than the physical surroundings."

"I should think that both would be important. Looking at the dirty walls, floor, and ceiling in some of these places does not stimulate my appetite. I recall one noodle shop where the proprietor admitted to me that he had not washed his pots in 40 years."

"Yes, that is supposed to improve the flavor of the meats, vegetables, and condiments which are cooked down into a rich sauce for putting on the noodles. I am sure the manager feels that by having such a rich and tasty broth he has gained much face."

"Yes, that is the only explanation I can think of," I agreed, "however I cannot help wondering how many American hamburger shops would try to convince the western consumers that by never cleaning the grill their hamburgers 'taste better', and much face is gained for all concerned."

"Probably not too many."

"Yes, the western consumers have very strong views about these issues."

"Certainly. And speaking of consumers, your essay has only barely touched on the relationship between the consumer movement in China and face," Sherman commented.

"Well, from what I read in the newspapers, the consumer movement in China is growing day by day."

"Of course, gains are being made. Nevertheless, face remains a serious stumbling block. For example, many government officials do not approve of consumer groups doing product testing and then publishing the results. They feel that this causes a serious loss of face for the manufacturers whose products perform poorly. Hence, many of these groups are very limited in the kinds of activities they can perform in terms of 'informing or educating the public'."

"Of course we would hope that such product testing is responsible and objective, but if the researchers stand behind their test results, it would seem to me that 'facts' and 'truth' are more important than face," I said.

"Well, I have no comment on that. However, I would guess that with your attitude you might even feel that false advertising is a serious issue."

"Of course, and according to my research, there are laws in China that prohibit false advertising."

"You legal research is good, however you should take a further step and investigate what sort of legal remedies are available to those who suffer damages as a result of any such advertising."

"Oh well, I did not look into that," I admitted.

"The remedies are minimal in most instances, and oftentimes non-existent. Certainly the prevailing Chinese feeling is that producers and consumers should conduct their relations in harmony, and not lose face for each other by getting into long drawn out arguments or legal battles."

I paused to think for a long moment. "It seems that Chinese social relations tend to stress a harmony achieved by an active avoidance of conflict, whereas western social relations are not adverse to a harmony achieved after conflict."

"Yes. Even with harmony as a premise, the entire approach to achieving it is quite different, so that is one possible explanation."

## Face for Everybody

I had a further discussion on my face essay with an American who worked for a large western pharmaceutical company, Mr. Felix Betterman. He had been in China not quite two years, and was involved in the marketing of several products which were new to China, although already well-established in the west. Several months earlier he had asked my advice on the promotion strategy for the company's new deodorant. It was designed to be used by men or women, and was available in three fragrances.

At that time he had wanted me to brief him on the peculiarities of Chinese thinking regarding "underarm smell", and so I had arranged to meet him at 2:00 one afternoon outside a large and well-stocked Chinese herbal medicine shop. When Felix arrived we went in, and I explained in Chinese to the staff that my friend suffered from underarm odor, and needed something which he could apply to the area in question. We were greeted with surprised embarrassment. When pressed for advice, the the proprietor admitted that he had no powders or salves suitable for this purpose, and suggested more frequent bathing as the best answer, perhaps with the use of a more heavily scented soap. He continued to say that if my friend felt the odor was serious enough, the best solution would of course be surgery. I thanked the proprietor for his time and assistance, and translated the course of our discussion for Felix as we walked out of the shop and back into the street.

Felix was so incredulous at my translation that he almost stumbled over the curb. His mouth was agape, and asked for further clarification.

"The Chinese take a peculiar view toward the subject of underarm odor," I said. "They regard it as a disease. While not being generally held to be contagious, it is assumed to arise for largely unexplained reasons and then may become hereditary. In order to combat this underarm smell, Chinese historically have limited their efforts to bathing. In a wide variety of Chinese magazines and newspapers, one may see advertising for clinics and hospitals that deal in the surgical procedures necessary to combat this disease, i.e. surgical removal of the underarm sweat glands."[1]

---

1. This type of surgery, although common, appears in direct violation of an important Confucian tenet in the *Filial Piety Classic*: "The body with its hair and skin is received from parents; do not cause it harm."

"Do the Chinese have a word for 'deodorant'?" Felix asked.

"Yes they do, but normally that expression is only associated with those sprays or other mixtures used in restrooms, kitchens, or other areas in the home or industry. They have not traditionally used anything of this type in conjunction with the human body, and I believe this is another reflection of Chinese naturalism."

"Are they aware of the smell?"

"Some Chinese say that it is similar to the smell of a fox, however I believe that is only in the most extreme cases. Due to the western diet which abounds in beef, pork, and other heavy meats, as well as milk and cheese, the westerners seem to give off more body smell than the Orientals. Their diet has traditionally been more abundant in vegetables."

"How common is it for Chinese women to shave their underarms?" Felix questioned further.

"That is primarily North American culture," I stated, "and largely unknown in the rest of the world. Of course there is some cross-cultural influence, but it is quite limited. Actually I believe most Chinese girls or women are scared at the thought of using a razor."

"That does present some problems for our advertising strategy," Felix admitted, "since as you know most of these 'considerations' are taken as understood in the west, and our deodorant advertising tends to be a bit more 'indirect' than the advertising for toothpaste, face cream, or shampoo."

"I am quite aware of that, and let me say that your strategy will have to be changed for entrance into China. If your advertising shows someone spraying deodorant on their forearms the Chinese will take it literally, and since they do not have smelly forearms, no one will buy it."

"So you think that our advertising should show the deodorant being sprayed directly on the armpit?" Felix seemed to cringe slightly as he posed this question.

"Obviously that is the only answer, however it does present a whole new range of problems. Since the Chinese consider underarm odor to be a disease, they will no doubt feel that anyone who buys this product has no face."

"What?"

"Well the Chinese concept of face is very complicated, but in this situation the person who admits to having this problem, and buys your product, could be said to have lost face. For someone to suggest that he needs to buy it could also be interpreted as a loss of face."

"It appears that we do not need an advertising campaign, we need an educational campaign," Felix shook his head sadly.

Felix and his staff later organized an entire entrance strategy for his company's deodorant into the local market, elaborating in a separate brief the difficulties of gaining acceptance for this product in China, due to the Chinese cultural background. He recommended "directness" in explaining and illustrating its use.

After lengthy review in the New York home office, Felix's plan was found to be unacceptable and scrapped. An advertising campaign which had proved effective in the USA market some fifteen years previously was brought in. Substantial budgeting for promotion was allowed, but over the course of the following year sales were disappointing. Chinese consumers who were interviewed expressed awareness of the product, however they explained that they washed their bodies regularly, including their forearms, so they had no use for it.

As Felix came to know more about the Chinese perception of reality, and was able to relate this to his western background, he told me that the New York home office had no doubt felt it would be a loss of face to be the first maker to come out with such explicit advertising. He regarded that as the real reason why his plan had been vetoed.

Some time later I was having dinner with Felix, and he told me that he had been born in north central Ohio, but moved at the age of five with his family to West Orange, New Jersey, and had been raised there. He asked if that biographical background was similar to anyone I could think of.

Pausing to think for a moment, the significance of that locality in New Jersey struck me. "That was where the world-famous inventor Thomas Edison had his largest laboratory!"

"Yes, that's right." Felix nodded. "As you can imagine, I am quite proud of being from West Orange. Our famous citizen Thomas Edison spent the better part of his life there, using it as a base to reshape mankind's destiny. He acquired over 1,000 patents during the course of his illustrious career, including those for the phonograph, the moving picture camera, and the incandescent light and electric system—inventions which have had a profound influence on human civilization."

"Yes, without those inventions, the world would be a far different one today."

"And yet you know, I have never been offered a discount or any other preferential treatment when purchasing record players, records, movie cameras, or light bulbs, etc., even when I presented proof of being a native of West Orange, New Jersey."

"That is puzzling," I said, slightly amused, "what sort of preferential treatment were you expecting?"

"Well, some recognition of the fact that I am part of these inventions, or related to them, or otherwise a more noble person because of them, or something." Felix paused for a few moments. "But whenever these inventions are brought up in any context, and I mention that I am from West Orange, New Jersey, the average reaction I get is 'So what?'."

I began to see where Felix's reasoning was leading. However, it seemed necessary at this point to clarify the issues involved from an economic standpoint before he got too far astray. "See here Felix, I agree that it is questionable to say that you are a better person because Thomas Edison invented the electric lightbulb. For you to insist upon that would just be empty pride. However there is I believe a certain level of significance to the city, state, or nation as a whole, especially to the extent that Edison's inventions resulted in economic growth, and improved the living standards of the people."

"It is true that Edison's inventions have fostered massive industries, originally in the United States, and later in other countries as well. In fact he was one of the co-founders of the General Electric Company," Felix stated.

"That is I believe where the true significance lies," I said. "Not in who invented it, but in who developed it and created economic growth as a result of it. Of course we offer the inventor a salute, and offer his hometown a bow, but in terms of purely 'inventive efforts' . . . well, before we could do anything more we would want to look at the number of useful inventions per million of population per millennium, or some other index of inventive intelligence."

"And yet somehow I cannot agree with you," Felix shook his head. "Just the other day we were having a discussion on new product packaging for a wide variety of our paper products. During the meeting one of the Chinese supervisors asked if I knew who invented paper. I was slow in replying, and he went on to recount the story. After explaining all about how the Chinese had invented paper he asked me what I felt."

"What did you reply?" I asked.

"I said that if he wanted to compare inventive intelligence, and make a list of inventions, I would match him one for one, China vs. West Orange, New Jersey."

"No doubt he would consider that as a loss of face," I surmised.

"Well, one of the other supervisors suggested that we move the conversation in another direction."

"That seems an excellent idea. What did you talk about next?"

"Some of our packaging design uses a compass motif, and several of the Chinese staff pointed out that the compass was invented by the Chinese."

"Certainly you did not reply 'So what?'[a] to that one?" I asked.

"No, I was about to launch into a discussion of the influence of British seapower on world history, in order to gradually lead up to asking exactly to what use the Chinese had traditionally put their compass, however again one of the supervisors suggested that we move the conversation in another direction."

"Yes, a discussion along those lines would have been regarded as not giving face. You are better off to offer a salute and a bow when these Chinese inventions are mentioned."

"In our company now I have suggested to the supervisors that we draw up some guidelines on what sort of comments can and cannot be made among our administrators, executives, supervisors, and all subordinates. I believe it is desirable to iron out certain things, such that comments about good and bad on-the-job performance should be solicited, and negative comments should not be taken as a loss of face."

"There is no clear agreement on what sort of statements are taken as a loss of face

---

a. 又怎麼樣？

in an office environment," I said. "And so I suspect that such an undertaking may be difficult. Remarks which some employees view as not giving face may be viewed neutrally by others, and if you get everyone together to hash out the issue it is most likely that all will agree that they have lost face." I thought for a second, trying to examine the concept of face from some other angle that would make it more clear to Felix. "Looking at it from a subjective point of view, I believe that the speaker's tone of voice may have a great bearing on the listener's impression of whether or not he is losing face. Naturally, there will not be total agreement among all listeners as to the meaning or intent of any one particular tone of voice."

"But why not look at it from the objective point of view?"

"If they did that, very little of this discussion would be necessary," I said, "I thought you would have realized that by now. Sometimes I really wonder about you people from West Orange, New Jersey."

## Living with Face

At the Barbershop: "Don't regard it as losing hair. Think of it as gaining face."
—— *Los Angeles Times Syndicate*

The following incidents illustrate further aspects of face in Chinese society with some comments on how the westerner might view, or deal with, such situations when they occur.

1. A Chinese singing star who was attending a large wedding banquet was asked on the spur of the moment to sing a song to wish the new couple a prosperous future. The star immediately realized that to refuse this request would be to not give face. Unfortunately, the star had a slight throat irritation that day. Only after several long explanations was the star able to decline this invitation, and it seemed advisable to leave the dinner immediately after this encounter. The star later told an acquaintance: "If I am asked to sing at any sort of private function and do not, then the parties involved take it as a loss of face. If I sing at one function, then go to another function and do not sing, the people there take it as a loss of face. For a person in my position it is not difficult to insult a minimum of 300 people per day."

The request to sing at a wedding is rather unusual, and probably only made to stars of established ability. However Chinese people in many types of informal gatherings (dinners, parties, camping trips, etc.) will take turns singing, in the best style of the Ted Mack Amateur Hour. The foreigner is well advised to carry around copies of the lyrics to some of his favorite English folksongs, country ballads, or other popular tunes, so that he can belt out a rendition of them when requested. For a foreigner to refuse to sing in one of these informal get togethers is considered lacking in group spirit.

2. A foreigner was walking down the sidewalk one day and bumped into a middle-aged man operating an illegal food stall. This man was carrying several plates of food to a group of patrons seated at a table illegally set up on the sidewalk, and obstructing pedestrian flow. When the foreigner tried to avoid responsibility for the overturned dishes, the man, his other employees, and the patrons took it as a loss of face, and got angry.

Clearly it is better in such situations to make a feigned show of generosity and sympathy. The foreigner should offer to accept all guilt, and pay for the cost of the upset items, broken dishes, etc. Chinese are generally always embarrassed to see the foreigner acting more politely than they themselves do, hence it is most likely that they will quickly feel the need to assume responsibility for the accident themselves. In fact the patrons at this point may even invite the foreigner to dine with them. If such a happy solution is not possible, it is still advisable for the foreigner to avoid argument or objective considerations of right and wrong until someone can notify the police to come and straighten the matter out. What you say may not be as important as how you say it, and efforts to save the faces of the illegal food stall employees, patrons, etc., should be made.

3. Many of the pricing examples in Chapter 3 are, in practice, actually further complicated by the fact that when the customer does not agree with the shopkeeper's view of the situation, it is seen as not giving the shopkeeper "face". The foreigner is thus advised to allocate his normal monthly budgeting with a bit more flexibility, and to avoid arguing over small sums, being content to chalk up some small losses to "cross cultural adaptation allowance". It may be desirable to give the shopkeeper or other personnel the benefit of the doubt in many situations, and forget the idea of trying (on the spot) to have them recognize the implied responsibility of having posted information conform exactly to the real situation. This is especially true if the organization in question deals primarily with the local Chinese community, who traditionally tend not to be very pushy or nit-picking.[1]

4. A foreigner once taught the students in his English class to sing "Ten Little Indians" in accompaniment with dancing and gesturing, and invited their parents to the performance. Since there were eleven students in the class, one was picked at random to stand by the side. After the performance, the mother of the child left out expressed much grief at this "loss of face". From that day forward, the institute established the rule that "When singing 'Ten Little Indians', all students in the class must participate, even if the student count is 11, 12, 13, or any other number." The foreigner should recognize that to the Chinese, being left out of the group may result in loss of face.

5. An American, who was expert in a particular branch of social sciences, was asked to participate in a lecture series with another Chinese scholar, who, although also being an expert, was largely self-educated. Since the American was unfamiliar with this

---

1. The Chinese public is also influenced by the phrase 吃一次虧 , 學一次乖 "if you suffer a loss you will be more careful next time". Clearly the attitude embodied in this maxim is at odds with a strong consumer movement.

gentleman, he asked the organizing body to arrange a meeting so that they could have a chance to talk first, before he made any decision in regard to the lecture series. Such a meeting was set up, and during the discussion the two men found that they shared many of the same views. However, there were some points upon which they did not agree, and the meeting was brought to an amicable close. The American later decided not to participate in the lecture series, and hence his name was removed from the advertising copy which was being prepared to be printed. When the Chinese scholar learned of this, he took it as meaning that the American looked down on his lack of a professional degree, and regarded it as a severe loss of face. He then used his connections in the Ministry of Foreign Affairs to try to have the American's letter of invitation from the sponsoring organization cancelled.

This entire situation appears most unusual, however it does show that just when you least expect it the entire issue of "face" will pop out of a dark corner and surprise you. For those of high academic standing involved in such encounters, some strategy for preventing this type of incident might be successfully formulated beforehand.

6. Chinese tend to take sports contests, local and international, as involving face. In international contests when the Chinese team wins, much face is gained, and they are treated by the news media and local citizenry as heroes upon their return. If they lose, much face is apparently lost. Although this type of feeling is not unknown in the west, the Chinese tend to take the entire issue much more seriously. Certain research projects in many universities in the USA have pointed to the conclusion that face is gained with a winning football team, and with winning teams in other sports as well. In North America this is reflected in a generally higher rate of alumni contributions in those years when the colleges or universities have winning teams.

Our observation would be that the Chinese are more inclined to agree with the adage "There is no substitute for victory", rather than the more sportsmanlike tenet of "It is not whether you win or lose, but how you play the game." In the business world, in a wide variety of organizational situations, many foreign observers have indeed noted that Chinese managers tend to have a low tolerance for failure.

7. Superior ability in a foreign language is often regarded as having face. Some Chinese employees of local magazines which publish in English (such as magazines which advertise merchandise for export) often feel that they have much face when they show a copy of their publication to their Chinese friends and relatives, and can point out their name on the Editorial masthead. However, as is often the case in smaller publications of this kind, many of the articles included therein contain numerous grammatical and typing errors. Hence the anomaly arises that for the foreigner who is working for such a publication to show a copy to his foreign friends (who are fluent in English) is to lose face, however for the Chinese to show a copy to his Chinese friends (who have very limited English language skills) is to gain face.

8. A Chinese businesswoman, Miss Ding, was visiting the home of a friend who lived some twenty minutes away by bus. Inquiring as to the custodial and public utility ar-

rangements her friend's four-story apartment complex building, the friend said "There aren't any." The building had no elevator, and they had to take out their own trash, and do all other minor repairs. There was no desk at which mail or other inquiries could be handled, and no security service was provided. Hence they were not charged any custodial fees over and above the monthly rent and the utilities for their apartment.

Miss Ding said that although her home was in a building twelve stories high which did have an elevator, she and her roommates also had to take out their own trash, and do all of their own repairs, as well as paying their own water, gas, and electricity bills. Although there was a main desk, the attendant was rarely there, and she always used her office address for mail, since the building's mailboxes were in a state of disrepair. When they had moved in, it was stated that the salaried attendant would provide some basic security protection, but this had not materialized. In addition to having been looted several times, they were frequently bothered by the operation of illegal hostels and gambling parlors in the building. The monthly custodial fee of some $60 U.S. equivalent was still collected regularly however, and as a matter of fact Miss Ding served as a member of the Building Committee which handled all affairs of the twelve-story building's operation.

A westerner in attendance suggested that she should complain to the effect "I am not getting any service for this custodial fee that I pay out every month". Miss Ding said that would be a tremendous loss of face for the Head of the Building Committee, so she did not want to bring it up.

Leaving Miss Ding and her friend to discuss the matter further, the westerner asked if they had any liquor in the house, and retired with the bottle to a quiet alcove, to begin reviewing his Chinese lessons.

9. A young Chinese woman, Miss Lee, was working for a large Chinese managed international hotel as Assistant General Manager, with a salary of US $1000 per month, well above what many people of her age group were making in similar positions of responsibility in other fields. She had been employed by the hotel for three years, rising up from an initial entry-level job (with an initial salary of approximately half this current amount) to her present position through hard work and good performance. Hotel policy stated that employees with outstanding work records would be sent abroad for further study after three years of service, and accordingly Miss Lee was sent to Switzerland to a famous international hotel school for a three month course, with the Hotel paying all expenses, as well as continuing to issue her salary each month, despite her absence.

Upon her return, Miss Lee was surprised to find that the employee who had been asked to take over her duties in her absence was earning US$ 1067 per month. Extremely angry at the loss of face that this represented, she resigned on the spot.

The foreign manager should be aware that unlike western employees, Chinese workers tend to discuss salary levels openly, while at the same time there is often fierce jealousy among them in regard to who is being paid more. Chinese employees often feel that they should be given raises for increased length of service, increased work experience, increased competence, etc. At the same time if another person in the organization is handling *the same*, or highly similar, *job duties* and being paid more, despite his additional qualifications, they feel this is grossly unfair.

10. A high ranking military officer in an Oriental country was convicted of consorting with the enemy, and sentenced to death by beheading. As was often the case in such punishments, the criminal would wear plain somber clothing to the execution yard. However, after pleas were lodged by the officer's family, it was ruled that he would be permitted to wear his full dress uniform to meet the end of his earthly sojourn.

Speaking to a foreign friend, the family members said "This way he will be able to keep his face." The foreigner was puzzled at this statement, and remarked to another foreigner "What is the good of keeping your face if you lose your head?"

How to Be a Good Peanut

A Chinese elementary school teacher told the story of a family which planted peanuts in an unused area of their garden. Several months later the peanuts were harvested, and the parents took special care to explain to the children all the good qualities of peanuts, including the fact that they taste good, can be used to make cooking oil, are important components in the manufacture of many types of soaps and cosmetics, and play an essential part in the processing of paints, varnishes, lubricating oils, furniture polishes, and nytroglycerin. Moreover, they are nutritious, inexpensive, and can be eaten by all people no matter what their status in life. "The moral of the story is," the teacher said, "that you should all be like peanuts. Peanuts are very useful, though they are certainly not good looking."

One of the students raised his hand. "But teacher," he said, "why are all Chinese people so concerned with face?"

The teacher quickly changed the subject.

*Conclusion of the Group Mentality:* Peanuts serve as a useful lesson to human conduct, but it is not proper to stretch the metaphor too far, lest you lose face for both the peanuts and the person who told you the story. Don't analyze it.

Don't laugh at a youth for his affectations; he is only trying on one face after another to find a face of his own.
―― L. P. Smith

# Immigration Problems

The Chief of Chinese Immigration was called on board an international airliner which had just arrived at a major Chinese metropolitan airport to deal with an arriving French passenger who had no passport. Quickly surveying the nearly 300 passengers on board, and wishing to take care of the matter speedily, he ordered her put under guard, to be held in detention until arrangements could be made to put her on a return flight to France. He asked his Deputy to take care of the details while he attended to some other matters.

The Deputy had studied some French in college, and while the passengers were waiting to come up to the arrival gate, he sang a French song over the loudspeaker, following it up with a Chinese song. When everyone was relaxed, he asked them all to search in their seats, and sure enough the French lady's passport was found in the crevice of another empty seat, where she had gone to relax several times during the flight.

When the Chief of Immigration came back and found that the Deputy had resolved the situation, he took this as a loss of face, indicating his own incompetence. He became quite angry with the Deputy and sent him off the flight.

At the next round of quarterly reviews the Chief made several pointed remarks about the Deputy's exceeding his authority, taking unauthorized measures, engaging in excessive conversation with incoming passengers, etc., which served to cancel any chances the Deputy had for a pay increase or promotion. Other immigration personnel heard of this incident and took note of its implications.

The reader may consider the following —

In a culture that stresses face saving and respect for elders, over time one would expect subordinates in all types of organizations

|  | yes | no |
|---|---|---|
| a. To develop creative and innovative methods in problem solving. | ___ | ___ |
| b. To actively try to deal with new situations which arise in the course of their duties, and willing to take on new responsibilities and new challenges. | ___ | ___ |
| c. To be unquestioning conformists to the established way of doing things. | ___ | ___ |
| d. To develop a fatalistic attitude toward life, feeling that "events control man" and that "change" is very difficult or impossible to achieve. | ___ | ___ |
| e. In dealing with responsibility, to try to "pass the buck" whenever possible, so as not to have to make a decision, and thereby run the risk of being held responsible for that decision. | ___ | ___ |

## The Answer is a "Yes, maybe"

One of the most disconcerting things about face is that because of it people will not say "No", but will go ahead and give a "Yes" answer to requests which they later do not fulfill. If the original asking party presses the issue, this can cause a loss of face.

*Harvey:* Mr. Chang, I understand you are an electrical engineer. I wonder if you could recommend some books to me to read about electrical wiring, and also if you could recommend some electrical companies to me. We want to do some special wiring in our auditorium.

*Mr. Chang:* Yes, I will be happy to do that. Please give me your address so I can mail the information to you.

*Harvey:* Yes, of course.

One week passes.

Harvey calls Mr. Chang's secretary. Mr. Chang has not mailed out the information yet, but in order to save face, he has the secretary inform Harvey that he mailed it out yesterday.

Another ten days pass.

Harvey calls Mr. Chang's secretary. He asks if Mr. Chang has been able to locate the information requested. She says that yes, he is getting it together, and will send it out the next day.

Another ten days pass.

Harvey calls Mr. Chang's secretary because he has not received the information yet. She says Mr. Chang has been busy, but he will certainly get to it.

When Mr. Chang comes back to the office that day, his secretary mentions Harvey's call. At this point Mr. Chang has a feeling, to which his secretary agrees, to wit: Harvey is very pushy. What is with him anyway? After all, Mr. Chang concludes: *"I don't owe him anything."*

*Notice Mr. Chang's rationale that assenting to do something is not equivalent to making a promise, and hence does not correspond to the existence of an obligation, especially if it is not convenient for him to carry it out. (In his own mind, he may feel that he had only assented to consider the matter.)*

Due to diverse ideas of the dictates of politeness, indirectness, and saving face in different cultures, there is easily much confusion generated in considering "when is a statement a promise" and "when is a statement only a statement". The reader may refer back to our distinction of a GWF Perception of Obligation and PSA Perception of Obligation in Chapter 1.

Advice: If two or three additional contacts with the original "promise-giver" fail to yield any results, the foreigner should consider this essentially equal to a cancellation of the "promise".

This clarifies that it is best to "put a time limit on your expectations." One should have an alternative plan in the wings, and put it into action when the pre-established time-limit runs out.

## The Rise of Face

In order to understand the origin and roots of face, as well as its usage and effects, we must consider some related psychological aspects of the Chinese mentality.

First it will be necessary to consider the importance of the acculturological term common-line culture.

Common-line culture: **the culture of the society as it is physically manifested in, bears relation to, forms an actual part of, or is illustrated through the daily life of the common man, without extrapolation of psychological or spiritual implications.**

Thus while the Crown Jewels and Buckingham Palace are part of British culture, they are not a part of British common-line culture, because outside of psychological and spiritual considerations, they do not represent, or have a relation to, the way the average Briton lives.

Face and Idealism

After travelling through a number of Chinese rural and metropolian communities, a foreigner was once asked: "Do you feel the Chinese have a strong appreciation for Beauty and Perfection?"[a] He thought about this for some time, and gave the questioner several puzzled glances. Upon further prompting he replied, in a rather low tone of voice, "No."

Asked to explain his remark, he said that it was based on the fact that many places they visited, including the streets, the beaches, the sidewalks, the mountain slopes, the riverbanks, etc. were littered with trash and broken bottles. At several of the rural homes he had been in, even when screen doors or windows had been installed, it was not uncommon to see torn-screening in evidence, or doors which were hanging crooked on their hinges. As a result, the mosquito population travelled freely from outside to inside, and when visiting these homes at night one was continuously attacked by these insect pests. One could not help but notice the wall area around light-switches was black from fingermarks, and no attempt had been made at cleaning. The kitchens appeared to have floors which were not very clean, and often with cobwebs on the ceiling as well. The woks and other pots hanging up were dirty on the outside. Stairways in apartment houses were generally cluttered with a variety of old bicycles, packing boxes, and other junk. The house exteriors were generally unpainted and peeling. Old equipment pushed off to one side of various lots, streets, or alleyways was abandoned and rusting. In fact, the remedying of any or all of these conditions could be accomplished with a little initiative and teamwork, and to the extent that money was needed it appeared well within the financial means of the families involved. Therefore the foreigner concluded: "Unless

---

a. 完美主義

I have mistaken the meaning of the phrase 'Appreciation for Beauty and Perfection', I would have to reply that they do not seem to have it."

No one doubts that the Chinese have thousands of years of exquisite art objects on display in their own, and in a wide variety of foreign, museums. Chinese painting, ceramics, weaving, woodcarving, jade carving, engraving, sculpturing, and other arts and crafts are world renowned. This foreigner's statement, by taking no cognizance of these facts, appears to be misdirected. However, if viewed specifically in relation to the more narrow confines of Chinese common-line culture, we may see that it does indeed have some validity.

Yet, the full essence of the Chinese appreciation for Beauty and Perfection lies a bit deeper, or is much more complex, than the foreigner here has perceived. Beauty and Perfection to the Chinese begin by being "without defect, shortcoming, or flaw". This is the ideal, but it is tempered by the fact that the people are very willing to resign themselves to destiny, and accept fate. Added to this is their "look to the past" orientation, since they believe the ancients possessed the best knowledge and the best society. Thus in relation to Beauty and Perfection in the world of today, there is a rather marked separation between the ideal and the reality.

The screen-door may be torn, but any repairs cannot restore it to its original blemishless, virgin state. Therefore there is little point in repairing it, rather it would be better to buy a new one. But to buy a new screen-door would look out-of-place in relation to the old exterior wooden door, and I believe it is still good for several more years of use. If we were to replace the wooden door, it would look out of place in relation to our living room decorations. If we redid the living room, that would be out of place unless we redid the bedrooms, as well. But if we were going to have all those rooms done, we should have the entire house redone inside and out. That would look out of place without redoing the chicken coop and other exterior buildings, etc. Having done all that, is that the structure in which I want to live? No, if I am going to go that far I will go ahead and buy a new house, and perhaps move into a better neighborhood . . . Since there is no end to idealism, there is no starting point for action. Or we may put it in another way – to the extent that there is action, it is done by overcoming idealism and fatalism. However silly or distorted this may sound to the westerner, it does represent a great deal of the reality of the situation.

Thus the westerner feels that "If I can do a little repair, or make a little improvement, I will."[1] The Chinese feels that "If I had the money, I would redo the entire house." Due to an idealistic and fatalistic Perception of Beauty and Perfection, the Chinaman still desires to give the appearance of good looks to others, so face is brought in as a substitute for his lack of action, and the existing imperfection.

---

1. This is the very attitude that stimulated the flourishing of the Industrial Revolution in the west.

### Face and Emotional Extremes

Another explanation of face is in relation to the extremes of emotions which the Chinese possess. For example, they have both emotions of modesty and extreme superiority. They feel China is the most remarkable nation, but they are often unable to validate their own actions or precepts. They see their society as being without fault and not open to criticism, while as the same time recognizing that the society is unfair and poorly organized in some respects, and backward in others. "Face" allows them to keep all of these factors in balance.

This was humorously illustrated once by the remarks of some Chinese civil engineers. Sent to the United States for advanced training, they were taken to one seemingly undeveloped area, and taught how to judge the nature of the soil, and how to dig building foundations with the latest technologically advanced equipment. A significant problem was that no matter where they dug, they continually ran into many underground communications cables, and dealing with these slowed down their work considerably. Returning to China with their American supervisors as consultants, they went to the suburban area of a major city and began digging the foundations for new houses and apartment buildings. During two weeks of work, not a single underground cable was encountered, and the work progressed smoothly. Commenting on this situation to his American cohort, one Chinese remarked that it was nothing out of the ordinary: "We Chinese had wireless communications long before they became common in the west."

The Chinese have inflated feelings of self importance, and want to establish a superior position of importance in the group, whether through the fact of the earliest discovery of some technology, the fattest hogs in the vicinity, or the biggest household, longest residence, most intelligent ancestors, etc. "Face" assures that only the good points of their situation will be mentioned and discussed.

### Face and Aristocratic Thinking

Face is certainly an element in the relationships between people in the upper class aristocracy, both on the domestic scene and internationally as well, and is related to maintaining a distinction between "inside and outside": between our own affairs and those of others. To put this in terms that the westerner could perhaps understand, if you were living in 1750 and your father was a nobleman, would you disagree with him at a banquet, in a town meeting, or at an international pageant? No, that would not be giving face. If you wanted to disagree with him, it would be best done behind closed doors.

The Chinese are descended from the Yellow Emperor, and have thousands of years of Imperial Dynastic history. The Chinese of all social levels today have retained many vestiges of aristocratic thinking in their mental makeup. Face is one of these.

### Face and Confucius

Diligently delving into the *Analects,* we clearly see that the main consideration is *jen* (as mentioned in the Introduction to this volume), and this word occurs in the text 105 times. Specific references to face occur zero times. Nevertheless, some sinologists have characterized Confucian culture as a "shame culture" (as opposed to a "guilt culture"),[1] because its morality centers on *li*.[a] The term *li* has often been defined as "ceremonious rites", and western scholars have further clarified it as being **all those outward prescriptions of behavior and demeanor, whether involving rite, ceremony, formality, manners, ritual, or general deportment, that bind human beings and the spirits together in networks or interacting roles within the family/clan, within the local community and the entire civilized human society, and with the numinous domain beyond.** That each person should fulfill his role, in order to have no reason for being ashamed, is a necessary precondition for life in society.

Hence, in traditional Chinese thought, the growth of a sense of shame, maturing into something like "a sensitivity for what is convenient and what is not," is viewed as a basic part of one's character development. We might conjecture that the scope of face has grown and expanded due to several millennia of contact with this brand of philosophy.

God has given you one face, and you make yourselves another.
— *Shakespeare, Hamlet, Act III, Scene 1*

The following questions have been asked by new arrivals, with replies made by foreigners of long residence in China.

Q: The Chinese seem very concerned with getting face and saving face. Do allow me to ask this question: What do they plan to do with all this face once they have it?

A: Face is honor, pride, dignity, self-esteem, status, etc. all rolled into one. If one cannot have face, there is little point in existing on this earth as a human being. Hence, face is all important. Face is happiness and social prestige, and having face means that I amount to something. To adjust the Biblical tenets:

*Blessed are the meek, for they shall inherit the earth.*

*Blessed are the merciful, for they shall obtain mercy.*

*Blessed are those who hunger and thirst for superficial pride and cultivation, for theirs is the Kingdom of Face.*

Q: As a newspaper reporter, I am seriously interested in understanding the Chinese political scene, especially in regard to who will be taking over some of the top spots in the national government when the present officials retire or pass away. I find there is generally a dearth of reporting or research on such topics in China. Why is this?

---

1. In this analysis, "guilt" is seen to arise from violating a divine law, whereas "shame" arises from violating some mere proscription of society.

a. 禮

A: Many Chinese privately tell us that to speculate, or forecast, on such things would be a serious loss of face for the officials now in power. The elders must be respected, so discussion of "succession" is generally considered impolite and possibly even defamatory. After all, if the leaders of the national government lose face, how can they lead the people?

Perhaps your readers would be equally interested to know about the succession questions in the leadership of many local trade associations, rural farming cooperatives, and other community organizations . . . ? In any event, we imagine those would be much safer topics to research and publish.

Q: I do not deliberately go out to insult other people, and I will try to avoid another person suffering embarrassment if I can. However, if it regards an issue of stated, and easily verifiable fact, and you tell me that in order to save someone's face I am expected to downplay, or ignore, the entire issue, then I think that is going too far. I would maintain that the correct stance is: "Facts first, face second".

A: Just think what would happen if there were a few people of your orientation in the Foreign Relations Committee of the US Senate? or the White House? If you would care to make some inquiries, you will most likely find that in international diplomatic circles, "face saving" tends to be a full time preoccupation. Looking back at the Asian domestic scene, if you can convince the Orientals to re-evaluate their traditional views on the subject, perhaps we could have you nominated for a Nobel Prize in "Realism". Good luck.

## Direct and Indirect Remarks

It is often said that the Chinese are indirect in their speech, and we will want to clarify exactly what this means, because different fields of scholarly pursuit have different meanings for the terms "direct" and "indirect". In an English grammar book we see the following examples.

Direct speech: He said "I have lost my abacus."
Indirect speech: He said that he had lost his abacus.

This is perhaps a relevant distinction when discussing sentence structure, however it bears little relation to our present cross-cultural commentary.

The Chinese tend to call relatives by their titles, such as "2nd older Paternal Uncle", "3rd younger Maternal Aunt", etc., whereas a westerner would be more comfortable with appellations like Uncle Bill and Aunt Helen. However it is debatable whether the Chinese usage here is more "indirect". Perhaps by being more specific it is indeed being more direct, albeit lacking in the simple informality to which westerners are more accustomed.

In many types of reporting or investigative work we differentiate sources or information depending on whether the speaker is an actual witness or not. "Ming-lin told me about the bank robbery he had witnessed" is first hand information. "Shing-mei told me about the hit and run accident her friend had seen" is second hand information. It might be reasonable to say that the former is direct speech (or data), and the latter is indirect, but this is not of major importance to the present discussion either.

Some would classify "He went to meet his Maker", or "He passed on to his just reward" as a more indirect way of saying "He died." However, such expressions more properly fall under the heading of euphemistic usage, and such usage, no matter how obtuse or circumlocutory, is clearly recognized by the native speaker (or fluent foreigner) as being equivalent to the more straighforward, simple idea which it intends to express. When we speak of indirect speech among the Chinese, we are not generally referring to euphemisms, although we can by no means ignore their existence entirely. Nor are we talking about using "riddles" to convey our meaning, a type of speech habit that occasionally comes into vogue in the west, and arguably is at odds with directness.

The indirectness of which we are speaking, in the most basic sense, is **a statement, comment, or question which is expressed in a way tangential to the speaker's intended meaning.** Examples:

If we want someone to turn off the radio, we say "Please turn down the radio."

If we want someone to help us move a desk or some furniture, we say "I have always thought that this room would look nicer if it were rearranged."

If we are asked by an artist if we like one of his paintings, and we do not like it, we say "I am not too knowledgeable about art myself, but I have a friend who likes this style of painting very much."

In some cases, the tangential nature of an indirect reply may be 180 degrees:
If we are hungry, and someone asks us if we would like something to eat, we reply "No, I am not hungry."

If we go to a lot of time and expense to prepare a meal for our guests, after loading up the table with food we say "I am sorry there is no food."

If we are expert in a particular branch of physics, and we are asked about our knowledge in this field, we say "I have studied it for a few years" or "I know a little bit about it."

This is one form of Chinese indirectness. It can be characterized as understatement or an attempt to be very modest, unprepossessing, undemanding, and uncritical. The listener is expected to infer the real meaning from the stated remarks.

Another form of indirect speech is in an attempt to divert attention to side issues. One common use of this is to let another party know that although we are unable to do something for them, this is not due to a lack of planning, ability, willingness, efficiency, etc. on our part. For example, if a friend asks if they can borrow our car tonight, rather than giving him a direct and abrupt negative reply, we say "I am sorry, I have to take it into the shop for repairs this evening." If someone asks to borrow some money, we may say "I am sorry, but my aunt is in the hospital and I am tight on funds right now." Instead of saying "I do not want to go" when we are invited somewhere this evening, we may say "I have an appointment to go shopping with my mother." In this way we avoid giving a direct refusal.

Indeed, many times a story needs to be invented to facilitate speaking indirectly. We recall the incident where a group of foreigners were on a tour to visit some famous archaeological sites and had now reached the restaurant where they were to have lunch in the town of Wing-bing. There had been some problem with the tour bus that morning, and the driver had had the engine hood open and his tools out working on some repairs, however it did not seem too serious. After lunch, the Chinese tour leader announced that the afternoon schedule called for driving to Gwan-gu, and staying in the Gwan-gu Palace Hotel there that evening. However since there was a serious storm in Gwan-gu, with a possibility of flooding, so they thought it inadvisable to travel on. The guide had therefore contacted the local authorities in Wing-bing who had arranged a walking tour of the local sites, including a visit to some local mounds which were thought to contain archaeological relics. They had been booked into the Wing-bing Resthouse for the evening.

The foreigners were most disappointed at this, since they had wanted to travel on to Gwan-gu, and in fact several of them were expecting some messages there in the hotel. Since one of the foreigners was a reporter, he called up his contact in Gwan-gu, and according to that fellow, the weather was fine in that town, however he had just learned from the Palace Hotel that since there was a storm in Wing-bing, so the busload of foreigners was now unable to come on as originally scheduled. When the tour guide was confronted with this discrepancy, he said that according to the weather report he had just received, actually the storm was halfway between Wing-bing and Gwan-gu. The truth of the matter was that their bus had broken down, however the tour guide was embarrassed, or thought it would be a loss of face, to say that. People who have been trained in using indirect speech since childhood would have perhaps easily "read between the lines" and understood the tour guide's real meaning, however these foreigners were unable to do so.

A foreigner bought a large desk lamp from an electrical store, and they said they would deliver it the following afternoon. When the foreigner reconfirmed this by telephone the next day, they said that their delivery man was sick, and so it would be another day or two before they could deliver the lamp. When the foreigner said he would be willing to come by and pick it up in person, the manager said that unfortunately there were some workmen nearby repairing the water lines, and the road was most difficult to travel. When asked how serious the delivery man's condition was, the manager said that actually it was the delivery man's sister who was sick, and he was at her bedside. The truth of the matter was that the lamp was out of stock, however the shop manager was embarrassed, or thought it would be a loss of face, to say that. He was trying to stall for time until he could receive delivery of the appropriate lamp from his

## Who Bought the Cakes?

A foreigner was working in a Chinese company. One day one of the secretaries came to his desk and said "Did you put those cakes on my desk? Thanks very much." The foreigner had no idea of what cakes she was referring to, however he framed his reply by saying "Cakes are good to eat in the afternoon, aren't they?" The secretary smiled broadly and walked away.

Two days later the secretary came back to confront him, stating "You said that you bought those cakes for us last time, but today Mai-ling told me that she was the one who purchased them and left them on my desk."

The foreigner looked up from his work. "That is probably true. I did not buy them."

The secretary replied "Why did you say that you did?"

Thinking back to the incident, the foreigner attempted to clarify the issue. "I didn't say any such thing. I said 'Cakes are good to eat in the afternoon, aren't they'."

The secretary said "Oh, that is the same meaning."

*Observation:* Due to habits of indirect communication, what the foreigner says and what the Chinese hear may be two different things.

---

wholesaler, and the fact that the customer could not infer this from his comments was most surprising (to him).

> **Frankness is the child of honesty and courage. Say just what you mean to do, on every occasion. If a friend asks a favor, you should grant it, if it is reasonable; if not, tell him plainly why you cannot. You would wrong him and wrong yourself by equivocation of any kind.**
>
> ———— *Robert E. Lee*

Saving face is certainly an important motive for making indirect statements in many occasions. If someone asks about what I think of their home decorations, even though I do not like them, I say "They are very nice." Asked to comment on a foreigner's Chinese language ability, even though his pronunciation is flawed and he has a very limited vocabulary, a Chinese will say "He speaks extremely well, just like a native." By avoiding making negative comments about someone else, we have saved them face. Likewise, if Ming-fai has an argument with someone in the place where he works and has now decided to resign, he may invent a story about his sick relative who lives in another city and whom he must immediately leave town to tend upon. When a high official accused with some gross dereliction of duty or violation of the statutes is found to be innocent, but actually guilty of another infraction several degrees less severe, one suspects the entire revelation of events and subsequent reportage in the Chinese press to be an exercise in indirection.

Chinese family organization tends to place much emphasis on *nei wai jr fen*,[a] which translates as "a separation of inside and outside". Internal family affairs are not to be broadcast, by word or action, to others, especially not to outsiders. One facet of this is that a Chinese husband and wife may be quarreling, but if guests come they will play the part of the amiable host and hostess, only resuming their quarrel after the guests have gone. Other facts or situations which might cause the family to lose face are also covered up as well as possible. The same considerations would apply to members of a government cabinet, and Napoleon Bonaparte had a similar idea in mind when he said "Even if I had done wrong you should not have reproached me in public – people wash their dirty linen at home." The indirection in this type of stance is clearly apparent.

## Indirect Speech

| *Actual* Intended Meaning | *Chosen* Form of Expression |
|---|---|
| Please move over there. | Would you like to move over there? |
| No, I do not think that would be a good idea. | Good, let me think about it. |
| Please stop doing that now. | Could you perhaps wait and do that a little later? |
| You are not qualified for this position. | Thank you very much for coming in. We will keep your application on file, and let you know soon. |
| We do not want to continue our English lessons. | We are busy these few weeks but we will call you up later and arrange to resume our lessons. |
| No, I do not want to go camping this weekend. | Well, I would like to, but I have to help my cousin prepare for a test. |
| We cannot do that. | There may be a little difficulty for us to do that. |

---

**a.** 內外之分

Indirectness may also be achieved by being deliberately vague, and this is a technique often used. To answer the question "What will you do this afternoon?" many Chinese will say "I have something to do this afternoon."

Failure to make any reaction at the time an incident occurs is also a form of indirectness, since the non-reacting person is generally saving up his/her complaints, criticism, and other comments for presentation at another time, or in another forum, when he/she feels they will be more appropriate, or carry more weight.

The Chinese idiom *jr sang ma huai*,[a] translates literally as "to point to the mulberry and then revile the locust tree". It is used figuratively however, and refers to scolding or cursing someone indirectly. Indeed this tactic is often used, for example when one party is mad at another, and curses his subordinates, or others close to him, instead of scolding him directly. Of course all those involved are supposed to recognize the reality of the situation.

Another form of indirect speech may be any expression of consent or agreement which is said in passing, in order to get off the spot. When someone asks me to look into some particular matter for them, rather than take the time to explain that I cannot, or do not have the time, budget, connections, etc. necessary to do so, I say "Yes, of course." When I have failed to perform within a reasonable period of time, the other party is supposed to be able to clearly and explicitly infer that I am now unable to complete this task. They will then not press me about it further, for to press me would be "not giving face". (Note: The original request, although phrased in the interrogative mood "Could you help me out to do such and such?", was actually regarded by the asked party to be a disguised demand, and it was felt that a quick and direct refusal on the spot would not have been taken lightly.)

Modesty is quite relevant to indirectness as well. Playing down one's own ability often serves to make others feel important, and this can be an important consideration in laying an "indirect groundwork" upon which further indirect statements may be based or promulgated.

A Chinese man was introduced by a matchmaker to a girl from a prominent local family. After their first meeting, the man decided that she was not his type. The next day when the matchmaker asked what he thought, he commented on all the girl's good qualities, and then mentioned that he had done some real soul searching recently and discovered that he had a number of personal failings and character weaknesses. In light of his own inadequacy, he felt that he was not a suitable match for the lady in question, and he said "She certainly deserves better." This is an excellent example of turning someone down indirectly. The matchmaker was not surprised when the gentleman's mother came back the next day and asked if the matchmaker had compiled a listing of other promising matches for her outstanding son.

---

a. 指桑罵槐

## To Be Hungry and Not To Be Hungry

My American acquaintance Roland was invited to stay at a Chinese friend's home one weekend. In addition to this friend, the household consisted of one brother, one sister, two cousins, two parents, and one set of grandparents. On Sunday morning Roland got up rather late, and after taking a bath, was treated to a substantial breakfast, which he finished eating at approximately 11:15.

At 12:15, the entire family sat down to lunch, and Roland was called from the living room to join in the eating. When he said "I am not hungry", this was considered impolite by the mother, father, and grandparents, and his friend insisted that he join in the meal so as not to cause further difficulties. Some days later the Chinese friend said that his mother had interpreted his "I am not hungry" as indicating that he didn't like the food, and didn't appreciate their hospitality.

*Observation:* Due to well-developed habits of indirect communication among the local populace, many innocent remarks made by the foreigner are assumed to have some greater underlying significance.

A foreigner was asked to edit a small newsletter concerning "English Teaching" and completed it with the help of several Chinese staff members. The blueprints came back from the printers in due course, and were checked over and finalized. Several days later when he arrived at the office however, the manager and director were examining the final printed newsletters that had been delivered, and complaining to the print shop manager who had delivered them: "This isn't what we expected", "This doesn't look right", "These headlines seem a little crooked", "The margins are uneven", and other comments. The foreigner looked at several copies, and felt that they were fine, but when he pointed this out, the manager gave him a discouraging glance, and told him to go into the office where there was an important message waiting from his relative. The truth of the situation was that the manager and director were engaging in fault-finding as an indirect way of asking the print shop manager to make a reduction in the printing charge. (There was of course no message from a relative.)

A tendency for indirectness also influences the meanings of many words. When discussing some action that was done, in explaining the reason for it, some Chinese people will say "We always do it this way." When asked why their performance varied from this norm on another occasion, they may reply "Many times we do it that way." It may be then seen that habits of indirect speech often rule out the possibility that words like "always", "invariably", "consistently", "100% of the time", etc. will be used in their exact and literal sense, more likely they may all tend to become synonyms for the terms "sometimes" or "generally". The Chinese mentality of inexactness certainly reinforces this. Seeing a selection of merchandise, we may be told that "These are all $100." However, when we pick one out, the salesman states "But these are $150." In this indirect and inexact social framework, the word "all" may tend to mean "most", or occasionally "some".

We offer the following summary and outline. Indirect talk may commonly be used by the Chinese in the following areas:

1) When explaining anyone's reasons for non-performance
                                non-fulfillment
                                non-compliance
                                cancellation or other readjustment of originally
                                    stated terms and conditions
2) When asking for assistance
                help
                cooperation
                aid
3) When explaining anyone's intention
                planning
                prospects
                desires
4) When stating or discussing anyone's expertise
                ability
                competence
                performance
                achievement

We have deliberately chosen here to use the word "anyone's", with the intent to convey the meaning of "one's own, or another person's".

Indirect talk may take many forms. Among the most common are understatements; evasive statements; statements designed to cause a slowdown or delay, delaying tactics; diversionary tactics; inexact statements; real modesty and false modesty. We may perhaps lump these all under the category of *roundabout remarks*.


"Then you should say what you mean," the March Hare went on.
"I do," Alice hastily replied; "at least, at least I mean what I say . . . "

———— *Alice's Adventures in Wonderland*, Lewis Carroll


In general, most westerners tend to assume that directness is, by definition, a presupposition for all concerns such as honesty, sincerity, truthfulness, integrity, etc., or in a broader sense, for human relations[a] in general. However, many Chinese feel that indirectness is in keeping, or compatible with, these concerns. Of course in the west we do find that in diplomatic circles and much of high society there is a more marked tendency for indirect speech than among the people of middle class orientation.

---

a. 做人的道理

Hence, upon doing some cross-cultural analysis, we can see that each society has retained the parameter of its most prominent or distinctive class. In China, indirectness is most typical of the speech habits in the traditional aristocracy, which historically has always represented the most prominent class in their Pre Industrial Revolution subsistence agricultural society. The western preferences for time-saving, simplicity, frugality, equal dealings with people of different social classes, etc. have developed historically and emerged as a tendency for directness. This represents the thinking of the middle class, which has been the dominant social class in the west in the Post Industrial Revolution age.

## Indirect Words and Action

We have spoken above of what falls into the category of "indirect speech". It would be incomplete for us not to consider the issue of "indirect action" as well.

Some would suppose that indirect action in the Oriental sense is when two people speaking to each other do not face each other directly. This is a notable peculiarity of Oriental interpersonal relations, which does not fall into the western norm. The foreigner is certainly advised to make allowance for it. However, the indirect action with which we are primarily concerned is not this. It is **not doing something yourself, but rather having someone else do it for you; using an intermediary.** We have outlined four possibilities below:

Variations of Action and Talk, and basic conceptualization or examples
1. direct     action     &     direct     talk
   Example: *No intermediary, and with remarks made straightforwardly*
2. direct     action     &     indirect     talk
   Example: *No intermediary, but with remarks made roundaboutly*
3. indirect     action     &     direct     talk
   Example: *Using an intermediary, but with remarks made straightforwardly*
4. indirect     action     &     indirect     talk
   Example: *Using an intermediary, and with remarks made roundaboutly*

In relations between two people, if Amy desires to speak to Bill and uses an intermediary, Cindy, to convey some message or otherwise make communication, this could be seen as a form of indirect action. The message conveyed could be stated in a direct fashion (variation 3) or an indirect fashion (variation 4). Of course if Amy tells Bill when she sees him, this would be more in the form of direct action, however her remarks could be stated in an direct fashion (variation 1), or an indirect fashion (variation 2). The indirect speech we have discussed in the initial part of this section, if spoken from one party to another without the use of an intermediary, would most probably fall under variation 2.

No doubt many westerners, steeped in the values of the middle class, would prefer variation 1, however many Chinese tend to shy away from the direct talk implicit in variation 1, and often the best that can be hoped for is variation 2. For the Chinese who needs to communicate some important and potentially sensitive information to a foreigner, if another Chinese is used as an intermediary, the decision to deal directly (variation 3) is often nullified, since the intermediary will tend to convey the communication in a roundabout fashion, (unless they are on extremely good terms with the intended recipient of the message). The result of this may be that originally intended variation 3 becomes in reality a variation 4.

No doubt the perceptive reader will realize that any explanation or discourse, being a collection of many sentences, is hard to classify as purely direct, or purely indirect. It might be more proper to classify its percentage of directness. Using 10% as a basic measuring unit, we can immediately see over twenty permutations.

Variations of Action and Talk

|   |   |   |   |   | % of direct talk |
|---|---|---|---|---|---|
| 1. direct | action | & | direct | talk | 100 % |
| ,, | ,, | & | ,, | ,, | 90 % |
| ,, | ,, | & | ,, | ,, | 80 % |
| ,, | ,, | & | ,, | ,, | 70 % |
| ,, | ,, | & | ,, | ,, | 60 % |
| 2. direct | action | & | indirect | talk | 50 % |
| ,, | ,, | & | ,, | ,, | 40 % |
| ,, | ,, | & | ,, | ,, | 30 % |
| ,, | ,, | & | ,, | ,, | 20 % |
| ,, | ,, | & | ,, | ,, | 10 % |
| ,, | ,, | & | ,, | ,, | 0 % |
| 3. indirect | action | & | direct | talk | 100 % |
| ,, | ,, | & | ,, | ,, | 90 % |
| ,, | ,, | & | ,, | ,, | 80 % |
| ,, | ,, | & | ,, | ,, | 70 % |
| ,, | ,, | & | ,, | ,, | 60 % |
| 4. indirect | action | & | indirect | talk | 50 % |
| ,, | ,, | & | ,, | ,, | 40 % |
| ,, | ,, | & | ,, | ,, | 30 % |
| ,, | ,, | & | ,, | ,, | 20 % |
| ,, | ,, | & | ,, | ,, | 10 % |
| ,, | ,, | & | ,, | ,, | 0 % |

Although the percentage of directness varies, the classification of many types of speech as basically direct or indirect is still generally feasible.

Arranged marriages are generally done rather formally through the employ of a matchmaker, and are certainly good examples of indirect action. That such marriages are far more common in China and Japan today than in the west shows that the Chinese and Japanese have a much greater tendency for indirectness.

The Chinese government is often surprised when foreign businessmen act indirectly. For example, since the government tends not to allow foreigners to own any Chinese buildings, land, houses, etc., knowledgeable overseas investors often invest in such real estate in an indirect fashion. This is done by supplying capital to local real estate and construction companies, and then receiving a return on this investment. Cries of "foul play" are often heard, however this is nothing which the Chinese do not engage in themselves, so one wonders what all the commotion is about.

## Telling Someone You Do Not Like Them

Some might think that "I do not like that man's behavior, and I told (or will tell) him so" is an honest expression of character, however the Chinese with their preference for indirectness would not condone such talk. It would be better to keep one's comments to oneself, or to discuss them with someone else who may, or may not, act as an intermediary in passing these comments on to the person in question. Of course it may happen that this intermediary in turn tells another intermediary, and on and on, with the result that much gossip is generated. Sometimes this may cause a westerner to feel that he is being talked about behind his back, and he may regard the failure to come forward and make comments or incriminations to him directly as a lack of character, honesty, integrity, etc. However this is merely another facet of Chinese indirectness.

## Beyond Indirectness

Beyond indirect action is non-action, which indeed may arise innocently enough, perhaps through spending too much time in locating or choosing a suitable intermediary. The result of this is that the message is not communicated, and some problem which could have been easily solved in its early stages has now gotten out of hand. This often happens because of real or assumed factional loyalty in a Chinese organization. If Manager Wang is favorably disposed to employee Robert Tsai, primarily because Manager Wang is good friends with Tsai's father, this will be recognized by other members of the organization. If Robert is not a good office worker, the other employees will hesitate to make any bad remarks about him, for fear that Manager Wang is "on his side", and will support him (Robert) in any argument or dispute. This being the case, the person making the bad remarks is only causing trouble for himself, and could easily end up being demoted, fired, or otherwise given a hard time. Obviously it is better to keep quiet.

For those employees who do not feel keeping quiet is the answer, good safety measures still require the use of an appropriate intermediary, someone very close to the recipient of the message, so that they can protect themselves by not relating the criticism or bad news directly. When lengthy consideration fails to come up with a suitable intermediary with whom they themselves are personally on good terms, the only feasible alternative is generally "inaction". If Robert then goes on to lose some big accounts or make other significant blunders, the Manager may see what is going on, and call the staff members in to review Robert's performance. When the real facts have come to light, the Manager will of course wonder why he was not told previously, and the employees can only offer mute silence in return to this question.

A company Chairman had worked in another organization some years back, and had just recently hired the son of his former co-worker. He was very proud of this new employee, Glenn Chang, and had big plans for him. Everyday he told the secretaries to take special care of Glenn, and make sure to show him all the procedures in the office, as well as where to go for lunch, how to catch the bus, etc. Shortly after Glenn had come to work, various female employees in the office had mentioned to each other that their purses "seemed to be a few bills short". One Saturday afternoon when only the Chairman, Glenn, and a few part-time secretaries were finishing up some work, one of the secretaries felt she had lost some money, and she reported it to a section chief by phone. He made a note of it, but thinking it was carelessness on her part, no further action was taken.

The secretaries continued to talk among themselves however, and by process of elimination it was determined that Glenn was highly suspicious. Knowing the Chairman's good feelings about Glenn, no one dared bring this to his attention however. Eventually the situation developed to the point where one afternoon the Chairman's wife came to the office, and upon preparing to leave happened to notice that her purse, the contents of which she had counted that very morning, was several bills short. After the whole story came out, the Chairman was very disappointed that he had not been told earlier. However, the employees said that they had been waiting to assemble "hard evidence" before presenting their case.

Certainly one reason why employees will not speak critically of someone whom their superiors favor, or who is related to their superiors, is the fear that the superior in question will view such comments, irregardless of their basis in fact or not, as a loss of face. In this eventuality it would be expected that the superior would support his favored worker in any dispute, in order to save face. The employee who spoke critically would then be in hot water.

A Chinese idiom which bears some relation to the present discussion is *tou shu ji chi*,[a] which roughly translates as "throw at the rat, regret the vase", [vase = jar] and is used figuratively to denote being afraid of injuring a third party. (In the story, the rat was hiding inside a valuable vase.) This phrase enjoyed wide usage historically, for example it characterizes the thinking of someone who is afraid of impeaching a corrupt official for fear of incriminating the emperor; broadly speaking it indicates "having a fear of the repercussions of some particular action". For example, in many organizations in China, if one accuses a certain clerk of being incompetent, when in fact this clerk is the daughter of the boss's younger brother (or has some other relation to powerful officials in the hierarchy), one would have "broken the vase". This kind of outcome is clearly unfavorable. Since the Chinese place a strong emphasis on family ties, it would be better to keep this type of negative or critical comments to oneself. In this way everyone's face is saved, and one does not run the risk of being transferred to the outer provinces or fired altogether.

One foreign manager in China hired his brother, Thomas, from the United States to work as a part-time electrician and handyman around their factory and offices. Several secretaries had requested some painting, cleaning, and general repair work in various places, and when these tasks had not been done after several days, one of the secretaries whose work had been affected spoke to Thomas about it one afternoon in somewhat of a harsh tone. Unexpectedly the manager walked in at this point. The secretary immediately stopped talking, and as if some giant weight had just been raised over their heads, all the Chinese employees in the office simultaneously seemed to get very ill at ease.

Quickly sizing up the situation, the manager said: "Tell my brother to get going on those projects. If he does not do a good job, tell him to do them again, and do not let him give you any backtalk." At this point he walked on into his office. Later the Chinese employees were talking among themselves, and their description of the manager's reaction varied from "hard to understand", "very unusual", etc. to "unbelievable".

Commenting on this and a host of similar situations in China, some observers would advance the hypothesis that "favoritism" to one's family, clan, friends, classmates, etc. is more the norm than the exception, (just as nepotism is more the norm than the exception), and it appears that many Chinese equate such favoritism with the demands of *chung* 忠 and *yi* 義. These are important Chinese philosophical concepts, which we may translate with the dictionary definitions of "loyalty and righteousness." The lack of objectivity in this stance is troubling, however only to the westerner apparently. What the Chinese immediately realize is the need for indirect action and indirect speech in order to deal with all the ramifications of such a value system.

Our discussion would not be complete without mention of the expression *yi twei wei jin*[b], which we may roughly render as "to move back in order to move forward", (or

---

a. 投鼠忌器
b. 以退爲進

in slightly more polished language "to pretend to move back in order to hide the intention to move ahead"). This is another broadly used tenet of indirect action in China, practiced by officials of all departments and citizenry of all occupations in a wide variety of activities. By contrast, Chinese who move or immigrate to western countries generally note that westerners conform more to the philosophy of *yi jin wei jin*[a], a careful conversion of which into English becomes "to move ahead in order to move forward."

Many successful approaches to problem solving, personnel relations, community action, etc., in China must take into account the Chinese cultural bias for indirect talk and indirect action in a multitude of situations.

### Justice, Righteousness, etc.

Although 義 is often translated as "justice" or "righteousness", (and occasionally as "integrity"), in fact it must be understood as proceeding from the basis of *loyalty to a cause* (whether the family/clan, an association or band, a group of cohorts, etc.) and indeed has a certain "Robin Hood" quality. As such, considerations of "justice" are frequently outside of, or above, the law, and become closer to 以牙還牙 "an eye for an eye, a tooth for a tooth". A Chinese description of 義 "justice" is 為朋友兩肋插刀 "willing to take two knives in the ribs for a friend." As to whether the friend's original action (which you are now defending) was legal or illegal is not an issue that is carefully weighed. 義無反顧 "righteousness will not look back" also ignores issues of legality.

Turning to the opposite consideration of 不義 "unrighteous" or "unjust", this is construed to mean ungrateful to your superiors, elders, teachers, friends, etc. or causing them trouble. The consideration of whether these people acted illegally is again largely unmentioned and undeliberated. The subordinate who exposes a superior of graft, corruption, illegality, etc. is therefore 不義 "unjust" and 不忠 "disloyal". He will probably lose his present job, and no doubt will have a hard time finding a job in another organization.

Confucius is on record as advocating that a son conceal his father's theft of a sheep. This is considered "uprightness," and further shows that a sense of *justice* or *fairness* is not necessarily related to following the law.

*Analects* XIII, 18:
葉公語孔子曰：「吾黨有直躬者：其父攘羊而子證之。」孔子曰：「吾黨直者異於是：父為子隱，子為父隱，直在其中矣。」

---

a. 以進為進

# Chapter 9 Language, Communication, and Non-Communication

The use of language is an important element in the relations between people. The foreigner in China is surrounded by Chinese, and frequently has much contact with locally-edited English-language newspapers, journals, books, menus, signs, catalogs, etc. as well as Chinese people who communicate, or attempt to communicate, in English. The overview of language in this chapter will begin by outlining some of the problems which occur when Chinese use English, and discussing some of the perceptual difficulties which Chinese people have in dealing with four different kinds of English language skills. Further commentary will be offered on many ways of comparing and contrasting the two languages, finally delving into the practical difficulties involved when foreigners strive to use Chinese on a daily basis.

In collecting material for this chapter, I have largely avoided including anything which is easily available from other sources, such as language textbooks, dictionaries, traveller's phrase books, traveller's guides, regular newspaper reportage, etc. I have attempted to dig a bit deeper, and concentrated on discussing many important orientations underlying the use of language which these books rarely mention.

**Detailed Contents:** Western speakers, writers, lecturers, negotiators, psychologists, etc. working in China have all been troubled at one time or another by the fact that certain English words and expressions carry significantly different "emotive content" in Chinese. The potential for misunderstanding or other ambiguity exists whenever we hit upon any of these sensitive terms or phrases, even when care is taken in translation. I have collected a large number of examples, and offer some guidelines for usage, so that the interested westerner can maneuver his way around numerous problems which often catch the unwary.

Although westerners who edit, write, or otherwise proofread a large variety of typed and printed materials are frequently familiar with western style proofreading marks, the majority of these are unknown in China. In order that the foreigner may deal more effectively with typed, printed, and other materials in his dealings with Chinese printers, designers, and others, I have collected the most commonly used Chinese proofreading marks and explain how they are used.

The "Integration of Concepts" which have been illustrated with various examples in previous chapters are now more fully summarized and analyzed. The idea of "Rationale Weight Indexing" for Chinese maxims, proverbs, sayings, etc. is introduced, leading us up to a discussion of what can only be called "Chinese-style Conversational Logic". Although baffling at first, its key foundational premises are quickly revealed.

Some examples of situations where fluent language skills fail to result in "communication with the natives" are illustrated, and the goal of total fluency in Chinese is examined in terms of its practical ramifications. Differing attitudes toward "the point of conversation" are divulged. Confusing points of medical terminology are considered, as are other important points of grammatical bias, verb tense confusion, and place-name adjectival descriptions.

Translation work is discussed from the point of view of western consumers, Chinese consumers, locally-run translation services, and foreign-invested translation services. It is by no means true that all take the same view of what constitutes "correct translation", "good value for the money", or the demands of "keeping our clients happy". The relation between quality and value in translation work is outlined and illustrated with several real world examples. Important considerations relevant to undertaking translation projects as a business are mentioned.

The difficulties for the westerner in learning Chinese as a second language, and dealing with Chinese data, (as compared to learning and using English as a second language), are categorized, so that at least the interested individual can have a coherent discussion on the topic with his Chinese friends and associates. The complexity and various restraints imposed when ordering Chinese data, whether with a manual system or a computerized database, are examined. The question of whether or not Chinese characters are "scientific", "logical", "exacting", etc. are delved into. Comparative language guessing games are outlined, which gives us frequent opportunity to make comments on the differing orientations of the educational systems in China and the west.

## English Language Difficulties

In dealing with Chinese who understand English, we must recognize some basic concepts. Among such Chinese, it is quite common to find differing levels of English competence in regard to differing types of English skills. This may be represented by three concentric circles, where the largest represents reading ability, the next smaller represents listening ability, and the smallest represents spoken ability. (Writing abilities vary widely, and are not easily outlined in a generalized fashion.) We should not be surprised then to see a Chinese person reading an English-language textbook on psychology, engineering, international relations, etc. and to receive nothing but a smile and a bow if we ask if there is a bus nearby that will take us to the train station. Reading, listening, and speaking abilities are all quite different matters.

Reading ability may be obtained through individual study, even when the "reader" is unsure of the correct pronunciation of the words or inflection of the sentences he is reading. Listening ability however is dependent on a number of factors which many people who have not had intensive exposure to the language, in the language's native environment, will not have fully mastered. Four are worthy of particular consideration: speed, accent, pronunciation, and terms of expression. Finally, spoken ability means that the person must be not only passively aware of these four factors, but indeed that he be able to actively deal with them, especially with the preciseness of pronunciation and the use of colloquial phrases, idioms, and other terms of expression to get his meaning across.

The speed at which most native speakers speak English[1] is generally a big problem in language comprehension for the Chinese, even though the person with many years of English language study might understand every word if spoken more slowly, or written down. One reason for this is that most beginning to high-intermediate students of a foreign language are, consciously or unconsciously, translating what their ears hear into their own language as part of the comprehension process. When listening to a foreigner speak, we may say that their minds are "in the translation mode". Added to this are their lack of experience in using the language and overly theoretical grammatical knowledge.

Different accents of different speakers also present a serious problem, whereupon a Chinese who understands American English fairly well is largely uncomprehending at the Australian, British, or even a southern U.S.A. accent. If he was trained in British English, he may of course have trouble understanding the "American accent". Also there are the idioms, popular expressions, place names, and historical references which the Chinese is not familiar with, and must pause to think about. While being aware of the problems of speed, accent, and pronunciation, we will not dwell on them here, for they are easily recognized, and training procedures, or replacement of personnel procedures, to deal with them may be quickly and effectively formulated if the task as hand so requires.

Further background information on the Asian student's difficulties in learning English is given in the following essay.

---

1. Experts tell us that normal English speech is approximately 140 to 160 words per minute. One hundred words per minute is considered an appropriate delivery speed if simultaneous interpretation is being done, roughly equivalent to something read at three minutes per double-spaced typewritten page.

# English and the Asian Student

## My Self Introduction

I come to introduction my family. We have four people in our family: father, mather, litter brother, and me.

Father is a Banker. Mather is manage in the family: I and litter brother is reading little school. Father is very like game tennis, baseball, and up mountain, also often carry our brother to travel in the Sunday or holiday. Mather is very kind, often buy new cloth and cooking good eat breakfast and dinner. I eating breakfast on 6:15 and dinner 7:00 more. Lunch take rice box is to school eat. I have a good lucky of family.

To the native Asian, English is quite a difficult language. English often has different forms for the noun and the verb, indeed we see our essayist in the above example has confused introduction with introduce. Forms of the verb "eat" have also given him trouble, and this is not surprising. Even the advanced Asian student may have difficulty making sentence examples of even a few of all the verb forms in English, although of course the native English speaker uses these instinctively, and without much thought. For "eat", in the active voice alone, we have: to eat, eats, do eat, eating, ate, will eat, have eaten, will have eaten, had eaten, would have eaten, was eating, would have been eating, will have been eating, etc. In the passive voice, we have: is eaten, was eaten, will be eaten, would have been eaten, will have been eaten, etc. By comparison, Chinese has no verb tenses.

More difficult yet are the many uses of verbs such as get, make, put, etc. Casual reference to a dictionary reveals different meanings for get about, get across, get ahead, get along, get around, get at, get away, get by, get down, get in, get nowhere, get off, get on, get over, get through, get up, get out, get on with, etc. That all of these separate meanings are related to "get" is rather baffling to many Asian students.

In private discussions with Chinese people, certain individuals have pointed out to me that rather than Chinese being illogical (as some western students of the language claim, much to the dismay of their Chinese friends), actually it is English that is totally illogical. I was given five examples of this illogic by a Chinese who had lived in the USA for many years, and offer them here for reference of any naive westerners in the reading audience.

1. A Chinese had collected a number of examples of English usage from his encounters with westerners. He said: "I understand it when you refer to a handful of beans, a handful of grapes, or a handful of paperclips. But when you say that there are only a handful of x-ray machines in one medical school, does that mean that there are none, or that all of the ones there are extremely small?"

2. A Chinese was watching the construction of a new road network in the United States. He went to research the cost expenditures for this project, and found that they ran approximately $3000 per foot. Neither the Chief Engineer nor anyone else on the construction crew was able to explain why it was called a "freeway".

3. Noting a large sign in a department store which said "Box Office", a Chinese was very surprised after making his purchases that the girl in charge there said they had no boxes for sale, nor would they have any in the future.

4. The clocks in an office had stopped due to an electrical power outage. Some time later, the manager happened to ask a Chinese employee: "What time is it?" The employee glanced at his wrist, and said: "It is eleven o'watch." He was surprised when told that this was unusual grammar.

5. Americans like to say that the majority of words are pronounced the way they are spelled. Reference to any map of Hawaii will show that this is a total fallacy. How do you pronounce "Laupahoehoe"? What about "Kealakekua"? Or "Mokuaweoweo"?

Pronunciation

Since North America is a land of immigrants, and many areas were originally inhabited by French, Spanish, Indians, etc., so the varying linguistic bases used in choosing place names is staggering. Actually, the best way to determine the correct pronunciation of the name of a river, city, town, county, state, etc. is to ask someone from that locality. In addition to the Hawaiian place names given above, other examples from the author's own experience are Gratiot Avenue in Detroit, the Schuylkill River in Philadelphia, the city of Albuquerque in New Mexico, etc.

However, beyond the difficulty of dealing with place names, a major conceptual problem to the Chinese studying English, and we suppose probably first on their list of complaints about the English language, is "the lack of a standard English pronunciation" among English speakers. For example, if we select an article out of TIME magazine, and ask 100 North Americans from different localities to read it aloud, even if we eliminate the heavier "deep south", "New England", and "French Canadian" accents, we are still left with quite a wide range of pronunciations for any given word, often due to a slight difference in enunciation of the vowel. If these are analyzed and cataloged in terms of correspondence to some reference table, such as an international phonetic alphabet, we find a lack of standardization. To the Asian student who asks: "Which pronunciation is correct?" The native speaker replies: "They are all correct."

Now when we add on the varieties of British pronunciation, Australian pronunciation, South African pronunciation, etc., we are left with an even more bewildering array of pronunciations for a great many words. Since the vast majority of these are perfectly understandable to the native speaker, he naturally considers them equally valid. Of course the Asian student generally carries over an accent from his native language into the speaking of English, and is therefore very concerned with "correct" English pronunciation. The native speaker has no absolute standards for "correctness" in this regard, and is happier talking about "understandable" and "not understandable". For example he says that after dinner, you may ask someone if they want "a dessert", and this should not be confused with "a desert". When you repaint your "house", do not tell people you repainted your "horse". When someone calls at your office, do not ask "What is your porpoise?", use "purpose" instead.

Unfortunately, these remarks are of very limited usefulness to Chinese students studying English. From an early age they have been taught that the Peking pronunciation is "standard Chinese pronunciation", and naturally they assume that other languages have a similar standard. Not only do the students feel this way, but their teachers agree. Thus in the English tests in the Chinese junior high schools, high schools, and colleges, various English words are dissected, the students are tested on comparative phonetic renderings of vowels, consonants, dipthongs, and other letter combinations.

Think of the "a" in apple. Consider if it is pronounced the same as the initial "a" in 1) apply, 2) aunt, 3) append, 4) apology, 5) able. According to the grammar books I have seen in China, only 2) corresponds to the "a" in apple. Any of the other choices would be marked wrong by the teacher. I have always wondered how the majority of native speakers would do in taking tests of this kind.

Further examples are given below:

In each question, determine if the underlined portion in each of the four examples are pronounced the same or differently from the underlined portion of the initial key word.

| | | | |
|---|---|---|---|
| A. r<u>ea</u>dy | 1. br<u>ea</u>k | 2. gr<u>ea</u>t | 3. f<u>ea</u>ther | 4. ch<u>ea</u>p |
| B. b<u>u</u>sy | 1. fr<u>ui</u>t | 2. b<u>ui</u>ld | 3. b<u>u</u>s | 4. exc<u>u</u>se |
| C. c<u>a</u>ke | 1. n<u>a</u>rrow | 2. st<u>a</u>tion | 3. sm<u>a</u>ll | 4. w<u>a</u>ter |
| D. t<u>al</u>k | 1. we<u>l</u>come | 2. <u>l</u>unch | 3. co<u>l</u>d | 4. ha<u>l</u>f |
| E. E<u>ng</u>lish | 1. a<u>ng</u>ry | 2. da<u>ng</u>er | 3. ora<u>ng</u>e | 4. stra<u>ng</u>er |
| F. c<u>u</u>te | 1. r<u>u</u>le | 2. p<u>u</u>re | 3. m<u>u</u>le | 4. ch<u>u</u>te |

Answers: Only one choice in each group of four actually corresponds to the underlined part in the key word. A. 3
B. 2
C. 2
D. 4
E. 1
F. 3

The other choices are wrong. Of course, to the native English speaker, such comparisons and analysis are nit-picking at best, and arguably of minimal real value in language study.

The concerned westerner may have hopes of resolving this situation by promoting "more valid testing procedures." He is quickly thwarted however by the fact that there is no "International Bureau of Teaching and Testing of English as a Foreign Language" or other such body which is the recognized authority on such matters, and whose determination on the validity or non-validity of certain types of testing procedures would be accepted as final. Making a quick overview of the English teaching situation in Asia today, the need for such an organization is all apparent. Ideally it would be associated with the relevant department of a prestigious western university or universities.

There is at the present time a Test Of English as a Foreign Language (TOEFL) for those non-native speakers who wish to continue their education in the United States. However, with the trend toward bringing English language instruction into the Asian junior high and elementary schools, the need for a multi-level Children's TOEFL is becoming more pronounced. Ideally it would be designed for all young students who were studying English, and not just those who might be planning further studies overseas in the near future. Such a test, recognized by a competent western educational authority, and sponsored by a Bureau such as the one mentioned above, would add much to continuing to promote English as an international language, by providing a structurally sound testing basis. Over time this would come to be recognized as an excellent guide for English teaching program development in these countries. The testing bureau could also provide models, guidelines, instructional tips, and other suggestions for use in schools in 3rd world countries, where English testing procedures are now largely without proper organization, direction, content, or validity.

In a related consideration, a Test Of Foreign Language English Teachers (TOFLET) should also be devised, so that the qualifications of local English language teachers in non-native English language countries and areas may be determined. The teachers' scores on such a test would enable local educational authorities to undertake remedial measures to deal with any weak areas, or to call in outside educational consultants to assist in the upgrading of teachers' skills. In this way much more effective English language teaching could certainly be promoted throughout the world.

## Dealing with the Language

Living in China, many foreigners often are overly quick to jump to the conclusion that if their skills in speaking (and to a lesser extent in reading and writing) the local language are poor, then they are at a decided disadvantage in communication. They then assume that if they were to vastly upgrade their ability in the local tongue, their communications skills would be significantly improved.

Indeed, it is seemingly redundant to state that the most effective communication with the Chinese people can be done by learning Chinese and "speaking to them in their language". The truth of this assertion, to the not-yet acculturated individual, lies in examining a wide range of simple everyday situations. For many things which we want to communicate or explain to the local masses, the difference between "comprehension" and "non-comprehension" lies in the choice of language used. Into this realm we may include all sorts of topics such as news of current events and other news of an informational nature such as weather reports, scheduling for trains, boats, and airplanes, operational instructions for appliances and machinery, safety manuals, training manuals, etc. The seasoned traveller is quick to point out that it is definitely advisable if not mandatory for the foreigner to learn an abundant selection of basic vocabulary items and simple commands in the local language when living in any foreign country. In fact, many foreigners make collections of multilingual flashcards for every conceivable purpose, and have remarkable ease in accomplishing a wide variety of everyday tasks and handling common transactions. This type of knowledge can be obtained in reference books, guidebooks, by taking a language course, or by structured questioning of local acquaintances, and is certainly useful, if not irreplaceable.

Yet there is a higher, or more complex, level of communication, which is considerably beyond the direct correspondence, or direct translation, of basic vocabulary items or sentence patterns from one language to another. For example, in regard to discussion of attitudes, ways of looking at personal relationships, ways of looking at the world, approaches to problem solving, conceptions of what constitutes fairness and honesty, what we consider to be acceptable behavior in different situations, even perhaps what we consider to be proper clothing — all of these various types of topics, as well as of course other types of topics where conflicts of interests might be involved, improving one's language skills is not always tantamount to improving one's communications skills. The reason for this lies in the fact that there is a "cultural gap".

In terms of acculturizing oneself to life with the Chinese people, we will want to examine certain concepts which may influence effective communication between Chinese and Westerners as a result of this cultural gap. We will then in this discussion largely skip over the introduction of any basic Chinese vocabulary or sentences, and proceed on to an examination of difficulties in dealing with cross-cultural communication, assuming that all parties involved have made adequate preparation, i.e. that we have eliminated 90% or more of the language barrier, and both sides seemingly have a very good grasp of the common language being spoken. For the purposes of our discussion on acculturization, we will want to assume anyone of three possibilities in an encounter between Westerners and Chinese: 1) that the persons involved in the discussion all speak and understand English to a well-above-average degree, or 2) that the English-speaking Westerner is utilizing a competent interpreter to translate his remarks into Chinese, or 3) that the Westerner has adequate Chinese ability to conduct a conversation or negotiation directly in reasonably fluent Chinese. In any of these cases, the initial obstacle of speaking different and mutually-unintelligible languages has been largely overcome. After this situation has been achieved however, there are still a number of significant problems which remain, and these will form the focus of our study.

## Assumed Cleverness

We often intermix clever expressions in our remarks to add some flavor and depth. However, some expressions which seem to be the most basic and uncomplicated to us, are often not readily understood by the Chinese, the reason being that they do not have the same expression in their language. Therefore, when the English speaker uses these expressions, he is more likely to be mis-translated or misinterpreted. At best the translator will have to go into several sentences of explanation to get this point across. An examination of several of these will be useful in clarifying that what we consider common sense is often nothing more than our standard form of expression.

One illustration comes from the story of a a Chinese college student who had applied to go study in Graduate School in the USA. He was informed that it would probably take him a month or two to adjust to the new environment and "learn the ropes". He couldn't understand what "ropes" had to do with it, unless it was that American students were required to take courses in knotting. Indeed in China, knotting is an art form, and his relatives agreed this seemed a reasonable explanation.

In the way of a more elaborate example, a group of adult Chinese in an advanced English class were asked to explain the phrase "10% down and the rest on time", which one of them had seen displayed in the window of a furniture store. Some thought that "10% down" meant that the furniture was built 10% lower in height than was standard, although others felt that this perhaps meant that there was a 10% discount on the price. The word "pay" was recognized as meaning "pay money". The word "rest" was examined in its various meanings including "to relax", "to become still", and "the remainder". "On time" was taken to mean either "promptly" or "at what time is convenient to you". One interpretation of this entire phrase then became "10% discount, and in order to relax you must pay your money promptly."

In the way of making a step-by-step examination of the concepts which influence effective communication between Chinese and Westerners as a result of the cultural gap, let us first deal with the simpler examples, so that we may gradually orient ourselves, by way of shedding some of our naivete, in preparation for the increasingly difficult topics that will follow in later chapters. Our initial attention will be devoted to differing forms of expression and phraseology, problems which are even stumbled over or misconstrued by highly capable linguists or translators.

## Categories of Confusion

There are a number of categories of confusion in dealing with the forms of expression in two languages as dissimilar as English and Chinese. This is true whether we are speaking to a Chinese person in English, who will often be "in the translation mode", or dealing through an interpreter (regardless of nationality). Let us first consider a number of items which an English speaker will want to keep in mind, and which are not listed for easy reference in any bilingual dictionary.

Category I
English – Chinese Usage
Notable Points of Difference & Similiarity

1. Words or expressions which are used one way in English, and used in an opposite manner in Chinese.
2. Words which are clear and precise in English but for which the Chinese equivalent is ambiguous.
3. Words and phrases which carry certain connotations in English which they do not carry in Chinese, and vice-versa.
4. Words and phrases which have differing emotive content in Chinese and English.
5. Forms of expression which exist grammatically in English but against which there is a Chinese bias.

Of course our discussion cannot end here, for the philiosophical Westerner quickly realizes that there is a higher level of Confusion or Disagreement beyond this one, which will include many topics relevant to personal conceptions and value systems which are different in a Westerner/Chinese cross-cultural encounter. These will include different viewpoints of rights, responsibilities, logic, fairness, reasonableness, propriety, good manners, honesty, the use of money, and many other concerns. We will want to be aware of this further category (Category II) of differences so that we may promote effective communication with the Chinese, with the intent of routing ourselves around potentially problematic or conflict-inciting areas, or at least cutting-short our losses. A specific listing of Category II problems would fill a book many times larger than the present one, but the present volume is striving to cover the high points, and describes many "potential conflict" areas of which the educated westerner will want to be aware.

Let us first look at Category I. Certainly we have touched on a number of examples in Chapter 2, and the reader should now be moderately aware of some of the potential for linguistic confusion which exists, while recognizing the general premise that there are a vast number of expressions in Chinese or English that when translated word-for-word into the other language will elicit no reaction beyond a questioning gaze, or puzzled smile.

Further examples may be seen in other areas beyond the realm of eating. For example, two Chinese employees, unknown to each other, asked the Personnel Chief of a large company: "May I get an advance of 1/2 of this month's salary today?" Since the company was newly established, the Personnel Chief referred these questions to the Foreign Manager for decision. The Manager being strapped for funds at the moment replied: "It is out of the question." This was translated back into Chinese by the Personnel Chief. Upon hearing this reply, the first employee thought for a few moments, rephrased his statement to: "May I get an advance of 1/3 of this month's salary today?" and the second employee said he would come to the payroll office at 5:00 to pick up his funds. The Personnel Chief dutifully remitted all this information to the Foreign Manager, much to the latter's surprise.

**Out of the question vs. _____:** When permission is asked for some course of action, many Chinese people with above average English ability cannot understand the reply: "It is out of the question." Many Chinese see this as being equivalent to: "It is not a question." This was the case in the above example, and that was the effect of the "translation" which the Personnel Manager incorrectly (though not intentionally so) offered the employees. In this case the first Chinese employee then just rephrased his remarks, assuming that perhaps the figure mentioned in his request had been a bit too high, or that his grammar, phraseology, etc. had been mistaken.

Since the Chinese often use the same word for "question" as they do for "problem",[a] the second Chinese reasonably understood "It is out of the question" to be "It is not a problem", thus indicating an assent to his request.

Why does such a difficulty occur? Certainly the Chinese have a word for "out" or "out of", as well as a word for "question". The phrase "out of the question" does not exist however. In order to avoid such misunderstanding, a simple substitute such as "No, it is not possible" is preferable.

Another example which comes to mind is "Thinking along parallel lines". Many Asians understand this expression to mean that our points of view will always be at some distance from each other, and that they will never meet or coincide. This indicates that our discussion has reached an impasse.

## Making the Choice of Words

We may want to strengthen our knowledge of language by seeking out and examining any idioms or other forms of expression which carry exactly the opposite meaning in English and Chinese. As a matter of fact, there are a number of such expressions. In speaking to Chinese people in English, or having our remarks translated, should we happen to hit upon one of these areas, we might want to consider that both sides carry the potential for significant linguistic ambiguity, and some remarks may be incorrectly rendered from Chinese to English or vice versa, with the resulting misunderstanding or impropriety.

---

a. 問題

**Yes vs. _____:** In terms of holding discussions, westerners must keep in mind that the Chinese word *shr* 是 (Japanese *hai*, Korean *nea*) which generally corresponds to the English "yes" does in fact carry other connotations. Consider the following dialogue.

First Speaker: Our plan is to move forth with this cooperative endeavour, if both sides are agreeable . . .

Second Speaker: Shr.

First Speaker: . . . to the whole idea, and if everyone feels that this is a desirable course of action . . .

Second Speaker: Shr, shr.

First Speaker: So when can I expect to receive confirmation from your Headquarters?

Second Speaker: We will let you know.

First Speaker: You do think it is a good plan?

Second Speaker: Shr.

As later events unfolded, confirmation was never forthcoming, and the Chinese party decided not to participate in the project. This confounded the foreigner, and he maintained in his reports to his Head Office that the Chinese representative had said "yes" all through the discussion. He therefore could not imagine why there was a sudden and 180 degree change in attitude.

Obviously, the second speaker did not intend to express affirmation each time he said *shr*. A better translation of his meaning would have been: "I am listening. Speak on." The word *shr* then may in fact in many contexts only mean that the other party is paying attention to what you say, and should not really be taken as an assent or agreement.[1]

In terms of body language, the Chinese nod their head to assert yes, and shake their head to mean no. This seems to be the same as we do in the west, however there is a slight difference which needs to be explained, not related to the body movement, but to the general concept of when to reply "yes" and when to reply "no". Consider the westerner who asks his secretary: "Didn't Mr. Jung call back yet?" and the secretary nods her head to indicate an affirmative reply. In a factory, a westerner points to a piece of machinery which seems to have malfunctioned for no apparent reason and inquires "Isn't it working?" To this the Chinese replies: "Yes." Or the foreigner who comes home to an empty cupboard and inquires of his Chinese roomate: "You didn't go to the store today?" and the reply he obtains is: "Yes, I didn't." Admittedly this causes some confusion at first for the native English speaker, but it is possible to adjust to it over time. The force of the way the Chinese view "Yes" is that they are agreeing to what you said, and the use of "No" then indicates disagreeing with what you said. Thus we may hear a number of Oriental-type grammatical constructions in our daily dealings, such as: "Yes, I don't want you to do that." or "Yes, he should not take

---

1. When dealing in Korean, we are told that if the other party pauses for approximately one second of silence, while looking off to the side with a distant expression, then turns back to us and says: *nea*, presumably indicating yes, the meaning is actually NO, and would always be understood as such by another Korean.

that document out to be translated." In either case the native English speaker would feel more comfortable using "No."

Please refer to the following chart.

### ORIENTAL "YES" AND "NO" USAGE

| question | Affirmative | Negative Answers |
|---|---|---|
| Are you going? | Yes, I am going. | No, I am not going. |
| Is it edible? | Yes, it is edible. | No, it is not edible. |
| Can you come with me? | Yes, I can. | No, I cannot. |
| Aren't you going? | No, I am going. | Yes, I am not going. |
| Isn't it edible? | No, it is edible. | Yes, it is not edible. |
| Can't you come with me? | No, I can. | Yes, I can't. |

| question | reply in Chinese grammar: | |
|---|---|---|
| Do you like it? | Yes, I like. | No, I not like. |
| Don't you like it? | Yes, I not like. | No, I like. |

In order to avoid confusion, simple (positive) questions would certainly be preferable to negative questions when talking to Oriental speakers of English, although this advice is admittedly difficult to follow. A question such as "Would you mind if I smoke?", where a one-word "yes" or "no" reply is still somewhat less than immediately clear as to the exact meaning intended, is less preferable to the basic "May I smoke?"

**Save vs. _____:** A westerner was camping out on a cold winter night, and accidently overturned a bucket of boiled water into the campfire. Being afraid that the fire would go out, he quickly yelled to his Chinese companion "Save the fire!", whereupon the Chinese poured another bucket of water on it, effectively drowning all embers. The westerner, though speaking English, unfortunately made a very poor choice of words in this instance. In Chinese, "save"[a] used in expressions such as to save a person's life, to save (relieve) the troops, to wear a save-life-clothing (lifejacket), etc. all have a similar meaning to English, but in connection with fire, the Chinese "save" means to "extinguish" and in the Chinese conception there is effectively no differentiation between such terms as "save the fire" and "put out the fire". Thus if the roof falls in on the Delphic Oracle, or the Olympic runner drops his torch, we would be wise

---

a. 救

to avoid the expression "Save the fire", although we may say "Do not let the fire go out!"[1]

**Female vs. _____:** For the trivia buffs in the crowd, it is notable that there are several characters in the Chinese language which have the "woman" radical and yet refer exclusively to men. In common usage are *jr er* 姪兒 (nephew), *nu hsu* 女婿 (son-in-law); more classical are *ya* 婭 (a mutual form of address between sons-in-law), and *jung* 嵸 (a wife's form of address to her husband's father or elder brother).

**No Flooding vs. _____:** Many people are aware of the fact that Chinese may be written in any direction, and there is one four character expression in Chinese 絶不淹水 which read one way means "Certainly no flooding", and read the other way means "Continual flooding". If one were renting a home or apartment, and this sign happened to be posted outside, it would be a good idea to make sure the translator was reading the sign the correct way.

**Diligently vs. _____:** The characters for "diligently" in Japanese 勉強 (pronounced *ben kyo*) carry the opposite meaning in Chinese, and hence indicate "poorly" or "ineffectively" (pronounced *mian chiang*). A Japanese student in China may make the Chinese statement "I am studying poorly", when his real meaning is "I am studying diligently".

**Open vs. _____:** In talking to Chinese electricians, one may come to the realization that when discussing circuits, the Chinese concept of "open circuit" is one with electricity flowing through it, and a "closed circuit" is one which has no electricity going through it. Anyone familiar with electronics will immediately recognize that this is exactly opposite the meaning of these terms in the West. Reference to the following chart will show why this is so, since the Chinese do not use the words "on" and "off" in talking about various electrical apparatus, but rather "open" and "closed", and then carry this usage over to circuits as well.

| *English usage* | | *Chinese usage* |
|---|---|---|
| Lights, Machinery, Appliances | | |
|   On | | Open |
|   Off | | Closed |
| | | |
| Circuits | | |
|   Closed | CURRENT IS FLOWING | Open |
|   Open | CURRENT IS NOT FLOWING | Closed |

---

1. "Save the fire" = "Put out the fire". While this is a bit confusing to the westerner, we do admit that it is much less serious than the fact that English accords "flammable" and "inflammable" completely identical meanings. This peculiarity of usage has certainly caused great confusion over the years, leading in some cases to injury or loss of life. Some scholars and consumer groups have even attempted to launch campaigns to have the word "inflammable" removed from the English language by statute.

| English usage | Chinese usage |
|---|---|
| Windows, Doors | |
| Open | Open |
| Closed | Closed |

If I was an American electrician working on some high voltage lines in China, I think it would certainly be advisable to agree with my local employers and co-workers on what terminology we would want to use.

**Pair vs. _____**: The use of the word "pair" can also cause considerable confusion in dealing between English and Chinese. Essentially, "pair" means two, but in English there are many exceptions. A foreigner asking for "a pair" of pants in some shops may end up with two pairs. It depends on how fluent the tailor's (or interpreter's) English is.

WHEN PAIR INDICATES ONE   Chinese usage is different

| item | English counting | Chinese counting |
|---|---|---|
| shorts | 1 pair, 2 pair, 3 pair, etc. | 1, 2, 3, etc. |
| pants | | |
| trousers | | |
| underpants | | |
| sunglasses | | |
| glasses | | |

Example: I am buying three pairs of pants.   I am buying three pants.

WHEN PAIR INDICATES TWO   Chinese usage is the same

| socks | 1 pair, 2 pair, 3 pair, etc. | 1 pair, 2 pair, 3 pair, etc. |
|---|---|---|
| shoes | | |
| sandals | | |

Example: I bought two pairs of shoes.   I bought two pairs of shoes.

**Miss vs. _____**: It is common practice for Chinese women to retain their maiden names after marriage, along with the prefix "Miss". Many Chinese will of course carry this usage over into English. The foreigner is often surprised to be invited by Miss Wong to "Come home for dinner and meet my husband". It is therefore apparent that "Miss" spoken by the Chinese may mean something closer to "Ms." by the average western perception. The foreigner is advised to redefine his thinking so that the term "Miss" includes two types of women: married and unmarried.

Non-Similar Similarities

In English we know that the opposite of heavy is "light", and the opposite of dark is "light". It would of course be extremely naive for us to assume that the same relationship exists in Chinese, and that the Chinese would see any conceptional similarity between a light blue dress and the weight of a carton of sponges. When we cross from English to Chinese, the words which are the same are different, and of course this should be kept in mind. Certainly western speech writers, advertising copy writers, visiting lecturers, and others will want to attune their unconscious thinking to the reality of this difference, so that they will avoid liguistic references or plays-on-words which lose all their meaning when seen through the Chinese consciousness. (Instead, they may be able to organize their remarks in another fashion to achieve greater effectiveness. Indeed it is always true that the more simple and straightforward one's remarks are, the easier it is to translate them into a foreign language.)

Consider the following examples. Although the English word is the same in each pair of expressions, and therefore we unconsciously consider these concepts to be the same or very similar, they are different in Chinese, and would not be considered by the Chinese to be even vaguely related.

(A) Asleep: My father is alseep. My foot is asleep.
(B) Race: He is a member of a minority race. She got first prize in a race.
(C) School: I go to school every day. He saw a school of fish.
(D) Hot: That molten iron is very hot. These peppers are very hot.
(E) Change: I want to change my clothes after I come back from the picnic. I hope you can give me some change for this $100 note.
(F) Customs: I had to pay $50 when I came through customs at the airport. The customs of the natives in Central Africa are different from those of the Australian aborigines.
(G) Fire: I will light a fire with these matches. If you do not work harder the boss will fire you.
(H) Order: He wants to order five of these and seven of those. I gave you an order and I expect you to obey it.
(I) Horn: That cow has long horns. This lighthouse has two fog horns.
(J) Bank: There are two new banks downtown. Rice fields usually have low banks of earth around them.
(K) Party: I joined a party last night. (This would appear to indicate some celebratory gathering, although it could refer to a political party.)
(L) Cases: We know of a total of five cases of trademark infringed merchandise which were seized last year. (We would normally assume this to mean "instances", although it could mean "cartons".)

This concept is fairly easy to grasp, but on a slightly higher level of language usage we may realize that we are quite used to making comparisons or implied meanings with individual words when speaking English, but rarely consider that these are not so readily understood in another language such as Chinese, even though the English words themselves are quite familiar to a large segment of the Chinese population, and the forms of expression seem quite simple. Certainly a large number of these were introduced in Chapter 2, and further analysis is given in the following pages.

## Contrasting Emotive Content[a]

One significant problem for anyone dealing in another culture is the differing emotive content of words and expressions. A foreigner may have his remarks translated, and be unaware that certain items are being misconstrued, specifically because some words carry different overtones in English than they do in the local language. Among foreigners who speak the local tongue well, it is not uncommon to find a great deal of perplexity regarding some sensitive words, and indeed the dictionaries rarely provide any explanation which would clarify the points involved.

The following summary is divided into three parts: Bad, Neutral, and Good. Each Part is further divided into Opposites, Polarities, Neutralities, and Similarities, as appropriate. A further summary at the end outlines a number of other sensitive words, which carry different emotive content from English in some circumstances, or whose usage is different enough to warrant special attention.

It is often hard to draw a strict and hard line of demarcation with some expressions, and the reader may be advised to make further inquiries as the need arises. The following explanation will clarify how we have categorized our entries.

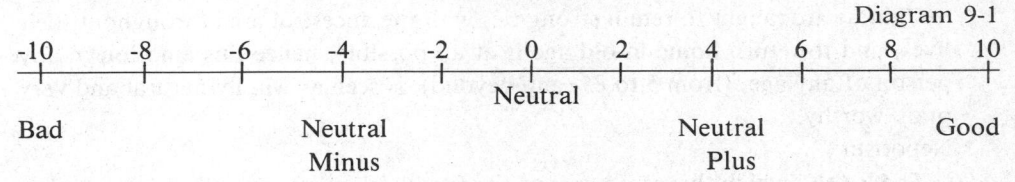

Diagram 9-1

```
-10     -8     -6     -4     -2      0      2      4      6      8     10
 +------+------+------+------+------+------+------+------+------+------+
                                  Neutral
Bad                  Neutral                    Neutral              Good
                      Minus                      Plus
```

Five designations have been marked on this Emotive Content Diagram, i.e. Bad, Neutral Minus, Neutral, Neutral Plus, and Good, covering a theoretical range of -10 to +10. The diagram is conveniently divided into three "categories", namely:

Bad to Neutral Minus
Neutral Minus to Neutral Plus    (Neutral)
Neutral Plus to Good

Regarding the English words we have selected for analysis, we will try to place each of them into one of these three Emotive Content Categories, so that they may be contrasted with their Chinese "value".

Part. 1
**BAD to NEUTRAL MINUS in English**
but carrying essentially Good Emotive Content in Chinese   (Opposites)

* Mother's boy
    Chinese immediately equate this with "the filial son" and hence hold it in high regard.

---

a. 中英文的文字在感情成份上的差異

* Conformity (to the group)

In Chinese thinking this is almost a duty – to consider the needs of others (especially family, relatives, close friends, etc.) before one's own personal needs, to be cooperative to the point of denying one's desires or legal rights, not insisting on one's own point of view, etc.

* Conservative

This is basically commendable, since it indicates that one is following the established patterns of thought and behavior, continuing in the practices of the ancestors, persevering in the **old-fashioned** ways, not experimenting with untried methods, etc. Conservative habits in dress, words, and conduct always find the most supporters and gain the most approval, and as one's age advances, an increasingly conservative outlook is expected. Hence older Chinese people will not participate in many activities which they deem "only suitable for youth", because they feel this will degrade their status. For younger people in society to make older people the butt of a joke, or to make fun of their thinking, methods, outlook, etc. is considered improper.

* Homesick, Homesickness[a]

Chinese are taught to retain strong ties with the ancestral area throughout their lives, and to return home in old age if at all possible, hence this emotion in any person of any age, (from 5 to 85, and beyond), is seen as wholly natural and very praiseworthy.

* Nepotism[b]

The loyalty which this represents to the family/clan is essentially praiseworthy, and from the point of view of human affection nepotism is regarded as good. Cronyism may be regarded in a similar light.

* Dragon

In western literature, the hero often slays the dragon to rescue a maiden in distress. Dragons are generally viewed as evil beings, as monsters. However, in China the dragon is a very auspicious symbol. The Chinese often consider themselves "Descendants of the Dragon" and are very proud of the fact. Dragon motifs were often used in the design of clothing for the Emperor. As such, the Chinese regard dragons as representing celestial power, magnanimity, and many other good things.

## BAD to NEUTRAL MINUS in English

but may carry Good Emotive Content or Bad Emotive Content in Chinese, depending on usage   (Polarities)

* Concealed Payments of Money

In Chinese, this is commonly called "red envelope". If given to a child during

---

a. 思鄉・想家・所謂之落葉歸根    b. 家族觀念，喜歡任用親戚，所謂內舉不避親

the Chinese New Year, it is good. Given to a person of power in an organization, it may be seen as a form of *yin shuei sz yuan*, [a] reciprocity for "favors rendered", etc. in which case it is still seen as good. If it is recognized as a kickback or under-the-table commission, it is bad. Whether or not this view of its being bad requires that it be publically exposed will depend on many factors however. See related discussion under OP Perception of Value in Chapter 3.

* Dogma

  Dogma[b] usually arises out of highly authoritative and non-democratic leadership. As such, it would be expected that Chinese society, with a lengthy authoritarian history, regards dogma as more "the natural state of affairs" than in most western societies. The Chinese have described their educational system as "dogmatic" for thousands of years, and this refers to not only the instructional methods, but the military style organization and functioning of the schools themselves. If this description carried the unpleasant emotive content of the term in English, we cannot imagine how they would have put up with such as system. Therefore, it appears that dogma is considered quite the standard operating procedure in many situations.

* Propaganda[c]

  Research into the history of this word shows that in the early 1900's, before WWI, propaganda, promotion, promulgation, publicizing, were essentially undifferentiated in English, and this is the situation that we currently find in the Chinese language. Hence the term propaganda exists in the Chinese conception without necessarily carrying overtones of "stretching the truth", "deception", "deviousness" or "distortion". It takes on different emotive content according to how it is described."Tourist propaganda" is normal and good. The "enemy's propaganda" is bad.

## BAD to NEUTRAL MINUS in English

but carrying essentially Neutral Emotive Content in Chinese (Neutralities)

* Fat

  The Chinese will often remark that an overweight person is fat, even in his/her presence, and this comment is essentially neutral in emotive content.

* Censor[d], Censorship

  The sense of this term in Chinese is basically **to inspect, to examine.**

* Mr, Miss, Mrs. + *first name*

  In addressing a person called Kevin Hortman, the appellation "Mr. Kevin" is not considered polite in English among most people, or indicates that the speaker is in the position of servant or slave. Likewise, Amanda Smith is not normally called "Miss Amanda". In Chinese however, the terms Mr., Miss, Mrs. etc. may be used with either first or last name.

---

a. 飲水思源　　　b. 教條，教條式的　　　c. 宣傳
d. 檢查，檢查制度

* Old [a]

Calling a man of advanced years an "old Mr.", an "old grandfather", etc. is quite acceptable in Chinese. Likewise, an elderly woman may be called an "old Mrs.", an "old grandmother," etc. The word "old" in this usage is of essentially neutral connotation, or perhaps even slightly favorable.[1]

* Idolatry [b]

Since traditional Asian religions are polytheistic and have various ceremonies that include bowing down to graven images, the entire issue of idolatry is treated favorably, or at the least neutrally.

* Moonlighting

Translation of this term into Chinese is *pi shing dai yue* [c] "covered by stars and wearing the moon", meaning that one works very late into the night. The idea of working more than one job is not frowned upon, nor is it something avoided from polite conversation. It indicates that this person is very diligent and hardworking. Not limited strictly to jobs, this expression could also describe students who attend extra classes after normal school hours.

* Uncoordinated [d]

Westerners often make fun of classmates or friends who are poor performers in athletic games, and often equate this with being uncoordinated. This type of comment is very rare among Chinese speakers. Whether talking of uncoordinated movements of the human body, or uncoordinated management policies between departments, the sense of the expression "uncoordinated" tends to be neutral.

Notes: Although many Chinese will assert that "lack of coordination" among departments in an organization, in the government, etc. is bad, nevertheless the continued existence of this lack of coordination for years, decades, etc. seems to deny the validity of such an assertion. Apparently the bulk of the Chinese population views such a lack of coordination as normal. Indeed, if an affected individual gets caught in the middle between the uncoordinated policies of two departments and becomes angry, the Chinese bureaucrats involved consider such a reaction unreasonable. This viewpoint further supports the consensus that such uncoordination is nothing to get excited about. See further remarks on Departmentalism below, and examples of Conflicting Regulations in various chapters of this volume. Tangentially related to this, see additional comments in Chapter 10 on the difference between striving for "synthesis" or "analysis", and the differing views on "the need for coherence" in theology, a world view, organizational directives, etc.

---

1. Chinese has two words for old: 老 and 舊. The former is a better term, and carries the connotations of: reliable, experienced, suitable, antique, long-standing, etc. The latter refers to something that is: out-of-date, old-style, no good, already used, past, etc. By contrast, we consider 古 to primarily indicate "ancient".

a. 老  b. 崇拜偶像  c. 披星戴月
d. 未經協調 or 不協調

* Naive [a]

This word is defined in the English dictionary as **1) unaffectedly or sometimes foolishly simple; childlike; artless; unsophisticated. 2) implying a genuine, innocent simplicity or lack of artificiality.** When speaking of a girl, a child, etc. in English, it means that he/she has an almost foolish lack of worldly wisdom, and hence will easily be taken advantage of. In Chinese the connotation is more neutral, and merely means that he/she will not take advantage of someone else.

## BAD to NEUTRAL MINUS in English
and carrying the same Emotive Content in Chinese   (Similarities)
(We would expect this in the majority of word usages, and of course the examples are too numerous to mention. Three are given for reference.)
* Pedantic [b]
* Barbarian
* Crazy

Part 2.
## NEUTRAL in English
but carrying Neutral Plus to Good Emotive Content in Chinese (Opposites +)

* "Not Bad" [c]

This is generally a favorable term in Chinese. "This food is not bad", "His Tibetan is not bad", etc. are all favorable statements.
* Standard [d]

This has overtones of the best, top-grade, A number 1, etc., in Chinese. Perfectly spoken Mandarin is referred to as standard. Machine parts which are standard would be of exact specifications.

## NEUTRAL in English
but carrying Bad to Neutral Minus Emotive Content in Chinese (Opposites -)

* Reorganize, Reorganization [e]

This appears to carry overtones of "having impending financial problems" in Chinese. Rather than saying that one's company is being reorganized, a preferable substitute would be to say you are having a personnel adjustment. [f]
* Change of Tradition [g]

Westerners continually question tradition, discarding those practices they feel no

---

a. 天真
b. 喜愛賣弄學問
c. 不錯
d. 標準
e. 重組or重整or改組
f. 人事調整
g. 改變傳統，創新作風

longer valid. Chinese tend to follow tradition because it is tradition, and may commonly object to innovation if it involves a change in the traditional methodology.

* Mixed Blood,ᵃ Mixed Ancestry

China is ethnically very homogeneous, and the Chinese tend to take pride in this idea of racial purity. For the Chinese who have married westerners, mixed blood may be a fact of life for their children, however it is rarely mentioned in polite conversation. The United States is an immigrant country, hence mixed ancestry is considered normal.

Notes: There is not always agreement between Chinese and westerners on the sense of what constitutes "mixed blood." If people native to Shandong and Hubei marry, the Chinese may consider their offspring pure Chinese; whereas if people native to Spain and Germany marry, the Chinese may consider their offspring mixed. Some westerners might say that in the latter case both parents are Europeans, and therefore the blood is not mixed; furthermore if a Chinese and a Japanese marry, both parents are Orientals, and therefore the blood is also not mixed. (Most Chinese disagree with this statement.) The primary races, with their major number of divisions in parentheses, are the Caucasian (4), Negroid (6), Mongoloid (5), Indian subcontinent (2), and Australoids (1), however this analysis does not clarify how the Chinese view the entire issue.

* Speculation,ᵇ Speculative, Speculator

This is generally associated with "reward without effort" in the Chinese conception, and hence speculative investments and speculative financial dealings are frowned upon. For the westerner who desires that bad or dishonorable overtones be be avoided, another choice of terminology, or an alternative explanation of one's motives, is definitely recommended.

Notes: Reading through the speeches of Andrew Jackson and Martin Van Buren given in the 1830's, we do see that speculators were frowned upon because they "live nimbly by their wits". Certainly this word has only taken on neutral connotations in the last hundred years, or less, in the west.

To the extent that the words "opportunism", "opportunist", etc. carry similar overtones, their use is best made with caution as well.

* Forget Your Rootsᶜ

In the great melting-pot of the United States, this elicits little comment under most circumstances. Canadians perhaps stress greater awareness of their "roots", and some Europeans even moreso. However, it is rare that a westerner who felt his ancestry was an insignificant issue would be criticized or held up to scorn. Not so in the Orient. Since the Chinese have a religion of ancestor worship, for one to forget his roots is an serious offense.

---

a. 混血　　　b. 投機　　　c. 數典忘祖，忘本

* Thick skinned

In English this tends to suggest someone who is insensitive to criticism, insults, etc., in which it might be a good character trait under some circumstances, or one who was callous, unfeeling, insensitive to the suffering of others, in which it might be a bad character trait. As such it might have differing emotive content depending on how it is used. In Chinese however, "thick skinned face"[a] refers to someone who is shameless, immodest, etc., hence it is clearly bad. A related phrase "the horse does not know that his face is long",[b] is also used to describe someone who is shameless or immodest.

However, there is a rather humorous usage in that people say if you want to study language you must have a "thick skinned face"— you cannot be afraid of making mistakes. This is acceptable usage.

## NEUTRAL in English

but may carry Good Emotive Content or Bad Emotive Content in Chinese, depending on usage (Polarities)

* Privilege[c]

In the west, the privilege of equality for all would seem to be taken for granted. Westerners say "It is my privilege" in response to a request for some minor help or assistance. School alumni may have the privilege of buying football tickets at a special discount. None of these uses of the term is particularly sensitive. If the President of the United States, a Senator, or Congressman is on vacation, he is expected to obey parking regulations, and if his son starts a company, he is expected to pay taxes. There is no privilege in these situations.

However in Chinese there are definite overtones that "privilege" is something which is outside of, or above, the law. It exists for some highly placed people, and enables them to enjoy special advantages, favors, and treatment unavailable to the common man. An example would be a de facto exclusion of high officials (congressmen, legislators, etc.) from paying any inheritance taxes, from the need to obtain licenses to operate businesses, immunity from arrest or punishment in some types of civil actions, etc. It may also include not being subject to regulations forbidding the establishment of gambling halls, houses of prostitution, etc., and a de facto exemption from the responsibility of paying taxes on any of the profits earned thereby. Further ramifications are numerous, for example the children of highly placed officials may be able to be appointed to choice jobs in the foreign service without going through any of the testing or interview procedures required for regular applicants, and/or they may be promoted much more rapidly.

a. 厚臉皮　　b. 馬不知臉長　　c. 特權

Monopoly rights to deal in the importation or sale of certain products, granted to friends and relatives of those in power in the government, thereby conveniently circumventing antitrust regulations, are further examples of privilege, similar to sinecures. When the profits from these monopolies go to private individuals, as opposed to going into government coffers, it is a situation that borders on **legalized corruption.**

* "See Again"

Most foreigners quickly learn the Chinese expression "See again" *zai jian* 再見 , which means "see (you) again", and is commonly regarded as the Chinese equivalent for "good bye". Few are aware that this term may be regarded as highly inauspicious, or even somewhat equivalent to a curse in some circumstances. To cite specific examples, to say *zai jian* to people when leaving a funeral suggests that you will all meet again at a funeral in the near future, or more particularly, at a funeral of the same family. To say *zai jian* to people when leaving a hospital after visiting a sick person suggests that you will all meet again in the hospital in the near future, most likely to visit a sick person of the same family. It will not be difficult to imagine what may be thought if one says *zai jian* when leaving the scene of an accident, or when leaving the home of some friends' house after they have just told you of some great misfortune which has befallen them, etc. In all of these types of cases, the expression *bao jung* 保重 , roughly translatable as "take care", is highly preferable.

On the other side of the coin, it appears that saying *zai jian* when leaving someone who has just received good news, or who is now in a much improved position as compared to previously (however measured), will be regarded as especially auspicious.

When in doubt, we suggest using the English expression "good bye" directly, and not speaking Chinese.

## NEUTRAL in English

and carrying the same Emotive Content in Chinese (Similarities)

(We would expect this in the majority of word usages, and of course the examples are too numerous to mention. Three are given for reference.)

* Normal
* Adaptable
* Ordinary

Part 3.

## NEUTRAL PLUS to GOOD in English

but carrying essentially Bad Emotive Content in Chinese (Opposites)

* Pride[a] (in one's own accomplishments)
   This is equated with arrogance and a lack of humility. It is more acceptable to speak of pride in another's accomplishments, and to have someone else speak of pride in your own accomplishments.
* Break with Tradition [b]
   Westerners tend to be iconoclastic, Chinese much less so. Using a "Go With the Flow" methodology, Chinese tend to allow things to change slowly over generations without conscious decision, without making a clear break with the past. Westerners prefer more forceful decision making action.

## NEUTRAL PLUS to GOOD in English

but may carry Good Emotive Content or Bad Emotive Content in Chinese, depending on usage   (Polarities)

* Popular [c]
   Popular has the same usage as in English when referring to songs, clothes, hairstyles, books, refreshments, sports, interior decorations, etc. However, it must be noted that Chinese has no word for "epidemic", and "popular" is used in this sense as well. Hence scarlet fever, cholera, small pox, measles, bubonic plague, rickets, etc. have all been popular in one era or another, and hepatitis continues to be so. Certainly, other diseases may reach this status at various times.
   "Popular" may also be used to denote "widespread", although there are other terms which express this idea in Chinese. Among the elderly, arthritis is a popular malady, and the Chinese recognize that acupuncture is a popular cure for it. In Chinese medical shops, there are many popular remedies for popular diseases.
* Practical, Practically Minded [d]
   Practical exists in Chinese in essentially all the senses of English, (see note), however it carries additional overtones of "flattering someone else with the hope of receiving benefit", "interested more in money than friendship", "concerned more with material gain than family relations", etc.
   In the Chinese sense, when someone returns from abroad (or faraway) and we ask (or think) "What presents did you bring me?", we are being practical. When we treat someone much better after we learn that their father is an important businessman, we are being very practical. When we are hired for the day, and insist on being paid for the day, even though the company's equipment developed problems, the weather turned bad, etc. and the job could not be completed (or even started perhaps), we are being quite practical, from the Chinese viewpoint.
   Note: The English language expression "a practical joke"[e] is not seen as having

---

a. 驕傲           b. 打破傳統        c. 流行
d. 現實or實際    e. 惡作劇

any relation to anything practical in the Chinese idea, and is commonly described as bad or evil, although of course the degree of damage caused, or the amount of face lost, would have to be taken into account.

To the extent that "pragmatic" is a synonym for practical, the same considerations would apply to it as well.

## NEUTRAL PLUS to GOOD in English
and yet having essentially Neutral Emotive Content in Chinese (Neutralities)

- Try My Best [a]

"I will try my best", in Chinese, may be an indirect way of saying that I will probably not be able to help at all. In another sense, it may imply that although I can help, I am not the most qualified person to do so. Hence "my best" may not be very good in the final analysis.

A more definite reply would be "I will do it and I will notify you of the results on [such and such a date]."

* Good

When we say "He is a good man", without specific reference to what qualities he possesses, the immediate thought in Chinese is "Well, of course he is a good man. You don't think he is a bad man do you?" Thus, with regard to this rather vague usage of the word "good", it appears that in Chinese it has, at best, a neutral plus emotive content.

In English, when asked what we think of the President, we may say "He is a good man". However, in Chinese, in describing high officials, "good" will invariably be translated by the press corps as "great and wise". This also shows that the emotive content of "good" in Chinese is not as strong as in English.

If we desire more specific use of the word "good", it must be considered in relation to traditional Chinese values. The issue of what constitutes a "good man" in the west in specific terms will probably consider legal obligations quite heavily, i.e. whether or not he is law abiding. However, the traditional Chinese view would see a "good man" as a good husband to his wife, a good father to his children, and a good son to his parents, and the "good" in each of these instances is related heavily to providing financial support, respecting the elders, and promoting harmony in the environment, providing for the children's food, lodging, schooling, etc. The fact that one's business consists of operating an unlicensed restaurant, office, or factory, manufacturing counterfeit merchandise, reprinting copyrighted material, using other's brand names without a license, etc. is essentially irrelevant, and few would describe this person as "a bad man".

---

a. 盡力而為

**NEUTRAL PLUS to GOOD in English**
and having essentially Good Connotations in Chinese (Similarities)
(We would expect this in the majority of word usages, and of course the examples are too numerous to mention. Three are given for reference.)
* Generous
* Happy
* Wealthy

Other words which should be used carefully, in regard for their special overtones when translated back into Chinese in some circumstances, and differences in conception which Chinese speakers of English may attach to them:
 * Little. The use of this word is not generally restricted, little books, little toys, little shirts, etc. are all acceptable, however "little movie(s)" are regarded as referring to pornography.
 * Dozen.[a] This is generally used only to refer to inanimate objects, and not in referring to people, animals, etc. in Chinese. In English we speak of "several dozen" of something, but the Chinese will tend to say "several 10's" of something.
 * Introducer.[b] This word may sometimes have overtones of "taking commissions".
 * White. In China, many types of white clothing are acceptable for daily wear, however it should be remembered that white (undyed) is the color associated with mourning. White flowers, white candles, white hats, white bonnets, white headbands, and pure white wrapping paper are all best avoided, since they designate recent death in the family/clan. Interior decorations of cut-out white paper snowflakes at Christmas time are a definite no-no. In terms of being invited to attend a wedding or a funeral, for a man to wear a full white suit appears inappropriate. (In a wedding, the groom may be subject to a different set of rules however.)
 Many scholars in China maintain that black is the color associated with death, and indeed many people will wear a swatch of black on their clothing when a parent passes away. Additionally, there is increasing western influence in China, and the western tradition has been to associate black with funerals. As a result, either black or white may be sensitive in many situations, because they may carry overtones of "death".
 * Green. A foreigner walked into the office where he worked. He was wearing a green suit. He remarked "I originally had a complete set: a hat and a suit, but I seemed to have misplaced my hat. Has anyone seen it?" All the Chinese laughed. Why?
 The Chinese say that a man is wearing a green hat to mean that his wife is stepping out on him.
 * Open. In English, this word is often used to describe another person. It exists in the sense of **free from prejudice or bigotry, not closed to new ideas**, as an open mind; **frank,**

---

a. 一打      b. 介紹人

**candid, direct, honest,** as an open manner. However, in Chinese the description of a girl as "very open"[a] almost always carries sexual overtones.

* Open-minded.[b] Among Asian speakers of English, this adjective is often used, for example when describing various officials or others in positions of power. This may mean that they are willing to adopt more progressive strategies in organization, management, administration, etc. Clearly it is related to the idea of being **unbiased**. However, the Chinese are often quite conservative, and the base-line for evaluating terms such as these generally reflects this conservatism. Hence, the actual behavior of the people in question may still fall well within what the foreigner would categorize as conservative and/or biased.

* Politician vs. Statesman. The distinction between these words tends to be highly stressed in Chinese. "Politician"[c] is often seen as an essentially derogatory term, with implications of seeking personal or partisan gain, scheming, opportunism, etc. "Statesman"[d] is seen as denoting uprightness and propriety.

* Fate vs. Destiny. In English, fate refers to the inevitability of a course of events as supposedly predetermined by spirits or some other agency beyond human control, as in "He was fated to be on that ferry the night that it ran aground." We often speak of fate as being "blind". Destiny also refers to an inevitable succession of events as determined supernaturally, but often implies a favorable outcome, as "He was destined to be elected to Congress." We rarely speak of destiny as being "blind".

Fate and destiny are rarely viewed as separate concepts in Chinese however, and both are commonly translated as *ming*[e], which appears to be a handy catch-all for what the Chinese see as "the will of heaven".[f] *Tien*[g], the guiding force in the universe, is a concept somewhere between "the actions of gods" and "fate".

A separate term exists for fortune or luck.[h]

* Original Thinker. "Original"[i] exists in two senses in English: we say "The original plans were later changed", and "He has many original ideas". The first usage implies **previously existing, or old**, the second implies **not previously existing, or new**. The Chinese are far more familiar with the first usage, and hence may easily take "original thinker" to mean "conventional thinker". If this is not the foreign speaker's intention, a substitute such as "creative thinker" is perhaps preferable.

* Gregarious.[j] This is generally taken to mean having a preference for the group, being group-oriented, feeling at home in a crowd, etc. with all the connotations that such preferences bring to mind in the Chinese consciousness. A foreigner who prided

---

a. 很開放　　　b. 無偏見的，能接納新思想的　　　c. 政客
d. 政治家　　　e. 命　　　f. 天命
g. 天　　　h. 運氣　　　i. 原來的
j. 合群的，喜好群居的，群集的

himself on his "gregarious instinct" surprised his Chinese wife when he said "No I do not think it is fitting for your mother, father, grandparents, aunts, and uncles to all move in our house and live together with us."

Clearly the overtones of 1) (generally inebriated) sociality, 2) in a party, get-together, or pub environment, 3) for a limited number of hours per day, etc. do not come through in the translation of this term.

* Dialect.[a] It should be remembered that whereas the various dialects of English worldwide are 95% mutually intelligible, the numerous dialects of Chinese are perhaps only 5% mutually intelligible when spoken. Certainly this appears to be the case between Fukienese, Cantonese, Hakkanese, Mandarin, etc. Hence the force of the term "dialect" is considerably different.

* Provincialism.[b] This word carries the sense of loyalty to one's hometown or ancestral area, and may often be regarded as a good term by the Chinese. They may not immediately associate it with "narrowness of outlook", or otherwise regard it as having any bad emotive content. Parochialism[c] may often be regarded in a similar light.

* Departmentalism.[d] This term carries an emotive content of neutral to neutral minus, when it is pointed out as existing in a bureau or ministry. Oftentimes it is not recognized by the westerner, and hence is not pointed out. A definition would be: **requiring strict following of one's own departmental rules, regulations, etc., without regard for the requirements, stipulations, or superseding directives of other departments (bureaux, ministries, etc.), with whom one's regulations may (or do) conflict.** As such, it is often equivalent to Catch-22ism. In a regulating body, the lack of communication between departments is certainly a major cause of departmentalism.

Uncoordinated regulations and conflicting regulations are certainly outgrowths of departmentalism. Often seen is the situation that certain activity is allowed, according to the announcement of one bureau, but the ramifications of it are not, according to the stated regulations of another department. An example of this is where travel to formerly restricted or off-limits areas is now allowed by the Ministry of Interior. When travellers return from these areas, all photographs, film, postage stamps, clothes, medicines, etc. purchased during their trip are confiscated, because they are prohibited items, according to the view of the customs authorities.

* Individualism.[e] The use of this word is not restricted, however there may be a great deal of difference in what the Chinese mean by it, and what the westerner does. For example, in discussing what course of action should be taken in any particular instance, it may be desirable to consider personal preferences, however if we have to ask the question: "Are you going to run your own life or or are you going to let someone else run it for you?", we have crossed the proverbial cultural borderline. Before we get down

a. 方言
b. 鄉土主義，地域觀念，省籍偏見
c. 地方觀念，眼界狹小
d. 官僚化的本位主義，各自為政
e. 個人主義

to the nitty-gritty, we should remember that in the west, before the revolutions of the late 1700's, "individualism" carried a bad emotive content. This has only changed since that time.

Due to the western influence in the last fifty years, there is much use of this term in the Orient today, however the westerner is open to surprises if he accepts this usage at surface value. In terms of citing individualism as the rationale for certain types of specific decisions, or actions, it may quickly be associated with selfishness, greed, lack of sympathy, etc. in the Chinese mind, and hence denied any validity.

For the foreigner who feels strongly about this issue, he is generally well advised to explain the meaning of this word when he uses it, and clarify why he feels it represents a sound concept.

* Tolerance, patience, acquiescence, fear. The Chinese often see themselves without the ability to change various social ills, and so "tolerance"[a] has become regarded as something of a virtue (one supposes out of necessity), especially for the people who are low in the hierarchy or without participation in various decision making processes in an organization, or in the society at large. Hence, contradictory regulations, selective enforcement of laws, departmentalism, etc. are allowed to continue or expand, rather than being contained. If we view the Chinese society as a pyramid, it appears that the people on the bottom-most level are the most tolerant (due to the crushing weight of all the more powerful people above them), but tolerance (or the necessity for it) decreases as we reach the peak.

This is easily seen in the educational system. While cries for change are heard from every quarter, the educational authorities say that they are reviewing the matter. However, as the years pass by only one trend is apparent, the students workloads get heavier, and the testing procedures become more frequent and rigorous. The population is urged to be "tolerant", so that a more meaningful educational program for the nation's youth can be devised. At the same time, the high ranking government officials, wealthy businessmen, and even many educational administrators in private colleges and universities have long since pulled their children out of the local Chinese school system and sent them to the USA to study.

* Chauvinism, Chauvinistic. The expression "male chauvinism"[b] has come into wide usage in the west, to the extent that many have forgotten the meaning of the basic word, and it is perhaps best clarified in the dictionary viewpoint: "chauvinism" refers to a **blind patriotism,**[c] **support of the country right or wrong.**

* Dramatic, Theatrical.[d] These are generally regarded by the Chinese as the same concept, however in English the word "dramatic" may just be a simple substitute for vivid, exciting, significant, full of action, etc. In many daily topics of discussion out-

a. 忍，容忍　　　b. 大男人主義，沙文主義　　　c. 愛國狂，盲目的愛國主義　　　d. 戲劇化

side of the theater, the English speaker would rarely equate "a dramatic illustration" with "a theatrical illustration", or "a dramatic increase" with "a theatrical increase", however such may often be the force of this phraseology when translated into Chinese.

* Strategic, Strategy,[a] Strategist. The westerner should be aware that these terms are primarily, if not almost exclusively, used in Chinese in the military sense, and have decided overtones of warfare. As such, expressions like "strategic economic planning", "strategic use of natural resources", "strategic lighting in a bachelor's apartment", etc., may all require some additional explanation.

A useful technique is perhaps first to compare the activity in question to "fighting a war", and then proceed from this metaphor into the main discussion. Example: National economic management may be compared to a "war" for national growth and prosperity, hence it is proper to speak of "strategic" economic policies, etc., etc.

* Yellow Journalism. In the west this refers to "sensationalism", in China it refers to sexually explicit journalism. In general, reference to yellow clothing, yellow flowers, and yellow interior decorations will elicit no comments in China, but yellow movies, yellow magazines, & yellow reporting will all be regarded by the Chinese as referring to pornography. Picking up an old book and remarking that "It has yellowed with age" will certainly be misunderstood.

There is no easy dividing line for which kinds of references to yellow are sensitive, and which are not, and the interested westerner is well advised to ask his Chinese acquaintances for further details as the need arises.

* Protestant, Christian, Catholic. With the Chinese stress on harmony, the term Protestant, denoting "one who protests", has never come into wide usage. As a result, the term "Christian" tends to be used to denote "Protestant", and the Chinese will commonly ask a foreigner "Are you Christian or Catholic?"

Some clarity may be gained by translating Protestantism as "New Religion", however in any case the reality that Protestants and Catholics are both Christians is generally hard for the Chinese to understand. If we continue in this sloppy Chinese usage, we then arguably have no word in Chinese for "Christian", (since this has been taken to denote Protestant).

The confusion is multiplied when we consider that the early preachers and gospelmen did not coordinate their linguistic endeavors, hence the word "God" was translated differently by the early Protestant and Catholic Missionaries. Add to this the renderings of such terms as "Heavenly Father", "Master on High", "Omnipotent Spirit", etc. and we have five or more terms for what the westerner would regard as an identical concept. The Chinese are easily confused by this multiplicity of deities in what is purported to be a monotheistic religion.[1]

---

a. 策略

1. Debates over the most fitting translation of "God" into Chinese have raged in Christian religious circles for centuries.

See our comments later in the chapter as to whether this violates the need for Rectification of Names, as stressed in traditional Chinese philosophy.

\* Desire for Privacy. This is regarded as normal in the west, however with the Chinese group mentality it may often be seen as unusual.[1] Certainly China and the west have differing views of "rights to privacy", for example in many Chinese homes the parents will actively screen children's telephone calls, open their mail, etc. even up through their teenage years.

\* Today Cannot Compare with the Past.[a] In the west, this expression tends to infer that "today is better than the past"; progress is admittedly a mixed blessing, yet we generally consider progress desirable. Chinese have an orientation of looking to and idealizing the past, hence this expression is generally taken as meaning "the past is better than today".

> We talk about fate as if it were something visited upon us; we forget that we create our fate every day we live. And by fate I mean the woes that beset us, which are merely the effects of causes which are not nearly as mysterious as we pretend. Most of the ills we suffer from are directly traceable to our own behavior. —— *Henry Miller*

> We have already had to re-think so many of our conceptions of motion, we will also gradually learn to realize that that which we call destiny goes forth from within people, not from without into them. —— *Rainer Maria Rilke*

## Being Conservative

Upon seeing the lack of privacy in many public restrooms, which often results in a clear view of the occupants' activities; the common bathing arrangements with children in some families, or where older children are assigned to bathe younger ones; the frankness with which some Chinese speak of having multiple wives; the open discussion of Chinese men visiting prostitutes; Chinese girls discussing the lives of men in various dynasties who made the decision to become court eunuchs, and the ceremonies regarding the burial or final disposition of their private parts, etc., some foreign observers have claimed that the Chinese are not "conservative". In fact, these facets of Chinese life are much more closely related to the subsistence agriculture foundation of the old society, and the common social structure which was then prevalent, than to any conscious decision of the present day Chinese to be "sexually open".

A famous western comedian commented: "I don't trust any country of one billion people who claim that their favorite indoor sport is ping-pong." This comment also suggests that the Chinese are more sexually liberated than they appear on the surface. However, China's large population is most closely related to the state religion of ancestor

---

a. 今非昔比

1. Chinese like a 熱鬧 "bustling, thronged, noisy" environment.

worship, and the desire to carry on the family name which has arisen from this. The predominately agrarian nature of the economy has also required the procreation of many people in order to work the land. Neither of these factors has any real connection with liberal sexual norms.

The dictionary definition of conservative is: **1) keeping, conserving, or tending to conserve; preservative. 2) tending to preserve established traditions or institutions and to resist or oppose any changes in these. 3) of or characteristic of a conservative person, point of view, etc.**

See further comments later in the text in the essay **Rejection vs. Acceptance of Orthodoxy**.

## Integration of Concepts

In previous chapters we have occasionally spoken of various concepts which tend to be separated in English, and yet for which a high degree of integration exists in the Chinese conception, i.e. the dividing line between them tends to be very vague, or perhaps non-existent. A more complete listing of these will be useful for reference of all westerners dealing with the local people in China, and is presented herewith.

1. Personal Relations, Business Relations

The Chinese tendency is to treat business, commercial, or professional relations on a personal level, and to develop a close personal relation. Due to the ideal of mutual dependence, in dealings with foreigners it is often felt that if problems develop, the foreigner will be understanding and accomodating, due to the personal relation involved. For example, a Chinese would generally view it reasonable to ask a foreign (or native) lawyer, doctor, accountant, etc. for professional advice "off the record" at a dinner, or party. In a similar fashion, in return for personal favors rendered by a Chinese acquaintance (such as an expense-paid weekend at a resort), a request for business or professional work, advice, favors, etc. in return might be made to the foreigner.

The idea that "Friends are friends, and business is business", or such rejoinders as "I am resting my brain today, come see me during office hours", etc. are all clearly opposed to this.

If the foreigner finds himself in an awkward situation, some hint at a solution may be had by clarifying to all parties involved the difference between help and favor. "Help" is to give one in need something necessary, or to do part of the work of, or share the labor of. It tends to imply the existence of a problem. "Favor" is merely a kind, obliging, friendly, or generous act. Personal help, personal favors, business help, and business favors are four distinct quantities in the western view.

2. Cursing, Criticizing

The dividing line here tends to be very poorly defined. Many remarks which the foreigner regards as constructive criticism will be taken as an affront by the Chinese, no doubt due to the loss of face involved. This causes the foreigner to feel that the distinction between criticizing and cursing is not being made.

Further insight into this problem will be gained by reading the **Strategies and Responses** Chapter.

3. Self Confidence, Arrogance, Pride, Conceit

The Bible says "Pride goes before a fall". The Chinese agree with this. Tennyson's comment was "True humility, the highest of virtues, mother of them all." The Chinese agree that humility is very important, but of course would not agree that humility is the highest virtue, or mother of virtues; nor would Aristotle (384–322 BC), who said "in justice is every virtue comprehended."

Nevertheless, the dividing line of where self-confidence ends, and pride/arrogance begins is culturally defined. In the Chinese value system, it appears that there is very little room for the expression of personal self confidence or proper pride, at all. Almost any statements which stress that one's abilities are superior to those of others are regarded as arrogant, and indicating excessive pride.

Aristotle said "with regard to honor and dishonor, the mean is proper pride, the excess is known as a sort of empty vanity, and the deficiency is undue humility." Clearly Aristotle's view of excess and defect being characteristic of vice, and the mean being characteristic of virtue, is at some variance with the Confucianists' "Doctrine of the Mean". This Doctrine says that the supreme attainment in our moral life is "to be central in our moral being and to be harmonious with all."

4. Disagreement, Disrespect

Due to the stress which Chinese place on conformity to the group and maintaining harmony, many westerners have noted that it is difficult to clarify for them that disagreement is not necessarily reflective of disrespect. The Chinese traditionally tend to equate one with the other.

Hence, in the statements "I respect my father, but I do not agree with him", "I respect the school principal, but I do not want to follow his advice", etc. the second part of the sentence may be regarded as a non-sequitur to the first part by many Chinese. They gravitate toward the view that respect equals acceptance of the superior's stipulated terms and conditions.

See additional comments in Chapter 11 in the discussion of TOPIC and Organizational Behavior.

5. Respect, Agreement, Obedience, Acceptance

Even though this is just the corollary of the integration of "Disagreement, Disrespect" mentioned above, it is highly important, and deserves specific clarification. Many times the westerner will come to recognize that our first impressions of the meaning of many Chinese philosophical maxims are inaccurate, and will be changed considerably if we later recognize that respect = agreement = obedience. Without this recognition, it is unlikely we will grasp the full force of "Respect your elders," "Respect your teachers," and other such tenets.

This is certainly one reason why Chinese students are so reticent to ask questions.[1]

### 6. Task Fulfillment, Loyalty

In many Chinese organizations, task fulfillment is the only non-debatable measure of achievement. This is because roles are often poorly defined, and there are few criteria of proper behavior. In this environment, it is much easier to follow present methods than to try new ones, since such efforts may produce accusations of disloyalty.

This entire attitude would appear to be at odds with promoting creativity.[2]

Task fulfillment may often be rather generally defined, and assumed loyalty will frequently be regarded as more important than expertise or competence in a particular area. Hence the Chinese preference for family run organizations, and the often seen practice of hiring relatives and clan members first, even if they are unqualified for the task at hand. These people are presumed the most loyal to the organization, and most able to understand and follow the leader, who occupies his position, in the classical Chinese notion, due to his superior virtue. Hence it is felt that such employees will learn the necessary skills if given enough time for observation. In a related situation, the young intern in a Chinese hospital who marries the daughter of the Head Surgeon or other established member of the hierarchy, is also maneuvering (through the building of blood relationships and the resulting upgrading of his loyalty quantification) to assure his future success in the organization.

Examples of appointments of Chinese government officials to their posts based on their loyalty to those in the upper echelons of power, as opposed to their competence in the field in question, are too numerous to mention.

### 7. Lack of Homesickness, Forgetting your Roots

Neither of these considerations elicits much comment in progressive western society. The Chinese are much more tradition-bound, and tend to idealize the past, retaining strong emotional ties to the ancestral areas, as well as the parents/family/clan. Individualism and independence (in the western sense) are rarely goals in one's life.

Hence a lack of homesickness tends to be equated with forgetting your roots, and both of these are bad in the Chinese idea. Further ramifications such as "You don't

---

1. It is true that in the west there is a body of opinion that says "it is better to be seen and not heard." However, the author of this book having lived in the Nashville, Tennessee, area for many years, and come in contact with many country music stars, has come to regard this with considerable suspicion. Country music entertainers continually stress that you must be "seen and heard" in order to be successful, and it appears this advice is valid in most fields of endeavor.

2. Authoritarian organizational structure is not conducive to new ideas. An American political analyst commented "Many of the Asian countries are telling their people to go all out and invent, create, and be innovative, but then expecting them to close their minds when it comes to politics. That doesn't work."

love your mother", "You don't love your father", etc. seem to quickly form in the Chinese consciousness too.

## 8. Reason, Rationale, Excuses

The Primary Sympathetic Orientation deals with issues by first stressing Sympathy (generally for the underdog), second by referring to the reason given for this behavior, and third by referring to the legal facts of the matter. The "reason" spoken of here is not to be confused with "reasonable", but is rather "a reason", any reason, which the person involved cares to offer. As such it corresponds to "rationale" in some vague sense, yet there is little attempt to differentiate it from "excuses".

Any reason given constitutes "a reason": "I took the money from the company's account to loan to my brother for a week because he has a business problem, and anyway we were not using it for the time being" is a good reason for misappropriation of company funds, and deserving of some degree of sympathy, in this orientation. In a similar fashion: "He was in a hurry so he drove the wrong-way along the curbside of the road; you should have been more careful so as not to have hit him" is a reason for certain types of behavior discussed in Chapter 5.

## 9. Lack of Consideration for the Group, Selfishness

The "group" referred to here is "others" or "others with whom one is associated", hence any members of the collection of one's friends, relatives, co-workers, etc. The Chinese tendency to share food, money, and to some extent possessions in general tends to arise from the perception that not to do so is being selfish and stingy.

## 10. My problem, Our problem

The consideration of the authoritarian structure of many organizations will certainly come into play in seeing how and when these two concepts may be linked. The lower level employee who forgets to lock the warehouse, resulting in the theft of much valuable equipment, may be unable to convince the company managers that he should not be held financially responsible all on his own (thus being unable to equate "my problem" with "our problem"), however he may very well be able to convince many of his friends and relatives that they have a certain obligation to share in helping him make reimbursement to the firm.

The accounting department official Mr. A who expects the worker to be understanding when he (Mr. A) has mistakenly deducted an excessive percentage of tax monies, and who feels it is unfair if he is asked to do all the paperwork over again, seems to be equating my problem with our problem. Using Whither-To Reasoning, Mr. A may try to spread the responsibility for problem solution among multiple individuals, or the group in general. Since the other accounting department personnel support him in his stance (i.e., that it is a great inconvenience to redo all the paperwork), they feel that the worker should go along with the group's determination.

## Rationale Weight Indexing

In reading through large collections of scholarly papers written by westerners, or western educated Chinese, on the subject of Chinese philosophy, one is often confronted with accumulations of sayings of the great sages,[a] which are used to fill out very well-rounded analyses of classical Chinese thinking, methods, orientations, sanctions, and proscriptions. For example, Confucius is on record as encouraging "the investigation of things", encouraging his students "to ask questions", encouraging the desire to learn thoroughly and then "to be confident of one's abilities", etc. Various quotes from Confucius' collected sayings may be given to support of these types of conduct, and of course this is the kind of structured exposition which appeals to Americans and Europeans.

However, this type of "proof", which relies on assembly of various quotes in the classical Chinese texts, starts with the assumption that all statements in these texts have "equal philosophical weight", when considered by members of the local populace. This assumption unfortunately only exists in the theoretical model constructed in a vacuum (i.e, one which contains no competing doctrines, precepts, or teachings). In the real world it is a highly doubtful postulate, and is certainly not borne out by observation of goings-on in the society.

As old China hands will tell us, Chinese education tends to stress memorization and conformity. Chinese companies, in the majority, tend to be small or medium sized, with very low, or perhaps non-existent R&D budgets. Strike one for "investigation of things." Western and Chinese teachers in the commercial schools, colleges, and universities in China will tell us that the Chinese students are very reticent to ask questions. Strike two on this issue. Chinese Nobel Prize winners, established singing stars, and many types of artists are all often heard to actively play-down, or even deny, their knowledge and skills when questioned by the press, or even by others in the field, visiting dignitaries, local civic leaders, etc. Strike three for being "confident of one's abilities."

The acculturator must be aware that in reality, without some sort of indexed ranking of the weight or "influence" of various classical maxims or rationale, it is impossible to gauge how they will be interpreted and put into use by members of the local cultural group.

I have frequently proposed a Rationale Ranking Index of 0 to 10, with 0 being the lowest ranking, and 10 being the highest. On this scale, encouragement of the investigation of things, which is perhaps a 4, is easily cancelled by the maxim *wan wu sang jyr* 玩物喪志 , which is about an 8. This latter phrase is translated as "to apply oneself too much to trifles, petty amusements, etc., so that one's fortitude and will power are eroded away," which is a lengthy explanation of a reasonably simple Chinese idea.

In a similar fashion, the encouragement of students to ask questions is approximate-

a. 引經據典

ly a 3, and is easily overridden by other maxims which stress respecting the teacher and being obedient, which I suspect are both 9's, and conforming to the group, which is probably an 8. The advice to be confident of one's abilities probably also ranks a 3, and is easily overridden by other considerations.

I regret that I have never seen any sinologists elaborate on this kind of Rationale Weight Indexing problem in any published works, and most researchers tend to start with the premise that any one statement made by an ancient sage is of equal weight with any of his other statements. This is most unlikely, (and can only be said to be the result looking at the ancient texts and "reading something into it"[a]). Although I have seen some partial indexing lists assembled by old China hands, in general we find that there is a great lack of analysis or data in this area.

Is there a solution? One suspects that the more time we can spend observing the local people in the present era, the more we will be able to route our way around this problem. In the study of acculturology we orient our primary focus on the examination of real-life happenings in the society, and turn back to the weighty philosophical tomes for reference as necessary, but not as an initial a priori source for building elaborate theoretical models. In this fashion, some ways of discovering the "big values" or "big tenets" (i.e., those considerations that would rank a 7, 8, or above on our Rationale Weight Index) may become immediately apparent, and we may deal with consideration of the other values when the appropriate occasion arises.

Notes: "Rationale" is defined as 1) **the fundamental reasons, or rational basis, of something. 2) a statement, exposition, or explanation of reasons or principles.**

"Indexing" is here used in the sense of indexing records in a database, hence means **to be in order or in sequence.** For example, our database might be set up in the following manner.

```
         Structure for database: rationale.dbf
         Number of data records: 10000
         Date of last update : 09/28/1775
         Field Field Name      Type              Width
             1 RATIONALE       Character          254
             2 WEIGHT          Numeric              2
         ** Total **                              257
```

Currently Selected Database:
Select area: 1, Database in Use: B:RATIONALE.DBF    Alias: RATIONALE
    Master index file: B:RW.NDX    Key: WEIGHT

We would establish an index on WEIGHT so that the records would be in order.

---

a. 望文生義 or 斷章取義

## Conversational Logic

The failure to have any conception of an RW Index is also the cause of a major difficulty in understanding Chinese logic. Consider the following conversation, discussing behavioral Actions X and Y, approval for which is found in some Book, B1, written, compiled by, or attributed to a sage, S1. Note: **Actions X** and **Y** could be anything mentioned in any classic of Chinese philosophy. For the sake of discussion, we may examine:

**Action X** could be the stipulation that food be put out as offering to dead spirits at certain times.

**Action Y** could be the stipulation that the exemplary person leaves a feast immediately after the elderly folk have gone.[1]

Another action or conception, **Action Q,** is also introduced for comparison. This might be the idea that if a wife earns more money than a husband, the husband loses face.

### Round 1

Westerner: Why do you do Action X?

Chinese : It is written in Chapter ____ of our classic book B1, as stated by S1, that we should do this.

Westerner: Do you believe that everything written in book B1 is correct?

Chinese : Yes, of course. We have a long and glorious tradition.

Westerner: But I recall in Chapter ____ of that book that it says you should do Action Y.

Chinese : Oh, I see.

Westerner: Are you going to change your behavior in the future and start doing Action Y?

Chinese : No.

Westerner: Why not?

Chinese : We Chinese don't do that.

### Round 2

Westerner: Well, moving along, I notice that you adhere to the dictates of Action Q.

Chinese : Yes, our social convention follows this pattern.

Westerner: Is that written in Book B1 also? Did S1 specify that you should do that?

Chinese : No, he did not.

Westerner: Is it written somewhere else?

Chinese : Not that I know of.

Westerner: Then why do you do it?

Chinese : This is our custom.

---

1. Reference: *Analects*, Chapter X. 鄉人飲酒，杖者出，斯出矣。

If we take as a given the existence of an RW Index in the subconscious mind[1] of the Chinese,(in accompaniment with all the Chinese sayings, maxims, philosophical tenets, traditional beliefs, religious dictates, etc.) it is not hard to understand the reasoning or logic of the Chinese person in this type of conversation.Action X is perhaps an 8, Action Y is perhaps a 2. Action Q is possibly a 7. The workings of the Chinese intellect are clearly revealed in this fashion.

Whether or not this type of Chinese reasoning is accurately described as "of the custom, by the custom, and for the custom" is a consideration we will leave to the reader.

## Contradictory Regulations
## Registration Requirements

A language academy which trains students (of high school age and above) in English and Japanese, and helps them organize their overseas study plans, is located on the 6th floor of a 12 story building, in office space which it owns. It applies to register as an official school. The Bureau of Public Works is first consulted and the Department of Building Administration (DBA), takes the school's application, and arranges for an inspector to visit the building. When he does so, he says that according to regulations, the basement of the building must be used as a parking lot, but now it is being used as a restaurant, and this is illegal. In the back of the building, in the required open space for emergency and Fire Department use, the first floor shops have built extensions on to their shop space (with cement and bricks), therefore illegally blocking the area. On the sixth floor where the academy is located, one of the fire escape exit routes as per the original blueprints of the building has now been blocked off by the owners of another office, and made into part of their office, and this is illegal. Unless these problems can be solved, no approval can be obtained from the DBA.

The academy checks with the management of the building, however they are unable to offer any advice except to say that these other tenants are old and well respected, and it would not be nice to cause trouble for them. The academy contacts the DBA and says it cannot solve these difficulties, and asks the DBA to enforce the law in these problem areas. The DBA however maintains that it is a regulatory agency, and enforcement is the concern of another separate Department in the Bureau of Public Works, and the academy is free to contact them as it sees fit.

When the academy does report or otherwise make formal complaint of these illegal goings on, the owners of these shops and other dwellings get word of it through their contacts in the various bureaus and departments, and use all the connections and power-pulling they can to get sympathy for their situation, and as a result, one year later still

---

1. in the subconscious mind: **intuitively felt, not actively analyzed or systematically researched, lying below the level of conscious perception.**

no action has been taken. When periodic inspections by other bureaus reveal that the academy is unregistered, it is given a stiff fine.

Inquiries with registered academies reveal other problems however, for example it is necessary to commit perjury every year by filing two sets of different income and expense documents with the Ministry of Education (MOE), and the Tax authorities. This legal requirement has arisen from the MOE's formal establishment of a scale of hourly tuition fees per student, and private academies are forbidden from charging in excess of these fees. The Tax authorities however state that this scale of fees was promulgated over 35 years ago, and is totally out of line with current tuition charges in the marketplace. Therefore they admit that "Nobody follows that regulation anymore", nevertheless they also admit "That regulation is still in force, and you had better follow it when you do your reporting to the MOE."

When questioned whether they will accept the same set of figures as on the documents submitted to the MOE, the Tax authorities say "Certainly not. Those do not reflect the true picture of your operations. We want to see the real income data in line with the tuition fees that you really charge."

Asked by a private academy if by filing two sets of different figures an academy owner who in some way had angered someone in the government hierarchy could be picked out for "special treatment", convicted on perjury, fined, jailed, etc., the Tax authorities replied "That is your problem."

(Review remarks on Departmentalism in the latter portion of the **Contrasing Emotive Content** essay).

## Unknown and Unadopted

We have spoken in various chapters of English language terms, expressions, idioms, etc. which are unknown in Chinese, or Chinese language expressions which are unknown in English. What exactly does this mean?

It must be remembered that we are discussing unknown as "unknown in language", and not "unknown by people": as a basis, we expect that Chinese people are familiar with all common forms of expression in their own language, and if the Chinese language lacks a particular expression, we expect that most Chinese will be unfamiliar with it.

Consider the expression "a white elephant". This does not exist in the Chinese language, and most Chinese are unaware of its meaning. Certainly however there are some Chinese with advanced English language ability who understand its implication.

How can we explain the idea of "a white elephant" to other Chinese people? In an approximate fashion, we may say it is "something big and cumbersome, and valuable, and hard to get rid of, and expensive to maintain". Will they then adopt the expression "a white elephant" into Chinese?

No, they will not. The reason is a circular one, to wit: *They will not adopt it because it does not already exist in the language.*

Collecting Bugs

A western entomologist had heard from an archeologist that the world's most colorful dragonflies were found in one southern Chinese province. He went to investigate. Making the rounds of towns and villages in that area, he asked where he could find "dragonflies". Some of the populace had studied some English, and could read the words he wrote out on the paper. They knew what "dragon" meant, and they knew what "fly" meant. They had no idea what the entomologist was referring to however.

As he stood before them in his hard hat, backpack, camping shirt, shorts, and boots, with an insect net in one hand and a a collection of jars and boxes in the other, he did appear to be ill equipped for chasing "flying dragons". Glancing again at his small net, the Chinese asked "What do you plan to do if you catch one?"

The foreigner confidently replied "I will stick a pin in it and put it in my specimen box." This received quite a few stares and shocked expressions of surprise from the assembled local multitude, and several paused to consider if perhaps all foreigners shared this same degree of mental disorientation.

He later went out searching on his own, and found some dragonflies in a rural area. Unfortunately, they were of a uniform dark appearance, not brightly colored as his archeologist friend had suggested. Returning to the natives, he asked "Do you suppose he was pulling my leg?" When he wrote this sentence out on a piece of paper, the Chinese considered it at length. Those who had studied English knew every word, yet they could not understand the meaning. Perhaps his leg had muscle spasms after walking around for so long, they pondered, and now he needs a massage?

These examples provide two more illustrations of what we mean by "unknown in the Chinese language": the words, when translated directly, do not carry the same meaning, often as not they do not carry any meaning.

What we call "dragonfly" the Chinese call *ching ting*.[a] In their idea, it is totally unrelated to dragons. The expression "pulling one's leg" does not exist in Chinese. The closest we can get is "making a joke".

Linguistically Speaking

Some linguists have dealt with the issue of how language conveys meaning by stating that sentences in language are constructed and composed of two modes:

1. The inner-mode, or deep structure. The inner-mode is the underlying train of thought that holds meanings and ideas.

2. The outer-mode, or surface structure. The outer-mode is the way in which the language expresses these meanings and ideas.

---

a. 蜻蜓

In terms of outer-mode, different languages use different imagery and different allusions to convey similar ideas.

For example, sometimes someone will go out to buy something in the morning, and when they come back we may ask them "How's the weather?" An American might reply "You could fry an egg on the sidewalk." Of course, this may be expressed in Chinese, however the Chinese people will be puzzled by it. "Why would you want to fry an egg in that manner? Wouldn't that be unsanitary? And anyway, what about the weather? You didn't answer that question."

A western government official might make some remarks in a press conference that were "tongue in cheek". After the remarks were translated, when a western spokesman pointed this out to the Chinese press corps, they could easily take it to mean that the official spoke English with a peculiar enunciation, accent, speech impediment, or that his English was not fluent. His translated statements would probably still be taken at full value however. Some other rendering of the phrase "tongue in cheek" into Chinese would certainly have to be found if the spokesman hoped to keep his job. More appropriate, we suspect, would be to speak straightforwardly, since such remarks are always much more easy to translate; cliches and indirect or colloquial remarks are frequently difficult if not impossible to translate accurately.

If we announced to our Chinese friends on the day of the wedding that the American groom "had gotten cold feet", this would not be understood except by those extremely fluent in English. An attempted sidetracking of the discussion at hand, such as "he is having an attack of appendicitis" might be better received. More plainly speaking, we would say "he wants to call it off and give back the presents."

In the course of talking with many foreigners and Chinese over a period of years, we find that there are some conceptions that exist in English, and for which there is no Chinese equivalent, nor any Chinese approximation. For example, I have always had difficulty in trying to express the seemingly simple phrase "beyond a reasonable doubt" (an important legal concept used in jury trials) in Chinese. Other examples are those expressions which involve philosophical patterns of reasoning, or double entendres, different ideas of humor, propriety, etc. The reverse consideration is also true, some Chinese concepts are not expressable in English. However, these are the minority.

The westerner can generally assume that for most all of our written or spoken comments, the inner mode can be rendered into Chinese, however the outer mode of many figurative expressions will often have to be simplified, transposed, interchanged, or otherwise reformulated.

## Alligators, Crocodiles, and Other Topics

It may seem like a small point, but the fact that the Chinese use the same word for alligator and crocodile has always struck me as extremely convenient. I never did understand the difference anyway. According to the writings of some learned zoologists I have heard of, the distinction lies in a differing arrangement of teeth, but I was never close enough to one of these animals to check that out, and I do not plan to get that close in the future either.

In a previous chapter we outlined some words which are normally differentiated in English, but are not in Chinese. We will round-out our discussion of this linguistic aspect by listing some other important items below. Whether or not this analysis shows a problem with the Chinese language is something upon which the reader may form his own opinion. To adjust Shakespeare's wording: "What's in a name? That which we call a *mei guei*, by any other name would smell as sweet."[1]

(CC) indicates that while different words exist in Chinese, the terms are nonetheless commonly confused.

## Undifferentiated Terms in Chinese

| | |
|---|---|
| Animals and related items | 1) alligator, crocodile<br>2) wild cow, bison, buffalo<br>3) cheetah, leopard<br>4) jaguar, tiger<br>5) rat, mouse<br>6) guinea pig, hamster, gerbil (CC)<br>7) cow, ox<br>8) deer, elk, moose<br>    However, there is recognition of "antelope" as a separate kind of animal.<br>9) hawk, eagle, falcon<br>10) elephant teeth, elephant tusk, ivory[2] |
| Food items | Listed separately in Chapter 2 |
| Things around the Home and Workshop | 1) ice skates, roller skates<br>    A distinction is obtained by saying "ice skates with blades" or "ice skates with wheels".<br>2) rope, cord, string, twine[3]<br>    There is an expression for "cable" however. "Dental floss" in Chinese is simply called tooth string.[a] |

---

1. Reference: *Romeo and Juliet*, Act II, Scene 2.
2. The expression "ivory tower" exists in Chinese: 象牙塔．
3. A sample of the thing desired is very helpful when going to purchase one of these items, even if one speaks pretty good Chinese.

a. 牙線

3) thread, line, wire
   There is a separate term for "ribbon".
4) toilet paper, tissue paper, facial paper (CC)
5) big clock, big bell[a]
6) hairbrush, comb
7) tweezers, pliers (CC)
   To aid in communication, the former may be called "pull hair machine".
8) pliers, vice, claw (of a lobster, crab, etc.)
   There is another term for the other type of claw(s): i.e. of birds, cats, wolves, tigers, lions, etc.
9) electric stove, hot plate
10) binoculars, telescope (CC)

**Behavior**
1) sin, crime
   It is often possible to commit a sin without committing a crime, however the general distinction is unclear in Chinese. Guilt is also regarded as essentially the same concept. A Chinese girl who visited a Christian church service was heard to comment "I am not a sinner, I never committed a crime."
2) hiccup, belch (CC)
3) scolding, cursing (CC)

**Metals**
1) copper, brass (CC)

**Weapons**
1) catapult, sling-shot

**Locations**
1) porch, entranceway, doorway (CC)

**Actions**
1) dive, jump
   There is no separate term for dive in Chinese.
2) hop, skip, jump
   Chinese only has the conception of "jump", there is no separate expression for "skip", and a hop is merely a "small jump". In track and field, "hop, skip, & jump" is one event, often rendered as "three-grade jump far".
3) paint, draw *(a verb)*
   Words exist for different types of "paint" *(a noun)* however.

---

a. 大鐘

4) ice skating, roller skating
Apparently ice-skating was known in China long before roller skating, and no new terminology seems to have come into the language to denote the latter.
5) spanking, beating, hitting

| Grades in School | American usage | Chinese usage |
|---|---|---|
| | 1st grade | 1st grade |
| | 2nd grade | 2nd grade |
| | 3rd grade | 3rd grade |
| | 4th grade | 4th grade |
| | 5th grade | 5th grade |
| | 6th grade | 6th grade |
| | 7th grade | 1st grade |
| | 8th grade | 2nd grade |
| | 9th grade | 3rd grade |
| | 10th grade | 1st grade |
| | 11th grade | 2nd grade |
| | 12th grade | 3rd grade |
| | 1st year | 1st grade |
| | 2nd year | 2nd grade |
| | 3rd year | 3rd grade |
| | 4th year | 4th grade |

As this chart shows, the Chinese language uses the term "3rd grade" with considerable ambiguity. Many Chinese people will carry this usage over into English, and in the American conception four different grade interpretations are possible, i.e. 3rd, 9th, 12th, or the 3rd year of college. A similar ambiguity exists with "1st grade" and "2nd grade" in Chinese.

**Rectifications:** At this point the western reader may be wondering if the confusion or ambiguity in the use of all the terms listed in this section essentially violates the doctrine of "Rectification of Names", or "Ordering Names Appropriately", as espoused by Confucius, Hsun tse, and others, and whether this represents a further failure to bring theory and practice together. To the knowledge of our study group, there is no consensus on this entire issue in modern Chinese scholarly circles.

| | |
|---|---|
| Printshop & Grammar terms | 1) sentence, phrase, word 句子
2) letter, word, character 字 (CC)
3) paragraph, section 段
4) chapter, section 章
5) printed, handwritten 印刷體 (CC)
The confusion existent in English has been to some extent carried over into Chinese: the use of the term "print" in the sentences "The stationery shop called to say they will print our forms this afternoon" and "Please print this application in a clear and legible fashion" is clearly different. Asked how to describe the method of writing ABC's in a beginner's handwriting copy book, many Chinese will say they are "printed", and after a student copies these down, his work may be described as "printed" as well. |
| Other terms | 1) weekend, Saturday, Sunday
The Chinese work-week is more commonly six-days, or five-and-a-half, so "weekend" rarely means "Saturday & Sunday." It may mean "Sunday", it may mean "Saturday", it may mean "Sunday and half-of-Saturday", etc.
2) first place, honorable mention (CC)
The problem exists with 優勝獎 *yeou sheng jiang,* since in one contest this may mean one thing, and in another contest it may mean something else entirely.
3) first name, last name
Since the first character of a Chinese name is the family name, the Chinese often equate "first name" with "family name." In western usage, "family name" is last name.
4) soft wood, cork
American customer: "Do you have any cork?"
Chinese shopkeeper: "Yes, this wood is soft."
5) stone dust, lime
Spreading lime around the perimeter of a campsite is reputedly helpful in keeping snakes away, but it is doubtful if spreading stone dust will have any effect.
6) down, feathers
Some clarity may be gained by calling the former "small soft feathers". The latter are merely "feathers".
7) statue, photograph
林肯像 may be translated as "Statue of Lincoln" or "Photograph of Lincoln". In any event, it is true that most Chinese photography shops do not sell statues, so this confusion is largely avoided in most |

daily dealings.

8) on top of, on, above, up 上，在上面

For example, in Chinese there is no difference between saying "Write the letters A to Z on the line" and "Write the letters A to Z above the line".

9) in front of, the front of 之前，在前面

In English, the statements "He is looking in front of the car", and "He is looking at the front of the car" are different, however this distinction is lost in Chinese.

in back of, the back of 之後，在後面

Such sentences as "She is looking in back of the bus" and "She is looking at the back of the bus" are the same in Chinese.

10) ripe, well-done 熟

If, instead of picking the apples, we light a fire under the tree, all of the apples will be ripe and well-done too. This will take a bit of explanation.

**Facial Expressions**

1) laugh, smile

The Chinese have several words for "sad" and several more for "disappointed", but no word for "frown". The same word is used for "smile" and "laugh" (most commonly it means "laugh"). It is usually further differentiated by adding an adjective, and some English usages are effectively cancelled out.

| English usage | Chinese phrasing |
|---|---|
| smile | little laugh 微笑 |
| laugh | laugh 笑 |
| | |
| little smile | — |
| big smile | — |
| little laugh | little-sound laugh 小聲地笑 |
| big laugh | big-sound laugh 大聲地笑 |

**Facial Additions**

1) beard, mustache (CC)

**Notes for Copywriters and Editors**

1) The sign for "start a new paragraph", ⸿ or ⸿ is not understood by many.

2) A triangle is used to denote that a word previously crossed out should now be retained. The triangle is placed next to, or above, the word in question.

*Language, Communication, and Non-Communication*

3) Chinese has no handy way of expressing "single spacing", "double spacing", "triple spacing", or their opposites, such as "no double spacing". A sample, for reference, is always helpful.
4) Circling a word and drawing a curly pig's-tail type line generally is taken to denote "delete this". Crossing out the item in question is also acceptable.

Scholars who submit reports in various academic, business, agricultural, and other conferences may occasionally be confronted with the task of correcting a proof-copy with some sort of notation which the Chinese printers or typists will understand. Even when the conference organizers are quite fluent in English, it is quite conceivable that their typing or printing service may not be. To see some of the problems which may develop, please refer to the following example of data which was proofread by a westerner untrained in Chinese methods.

There has been a recent statistical movement (in the) increased demographic stability of hill tribes in the provinces. This appears to represent a concrete reaction to an often mentioned General tendency to stay put in traditional localities or ancestral regions, which in turn is an outgrowth of a highly conservative attitudinal backlash recently apparent in these remote (r)egions.

There is, we suspect, no need to mention certain restrictive provisions and clauses of the 1986 Tribal Areas Investment Law which the government has now formally decided to delete in that document, since these have been well publicized in the press. It is believed that this policy has also had a contributing effect to (population overall) and migratory patterns.

The Threat from the Extreme Right
In the past year, certain social factors have been affecting the daily availability of (Chinese) (labor) in the nearby villages. Among these are the emergence of power factions described as "rightest" among the aborigines, and which aer re advocating a return to old-style, traditional

agricultural occupations as a way of appeasing the local earth gods, in light of a recent fourteen month drought.

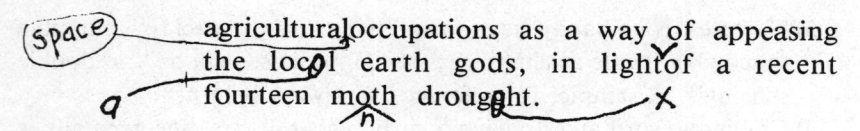

Whether or not the Chinese organizers of the conference understood the proofreading marks in these few paragraphs is an open question, however the final copy printed in the conference manual showed some significant errors. Comparison of this "corrected" copy below with the original will reveal how the typists, no doubt with English dictionary in hand, misconstrued the proofreader's intention in a number of areas. Contrastingly, the significance of most of the simpler marks was fully grasped.

> There has been a recent statistical movement down in the increased demographic stability of hill tribes in the provinces. This appears to represent a concrete reaction to an often mentioned small general tendency to move their homes in traditional localities or ancestral regions, which in turn is an outgrowth of a highly conservative attitudinal backlash lately apparent in these remote regions.
>
> There is, we suspect, no need to mention certain restrictive provisions and clauses of the 1986 Tribal Areas Investment Law which the government has now formally decided to retain in that document, since these have been well publicized in the press. It is believed that this policy has also had a contributing effect to overall population and migratory patterns.
>
> The Threat from the Extreme Left
> In the past year, certain social factors have been affecting the daily availability of Chinese capital in the nearby villages. Among these are the emergence of power factions described as "rightest" among the aborigines, and which are advocating a return to old-style, traditional agricultural space occupations as a way of appeasing the local earth gods, in light of a recent fourteen month drought.

Another example, corrected by a foreign scholar with some basic knowledge of the Chinese way of doing things, fared much better.

As mentioned in the preceding paragraph, a public prosecutor's investigation is private and confidential. The victim's complaint for search are available not to the accused. On the other hand, a private prosecution is a public process. The law requires that a duplicate copy of the indictment be delivered by the court to the accused.

The past five years have seen the judicial practice of more severe intellectual property sentencing for offences. Nevertheless, the percentage of suspended sentences has also increased, as the courts struggle to deal the legil and moral issues involv ed.

Corrected copy received back from the printer's was as follows:

As mentioned in the preceding paragraph, a public prosecutor's investigation is private and confidential. The victim's complaint or application for search are not available to the accused. On the other hand, a private prosecution is a public process. The law requires that a duplicate copy of the indictment be delivered by the court to the accused.

The past five years have seen the judicial practice of more severe sentencing for intellectual property offenses. Nevertheless, the percentage of suspended sentences has also increased, as the courts struggle to deal with the legal and moral issues involved.

## Chinese Proofreading Marks

The above example shows us that the following marks are commonly recognized in Chinese printshops, typing services, etc., among staff members with limited English ability. There is often little need for accompanying explanation or gesticulation.

| type of mark | meaning | type of mark | meaning |
|---|---|---|---|
| ℓℓℓℓℓℓ | eliminate, delete | ⌒ | combine, bring together |
| ≡ ✠ ✠ | eliminate, delete | ∽ | transpose |
| ≡≡≡ △△△ | triangles indicate that originally crossed out material was mistakenly crossed out, and should be included in the final corrected copy. | | |
| ∧ | insert (if no word or expression is indicated, then the meaning is that a space should be inserted.) | | |
| 小 | small, lowercase | ∧̈ | insert double quotes |
| 小 e | small "e" | ∧̄ | insert hypen |
| 小 p | small "p" | ∧: | insert colon |
| 大 | big, capital, uppercase | ∧) | insert parentheses |
| 大 O | capital "O" | ∧i | insert small "i" |
| 大 P | capital "P" | 移 | move |

Other corrections, additions, etc. may be made directly on the typed or type-set copy in pencil or red ink if it is to be retyped, otherwise a proof or xerox copy may be marked with the corrections, as appropriate.

## Advanced Proofreading Marks

The following Chinese notation is given for those who are dealing with more difficult printing or typing problems. The Chinese characters may be transcribed by hand to an appropriate place on the material being proofread, the item in question may then be circled, or an arrow drawn to it. In the case that movement is desired, the arrow should be drawn in the desired direction of movement.

| | | | |
|---|---|---|---|
| 往左 | toward the left, move left | 往下 | down, move downward |
| 往右 | toward the right, move right | 往上 | up, move upward |
| 居中 | center in the middle of the line | | |
| 标题居中 | center the title in the middle of the line | | |
| 行间加大 | increase the spacing between lines | | |
| 齐尾 | even right margin, make the right margin even | | |
| 勿齐尾 | ragged right margin, don't make the right margin even | | |
| 另起段 | start a new paragraph (here) | | |
| 字体 | typestyle | | |
| 粗体 | boldface, type in boldface, set in boldface | | |
| 斜体 | italics, type in italics, set in italics | | |
| 空一行 | insert a blank line | | |

## Typesize

The size of English language type is spoken of in "points".[1] On a computer assisted typewriter or typesetting machine the standard size for typing most reports in academic conferences is 11 point. Using this standard, 9 point would be type which is two sizes smaller, 10 point would be type which is one size smaller. 12 point would be type one size larger, 13 point would be type two sizes larger.

Most Chinese typists who deal with this type of technically advanced equipment are familiar with the abbreviation **pt**. to stand for point. The Chinese translation for this word is 磅.

---

1. The size of (movable) Chinese character type is spoken of in terms of 號, or on an electric photosetting machine in terms of 級.

改為9pt. change to 9 point      改為13pt. change to 13 point

全大寫 ALL CAPITALS      全小寫 all lowercase

並     and, moreover (This may be used to combine various terminology.)

## Arabic Numerals and Chinese Characters

Some items of confusion when dealing with Chinese characters and so-called Arabic numerals are worthy of mention. All of the latter are recognized, and they are compared here with their written Chinese style for reference.[1] Arabic number "5" is easily mistaken for English capital "S" if the top portion is not written as the final stroke.

If the loop of a six passes through the stem 6 the Chinese will probably read it as a 4.

| Chinese written style | 一 | 二 | 三 | 四 | 五 | 六 | 七 | 八 | 九 | 十 |
|---|---|---|---|---|---|---|---|---|---|---|
| normal style | 1 | 2 | 3 | 4 | 5 | 6 | 7 | 8 | 9 | 10 |
| Chinese variation |  | 兩 |  |  | 5 |  |  |  | 夕 |  |

Certainly all Chinese accounting, mathematics, surveying, and other related activities use the Arabic numerals. However, in terms of jotting down the quantity 1, 2, and 3 within some accompanying Chinese character text, these three numerals written in this fashion are perhaps easily confused with other characters in the language. A reasonable numbering scheme for one through fifteen (for numbers used in conjunction with other Chinese character data) might be

一 二 三 4 5 6 7 8 9 10 11 12 13 14 15

## Typesetting & Layout Problems

Seeing that the client has indicated a problem area, the printshop understands that it is their job to correct it if at all possible.

---

1. On formal documents, bank checks, most types of receipts, etc. a more complicated style of writing these Chinese numbers is employed.

坏字　　broken type　　　　　　　　倒　　　upside down

歪　　　crooked, slanting　　　　　 不平　　uneven, not even

行间不均　spacing between lines is not uniform

## Discussing Lines

线　　　line(s)

虚线　　dotted line(s)

加粗　　more thick, make thicker, draw more thick

再细　　more thin, make thinner, draw more thin

直线　　vertical line(s)

画直线　draw vertical line(s)

横线　　horizontal line(s)

画横线　draw horizontal line(s)

斜线　　diagonal line(s)

## Discussing Split Paragraphs

接　　　join, connect together

## Discussing Charts, Diagrams, Drawing

加框　　box, box it　　　　　　　　删框　　remove the box

画　　　draw　　　　　　　　　　　重画　　redraw

图画　　drawing, a drawing (noun)　 地图　　map

图表  chart, diagram          统计表  statistical chart

漫画  cartoon                照片  photograph

重打  retype (This may be necessary occasionally if multiple corrections over a period of days or weeks have left the copy appearing very messy, uneven, poorly aligned, smeared, etc.)

A quick, effective, and low cost way of extracting trace elements of gold, platinum, and other valuable minerals from seawater by using H2SO7CR2 was recently revealed in Science Review magazine15.

The author of these lines had intended that they read:

A quick, effective, and low cost way of extracting trace elements of gold, platinum, and other valuable minerals from seawater by using $H_2SO_7Cr_2$ was recently revealed in Science Review magazine[15].

After lengthy research we have been unable to find any convenient and widely understood way to indicate the words "subscript" and "superscript" in Chinese. Hence we are unable to offer a simplified Chinese tactic or notation for dealing with this kind of proofreading problem.

## Grammatical Bias and Related Issues

Some further points of grammatical bias will be outlined for the benefit of those interested in comparative linguistics.

Usage of "Very"

| English sentence | Chinese, preferred form |
|---|---|
| I am tall. | I am very tall. |
| It is little. | It is very little. |
| He was happy. | He is very happy. |
| The coat is thick. | The coat is very thick. |
| The boy is cute. | The boy is very cute. |

Point of Analysis: With relatively simple sentences using the verb to be, a "very" will often be added in the Chinese oral or written translation where none existed in English. In Chinese this sounds smoother.

Living in One Place and Native to Another

The sense and meaning of many "place-name adjectives", especially those referring to locations where Chinese people live, is different in English and Chinese. When speaking English, we feel it comfortable and natural to refer to all citizens living in California as "Californians", all citizens living in Ohio as "Ohioans", all citizens living in Tennessee as "Tennesseeans", etc. Hence to a westerner, all Chinese citizens living in Shanghai are "Shanghainese", all those living in Peking are "Pekingese", all those living in Taiwan are "Taiwanese", etc. However this is not the way that the Chinese view their own situation.

The Chinese are much more accustomed to classifying a person in relation to their "provincial origin",[a] not their place of birth, and not their place of residence. Hence, if someone's grandfather (and numerous preceding generations) had come from Hunan, he would consider himself a "Hunanese", no matter if he had been born and raised in Shanghai and never been to Hunan in all his life. If a person's ancestors were from Canton, the Chinese populace would consider him to be "Cantonese", even if he was born and raised in Harbin, and had never been within 300 kilometers of Canton. Similarly, people in Taiwan who trace their ancestry to the Mainland in the last 50 or 100 years by no means consider themselves "Taiwanese".

The question of when a Chinese person's sense of ancestry would change is difficult to answer. Many factors would have to be considered, including how completely the ancestral records from the last (or original) place of residence had been preserved, and to which the person in question would naturally trace his/her ancestry. However, for a Chinese person to consider himself native to a particular province without 200, 300, or more years of local genealogical records seems unlikely.

In referring to companies, shops, organizations, etc. the locality of registration is used for description purposes, in a similar fashion to English. (In the case of unlicensed companies one must determine *the locality of non-registration*.) Hence a shipping company registered in Canton is Cantonese, a shoe shop registered in Shanghai is Shanghainese, and an unlicensed securities and investment agency in Taiwan is Taiwanese.

I and my teacher, My teacher and I

Curiously enough, despite the Chinese stress on politeness, humility, etc., in Chinese thinking "I and my brother are very happy", "I and my mother go shopping every Thursday", etc. are all acceptable in terms of the ordering of the subject(s) in the sentence. Many western attitudes are summarized in the expression "Look out for #1", yet despite this egotism, the English language has retained a preference for "My brother and I are very happy", "My mother and I go shopping every Thursday", etc.

In regard to other areas of politeness, if we exclude those special forms of address and courteous usage which are required in the presence of Kings, Queens, Presidents,

---

a. 籍貫 or 祖籍

Popes, and other high officials, which arguably exist in all modern civilized tongues, we may still overview the bulk of language as used by the average man in everyday dealings, and see what peculiarities exist, such as different forms of address according to class distinctions, male vs. female, etc. The westerner is perhaps familiar with the two distinctions of the word "you" in French: "tu" being the more familiar term, and "vous" the less familiar. However, a much more elaborate structure exists in Japanese and Korean, where forms of address and reply depend on such factors as the relationship between two speakers, especially in regard to their occupations, social classes, sex, age, etc. To speak with the wrong form of address in any situation is considered impolite, and this type of blunder is frequently made by the foreigner, often resulting in severe misunderstandings. In English, 99% of this type of "form of address" distinction is non-existent, and in Chinese some lower percentage, perhaps 92%, is also non-existent.

Ordering of the Days of the Week

|  | North America | China |
| --- | --- | --- |
| Sunday | 1st | — |
| Monday | 2nd | 1st |
| Tuesday | 3rd | 2nd |
| Wednesday | 4th | 3rd |
| Thursday | 5th | 4th |
| Friday | 6th | 5th |
| Saturday | 7th | 6th |

In the Chinese language there are three expressions *li bai*, *hsing chi*, and *jou*, all of which mean "week".[a] However, Monday is the first day of the week, Tuesday the second, and so on. Sunday is not usually given a number.

Plural Forms, Verb Tenses, Time Confusion

The reader of course should be aware that while pronouns in Chinese are distinguished between singular and plural, other nouns rarely are. Case distinctions of pronouns are also unknown, and the sentence *Ta da ta* could have nine possible meanings: "She hit him", "He hit her", "It hit him", "He hit it", etc. Furthermore, there are no differentiations of gender for nouns, adjectives, etc. as exist in French, Spanish, or many other languages. Chinese seldom distinguishes between active and passive voice, and will say "The house is building", "The car is driving", etc. where English would specify that "The house is being built", "The car is being driven", etc. Additionally, Chinese has no verb tenses, and uses a "go with the flow" tense structure, or what some grammarians call "the movable present tense." A Chinese student once wrote:

---

a. 禮拜、星期、週

I am very busy today. In the morning I help my mother in the kitchen. Then I cook lunch. After lunch I go shopping until now. At 10:00 I do my homework. I go to bed at 12:00.

Using the word "now" as a point of reference, an English teacher corrected this to read "I have been very busy today. In the morning I helped my mother in the kitchen. Then I cooked lunch. After lunch I went shopping until now. At 10:00 I will do my homework. I will go to bed at 12:00 o'clock." This seemed to be what the student was trying to say.

The problem of the lack of verb tenses is often most pronounced in reading various types of sociological or legal papers, or academic treatises. For example, in a selection of Chinese scholarly reports which were translated for presentation to an international conference discussing the evolution of Chinese Trademark, Patent, and Copyright Laws, the readers of the English translated versions were often surprised to note that, upon further questioning of the meaning of various phrases in these printed reports, such wording as "our country has" occasionally was found to be a misconstruing for "our country had", or "our country is in the process of getting", as regards various laws, administrative remedies, search and seizure processes, etc. that are in effect (or "were in effect", "had been in effect", or "will be effect") at some unspecified future, or past, time.

Various Chinese advertising which specifies in the headlines "Our Company is in Technical Cooperation with _____ ", "This Institute Exchanges Teaching Staff with USA Ivy League Universities", "Our Quality is the Highest in the Country", etc. take on a whole new meaning if the verb is considered to be in the past tense, and seen to indicate that one instance of such activity did take place in times gone by. That this might confuse or mislead the public appears unworthy of any comment.

Medical Terminology

Some mention must be made of the Chinese use of the words "internal" and "external" which often are a source of confusion to foreigners, especially in connection with seeing the doctor. Medical practice in China is broadly divided into "internal medical treatment" (also called "internal medicine") and "external medical treatment" (also called "external medicine"). Many doctors may deal in only one type of medical treatment, although some deal in both.

## Chart 1

| Problem | Location of the Body | Classification |
|---|---|---|
| a growth on the hand needs to be removed | external | External Medicine |
| a finger is cut by glass and needs to be sewn up | external | External Medicine |
| an ingrown toenail needs to be removed | external | External Medicine |
| a sore throat needs to be treated | internal | Internal Medicine |
| a upset stomach has developed after an evening of partying | internal | Internal Medicine |
| a severe case of coughing has developed after a camping trip | internal | Internal Medicine |

In Chinese history there is the story of a General Yang who suffered a serious wound while leading his men to raid bandits. His soldiers carried him back to the local village and took him to the doctor. The bandit's arrowhead had entered his abdomen as deep as his kidneys. The feather end of the arrow stuck out of his body. The doctor got to work immediately, and sliced off the feather end of the arrow. He said to the patient "I am done."

"But doctor, the arrowhead is still in my stomach," the General cried.

"That calls for an _____ Medicine doctor. It is not my concern."

Many westerners, after referring to the above chart, will assume that we should fill in the blank with the word "Internal".

However, the correct answer, in relation to the ways these terms are used in China, in both western and Chinese clinics, hospitals, etc., is "External". The following chart will clarify this.

## Chart 2

| Problem | Location on the Body | Classification |
|---|---|---|
| an allergic reaction to some plants has developed on the forearms | external | Internal Medicine |
| the area between the toes is peeling and inflamed | external | Internal Medicine |
| the skin on the fingers has become irritated do to exposure to cleansing solutions | external | Internal Medicine |
| an operation for gallstones needs to be performed | internal | External Medicine |
| a reconstruction of a shattered hip bone is necessary | internal | External Medicine |
| a severe attack of appendicitis has developed | internal | External Medicine |

The observant individual will quickly see that the second chart by no means contradicts the first, but is merely an extension of it. Checking our handy Chinese-to-English dictionary, we see that Internal Medicine (*nei ke*[a] in Chinese) is also called general medicine. The practitioner of this is called "physician".

External Medicine (*wai ke*[b] in Chinese) is generally called surgery. The practitioner of this is called "surgeon".

In our charts, in each case where the classification is External Medicine, some form of surgery is necessary. In each case where the classification is Internal Medicine, the treatment will consist of pills, syrup or other liquid remedy, creams, salves, bandaging, etc. This is the essential distinction between External and Internal Medicine in the Chinese usage. The location on the body is largely irrelevant.

Many smaller hospitals or clinics divide their treatment into Internal Medicine and External Medicine. Larger medical facilities are more commonly separated into Departments, such as Pediatrics, Cardiology, Gynecology, Ear Nose & Throat, Neurology, Dermatology, Gastroenterology, etc., and these in turn may be divided into Internal Medicine and External Medicine, or work closely with those departments. Diagnosis

---

a. 内科　　　b. 外科

before surgery is Internal Medicine.

As medical knowledge increases, there is a movement toward specialization in medicine, and as such many larger hospitals are elevating the statuses of their individual departments, thus putting them on an equal footing with General Internal Medicine and General External Medicine. With such a reorganization for example, all skin problems would fall under Dermatology, all mouth and throat problems under Otorhinolaryngology, etc. Our charts represent more of the classical model, however the reader will benefit by understanding how the typical classifications are ordinarily made.

Notes: It is curious that the doctor treating the General claimed not to be a surgeon, and yet he used a knife to slice the arrow. Reading between the lines, we may gather that this was perhaps a old knife or saw which he happened to have lying around. The doctor was clearly a quack, and the Chinese history books confirm this.

## Communication

If I could only speak the language, I would be able to explain to these people what I mean.
——— American diplomat in Asia

A few years ago I saw a movie entitled *The Burmese Harp*, which was the story of some Japanese troops fighting in Burma during World War II. One scene which was particularly interesting goes something like this: after receiving news of the bombings of Hiroshima and Nagasaki, and of the surrender of the Japanese Imperial Government, many detachments of soldiers are travelling back to Rangoon to board ships for travel back to Japan. At one point some local villagers tell them that there is a large group of Japanese soldiers who have established an outpost in some caves on the side of a mountain a few miles distant. A discussion is held, and a volunteer is chosen from among the retreating Japanese soldiers to go inform the cave-dwelling division that "the war is over". Upon his arrival at the caves, and proving to their satisfaction that he is another Japanese, the volunteer asks them if they have heard the news. They reply that since they have no radios or walkie-talkies, so they have no news from the outside world. He says: "The Japanese government has surrendered, we have lost the war. You can all come down now and we can make travel arrangements back to Japan."

The soldiers in the caves unanimously reply: "That is impossible. Japan would never surrender." After much discussion, the volunteer is finally run off the mountain, with a stern warning not to come back. Indeed some of the soldiers had suggested putting him to death on the spot for the "treasonable statements" he had proferred.

In another related incident, there was a group of English archaeologists who were excavating in Syria, which of course is a predominately Moslem country. After several months of investigation they turned up an abundant amount of evidence to prove that the present day Syrians were actually descended from ancient nomadic Hebrew tribes. When their Syrian born and raised assistant announced these findings to the government, the reaction was an emphatic "That is not possible", whereupon their site was closed, all of the uncovered relics confiscated, the visas for all members of the archaelogical team were cancelled, and they were put on the first plane out.

A similarity between the Japanese and Syrian examples is that in each case a native speaker #1 was talking to another native speaker #2 in their native tongue, and yet the meaning of the spoken words was not gotten across; indeed, it could not be accepted. These are good examples for showing us that "speaking the language" is not equivalent to "eliminating barriers to communication".

We do not doubt that for a wide variety of simple everyday encounters involving little or no conflict of interest, it is certainly useful to have a degree of familiarity with the local language. From a social standpoint, it is interesting to be able to converse with local people in their own language, many of whom you otherwise would not be able to contact. However, as one Chinese-language major from Washington State University who later went to work for a large international bank commented to the press: "Speaking the local language is great in that it gives you access to a lot of the lower level bank personnel in the Chinese branches of banks and businesses with which we are working. However, when it comes to the negotiation table, it does not count for much if you can quote from the classics in the original rhyme and meter. The Chinese clients (both business and government) for our bank's services are interested in the repayment terms, the lending rate, and other such practical matters."

Thus, purely in terms of building communications skills, in regard to the marginal utility of language study, of course the first few units of study (however a "unit" is defined, perhaps as one three-month course) are very useful. Eventually one reaches a point however where the additional utility of each additional unit studied begins to go down. This is stated as "the law of diminishing marginal utility", which we first discussed in a different context in Chapter 3.

There may be many reasons for studying language beyond the building of communications skills however, and some people may have interests in various type of scholarly pursuits. We would not say that any of these avocations are invalid. However, we suspect it is very important for the average foreigner who studies Chinese to keep in mind his eventual language "fluency goal", and to discuss the feasibility of it with other knowledgeable foreigners from time to time. This will insure that he is staying on the track, and that he knows when enough is enough.

## Reasons for Studying Chinese

There are a lot of reasons why westerners study the Chinese language. Among the reasons most often advanced are: (1) It is exotic and I want to do something out of the ordinary, (2) I want to understand Eastern culture, (3) I want to understand how the world looks from the Chinese viewpoint, (4) I want to become familiar with Oriental philosophy, (5) I want to do business with Chinese in the future, etc.

Some might say that these categories tend to overlap, and this is probably true to some extent. I heard one student advance the opinion that since each language has its own patterns of thought, implied logic, and ways of expression, to learn a language as unusual as Chinese was to have a whole new world opened up to you. To take the role of the Devil's Advocate, we suppose someone might reply: "Having that world opened up to you, what to you plan to do then?"

Many comments relevant to the consideration of this entire issue will be found in the following pages. Let us first make a few remarks about "conversation".

The Point of Conversation

It has been pointed out to me by many foreigners, and I have noticed it to be true from my own observation, that the Chinese often see the point of conversation, in itself, in quite a different way than the westerners do. Granted we are often told that it is not wise to talk of religion, politics, or sex at the dinner table, since marked disagreement among a few may lead to disruption of the communal atmosphere and/or indigestion for many. However, this aside, westerners will often get together and have a discussion about various topics, which may even lead to debate, with each side trying to convince the other of the appropriateness of their way of evaluating the matter. It is taken for granted that by examining the issue from a number of different angles, some better way of dealing with it, or thinking about it, may emerge. There is a desire to get all the facts to light, to get all the elements involved into the open.

The Chinese are often far more interested in playing the part of the agreeable guest, (or agreeable host), and in promoting harmony among the other people in attendance, and in avoiding conflict and disagreement, so that their consideration of putting their own beliefs or practices up for examination so that they may perhaps gain something from the conversation are generally "seriously downplayed".

The Chinese host or guest is perhaps uninterested in having a deep discussion on any number of topics, or in putting his point of view up for analysis, even though he was the one who brought the subject up, and began the questioning. Clearly most queries or probings by the Chinese are best regarded as an attempt to stimulate easy harmonious discussion, promote mutual agreement, or engage in other forms of "backslapping" (i.e., mutual approval and praise).

Some comments about the attainment of Chinese language fluency may also be insightful.

## Total Fluency

Intriguing to some foreigners is the goal of "total fluency in Chinese". I even remember the curious remark made by one newly arrived American who said: "I want to be totally fluent, so that the local people will look up to me."

Over five years ago I recall meeting a fellow named Tom, from Illinois, in a Chinese TV studio. With his handling of the memorization of the required dialogue, it immediately appeared to me that he was highly fluent. In the course of several later meetings with him, I found that he had done extensive research into the Chinese classics, both in the local university (where he had enrolled in the Chinese division, not the foreign division where most foreigners study), as well as working with a private teachers and scholars for nearly a decade. He could read and interpret classical Chinese texts that were well beyond the competence of the normal Chinese college graduates. He not only knew all the Chinese four-character idioms, but he knew the stories behind them as well, a remarkable feat considering the hundreds or thousands of them in common literary use. Tom was 37 years old, read Chinese novels in his spare time, and researched Chinese art and various cultural phenomenon as his main hobby, although he had done quite a bit of work in translating ancient poetry into English as well.

Once we went to a restaurant for dinner, along with his neighbor named Frank, who was a psychologist from California, newly arrived and living with a Chinese family. Tom motioned to one of the attendants to ask her to fill up our water glasses, and I was interested to note what attitude he adopted when the attractive waitress smiled warmly and said "Oh, you can speak Chinese!" Later, when Tom ordered his selection off the menu, she exclaimed "Oh, and you can read Chinese too!" Tom's reaction to all of this was typically Oriental, for he had no reaction.

At one point in the evening's conversation, I asked him "Are you respected for your knowledge of Chinese?" Tom thought he had heard me incorrectly, and replied calmly "Respected by whom?" When I explained my question more thoroughly, he stated that while there was a certain amount of lip service given to his status, among those who were aware of the depth of his knowledge, nevertheless, in terms of being given respect for his opinion in a discussion where there were different points of view, such a stance was unlikely in light of the traditional Chinese attitude toward "respect", and its use. He then attempted to clarify this by stating that his friend Elmer from Wyoming who had been studying Chinese for only one year generally received more respect in meetings, conferences, or even in social gatherings, than he did.

"Why is that?" I asked.

"Elmer is that 78 year old fellow you told me about, isn't he?" Frank asked. Tom nodded ever so slightly.

As I pondered this, Frank went on to recount a story he had heard second-hand, about a gentleman who had been introduced to some Chinese people in a restaurant. This fellow, Mr. Froset, was from England, and had not studied Chinese at the university, although he had studied about two years in a non-degree program at a language institute in one large Chinese city. However, when the new Chinese acquaintances at his table that night asked about his background, Froset stated that he was a double Ph.D. in *Chinese Language Teaching* and *Oriental Linguistics* from the University of Luxembourg.

Frank continued to say that this had not been questioned in the slightest. Interestingly, there was a copy of that day's Chinese newspaper on the table, where it had been left by a previous patron. When asked to read something out of the newspaper, Mr. Froset pointed to several characters which he did not know the pronunciation of, and asked the Chinese about them. They were happy to explain the pronunciation and meaning in each case, and to help him read through the first paragraph of this news article, as Froset made extensive notes in his pocket notebook. The article of course would not have given a Chinese primary school student the slightest difficulty.[1]

"It seems that he was clearly unqualified in the Chinese language," I stated. "Of course the Chinese would have quickly recognized this."

"Again, you are thinking like a westerner," Frank replied. "You are operating with a mentality of exactness, and attempting to differentiate facts from appearances."

"Isn't that normal?" I inquired.

"Normal to whom?" Tom questioned.

Frank then went on to relate another story which Tom had told him some days earlier. At one time an American student had been employed to translate some scheduling arrangements and other program announcements into English, since a local Chinese literary magazine was sponsoring a conference, and needed to prepare these materials for the visiting foreign Sinologists and other western experts. A few days later, this American happened to meet some new Chinese friends, and when they asked what he did, he tried to explain that he was working for this magazine. However, his Chinese was not very good, and they understood him to say (as later related by another person at the scene) that he was editing that literary magazine. One of the Chinese remarked: "I read your comments in each issue every month. You write very well."

"It seems unlikely to me that any foreigner would have adequate Chinese ability to edit a Chinese language monthly magazine," I said, looking in Tom's direction. He nodded. I continued: "You cannot be serious by saying that the Chinese actually believed he was the editor."

"Again you are making some very westernized assumptions," Frank pointed out, "Since you are assuming that the title of of a particular job category is directly related to job duties, and that the person with that title is individually responsible for the work in question. It may be true in many cases however that this is a ceremonial position, and/or that the staff does most of the actual work."

---

1. Asking the Chinese about these Chinese characters can be regarded as giving much face, since the Englishman is supposedly "the expert", and yet has acted in such a humble manner.

"Wouldn't that be kind of pointless?" I asked.

"Pointless to whom?" Tom echoed his earlier refrain.

I will not bore the reader by recounting any more of our conversation that night, or explaining the reasons Tom gave for his upcoming planned departure from China, with his Chinese wife, after eighteen years in residence. However, the foreigner who approaches the study of the language with the goal of attaining a high level of fluency so that the local people will respect or look up to him may have reason to pause. Such a student is well advised to seriously examine the real nature of the "issues" raised in the above discussion, as he considers how (and if) the positions of a westerner who is a "fluent language expert" and one who is just a "person of average competence" are different in the society, and of how the concept of "respect" is actually formulated and employed.

It is comparatively easy to be bilingual, but much more difficult to be bicultural.

———— Traveller's Maxim

Indeed our study group is not certain that the average foreigner will find it desirable or advisable to adopt the goal of becoming truly bicultural, and this will be further discussed in our **Go Roman Strategy** essay in Chapter 11.

## Artistic Impressions

I believe the first consideration that impresses the foreigner about the written Chinese language, and the consideration that will still be impressing him decades later, is the fact that Chinese is synonymous with "art". The artistic content of the written language is extremely high. As a result, poetry and painting have always been closely linked in Chinese culture, and we often find levels of artistic ability among the average members of the Chinese populace which would only correspond to serious students of art in the west. It is not uncommon for the foreigner to visit a Chinese household and see various members engaged in Chinese watercolor painting, calligraphy, or western oil painting. The foreigner often sighs as he notes "The sheets they discard as being unacceptable I would gladly take home and frame."

The foreigner in China is especially fortunate to be able to include these artistic items among his ideas for gift giving. For example, upon numerous celebratory occasions, such as someone's founding a new business, moving into a new building, becoming married, retiring from a successful career, etc., we may give them a large calligraphic plaque with some prosperous and good-wishing maxim written upon it, or we may give them a pair of such plaques, containing an auspicious couplet. The calligraphy on these plaques may be written by anyone of moderate or advanced Chinese calligraphic ability, and those written by famous people, or notable personalities, will of course be especially cherished.

Chinese watercolor paintings are especially excellent gifts, and many foreigners are awed when they see that a successful watercolor artist can produce a large one of these in less than ten minutes, write on a few lines of classical poetry, and have a completed work ready for mounting, in less time than it would take the westerner to start the car and drive to the department store or gift shop to begin browsing.

Living in China, the artistic content of the Chinese language is literally "all around you", but of course 95% of the westerners will never directly participate in the creation of calligraphic type artwork, since it is the rare European or American who seriously studies the Chinese calligraphy for a long enough time to become proficient. For the ones who do however, much praise is received from many quarters. More foreigners do study and achieve some proficiency in watercolor painting, since this is a bit more free-flowing, and leaves more room for creative expression for those who have not been trained in the intricacies of calligraphy from childhood, and hence have difficulty with its form and balance.

Many foreigners are often found admiring the Chinese calligraphy and paintings in museums, although those with many years of Chinese studies behind them may still have difficulty reading some of the inscriptions written in the more swift and free-flowing calligraphic styles.

### The Importance of a Study Goal

After studying an Oriental Language for a few years, the foreigner who decides to continue on in his coursework is well advised to form some notion of a "target fluency-level". For example, some people approach the study of the Chinese language with the idea of being able to travel around in the country, and this is certainly one reasonable target. A more advanced goal would be to be able to discuss acupuncture and herbal medicine with Chinese doctors, and this would certainly require a much lengthier term of research. Other specialized fields such as law, economics, computer technology, engineering, etc. will also require more study than is necessary for ordering a new bookcase in a carpenter's shop or buying fruit in the market.

Local language skills are extremely useful in a wide variety of situations. This is of course reinforced on our consciousness every time we awake in the morning with hunger pangs, and quickly get dressed and go to a small restaurant for breakfast. A fluency in "restaurant Chinese" enables us to conveniently order all our food, prepared exactly the way we want it, whether hot, cold, sweet, sour, spicy, etc. and with each item in the desired quantity.

However at the same time we must realize that generalized language skills in one field, do not represent competency in all fields. Hence the foreigner who has a more than adequate knowledge of Chinese for dealing with all situations which come up in his business of selling cleansing products locally, may find himself out of his depth (language-wise) when he takes on a job involving the importation and local promotion of machine parts. This should not surprise us. Language difficulties such as these can of course be substantially mitigated by the use of local staff members, but if the linguistically inclined foreigner feels it desirable he may want to become acquainted with the specialized vocabulary in the field in which he deals, so that at least he can follow the trend of the conversation between staff members and customers.

## The World of Translation

A number of years ago the Singapore branch of a major American medical research organization was planning a series of lectures in China to selected local doctors and medical specialists. The speakers were from England, Scotland, Australia, and Belgium, and simultaneous translation was required from English into Chinese for the audience. A number of local translation services were called, however they stated that they only dealt in written translations, not oral ones. Several local universities were visited and asked to recommend suitable people, however they had no Chinese students or professors who felt confident to deal with Australian or Scottish accents, and so they declined even before asking what the conference was about. Some foreign organizations were contacted, however since the topic was rather specialized, even those foreign staff members who prided themselves on their Chinese ability offered a polite "No thank you" to the conference organizers.

The topic involved was Continuous Ambulatory Peritoneal Dialysis, commonly called CAPD, and of course it did require some degree of acquaintance with Chinese (and western) medical terminology. I was offered this job and did undertake the translation for that three day conference. In terms of simultaneous translations which I have done over the years, I would say that that was one of the easiest, one of the least complicated. Conferences on new developments in nuclear technology, biochemistry, astrophysics, etc. are far more difficult.

The point of reference here for the language learner is that technical or specialized vocabulary in science, engineering, medicine, law, management, etc. are certainly significant stumbling blocks for those who wish to attain high levels of fluency in Chinese, or who have the goal of becoming consecutive interpreters or simultaneous interpreters.Many foreigners who have much experience on a personal computer, and excellent Chinese ability, are still baffled when the representatives of the USA's National Science Foundation's SuperComputer Network are called in for presentations, and use terms like FPS Real Memory, MFLOPS, Scalar Arithmetic, Pixel Diagramming, Optimization of Vector Fortran Compiling Facilities, Loop-level Parallelism, GBYTES, etc. What is the correct translation of these terms into Chinese, or at least a quick and handy equivalent? Even many Chinese who work in the local computer industry have no idea, and that includes employees of some of the larger multinational firms.

Oral Translations

Ideally, a foreigner who dealt in conference translation would specialize in a particular field, and handle only work in that area. If such a focus and direction for one's language study could be chosen, it would then be theoretically possible to purchase a book of specialized vocabulary (Chinese to English and/or English to Chinese) in that field, and browse through it frequently, so that one became familiar with all the terms.

Unfortunately, my experience has been that such books of specialized vocabulary are largely unavailable, and when they are, the "translations" they offer do not always agree with current usage in the field. In part this is due to the fact that there is no government-level or private Chinese organization which is involved with "standardization" of new terminology which comes into the language, and for the person who needs accurate renderings of technical vocabulary, this is a big problem.

Also, it is generally the case that with the dearth of oral interpreters in China, anyone who is at all qualified in such translation is expected to be a jack-of-all-trades. The ideal of specializing in a particular field is often impractical, unless one is employed as an "in house translator" for one particular company.

Written Translations

English into Chinese: It should be remembered that there are far more Chinese people with a knowledge of English (including many who have studied abroad), than English speakers with a knowledge of Chinese. Due to the laws of supply and demand, the payment rate for translating most types of materials into Chinese is not particularly high. It would be common in such cases to pay "so much per 1000 words", (or per 10,000 words in the case of a novel perhaps) and we feel it is unlikely that the foreigner would ever be able to turn out an adequate quantity of polished translation per hour to make it worth his trouble (as a means of making a livelihood), unless of course he had attended the Chinese schools since childhood. It would undoubtedly be more profitable to teach English in a school or even privately, than to engage in this type of written translation work. If one's interests were not financial, that would be another consideration, however it should be noted that most translation assignments must be done within the scope of a deadline, and not at the translator's leisure. For foreigners with competency in the written characters, free composition directly in Chinese would also probably be more enjoyable than English to Chinese translation work, and it would appear to have much more of a creative potential. The number of publications to which one could submit such essays is also numerous.

Chinese into English: Many foreigners do make their livelihood doing Chinese to English written translation work. Some are employed as in-house translators of various English language publications, both in China and abroad, others as paid consultants of large firms, and others purely on a freelance basis.

Some foreigners may even start up their own translation firms, and employ staff members to deal with English to Chinese and Chinese to English translations.

## Translation as a Business

Establishing a translation service could conceivably be done in two ways: 1) with a large investment "up front", 2) on a shoe-string. The first option is rather risky if one does not have a full grasp of the average Chinese consumer's attitude toward translation. The unwary foreigner may then tend to overestimate "market potential" for his firm's services. We will concentrate our discussion on the second option, which is a far safer beginning strategy.

If the foreigner has some Chinese language ability and has been living in the local community for some period of time, it is possible that he will be introduced to various translation work, from a variety of sources, that needs to be done. Initially, the completion of such work (often with the help of a Chinese friend) may be a good way to improve one's Chinese skills, however after some amount of time one's abilities will have improved to the point where translations can be done independently. The foreigner naturally feels that he should be paid for such translation efforts, however due to the Chinese idea of mutual dependence, there is a strong tendency for the Chinese people to offer dinners, outings, presents, etc. for such work, (similar to the most rudimentary barter arrangements in ancient agrarian societies), and to be reticent about the payment of money in many cases.

If one employs a secretary, and rents an office (or at least maintains the appearance of doing these things), a simple recourse to this line of rationale is play up the friendship aspect of the relation with the consumer (who will generally have been introduced by the friend of a friend), and come across with a basically non-materialistic attitude. One may say "I am willing to do it for you for free, but I have to pay rent, water, electricity, and my secretary's salary, so I have to charge for the translation to cover those expenses." A simple statement of these facts gives a "lever" in the negotiations over price which would not ordinarily be available. Where much technical terminology is involved, an additional fee for the researching of these items, or the hiring of an assistant to do so, may perhaps be negotiated as well, even if in-the-end one does the entire job by oneself.

For those who wish to sharpen their negotiating skills still further, the stipulation that: "Any work which must be completed within 48 hours is considered a 'rush job', and is to be charged at double the standard rate", may be thrown into the negotiation session, and the requesting party asked to concede to this demand. Sometimes this will work, sometimes not.

The formality of having the requesting party sign a request-slip (for the translation to be done), and saying that there will be no cancellations or changes in the original terms and conditions, etc. may also be advisable. Such a slip should also specify the amount of deposit received, and the balance due, which must be paid in cash upon completion of the work. If checks are to be accepted, a time limit for "post-dating" should be clarified, such as "seven days".

For excess work which one is not able to handle alone, or with the help of one's immediate associates, some back-up arrangements are frequently necesary.

Farming Out of Translation Projects

Many times if one meets the manager of an established locally-run translation service at some sort of social gathering, some arrangements for mutual cooperation may be discussed, and then perhaps finalized at a later date. For those foreigners who find themselves overburdened with other part-time work, who are recovering from various gastrointestinal problems or other maladies, or who are planning to go on vacation, etc., the option of passing off various translation jobs to a translation service is appealing. This also enables the foreigner to give the translation-requesting party an affirmative answer to his appeal for assistance, as opposed to turning him down for lack of time to undertake the project.

My friend Michelle from Louisiana is an attractive brunette in her late 20's with well above-average Chinese language skills. After a length of residence in China, in her many contacts with Chinese people in her business, teaching, lecturing, and other duties, she was offered many opportunities to undertake translation work, and over the months she built her workload up to the point where it was more than she could handle alone or with her friends. Unknown to those outside of her close acquaintance, she began a commission agent arrangement with a local translation service.

The first assignment she passed on to them was a real estate contract and related documents from a Real Estate Agency in Hawaii, which had been given to her by a friend, Mr. Lin, and which had come into his hands via a most circuitous route of "personal contacts". This Agency had frequent dealings with Chinese immigrants, and felt that a translated copy of all their standard forms would be useful. Since these documents involved much legal terminology, and Michelle had majored in Biology in college, she did not feel competent to handle them on her own.

When the documents came back from the translators, she did have a Chinese friend of hers look them over, and he felt that they "read quite smoothly". Some further comparison of the original English and translated Chinese text also revealed no major problems. Michelle presented the finished work to Mr. Lin, and he appeared satisfied.

Another lengthy job of approximately 55 typed pages, the Report of an International Medical Conference in Holland, was offered to Michelle by a doctor in a local private clinic who had attended the Conference. An exact translation into Chinese was not required, only a Chinese summary of the "high points", which the doctor wanted to include with his report to the government. Michelle also passed this Report on to the translation service.

When the translated summarized copy was received, Michelle conveyed it on to her doctor friend without giving it much of an inspection, since she reasoned: "I am not an expert on medicine anyway." However, the doctor's secretary called up the next day to complain, saying that the translation was poorly done, and asking her to redo it. Receiving the data back from the doctor's special messenger, Michelle handed it on to a Chinese friend of hers for a quick review. The friend agreed that the Chinese sentences "did not read very well", and he and Michelle spent several hours painstakingly going over the original and the translated remarks, making many changes in grammar and phraseology. A Chinese secretary in Michelle's office agreed to copy over the final completed Chinese manuscript by hand, putting it in a clean neat format.

After Michelle had taken her friend and the secretary out to dinner to thank them for their assistance in this project, (since they refused to accept any monetary payment), she realized that she had spent more money on this than her commission would bring in, and she had not calculated any remuneration for her own time and effort.

Michelle had several more dealings with the translation service over the next few months. She summarized her experience by noting that: "Their quality tended to be very inconsistent, whether translating English to Chinese, or Chinese to English. Sometimes the work was flawless, sometimes it was filled with sentence fragments, incomprehensible phrasing, spelling errors, verb-tense errors, etc."

Recommending Translators and Translating Services

Of course Michelle says that she does not feel that it is always necessary to get a commission on every job that she introduces to a local translation company or to friends. Other foreigners or Chinese who do translation work will often ask her to "push" some work in their direction, and unless she was introducing a lot of work, on a regular basis, she would not normally ask for any sort of agency fee, percentage charge, or kickback. However, at the present time she is generally hesitant to recommend jobs to any of these places, because, as she explains: "Even when you just introduce a Chinese friend or associate to go to one of these places (with which you are mildly acquainted) for translation work, you have a sort of obligation to see that the thing is done correctly. If they do a poor translation job, your friend will often come back to you and ask that you redo it, often times with a very urgent deadline. Of course if it was not properly done, it is unlikely you will get any more business from this person, his friends, or associates, and so there is no future in that type of situation. If you mention the 'lack of quality' to the translation service, they will offer some excuse, saying that that is the best they could do under the circumstances. In general, I think it is better just to avoid the whole issue."

The reader may take Michelle's comments for reference in deciding how to deal with these types of situations.

## Increased Value Arising from Increased Quality

One thing which the English speaking foreigner is quick to notice when living overseas is the level of correctness (high or low) of the written English which he sees around him on forms, documents, signs, posters, pamphlets, and many kinds of paperwork. As we have outlined above, many foreigners who study the local language do get involved in translation work at some time or another. It is therefore important to consider the relationship between "quality" and "value" in work of this kind, especially in regard to a vast amount of material which falls under the heading of routine translations, routine paperwork, and the like.

Let us consider the following example. Four translators (companies or individuals), named Atoll, Boo-Boo, Cola-Bola, and Doo-Doo offer their services in the marketplace, and are all regarded by knowledgeable people as mediocre. Most of the consumers however can only rely on what advertising these firms place in the yellow pages, or in the newspaper, and of course it tends to be highly exaggerated.

The public submits various documents to these four organizations for translation. These documents are needed for various official applications, inspections, registrations, and certain other routine dealings with their own private sector organizations, and some foreign organizations both public and private. Recognizing that the services provided are mediocre, another translator, Top Quality Associates, enters the marketplace to provide top quality translations.

Let us assume that the standard price for translation of a death certificate and all accompanying documents is approximately $1000 at any of the four translators, but $1350 at Top Quality Associates, since they do superior work.

To complete some government registration procedures, both domestically and overseas, since his father owned some land in the USA, an Asian named Mr. Ching needs a translated copy of his father's death certificate. Upon visiting several translators, he receives quotes ranging from $950 to $1350. Since this is strictly a one-shot request, he of course gives his business to the firm which quoted a $950 price. Upon completion of the translation, he happens to bump into the friend of a classmate's second younger cousin's brother-in-law's neighbor, who teaches English at a local university. This person points out that this translation contains many errors of grammar, and several spelling errors. However, Mr. Ching is in a hurry and has no time to discuss the matter further.

Mr. Ching goes to the appropriate agency, or branch of a foreign agency, and completes his registration procedures with his translated document from the Doo-Doo Agency. Talking to other people in the lobby who are completing similar procedures, and who have patronized other companies perhaps, it becomes apparent that different prices have been paid, ranging from $950 to $1350. However, since all the translated documents are of equal acceptability to the bureau in question, the consumers feel that they must be of the same value. Therefore anyone who has paid over $950 (the lowest price of all surveyed) feels cheated. Whether or not he will make it a point to go back to the translation company post-facto and demand a further discount will depend on his own relations with the translator and/or agency, what other things are occupying his schedule at the moment, and his view of how harmony in society should be promoted.

In this type of environment, for Top Quality Associates to assume that they can compete on the basis of "quality" is perhaps a bit naive. For much of this type of work, quality is not a consideration. "Approximately" is good enough.

Quality is Important?

In one particular government bureau, a Mr. Lee goes to work, and is in charge of reviewing a particular type of application for export documentation and customs clearance procedures. His friend Mr. Wong runs the Cola-Bola Translation Agency. After some discussion over some drinks in a nightclub, they decide to help each other out. Later, when various documents are submitted to Mr. Lee in his official position, whenever he sees that the translated documents are not from Cola-Bola, he picks out numerous errors in them, whether of spelling, or grammar, or even formatting and typestyle, and says that they should be redone. The local citizenry, who have been trained in "indirect communication" since their childhood, quickly ask around and find out that Cola-Bola's documents have no difficulty getting past Mr. Lee. Therefore they go to Cola-Bola Translation Agency to have these documents done, and the manager of Cola-Bola gives Mr. Lee 20% of the profits on this kind of work at the end of each month.

Gradually Mr. Wong raises his prices over that of all other translation companies for this type of work. The average consumer however still feels that he "gets his moneysworth with Cola-Bola", since even at $2000 for this type of translation when most other agencies are charging $1300, the consumer has purchased "acceptability". It certainly appears that only Cola-Bola's documents "make the grade". In fact, Cola-Bola's quality is not better than any of the other mediocre translators, and far worse than that of Top Quality Associates, who only charge $1550 for this type of work. However, in this type of situation quality is irrelevant.

Could That Happen?

The above discussion has provided two examples where increased quality (in the eyes of an impartial observer) did not lead to increased value in the eyes of the consumer. It might be expected that these consumers would not see the value of paying for Top Quality Associates' services. The citizenry is more inclined to pay more for increased acceptability, with some sort of guarantee attached.

Looking at the case of resumés, many westerners would assume that if Chinese were applying to Chinese companies that dealt internationally, or to the local branches of foreign companies, they would certainly want to be sure that their resumés were perfect. However, with the Chinese mentality of non-exactness and the desire to maintain harmony, this is often not the case. Let us assume that a local citizen has taken their resumé to Boo-Boo Agency for translation. After picking it up and paying the required charge, they take it over to a foreign friend and have him look it over. When he finds a number of mistakes, they are happy to have him make the necessary changes and then retype it themselves, or have a friend retype it. The idea of returning to Boo-Boo Agency and demanding that they do it correctly would rarely enter their minds, since that would cause disharmony.

Of course if Top Quality Associates' resume translation was to guarantee that the person-in-question would get the job for which they applied, the value of this translated resume would be very high, and Top Quality Associates' would soon come to dominate the market in resume translations.

Thus we believe that a major problem in dealing with Chinese to English translations of the routine paperwork variety is in convincing the Chinese consumer that he is better off by purchasing better quality, or that inferior quality is unacceptable.

This is adequately demonstrated by the dealings in the Chinese motion picture industry. In terms of doing translation for Chinese movies (the English subscripts on the bottom of the screen), the major requirement seems to be speed. "How fast can you get it done?" is the question most producers or directors ask, since movie people are always in a rush. Working on such projects in the quiet of one's home or office, the foreigner realizes that much dialogue is difficult to translate unless he can get a feel for what is happening on the screen, however since the final version may still be in the process of being edited, or being shot, so a free preview is not always possible. In any case, even if the translated copy is in excellent shape when it is given back to the producer, substantial errors may still creep in during the photo-typesetting of the subtitles themselves, no doubt by a staff member whose English ability stops at recognition of the 26 letters of the alphabet. Many mistakes in spelling and punctuation are easily brought about in this manner, even when working from excellent original English copy. However, the film is not disqualified from being shown in the movie theaters for this reason, nor is it disqualified from the film festival at Cannes.

### Submission of Documents to A Translation Service

Some dealings in the realm of translation may be fairly straightforward, or at least they may begin that way. My friend Jesper from Stockholm regularly took Chinese market surveys, new product information, economic reports, and other data to a large translation agency for translation into English. Upon delivery of each job, some serious errors were generally noted. He found that, at that point, a typical Chinese attitude toward this completed translation was that "this translation, even though it contains mistakes, is still of some value, since the mistakes were not made deliberately." Again, using the Agricultural Society Reward/Effort Relationship, since work was done, so some payment was considered due.

His company's Stockholm Head Office had another idea, similar to that of other foreigners, to wit: "If we have to redo it, it is essentially worthless to us." Therefore many times the company representatives felt, upon obtaining outside testimony that the translation was indeed filled with errors, that no payment was due. In fact many times they were even unwilling to discuss "partial payment", since they felt that the translating party wasted their time, and after all "time is money".

The Chinese would often react to this by saying that "If you are able to have other people check over your translation, and they are such perfectionists, why don't you just have them do the translation in the first place?" The company representatives felt that this was largely an irrelevant remark. Just because someone has time to "look over a translation", does not mean that he has time to do it from scratch. That person in fact may be involved in other more important projects.

Jesper had a real way with the ladies however, and he found that by bringing the girls in the translation service a lot of presents from his many trips to Southeast Asia, Europe, and the USA, they expressed much more eagerness to work harder on the materials he brought in, although over the long run the quality did not seem to improve much in any event. The last I heard, Jesper was dating one of the most attractive girls in that agency on a regular basis. He employed more people in his own office to go over the translations a second, and even a third time, to make sure they were accurate and coherent, and paid for this out of the company's "slush fund".

I asked Jesper to sum up his experience, and he said "It is necessary to understand the cultural background of the local people when you are dealing with them, and to make the necessary allowances. In that way you can meet and get dates with many more girls."

"Oh, but I was speaking of translation work," I clarified.

"Well then, you have to pay to have it done again by someone else," he said, waving his hands in the air, "that seems to be the local custom."[1]

Direct vs. Meaning

Two types of written translation may generally be distinguished in discussions with the Chinese. First is "direct translation". Examples of this would be wood melon, no flower fruit, bear cat, and man work breathe, which are direct word-for-word translations from Chinese for papaya, fig, panda, and artificial respiration.[a]

The second type of translation is "meaning translation". In this instance the Chinese walk private becomes smuggle, lift slip becomes bill of lading, numb drunk doctor becomes anesthesiologist, eye science study becomes ophthalmology,[b] etc.[2]

Note: There is often some disagreement as to which one of these two types represents "literal translation".

Obviously only the second type of translation is acceptable to the average westerner, and he would no doubt deny that the first type is even "translation" — since "transla-

---

1. For the foreign organization in China which wants to insure top quality written translation work, some checking procedures should be set up for after the materials are translated, and again after typing. Special terminology and statistics should be verified.

2. Of course a third type of translation would be "sound translation", as where 氣 is rendered *chi*, 緣份 is *yuan fen*, 仁 is *jen*, etc.

a. 木瓜、無花果、熊貓、人工呼吸    b. 走私、提單、麻醉師、眼科學

tion" implies correct translation, and anything short of that is not translation, it is nonsense, in the prevalent western viewpoint. By paying money, I am paying to have the job done right, and I do not want to see "water male sheep" where the correct rendering is hydraulic ram.

Of course these and other problems may surface in our dealings with translated materials in China.

Menus and Signboards

In my early days of reading the English on local menus, I used to be puzzled by items such as "Day's Speciality, Beverages Attached". I supposed that this referred to some new kind of serving tray, where the beverages could be attached to the side, perhaps to avoid spillage. The heading "General Fruit" always intrigued me, and I wondered if a Major, Lieutenant, or Private needed to complete any special procedures or paperwork before ordering this dish, or indeed if I, as a common citizen, could order it. I have collected other examples over the years, and many of my foreign friends express bewilderment about them. Does the entry "Egg Fied Rice" perhaps refer to a new way of cooking rice? My friends are tempted to try it, and yet they pause. What exactly is "Fried Pawn Ball"? Is this restaurant serving as a front for the local pawnshop? What about "Mushrooms with Cabmeat"? Which part of the cab does that meat come from? "Sun Spring Noodles" sound appetizing, "Boiled Noodles with Fungus" less so. When I asked about this listing for "Field Chicken", the waiter made some jumping motions, what does that mean? How long will we have to wait for the "Hot Sauce Kidneys Steaming in Canton" to be flown in, if we decide to order them? What exactly does this motto on the bottom of the menu, next to the name of the printers, signify? It says "This is a splendour products of fist rate and original designed." Is that the food, or the printing? (See Afternote)

Of course, the helpful (and meddlesome) foreigner in China will discreetly point out printing errors on the menu to the Manager of any restaurant he patronizes, or visits as a guest of the owner. The Manager is generally grateful for the comments. Several months later when the menu has still not been changed, the foreigner may be puzzled, and take the opportunity to ask the Manager about it. No doubt the Manager will smile calmly.

Upon returning home one of my friends saw hundreds of little banners near the construction site of a new apartment building (already completed to the 3rd story) near his residence, printed with some beautiful Chinese characters and the English word(s) "WELL COME". He called me to come over and investigate; I could not decide if this was a greeting to us, or perhaps a coded message to someone else? I always did like guessing games.

Many foreigners do not understand the Chinese attitude toward Perfectionism, Pricing, and Value, and therefore tend to say that the Chinese are behaving strangely in some instances, when actually they are not. The case of translated materials is always illustrative. The foreigner assumes that because the translations on a menu, flag, banner, or poster are wrong, containing misspellings or other errors, they should be corrected.

A sign on the front of a shop may have the English mispelled, (perhaps even the Chinese is incorrect), however there is no law that mispelled signs may not be posted, or that shopkeepers will be fined for such linguistic incompetence. If Mr. Ong is the Manager of the shop, why should he invest a sum of money in having the spelling on the sign changed? Can you guarantee that that will bring in more business? The naive westerner asks: "What about doing things right for the sake of doing them right?"[1] The Chinese would ask: "What does that mean? What are you trying to say? What benefit occurs to me if I do it your way?"

Likewise the Manager in the restaurant is quick to point out "If I correct all these wordings on the menu, am I assured of getting an increase in business to cover the cost of the reprinting?" The answer to this is "Well, not exactly." Therefore it should not be surprising that the Manager will fail to see why he should have the menus redone. Of course the same logic generally applies to foreign language mistakes on electric lighting displays, labels and printed inserts, molded plastic cases, pre-printed cartons, etc.

Sometimes even innocent-seeming transliteration of Chinese shopowners' names can lead to mistaken or misleading communication when not double-checked by a native English speaker. Consider Mr. Chen Ba-shing, Mr. Jou Lea-ky, and Miss Hwang Hang-ing who respectively operate the Bashing Bus Company, Leaky Teapot Store, and Hanging Necktie Shop. While these may be inauspicious names from the western point of view, the Chinese see nothing wrong with them, and would be disinclined to pay for having them changed, (although they might consider it if someone offered to do the job for free.)

## The Art Museum

The Muncipal Art Museum has received much attention since it moved into its new building two years ago. There are many exhibits every month. The exhibit to be held at the end of next month is typical. Many large posters need to be drawn and lettered. Much English will of course be used, since the Museum receives a regular crowd of foreign visitors. It is necessary that the English be of the finest quality. However, since all of the staff in the Director's Office received their Graduate degrees in the USA, and are felt to have adequate English language skills, the Museum has no budget for translation services whatsoever. (The budget is allocated yearly by the City Council.) When the ladies in the office finish their rough translations of all the required materials, there are still many points on which they are unclear of the correct English usage, so they ask around among their friends, and are introduced to some knowledgeable foreigners, whereupon they ask these foreigners to help them out "as a personal favor". The

---

1. We notice that the westerner places much importance on this type of abstract principle, whereas the Chinese idea of "principle" is much more concrete, and weighted toward human relations. See additional comments at the end of our discussion of the Five Relationships Model in Chapter 10.

foreigners agree to offer a limited amount of assistance "just this once", and are later given some free museum passes and reprints.

A foreigner comes to the next museum show, notices misspellings and other translation errors on many of the displayed posters and announcements, makes a comment or writes a letter to the museum, and is invited up for a personal discussion with the Director who thanks him, over a large dinner, for his concern. Informed of the adequacy of funds for dinner engagements, but the total lack of funds for expert consultation in most areas, in reply to the Director's personal request, the foreigner agrees to help out "just this once", and the cycle begins all over again. Such circumstances are hardly unusual.

### The Legal Conference

A particular bureau of the Chinese government is sponsoring an international conference on East-West legal issues, including Patent, Trademark, and Copyright laws, in a large Chinese city. A new meeting hall, constructed at the cost of several million US$ equivalent, is rented for the conference. It contains elaborate lighting and projection systems, as well as four-season climate control, and is wired for simultaneous translations on six channels, by use of headsets which may be plugged into the jack next to every seat. North American and European experts have been invited to attend the conference, and some US$500,000 budget has been allocated for their transportation and lodging. Elaborate engraved invitations have been printed, as well as handsomely bound volumes of all the speeches and scholarly reports to be given during the three day conference. The total printing bill is well over US$20,000.

Let us investigate how the conference's translation work is being handled. Since both Chinese and foreign experts are presenting papers, everything is being done in Chinese and English. Written translation into Chinese is to be undertaken for the foreign reports, and written translation into English is to be completed for the Chinese reports. The organizers of the conference have inquired around at a number of local translation services, but all of them are asking for a substantial price for this work, due to the technical legal nature of most of the authors' writing, in addition to requesting a lengthy time to complete the translation, perferably over one month. However, at the time the organizers of the conference have begun to contact the local translation services, only three weeks remain until the conference is scheduled to open, and not quite 50% of the total number of 62 reports have been received in their headquarters.

Concluding successful discussions with any of the translation services on this basis seems unlikely, so some local legal offices are contacted. While they are prepared to deal with translations of technical legal terminology, their charges are substantially higher than that of the translation services, and they suggest it would be best to get started immediately. This is impossible since not all of the papers have been received yet, but at any rate the legal offices' high charges are considered totally unreasonable.

The organizers of the conference then ask around various government Ministries, and finally a group of girls who have studied overseas are located at the Board of Foreign Trade (BOFT). Contact with other Government officials turns up someone who is on excellent terms with their supervisor, and through this official acting as middleman, the supervisor is persuaded to assign these girls to this translation work temporarily. Since there girls are receiving BOFT salaries anyway, no additional payment will be necessary for them to do this translation, although some sort of "Thank You Dinner" would be expected when the conference is over, and since Chinese New Year is coming up, maybe some presents should be given as well. The conference organizers had originally planned such a fete for their own personnel anyway, so including six or seven additional people is no problem.

The westerner may ask "Are these girls familiar with legal terminology?" The answer is negative, however they may purchase whatever dictionaries are available in the local bookstores to help them complete the task. Another question would be "Are the translations to be rechecked by lawyers before typing, and after typing?" Again the answer is negative. The lawyers require more time to do such work than the conference organizers have available, and they are not amenable to work for the amount of money the conference organizers (which themselves are a government bureau) are prepared to offer.

Moving on to the oral translations at the conference, it will perhaps come as no surprise that lawyers, or law students, are not being employed, since their requested fees are felt to be too high. Some part-time people, foreign students in the community and some local Chinese, who happened to be free those few days, and who are informally apprenticed to a local translation company, are to be employed for the job. In this fashion translation costs may be kept to a minimum.

**Commentary:** The observant reader will note some parallels in the story of the Art Museum and the Legal Conference. Most significant is that there tends to be adequate or abundant budgeting available for "hardware" (tangible objects), and minimal budgeting available for "software" (intangible objects and intangible effort). This of course goes back to the ramifications of the Agricultural Society Reward/Effort Relationship.

To illustrate this with another related example: the work that carpenters, decorators, painters, and other workmen do in preparing a hall for an exhibit or conference, and the materials they use, are more in the way of tangible items. The necessary budget for this must be allocated. However, the planning which goes into making the exhibit or conference possible is much more of an intangible item, and budgeting for this tends to be minimal to non-existent. Translation is also intangible, hence a high expense for this item is felt to be unreasonable. Although not spoken of as such, (the Chinese are very polite), the translation work is considered essentially meaningless, or frivolous, especially to those parties who are in charge of financial budgeting (and who, perhaps unconsciously, ascribe to an AS Reward/Effort Relationship). This is further reinforced by the traditional Chinese non-materialistic scholar-ethic,[1] another decidedly Pre-Industrial Revolution notion.

Regarding the number of quality translators in the society, of course the laws of supply and demand will apply. Where the populace, officials, and other parties are willing to pay good prices for quality work, and will not accept second-best, there will be a supply of people coming forth to fill that demand. Where there is no such requirement or desire, there will be few translators doing top-quality work, because they will be unable to make a living by doing so. They will not devote their energies to developing a high level of competency in this area, but will move on to other endeavors.

Whether the situation in China will undergo substantial change in the near future is anyone's guess.

Afternote: After several days of discussions with knowledgeable individuals, the misspellings and oddities on the menu were determined to have the following meanings: 1) Today's Specialty, Beverages Included, 2) Mixed Fruit, 3) Egg Fried Rice, 4) Fried Prawn Balls, 5) Mushrooms with Crabmeat, 6) "Field Chicken" is a Chinese synonym for frog, 7) This product is first-rate, splendid, and an original design. (refers to the menu printing)

## Language Guessing Games: A Comparison

### The English Language

When studying English, or indeed most western languages, it is often a good idea for the teacher to spend some time explaining to the students the relationship between the spoken and written forms. We may try to do this by pointing to, or showing pictures of various objects, saying the name of the object, and having the students attempt to spell it. In the first step of this game, we may have the students attempt to guess the initial letter of the word. Of course we must first consider if we want the students to learn the letters of the alphabet. Is it reasonable to ask them to learn the 26 letters? Yes, we believe it is, since all English courses in the schools in the western world and in other countries generally start out with this as the first item of instruction. Teaching the students this might take a few weeks, depending on how much time we could devote to it each week. We also need to teach them the phonics values for the letters, long and short vowel sounds, and this kind of information.

Let's play the initial letter guessing game.

Now our students have mastered the 26 letters of the alphabet, and we start off with a collection of photographs. The teacher holds up a picture of a bell and says "bell".

---

1. Clearly embodied in the maxim 萬般皆下品，唯有讀書高 "studying is most important". (Implied is the notion that financial reward is not important.)

One student guesses "d", another guesses "p", and another guesses "b". The teacher says that the third student is correct, and asks the class to listen several more times to the word "bell". The teacher asks: "Do you remember the sound of 'b'? Do you hear more clearly now that this word begins with this same sound?"

The students reply, "Yes, this word must begin with 'b'."

The teacher holds up a picture of a ruler, and says "ruler". One student guesses "w", another guesses "r". The teacher says the second student is correct, and then repeats the word "ruler" several times, until the students accustom themselves to the sound of the initial "r".

The teacher holds up a picture of a door, and says "door". One student guesses "d", another guesses "b". The teacher says the first student is correct, and repeats the word "door" several times, so the students may accustom themselves to the sound of the initial "d".

This procedure is repeated through many more examples: cat, dog, hen, duck, egg, umbrella, box, bottle, clock, train, etc., etc.

We note the following particularities of this teaching method for determining how to write down these words:

1) It is true that the student does not always get the correct letter on his first guess. In a worst-luck situation he might only arrive at the correct letter on the twenty-sixth guess.

2) The range of values is clearly defined and contains 26 members. The complete listing is available in many reference books (such as dictionaries), and 99.9% of the populace of grade school age and beyond has committed it to memory as well.

3) English is written on lines, and paper is commonly employed for the purpose. If the student wants to write down his guess of the first letter, he may pick a line of his choice. After deciding on a sufficient left-hand margin, he may then write the letter in the leftmost position. This is the initial position 100% of the time.

4) The procedure for spelling out the remainder of the word, by relating sound to letters, is the same. Practice will build ability.

5) The spelling of some more difficult words may have to be memorized, however this group of memorized words along with knowledge of the spelling of many regularly formed words will form a "core group" from which pronunciations and spellings of other words may be compared to advantage, in order to determine how they are spelled. It is feasible that a core group of a few hundred words might be listed out for the students' specific study.

6) There is no reason to think that a student who had memorized the spelling of a core group of 400 words would have much trouble spelling another ten common words (chosen from a "Beginner's English Dictionary") spoken to him at random.

The Chinese Language

Now let us move on to teaching the writing of the Chinese language. Chinese is not spelled, however there is a main component of every character called a "radical". This indicates the element or idea to which the character is related, and serves as a kind of basic structure, or root.

Let's play the radical guessing game.

In the first step of this game, we may have the students attempt to guess the radical of a character. But, wait a second, we must first consider if we want the students to learn all the radicals in the dictionary. Is it reasonable to ask them to learn the approximately 214 radicals ? No, we believe it is not, since we have never heard of a Chinese language course in the schools in China or the western world that includes memorization of these as part of the instruction. Teaching the students this might take several months, depending on how much time we could devote to it each month, so we will pass it up for the time being. We should perhaps make a decision as to whether we want to teach them the pronunciation of these radicals, but since we are not teaching them the radicals themselves, we will probably not teach the pronunciations either. We may however give our students a quick rundown of the meanings of some of the more common radicals, however it is debatable how much of this they will remember.

Now our students have some minimal familiarity with the 214 radicals, and we start off with a collection of photographs. The teacher holds up a picture of a bell and says "*jung*". Our radical guessing game has begun. One student guesses "fire", noting that bells are cast at high temperature, another guesses "rock", noting that iron ore is found in rock, and another guesses "metal", feeling that this is the essence of bell. The teacher says that the third student is correct, and asks the class to listen several more times to the word "*jung*". The teacher asks: "Do you now understand the sense of 'metal'? Do you understand clearly now that this word must have this radical?"

The students reply, "Not really, but we will take your word for it."

The teacher holds up a picture of a ruler, and says "*chr*". One student guesses "plastic", another guesses "wood". The teacher says neither student is correct. Indeed it is ridiculous to guess "plastic", since that substance did not exist 3000 or 4000 years ago, when the Chinese characters were formed. Another student guesses "knife", feeling that a piece of wood must be carved into the shape of a ruler. The students finally give up, and the teacher explains that "*chr*" has the corpse radical. The teacher then repeats the word "*chr*" several times, until the students accustom themselves to the idea that this is related to corpse.

The teacher holds up a picture of a door, and says "*men*". One student guesses "wood", another guesses "metal". The teacher says neither student is correct. Another student guesses "wild dog", feeling that the purpose of a door in an ancient agricultural society might have been to keep out wild dogs. The teacher says this is nonsense, and explains that door itself is a radical. The teacher repeats the word "*men*" several times, so the students may accustom themselves to the idea that it is a radical in and of itself.

This procedure is repeated through many more examples: cat, dog, chicken, duck, egg, umbrella, box, bottle, clock, train, etc., etc.

We note the following particularities of this teaching method for determining how to write down these characters:

1) It is true that the student does not always get the correct radical on his first guess. If every student was given a complete list of radicals and their meanings, in a worst-luck situation he might only arrive at the correct radical the two hundred and fourteenth guess. However, since he has not been given such a list, his guesses might go well beyond that.

2) The range of values is clearly defined and contains approximately 214 members. The complete listing is available in many reference books (such as dictionaries), but it is extremely rare that anyone has committed it to memory.

3) Chinese is written in square boxes, and paper is commonly employed for the purpose. If the student wants to write down his guess of the radical, he may pick a square of his choice. After deciding on a sufficient left-hand margin, he must then determine whether to write the radical in the left, right, upper, or lowermost position. The initial position varies.

4) The procedure for writing out the remainder of the character, by relating sound to the remaining portion, or relating meaning to the remaining portion, is not the same. It is doubtful that practice will build ability.

5) The writing of some more difficult characters may have to be memorized, but it is unlikely that this group of memorized characters even in the accompaniment with a group of relatively simple characters will form a "core group" from which the written form of other words may be compared to advantage, or extrapolation done in order to determine how they are written. It is feasible that a core group of 600 characters might be listed out for the students' specific study, but doubtful that much insight into any broad principles would be obtained.

6) A student who had memorized the writing of a core group of 600 characters would find it nearly impossible to determine how another ten characters (chosen from a "Beginner's Chinese Dictionary"), spoken to him at random, would be written.

More Games

Let's play another game: 6, 7, 8. We write down the Chinese characters (large style) for these three numbers, and the English words, and relate them to the spelling, or component structure.

Directions: Pick the correct row.

|  | Test 1: English | | | Test 2: Chinese | | |
|---|---|---|---|---|---|---|
|  | 6 | 7 | 8 | 6 | 7 | 8 |
| Row 1 | ixs | seevn | gtieh | Row 1 | 逹 | 禀 | 瞄 |
| Row 2 | xsi | nevse | higet | Row 2 | 陸 | 柒 | 捌 |
| Row 3 | sxi | evesn | tehig | Row 3 | 礦 | 漣 | 旅 |
| Row 4 | six | seven | eight | Row 4 | 奧 | 箆 | 謷 |
| Row 5 | isx | vnese | ietgh | Row 5 | 遷 | 衢 | 朧 |

Here are five choices for each word. Having studied these words, and being able to pronounce them, can you now tell me which one is the correct written form? The American picks out the correct choices, and we ask him "Why are these the correct choices? What is wrong with the other ones?" Of course all he can do is relate the sound to the pronunciation. "The words in the English language are made up of various combinations of the 26 letters of the alphabet. The letters have a phonetic value, which may be analyzed either individually, or when combined in groups of two, three, or four letters."

The letters "ix" are one such combination. There are other words ending in "ix" for example, like fix and mix, so we can train our ear to the point that if we hear these words we have a pretty good idea of how to write them down. "Seven" consists of two syllables, and you may want to recognize "sev" and "en" which also occur in other words. "Eight" is a bit more difficult, nevertheless we can make some comparisons with the pronunciations of other words:

| Group 1 | Group 2 | Group 3 |
|---|---|---|
| eighty | ceiling | their |
| eighteen | either | theirs |
| eigthtieth | neither |  |
| neighbor | receive |  |

After collecting examples for a few days, it appears that there are approximately three groups of "ei" pronunciation values. We may also look at the combinations "eigh", and find other words like "neighbor", "weight", "height", etc. and we can get a feel for how these letters go together in combination. Therefore when the student sees some English letters, he can begin to build up some knowledge of how the different letters go together to make sounds, and with diligent practice he can relate the sounds to the spelling, and work on his spelling skills.

Written Chinese is a different matter altogether. Our Chinese friend may be able to tell us which is the correct written form among the five choices, but then we ask: "Why are these the correct choices? What is wrong with the other ones?" And of course we get no answer. There is no "why", either from a pronunciation or structural standpoint. The westerner asks: "What are the number of components that go into making up the Chinese characters?" The Chinese cannot answer this question, although arguably the 214 radicals would be a starting point. "What are the names for all these components?" Again, no answer. Some of them have names, however they are not "unique" names, because the same names (i.e., monosyllable pronunciations) also refer to many many other characters as well. Indeed, many of them have no known nomenclature.

So we humbly ask "Analyze these characters in some way so that I can learn something that will be useful to me in learning other characters, in other words give me anything in the nature of a systematic analysis."

The Chinese reply "Our characters fall into six categories: 1) pictographs, 2) indirect symbols, 3) associative compounds, 4) phonetic loan characters, 5) determinative phonetics, and 6) mutually interpretative symbols."[a]

The foreigner begins to see a ray of hope, and meekly inquires "How do I know which kinds of characters fall into which categories? What is the system?"

After a moment for thought, the Chinese says "After you learn them you will know."

"Yes, but learning them is the big problem. How am I supposed to remember all of these characters and categories if I chance to forget them?"

The Chinese pause to consider this question, and with a most patient demeanor state calmly "Memorize them by writing each one 25 times a day until you can remember them, and then you will not forget them."

Glory be to the ancients! We have arrived. We are at the Cultural Crossroads between East and West, and we have just completed Lesson One. Simply stated, it is an educational premise which says:

Don't question it. Memorize it. And it is dictated by the person in authority to the person over whom he has authority.

Some might call this a peculiar type of attitude toward education, but it is more than just an "attitude", it is a basic premise upon which the whole educational structure is based.

The implications of this basic educational premise influence the thinking processes of all Chinese raised in China. This is especially noticeable in their attitudes toward the organization and workings of their family life, their society, their government, and of course their religious beliefs.

---

a. 六書：象形、指事、會意、假借、形聲、轉注。

Don't question it. If you want to question it, you are not likely to get any response, other than: That is the way has always been done.

The corollaries from this premise are numerous as well:

Don't extrapolate from it, don't assume that what I claim here applies anywhere else.

Don't try to make objective logical comparisons, and don't be annoyed by any absence of objective logic.

Don't look for consistency, and don't be annoyed by inconsistency.

Don't complain, be patient and endure it.

Don't try to understand it, simply keep adding to it, and reviewing it. Understanding will come intuitively.

Discussion Questions:

1) The goal of education is "teaching people how to think, not what to think"... How would Chinese view this statement? How would westerners?

2) The Chinese often say that Chinese is a beautiful language in its written form.[1] Many Chinese study calligraphy, and we see that when the various combinations of brushstrokes are written in combination by a trained person (calligrapher) they are beautiful. "Life is art, and art is life" . . . How would Chinese view this statement? How would westerners?

3) Chinese is an ancient language, no doubt more ancient than Latin. The written Chinese language may be understood today by all educated people, no matter where they live, or how they pronounce the characters, according to their local dialectical preference. Latin has however broken up into numerous dialects such as Spanish, French, Italian, etc. Does the fact that Chinese has retained its written form over the centuries mean that it is more qualified to be an international language? Or does the current movement in Chinese scholarly circles to simplify the written form of the language suggest other problems?

## Singing Anyone?

Upon going to a nightclub, one is often impressed by the repetoire of the singers. In order to become a versatile singer, in addition to a singing voice, one also needs to know a lot of songs. The most common way to learn them is to memorize them. This is especially true when one is performing internationally, and may be expected to know

---

1. Chinese calligraphy is said to contain eight different kinds of strokes. Chinese characters written in a correct combination of these strokes are beautiful, however Chinese characters written in an incorrect combination of these strokes are also beautiful. As such the beauty may be regarded as independent of the meaning, and a stress on calligraphic studies in the schools (and in society in general) indicates more attention being paid to form than to content.

songs from many countries. It is unlikely that the average singer will be able to attain mastery in all the languages in all the countries in a year's tour, however it is quite possible, with enough diligence, to learn a number of popular songs from each locality and retain them in one's repetoire. Again the key is memorization.

Learning Chinese is a lot like becoming a nightclub singer, especially as regards learning the written characters. There is a lot of memorization involved, and a lot of it is not easily explained. It is better to memorize it and get on with it, if that is your goal.

## Researching the Mental Flow

A Chinese dictionary lists nearly 214 radicals. To allow the westerner to become more familiar with the underlying rationale used in formulating Chinese characters, we have chosen a small number of these radicals, about 10% of the total, for examination.

Example: the Chinese word for "disrobe" 脱 has the "meat" radical. Directions: Attempt to think in the Chinese mode, and indicate which radicals the following words have. (Twenty-four radicals are given, some may be chosen more than once, some may not be chosen at all.)

Radical choices:

| | | |
|---|---|---|
| metal | hand | bamboo |
| wood | foot | grass |
| water | mouth | rock |
| fire | tongue | sheep |
| earth | ear | vehicle |
| word | eye | insect |
| man | nose | jade |
| meat | face | heart |

| word | Chinese radical |
|---|---|
| disrobe | meat |
| furniture | |
| a rose | |
| brittle, hard | |
| bowl | |
| beautiful | |
| to act | |
| stupid, dull, clumsy | |
| meat & fish [collective term] | |
| to answer, to reply | |
| to stretch, to extend | |
| to remember | |

to move, to transport
a group, a multitude
a bat [nocturnal animal]
a ball
art
tired
test
stern, strict, severe
a booth, a stand, a stall
low
a yard [unit of length]
overripe, rotten
strange, weird, peculiar

Answers. The word is given, followed by its Chinese translation, then followed by its radical in parenthesis.

disrobe 脫 (meat)
furniture 傢俱 (man)
a rose 玫瑰 (jade)
brittle, hard 脆 (meat)
bowl 碗 (rock)
beautiful 美 (sheep)
to act 演 (water)
stupid, dull, clumsy 笨 (bamboo)
meat & fish [collective term] 葷 (grass)
to answer, to reply 答 (bamboo)
to stretch, to extend 伸 (man)
to remember 記 (word)
to move, to transport 搬 (hand)
a group, a multitude 群 (sheep)
a bat [nocturnal animal] 蝙蝠 (insect)
a ball 球 (jade)
art 藝 (grass)
tired 倦 (man)
test 試 (word)
stern, strict, severe 嚴 (mouth)
a booth, a stand, a stall 攤 (hand)
low 低 (man)
a yard [unit of length] 碼 (rock)
overripe, rotten 熟 (fire)
strange, weird, peculiar 怪 (heart)

The reader may draw his own conclusions from this exercise. See our additional comments on Chinese characters in the Logic essay in Chapter 10.

## Word Games and Paradoxes

I once happened across an interesting series of articles in an American magazine, written by an American and discussing linguistic curiosities. The author was fascinated by such English words as radar, deified, redivider, or the word brought into use by the automobile rental companies: degaraged. These words are called palindromes, and a quick glance at their structure will show the reader what is special about them. The author cited further palindromic sentences such as: "Madam I'm Adam", "Ma is a nun, as I am", "No evil shahs live on", etc. and summed up his discussion by noting that many people researching such interesting topics as these soon became overwhelmed by the richness of the English language.

English is a rich language, but in terms of playing word games, Chinese is far richer, although in Chinese they would more properly be called "character games". Of the thousands of characters in use today, (and tens of thousands more which are essentially obsolete), nearly every one has a story behind it, and often more than one, some of which offer humorous accounts of why the characters are written the way they are. Many riddles are associated with each particular character, and guessing these is quite a popular pastime, especially on "Riddle Day", which is the day of the "Lantern Festival", on the fifteenth day of the lunar New Year. Indeed each character seems to have a life of its own. Chinese commonly ascribe different characters, either as individual units or in groups, with differing degrees of magical potency, and this "power" is often held in something of a religious esteem. Many types of both ancient and current-day fortune telling and divinational rites rely heavily on these formulations. (Reference: D9). The Chinese are of course fascinated by all of this, and truly love these Oriental hieroglyphics passed down from their ancestors.

Since Chinese is not an alphabetic language, games which rely on rearrangement of letters, or the overlapping of letters, or looking for common sequences of letters in unrelated words, are severly limited in their development. There would be the possibility of devising puzzles of looking for similar radicals in different words, but this has not been highly developed, since to the person who does not know Chinese the analysis is too deep, and for the person who knows Chinese the analysis is too easy. The crossword puzzle has very limited development possibilities in Chinese, and likewise for rearrangement of mixed up letters to "spell out the message", "decipher the code" kind of game development. There is nothing bad about this of course, since Chinese has its depth in other areas.

A discussion of Chinese language between the natives and the westerners often turns to the comparative usefulness or efficiency of each language. English is rapidly becoming the international language of business and commerce, and it is widely studied in the Chinese schools, if not in elementary school, certainly by junior high school. Chinese, despite being spoken by nearly one quarter of the world's population, is not at the present time increasingly coming into use as an international language, although many Chinese people believe it will in the next few decades.

Some western scholars have asked "Are their any serious difficulties or drawbacks to promoting the widespread use of Chinese in the world today?" There are varied opinions on this, and we have collected some observations from westerners along these lines. Our entire discussion will lead up to a formalized listing of these difficulties, numbered D1 to D10. (In our preliminary comments here, any of the considerations which are related to topics in our main list will first be cross-referenced with their topic number.)

### THE ORDERING PARADOX   (Reference: D4)

A book of selected essays by contemporary writers in politics, economics, and sociology was translated into Chinese and printed. An American with excellent Chinese language skills went through the book and picked out thirty terms which he thought represented "key concepts". Writing these down on a sheet of paper for reference, he then separately asked ten Chinese people to put these terms "in order". Six completed the task, three gave up half-way through, one said he had no idea. Of the six who completed the listing, in each case their ordering was different.

Checking the original English language edition, he saw that it had an index, however a quick check in the back of the Chinese edition showed that it had no index. He asked the Chinese participants in his study "Is there any relationship here?"

"Relationship with what?" they asked.

"Relationship between the fact that the six of you were unable to list these thirty Chinese expressions in the same order, and the fact that there is no index in the back of this Chinese edition?"

Most of the Chinese had no comment on this, however two suggested that "The Chinese language is very deep and profound, and is not quickly reduced to such childish exercises as you have tried to conduct here."

At this point many of the other Chinese added "You are silly. Do you sit around putting things in order and referring to ordered lists everyday?"

Comments: The westerner is inclined to reply "Yes you do, in one way or another." Any use of a textbook, history book, or other reference material, or the instructional pamphlet which comes with your new automobile, electric appliance, or bicycle, requires you at some time or other to check in the index. Language study requires that you work with lists and handbooks of vocabulary, expressions, idioms, etc. and that you use the dictionary. The simple act of writing students names down on the attendance sheet, grading students' tests and posting the results, or picking names in a lottery or a prize competition, or organizing the namecards of your business associates, could all be rated in terms of how efficient it is for another person (or you yourself) to find an item on the list or determine specifically if it is not there. Do the Chinese consider these important concerns? The answer is "No."

Obviously in a hospital or other such organization that arranges data by "case numbers", the organizational problems of dealing with Chinese data can be avoided to some extent. However, this does place a burden on the patient, consumer, customer, etc. to "know his number", or "know his code", and this is not desirable in some applications.

## An Exercise in Ordering

If we are given the names of fifty types of flowers, let us consider for a moment how we could arrange them "in order". The following possibilities come to mind:

1. In terms of flower size, from smallest to biggest.
2. In terms of the dates when they normally bloom, in a January to December progression.
3. In terms of the height of the grown plant, from shortest to tallest.
4. In terms of their geographical distribution, beginning with those found in the Pacific Islands, and then moving westward around the globe.
5. In terms of the average density of their root systems, from most dense to least dense.
6. In terms of what entomologists have determined as an order of "taste preference" by honeybees.
7. In terms of their popularity ranking for use in floral arrangements by florists.
8. By assigning each flower a number from one to fifty, based on its age as a species, from oldest to youngest.
9. In terms of a popularity ranking of the sales of their seeds. This information could be determined by conducting a survey of famous plant nurseries and seed mailorder houses.
10. In terms of the weight of the grown plant at the age of one year, from heaviest to lightest.

These are all nice systems for ordering our flower names. If ten average citizens are chosen, and each is given one of these lists (flower names only, no specification as to how the listing is ordered), we may then ask a question: "Determine if the flower edelweiss is on your list, and if so, what is its number?"

Any one of these systems of ordering our data is rational, and hence, one supposes, equally valid. However, to the average citizen, they are by no means equally "workable". One supposes that the holder of each list is generally forced to look at each entry from flower #1 to flower #50 in a sequential fashion to determine whether any particular flower name is actually on his list. If he replies that it is not, and we ask "Are you sure?", his only way of checking is to look at each entry again.

If we increase our number of entries to 100, 500, 1000, or more, the unworkability of these ordering arrangements, in terms of our need to locate the names of particular data entries, increases geometrically.

What we need is a "Primary Ordering System". Hopefully, this ordering system would be well-known to all members of the populace, with one established ranking and minimal ambiguity. Secondary keys, tertiary keys, etc. should be provided so that ordering may still be done where the initial value is the same. Ease and speed of use are necessary considerations. Ideally, there would be a marked preference among the populace for the use of this system in any and all situations.

In English we have such a system, it is called "Alphabetic Ordering". The reader certainly needs no further explanation as to its theoretical structure. If we give eight average Americans a collection of our fifty flower names, and ask each of them to put the names in order, they will of course put them in alphabetic order, and the eight lists will be the same.

The situation using the Chinese language may be different however.

## THE COMMUNICATION PARADOX   (Reference: D5)

A foreigner once expressed some bafflement in regard to his progress in Chinese language studies. He claimed that although he had gotten to the point where he could carry on a pretty good conversation with the Chinese in person, and he could write down the characters he knew when they were given to him by the teacher during a dictation, and copy any sentences he wanted out of the newspaper, nevertheless he was unable to efficiently communicate things over the phone when it came to the matter of leaving a message, or taking a message. Names, places, and street names, hotel names, etc. were all stumbling blocks for him.

Upon discussing this phenomenon with other students of the Chinese language, we found that it was by no means an isolated feeling of frustration. It appeared that everyone had the same complaint--there appeared to be some kind of barrier beyond reading and writing--and before basic communication could take place. In other words, there is a lag between what you can read, what you can write, and what you can communicate to someone who is not standing within close enough range to see you. We have come to term this obstacle as the major "Plateau" to be crossed before true spoken fluency in Chinese can even be evaluated.  It is a barrier that does not exist in English.

What is this barrier? Again it is rooted in the alphabetic vs. character nature of the two languages, and the overwhelming "complexity" (or "depth", depending on your point of view) which this gives to Chinese. In English we may communicate messages to people who are not within our view by spelling out the letters of the words we wish to communicate, and a system may even be easily devised among two individuals to transmit information across large distances, through means of smoke signals, or some similar system to the morse code, etc., where each letter is represented by a symbol or combination of symbols.

Suppose that we have three individuals: the communicator (sender of the message), communicatee (receiver of the message), and an intermediary. We will assume that the communicator is fluent enough in the relevant language to compose his message. We will also assume that the person for whom the message is intended is fluent enough in the language in order to understand it when it has been written down and handed to him. However, in actual daily dealings there is no requirement that the two individuals communicate directly, and in many cases this would not be the case. Either one or both sides may have an assistant or intermediary acting in his behalf. Let us assume one intermediary on the side of the communicatee for this example. What skills does this intermediary need to work with the English language? Knowledge of the alphabet certainly, 26 letters, or 52 letters if both upper and lower case were considered. Does he need to be fluent in English? No, that is not a requirement for him to deal with transcribing the message correctly, and it is possible for him to write down a message which he has received when he has no idea of its meaning.

Chinese, being non-alphabetic, cannot talk about its characters in terms of an alphabet, nor do the radicals have mutually exclusive names by which you could describe the structure of the character by reference to its components. Indeed many of the components are not radicals, and in fact have no commonly agreed upon nomenclature. Let us repeat this—neither the Chinese characters themselves or their structural components have mutually exclusive, definitive names which can be used to specify which one we are talking about in dealing with the oral communication of written data.[1] Therefore what the Chinese tend to do is to talk in terms of similies, metaphors, and other types of comparisons. Unfortunately, this can lead to circuitous discussions indeed. In English, we might try to give similar examples of this methodology by doing the following: Assuming that the word "John" was four Chinese characters, we might communicate this word by noting—

The "J" of Joshua, the Biblical figure who took over leadership of the tribes after Moses. The "O" of Othello, as in Shakespeare's play. The "H" of Henry VIII, who ascended to the throne in 1485. The "N" of the Norman Conquest.

(Note: to make the comparison valid, the Joshua, Othello, Henry VIII, and Norman Conquest should be considered as "multiple character expressions", with which we assume that the other party is familiar, and the "J", "O", "H", "N" repesent the initial character in each expression).

Without any other way to communicate, one might say "Well, it is quite clear to you and me, right?" But consider for a moment what skills a student of the English language needs to to understand this explanation? A thorough knowledge of history, literature, geography, and all the famous places and personages associated with these and many other fields would certainly seem desirable. We assume that he is familiar with all of Shakespeare, and will know which ideograph is in the first position of "Othello". We assume that he is familiar with English history, and will know which ideograph is in the first position of "Norman Conquest", etc., etc. In a nutshell, with no other simple method at hand, in order to understand an explanation of this type, one has to be very fluent in the language.

Of course it is quite possible that someone else might transmit the same information in another way, to wit—

The "J" of Johnson, Andrew, 17th President of the United States and Governor of

---

1. Chinese sounds only have meaning in context, i.e. in combination with a group of other sounds. Clearly this shows that the group mentality is actively alive in the structure of the Chinese language.

Tennessee 1853-57. The "O" of Okeechobee, a lake in central Flordia. The "H" of Halloween, when everyone says Trick or Treat. The "N" of Neanderthal, a type of prehistoric man/ape.

The possibilities are quite numerous, and with 5,000 Chinese ideographs in a common use, and another 10,000 less commonly used, you would not expect that these linguistic allusions have been standardized for the populace in their daily usage. Indeed there is no "Bureau of Speech Comparisons" doing such standardization work.

WHAT'S YOUR NAME? CAN YOU DESCRIBE IT?   (Reference: D5)

Two people met at a party. The first asked the second "What is your name?" After hearing the reply, he was still not sure, so he asked "How do you write it?"

The second man said "Well, I guess I could describe it like this: it has a straight line, then a line sloping down to the right, then another straight line down and connecting at the bottom. Then one vertical line, and another one with a loop from top to middle, and from middle to bottom. Then another vertical line with the same two loops. To the right of that is a vertical line, with horizontal lines stretching out top, bottom, and middle. Then a horizonal line, and another one from the middle down . . . "

The first man said "Oh, I see. Well, thank you." Of course in reality he saw nothing, and was unaware of what the other gentleman was trying to describe to him.

Actually, the second man's surname was NIBBETS. He had not gotten to the S yet, but he had described the writing of the other letters already. This is what we might call a structural description.

Imagine that we had no names for the letters in the alphabet, and could only describe them structurally.It might be a problem for communication, until someone came up with good structural descriptions for all the letters. With a total of 52 elements in upper and lower case, there is an excellent chance that someone could come up with good descriptions for all of them, and then these descriptions could be standardized for use among the populace.

But what if you were dealing with a language that had 5,000 or 10,000 or more elements?

Once at a party, I overheard the following brief conversation, between a foreign man and a Chinese lady, Miss Shr.

"Have you chosen a Chinese name?" Miss Shr asked.

"Yes, I talked to some of my Chinese friends and we came up with Fu Tao Tsung."

"*Bu*? Is that the character for cloth or step?" an American standing nearby inquired.

"No, not *bu*," the original speaker clarified, "*Fu*."

"Oh, I do not know any *fu's* yet," the American said.

Miss Shr smiled. "*Tao Tsung?*" she asked curiously.

"Yes, you know, *tao* like in a big ocean wave, and *tsung* means intelligent."

"Is that the same *tao* that is used for pottery?" the American asked.

"I don't think so, but I don't know that one yet. My *tao* means wave, and it has the water radical."

"Like panning for gold? That is *tao* with a water radical I believe," the American tried to be more specific.

"Sorry, I didn't bring my dictionary."

"No, it is not the same *tao*," Miss Shr clarified. "Which *Fu* are you using for the family name?"

"Well, *Fu* is . . . "

The American concluded that it was unlikely he would learn anything more from this conversation, and wandered off.

"It is the *Fu* in *shr-fu?*", Miss Shr asked.

"Which one is that? Is that the same *Shr* you use?"

"Oh, no, not that one. *Shr-fu* means cook or chef."

"Oh, I haven't learned those yet. It might be that one . . . I am not sure."

"Does it mean to lean upon, or is it the character for buddhism or perhaps plentiful?" Miss Shr queried.

"I don't think so."

"How do you write it?"

"It is hard to describe. Do you know the *bwo* for museum? It looks something like that."

Miss Shr pondered this for a moment.

A South American who was standing nearby interrupted to say "Did you mention the character *tsung* for intelligent? How do you write that one? I always forget."

"On the left it has a . . . er, well, anyway on the right is a . . . ah, . . . but anyway there is a heart character underneath that."

Comments: Why couldn't our foreign friend Fu Tao Tsung give structural descriptions for the writing of the components of the characters in his name? As has been stated before, with over 70% of the components of most characters, there is no commonly recognized nomenclature, and when there is, often as not the monosyllabic names employed refer to many items, they are not unique names. Some of Mr. Fu's acquaintances have attempted to isolate the characters in question by means of comparisons and allusions. This has not proven very successful either, because our foreign friend is only a beginner in his study of the language. This again hints at the difficulty of basic communication in Chinese for all but the very fluent.

## THE INTENDED-MEANING PARADOX  (Reference: D6, D8)

I was having dinner with a friend. She began to eat a piece of fish, and to place the bones from her mouth on the table as is the Chinese fashion. She remarked that the bones seemed big, and I passed this off as simple conversation, whereupon she asked if I knew the Chinese term *she li ju*. I asked if it was some kind of pig, since *ju* is the word for pig. She said no, not that *ju*. Oh, then *ju* as in pillar or column, and she was perhaps referring to some architectural term, I suggested. No, she shook her head sadly, and then took another bite of the fish. Well, of course, I remarked: *ju* is the word for bamboo, and *she li* means to set up or establish, so this is perhaps some method of bamboo cultivation. The reply to this was more head shaking. Oh, I ventured, she must be referring to *ju* meaning cavity or hole, and this was a new dental technique for treating bad teeth. She was looking for a pen by this point, and wrote down *ju* on the edge of a newspaper. I could see it was the character denoting "bead". She added *she li* at the top, and I could see the first of these was the character for "inn", "dormitory", or "resthouse", and the second was the character for "benefit" or "advantage". I was unaware what the three characters could mean when put together.

As it turns out, *she li ju* is a Buddhist term, and refers to the round bead-like bones which are believed to form in the joints of highly practiced Buddhist monks, and which can be found in their cremated remains after death. The greater the number of *she li ju*, the higher was their knowledge of the Buddhist philosophy, so says one popular theory.

It is however in discussing terms in this fashion, that we see an essential problem in dealing with spoken Chinese data. It is a language of homonyms. Added to this is its non-alphabetic nature, which results in the fact that there is no easy relation between the spoken and written forms.

## THE STANDARDIZED TRANSLATION PARADOX   (Reference: D7)

From the earliest days of foreign presence in China, notably among the western missionaries, there has been much attention paid to the transliteration of Chinese sounds into English, i.e. the attempt to spell out Chinese sounds using alphabet letters. Three such systems which come to mind are the Wade-Giles, the Pinyin, and the Yale. Obviously, no such systems are free from fault, and the pronunciation values of each of the letters must be carefully annotated and explained in order for the western student of Chinese to use them with even a modicum of success. However, such efforts do show the orientation of the westerner to research a vast mass of unfamiliar data, organize it, codify it, and to as great as possible an extent to standardize the usage of it. Thus in western scholarly circles as well as the mass media, when Chinese data is mentioned, the author, editor, publisher, etc. generally take pains to consistently use one type of romanization, and clearly note if and where they have made deviation from it.

Yet during this same period of time, hundreds of years, we have yet to see any attempt which has come to fruition by the Chinese officialdom, scholars, or populace in general to set up some sort of standards for the translation of western data into Chinese. Thus when visiting congressmen, senators, or other western government officials visit a Chinese city, one may collect several copies of different Chinese daily papers, and it is not uncommon to find any one foreign official's name (usually only the last name is rendered into Chinese) represented by different Chinese character combinations in the news stories of different newspapers. In fact such inconsistency often occurs in different articles in the same paper on the same day, where the tour schedules, upcoming negotiation sessions, and overall implications of this latest foreign visit are discussed.

Sometimes the original alphabetic spelling of the person's name is given in the article, quite often it is not. For anyone doing research or collecting data, determination of exactly who the article is talking about becomes quite difficult, and translation of the article into a western language can only be done if copies of western-language press releases, newspaper reports, or similar data can be provided in order to determine the proper spelling of the names.

The same problems arise with dealing with "Chinese data", particularly people's names, which arrive in China via the international wire services, news media, or television, and are needed to be translated back into Chinese for use of the local Chinese media. Thus if an airline crash, ship wreckage, or other catastrophe occurs, or a number of overseas Chinese are awarded special honors for their work in some field in a foreign country or otherwise make the news due to their special achievement, problems in dealing with their romanized names which come in over the wire services immediately develop. Granted, Chinese characters each have a one syllable pronunciation, but there is no way to know what Chinese characters are represented by any particular spelling of some Chinese character data in the western press, unless you know someone who knows that person and can tell you exactly which characters they are.

This situation exists for a number of reasons. First, Chinese is a language of homonyms, and any one sound may relate to three, five, ten, or literally dozens of characters. Secondly, in applying for passports and other documents, the Chinese are generally free to spell their name any way they want to, and in the case where they have no opinion, the issuing officer is generally free to do as he sees fit. The phonetic rendering of any character is then also influenced by the local dialect, whether it be Fukienese, Shanghainese, Cantonese, etc., thus leading to different spellings for the same character by people in different parts of the country. There has been little attempt to deal with this problem in a systematic fashion in the past, and we seriously doubt there will be in the future either.[1]

---

1. Another translation problem is revealed in the attitude that Chinese take toward translation of a wide range of foreign novels and other material, which can only be described as "rather haphazard". For example, an English-language novel is divided into five or six sections, given to five or six people, and they translate it into Chinese. Speed is often a primary consideration. Whether it is translated correctly, no one knows, however when talking to many of these "novel translators", or going over various articles in an advanced English Reader with them, and noting their English language ability, I would say it is extremely unlikely. The publisher rarely takes note of this however, he merely puts together the various sections, and publishes the book.

On the other hand, in my rounds of the Chinese newspaper offices I have met a few translators who are highly experienced in doing written work, and whose grasp of the written English material they were working with was absolutely A number 1. It is unfortunate that they are in the minority.

## THE ORDERING PARADOX   Revisited   (Reference: D4)

A secretary in a business office in New York was asked where she placed the papers concerning the contract negotiations with N.A.S.A. for redesign specifications of the Space Shuttle. She replied: "I put them in the files under 'T'."

Her manager was puzzled, and asked: "Why did you put them under 'T'?"

She replied: "Because our last meeting with them was held on a Tuesday."

We laugh at such stories, because the average individual knows that that is not the proper filing procedure. Everyone would seemingly agree that an efficient filing, listing, or cataloging system is extremely helpful when we have to find various items of data.

Yet when dealing with Chinese data, we are not much better than the secretary depicted above, because there is no one widely used, efficient, exact, easily learned, consistent way of ordering Chinese data. Give some Chinese a list (or a collection of 3 x 5 cards) of a hundred names of common fruits, vegetables, spices, and herbs seen in the local Chinese marketplace and ask them to put them in order. To those who even have the ability to map out a strategy and complete the task (many do not), you will generally have as many different lists as you have people composing them.[1]

This is not to say that the people who have spent some time researching the ordering of Chinese data cannot do so. Most Chinese dictionaries require that you look in an index first, whereupon the number of the character you want (as assigned by the editor), or its page number in that volume, is given. You may then look it up in the main part of the dictionary. Chinese telephone books tend to be ordered on stroke counts, and on a sequence of "first stroke orderings" within identical stroke counts. Computerized Chinese character data may be ordered on the "internal number" assigned to each character, however the resulting "order" may mean little to humans.

I received an advertisement for a new Chinese dictionary in the mail the other day, the dictionary contains 9,000 of the most commonly used Chinese characters, and five indexes: 1) radical, 2) Mandarin phonetic symbols, 3) Wade-Giles with accent marks, 4) another type of romanization without accent marks, and 5) a two-corner method.

The fact is that there is a considerable gap in ordering orientation between the Chinese telephone book editor, dictionary compiler, or librarian, and the average secretary, sales girl, herbal medicine promoter, or hardware store manager.

When asking the accounting staff in a Chinese company to put the names on the salary list "in order", one is generally given a blank stare along with the question "What order?"

Therein lies the problem.

## THE COMMUNICATION PARADOX   Revisited   (Reference: D5)

---

1. Suggestions to Foreigners: The message of this section should be quite clear. In dealing with Chinese people using Chinese character data and a manual system, you are going to have to be more patient than you are previously accustomed. Be prepared to fill out a second set of forms if they cannot find the ones you filled out before. Keep smiling.

Without an alphabetic base, and with no mutually independent, unique, commonly known sounds for the parts of the various Chinese characters, communication of character data over the telephone is extremely difficult for the non-fluent speaker and writer. I know of no studies that have been done to determine the amount of characters and character combinations a foreigner needs to know before he can effectively function as a transcriber of written data given to him by a person who is out of his seeing distance, (and hence can only communicate orally), but I would guess that the number is well in excess of 1500. Studies on such a topic in the English language do not need to be done, for the answer is 26 letters, namely those of the alphabet. If capital and lowercase are both included, then 52. At the most we would add some punctuation marks to this – comma, apostrophe, parentheses, quotes, dash, space, period, etc., – and these seem unlikely to exceed ten elements, most of which are used in modern Chinese as well.

As a further extension to this problem, we have the whole issue of how to transcribe the "spoken" sound of Chinese onto the paper in the form of characters. (Reference: D6) Again we know of no research that the Chinese have done into conceptualizing and analyzing the mental flow[1] from "sound" and "meaning" into "written components" and finally into the modern day written form. The foreigner generally attempts to do this as he learns Chinese, and may have some initial success in his first few hundred characters. If he continues on to the 2,000 or 2,500 character level, and beyond, he is often faced with the problem of writing down a character which he can pronounce and use in conversation, but which he has suddenly forgotten how to write. At that point the problems of this mental flow come into play. The word he wants to write down is related to talking, does it perhaps use the "word" radical, or some other radical? How is he to analyze it? The conceptual difficulty of this is that even having learned 1500 characters, he is still unable to determine by his own analysis, logic, or divination how any other new character, given to him at random, would be written.

In English, having learned the exact spelling of 250 words, the student is certainly able to make a pretty good guess at how to write down another one given to him at random, because the system, although not without its faults, is clear, and the challenge is for the student to gain practice in transposing sounds to written words by using different combinations of letters. According to studies we have seen, it is estimated that 83% or more of the words in the English language can be spelled accurately according to spelling rules which are given in the normal course of English language study, and other generalizations which the teacher may point out, or the student notice on his own. In the realm of such rules I include such large categories as all the ideas contained in a good Phonics course, including complete analysis of the short and long vowel values of a,e,i,o,u, as well as the three pronunciations of "y", the generally accurate rules covering soft and hard "c" and "g", as well as such minor points as "f" being also spelled "ph", the silent "k" in words such as knife, know, and knuckle, and the special

---

1. The author has attempted to offer some insight into this problem in a previous essay in this chapter.

pronunciation of the letter combinations "tion" and "sion" at the end of many words, etc., etc.

By way of comparison, the number of even general ideas existing in language textbooks concerning how to transpose Chinese sounds into "characters" written down on the paper could probably be counted on one hand with several fingers left over. Our Chinese teachers will tell us that all characters with the metal radical have some relations to metal, but as we happen across many things in our daily lives that are made of metal, we see from our Chinese studies that they do not have the metal radical.[1] Why is this? Where is the analysis? Our teachers say: Memorize it and then you will know. "What happens if I forget?" asks the interested foreigner. The Chinese reply is "Then you didn't memorize it very well did you?"

Chart 9-1

## COMPARISON CHART
### Written Language Components

Considering an important function of language, which is to serve as a basis for (1) WRITTEN COMMUNICATION, or (2) ACCURATE ORAL TRANSMISSION OF INFORMATION where the receiver must keep a record

|  | English | Chinese |
|---|---|---|
| total number of possible separate components in the whole of the written language | 26 pairs (Upper & lowercase letters) | unknown, certainly over 300 |
| number of distinct pronunciations of the components (as in spelling them out, one by one) | 26, thus 100% of the total | unknown, probably less than 150, thus 50% of the total |
| ways in which the components are combined to form words or characters | one, i.e. left to right | unknown, probably more than five, anything goes |
| Possibility of transmitting a word (character) only by reference to the word's components and how they are written (no metaphors or comparisons with other combinations) | very high, possibly 97% (some allowance for bad pronunciation, static in transmission, etc.) | low, probably below 22%, all factors considered |

1. Examples are: electric wire, tea kettle, knife, water faucet, kitchen sink, signboard frame(s), various types of handles, knobs, lids, etc.

## Chinese Language and the Westerner

A number of years ago a certain USA West Coast University organized a "Semester in Singapore" program for their students to live and study in the Lion City. This was in the days before the Singapore government had formally adopted English language instruction in the schools, and so there was still considerable Chinese influence in the educational system. Nevertheless, while Malay, Indonesian, Tamil, and Tagalog were offered as possible elective courses in language study, Chinese was not. In the program catalog, the reason given was "The western student cannot learn any useful amount of Chinese in three or four months."

Of course one supposes that the statements in this program catalog do not qualify as the final word on the subject, nevertheless they are useful for reference. Indeed, we still frequently see newly organized study tours to China, where the students are given the opportunity to live and study in the country for a semester, or perhaps two. Realistically speaking, such a short term study of the Chinese language will not yield the westerner with any degree of competency in Spoken, Listening, Reading, and Written (SLRW) skills. Its value would lie primarily in serving as a wonderful foundation on which to do further language study, either in one's home country, or in China.

In speaking of the tendency among westerners to underestimate the seriousness of the problems involved in tackling the study of Chinese, we are reminded of the story of an East Coast tour group visiting a nuclear power plant some distance from Reno, Nevada. At one point during their visit to the Main Control room there was a noticeable vibration, and several members of the tour group asked if there was any danger. One of the officials shook his head, but then glancing at the dials and reconsidering the situation, said: "Well, I suppose there is some chance of a meltdown, perhaps everyone should step back."

"How far should we step back?" the tour leader inquired.

The men in the control room conferred for a few moments, and gave a confident reply: "The Fiji Islands should do it."

Thus, what appeared to the experts and other knowledgeable individuals as a reasonable estimation of the seriousness of the problems at hand, was regarded by the newcomers with incredulousness, shock, and incomprehension. Quite frankly, I believe this is the same situation that occurs when unknowing westerners are apprised of the necessary effort required to gain fluency in Chinese SLRW skills.

### Beginning on the Chinese Language Journey

Some would advance the proposition that after a semester or two of Chinese study, the westerner would at least have grasped the basic structural basis of the language, and have most of the basic orientations, thus being at the least "able to grasp the extent of the difficulties before him". This statement, our study group concludes, is unfortunately invalid. The real difficulties of the Chinese language do not present themselves until one reaches the 1500 character level and beyond. Even assuming complete mastery of 15 characters per week, which is a "back-breaking pace" for most westerners, the 1500 character level represents two years of full time study, (assuming a "perfect" review system). Only at this point we believe does the western cranium begin to see the true nature of the difficulties which must be surmounted. There is little comfort to be gained from the recognition that another 2000 or 3000 characters lie between this level, and the fluency necessary for dealing with a wide variety of newspaper and magazine articles, reports, novels, and other Chinese data with which the average Chinese person is in contact every day.

Since reading and writing of the Chinese characters is difficult, many westerners, including some of the professors in charge of Chinese language training programs in US, Canadian, and European universities, have adopted a restricted approach, at least for the first eight months to a year of study. This approach confines itself to speaking and listening skills exclusively, thus keeping the development of reading and writing skills temporarily in limbo. This I believe violates the first Chinese language study orientation, which I would formulate as follows.

## CHINESE LANGUAGE STUDY ORIENTATION, RULE 1
The characters do not get any easier just because you put off studying them.

In a similar category to those who initially adopt the "speaking and listening" approach deliberately, are those who end up adopting this approach over the long run, thus letting reading and writing skills fall by the wayside. In terms of a goal of fluency, such a restricted methodology does suggest resignation, and is perhaps an admission of defeat before the battle has even begun.

Adopting a purely speaking and listening approach, some foreigners can communicate adequately in an oral fashion on a number of everyday topics after a six months of serious study in China. These are the individuals who are actively striving to immerse themselves in the Chinese environment, cultivating many Chinese friends, and avoiding speaking their native language whenever possible. For the person who spends most of his time with other expatriates, six months could yield very little in the way of results.

## Difficulties of Dealing With Chinese Information

An outline of various basic orientations in regard to the difficulty of dealing with Chinese data may be of value to all people interested in cross-cultural communication, the search for a "world language", as well as to students of the language itself, and is presented herewith. Ten aspects have been outlined; some of them may overlap to some extent. Others could no doubt be formulated. Many of these aspects have been treated in more depth earlier in this Chapter; this is designed to be a final summation. These comments have all been gathered from westerners who have studied Chinese for between seven and sixteen years.

Although the tone of these remarks may seem a bit negative, this is not our study group's intention. We are not attempting to deal with the issue of whether the Chinese language is an excellent means of communication among Chinese native speakers. That is something most properly discussed among the Chinese themselves. What we are dealing with here is consideration of the difficulty of "non-native speakers using the Chinese language." Our point of reference of course tends to be what we feel is an objective one for the basis of comparison, namely the comparative difficulty of "non-native speakers using the English language."

Natives vs. Non-Natives

In any culture, it is important to remember that the child grows up fluent in his own language. At every stage in the child's development, he/she is fluent, although different ranges of vocabulary and forms of expression are of course the norm for different age groups. For the foreigner who arrives on the scene, "fluency" is a goal.

Let us assume that on the average, the child of 10 years old has already attained 80% to 90% of the fluency in basic grammatical structures, pronunciation, voice inflection, and basic vocabulary which he needs to communicate in a simple understandable fashion in his own language. We may compare this to the building of a mosaic one hundred feet high, and ten feet wide. The native child builds from level zero, effectively filling each foot of space before preceding on to the next. Hence each piece of the mosaic is connected or linked to others. The foreigner who comes for language study however fills in his "mosaic" in a disjointed and sporadic fashion, yet this is perfectly natural. He may learn the word for "chemistry" before he learns how to say "palm of the hand", "belly button", or "wrist". He may learn technical legal, medical, psychological, etc. terminology before he becomes acquainted with the names of all the common foods sold in the marketplace, or the descriptions of common cooking methods. He may be unacquainted with many children's stories, mythological tales, popular folklore, or historical incidents. This is certainly not the case with the native speaker.

As a result, the foreigner's language knowledge can be expected to be rather poorly linked together. As we will see in much of the following commentary however, in order to communicate Chinese data in an oral or written fashion, a high degree of linkage is required.

Difficulties for non-native speakers in using the Chinese language are due to —

**D1) The lack of a "starting point" for reading signs, posters, announcements, etc.**

We may refer to the following diagram, where each star represents a Chinese character.

```
          * * * * *
          * * * * *
          * * * * *
          * * * * *
          * * * * *
```

To the western student of Chinese who sees this sign posted, before he can attempt to "read" it, he must determine a starting point. There is no rule to this, hence the sign could be read in any of the following ways: (We will retain a star to designate the first character to be read, and use arrows to denote the direction of reading.)

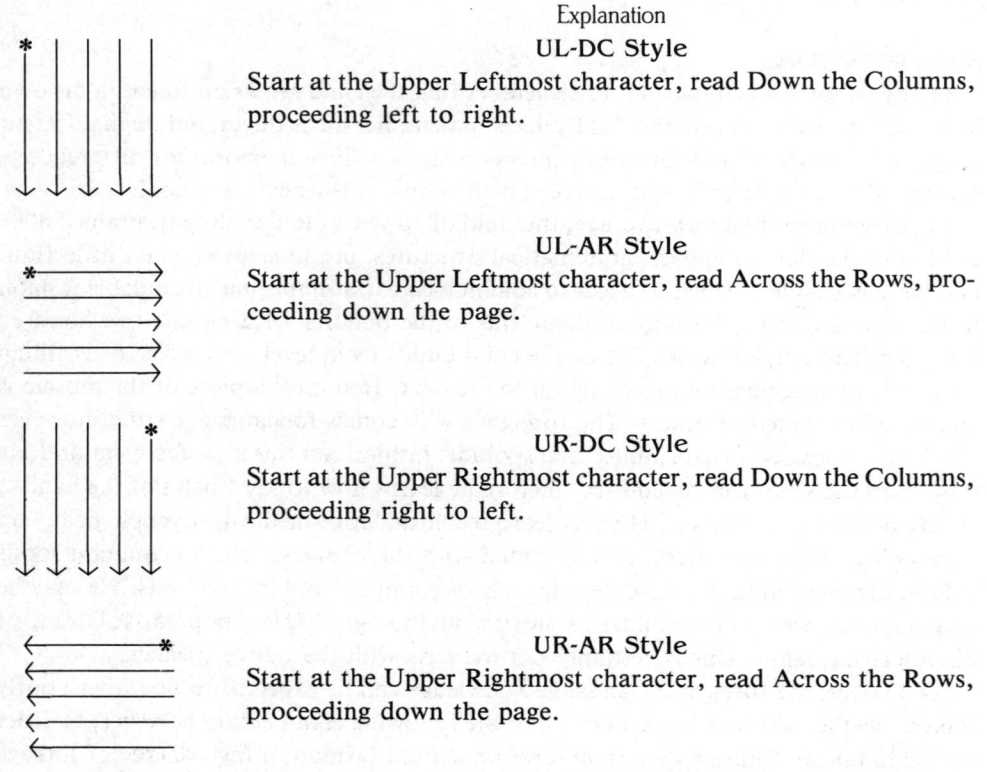

Explanation
### UL-DC Style
Start at the Upper Leftmost character, read Down the Columns, proceeding left to right.

### UL-AR Style
Start at the Upper Leftmost character, read Across the Rows, proceeding down the page.

### UR-DC Style
Start at the Upper Rightmost character, read Down the Columns, proceeding right to left.

### UR-AR Style
Start at the Upper Rightmost character, read Across the Rows, proceeding down the page.

Observation: To the Chinese, who are fluent in their own language, or who have someone nearby at all times who is fluent, we are told that this does not present a problem. The westerner's feeling can perhaps best be summarized by the incident involving a three-year student of Chinese, a fellow from Los Angeles (a town of freeways and innumerable roadsigns), who was riding in a tour bus on the highway in one Chinese province. Asked to decipher the various signs posted by the side of the highway, he continually failed. Later, commenting to his Chinese teacher, he said: "By the time I had begun to see which way a sign should be read, we were already past it." The other westerners in the group were heard to comment: "It is a good thing he wasn't driving."

By comparison, this type of difficulty is unknown in any alphabetic language, and one style, be it UL-AR (as in English, French, Spanish, German, etc.) or UR-AR (as in Arabic) is standard in 99.9% of all reading material.

MENU SELECTIONS
in various restaurants

鍋火大肉鹿
吃三烤魚活
湯飩餛州溫
辣不甜式日
淋淇冰奶牛

什 糖
錦 醋
炒 排
飯 骨

海 鮮
山 產
牛 肉
土 雞

UR-AR style  UR-DC style  UL-AR style

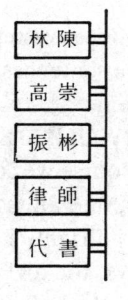

林 陳
高 崇
振 彬
律 師
代 書

These five plaques were seen on the side of a building. The top three plaques are UL-DC, and the bottom two plaques are UL-AR. This is the office of two lawyers.

P 794183207
易美鐘

This is the name and number on a child's school uniform. The top line is read left to right, however whether the bottom line is left to right, or right to left, is anyone's guess.

Figure 9-1

易不・賊防門名珍貴先祖保
德缺・賣盜財貪物古化文偷
→ UR-AR style

應有使用對策  新式食品包裝
← UR-DC style

西德商業產品大展
本省百貨公會協辦
UL-AR style

Three styles on the same page of a newspaper.

**D2) The lack of initial-letter capitalization or other indication of proper nouns, place names, brand names, etc., and lack of spacing between words.**

One student of my acquaintance made the following comparison of how a westerner might view the layout of Chinese data on a page, by taking some sample sentences out of an beginning English reader, and placing them in more of a Chinese mode, to wit:

THISISABANANAANDTHISISACOOKIE.IMADETHEMBOTHMYSELFANDIHOPEYOULIKETHEM.

This layout corresponds to the UL-AR Style as outlined above, but of course we could just as easily have written these sentences in one of the other three styles, and all would be equally valid. Some beginning students are inclined to say "That is alright, I will get used to it." However, as the complexity of the reading material grows, the difficulty of dealing with this type of arrangement increases geometrically, as the following example will serve to illustrate.

ASENIORMINISTERINSINGAPOREPRIMEMINISTERLEEKUANYEW'SGOVERNMENTCOMMITTEDS
UICIDEAFTERPOLICEBEGANINVESTIGATINGHIMFORALLEGEDINFLUENCEPEDDLING.THEMINISTE
ROFNATIONALDEVELOPMENT,TEHCHEANGWAN,DIEDDECEMBER14THFROMANOVERDOSEOFTHEBARBI
TURATEAMYTAL,ACORONER'SCOURTWASTOLDTUESDAY.MAGISTRATELIMKENGSIONGRETURNEDAVE
RDICTOFSUICIDE.AUTHORITIESARECONTINUINGTHEIRINVESTIGATIONINTOTHISSTRANGECASE

Some would say this is "Go with the flow" taken to the extreme.

Observation: To the Chinese, who are fluent in their own language, or who have someone nearby at all times who is fluent, we are told that this does not present a problem. To the westerner with meager Chinese language ability, even the attempt to use the dictionary is thwarted since he is unable to determine which characters go together (to form combinations), and where place names, people names, and other proper nouns leave off, and where other ordinary nouns, adjectives, verbs, and adjectives begin. (In beginning Chinese reading texts, proper nouns are underlined, or perhaps in quotes, but they are not "in the real world", i.e. in the regular magazines and newspapers sold to the populace.)

For those westerners who like to experiment, some articles out of intermediate English language textbooks may be typed-up in this fashion, and presented to one's native Chinese friends, acquaintances, and students for practice reading. The reactions obtained may then form the basis for an interesting discussion.

By comparison, this type of difficulty is unknown in any Roman-alphabetic language. Spacing between words and established rules for capitalization facilitate the identification of place names, people's names, titles, chemical terms, and other proper nouns, enabling us to separate these items from the run-of-the-mill nouns, adjectives, adverbs, verbs, prepositions, etc., and allow us to recognize where one word leaves off and the next one begins.

**D3) A conceptually difficult and non-exact method for finding characters in the dictionary.**

The standard method for locating any character in the Chinese dictionary is by means of its radical, of which there are approximately 214, and thus we may say that the standard Chinese dictionary tends to be separated in 214 uneven sections. Each dictionary includes a radical index, and often a pronunciation index (or indexes), a stroke-count index, a four corner index, etc. The user of the volume must find the character he wants in an index first, and then look it up according to its page number or other reference number. For the foreign student who is unaware of the pronunciation of most of the characters he looks up, the radical index is most commonly employed. We may find a multitude of characters we do not know in the newspapers or other books, however when we go to look them up we are confounded by the fact that there is no precise system for exactly determining the radical of any character, and therefore it must be guessed. Although a wealth of experience in using this formulation is quite valuable in aiding one's guess, even a lifetime of experience does not enable the average Chinese to determine the radicals with 100% unfailing accuracy. If we fail to find a character listed under the first radical we have guessed, then we must guess a second, a third, and on and on.

The stroke-count index is often used by the foreign students of Chinese as well. However, the counting of the strokes of many of the more elaborate characters is not an easy task, and even many Chinese are heard to say "I think it is eighteen, or perhaps nineteen." Within the characters of the same stroke count, the secondary ordering system tends to be haphazard. In short, the goal of preciseness is not achieved with this method either.

In recognizing these facts, the beginning of most Chinese dictionaries includes a listing of "Characters Difficult to Locate", (CDL), and it is not uncommon to find over 1400 characters listed therein, with their exact radicals specified, so that the user may find them.

Observation: After several years of research, we fail to find a similar CDL listing in the dictionary of any other Asian or world language. Noting this situation, one linguist of international standing was heard to comment "If the editors still need to put a 'List of Words Difficult to Locate' in the beginning of the dictionary, they must be poor editors." Many foreigners have suggested certain cross-indexing schemes which would solve this problem, however the Chinese dictionary editors appear content with their traditional editing policy.

By comparison, this type of difficulty is unknown in any alphabetic language. Considering that an English dictionary is divided into 26 sections, a Chinese student who has studied English for only six months or less, when seeing any English word, can determine with 100% unfailing accuracy in which section it will be found. Given another word of the same initial letter, he is also immediately able to determine if this word lies before or after his target word in the dictionary.

**D4) The lack of one primary, standardized, uniform, and commonly-accepted system for ordering Chinese data.**

There are more than five commonly-used systems for ordering Chinese characters in dictionaries and other scholarly works, none of which is totally free from ambiguity. Moreover, all of these are quite tedious, and far more difficult to use than the simple alphabetic arrangement to which most westerners are accustomed. Often times, when listing a few hundred items of data, the Chinese tend to do it randomly, simply because there is no one handy standardized system.

Observation: This type of problem is not easily solved. In many Chinese scholarly texts which deal with western data, or which are geared toward a western audience, the index provided may be based on alphabetic ordering of the English pronunciation of the initial Chinese character. This represents still another ordering system (not included in the "five" mentioned above), probably not practical out of scholarly circles, or among those who are very fluent in romanization and/or English. It is not a system that is widely used among the native Chinese themselves, no doubt because it is simply "not Chinese".

Computerized Methods: When we use a computer and run under the Chinese mode, it is essentially similar to dealing with a giant graphics program. As such, in terms of handling a database, when we want to order our data we cannot index on stroke counts, radicals, corners, Mandarin phonetic symbols, one of the romanization systems, etc., because such systems are not inherent in the Chinese character (graphic) data. In our character database, these items would have to be established as separate fields, and keyed-in manually.

The "internal number"[a] assigned to every Chinese character in the typical Chinese computer program is not standardized, and several versions circulate in the marketplace. One main cause of this, we suppose, is that there is no agreement in Chinese scholarly circles on the exact number of characters in the language. To our knowledge, there is

a. 內碼

no definitive study on this issue.

By comparison, this type of "ordering" difficulty is unknown in any alphabetic language. When using alphabetic data in a computer, the ordering of every letter, number, or symbol on the keyboard has been universally standardized according to the ASCII code (American Standard Code for Information Interchange). The number of characters (letters) in the language has been completely standardized for over 100 years.

**D5) The lack of precise nomenclature or systematic descriptive structure for transmitting Chinese character data through oral communication.**

Observation: Given present Chinese habits of speech in this regard, and the preference for simile, metaphor, and allusion, this would be an extremely difficult problem to overcome. It makes dealing with character data extremely difficult for any but the very fluent foreigners, and certainly far more difficult than an alphabetic system where all the elements are specified and uniquely named.

The problem is easily illustrated if we pick a paragraph of text out of the Chinese newspaper, and ask a Chinese to communicate this orally to a foreigner who has been studying the language for one or two years, and who is out of his line of sight. For experimentation purposes, we may even place both of these people together in the same room, separated perhaps by a simple room-divider or screen. Success in such an undertaking is rare.

It is perhaps redundant to state that this type of difficulty is unknown in any alphabetic language, nevertheless it is true. In a "worst case situation" the transmitter of a message in English (or another romanized language) merely spells out the data letter by letter, and the receiver may then transcribe it.

**D6) The lack of any easy relation between the spoken and written forms.** We might say this is an additional consideration to item #D5 above. Knowing the exact pronunciation of Chinese data is often of little help in getting a detailed message across.

This is illustrated by the situation of a foreigner named Jack Robertson who met a Chinese at a party. The Chinese introduced himself as Cheng Jyr-yuan. They had a delightful discussion. Mr. Cheng said that he had forgotten to bring a namecard, but said that his phone number was listed under his name. He mentioned that his office was in such and such a building, and he welcomed Jack to come visit him sometime.

A few days later Jack wanted to get in touch with Mr. Cheng. He called Directory Assistance, and asked for the number of Cheng Jyr-yuan. The operator asked: "Which *cheng*? Which *jyr*? Which *yuan*?"

Jack had been studying Chinese for two years, but he could only reply "I don't know."

"What are the tones?" the Chinese operator queried, trying to be helpful.

"I am not sure," Jack stated. His inquiry with Directory Assistance ended on this note.

Chinese is a language of homophones, monosyllables, and of tones. In order to even begin a search for a character, as with Directory Information, (1st) you must know the tone. To non-native speakers, this is a big problem. However, even a perfect grasp of the tone is not enough, (2nd) you must know the exact character used in order to convey your request to someone like the Operator, as in this case.[1] And yet, (3rd) "passive knowledge" of the exact character in question is not enough. For example, given any particular character, you have perhaps seen it written down or printed in a textbook, you may even remember it, you could jot it down to show to someone else, etc., however this type of knowledge of the character is still passive, and not enough to facilitate message transmission. You must be actively able to talk about it, to discuss its use in combination with other characters (in relation to historical places and personages in many cases), to compare its structure to other characters, etc. For the less than totally fluent foreigner, this is often a highly difficult task.

Observation: Communication in any alphabetic language is vastly simplified by use of the letters of the alphabet, all of which are uniquely named. Any student with adequate training in Phonics can make a guess at the spelling of a word he hears, and there is no need to differentiate tones.

**D7) The lack of any rules for translating foreign brand names, people's names, and other terminology into and out of the language.**

Observation: Even such world figures as Ronald Reagan, Jimmy Carter, and Woodrow Wilson find their names rendered into Chinese differently in different provinces, due to the vagaries of local pronunciation, as local editors and other translators try to render what they feel is an appropriate transliteration, i.e. one that bears a similar sound to the original, while at the same time having a favorable connotation. Of course, for personages of this stature, present or later readers of news reports can probably guess at who is being talked about, but for the multitude of minor officials in foreign governments who visit China, or foreign scholars, businessmen, athletes, etc. who come, or

---

1. Suggestions to Foreigners: We use the telephone frequently in our daily lives. However, do not expect that flawless pronunciation will be your trump card in transmitting Chinese information with the use of this device. Additionally, you may have the diligence necessary to memorize all the strokes that compose each character your teacher has taught you, to the point of getting 100% on all your dictation exercises, and being declared brilliant. However do not be so bold as to expect that this diligence and brilliance will transfer over to ease of communication with the telephone, if you have specific Chinese names, places, references, etc. that need to be communicated. That is another level of skills entirely, something which is gained from vast experience, and is not covered in the Chinese language textbooks.

If you are telephoning a home or other location where the telephone is answered by a young child, or other individual of limited schooling (grandmother, grandfather, etc. in many instances), do not expect that you will be able to leave a message with much accuracy, regardless of the urgency of your plight. Even under ordinary circumstances, where the other party has a full grasp of the written language, it is a good idea to adopt the group approach, and have one or more Chinese people handy to explain, rexplain, compare, and recompare those points of your Chinese dialogue or message to which the other side is rather unclear, or very confused. This will probably be true whether you have been in China for one year or twenty. Be patient and keep smiling.

otherwise find themselves being reported about in the Chinese press, a determination of the "spelling" of their name from reference to the Chinese data is totally impossible. The Chinese media's habit of generally only transliterating the last name of these foreign personages into Chinese assures that there will be much ambiguity between persons of similar sounding surnames, such as Mr. Harvey Meenes, Mr. Oliver Means, and Mr. Rhodesia Meinnes, or such figures as Theodore Roosevelt and Franklin Roosevelt. When rendered into Chinese, even such names as Churchill and Thatcher often sound nearly the same.

In regard to the cross-cultural "correspondence" of various data, the foreigner should be aware that given the English name of a Chinese company, there is no handy way to determine the Chinese name, unless one consults some sort of trade directory. The romanized names of hotels, restaurants, clubs, etc. may be at a wide variance with their Chinese names; indeed there is no required correlation. Some people would say that there is a certain degree of freedom in such arrangements, and we do not deny this. However, we often regret the lack of any system to transfer romanized data accurately into and out of Chinese when any reporter, scholar, diplomat, or other person specifically desires to do so.

**D8) The lack of independent pronunciation.** No doubt 95% of individual Chinese characters cannot be understood when spoken individually, even by fluent native speakers. They must be spoken of in context to achieve any meaning. The chemical elements are good examples of this. Any random words such as argon, aluminum, helium, hydrogen, plutonium, potassium, tin, titanium, uranium, xenon, zinc, zirconium, etc. cannot be understood, even if perfectly enunciated. Their written form must be described, they must be spoken of in some sort of context, or other explanation must be offered before the meaning is clear. An an example, the pronunciation for hydrogen, *ching*, is also the pronunciation for seven other characters in common use, ranging in meaning from frog, clear, nobleman, all the way to mackerel. If the tone is not clearly communicated, another fourteen meanings, of other characters pronounced *ching*, could be arguably added to this listing. The situation for most other single characters is equally ambiguous.

Observation: Homonyms in English are fairly limited, and this type of problem rarely comes up. In 95% of all cases, English words have a pronunciation by which the meaning is understood when a word is spoken independently, or individually, with the correct pronunciation.

**D9) The widespread belief among the populace that "Words have magical powers."** This is in violation of a basic rule of Semantics. The Chinese tend to be very superstituous about the use of the various characters, and much related consideration goes into the choice of a child's or company's name, including examination of the tonal combination and stroke count, to determine whether it is "auspicious" or not. Many Chinese fortune tellers base their predictions on analysis of the characters in one's name, native locality, or favorite slogan. The continued promulgation of this custom hardly seems praiseworthy, and certainly is at odds with a rational methodology, as well as unnecessarily complicating many otherwise simple matters. However, the intricateness, artfulness, and inherent complexity of the characters themselves tend to promote these types of investigations, extrapolations, and long drawn-out etymological divinations in all quarters.

Observation: The rather simple and unexciting nature of English word formation has largely caused this type of ancient superstition to die out in the west.

**D10) The extreme difficulty of mechanizing the use of the language in a wide variety of daily activities, resulting in the need to deal with much handwritten data, which is difficult to read.** The Guinness Book lists the Chinese typewriter as "the world's slowest". Due to the extreme complexity of the language, as characterized by the cataloged listing of nearly 15,000 characters in daily use by organizations that maintain Chinese mailing lists, the average Chinese citizen deals with most daily activities in the same fashion that his ancestors did 500 years ago: writing by hand. College reports, essays, and other student submissions are still primarily submitted handwritten, as are entries in literature or essay contests. Extremely rare is the Chinese household that has a typewriter, unless the family is engaged in the printing and typing business. Indeed, it is generally quicker for the average Chinese person to write out documents by hand than to type them, even if he has been trained in the necessary typing skills, and/or has access to a computerized Chinese word processor.

Observation: The use of the English language is highly mechanized, and a large portion of the populace possesses typing skills. Documents, reports, essays, etc. written out in longhand are not generally preferred, because of the difficulty of reading many people's handwriting. The use of typewriters in communication adds much clarity and exactness for all concerned, both for native and non-native speakers.

Interestingly, the foreigner who admires the beauty of the complex calligraphic scrolls in libraries, museums, schools, and other localities, praises the depth of this art, even as he strives to comprehend it. The foreigner who works in a Chinese organization and is forced to deal with hastily hand-written Chinese memos,documents,interdepartmental correspondence, proposed advertising copy, and other data, frequently complains of the incomprehensibilty of so much of this written material, as he struggles to decipher it. This certainly represents a PC Paradox in the realm of Chinese language study.

## CHINESE LANGUAGE STUDY ORIENTATION, RULE 2

The vocabulary needed to read the newspaper is vastly more than that needed to converse effectively.

## CHINESE LANGUAGE STUDY ORIENTATION, RULE 3

Just because the Chinese say that their language is easy for them, does not mean it will be easy for the foreigner.

Actually, many experienced westerners have commented that the Chinese language is not "easy" even for the Chinese people. Considering that they have the social and household environment to hear the language used in a natural fashion since childhood, "speaking" of course comes naturally. Yet in terms of mastering the written form, it is no exaggeration to say they easily spend two to three times more effort in learning the characters than the westerner does in his home environment learning the written form of his native tongue. This is reflected by the fact that it is normal for the Chinese children at all grade levels to have substantial homework assignments over summer vacations, and to report back to school once a month or more to verify their progress. Other vacations often see the students being assigned significant amounts of homework as well.

For the Chinese who study English, some ability in composition and letter writing is normally expected to be achieved. For the foreigners who study Chinese, it is comparatively rare that they learn to write in the language fluently, and it is highly infrequent that instruction in Chinese essay writing for foreigners is part of any language school's regular curriculum, although of course such topics may be studied in an individual class (one teacher, one student). Certainly this is due in a large part to the difficulty of mastering the characters.

Westerners have often been heard to complain that Chinese Characters are unscientific. Debate on this subject still rages, however if asked to produce five considerations in support of this contention, we would point to aspects D1, D3, D4, D5, and D7 outlined above. In addition, the following aspects D11 — D13 are worthy of mention.

**D11) The inability or, at best, comparative difficulty of contracting or condensing much common terminology.** In a conference, report, or other data given in English, we may refer to Gross National Product one time, and later simply refer to it as GNP. Newly Industrialized Countries may be referred to once, and then called NICs. The Board of Investment quickly becomes the BOI, the World Health Organization becomes the WHO, and American Automobile Association is quickly shortened to AAA. Tuberculosis is TB, Electrocardiogram is EKG, and Cardio-Pulmonary Resuscitation is CPR. Among professionals in many different fields, there is much use of this type of shortened terminology, and much paper, ink, and time is saved in this manner. In chemical formulations, its use is especially widespread, as when potassium carbonate becomes $K_2CO_3$. In dealing with a wide variety of data, Chinese lacks this type of condensibility, and this certainly appears a drawback for advocating its use in scientific or technological endeavors.

**D12) The lack of easily formed opposites.** In English, many useful technical, scientific, or even political and economic terms have easily formed opposites with the addition of the prefix "di" or "de", such as oxidization, deoxidization; magnetize, demagnetize; aquify, deaquify; control, decontrol; mobilize, demobilize; glaciation, deglaciation; inflation, deflation; investment, divestment; regulate, deregulate; centralize, decentralize; flower, deflower. In Hegel's philosophy we find references to alienation and dealienation. In English history we find mention of kings and queens, as well as use of the people's mandate "to throne" and "to dethrone". The linguistic capability to form and use such opposites can often facilitate much communication.

> People ask you for criticism, but they only want praise.
>
> ———— *William Somerset Maugham*

My American friend once visited a Chinese shipyard, and noted that the gauge of steel being used on the construction of the hull of a new vessel was incorrect. As the reader may be aware, when touring or doing on-site inspections with the Chinese, one is invariably told "Please give us all your comments and suggestions", and when the Head of the shipyard came out with this phrase, my friend suggested that if the vessel were expected to prove seaworthy, the correct procedure was not to rivet, but to derivet; not to weld, but to deweld; not to continue, but to stop.

After this was laboriously explained, the Chinese foremen conferred for several minutes, thanked him for his comments, and went on with their work. They claimed that they had been given orders to use the remaining steel in the warehouse before ordering more, of a greater thickness, from the national steel corporation.

Of course we suspect that such failure to communicate is based more on authoritarian organizational structure than language difficulties per se. Nevertheless, the lack of simple and quickly formed positive/negative terminology is often a real hurdle for language students and translators working between Chinese and English in a variety of situations.

This is true even in the simplest cases, for example consider the city of Anadyr on the Bering Sea in western USSR near the Artic Circle, which is seeking to attract investment through its Anadyrian Industrial Development Service, (unfortunately afflicted with the acronym of "AIDS".) When the Service gives a presentation in Anadyr, the first statement is "Welcome to Anadyr!", which the MC can learn how to say directly in Chinese to visiting tourist and trade groups, in order to break the ice. When the Service gives a presentation in China, the first statement is "Welcome from Anadyr!". This is not an easy opposite to the first phrase, and becomes much more lengthy when rendered into Chinese, hence we doubt the Anadyrian MC can master it. (Chinese is not a language that can be picked up just by doing diligent repetition of various phrases, for without the proper tones, it is just gibberish.)

**D13) The lack of a "leading expert" mentality or "authoritative reference work" mentality.** It is not uncommon to meet a Chinese parent who expresses difficulty with keeping up with the Chinese teaching which their children are being taught in school, especially as regards how the characters should be written, or which ones should be used in which combinations. Since the total range of components of which all Chinese characters are formed has never been accurately put down, and the structure of each character has never been specifically put down in terms of these components, so there is room for quite extensive debate on whether "this stroke should just touch this line here, or should go through it slightly, or go through it more significantly." English alphabet letters are far too simple to give an illustration of this, since none have a stroke-count exceeding four, whereas the stroke-counts in Chinese characters may exceed 20. However, perhaps we could compare this to a discussion of the correct length of the middle bar on a capital H. Should this extend through the right side vertical stroke, or just touch it? What about on the left side?

In English, if such a conflict arises, in regard to the hand-printed style anyway, reference to a child's copybook seems to solve the problem to the satisfaction of all parties. In Chinese, due to its extreme complexity, and lack of defined parameters, no such simple solution is attained, and no matter what evidence the student or the student's parents care to proffer, including copybooks, dictionaries, usage manuals, etc., the teacher is free to deny their validity, claiming that his/her version is the correct one, because "I say so." There is no final authority on the matter to be found in the bookstore or library, so much discussion may ensue unless the Ministry of Education has made a recent pronouncement on the character in question. In line with Confucius's doctrine of "Respect your Teachers", the dispute is usually settled in favor of the teacher.

This puts the student, or younger members of society in general, (or foreigners with advanced Chinese skills in particular) without any absolute and irrefutable knowledge about the use of the language, so that they can, or could, stand up and say "No, this is the correct usage (or form) in this instance, and I have proof of my convictions," since no absolute proof can be obtained. A stack of newspaper clippings discussing the usage in question, plus corroborations from several dictionaries are all rather futile when up against a teacher, editor, or elder who has another opinion.

The existence of this type of situation appears at odds with any sort of exacting or scientific approach to linguistic study, usage, or development.

Suggestions to Foreigners who have been studying Chinese for five years or less: *Keep working.*

# PART 4  Bases for Action and Non-Action

## Chapter 10  Opposing Explanations & Varying Worldviews

### The Five Relationships Model

From ancient times, the Chinese have tended to view all human relationships as falling into five categories. This is called the *wu lwun* [a], and is succinctly outlined in the *Book of Mencius*, Chapter 3A [b]. The five relationships are:
1. Between sovereign and subject
2. Between father and son
3. Between husband and wife
4. Between brothers
5. Between friends

From the Chinese point of view, this is a complete formulation of all relationships between all people in the society. In our discussion here we will call these "The Five Relationships", and any one of them as "A Relationship". Differentiated from this, and written in the lower case, "relationship" will be used more generally to mean: a **connection by blood or marriage, kinship.** More narrowly, also written in the lower case, "relations" is used to mean: **non-kinship connections, the connections between or among persons in business or private affairs, and many types of public dealings.**[1]

Building Family Ties

Obviously, any man and woman who marry can initiate the production of a vast number of descendants over the generations. All of these descendants are related to each other, and all of them fall into the scope of The Five Relationships, since they exist as recognized patterns of interaction in the family/clan.

Thus, in order for the westerner to understand The Five Relationships formulation more clearly, it must be recognized that there are many relationships which are implied

---

a. 伍倫    b. 藤文公上

1. Unfortunately it is not always possible to draw a strict line of demarcation between usage of the terms "relationship" and "relation". This is especially true when we consider that the 5th Relationship is more properly viewed as a mere relation, according to the definitions we have advanced here.

but not specifically listed. These generally fall into major and minor categories. In general, relationships with females (except in the case of a wife) are considered minor; relationships between males are considered major.

We will distinguish these as follows.

**Major Auxiliary Relationships:** These are subsidiary to the main relationship, and assist it. The degree of bond could vary. Without the main relationship they would not exist. If the main relationship ceases, this relationship could rise to prominence in the lives of the individuals concerned. Abbreviated "Major AR".

**Minor Corollary Relationships:** These are variations on the main relationship, and follow its pattern, but are considered of minor importance. Normally they would have a much lower degree of bond, especially in a Pre Industrial Revolution agricultural society of very limited geographic mobility. They could exist without the main relationship, but are not viewed as highly significant. Abbreviated "Minor CR".

By viewing the entire scope of this Five Relationships model, and the Chinese understanding of it, we can gain some valuable insight into Chinese thinking. Let us consider further examples of "relationships" which appear at first glance to be absent from the five, and see how in fact they are inherent in this formulation. (The relationship type is distinguished in parentheses, as a Major AR or a Minor CR to one of the Five Relationships.)

It is hoped that by considering all these examples the reader may be able to extrapolate how the Chinese would view other relations and relationships in society.

Examples
*Kinship Relationships*
**Major Auxiliary Relationships:**
  A. Uncle and nephew. (Major AR to 2).
  B. Grandfather and Grandson. (Major AR to 2).
  C. Mother and son. (Major AR to 2).

**Minor Corollary Relationships:**
  D. Between sisters. (Minor CR to 4). Girls [are considered to] marry-out of the household, (hence marrying-into the household of their husbands). In the old society sons who married brought their wives home with them and all lived together in one large family, often with several generations together. Entire communities of patrilineal relations would be formed in this manner.
  E. Between brothers and sisters. (Minor CR to 4).
  F. Mother and daughter. (Minor CR to 2). In traditional thinking, raising a daughter is doing the work of someone else, (since the family into which she marries will receive the benefit). Accumulating the required dowry monies for marriage has always been regarded as a money-losing proposition.
  G. Father and daughter. (Minor CR to 2).

H. Aunt and niece. (Minor CR to 2).
I. Uncle and Aunt. (Minor CR to 4).

Others:
J. Adults of the opposite sex. (5) or potentially (3). In the old society, polygamous marriages were common, and much influence of this traditional behavior still affects thinking today, if only subconsciously. Much reportage in newspapers and magazines in the present era discusses the issue of a husband stepping-out on his wife, and this is known as *wai yu* [a].
K. Fiance and fiancee. A potential (3).

### Divine Relations
L. Man and God. ( — ). This is missing, however one supposes that Christian missionaries might want to redefine (1) to include the idea of "sovereign on high" and "subjects on the earth". Many Christians believe that a more proper application of "filial piety" would be to extend this devotion back to God as the source of all life.

Many Chinese may view this as a (2), and in fact many local gods are regarded in this manner. The relationship between man and ancestors is also viewed as (2).

In the dynastic eras, the Emperor was called *tian tse* [b] "son of heaven" and was viewed as something of a god. This appeared to take the place of a relationship with any other sort of "god".

Outside of kinship relationships, there are also many relations which are not listed, but they are often equated with one of the existing five.

### Non-Kinship Relations
In the following examples, some of the relations (a) normally occur in the course of our lives in society, or else (b) are the result of an active effort by one or more parties to initiate.

In this latter instance, it would be expected that the Chinese person who needed to establish this type of relation (for assistance in some matter[1]) would prefer **a)** to deal with a member of his family/clan first. If no qualified person was available, then he might **b)** look and inquire among his own friends and acquaintances. It would also be common to **c)** ask the relatives to recommend one of their friends, and this individual would be considered as a (5). All of these types of relations fall within the known patterns. If it was still not possible to locate the necessary person in this fashion, we are in the situation of *"Being Without a suitable person in the Five Relationships structure for the establishment of this relation"*, which we will abbreviate as BW. The following

---

a. 外遇    b. 天子

1. Even in terms of hiring a person for a position in a company.

ways of categorizing or dealing with these relations would then most likely apply.
M. Between doctor and patient. BW, try to establish (5).
N. Between farmers. BW, try to establish (5).
O. Between head official (of Department, Ministry, etc.) and subordinates. (1).
P. Between teacher and student. (2). We note the existence of a Chinese phrase "Teacher for one day, Father for life."[a]
Q. Between shopkeeper and customer. BW, try to establish (5).
R. Between shopkeepers. BW, try to establish (5).
S. Between company head and employees. (2) or maybe (1).
T. Between scholars. BW, try to establish (5).
U. Between section chief and employees. (2) or maybe (5).
V. Between government and citizens. (2) or sometimes (1). We note that a traditional appellation for County Magistrate was "parental official"[b], and policemen are often called "Baby Tenders for the Society"[c]. In the fashion of a father who forbids his children to read certain types of books, magazines, etc., the government feels justified in many types of censorship.
W. Between artisans. BW, try to establish (5).
X. Between students or classmates. (4) or (5). We note that the Chinese use terms such as "younger sister classmate"[d], "elder sister classmate"[e], "younger brother classmate"[f], "elder brother classmate"[g], etc.
Y. Between members of a business association. (5).
Z. Between military officers and soldiers. (1) or (2).

Obviously, without a relationship that can be equated to Relationships (1), (2), (3), or (4), the tendency is to build "Close Personal Relations"[h] (which we have abbreviated previously in the text as C.P.R.), in an attempt to achieve Relationship (5). Certainly in Chinese banking circles we often hear that bank officers are more amenable to loan money to friends, relatives, and other members of society recommended by any of these people, than to unknown outsiders. Reviewing the Chinese philosophical basis for such preferences, their existence should come as no surprise to us.

a. 一日爲師終生爲父  b. 父母官  c. 社會的褓母  d. 學妹  e. 學姊  f. 學弟
g. 學長  h. 關係

### Behavior

Ten types of behavior can be delineated.

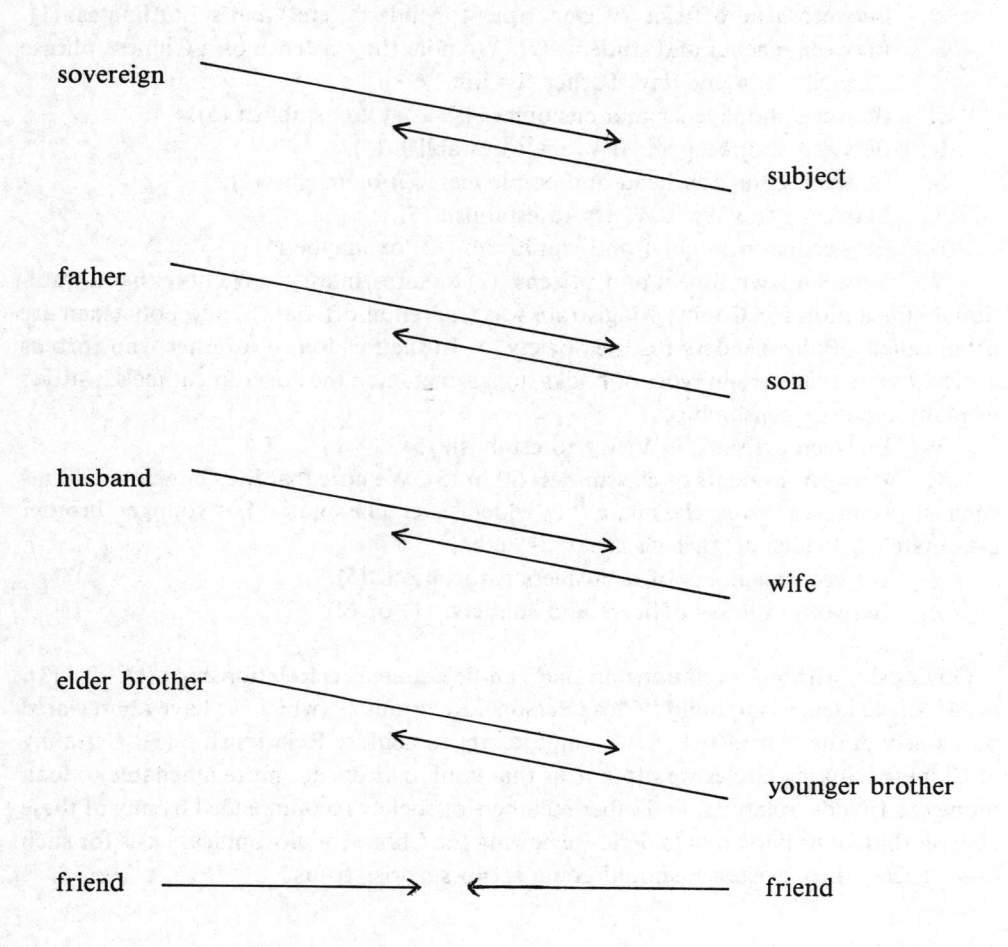

sovereign ⟷ subject

father ⟷ son

husband ⟷ wife

elder brother ⟷ younger brother

friend → ← friend

Notice that for the first Four Relationships, they are typically hierarchical and are represented on the horizontal plane. However we do not speak of a vertical relationship in either direction (up or down). Hence a Chinese person feels comfortable behaving differently depending on which role he is fulfilling at the moment.

Each arrow indicates a type of behavior, which gives a total of ten types. Of course, there could be many hundreds or more styles of each type of behavior, however they still fall within the established patterns of interaction, as delineated by the Five Relationships model.

## Stories

Let us consider the following stories which appeal to different types of humanitarian and moral motives, or represent a type of altruistic heroism.

A) A passenger on a late night train to a large metropolis sees a fire break out in a small village, and jumps out to warn the residents of the impending confligration, breaking his arm in the process.

B) Due to heavy rains, a reservoir has risen to the danger level. Telephone lines are out, and the guard on duty rides his bicycle through the storm to tell the people in a nearby village of the danger. The people begin to leave, but the guard is swept away by the flood when he goes to tell some neighboring homes in a small valley.

C) Two teenage girls, serving as assistants to the local fire department, notice that a farmer near a highway is burning much trash, and that the smoke is billowing over the highway. As they walk near, they hear the sound of a collision, and then another, and another. One girl sees some water nearby and starts to put out the fire, while the other runs onto the highway waving her arms, to warn oncoming traffic that there is a chain collision ahead. When a large truck stops too late and runs over her, she is crushed, but dies with the satisfaction of having done her duty.

D) A boy participates in a complicated ritual and wilderness chase as part of the procedure for initiation into a college club. During these activities he has a fall, sustains serious injuries, and dies. His mother spends the next three years writing letters to local and national senators, congressmen, and other elected officials, and finally succeeds in having a national law enacted forbidding such initiation ceremonies in college clubs.

E) A husband is conscripted into the Army, and sent to a distant region. He writes letters back for three years, but then no more is heard. Army records list him as missing. His wife remains celibate until her death 46 years later.

F) A high government official supports the ruler's innocence in an influence-peddling racket which comes to light.[1]

G) An engineer gives up his plans to purchase a new house when his former high school teacher is injured in a car accident, and contributes the money to the teacher's health care.

H) An elderly mother refuses to take the pills which the doctor prescribes for her liver ailment, and prefers a more traditional remedy of herbs and a special kind of vegetable, which must be freshly brewed every day. Her eldest son gives up his successful business in a distant city and returns home to take care of her. He sells all of nis worldly possessions to buy the rare herbs which she feels are most appropriate for her illness.

Certainly stories E), F), G), and H) have traditionally received the most praise from the Chinese populace, and indeed stories of this nature have found their way into popular literature, plays, movies, school textbooks, scholarly treatises, etc. Stories A), B), C),

---

1. This is certainly related to the Chinese concept of 官官自衛 "officials protect one another."

and D) are much more uncommon in China, and when they do occur they do not receive near the amount of praise as the other four.

Why is this? Clearly E), F), G), and H) fall within the framework of the Five Relationships model, and A), B), C), and D) do not. In order to widely recognize the true laudability of the former four, there would have to be a widespread recognition of "a Sixth Relationship" in Chinese philosophy. This relationship model problem is discussed more thoroughly in the **Sympathy** essay, where we examine the 6th and 7th relationships, however for now it is adequate for us to recognize that as a general rule, the Chinese sense of altruism in a group context must be understood in Chinese terms, and not in western ones.

The following two versions of a traffic situation provide a further illustration of this.

**The Situation:** A car and a pedestrian nearly collide in the crosswalk near the corner of a major road in a Chinese city. Both the driver and the pedestrian are Chinese. The pedestrian is walking "with the light", and has the right of way.

*Version 1.*
Chinese Pedestrian: (Startled) Why don't you watch where you are going?
Chinese Driver: Why don't you make way, I am in a hurry.
Chinese Pedestrian: I am walking in the crosswalk.
Chinese Driver : Then you should move quickly so as not to hinder traffic.
An argument ensues.

*Version 2.*
Chinese Pedestrian: (Startled) Why don't you watch where you are going?
Chinese Driver: Why don't you make way, I am in a hurry.
Chinese Pedestrian: Excuse me, what is your surname?
Chinese Driver: My surname is Chou.
Chinese Pedestrian: My surname is Chou, too. Please be on your way now. You go first. (He gestures and bows.)
Chinese Driver: No, you go first. (He gestures and bows.)
The pedestrian walks across the street and nods back to the driver, who smiles warmly and then drives off.

The situation is the same, but the handling of it is different. With the lack of a 6th Relationship, the result in Version 1 is an argument. In Version 2, the men are found to have some degree of blood ties, and this is construed as falling within the Five Relationships model. They treat each other as brothers, and harmony is maintained. The same result would be obtained if the two recognized that they were of a former employer-employee relation, teacher-student relation, neighbors (friends), etc. All of these fall within the Five Relationships, upon which the Chinese mentality is organized.

Natural Disasters

Of course it is true that in China we often see collections of money taken up for victims of floods, earthquakes, typhoons, and other natural disasters, and all people far and wide are asked to contribute. To many observers this appears to indicate the emerging of a 6th Relationship. However, when pausing to think for a moment we can see that this type of "one-shot treatment" actually denies the 6th Relationship. Why? There is essentially no government body (or none with adequate funding) established to deal with these natural disasters as there are in most western countries, and no social insurance schemes have developed over the centuries, so the populace is urged to "be sympathetic" and "give generously" to make up for this lack.

The words of Arthur H. Smith, written in the 1890's, showed a similar story:

> When a vast calamity occurs, like the great famine, or the outburst of the Yellow River, the government, local or general, often comes to the front with the greater or less degree of promptness, and attempts to help the victims. But instead of doing this on any uniform and extensive scale, such as the perpetual recurrence of the necessity might seem to suggest, it is done in a makeshift way, as if the occasion had never before arisen and might never arise again.

Clearly what is needed to deal with all these types of natural disasters is long term planning, systematic action, established government procedures, disaster relief insurance, etc. and yet these have yet to be formulated.

Ramifications of the Five Relationships model

1. Relationships are not viewed as equal, they are hierarchical. **In the family:** there is much stress on titles and forms of address in the family and clan structure. As examples of this there are four different expressions for "uncle", differentating between whether he is the father or mother's older or younger brother. Aunt is similarly differentiated. Further distinctions are made by adding a numerical designation, such as "third eldest paternal uncle", "second youngest maternal aunt", and indeed these people are generally addressed in this fashion, as opposed to calling them by their first names: Uncle Hsiao-ting, Aunt Mei-ling.

**In society:** Chinese are very much aware of, and sensitive to, their position in a hierarchy, i.e. to "context". Chinese feel "you must fit the role", hence there is much of what the westerner might see as "stereotyping" — if you are a professor "you must act and dress like one"; if you are a government official "you must act and dress like one", etc.; if you are of marriageable age "you must get married",[1] etc., and this of course dovetails very nicely with Chinese group mentality norms.

Westerners do not "act the role", and this often confuses Orientals.

2. The traditional way of teaching most trades, crafts, and other skills has been through the master and apprentice system. The master takes care of the apprentice like a son.

---

1. Much stress is placed on the Third Relationship, and many social commentators have argued that the viability of "the single lifestyle" is not recognized in the Five Relationships model. Indeed all observers have reported that in Chinese society "there is much social pressure to get married."

The apprentice is obedient and unquestioning.

3. Company officers and subordinates tend to have relations that continue even after the employees have left the company. A similar situation often exists between teachers and students after the students have left the school, etc.

4. Relations between many local gods and the people are viewed as being of the "father-son" type, hence in keeping with the traditional Chinese notions of being thankful and obedient to parents, there is a feeling of mutuality: You do something for me, so I do something for you in return. For example, if a person beseeches a local god to grant the birth of a male child, and a male child is born, this person will normally contribute a sum of money to the local temple in thankfulness, or sponsor the showing of a play, opera, or movie at the temple, "to thank the god" for the wish that was granted.

This mutual aspect is carried over to relations between people in society, hence social interaction is viewed as a two-way street. Chinese people treat others generously not only from the motivation of "gaining face", but also in the expectation that they will be treated generously in return. Such "investment" in building personal relations, with some expected "payoff date" far in the future, (which will yield direct or indirect benefits to the giver and/or his group), is considered good strategy for life.

5. A high integration between business affairs and personal affairs appears to be a direct outgrowth of the Five Relationships model. Note examples Q, R, W, and Y in the Non-Kinship Relations discussed above. Contrastingly, the westerner tends to view business affairs and personal affairs as separate.

Other Considerations and Conclusions

1. The husband and wife are viewed as a unit. Hence, in Asian politics, in the leadership of civic organizations, etc. if the husband dies, or is otherwise put out of the picture, the wife often steps in to take over, (without consideration of her ability to do the job, or fill the office, in question.) In western society this is extremely rare.

2. Asian soldiers are loyal to their general, as opposed to being loyal to their government in some abstract sense. If the government authorities discharge the general from his duties (for failure to obey the instructions of the government, or for corruption, etc.), it would be expected that he would take most of the soldiers with him, thus resulting in a "power conflict" in the nation.

3. Because of this classical five-tiered formulation, Chinese have traditionally viewed personal relationships as more fundamental and important than abstract doctrines. They are more unquestioning, unanalytical, and hence generally disinclined to argue or debate different (or even opposing) ideas when such ideas are presented. This gives foreigners the initial impression that Chinese are very tolerant, and willing to temper "traditional views" on many issues. The Chinese value the appearance of tolerance, especially when it contributes to harmonious human relations, even if the harmony is only superficial or temporary, or is achieved through actions which are not thorough and complete, but only indicative of "tokenism".

4. Chinese principles are human-relations based, western principles are more likely to be abstract-doctrine based.[1] Chinese could sacrifice the determination of right and wrong 1) when discussing the questionably graded items on a child's test paper, 2) when considering the legality of burning paper-money inside an apartment building, 3) when dealing with the violation of health and safety standards by local factories, etc. In each of these types of cases, and many others, Chinese people generally prefer to preserve harmonious relationships with the people involved. A westerner would more likely feel that the relationship with any of these people should be secondary to a determination of right vs. wrong, legal vs. illegal, compliance or non-compliance with relevant codes, etc.

**Example:** In discussing the interaction between a child and a teacher, the Chinese generally see the human relations as more important over the long run, as opposed to arguing about the correctness of grammar, phonetic analysis, etc., on a particular examination, or the validity of particular testing formulations in general. Taking more of a concrete, personal view, a Chinese might ask himself "What does it get me if I argue and I have the testing procedures (or other procedures, regulations, etc.) changed? If I can get more favorable treatment for me (and my clan), or have the rules bent in our favor, or get some sympathetic treatment this once, that is enough."

In order to recognize the importance of striving to achieve benefits for all members of the society, over the long-term, it would be necessary to have some regard for the needs and interests of strangers. However, the 6th Relationship does not exist.[2]

5. Westerners can argue about a point of law, strategy, planning, ethics, propriety, etc., or an abstract or hypothetical idea, without taking it personally, as an affront, insult, or loss of face. Chinese, both ordinary citizens and government officials, tend to take it personally.

## Sympathy: A Primer

It is necessary for the western reading audience that we explain in more detail exactly what is meant by the Chinese sense of a Primary Sympathetic Orientation. This is a particularly important item outside the realm of topics covered in most sociological,

---

1. Abstract: 1) thought of apart from any particular instances or material objects; not concrete. 2) expressing a quality which is thought to be apart from any particular or material object; as *correctness* is an abstract word.
   Doctrine: 1) something taught, teachings. 2) tenet or tenets. 3) belief or precept.
   Abstraction [in the study of philosophy] is defined as the act of forming general ideas or universals. The attention to "abstractions" in western thinking certainly goes back to the writings of Plato (428–347 BC), and his development of the Theory of Forms. He conceived universals as eternal forms that are more real than the transient particulars of sense experience. This school of thought was further developed by Aristotle, John Locke, David Hume, John Stuart Mill, and many others.
2. Such an analysis also shows why the Chinese tend to lack "a crusade mentality".

psychological, or anthropological studies. However it is a announced fact of which every Chinese is cognizant: the Chinese are a sympathetic race.

Let us look first at the following basic definitions.

Sympathy: 1. sameness of feeling; affinity between persons or of one person for another. 2. an action or response arising from this. 3. agreement in qualities; harmony; accord. 4. a mutual liking or understanding arising from sameness of feeling. 5. the entering into or ability to enter into another person's mental state, felings, emotions, etc.; especially, pity or compassion for another's trouble, suffering, etc.

Sympathetic: 1. of, expressing, resulting from, feeling, or showing sympathy; sympathizing. 2. sharing or understanding the feeling or ideas of another.

It is important that we outline various usages of "Sympathy" in the English language which are not relevant to our discussion here as well.

========== **Sympathetic, Sympathize, Sympathy** ==========
Sentences and Senses

Not Relevant to our discussion of "Chinese Sympathy" are the following usages of the term
*Sentence Example*                                     *(synonym in parentheses)*

The staff of that company works best in a sympathetic atmosphere. (harmonious)

He is sympathetic to the project.                                    (approves of)

His parents do not sympathize with his ambition to be an astrobiologist.
                                                                    (not approve of)

The sympathy between the brothers was so great that they always laughed or cried at the same things.            (mutual feeling, ability to understand each other)

He is a man of wide sympathies.                              (interests, compassions)

[physics] sympathetic vibrations
[physiology] sympathetic disorder in the body
[anatomy] sympathetic nervous system
[ophthalmology] sympathetic ophthalmia

=========================================

The Chinese term we are dealing with here, 人情 *ren ching*, some people would no doubt take exception to translating as "Sympathy", saying that a better translation would be "sentiment". "Sympathy" is closer to 同情 *tong ching*. It is therefore relevant that we consider the following definitions as well.

Sentiment: 1. a complex combination of feelings and opinions as a basis for action or judgment; general emotionalized attitude. 2. a thought, opinion, judgment, or attitude, usually a result of deliberation but often colored with emotion. 3. sensibility; delicacy of feeling; susceptibility to feeling or to emotional appeal; tendency to be influenced by emotions, not reason.

Sentimental: 1. having or showing tenderness, emotion, delicate feeling, etc. 2. affectedly or superficially emotional; pretending but lacking true depth of feeling. 3. influenced more by emotion than reason; acting from feeling rather than from practical and utilitarian motives; moved by emotional factors.

It is necessary to be aware of the fact that the "Sympathy" we are speaking of when we introduce the term Primary Sympathetic Orientation contains the idea of "sentiment". The major drawback in changing our terminology to read Primary Sentimentalistic Orientation is the overwhelming overtone of "nostalgic feeling" which this latter term suggests to the western ear, and which serves to confuse the issue at hand. (The Chinese do entertain strong nostalgic feelings about the past, but that is not our concern at the present moment.)

=============== **Sentiment** ================

I am unaware of his sentiments on racial discrimination in Nigeria.

There was much protectionist sentiment in Congress when it reconvened.

=================================================

These usages of the term sentiment(s) appear to correspond to our Sentiment definition, #2. As such they are of borderline relevance to our present discussion.

Having decided on our choice of terms, we may note several characteristics about the Chinese sense of Sympathy:

**Direction** — the following are stressed

A) "forgiveness" (different in some important ways from the traditional Christian conception)

B) giving aid and assistance to others

C) helping others to obtain an opportunity (putting yourself in someone else's debt)

**Quality** — the following are important aspects

D) In an accident, Sympathy is generally extended to the underdog, regardless of who is at fault. Refer to our discussion of the "Ability to Pay Perception of Liability." In a disagreement, or in regard to a change in original terms and conditions, etc., Sympathy is generally given to the party whom the group feels is at an economic disadvantage, and all the Chinese conceptions of fair pricing, Agricultural Society Reward/Effort Relationship, saving face, etc. apply. Considerations of objective right and wrong are often ignored.

E) Sympathy is generally limited to the traditional Chinese philosophy framework, especially the Five Relationships model. In practical usage, the application of item C above is especially pronounced in helping others who are from one's home (or ancestral) area, who have the same surname or are otherwise related, who went to the same school, who are co-workers, friends, etc. All of these people are seen as part of one's own group, thus the clear preference is to "help one's own people first".

F) Sympathy is considered outside of, or superceding, relevant regulations, contracts, promises, etc. all of which are seen as part of "law", or a legal orientation. Contractual obligation is often ignored, or severely downplayed.

All of these considerations are clearly related to the cornerstone Confucian doctrine of benevolence 仁 .

## Laws are Not Always Fair

Due to the influence of China's long autocratic history, there is a general feeling among the populace that "Laws are without Sympathy." It would be far less common for westerners, having several hundred years of democratic tradition behind them, to make such a statement, or have such a feeling. To a great measure this is due to five aspects of law in the west: 1) Democratically established, 2) Consistently and uniformly enforced, 3) Mutually compatible and non-contradictory, 4) Existing within the framework of an independent judiciary, and with enforcement separated from the day-to-day influence of other governmental bodies or officials, 5) Reflective of the general moral code in the society. To the extent that any of these conditions are not met, the populace (of any country) will no doubt fail to feel that "Laws are fair".

\* The reason for laws failing to be democratically established is the presence of largely authoritarian rule.

\* Failure to enforce laws consistently and uniformly[1] is, at the most basic level, due to inadequate allocation of manpower in the enforcement agencies, although it is complicated by the existence of corruption among the bureaucrats therein, as well as the presence of many privileged and powerful people in society who can exert control over (or swap favors with) officials in the relevant agencies. The Chinese tendency to deal with violations of administrative law only upon complaint, as opposed to taking a more

---

1. It should be noted that it cannot be said that "Since we do not enforce the law, so having it on the books makes no difference." Such a statement (1) ignores the basic purpose of law which is to serve as a guideline for human activity, (2) destroys respect for law, since the law is not held to have power or influence, (3) confuses the public, since they do not know which laws are in effect and which are not, and (4) leaves this law subject to selective enforcement by the government.

The only correct course of action is to repeal the law if the enforcement agency cannot, or will not, enforce it consistently.

In addition to laws, the regulations of any government body upon the citizens should be viewed in a similar light: enforce them or repeal them.

Contradictory Regulations
Licensing Requirements

A restaurant is located is the first floor of a building, and rents its location. It desires to register as a licensed restaurant and therefore applies with the Muncipial Government's Bureau of Public Works, which is divided into a number of departments, two of which are the Department of Building Administration (DBA) and the Department of Land Use (DLS), and with the Bureau of Sanitation and The Tax Department, the four regulatory agencies involved. The DBA says that according to the regulations, the 1st or 2nd floors of a building in a residential area may be used to open a restaurant or shop. The DLS says that according to regulations, no business establishment of any kind may be registered in a residential area. Further inquiry with the personnel in these departments by the restaurant owner Mr. Wu yields the result "That is your problem, you may sort it out as best you can." Each department maintains that its statement of the regulations is "the correct one". The Bureau of Sanitation says that the owner must accompany his application with the approval of the DBA and the DLS. (See our previous comments on "departmentalism.")

The Chinese restaurant owner invariably thinks that "arguing" with these departments will have no good result, and only wastes his own time. If he were to instigate legal action, this would cause much bad feeling in the officials involved, and even if he won, they would certainly give him a hard time in the future.

Furthermore, even if this case were decided in his favor, that is meaningless for the next person who applies, since it will be said that Mr. Wu was a special case, and other cases are different. So the majority of people, if they really desire approval, will try to find someone in the department who is a former classmate, or former schoolmate, or neighbour, or friend of a relative, or born and raised in the same province, etc., and try to convince him/her to have sympathy on his case. This often works, but of course has no effect on clearing up the contradiction in the regulations.

active role in supervision, inspection, regular issuance of violation notices, etc., also insures that enforcement will be spotty. (Please refer back to our **Law, Ethics, and Business Philosophy** essay in Chapter 4, and to the **Basic Organization of Chinese-style Continental Law System** comments in this Chapter.) Of course, if the compelled observance of some laws results in circumstances which violate the moral code of the society, high efficiency in enforcement will probably not be a very high-priority goal of those in power, and this observation is certainly relevant to legal goings-on in China in the current era.

Notable is that in *Ideas and Opinions*, Albert Einstein said "Nothing is more destructive of respect for the government and the law of the land than passing laws which cannot be enforced."

* For laws to be mutually compatible and non-contradictory often requires much coordination between the relevant government bureaus, especially in the initial consensus-taking, conceptualization, and actual wording of the statute, and later in its periodic amendment in light of new conditions. However some governments are well-known for their lack of coordination between departments and bureaus, and the resulting collec-

tion of contradictory statutes on the books is enough to confuse the most conscientious citizen. Such contradictions also allow the relevant departments to dole out Sympathy to those whom they see fit, usually meaning to those with the best connections or largest expression of "appreciation," monetary or otherwise.

A Chinese expression says that "If you eat food of another your mouth will be soft, if you receive things from another your hands will be soft."[a] The implication here is that when a person (Mr. A), perhaps an official, has benefitted from the hospitality or largess of someone else (Mr. B), he will tend to speak of Mr. B warmly and pleasantly, and to treat Mr. B in a gentle, mild, agreeable, and sympathetic manner, and certainly not "attack him", or cause trouble for him. Hence, accounts of important officials granting exceptions to friends and other special people are often heard, and this of course reflects the reality that the enforcement of many laws is being stymied, and that detours are being taken.

* The lack of an independent judiciary is suspect in any country that forbids the formation of new political parties, is without a multiple political-party government structure, and which has essentially no balanced multiple party participation in elections. Pluralistic politics have of course never flourished in Chinese history.[1] What the future holds is an open question.

In terms of how one becomes a judge, it is generally necessary to pass a series of tests, and there is certainly always a quota of "available openings" in any particular year, which will theoretically go to the highest scoring applicants. However, some countries may adopt multiple-tiered judgeship qualifying procedures. For example, a double-tiered scoring procedure may be used whereby present (perhaps on the verge of retirement) or former military officers (of known loyalty) are given bonus points and thus consistently have higher scores. This may be complemented by a double-tiered selection procedure where some high percentage (perhaps over 90%) of the quota of available judgeship openings are, by statute, to be given to the highest scoring present or former military officers, with the remaining percentage open to all others of a qualifying score. This would tend to assure that the vast majority of judges are loyal to their superiors in the other branches of the government, and would cast doubt on their independence, especially in a one-party government structure.

* The 20th century Chinese legal system was originally fashioned after the German model, and has continued to be influenced by Post Industrial Revolution western legal systems over the decades. However, a great deal of the Chinese citizenry's thinking (in-

---

a. 吃人家的嘴軟，拿人家的手軟

1. Even in the Chinese high schools, colleges, and universities, students may take time off to participate in assemblies, rallies, marches, parades, etc. of the party-in-power, (and indeed are often encouraged to do so). This is excused as a public absence 公假 , but participation in any other competing political party activities is strictly forbidden. Chinese school campuses also have a Party Office 黨部 to coordinate the party-in-power's activities, and representative offices of competing political parties are banned from the campuses.

cluding moral thinking) has remained in the Pre Industrial Revolution subsistence agricultural society mode, and has not adapted itself to Post Industrial Revolution society. Hence there is a legal/moral gap, in that enforcement of the law in many situations (as illustrated with various cases in this volume) is viewed as immoral by the citizenry. Often we see that the Chinese feel that enforcement of the law should capitulate to (i.e., be Sympathetic to) "poverty", for example: illegal factories should not be closed because the employees have no other way to make a living and support their families, hence they will starve, and to allow them to starve is immoral[1].

When laws are not reflective of the general moral code in the society, there will exist a legal/moral gap: this gap reflects a difference of opinion in what the legal code stipulates and what the populace feels is correct. Two types of contradictory situations are 1) Where the legal determination returns a "not guilty" verdict for the actions of a particular person, the populace view this person as "guilty." 2) Where the the legal determination returns a "guilty" verdict for the actions of a particular person, the public opinion favors a "not guilty" verdict. If there is an abundance of such contradictory situations in the society, we describe the legal/moral gap as large, if there are very few we describe the legal/moral gap as small.

Consider one driver proceeding up a superhighway entrance ramp who hits a second vehicle which has turned around and is going the wrong way down the ramp. When this accident results in the second driver's serious injury or death, the law returns a verdict of "not guilty" for the actions of the first driver, whereas the moral code of the Chinese society generally returns a verdict of "guilty," and the victim's family would then demand compensation.[2] The first driver might be heard to exclaim: "I obey the law, but I am not protected by the law."[3] Hence, the legal/moral gap clearly serves to destroy respect for law in the society.

---

1. In speaking of the law capitulating to poverty, the reason often given is that if such factories, street stalls, hawkers, etc. are closed, or put out of business, many or most of the unemployed workers will (either individually or in bands) engage in robbing, stealing, or other nefarious activities. It is interesting to note that since many third world governments have little or no unemployment benefits, welfare programs, etc., so the issue of starvation is a very real concern for people suddenly put out of work. The well-intentioned analysis to the effect that "It is the job of the enforcement agencies to enforce the law, not to give sympathy. If the citizens affected have other problems of a social welfare nature, they should apply to the relevant government agency . . . " etc. is seemingly worth very little, because apparently everyone knows that there is no relevant agency with which to apply.

However, to reiterate what Albert Einstein said: "Nothing is more destructive of respect for the government and the law of the land than passing laws which cannot be enforced."

2. Refer to our discussion of liability in Chapter 5.

3. This is certainly a problem for most Asian citizens and organizations, since they tend to be undercapitalized and often carry no insurance, preferring to be "self-insured". They commonly have no insurance agent, lawyer, financial advisor, etc. to help them sort out such problems.

## A Fair Standard

Further difficulties in the Chinese person's ability to accept "Rule by law" as a fair standard arise when we consider differing ways of dealing with constitutional rights. In the United States, the formal written constitution is interpreted and enforced by the federal judiciary, and ultimately by the Supreme Court. Citizens who feel their rights have been violated by some regulations, legislation, school rules, etc., may take their cases through the different levels of local, state, and national courts, and the Supreme Court is the last court of appeal. Many citizens have been known to file such suits, and those cases which actually reach the Supreme Court are frequently reported in the press. Hundreds of legislative actions have been declared unconstitutional in the last 75 years.

However, if a Chinese citizen felt that his constitutional rights had been violated by some regulations, legislation, etc., to which he was required to conform, he might first file a complaint or administrative appeal with the different levels of superior agencies (of the relevant bureau, department, ministry, etc.) in the government. These superior agencies could often yield little remedy, since the officials could maintain that his failure to conform to regulations "violated the regulations." If indeed no satisfaction was obtained in this manner, he might file a suit in the administrative law courts. Further application could then be made to the Constitutional Court, or Council of Grand Justices. However, for a suit of this nature to be entertained at this high level, where the attorneys argue in behalf of a private client that a particular regulation is unconstitutional, is extremely rare[1], and for this private client to win such a case is even more rare. Hence, it is difficult to find even a few Chinese legislative actions which have been declared unconstitutional in the last 75 years[2].

In the Anglo-American legal system, a parent who thought his child's rights (in regard to clothing requirements, hair style, participation in school activities, etc.) had been violated by various school regulations could take the school to court. In the Continental legal system used in China, such an action would not fall under the jurisdiction of the Civil Law Courts, nor would it fall under the jurisdiction of the Criminal Law Courts[3]. It would apparently only fall under the jurisdiction of the Ministry of Education, and its superior agency the Executive Yuan, which could choose to offer no comment, or "not entertain", the matter[4].

---

1. Government Ministries, Bureaus, etc. are much more commonly able to apply to the Chinese Constitutional Court, or Council of Grand Justices, as court of last appeal; individuals vastly less so.
2. Some Chinese legal scholars have pointed to this fact, in comparison with the United States Supreme Court figures, as justification for claiming that the Chinese legislative bodies do a much better job in interpreting the Chinese Constitution than the US legislative bodies do in interpreting the US Constitution. Western legal scholars have suggested other explanations for this "discrepancy" however.
3. It is possible that if a teacher took students on an outing and some accident occurred, the parents might file civil, criminal, and even administrative actions.
4. Another technique often seen is that the relevant government body says that it neither has nor knows of any such regulation, and/or that is not authorized to deal in such matters. This is called "kicking the ball."

Hence for the average citizen, China has little effective judicial review of legislative or executive actions which could return a verdict of "unconstitutional," and therefore render them null and void. Chinese citizens are guaranteed certain rights by their constitution(s), but to the extent that laws are passed or official procedures instituted (often stipulated to be "temporary measures") that take those away, there is little recourse. Indeed the Chinese constitution has certain catch-all provisions which stipulate that the the government may make restrictions on constitutional rights and liberties in order to 1) prevent a person from violating another liberty, 2) avoid pre-eminent emergencies or risks, 3) maintain social order, 4) promote the public interest. In the Continental law system, the exact determination of the meaning and scope-of-application of these types of provisions are up to the determination of the judges, since there is no use of juries.

Laws in China tend to be enforced in movements, and this of course negates much of the sense of a "consistent uniform standard". If, for example, it is illegal for local people to dig wells, bring up underground water, and construct fishponds for the commercial raising of fish, when the first person in this area does so, he should be informed of the law and stopped. If this is not done however, his neighbor may build a fishpond, and another, and another, until there are many people raising fish in fishponds in this area, and supporting themselves in this manner. At this point the government sees that the situation has gotten out of hand, and sends in the authorities to fill-in all the fishponds and stop this illegal activity. When the local people riot, throw bricks, etc. the government says that "They refuse to obey the law," and offer this as an explanation to all interested outsiders as regards the government's difficulty of dealing with the unruly populace. The fact that prompt and efficient enforcement at the initial stage would have avoided this type of mob-reaction is not mentioned[1].

Another important historical fact has been that since western type legal thinking began to become influential in China, and in Chinese communities abroad, generally during the mid-part of the 19th century, the Chinese people and government have continually found themselves "being regulated", as opposed to "doing the regulating." For example, the British had made efforts to obtain better trading arrangements with China, and establish formal and equal diplomatic relations as early as the 1790's, but were invariably rejected by the Ching Dynasty. After the Opium War of 1839-1842, The Treaty of Nanking was forced on the Chinese by the British, and included opening the five ports of Canton, Amoy, Foochow, Ningpo, and Shanghai to residence and trade; ceding the island of Hong Kong to Britain; establishing equal diplomatic relations; and other terms. Western naval supremacy also forced the making of further treaties over the next few decades. The staunchly patriotic and traditionally conservative Chinese were naturally outraged, and regarded these treaties as highly insulting. A simple conclusion in their

---

1. Mencius said: "Only kindness is not enough to govern the nation; legal rules cannot be executed by themselves." 徒善不足以爲政，徒法不能以自行

eyes is that "treaties are unfair."

The lack of a free market, which results when import or sales monopolies (to deal in various essential commodities) are granted to friends and relatives of those in power, also causes the populace, who by statute are forbidden from competing in these areas, to feel that laws are prejudiced, inequitable, and unjust.

In the current era, in overseas communities abroad, especially in Malaysia, Thailand, Indonesia, and other Southeast Asian countries, the local and national laws place a wide variety of restrictions on people of Chinese ancestry in regard to educational opportunity, ownership of land, operations of businesses, etc. The effect of these policies has been to further destroy any possibility that the Chinese will regard laws as "just and equitable." For example, a writ of habeas corpus may be denied because the person in question was arrested under some Internal Security Act or Anti-Rebellion Provision, hence cases of arrest without trial are frequently reported. Unfortunately, the Chinese government at the present time appears to lack the international diplomatic clout necessary to have such unfair regulations abolished.

Historically it was true that Chinese officials depended on the pleasure of their superiors for security of tenure, and that they could be dismissed arbitrarily, for any of a number of reasons, trumped up or otherwise. As a result, the officials felt it necessary to accumulate all the money they could, and to do their best to please their superiors by sending them substantial gifts on all important occasions. Hence, money and valuables flowed continuously from the lower level officials to the higher ones, who in turn gave substantial gifts to the imperial household. Every single gift which travelled through the ranks of officialdom came from the extractions the officials placed on the common people. To supplement their meager salaries, and in light of the heavy financial burdens posed by the requirements of such gift giving, officials at all levels of government sold justice, offices, and favors to the highest bidder. With such a historical background, fully described in Chinese history texts and much of the historical literature, it is not unexpected that Chinese would cast a skeptical glance on "law" and "legal standards".

In the present era many countries find their courts seriously backlogged, and the inability of the citizenry to obtain a speedy trial often leaves many with the feeling that "law not speedily administered is not justice", since they may be held in jail, or otherwise have limits set on their movement and actions, pending their trial. The high cost of legal fees has also caused many people to feel that the price of justice is unreasonable, hence "laws are unfair."

## Qualifications to Avoid Misunderstandings

There is a certain amount of western misunderstanding about Sympathy in the Middle Kingdom. We are aware of a collection of essays published in Shanghai in 1890 which devoted an entire chapter to "The Absence of Sympathy" of the Chinese. Before we look at a number of the author's observations, we must consider the fact that the Sympathy of the Chinese is qualified, or limited, in several important respects, which tend to give it a different nature from Sympathy in the West.

The Chinese concept of the scope and types of "human relationships" traditionally includes only five.[a] At least two notable ones are missing, i.e., #6) the Relationship between Strangers,[b] and #7) the Relationship between Man and (animate) Nature.[c] (We shall refer to these as "Relationships #6 and #7".)[1] Therefore in actual practice, the Chinese tend to limit their Sympathy, pity, compassion, sentiment, etc., primarily to the group which consists of a) their friends and relatives, plus b) various extensions of this basic number, such as alumni of one's same school, co-workers in one's same office, neighbors of good acquaintance, and to some degree c) the relatives and friends of any of these people. This is in keeping with their view of the proper scope of the "human relationships" as defined in their philosophy.

In the following description, we shall use the term "Dependence" to denote: "dependence on the fact that the traditional scope of Chinese relationships numbers only five, and two notable ones are missing."

The author mentions that at the time of his writing (late 1880's) —

**a)** the Chinese tend to have a lack of Sympathy toward those who are in any way deformed. Comment: There seems to have been some improvement in this attitude in the last one-hundred years, no doubt in large part due to western influence. This would rate a Medium to High Dependence, with the added note that the Chinese frequently exercise a much greater frankness in speaking of people's physical defects, deformities, or blemishes than do westerners, and this is not considered impolite.

**b)** the Chinese tend to have a lack of Sympathy toward those who are seen as dim-witted. Comment: essentially similar to that of part a), above. Many westerners maintain that remarks made to others about their lack of intelligence, obedience, skills, etc., can influence their subconscious with the effect of bringing about an exact manifestation of that lack. This is a relatively unknown concept in Chinese thinking. It is in more in the realm of western psychology.

**c)** the Chinese tend to treat daughters, and daughters-in-law, poorly and without Sympathy. Comment: Since daughters marry out of the household, and into another household, they are generally omitted from family registers. They belong to the family of their husband. The role of daughter-in-law was traditionally close to that of "servant" for the family into which she had married. To the extent that this attitude causes suffering or hardship for others not of one's acquaintance, this would rate a Medium

---

a. 君臣、父子、夫婦、兄弟、朋友    b. 陌生人之間    c. 人和(生)物之間

1. By including these, we can realize 民胞物與的理想 "the ideal of being kind to people and animals", and no doubt come closer to 墨子 Motse's doctrine of 仁愛 "universal love".

to High Dependence. To the extent that this attitude causes suffering or hardship for one's own family group, it is of course explained away as being the traditional custom. The demands of Filial Piety are more important than the daughter's, or daughter-in-law's, individual happiness.

**d)** the Chinese tend to neglect minor maladies, allowing them to become major ones. People with a wide variety of diseases are dealt with without Sympathy, and often viewed as objects of curiosity. Comment: Again, there seems to have been some improvement in this attitude in the last one-hundred years, no doubt in large part due to the inflow of western medical technology, research, and teaching about causes and treatment of disease. To the extent that this attitude is manifested toward others not of one's acquaintance, this would rate a Medium (or greater) Dependence.

**e)** the Chinese tend to not to be Sympathetic to the plight of a traveller who has lost his way, or who needs other assistance. Comment: I have talked to hundreds of foreigners with varying lengths of time in China, and no one was willing to agree with this statement, nor would I agree to it as a result of my own experience. I would have to say that the author's comments in this regard are largely invalid in the present day.

**f)** the Chinese tend to display an indifference to the sufferings of others which is probably not to be matched in any other civilized countries. The author mentions this chiefly in regard to the punishments inflicted on students in school who fail to memorize their lessons properly, or who break other regulations. Comment: While this type of punishment has apparently tapered off somewhat from that common in the 1880's, it is still frequently heard that in many elementary school, junior high school, and other educational institutes, teachers will beat the students who perform poorly. The Chinese do not associate such punishment with a "lack of Sympathy". Many Chinese parents have the traditional view that "passing examinations is the road to success", and therefore their view of education is primarily oriented toward passing tests. The content, relevance, usefulness, or correctness of what is tested is of much less importance, and the fact that a Chinese education, by definition, requires huge amounts of memorization is accepted without question. Thus many Chinese feel that the student who does not learn his lessons properly (as signified by poor test marks) will never amount to anything, so it is better, and certainly in the student's best interest, to "suffer" now. The unthinkable alternative is to grow up without an education and to become neither a productive member of society, nor a source of financial support for the parents in their old age. This view accepts that such punishment be inflicted on all who are not up to par, no matter whether members of one's relative and friendship group, or not, and therefore is not related to Relationships #6 and #7 above, and would be rated Zero Dependence.

In relation to Sympathy and Discipline in general, one traditional Chinese maxim is of relevance: "If the discipline is not strict, it is the father's fault. If the teaching is not strict, it is the teacher's fault."[a]

---

a. 子不教父之過，教不嚴師之惰

Other Concerns

The author does not mention some other types of activities which were probably not a concern in his day, namely — air, water, and soil pollution, killing of endangered species of wildlife, marine animals, etc., various forms of poaching, off-season killing of game, and other related issues. To the extent that these activites show a lack of Sympathy to nature, this would probably not be recognized by the Chinese in their definition of the proper scope of Sympathy.

Community services (or the lack of) were not mentioned, and indeed these have traditionally been underdeveloped in Chinese society. The coherent formulation of a national policy to deal with refugees (from other nations) was not discussed, and the Chinese have also traditionally neglected this topic. Either of these items could be related to the lack of a Sixth Relationship.

The author also seems to have had limited contact with the government bureaucracy. Some writers over the years have accused the Chinese of bureaucratic rigidity in many situations, and stated that this shows an absence of Sympathy. However, the fact is that such rigidity has always been accompanied by an informal, quasi-legal system of old-boy networks, favor-swapping, gift exchanges, and private understandings, which enables those with connections and savvy to obtain special treatment. This has often been called "going through the back door", and indeed the existence of such "backdoorism" is a direct reflection of the Chinese propensity to be Sympathetic. In one case which came to light recently, a Chinese man had been wanting to sell a four-story building for nearly 15 years, but due to a complicated land division and title problem, which the local government bureaucrats said must be resolved first, he was unable to make any headway. After his son was graduated from college, it was found that one of his classmates was the son of a high ranking official in the relevant department. A private appeal for special treatment was put forth on this basis, and the entire issue was resolved in less than two months.

## Religious History as Related to Sympathy

In the discussion below, in order to reiterate our main point, we will use the abbreviation "(PSO!)" for the sentence "Thus we see that the Chinese have a Primary Sympathetic Orientation."

We must also consider the different nature of western Sympathy which has arisen due to certain historical peculiarities of western religion. It will be necessary to do a brief overview of some early Old Testament history to make this clear.

**Historical Overview:** To trace the history of the Hebrew people from whom the Old Testament eventually emerged, we must go back to a group of Semitic tribes which inhabited the region referred to as the Fertile Crescent, a strip of land lying between the Tigris and Euphrates rivers, well before 2000 B.C. At some point, some of these tribes migrated to Egypt, and lived there for three or four centuries. Eventually their presence came to displease the Pharoah, and he inaugurated a program of harsh measures toward them, forcing them into a condition of servitude and slavery: referred to in the Old Testament as the period of Egyptian bondage. With the gracious help of the Hebrew God, known to them as "Yahweh", Moses was able to lead the tribes out of Egypt and journey to a new territory where they could make their home.

It was this exodus from Egypt that marked the turning point in the history of the Hebrew people, enabling them to become a separate nation. The date usually given for the exodus is about 1250 B.C. After leaving Egypt the tribes are said to have spent forty years wandering in the wilderness prior to their entrance into the land of Canaan. Two important events occurred during the Wilderness Journey: First, the proclamation of a code of laws which, according to the tradition, Yahweh revealed to Moses on Mount Sinai. (Exodus 20:01–20:22). Second, the establishment of a covenant, or contract, between Yahweh and the people of Israel. (Exodus 20:23–23:19).

The basis of the covenant was the body of laws which Yahweh had given and which the people had agreed to obey. Yahweh's part of the contract consisted of his promise to care for them, supplying their needs and protecting them from the ravages or attacks that might be brought on by their enemies.

This covenant-based, essentially contractual, relationship between Yahweh and his people is one of the dominant ideas throughout the entire Old Testament. (The word "Testament" itself means covenant or agreement.) It served to distinguish Yahweh from the gods of the surrounding nations. These gods were, as a general rule, believed to be related to their peoples by their natural ties of physical descent. In other words, they were bound to their people by ties that were not dependent on any contractual agreement or on any type of moral qualifications. Consequently, they could not abandon their people because of any failure to uphold a contract (since they had none), nor because of any moral delinquency (because that was not a specific requirement of their relationship). But this was not true of Yahweh in his relation to the Hebrew people. His promise to remain as their god was conditional on their living up to the terms of the agreement. Whenever they failed to obey the laws he had given to them, he was no longer bound to protect them or even to claim them as his own people. The prophets of later generations would call attention to this fact and thus remind their contemporaries that security for the nation could not be expected so long as they failed to fulfill the requirements of the covenant to which they had been committed.

Many western ideas and attitudes in regard to "contractual relation" which are based on "laws" may be traced back to this Old Testament history. If the tribes broke the terms of the contractual relation, whether deliberately or by oversight, Yahweh was not disposed to be Sympathetic, and they would certainly be punished. Indeed they were punished on several occasions, by natural disasters or calamities, by their enemies, etc. This was considered fair, and there was no reasonable claim to Sympathy under the circumstances. In the present day, westerners in their dealings tend to stress the sense of "contractual obligation", and when the contract is broken it is not uncommon for them to feel that the party that broke it should suffer the consequences.

By contrast, the Chinese have historically had, and to the present day do continue to have, an effective state religion of ancestor worship, and thus their "gods" are related to the people by their natural ties of physical descent. There is essentially no notion or conception of "contractual obligation", from the standpoint of religion, that exists and that could or would be carried over in regard to defining some basic premise which underlies the dealings between people.[1] (PSO!)

This is not to say that the Chinese never enter into specific contractual relations with each other, or with foreigners. However, in any event, whether the sense of "contractual obligation" is implicitly or explicitly present, if one party breaks the terms, whether deliberately or by oversight, and asks for Sympathetic treatment of his situation (i.e. "Please do not enforce the terms of the contract"), he would indeed be entitled to such treatment under the basic Confucian cornerstone doctrine of benevolence.[2] To not give Sympathy when it was asked for in this manner (i.e., to not offer forgiveness) would be considered "unfair", although to the westerner with his Old Testament background, it could be seen as "fair." This is another important way in which Chinese Sympathy differs from that of the west. (PSO!) Mencius said "The feeling of commiseration is what we call humanity." (humanity = *jen*) As a component of this *jen*, the concept of *shu* 恕 is very important, and some sinologists have rendered this into English as "intensive empathy," or "reciprocatory sympathy".[3] It holds that we should care about other's thinking, and care about other's feelings, before our own.

A western lawyer with much experience in China summed up the situation by saying "The theory in this part of the world tends to be that a contract is only good if both parties want to go on with it. When problems arise you are expected to enter into 'amicable discussions', which means the westerner is expected to sit there and smile as they breach the contract."

## Linguistic Peculiarities

Another significant factor which comes into play in considering Chinese thinking is the lack of the expressions "to draw the line" or "the last straw" in the Chinese language. Western scholars have often mistakenly equated the former with *yeou fen tswun*,[a] which it is not, and the latter with *ren wu ke ren*,[b] which it is not.

---

a. 有分寸    b. 忍無可忍

1. Likewise, the relationship between the Chinese Emperor 天子 and heaven was never to our knowledge viewed as a contract. More commonly it was considered to be "fate".
2. By contrast, the term "benevolence", or "benevolent humanism", is not mentioned in the Old Testament.
3. Sometimes very broadly rendered as merely "reciprocity".

In many situations where the Chinese expect Sympathy to be given their point of view, the foreigner may regard the issue at hand as quite important, and perhaps setting a bad precedent if he follows their advice. He may then be attempted to wonder: "Where do you draw the line?" The Chinese answer is "We don't." The situations which we have given in the Filial Piety section are good examples of where the foreigner would be tempted to "draw the line" on the application of a particular doctrine (the need to be filial, in this case), and the Chinese would not. The Chinese (represented by the family, clan, elders, etc.) expect Sympathy to be given their point of view in these situations, (PSO!) and for the foreigner who marries into this family, the possibility of some related type of situation developing should be taken into account. It may be clearly seen that the Chinese idea of what constitutes the correct direction and functioning of "principle" is in terms of Confucian doctrine (respect for elders, respect for teachers, respect for parents, a generally benevolent attitude, etc., being main components, and clearly showing a weighting toward "human relations"), whereas the westerner's idea of what constitutes the correct direction and functioning of "principle" is often more closely related to an attempted determination of some objective good (which is an essentially abstract concept). This arises from Aristotle's view that 1) every inquiry and action aims at some end, and the *good* is that at which all things aim, and 2) the proper direction of man's thinking is the contemplation of truth. Obviously the Chinese and Western views are separated by some distance.

Whenever the foreigner is tempted to respond to a situation by saying "That is the last straw!", he may be again quite certain that the Chinese would not consider this an appropriate reaction, since they lack this expression/concept. Thus in many situations they would plead for the foreigner to maintain a continually forgiving attitude, whereas in his own mind he could have already reached the point where the camel's back had broken. Repeated violations of contractual arrangements, where the violating party repeatedly asks that stipulated penalties not be enforced, (i.e. "Give me Sympathy") would certainly be excellent examples of this. To NOT give Sympathy in such cases is generally seen by the Chinese as immoral. (PSO!)

Consider the group of Chinese college students who were watching a TV show. The main characters were an American husband and a Chinese wife in their late 20's, and the wife's older brother. In one scene the older brother wanted to borrow a sizable amount of money from the couple to buy a taxicab and go into business for himself. This was agreed to, however it was later learned that the brother had taken the money and gambled it away. The reaction of the Chinese students to this was: "Oh, that is bad."

In a later scene taking place some years later, the brother came back and said he had now decided to open a restaurant with some friends, and felt sure that this would enable him to have a promising future. He therefore needed to borrow more money. After some brief consideration the wife agreed, but the husband, considering that the previous loan had not been repaid yet, the older brother had lied to them before, etc., disagreed, and resolutely refused to loan him the money. The reaction of the Chinese students to this was: "Oh, that is bad."

Experience in talking to Chinese outdoorsmen, mountain climbers, and filmmakers who do a lot of travelling confirms that many Chinese feel it proper that a rescue team be sent up to help climbers who have gotten into distress, even on those slopes or faces which have been posted, bannered, marked, flagged, registered, proclaimed, published, and listed, on the scene and in guidebooks, to the effect: "Extremely dangerous. Experienced climbers are advised to proceed at their own risk. The Mountain Rescue Teams WILL NOT aid or assist injured, trapped, or otherwise disabled parties on this route!" Of course, the north wall of the Eiger in Switzerland, and many routes in the Himalayas come into mind immediately in this regard. The foreigner who maintains that the Rescue Teams should indeed not be sent up is quickly labelled by the Chinese as unsympathetic, or worse, immoral.

Educational Levels and Sympathy

In societies with no food surplus, all hands are needed to help at harvest time, including children, who must take time off from school. For other children who live far from school and are without geographic mobility, attendance therein is also often impossible. These factors result in widespread illiteracy. When members of the populace instinctively take illiteracy into account in their discussions of the appropriateness of others' actions, they may regard the failure to heed signs or written warnings as within the range of accepted normal behavior. They may then, when some violation has occurred, feel themselves perfectly sensible in asking for Sympathy on this basis: "I/She/He didn't know about that." Such an attitude, often seen even today in China, clearly reflects the mentality of a Pre Industrial Revolution society of subsistence agriculture. The reader may be interested to contrast this with common thinking in the west, to wit: "Ignorance of the law is no defense."

## Sympathy and Honesty

As a further clarification on Sympathy, we should consider the view which Chinese take of honesty. Many westerners might feel that no Sympathy is due to someone who has acted dishonestly, however there is considerable difference of opinion in what types of behavior the Chinese consider dishonest, and what types the westerners do. In addition to different Perceptions which have been discussed in this volume, one fact stands out. The Chinese view of honesty appears to pivot on the belief that the results of behavior *not done deliberately* are not within the honesty/dishonesty spectrum.

Hence, intentional misrepresentation is seen as dishonest. However the burden of proof to show that it was "intentional misrepresentation" is generally on the party who feels "injured". With this qualification, we may say that the Chinese view in regard to responsibility is close to "A person is responsible for his acts if they were deliberate."

Unintentional misrepresentation is not seen as dishonest, rather it is outside the honesty/dishonesty spectrum. Thus there is the view "A person is not responsible for his acts if they were unintentional."

An illustration of this is considerably complicated if we deal with a case involving liability, physical injury, or damage. A simpler case, such as a pricing problem, where a large bowl of congee which is marked on the menu or signboard as $95, but which the restaurant personnel claim should correctly be marked $125 (with no announcement to that fact posted anywhere), is illustrative. Is this dishonest? With the customer being unable to offer any proof that the restaurant personnel had acted deliberately with the intention to cheat, the Chinese reply would be "No, this is not dishonest." Again, the double negative 'not dishonest' does not imply that the behavior is honest, rather it is outside the honesty/dishonesty spectrum. The Sunglasses Incident described previously is another example of behavior which the Chinese would not view as dishonest. Having not acted dishonestly, the Chinese would naturally expect that Sympathy be given their point of view, and that their statement of the situation be accepted. (PSO!)

The westerner's view of the situation is more likely to be in terms of corresponding rights and obligations, (an essentially legal approach), whereby each party must accept the responsibility of its own, or its agent's, actions. The issue of deliberateness, or lack of deliberateness, is essentially irrelevant, or only comes into consideration in far more serious actions, such as manslaughter.

Certainly the issue of "not being deliberate" is often a very subjective matter, and the westerner would feel that in dealings between S and B, Seller and Buyer for example, the obligation to prove that S's actions were not deliberate rests with S, rather than saying that B has some sort of reverse burden of proof (to prove that S has made intentional misrepresentation with a desire to defraud). In the absence of either party being able to offer any "proof", the objectively verifiable facts could easily point to one party being at fault, and for him ignore this responsibility would be to act dishonestly in the western view. To ask for Sympathy in such a situation is easily seen by the westerner as unreasonable.

In many situations presented in this volume, we may attempt to put the Golden Rule (Do unto others as you would have them do unto you)[a] into practice and see what happens. We may ask ourselves: "What if someone dealt with me this way? How would I feel?" We may obtain an answer: "That would be acceptable" or "That would be expected under the circumstances." However, oftentimes our behavior is still not proper in the Chinese viewpoint. Final determinations of propriety in these types of situations rest on a some degree of subjectivity, yet we are lead to suspect that the Golden Rule can break down as a guide to behavior in many types of cross-cultural dealings. For ease of reference this phenomenon may be referred to as a "Golden Rule Applicabili-

---

a. 己所不欲勿施於人

ty Dysfunction", or GRAD.[1] The foreigner in China may collect his own examples.

## Facts vs. Emotions

Westerners tend to look at facts, weight evidence, and attempt to determine what constitutes objective reality when they are deciding an issue at hand. The determination of whether or not Sympathy should be extended in any particular case goes through a similar mental process of "evaluation". The Chinese have a pronounced preference for giving Sympathy to the "underdog" (the weaker party) in any situation. The emotions which this party's plight elicits are more important to them than other considerations. (PSO!) Not surprisingly, in the west when we think of the verb "think", we associate this with "think with the brain" or "think with the mind". The Chinese grammatical preference leans toward "think with the heart,"[2] and indeed "think" has the heart radical.

The tendency to say one thing and do something else is often related to the Primary Sympathetic Orientation, as the following simple diagram shows.

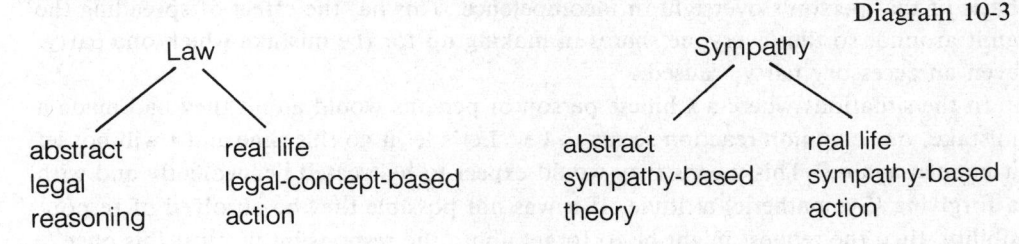

Diagram 10-3

```
         Law                        Sympathy
        /   \                       /      \
abstract    real life         abstract      real life
legal       legal-concept-based  sympathy-based  sympathy-based
reasoning   action            theory        action
```

For those of a more legal orientation, we would not be surprised if abstract reasoning about legal theory and real life action based on legal notions corresponded very closely. For those of a Sympathetic orientation, when we try to discuss "abstract Sympathy-based theory" and compare this with "real life Sympathy-based action", we often see that the former is essentially a contradiction in terms: since no emotion is elicited, no such accurate "theory" is possible by the natives. Hence, it may be highly faulty to ask people of such an orientation "What would you do in such and such a situation?" if we are looking for replies that correspond to reality. See our discussion of Remeliorated TOPIC later in the text.

---

1. In relations between A and B, in trying to apply the Golden Rule, Party A attempts to mentally put himself in Party B's position, and then estimate what "treatment" he would "expect" in such circumstances. This yields a "Do unto others as you would have them do unto you" determination. If A's mental exercise yields the response (treatment, behavior, etc.) that B indeed considers appropriate, there is no problem. If it does not, we are in a GRAD situation.

2. In considering a difficult or puzzling situation, the Chinese will often express themselves by saying 我心裡想，這應該怎麼處理？ and never by saying 我腦裡想，這應該怎麼處理？

## "Admission of Error" and Sympathy

In addition we often see in the North America and Europe that truthfulness and frankness elicit Sympathy. The western government official who admits his mistakes and says that he will try to do a better job in the future is likely to get far better (i.e., more Sympathetic) treatment in the press than the official who maintains his air of innocence and infallibility, while hard evidence of his mismanagement and other signs of guilt amass about him. The accused lawbreaker who admits his crime in front of the judge and jury is generally entitled to a reduced sentence. George Washington chopped down a cherry tree and was apparently forgiven by his father, because young George told the truth. While we find no similar story to that of young George's in the long history of China, nevertheless the Chinese do appear to accept the general premise that children up to a certain age are not responsible for their actions.

However, in general terms, with the Chinese concept of "face" it is much more difficult for people to admit that they have acted unwisely or improperly. More likely, they will try to pass the blame off on someone else and then ask for Sympathy on the basis of that person's oversight or incompetence. This has the effect of spreading the guilt around, so that everyone shares in making up for the mistake which one party, even an accessory party, caused.

In the situations where a Chinese person or persons would admit they had made a mistake, one common reaction seems to be "Let's let it go this time and I will not let it happen again." This means they would expect to be treated benevolently and with a forgiving (Sympathetic) attitude. If it was not possible they be absolved of responsibility, then the request might be to forget about the responsibility "just this once".

If the Chinese party were to refuse to admit any wrongdoing, even when confronted by hard evidence, they and their comrades would consider it grossly impolite to "push them in the corner" by continued accusations and/or demands for a change in their stance. They fully believe that since everyone "knows" the situation, it is not necessary to state it directly. As a result, the guilty party or parties still expect Sympathetic treatment, because they can maintain that they acted in the best of intentions, even though they botched it up. They would not expect to be taken to task for something that was not done deliberately or with specific intention to harm. (PSO!)

Beside the concept of "face", there is also another factor at work in making many Chinese, especially elderly Chinese, reticent to admit any wrongdoing, and for the public not to push them into admitting it. Whereas the westerners tend to engage in "hero worship",[1] the Chinese engage in "leader deification",[2] which means that anyone in

---

1. The word "worship" is used loosely here to denote a strong admiration.
2. The word "deification" is used here in its literal sense: 1) to make a god of; rank among the gods. 2) to look upon as a god.

a position of high leadership tends to be deified, and therefore by definition "can do no wrong." If he admits wrongdoing, he is no longer qualified to be the leader. This is of course a direct outgrowth of the traditional notion that the leader is of perfect virtue, and can be viewed as a temporal extension of ancestor worship.

## The Iceberg Model

Due to the dissimilar historical development of western thought and Chinese thought, the westerners expect sympathy/sentiment to be given (or not given) from the structural basis of promises, regulations, covenants, testaments, laws, contracts, and other stipulations, whereas the Chinese see sympathy/sentiment, benevolence, compassion, etc. as a basic foundation for dealings between people, and consider these elements as more important than the restrictions imposed by promises, regulations, laws, contracts, and other conditions. The following Iceberg diagram (Diagram 10-1) will aid us in our understanding of this.

Diagram 10-1

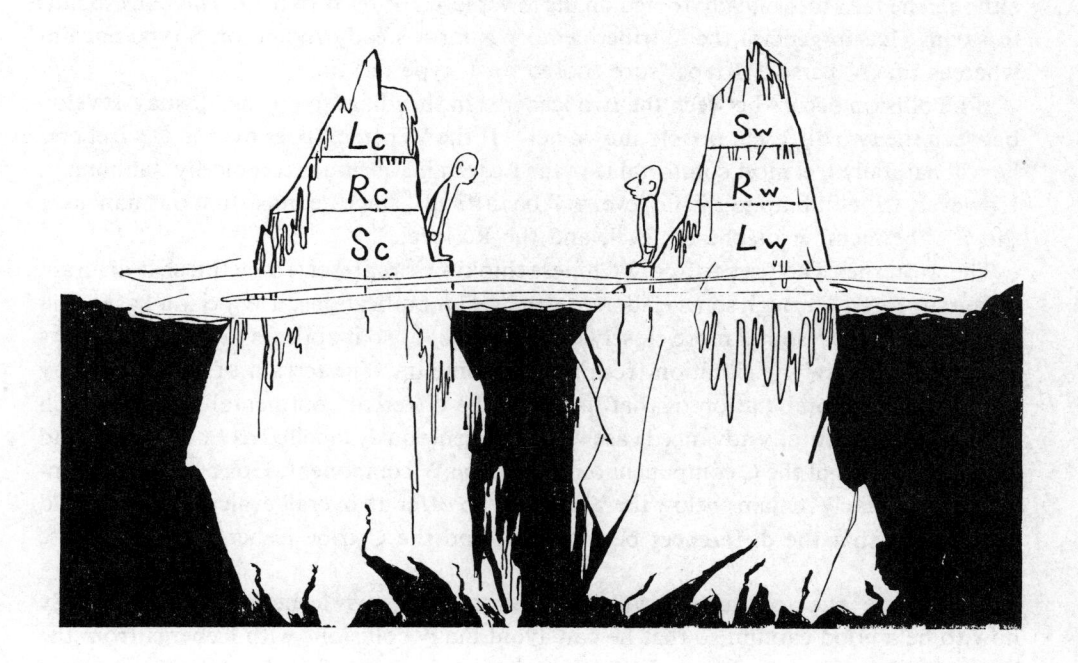

On one side is an iceberg from the C Continental Shelf, inhabited by a member of the C tribe (a C person). On the other side is an iceberg from the W Continental Shelf, inhabited by a member of the W tribe (a W person). The water line is represented by the wavy line. Each iceberg appears to be roughly the same size in this two-dimensional diagram, however a three dimensional diagram might reveal differences. Although represented here as physical quantities, the icebergs are more properly seen as mental states. The part below the waterline is the subconscious, the part above the waterline the conscious.

Although to the casual observer each iceberg is completely white, a more thorough inspection would reveal that each iceberg is essentially composed of three levels, which can be said to be terrain of the L, R, and S type, (Law, Reason, Sympathy. See further explanation of "Reason" under the Integration of Concepts discussed in Chapter 9.) However, in the case of C's iceberg, the S type terrain extends well below the waterline and provides the foundation for the entire berg. In the case of W's iceberg, it is the L terrain that extends below the waterline and provides the foundation.

Even though the terrain of each iceburg is divided into three types, it does retain some differences peculiar to itself, thus each is properly sub-labelled with its continental shelf designation, hence Lc, Rc, Sc, and Lw, Rw, Sw.

Each tribe member is quite intimately familiar with the terrain of his own iceberg, although he feels most steady-footed on the lower levels of his own berg. This corresponds to saying that in general the C tribe member is most steady footed on S type terrain, whereas the W person is most sure footed on L type terrain.

If a collision occurs between the two icebergs in this diagram, a scuffle may develop between the two different people shown here. If the W person goes over to C's iceberg, he will naturally feel most comfortable in the Lc terrain, abeit not completely "at home". However, the climb up to the Lc level will be difficult, since he must first outmaneuver the C tribe member on the Sc level, and the Rc level.

The westerner who tries to adopt Chinese thinking is represented by the next diagram (Diagram 10-2). Through some elaborate structural modifications, a W person has rebuilt his iceberg to correspond more closely to the C type, or so it appears to many observers who can only view the situation from the waterline up. The terrain of each level may be said to be a combination of that native to the different continental shelves, which in the most structurally advanced case would be generously labelled as Lc-w, Rc-w, and Sc-w, meaning that the C component outweighs the W component. However, an L foundation most likely remains below the waterline. To offer an overall evaluation, we would have to say that the differences between this and the C tribe icebergs are still quite pronounced.

Comments: The acculturator will want to retain his own iceberg model, and study how to be a good captain so that he can avoid many collisions with icebergs from the Entry Culture. He will also study the experience of others of his Background Culture in dealing with past major and minor collisions, so as to learn how to deal with these most effectively when the need arises.

Diagram 10-2

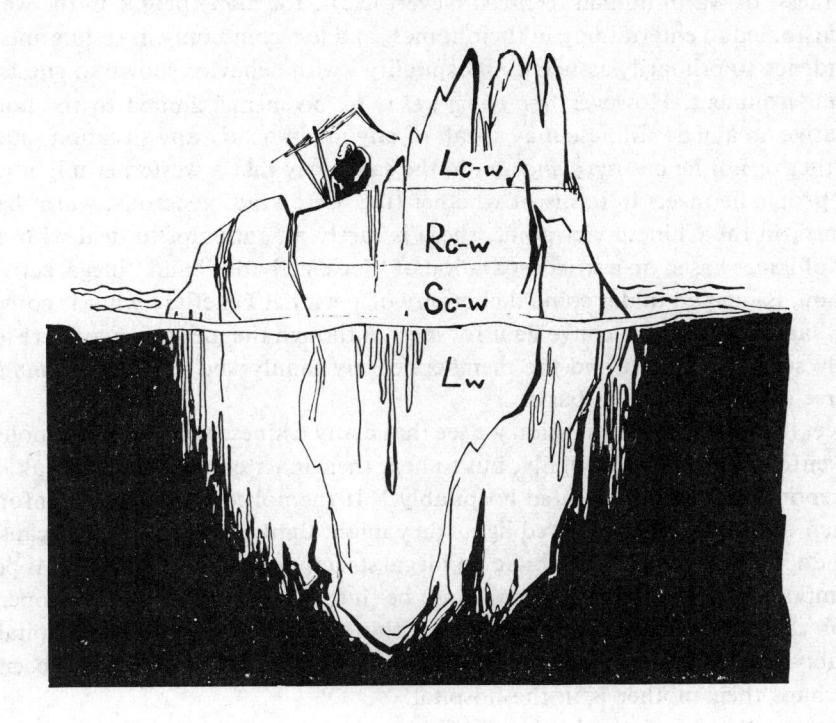

## Hospitality and Sympathy

Hospitality is also closely related to Sympathy in the Chinese conception. In reply to the question of "What do you think of Chinese hospitality?" It would surprise some newly arrived foreigners to hear a westerner of long residence state "Chinese hospitality is great. However I think that if there is a contradiction between hospitality and law, we should obey the law."

## Debate Topics
*(continued from Chapter 5)*

3. Resolved, the traditional ways of Chinese thought and behavior are most fitting and proper, and their stress on the tenets of "humanity", "benevolence", "kindness", etc. are fully compatible with the demands of justice, fairness, and an objective determination of right and wrong, in the world of today.

The problem is that the term *ren ching wei* [a] in Chinese is generally used to translate the English term "hospitality", and it also carries the meanings of having human touch, friendliness, or warm human feelings. Nevertheless, for many people in the west who are accustomed to entertaining in their homes, and less commonly in restaurants, there is a tendency to primarily associate "hospitality" with behavior shown to guests in the home environment. However, *ren ching wei* is by no means limited to the home, or even native area. The Chinese may speak of anyone in nearly any situation, and refer to whether or not he has *ren ching wei*, in the same way that a westerner might classify all the people he meets in terms of whether they were kind, generous, warm hearted, etc. Since, in the Chinese viewpoint, there is rarely any attempt to deal with a great variety of issues based on a strict separation of "legal activities" and "illegal activities", everything is lumped under some dichotomy of personal benefit: "what is convenient for me" and "what is not convenient for me", although the me spoken of here is more properly seen as "myself and the members of my family and clan". *Ren ching wei* is of course evaluated on this basis.

Hence, through long observation we see that many Chinese will feel that a policeman should enforce the law thoroughly, but to hear their inner consciousness speak: "I am the exception, I should be treated hospitably." If the policeman wants to enforce the law when they drive through a red light, they might think that is not fair because they did not do it on purpose. If they build an illegal structure on their premises, it is perhaps only temporary, so they feel they should not be fined. If they fail to obtain proper licensing for their fruit stand, certainly it is within the realm of normal hospitality to reasonably request a time exension, in their rationalization, because they have been busy, and perhaps their mother is in the hospital.

*Ren ching wei* comes into play in all of these situations, and the Chinese will praise those officials who have *ren ching wei*, while expressing their displeasure with those who do not, calling them "inhuman."

Certainly the Chinese are very hospitable[1] toward guests in the western sense of the term. The Chinese enjoy inviting foreigners into their homes, whether on the spur of the moment, or with some advance planning, and asking them to share in dining. Often they will even give them presents. In traditional philosophy, the guest is first, and by treating him in this way the host will feel that he has gained much face.

Further Connections

The connection between hospitality and law is further complicated by the peculiar lack in the Chinese mental makeup of certain types of replies or rebuttals in ordinary conversation. This is easily illustrated by a "Typewriter Story" that I heard from an American friend some years ago.

---

1. The Chinese tend to feel that they are the most hospitable race bar none. However, rare is the Chinese person who can objectively compare Chinese hospitality with that of the peoples in other Asian or European regions. Many westerners with broad travel experience claim that the Chinese have no monopoly on hospitality.

a. 人情味

Daniel was from Las Vegas and was teaching an advanced English class in a private academy in China. A topic had been chosen for each class, and that week the discussion had gotten around to "movies". The students talked about the movies they had enjoyed in the past, compared foreign and Chinese filmmaking techniques and common themes, stated their views on the acting abilities of various actors and actresses, etc. Daniel asked if there were any questions on movie dialogue from western movies they had seen recently. Most students said that they usually just read the Chinese subtitles on western movies, but one girl spoke up and said that she had recently seen a movie where a disgruntled secretary resigned from her job, and told her boss "You can take this typewriter and all of the office equipment and shove it." The student was curious as to what this phrase meant. She had checked all the words in the dictionary, but she still could not catch the meaning.

Daniel cleared his throat, and said that her question was very good, very good indeed, however it was perhaps a bit too involved for discussion in class, so he thought it would be best to handle it after their lesson was over.

Quite a number of the students stayed after class that evening, and everyone decided to go out for fruit juice and treat the teacher. Over their drinks, Daniel tried to carefully explain the meaning of the phrase "shove it", and how exactly this would apply to typewriters and office equipment.

The students were most confounded by this explanation however, and one of the Chinese boys asked "Wouldn't that be painful?" One of the girls commented "I don't see how it would fit."

This and several similar encounters among the Chinese people, along with discussions with many other westerners who had done research on the topic, confirmed for Daniel that the use of "stick it", "cram it", "shove it" or other related retorts does not exist in Chinese. When such English usage is explained, most Chinese do not even understand it, and will perhaps reply "Why would you want to do that?" The Chinese are simply without this conception.

Related to "cram it" are certain finger gestures, such as the one employing an upright middle digit, and suggesting (to the westerner) a certain attitude of displeasure, with the intent to inform the "recipient" exactly what he/she can do about the issue under consideration. This gesture and its significance are also unknown among 97% of Chinese people.

Recognizing this fact, many elderly westerners, who object to such pointed oral exclamations and nasty sign-language anyway, will no doubt say "Glory, hallelujah!" and praise the Chinese because they do not use such vulgarities.

However, when we step back for a moment and examine many of the dealings between people in society, it may become apparent that some problems in expression have now arisen. If we eliminate such phrases as "shove it" from our speech, we will of course have to eliminate related phrases such as:

> If you don't like it that is too bad
> you can lump it
> that's tough
> that's your problem

Consider the policeman who finds that a motorcycle shop, appliance shop, or general merchandise store has a lot of things parked, stacked, displayed, etc., on the sidewalk, seriously blocking pedestrian traffic. When he asks the manager to move them, the reply he is given is a request for sympathy such as "I have only put them there temporarily, I will move them soon, the customer is coming to pick these up very shortly, etc."

A western policeman might reply "I am not interested in excuses. Move this stuff out of here in ten minutes or I will have it hauled away." A Chinese policeman would probably be much more polite in making such a request.

The shop personnel may reply "That is not fair. You should help me out. Since when are policemen so lacking in hospitality?"

Having eliminated the above mentioned phrases from our speech habits, how are we to reply to this? We might say "No, you did not quite catch my meaning, I said . . . "

As we grope for an appropriate reply, the manager innocently says "Where am I supposed to put these things anyway?"

To this we reply "Well, perhaps you could just . . . maybe make a passageway through here . . . or move them back . . . no, I guess . . . "

Hence we commonly see that Chinese are much more sympathetic, or hospitable, in the enforcement of law than westerners would consider feasible or reasonable. The lack of certain western habits of speech (and thought) may also be pointed out as one of the reasons for this.

Foreign Impressions

Nevertheless, it is often true that many foreigners who are confronted in their dealings by seemingly intractable Chinese bureaucrats come away with the impression that the Chinese attitude is "If you don't like it you can lump it." This, we believe, is some confusion arising from the essentially authoritarian nature of much Chinese decision making. The officials in power often assume that since they have the capacity to give orders, those orders will be obeyed without question, in the traditional Chinese fashion of superior-to-subordinate dealings. Since they are in the position of leadership, they are able to tell other affected parties "You do not have to make the decision, we make it for you." In this way they feel that they are doing the other party a favor, or at least providing him with a solid reason as to why he must do the action in question: "We are ordering you to do it."

For those persons who have more of a Group Orientation, and are much less questioning of orthodoxy or authority than a typical westerner, this is not regarded as an issue of "lumping it", but rather as an additional opportunity to show one's good character and harmonious disposition by being obedient.

## Sympathy and Legality Test

The reader is invited to take the following test to determine the components of Sympathetic and Legal thinking in his own mental makeup.

It may be illustrative to take the test two times. The first time, the Chinese point of view should be adopted. In this manner the reader may gauge the amount of knowledge he has gained from reading this volume so far.

The second time, the reader may revert to his original personality, and give his answers according to his customary habit or inclination.

Comparison of the two scores may then be made, and some further enlightenment may be forthcoming.

One answer should be selected for each statement, and points scored: zero, one, or two, as indicated.

| Would you ever say this if confronted with a suitable situation? | Never at all | Rarely, or sometimes | Frequently, or always |
|---|---|---|---|
| points: | 0 | 1 | 2 |
| **1)** "No, I want you to come and install it on Thursday at 2:00 just like you promised." | ____ | ____ | ____ |
| **2)** "Here, I think you can read this regulation: there is no burning of paper allowed in the building. I want you to stop and desist, now." | ____ | ____ | ____ |
| **3)** "I do not care if this is the way you have been making your living for decades. The hunting of these animals is now illegal. You must stop and desist immediately, and never engage in this activity again." | ____ | ____ | ____ |
| **4)** "I do not care if it is only for ten minutes. This area is posted as No Obstructions, and that is what it means." | ____ | ____ | ____ |

**5)** "It is true neither you nor I forsaw this eventuality when the contract was signed, however according to the delegation of responsibilities outlined in the contract, this is your responsibility. In no way can it be construed to be mine (ours)."   _____   _____   _____

**6)** "This is not what it says on your advertising. What do you mean it was a mistake? I want the advertised terms and conditions."   _____   _____   _____

**7)** "If you want me to follow the rules, that is fine. Tell me what they are first, write them down."   _____   _____   _____

**8)** "No, that is not what the sign says. If there was any change in the posted data, you should have marked it. I am not responsible for your oversight."   _____   _____   _____

**9)** "Wait a minute, that was not the deal. That was not what we agreed upon. You cannot change the stipulations now just because you are inconvenienced. Here is our agreement, read it."   _____   _____   _____

**10)** "No, I want it delivered within two days as per our original stipulations. I am not willing to give a time extension."   _____   _____   _____

*Scoring:* After calculating your point total, refer to the following analysis of your mental makeup, which will compare your views with the Chinese "Primary Sympathetic Orientation". Major components of P.S.O. include benevolence, kindness, maintenance of harmony, concern for our fellow man, go-with-the-flow reasoning, and giving face.

**First time.** If you have adopted the Chinese point of view to take this test, refer to the following scoring and commentary.

## Opposing Explanations and Varying Worldviews

18 to 20 points      You have misconstrued most of the essays in this volume, and are totally unable to "read between the lines." Go back to Chapter 1 and start over.

12 to 17 points      Although you have some recognition of the Chinese mentality and group norms, your knowledge is still inadequate. Go back to Chapter 3 and begin again.

7 to 11 points      With your attitude, it is sure that you will embroil yourself in much needless argument and conflict every day. Reread Chapter 8 before continuing on in the text.

3 to 6 points      You are beginning to see the light. You may proceed on and finish up this volume, however pay special note to all comments about avoiding conflict and promoting harmony.

0 to 2 points      Congratulations, you are an expert on cross cultural human relations. You should write your own book.

**Second time.** If you have adopted the western point of view to take this test, refer to the following scoring and comments.

18 to 20 points      You are totally legally oriented, and without any sense of P.S.O. If you read Chinese philosophy with this orientation, you will misconstrue nearly every sentence.

12 to 17 points      You retain a very legalistic view of human relations, and lack a great deal of P.S.O. Your body may be in China, but your head is still in the west.

7 to 11 points      You have a generally legalistic outlook, and lack a significant amount of P.S.O. Try more to elevate your heart above your head.

3 to 6 points      You have legal leanings, however with effort you may strengthen your P.S.O. You are well on your way to living harmoniously in the society.

532                         Bases for Action and Non-Action

0 to 2 points               You have a highly developed sense of P.S.O., and will find
                            that your relations with Chinese people over the long term,
                            whether neighbors, local business people, cooperative ven-
                            ture partners, associates, etc. will function very smoothly.
                            However, you may find that your relations with other
                            westerners will suffer.

Further insight may be obtained by completing the following exercises.

*Round Three:*
The reader is now invited to find a close Chinese friend and lead them in taking the test. Ask the Chinese person to to answer all the items from the point of view of Chinese law, as he/she is aware of the laws, and as they relate to the incidents in question. An "expert" analysis is not necessarily required.For example "According to the Chinese law as you understand it, is it reasonable for a person when confronted with a suitable situation to state this?"
The scoring procedure is identical.If further examples or explanations are needed for any item, the reader may get them from the pages of this volume.

*Round Four:*
The same Chinese person who assisted in Round Three may be asked to participate once more, or a different Chinese person may be asked to help. Ask the Chinese person to answer all the items in what he/she feels is the way most Chinese would answer, reflecting the attitude most Chinese would employ in dealing with a likely situation in the present day. For example "According to the mentality of most Chinese people as per your observation, is it likely someone would make a statement like this when confronted with a suitable situation?"
*Compare the answers in Round Three and Round Four. What does this indicate about the society? If you saw a headline in the Chinese newspaper saying that "China is a country ruled by laws", would you agree or disagree based on your findings here?*

## Harmony as a Social Basis

Some western observers have recently commented on various aspects of *disharmony* between Chinese people in Chinese society, and would therefore tend to question the claim that "harmony" is an underlying premise of the Chinese social structure, and of Chinese social relations in general.

Certainly it is true that times are changing. Nevertheless, in viewing any disharmonious situation between Chinese people in Chinese society, the following points are useful for reference, in comparing the relative weight which Chinese and westerners place on "harmony".

In speaking of disharmonious incidents —
1. What are the real facts of the situation? Would westerners react to this situation in the same way?
2. Would westerners have let the situation develop this far before instigating conflict?
3. Is the present conflict the direct result of western influence? Have similar incidents recently occurred in western countries?
4. Is this small conflict in fact a search for a greater harmony?
5. Is this behavior the norm for Chinese society, or is it quite unusual?

Many Chinese social scientists have commented that the Chinese often tend to engage in much slogan shouting, so called "sloganeering",[a] and this occasionally gives foreigners the impression that there are various disharmonious elements in the society. However, such activities tend to be conducted "with the head of a tiger and the tail of a snake"[b], and society reverts to its original functioning style before long.

The following ten idioms show the importance of harmony in Chinese society.

①息事寧人　　②隨遇而安　　　　　③逆來順受
④家和萬事興　⑤和氣待人，和氣生財　⑥敦親睦鄰
⑦委曲求全　　⑧以和為貴　　　　　⑨天下本無事，庸人自擾之
⑩不了了之

## Basic Organization of Chinese-style Continental Law System

**CIVIL LAW** 民法
Chinese laws relating to the private rights of individuals and to legal actions involving these, such as contracts, transactions, relationships, property damage, etc. where an injured party brings action against the the injury-causing party for damages.

Punishment: civil punishments such as monetary damages, court costs, restoring of property to its original condition, etc.

There are no class action suits (which are characterized by the fact that all the plantiffs need not be specifically defined.) However, if all the plantiffs are named, representative action suits may be filed.

Jurisdiction: Chinese Civil Law Courts 民事法庭

**CRIMINAL LAW** 刑法
Chinese laws relating to tortious conduct. bodily injury, mental injury, and injury to nation or society

---
a. 喊口號　　b. 虎頭蛇尾

Punishment: criminal punishments such as fines, imprisonment, denial of civil rights

*types of prosecution:* **1)** if the injured party institutes action, it is a private prosecution.
**2)** if the public prosecutor institutes action, it is a public prosecution.

In enforcing this criminal law, action will be instituted only upon complaint[1]. The public prosecutor will usually not take the initiative unless in the event of a major offense[2], of which the most important is an offense against the nation, and second most important is an offense against society, and least important is an offense against an individual[3].

Procedure: An injured party may institute proceedings under criminal law (whereupon the case is decided before a judge directly), or try to convince the public prosecutor to take action[4].

Jurisdiction: Chinese Criminal Law Courts 刑事法庭

## ADMINISTRATIVE LAW 行政法

Chinese laws relating to government bodies and the persons or organizations which they regulate, as well as the relations between government bodies

Punishment: **1)** administrative punishment, or
  this administrative punishment can be imposed by a government agency
**2)** criminal punishment
  the government agency must take this action to court, and criminal punishment must be imposed by the criminal law courts

*types of prosecution:* In enforcing this administrative law in the private sector, government bodies must initiate action uniformly against all violators (persons, companies, etc.) However, due to a claimed lack-of-manpower in the enforcement agencies, action is often only instituted upon complaint[5] by a citizen or other private party.

Jurisdiction: Chinese Administrative Law Courts 行政法院

---

1. The famous *gao su nai lwun* 告訴乃論 : action will only be taken upon complaint.
2. In criminal suits, if the prosecutor takes action on his own initiative it is considered *fei gao su nai lwun* 非告訴乃論 . Crimes against society such as poisonings, arson, etc. certainly fall in this category. [*fei* = not]
3. Criminal penalties for patent, trademark, and copyright infringement clearly fall in this least important classification.
4. The public prosecutor will often ask to see proof that the complaining party has suffered damage, i.e. that the complaining party is "an interested party".
5. Amounting to a de facto *gao su nai lwun*, hence — selective enforcement.

*Notes for concerned westerners:*

**a)** Complaints about a lack of thoroughness or uniformity in enforcement should be made to the Control Yuan, which is empowered to take disciplinary actions against government officials or agencies.

**b)** Any one kind of legal problem could have elements of civil and criminal law, thus resulting in two suits.

**c)** If damage and injury were received due to the action of a government body, this might have elements of civil, criminal, and administrative law, thus resulting in three suits. One would be the main suit, the other two would be filed as accompanying suits.

## Conflicting Views of Naturalism

It is often seen that there is a strong undercurrent of naturalism in Chinese thinking. The words "natural" and "naturalism" have specific uses in a number of fields, most notably literature, painting, religion, mathematics, music, and western philosophy. However, outside of some overlapping with the usage in the area of religion, the "naturalism" we are discussing in this text is not related to these specific fields. The "naturalism" we are referring to is a rather generalized concept, and arises from the most basic definition of "natural", which is: **of, forming a part of, or arising from nature; in accordance with what is found in nature; true to, or showing fidelity to nature.** This naturalism brings to mind phrases such as "Go Back to Nature", "Do What Is Natural", "Follow the Natural Path in Behavior and Thought", "Consider the Original Nature of Human Beings", "Act in Accordance to Natural Laws", etc. In Chinese, "the way of heaven"[a] (which must be understood with regard to the fact that Buddhism, Taoism, Confucianism, etc. do not deal with or recognize the existence of a supreme deity), is often a synonym for "naturalism". Much of Chinese ethics begins from a so-claimed "natural manifestation of human nature", and The Doctrine of the Mean says "Following nature is called the way."

In speaking of this naturalism in the West, we are tempted to start our discussion by turning to the pages of *Walden*, Henry David Thoreau's account of his two years (1845–1847) spent living simply, frugally, and very close to nature in a cabin by Walden Pond, Massachusetts. In chapter 1, Thoreau tells us that while living at the pond, he had the opportunity to view society from the outside and see that, in contrast to his happy situation, most men were leading lives of quiet desperation. All men may confidently hope for a better life, he stresses, and they need only take the first step toward perfection: self-criticism.

Thoreau states his belief that once a man critically reviews his life he will immediate-

---

a. 天理、天道

ly discover a major hindrance to personal growth and happiness: the blind acceptance of traditional, conventional ways of living as handed down by previous generations. He feels that too many individuals unquestioningly accept what their parents and grandparents believed to be the meaning of life; this is the root of man's present predicament. Later on he continues on this theme, and rejects the old vision of man's relation to the universe, which held that an individual was suposed to fit into his preordained place and conform to a pre-established plan for his role in life, most commonly determined by tradition and authority. Thoreau makes a declaration of independence, stating that he will not fit into the world; rather, the world will fit around him, the world will exist in relation to him.

All of the above statements from *Walden* form a part of Thoreau's view of naturalism, however the long-term foreign resident of China is immediately struck by the polarity of these comments from what the Chinese regard as naturalism. The Chinese are quick to point out that the ancients were closer to nature than we are today, hence acceptance of traditional, conventional ways of living as handed down by previous generations is most natural; indeed the customs and traditions which have survived down to the present day are valid, and natural, by definition. To the extent that we can make our thought and behavior conform to the ways of our ancestors, we are getting closer to nature. For an individual to fit into his preordained place and conform to a pre-established plan for his role in life is most natural, since that is the way it has always been done.

In a general sense we must recognize that the Chinese regard "civilization" as a baseline for any discussion of this whole topic, hence men and women dressed in leaves (or less) running around in the forest would not correspond to the Chinese view of naturalism. We suspect Thoreau would have few reservations about this type of baseline, although he might disagree with much else.

Of course there is no exact consensus among the citizenry of western countries as to what is the most natural course of action to take in any situation. In relation to eating, some would say that consuming raw vegetables is most natural, others would maintain that since fire is naturally occurring, cooking vegetables over a fire is also quite natural. Due to the natural occurrence of mud, rocks, metals, etc., other people could also maintain that baking vegetables in brick ovens, forming vessels to cook them in, etc. are all natural actions. It may be expected that a great deal of divergence will be encountered in this and other areas when people of different cultural groups are discussing naturalism. In terms of eating, many Chinese have not traditionally viewed the consumption of raw food as natural, but as barbaric. This is only slowly changing in the present day.

Whether listening to lectures by learned western or Chinese scholars, the audience is often asked to accept the premise that "Naturalism is the best course", or "The Natural Way is the Best Way." Upon consideration it will be seen that these statements could be interpreted by the speaker to mean just about anything. This is especially true when discussion of various cross-cultural issues arises, and each side stresses that its views are the most natural, and therefore have the most validity. With this problem in mind, we have felt it illustrative to collect many aspects of Chinese naturalism, and mention how they diverge from western views.

We do not expect that all western readers will agree with all the comments under the "Alternative View" sections, however they do represent a point of reference. The contrast of Thoreau's views with those of the Chinese will serve as #1. We will start our listing at #2.

2) **Ancestor Worship.** If our parents had not created us, we would not exist. Parents have given us everything we have, hence we should give them total obedience, honor, and respect. We should cherish their memory after they pass away, and carry on the family name line by having male heirs. If our ancestors had not created our parents, none of us would exist, hence by extension it is completely natural to worship our ancestors.

*Alternative view:* in the Christian tradition, worship and obedience are naturally given to God. The commandment "Honor thy father and mother" has never been interpreted to mean one should worship one's parents or ancestors. Since the children, parents, and ancestors are equal before God, it is unnatural to worship or offer sacrifices to ancestors, for they occupy no special position. Since boys and girls are equal, there is no natural necessity to have male heirs. Preservation of the race is important, preservation of the family name line is considerably less important. Moreover, nature's most outstanding characteristic is that it is living, growing, and moving forward. To dwell on that which is dead is improper, since the natural direction of our thoughts is toward the present and future life of the living.[1]

Although many Chinese commonly believe that Mormons worship their ancestors, actually the Mormons are a "Restored Church" of Christianity, and offer worship to God, not ancestors or idols. They do hold that family relationships extend beyond the grave, and that Mormons can make salvation possible for their non-Mormon ancestors by performing certain ceremonies for them. Salt Lake City has the world's largest collection of genealogical data, international in scope.

3) **Filial Piety and Government Control.** Parents gave you life, hence have given you the totality of your being. It is natural that their dictates be obeyed always, and that parents' wishes and dictates are more important than those of one's spouse. Parents control all aspects of the child's life, hence children are not entitled to self-determination, but may only do what is specifically permitted. Government behaves the same way: the government rules the country as a result of winning the revolution, and they have the

---

1. There are a number of important differences between Christianity and Confucianism. Among the most important are that Christianity 1) is monotheistic, 2) stresses abstention from all idolatrous practices, 3) has a strong sense of essentially "contractual relation", and recognizes the appropriateness of punishment for violations, 4) does not limit its definition of the proper scope of important human relationships to five, 5) actively looks toward the future and does not idealize the ways of the ancients. As such it does not look for the definition and scope of relevance of important terms in relation to a society of 1000 or 2000 years ago, e.g. no one would define "Christian charity" based on a social outlook of 1000 AD, or 100 AD, etc. However the Chinese do frequently define many of their terms in this fashion: "benevolence" is one example.

mandate of heaven. Hence it is natural to say that the citizenry owe them everything, including their lives, homes, businesses, land, etc., and no criticism of the government should be tolerated. The citizenry are not entitled to self determination, rather the government controls all aspects of the citizens' lives, and citizens may only do what is specifically permitted. Business is subject to complete government control, and the government may grant business licenses, or monopoly licenses, for various industries to those to whom it sees fit, according to its own criteria which need not be publically announced. The government can require that the citizens stay at home to assist in national construction, and deny permission to travel domestically or overseas. Mineral wealth belongs to the government, and land which is found to contain minerals may be purchased by the government at whatever price it deems appropriate.

*Alternative view:* Any statement of the natural rights of man stresses that men are free and independent, and this would certainly apply to children after they have reached legal age. As such, they may decide on their own course of action, engaging in any activity not specifically disallowed. Men are naturally competent to take care of their own affairs, the citizenry may engage in any activities not specifically forbidden, and not specifically delegated to the national and local governments. Government naturally exists for the convenience of the people, and through consent of the governed, hence it is natural that the government officers owe a debt of gratitude for their jobs to the tax-paying citizens, who should be entitled to decide who is elected to which office. The citizens are also free to criticize the actions of the government whenever they see fit. To say that the people are in eternal debt to the government for everything they have denies the reality that the most natural government is merely an extension of the citizenry, and the best government is the least government. If the present government were to disappear tomorrow, the citizens could elect new representatives and go on with their affairs. Regulations which apply to the licensing of all industries must be fully promulgated. The government should stand in a position to help and assist business, while protecting the interests of the public at large, but has no right to absolute control. The citizenry may travel wherever they wish. Purchase of private land or property must be made at the market price; the government is not entitled to a special right in this regard.

**4) Intuitive Perception of Knowledge.** A child learns to walk and run not through elaborate explanations, but through observation and personal insight. Order in the universe is complex, however it exists without our interference, without our investigation or manipulation. The natural way to obtain knowledge is through calm observation and quiet contemplation, not through questioning. If one observes steadily, learning will come naturally through osmosis, in a spontaneous manner, and often through sudden intuition.[1,a]

---

1. Resulting in the often heard statement: "I know it, but I cannot explain it." 只可意會，不可言傳。
a. 頓悟

*Alternative view:* Knowledge must be systematically researched and investigated in order for us to achieve understanding, and indeed this is the course of action which results from natural curiosity. Induction and deduction are useful methods for dealing with precepts, but proof must be offered in order to establish the validity of a conclusion. The "Intuitive Perception of Knowledge" theory is valid to the extent proof and reasoning may be given for some premise, but without proof such Perceptions are often dangerous, and are at odds with an evidential bias and scientific methodology, both of which are concerned with naturally-existent facts, and hence are wholly natural. Beliefs founded on imagination, traditional reasoning, and the appearance of things, usually inherited from ancient philosophers, are considered superior to experimental evidence generally only in a Pre-Newtonian world.

5) **Harmony.** The Universe exists in natural harmony and balance. The proper social relations for man should naturally stress harmony first. Improper conduct by man can throw the world of nature out of joint.

*Alternative view:* Conflict is the natural order of the universe, and the resolution of conflict is the history of the universe. Man is a part of the universe, and resolution of conflict is properly seen as a natural concern of man in society. To say that harmony is the natural order of the universe is Pre-Darwinian. Darwin was an eminent naturalist, and his theories cannot be ignored.

**The exaggeration of the harmony attributed to Nature aroused men to note its disharmonies. An optimistic view of natural benevolence was followed by a more honest, less romantic view of struggle and conflict in nature. After Helvetius and Bentham came Malthus and Darwin.**

———— *John Dewey*

Nature is not static but in turmoil. If our life span was 10,000,000 years, we would see rocks turned into sand, old species of life die, and new species of life evolve. Just because some people cannot see change does not mean there is none, only that they are not aware of it.

The premise that the spirits of the land, wind, and water play an active role in man's affairs (and vice-versa) is not naturalism, but primitivism. To the extent that harmony in social dealings and dwelling arrangements is viewed as a premier consideration due to the typically overcrowded living conditions in most population centers, the encouragement of more individualism, of the single lifestyle, and of late marriages is the natural solution.

6) **History is Cyclical.** Like the seasons, history moves through natural cycles, and everything that happens has happened before. The future is determined by fate. The ancients had a much more perfect and natural society than we do today, and encountered every type of situation and circumstance. For knowledge we should look to the past, to the ways of the ancients.

*Alternative view:* Although there are similarities, history does not repeat itself all the time. The Industrial Revolution had never happened before. Progress is a result of man's effort and inquiry, and hence is perfectly natural. Man controls his future through his thoughts, actions, and plans. To say that we should live today in a manner similar to the ancients denies progress, and hence is exceedingly unnatural. The teachings of the ancients must be tempered in the light of the changed world situation of today, and the requirements of meeting the challenges of tomorrow. While being aware of the past, we should look to the future.

7) **Go With The Flow.**[a] The standard course of all activity in nature is like that of the flowing stream, and it is natural that man organize his activities in the same fashion. We should not try to manipulate nature for our own purposes, or make rigid plans, but rather recognize that nature controls man.[b] In society, the relationships we make are predestined by fate, and in determining proper behavior we should go along with custom as dictated by the society (the group).

*Alternative view:* The demands of civilization require that man plan his activities, moreover, nature was given as man's dominion to control, and to deny these facts is not to revert to naturalism, but to hermitism, or in the extreme, to live like the wild monkeys. Man is naturally entitled to exercise planning and control, doing what feels right and proper according to his own standards, while being careful not to violate the rights of others. Man makes his own destiny.

8) **Respect and Obey Elders.** Our elders have more experience in the world, and therefore it is natural that they are more knowledgeable than we are, hence we should respect them. Advanced age is naturally equivalent to advanced knowledge. We owe them our total respect and obedience. The elders dictate what actions are appropriate for children, and the elders in an organization have full authority over younger staff members.

*Alternative view:* In the democratic tradition, all people are created equal, and have a right to express their opinions, to vote, to petition, etc., regardless of whether these opinions conform to those of the elders. After attaining legal age, a child may act independently. In an era before the specialization of sciences (pre-1700), advanced age equaled advanced knowledge, however this is not true in a Post Industrial Revolution society. It is only true if knowledge is assumed as a fixed quantity, and virtually unchanging from generations to generation. Therefore there is no natural claim to saying that elders may dictate what actions are appropriate for their offspring, or subordinates. Plautus said "Not by age but by capacity and disposition is wisdom acquired."

9) **Polytheism.** In the view of most traditional Asian religions and philosophies, polytheism is natural, and a large pantheon of "gods" is recognized.[1]

*Alternative view:* The western tradition has been predominately Christian, and hence recognizes one supreme deity as the creator of the universe. Polytheism is not considered naturalism, but is rather is associated with the pagan rituals of uncivilized tribes. The

---

1. The outgrowths of this attitude appear in many forms, and serve as both cause and effect of the Group Mentality.

    a. 聽其自然         b. 生死有命，富貴在天

statement or implication that men can rise to the position of gods after death is blasphemy.

**10) Complete Corpse Concept.** A person's body belongs to his parents, ancestors, and clan, and should be carefully preserved after death, not mutilated in any way, subject to surgical investigation, or autopsy. It is natural that the body being prepared for burial should be retained in the same complete fashion in which it existed in life, so that it may keep its integrity when it becomes a spirit/ghost. The consideration of this entire issue is largely unrelated to humanism.

*Alternative view:* After a person has died, their body is of no further use to them. The request that various useful organs be donated for medical research, or that autopsies be done to extend medical knowledge, with the future goal of saving and prolonging other lives, is perfectly natural. Likewise, if some organs may be donated immediately for transplantation to needy individuals, this is a very humanitarian gesture, and eminently in keeping with a proper definition of humanism. Many people desire that inoperative organs be replaced with properly functioning ones, and this is the natural direction of medical practice.

Additional Considerations and Summary

The Chinese philosophy of Lao-tse has a strong undercurrent of naturalism, as when the sage says "The natural way is to support things in their natural state and thus allow them to transform spontaneously." "The Way" spoken of in these writings is often clarified as "the way of nature". In general the Taoist philosophy of "Do nothing, and all things will be done"[1] is considered naturalism, (as well as being an underlying premise of "indirectness"), and a "Go with the Flow" type of reasoning is an outgrowth of this. In many types of daily dealings, most westerners would often consider it more natural for man to be organized, systematic, and direct.

Western historians consider the development of a nation's naval power as a natural phenomenon, and often puzzle over why the Chinese never developed in this direction. Chinese historians maintain that this simply was not the natural direction for their country's development to proceed.

Those familiar with international economic theory will recognize that the citizens and officials of the communist and socialist countries can, through elaborate historical analysis, show that those doctrines are the natural outgrowth of historical trends and human needs. Most educated individuals in democratic free-enterprise capitalistic societies can also show that democratic capitalism is the natural outgrowth of historical trends and human needs. It is not the point of this discussion to determine who is right or wrong in this type of "economic system" argument, but merely to note that both sides have proceeded from the premise of "naturalism", and have arrived at diametrically opposed conclusions.

---

1. Compare this to the maxim of 天下本無事，庸人自擾之 which also stresses inaction.

Another point of Chinese naturalism is the claim that "since we have done it this way since the beginning of recorded history, it is natural to do it this way." Reflection on this statement reveals that it would be an excellent justification for slavery (including the buying and selling of human lives in general), the autocratic rule of kings, the maintenance of rigid social classes, etc., and hence the westerner is forced to deny its validity. In the western view, it is proper to question anything, and continue to ask "Why?"

Indeed, the search for the answer to "Why?" seems exceedingly natural to the westerner, and the reply "because we have always done it this way" is not a natural reason, since it appears to assume the mind is incapable of reasoning. To a large degree this is due to the fact that the westerners 1) do not tend to idealize ancient society, 2) do not consider the ways of the ancients sacrosanct. These two aspects of western behavior and thought have arisen from a mode of thinking which does not include ancestor worship, and from a tendency, especially notable in the last 300 years, to be iconoclastic, and reject orthodoxy. A specific listing of westerners' "Rejections of Orthodoxy" is also included in this volume.

> The life which is unexamined is not worth living.
> ——— *Plato*

In summary we would say that among Asians and westerners there is often a difference of opinion on what constitutes "natural behavior", "natural desires", or naturalism in general, and that many doctrines which one cultural group considers in conformity to nature are often viewed by other cultural groups as "unnatural naturalism".

Discussion questions:

1. Thomas Jefferson said "A wise and frugal Government shall restrain men from injuring one another, shall leave them otherwise free to regulate their own pursuits of industry and improvements." Americans tend to believe that government should primarily serve one purpose — to create conditions favorable to the protection of the freedom of the individual. Is this related to naturalism in the western view? Is this related to naturalism in the Chinese view?

2. Life on the frontier is often viewed as an expression of individual freedom, self reliance, and the ideal of equality of opportunity. Frontier people tend to treat each other as social equals, and the highest importance is placed on what a person can do in the present, with hardly any importance placed on who his dead ancestors were. Frontiersmen say "What is above the ground is more important than what is beneath the ground." Would westerners consider these types of thinking and rationale natural? Would Chinese consider them natural?

3. In North America, Europe, and many other western regions, there is emphasis on raising children to be independent and separate from their parents. Some have said that

the western goal of parenting is "to make children competent and confident enough to leave the nest." People are expected to leave relationships for opportunities, and it is considered unreasonable, or somewhat unpatriotic, for parents to *cling*. Would this be considered a natural view in the more ancient societies such as China, India, or the tribes in Western and Central Africa?

## Discussions of Naturalism in Adam Smith's Wealth of Nations
### (published 1776)

Humanity consists essentially of sovereign individuals pursuing their self-interest in competition with one another. These activities, when left to operate largely unchecked, produce a "natural" social order, as opposed to an artificial one imposed by aristocratic vested interest, tradition, custom, conventionalism, opposition to human progress and enlightenment (so called "obscurantism"), etc. The pursuit of self-interest will lead to the most rapid possible increase in the wealth of nations, which will be reflected in the increased comfort and well-being of all men.

The basis of the natural order is the social division of labour. It is possible to prove with some relatively simple equations that the existence of a class of capitalists owning the means of production benefits all, including the labourers employed. In a similar fashion, it may be proved that the interests of both Britain and Jamaica were best served by one producing manufactured goods and the other producing raw sugar.

The increase in the wealth of nations is caused by the operations of property-owning private enterprise and the resulting accumulation of capital. Other methods of increasing this wealth are relatively slower and more innefficient.

The economically very unequal society which inevitably results from the operations of human nature is not incompatible with the natural equality of all men or with justice. Actually, it secures a better life than otherwise would have been had by the poor. Essentially, it is based on the most equal of all relationships, the exchange of equivalents in the market. Hence, no one becomes dependent on the benevolence of anyone else, because for everything that one receives, he gives an equivalent in exchange. Moreover, the free play of natural forces will be destructive of all occupations which are not built upon the contribution to the common good.

Progress is as natural as capitalism. All artificial obstacles to progress should be removed, and it follows that the progress of production will go hand in hand with that of the arts, sciences, and civilization in general. The way forward for humanity is through capitalism. A nation's prosperity can best be provided by allowing the uniform, constant, and uninterrupted effort of every man to better his condition . . . "It is not from the benevolence of the butcher, the brewer, or the baker that we expect our dinner, but from their regard to their own interest. We address ourselves, not to their humanity, but to their self-love, and never talk to them of our own necessities, but of their advantages."

Modern industry is made possible by the division of labour and the accumulation of capital, both of which are explained by self-interest, and are obvious ramifications of "the natural order". Unconsciously, a divine hand leads man so that, in working for his own gain, he is contributing to the good of the whole. It naturally follows that there should be minimum government interference with the economic order.

Observations: Smith was primarily concerned with production. He showed that every human being is motivated primarily by self-interest, although a desire for wealth is only one of its manifestations. David Ricardo, another early economic thinker, was concerned with distribution. Ricardo pointed out many contradictions within the system which Smith had overlooked, and other economists to this day have continued to refine Smith's classical theories.

The Chinese are also motivated by self-interest, however to the extent that the west has seen a greater and more rapid increase in the wealth of nations, and China much less so, this must be explained by recognizing the greater restrictions and limitations on the pursuit of the individual's self-interest in China. Certainly the entire Group Mentality orientation is one of these restrictions. In *The Development of Personality*, Carl Jung stated:

> What is it, in the end, that induces a man to go his own way and to rise out of unconscious identity with the mass as out of a swathing mist? Not necessity, for necessity comes to many, and they all take refuge in convention. Not moral decision, for nine times out of ten we decide for convention likewise. What is it, then, that inexorably tips the scales in favour of the extra-ordinary?
> It is what is commonly called vocation: an irrational factor that destines a man to emancipate himself from the herd and from its well-worn paths.

The denial of the vocation [a calling, summons, or impulsion to do something] which the individual feels, and the assumed highly superior position of the group, especially the family/clan, over the individual, is much less compatible with a true pursuit of self-interest, than the individualized orientation found among most westerners.

Related to this, the differing attitudes which Chinese and westerners take toward "orthodoxy" are significant, and will be discussed later in this chapter.

## The Implications of Positiveness

"Positive" is a very popular adjective in the west. In order to promote cross cultural communication, some discussion should be made of this word in relation to its use in the Chinese language and Chinese mentality. Let us first consider how we would rate an expression like "Positive Thinking" in terms of ethnocentric overtones. Is it a western concept, an Oriental concept, or is it neutral? Many Americans I have questioned feel it is an essentially neutral term. Additionally, we may pause to speculate how and if it relates at all to "Positive Action"?

Dictionary Investigation

In an English dictionary we can find nearly twenty distinct uses for the term "positive", including technical senses in bacteriology, biology, electricity, medicine, linguistics, mathematics, photography, etc. Certainly all of these meanings tend to go together to form the totality of what the native English speaker regards as positive. However, checking our English-to-Chinese dictionary, we see that the translation for most of these twenty usages of this one English word are rendered differently, and therefore bear no direct relation to each other.

As a result, in my many years of translation work, I have come to find that the use of Positive in reference to "Positive Thinking", "Positive Remarks", "Positive Measures" etc., is not easily rendered into Chinese. The standard translation is *jeng mian de.*[a] In this phrase, *de* is a possessive particle, *mian* means **side or face**, and *jeng* carries a variety of connotations, including: **obverse, appropriate, proper, just, pure, straightforward, honest,** etc. Obviously these synonyms or descriptions must be understood in terms of Chinese perceptions and standards, not western ones.

With these definitions in mind, it may be said that "Do not drive through the red light", "Do not spend more money than you make", "Be nice to your younger sister", "Study hard so that you can get into college", "You should do what your teacher says", etc. are all good examples of what the Chinese could see as characteristic of Positive Thinking (since they represent proper, appropriate thinking). However in the western point of view, these bear little or no relation to Positive Thinking whatsoever, since they lack the core idea of (as expressed in Norman Vincent Peale's book *The Power of Positive Thinking*): **having confidence and believing in one's own abilities, refusing to be defeated, making the most of what you have to deal with in life, never giving up, never giving in.**

By writing down this core idea, and then sitting back to look at it, we do see that some problems have been generated. To the extent that this core idea has overtones of individualism and self-reliance, this would be at odds with the Chinese ideal of mutual dependence, while its overtones of assertiveness and strength-of-convictions would be at odds with the Chinese ideal of humility. The implication that one's destiny is in one's own hands denies the traditional undercurrent of fatalism in much of Chinese thinking.

> Whatever you can do, or dream you can, begin it.
> Boldness has genius, power, and magic in it.
>
> ——— *Goethe*

Further confusion is generated when we consider that positive thinking, positive measures, etc. must be coordinated with effort, in other words they must be somehow

---

a. 正面的

carried out or put into effect. Indeed we often hear westerners say "Where there is a will there is a way," and this reflects a belief that we may move forward with our thinking, and turn it into reality. However, in the Chinese philosophy of Lao-tse, Chwang-tse, etc., are statements like "The sage manages affairs without action, and spreads doctrine without words", "The Way takes no action and there is nothing left undone", and "By following nothing, by pursuing nothing, the Way may be attained." Modern extrapolations of this are numerous, including "The best enforcement is no enforcement", "The best planning is no planning", and the statement "There is no way to guarantee winning a chess game, but one sure way to guarantee not losing: don't play." We might properly classify this as **Positive Inaction.** This type of approach to human endeavor must certainly be contrasted with **Positive Action**, with which the westerner is far more familiar. In dealing with Chinese thinking, we must be aware of these two types of action or conduct, and of their implications for the Chinese person's understanding of what Positive connotes.

> Victory belongs to the most persevering.
> ——— *Napoleon Bonaparte*

> No one knows what he can do until he tries.
> ——— *Syrus*

As with much other terminology which involves philosophical concepts, its use in conversation and lecturing is not restricted. However, what the westerner means when he employs this term may bear very little relation to the Chinese understanding of how it should be construed. A Chinese and a western party may be in full agreement on a premise, but arrive at completely different conclusions as to how this premise should be extrapolated into action and reality (or even if any action should be taken). For those westerners who desire clearer communication, it would certainly be advisable to give abundant examples, and to outline the way in which the recommended conduct or conclusion in each case relates to the original stipulations. Patience is certainly necessary in such an undertaking.

## Half-Empty or Half-Full

In order to determine another person's basic outlook on life, one favorite question to ask is: If you have a glass, and the water inside it is exactly at the mid-point level, how do you describe it? Many westerners with a knowledge of psychology claim that if the respondent replies "half-full", he is generally more of an optimist, and a positive thinker. If he replies "half-empty", he is perhaps more of a pessimist, and tends to look on the bad side. However, many Chinese have pointed out that this is not a valid distinction. We may consider a glass filled halfway, a grain-bin filled halfway, a warehouse filled halfway, etc., and in every case it is the very fact that it is "half-empty" that clarifies that it still has immediate usefulness. If it is full, we cannot put anything more in it, therefore it has ceased to be useful. Hence, in this view, "half-empty" is also a positive statement.

Lao-tse said: "Shape clay into a vessel, it is the space within that makes it useful. Cut doors and windows for a room, it is the holes which make it useful. Therefore profit comes from what is there, usefulness from what is not there."

## Individual vs. the Group

So-called "Positive Action" also implies that an individual is assuming the responsibility for initiating a certain series of events that will flow from this action. However, the people in many Oriental cultures tend to view responsibility in a group context, and shy away from individual responsibility. This aspect of organizational behavior is often noted in Chinese bureaucracies, and in family-run organizations.

For the westerner who desires the Chinese to take Positive Measures to remedy any sort of situation, it is most likely that an exact listing of the actions to be taken, as well as their method of application, the relevant time frame, etc. all be specified in much detail. In this manner we suspect a great deal of confusion can be eliminated.

Of course it is often true that the word "positive" is used a bit broadly in English, as a close synonym to other words. In a good thesaurus we find such synonyms as definite, explicit, express, sure, certain, precise, unequivocal, substantial, stated, assured, confident, etc. Sentence examples are numerous: "We want to encourage a positive relationship between our cousins", "The investigation will soon be made and is expected to attain a positive result", "More positive measures are needed to help the flood victims", "She is expected to make a positive contribution to our work in this committee", etc. To facilitate cross-cultural communication, it is advisable that we clearly outline what we mean by "positive" in each situation.

## Positive Considerations in *The Book of Changes*

In The *Book of Changes (Yi Ching)* is stated: "In the systems of change, there is the Great Ultimate (Tai chi), which generates the Two Modes, Yin and Yang. The Two Modes generate the Four Forms, major and minor yin and yang. The Four Forms generate the Eight Elements. The Eight Trigrams determine good and evil fortunes. Good and evil fortunes produce the great business of life." This is further explained in the following way: "The Great Ultimate through movement generates Yang. When its activity reaches its limit, it becomes tranquil. Through tranquillity the Great Ultimate generates Yin. When tranquillity reaches its limit, activity begins again. So, movement and tranquillity alternate and become the root of each other, giving rise to the distinction of Yin and Yang, and the Two Modes are thus established."

| Yang | Yin |
|---|---|
| Positive | Negative |
| Day | Night |
| Sun | Moon |
| Light | Dark |
| Masculine | Feminine |
| Soul | Body |

The conception of Yin and Yang can be traced to the remote past, when divination was the primary intellectual activity in China. In line with this theory, Yin and Yang must be in balance, in harmony, for the world to function properly. The balance of these two Modes (or Ethers) is then viewed as the natural state. Their interaction operates to produce all things, and these in turn produce and reproduce, so that the transformation and change continue without end.

Clearly this view reflects some degree of moderation over the long run, and a search for harmony through a balance of opposing forces. In this way it appears to bear some logical relation to the "positive" and "negative" spoken of in magnetism, yet the westerners rarely use magnetism as a model for human activity, except to say that boys and girls attract each other. Yin and Yang are extremely more broadly based as a theoretical model, being the Chinese people's basic underlying formulation to the structure of the Universe, the ordering of society, and the functioning of the human body.[1]

A continuous and non-relenting "Positive Approach" (indicating an excess of Yang) over the long term could easily be viewed as a violation of this desired state of balance and harmony. The failure of many movements in China which have strived for Positive Reform may perhaps be viewed more clearly in light of the Yin and Yang formulation, and with reference to the outlook of Lao-tse when he conceives of the Way (Tao) as both "is" and "is not".

The foreigner is now free to return our original question, and more carefully consider whether "Positive Thinking" is a western concept, an Oriental concept, or is it neutral?

Discussion questions:
1. Do the Chinese need more Positive Thinking in their daily lives?
2. Is Positive Thinking compatible with Buddhism? What about with other philosophical/religious doctrines?
3. What would be some indirect methods for promoting Positive Thinking? How could

---

1. The combination of Soul 魂 and Body 魄 is seen in such idioms as 魂飛魄散 "frightened out of one's wits".

one indirectly skirt possible objections to its application when and if such objections arose?

## Rejection vs. Acceptance of Orthodoxy

Much of the structure of the modern western economies, as well as their politics and ideology, were formed during the dual Revolutions of the 1780s: the Industrial Revolution in Britain, and the French Revolution in France. Many historians have pointed out that world politics between 1789 and 1917 were primarily the struggle for and against the principles of 1789, which were fully espoused in The Declaration of the Rights of Man. These Revolutions changed the habitation style, work patterns, and indeed the mental makeup of the majority of westerners.

The Industrial Revolution which began modestly in Lancashire, England, has been called the most important event in world history since the invention of agriculture and metallurgy, or the formation of cities. Speaking of the events of the following 60 years leading up to the establishment of the world's first Railway system, in Britain, we must recognize that they were not simply the triumph, in some general sense, of industry, of liberty and equality, nor of the modern economy. They are more properly viewed in specific terms, as representing the triumph of "capitalist industry", of "middle class liberal society", and of the economies and countries in a particular geographical region, centering on Great Britain, France, and a few sections of North America.

The French Revolution is considered the most fundamental of its time, even more fundamental than its precursor the American Revolution, for several reasons: It occurred in the most powerful and populous state of Europe, it was a mass social revolution immeasurably more radical than any comparable upheaval, and it was universal in its repercussions. Many American revolutionaries, visiting France in the 1780's, found themselves to be moderates by French standards.

Speaking of these revolutions, and their repercussions over the next half-century or more, social historians have noted that for the first time in history, men gained control over physical nature and threw off the control of men over men, which is to say men discovered science and political freedom. The creative energy, the abundance, the wealth, and the rising standard of living for every level of the population were dramatic, and unequalled in human history. Although there were low wages and harsh living conditions associated with the early years of capitalism, the Industrial Revolution was not the cause of poverty, but rather inherited it from the previous eras. What it did offer was the chance for the poor to survive, and this could only be contrasted with centuries of Pre-Industrial Revolution starvation.

## Social Results

Perhaps the greatest change caused by the Industrial Revolution was the transition from rural to urban life, and the influence of mechanization on increasingly wider aspects of daily life. As a result of the Revolution, man does his daily work in a different way, with different tools, at a different tempo, and as part of a different type of organizational structure. After work, the worker and his family consume different goods and services, according to new mores.

Immersed in the "Enlightenment" thought of the 18th century, people of that era believed that human history was an ascent, rather than a decline, and was not an undulating or cyclical movement about a level trend, (although later historians have noted that there is some degree of cyclical movement around this generally ascending trend). They were able to observe that man's scientific knowledge and technical control over nature increased daily. The Enlightenment was marked by a questioning of tradition. It developed many ramifications in the religious, political, scientific, moral, and even aesthetic spheres. The desire for progress was manifest, and the status quo was looked upon with doubt, as the movement's adherents struggled to free men's minds from the oppression of dogma and authority. Man was now held to have the right to direct his own destiny insofar as he was able, and given the impetus to make his life on earth and its betterment his highest goal, although the vague belief in the power of a guiding deity was retained.

Up to 1789 the ideology of progress had also been a strong component of classical bourgeois liberalism. Being rigidly rationalist and secular, it presupposed that men could solve all problems by the use of reason, and viewed traditionalism in all fields as having a tendency to obscure rather than to enlighten. Philosophically, since its force and methods were primarily drawn from the 17th century scientific revolution, it tended toward materialism, and empiricism, and had a pervasive undercurrent of individualism. In the course of pursuing his own self-interest, each individual found it advantageous in some cases, and unavoidable in others, to enter into certain relations with other individuals, and this complex of useful arrangements, which came to be viewed in the terminology of commercialism as representing a "contract", were what actually constituted society and socio-political groups. The job of politics was to reduce any and all interference in the individual's life to the practicable minimum, and social aims were viewed to be the arithmetical sum of individual aims. The greatest happiness of the greatest number of people was the goal of society. Many traditional institutions fell before the onslaught of utilitarianist questioning: "Is this rational?" "Is this useful?" "Does this contribute to the greatest happiness (or good) of the greatest number?"

Comments: the above discussion has mentioned a number of social movements which amounted to "Rejections of Orthodoxy" in the west, in that traditional ways of thinking and doing things were cast aside, and new ways were formulated. These include the Enlightenment, the Industrial Revolution and indeed the entire movement toward

## Newton and the Modern World View

The writings of Issac Newton made a fundamental break with the past by insisting that there is no difference between earthly and celestial phenomena. "Like effects in nature are produced by like causes," he stated, and he strove to mathematically prove that events in all corners of the cosmos are governed by the same rational laws.

Scientific advancement in the 20th century has revealed some degree of inadequacy in Newton's work. Nevertheless, the design of a 100 or 200 story building, the structure of a railroad bridge, the motion of a motor vehicle, the flight of an airplane or space shuttle, the navigation of a sailboat or supertanker, the measure of time in our daily lives, and other aspects of contemporary civilization still depend primarily on Newton's laws. The great Newtonian synthesis is inadequate only with reference to the ultra-refinements of modern science, such as when dealing with quantum theory, subatomic units of matter, or the Einsteinian conceptualization of time and motion in the universe. The engineer who is constructing a bridge, dockyard, astrodome, or underground bomb shelter does exactly what he would have done had Newton's system never been proved incomplete. The same is true of any electrical tradesman, whether he is fixing a FAX machine or designing a hydroelectric dam. The science of everyday life is still wholly Newtonian-based.

capitalist industry and global trading, the French Revolution, and the American Revolution.

Other rejections of the established order which have occurred in western history are numerous, and many will come to mind to the person with even a minimal knowledge of history. Starting our listing at #5, we will list several for reference, although in no particular historical order.

**5.** The writings of Copernicus, especially *De Revolutionibus Orbium Coelestium* (1543), Kepler's *Astronomia Nova* (1609), Galileo's *Dialogue* (1632), and Newton's *Principia Mathematica* (1687), which overthrew the traditional view of man's relation to the cosmos and the world around him, while specifically rejecting the Catholic Church's earth-centered view of the Universe.

Copernicus' influence on his contemporaries and on all subsequent thought have entitled him to a pre-eminent position in the history of science. As Goethe wrote "Of all discoveries and opinions, none may have exerted a greater effect on the human spirit than the doctrine of Copernicus. The world had scarcely become known as round and complete in itself when it was asked to waive the tremendous privilege of being the center of the universe. Never, perhaps, was a greater demand made on mankind—for by this admission so many things vanished in mist and smoke!" Unwilling to see these things vanish in mist and smoke, the Catholic Church placed the writings of Copernicus on the Index of prohibited books, where they remained for over 200 years.

Western scientists and Nobel-prize winners have commented that publication of Copernicus' work marked a turning point of such great importance as to influence every phase of human thought. It affords an outstanding example of the effect of scientific truth in the freeing of man's mind from outdated customs and superstitious beliefs, and in clearing his vision for future conquests of ignorance and intolerance. In breaking with a conception of the solar system that had stood for thousands of years, Copernicus initiated the whole modern method of scientific thought, and modified our thinking on all phases of human life. His work was carried on by several other investigators, despite official disapproval of the Church.

**6.** The Protestant Reformation, begun in Germany in 1517 by Martin Luther. The birth of Protestantism was a significant break with the past. Among other important promulgations, Luther rejected the idea that acts of wickedness can be forgiven by a priest acting in God's name. Accumulating data from the Bible and a wide variety of theological studies, he showed that individuals are left alone before God to improve themselves or suffer eternal punishment for their sins. To this day, Protestantism encourages a strong and restless desire for self-improvement.

**7.** The Pilgrims' rejection of the Church of England's authority, departure for Massachusetts on the *Mayflower,* and establishment of a new colony there in 1620. The Pilgrims came to a new land to begin new lives for themselves, leaving behind everything that was customary and familiar. Among all the immigrants who came to the New World, there was a basic hope for a brighter future, and a view of humanity perhaps best summarized by Nathaniel Hawthorne: "Human nature will not flourish, any more than a potato, if it be planted and replanted, for too long a series of generations, in the same worn-out soil."

**8.** The American frontier experience, the opening of uninhabited regions to commerce, agriculture, industry, prospecting, and settlement; epitomized by the struggle of man against nature. This generally westward expansion and exploration began on the east coast in the 1600's, and ended in about 1890 when the last western lands were settled.

**9.** The great "year of revolutions" in 1848 and its related repercussions. Louis Philippe was overthrown, the Second Republic proclaimed, and a new French constitution was promulgated.Prince Metternick fell, and revolt against Habsburg domination spread through Hungary, Bohemia, and Italy. King Frederick William IV promised a constitution to the Prussians and an assembly at Frankfurt discussed German federation. Further ups and downs in these and related developments were seen over the next seventy-five years.

**10.** The writings of Charles Darwin, especially the *Origin of Species* (1859), which introduced the concept of evolution through natural selection. Controversies have raged around Darwin's work for more than a century, and continue to rage in some circles.

Some scholars have also claimed that the United States matured in many ways as a result of the Vietnam War Era anti-war movement and student protests, and we suppose this could be added to our listing as well.

Chinese Influence

Yet we fail to see that any of these factors had much of a direct effect on the mental conceptions of most Chinamen, certainly not to the point of showing them any need for seriously reviewing traditional ways of thought and action, and rejecting such traditionalism in favor of new ideas. Looking for some historical movement, domestically instigated, that would have had this kind of impact on the Chinese, we find the 1851 Tai Ping Rebellion, which was an attempt to overthrow the Ching Dynasty. Its announced goals were to establish Christianity; create a more egalitarian society characterized by religious brotherhood. It also sought to overthrow idolatry and ancestor worship, and the Confucianism in state and society. This Rebellion was finally crushed in 1864.

The May 4th Movement in 1919, and the accompanying intellectual revolution seemed significant at the time, however its major themes of freedom, equality, and independence were bound together tightly with the desire to save China from the weakened international position in which it found itself in the early 1900's, which contrasted with previous centuries in which China was in a leadership position among civilized nations. Unfortunately, without a strong middle class, many of the Movement's liberal ideals never gained wide support among the populace. The desire for a strong state to resist foreign aggression came to surpass demands for freedom and independence. Anti-authoritarian feelings also began to run out of steam in the late 1920's.

The overthrow of the Ching Dynasty and establishment of the Republic of China in 1912 were of course very important, however various warring factions in the country continued to battle until the nation was reunified with the completion of the Northern Expedition in 1928. A decade of some stability was maintained before the all-out Japanese attack of 1937, which unsettled the nation again, and kept it in the throes of conflict until the close of WWII.

However, despite any number of movements or achievements which may be listed, it should be remembered that the Chinese politicians, teachers, intellectuals, etc. tend over the long term to seek justification for new developments in the classical tradition. Hence many, or most, Chinese reformers over the last few hundred years have looked for "sourcing" for their ideas or principles (often retroactively, one suspects) in the pages of the classics, and they have generally been able, by reinterpreting various passages, to find them. To the remainder of the Chinese populace, who have a strong emotional attachment to the ancient traditions, this seems to clothe such actions in a far greater air of acceptability and respectability.[1]

In summary it would appear that there are far fewer historical upheavals which have been brought to a successful conclusion in China which amounted to real Rejections of Orthodoxy, and this is certainly an important consideration in recognizing why the Chinese are more tied to tradition than westerners.

---

1. Indeed, surveying the entire span of Chinese history and the complex interplay of personalities over the millennia, many western historians have commented "There have been very many rebels but very few revolutionaries."

In speaking of Chinese history, the difference between "rebel" and "revolutionary" is not always easy to quantify. Some historians have suggested that while both openly resist authority, oppose the present government, and may hope to achieve positions of power in some future political hierarchy, a rebel is generally content in retaining most of the traditional structure and functioning of the present government in the "new order", while a revolutionary advocates drastic change in the entire governmental system.

## Chinese People Don't Do That

I received the following comments from an American ex-navy officer who had married a Chinese and lived in the country for several years:

> There is generally a hint of evil associated with being a non-Chinese. If Chinese people don't do it, it should never be done. If you do it, you are not Chinese, therefore *you are not*. There is no distinction between races of people here. You *are* or you *are not* Chinese. And if you are not Chinese, you just are not.

Indeed it may arguably be stated that the Chinese have no real word for "orthodoxy" as such, because they have always regarded their status quo as the correct and only viable one. In the *Book of Mencius* we read "Without transgression, without forgetfulness; follow the ancient canons. No one has ever erred through following the principles of the ancient kings." In *Future Shock*, Alvin Toffler categorizes this type of maladaptation to the changing world as "The Reversionist". This person is characterized by obsessive reversion to previously successful adaptive routines that are now irrelevant and inappropriate; he demands a return to the glories of yesteryear.

Since the Chinese have always regarded themselves as being at the center of civilization, other points of view or cultural perceptions seldom had any validity in their eyes, and therefore were rarely discussed in a serious fashion. Checking the dictionary, we see that "orthodoxy" translates into Chinese as **correct, proper, customary, or traditional.** The idea of questioning this, or of trying to define a "new orthodoxy", rarely enters into the Chinese thought pattern, indeed to question this makes one un-Chinese, makes one insulting to the sense of what is Chinese. *Change* in the Chinese mind appears closely associated to instability, but this puzzles the westerner who asks "Why can't you have change with stability?". Reference to Mencius' quote above indicates that the Chinese prefer to follow the ways of the ancestors, and dislike making a deliberate and forceful break with the past. Heterodoxy is strongly discouraged.

In *Self Reliance,* Ralph Waldo Emerson said "Most men have bound their eyes with one or another handkerchief, and attached themselves to some one of these communities of opinion. This conformity makes them not false in a few particulars, authors of a few lies, but false in all particulars. Their every truth is not quite true." To the extent that the Chinese people follow orthodoxy more closely than westerners, these comments would appear to be a greater indictment of their reasoning, than of western reasoning.

## Schools and Textbooks

The existence of local self-government is also a factor which will tend to cause the populace to develop different ideas on the way traditional ideology may be used, or not used, in solving present day problems, and which will have a mitigating affect on unquestioning acceptance of established orthodoxy in many fields. The teaching of subjects in the schools, through the use of approved textbooks, is a good example of this. In Japan, the United States, and most West European countries, local school boards have a wide degree of freedom in deciding which textbooks they may use for instruction in their schools, and different school districts may choose different texts which are weighted more toward history, science, classical or modern literature, liberalized or conservative sexual norms, etc., according to the general preferences of the people in the community. In China however, school texts in elementary through junior high school are 97% standardized, with one edition, edited under the auspices of the Ministry of Education, specified for use in each subject at each grade level, and local school districts have no say in the matter. This assures that the content and overtones of the teaching material all follow the national government line. In senior high school the percentage drops to perhaps 30%, with the schools making choices of other "approved" texts from the marketplace. This authoritarian textbook policy certainly reflects the acceptance of one and only one view of "orthodox education", and serves to assure that no alternative viewpoints find their way into the educational system.

The free, exploring mind of the individual is the most valuable thing in the world. And this I would fight for: the freedom of the mind to take any direction it wishes, undirected.
—— John Steinbeck

If we educate too abruptly, if we cram the mind with facts memorized for themselves alone, what comes? Pure atrophy.
——Thomas Edison

Additionally, Chinese education has tended to stress memorization, and not interpretation or analysis. Instead of asking the students to discuss varying interpretation of poems or essays, or even to explain the author's meaning in their own words, the major force of the lesson is for them to memorize various sections, so that they can "reproduce" these well-turned phrases on their test papers in an exact manner.[1] The historical progression of the Dynasties, Emperors, Prime Ministers, and other minor functionaries in each era must also be memorized, so that one may regurgitate this information effortlessly on an endless series of examinations, and term papers, as each student goes into elaboration on the accepted version of all the historical movements. The inherent support of orthodoxy, at a grass roots level, which this causes, is highly indicative of the importance which Chinese attach to making everyone think in the same manner, and making everyone march to the beat of the same drummer.

In painting, calligraphy, and other fields, how well a Chinese artist copies the content, form, and techniques of ancient masterpieces has always been considered a measure of his skill. This type of tradition in the art world assures that the greatest recognition, applause, and respect go to those who excel in being unquestioning conformists, and supporting the orthodox methodology.

---

1. Confucius said: "I transmit but do not create; I am sincerely fond of antiquity." (*Analects*, VII, 1)

> There are people who not only strive to remain static themselves, but strive to keep everything else so, and weep like Heraclitus to find that nothing ever stands still to be studied, understood, and described. Their grievance against the world is that it insists upon changing at every moment and destroying all their categories. Who that has lived at all has not sympathized with them at one time or another? And yet their position is almost laughably hopeless.
> ——— *Odell Shepard*

The westerner in China will often have occasion to see that the entire issue of how to blend the great traditional Chinese customs and value system with the demands of the economically and technologically advanced state of the modern world today, and still retain the sense of Chineseness, is often a subject that provokes heated arguments, even among the Chinese themselves.

## Logic and its Ramifications

Introductory Orientations

> If you call a tail a leg, how many legs has a dog? Five? No, calling a tail a leg don't make it a leg.
> ———*Abraham Lincoln*

What would the Chinese say? They would say "Well, what are the circumstances? Who said it? Was it a village carpenter? Was it the village elder? Was it a fisherman down by the river? Was it the Provincial Magistrate? Was it the Emperor? A statement made by a person in a position of authority is valid within their area of control."

**Determination:** If the Emperor said it, then a dog indeed has five legs and will continue to have five legs until another Emperor makes another declaration.[1]

The following story illustrates this mode of thinking.

The Second Emperor of the Chin Dynasty[a] undertook some massive construction projects, and burdened the people with conscripted labor, military service, and heavy taxes. Chao Gao[b], a senior minister, plotted to have control over the Emperor, and gradually took charge of all of the court administration. Li Si[c], the prime minister, tried to persuade the Emperor to stop the construction projects, as well as cut down taxation and conscription. The Second Emperor did not take his advice, and angered by his comments, had him convicted of various charges. Chao Gao took the opportunity to see that Li Si was found guilty and executed.

Soon thereafter, Chao Gao was given the post of Prime Minister, and tried to further increase his own power in the court. Fearing that the other ministers might not follow

---

a. 秦二世　　　b. 趙高　　　c. 李斯

1. The personalities involved in any decision are very important to the Chinese. Their determination of the correct course of action to take in any situation often rests on consideration of the people and faces involved.

his bidding or recognize his authority, he arranged a special situation to test them. Early one morning he presented the Second Emperor with a deer which he said was a horse. The Emperor was somewhat surprised at this, and turned to the other Ministers around him for confirmation. Some remained silent, some others insisted it was a deer, yet others went along and said it was indeed a horse in order to please Chao Gao. The Emperor decided that it was truly a horse, and thereafter referred to this species of animal as a horse. Chao Gao made note of those who spoke the truth and later had them convicted on trumped-up charges, which resulted in their executions.

—— *Chin Dynasty annals*

These two examples do give us some insight into what we are calling Democratic Equalitarian Logic and Autocratic Hierarchical Logic. Some would perhaps say that this is not a valid distinction in the realm of logic, therefore it is proper that we advance our reasons for making it. First we need to deal with the entire issue of "'What is logic?"

Logic and Premises

The example comes to mind of some teachers who were assigned to test a number of students in their knowledge of history. When a student got the wrong answer, Teacher A praised the student for his reply, and Teacher B punished him. For the correct answer, Teacher A punished the student, and Teacher B commended him. If the student raised any questions about the discrepancy, he was scolded. If he failed to raise any question about the discrepancy, he was beaten. Later Teacher C was introduced into the group, and he would arbitrarily punish or reward each student no matter what answer was given. The Teachers changed roles from time to time.

Regarding this method of instruction, an outsider was asked: "Is this logical?" After conferring with the Teachers, he replied: "Yes, the Teachers' behavior is perfectly logical." This surprised some other people who asked him to explain this "logic". He replied that it was quite simple: the Teachers wanted to cause the students to have mental breakdowns, and they were proceeding successfully along a planned course of action to achieve exactly that goal. In fact the story took place in a prison camp in Eastern Europe in World War II.

This story, crude as it may be, does serve to illustrate an important point which is of some significance in the present cross-cultural discussion: in order to evaluate whether methods, processes, procedures, courses of action, etc., are logical, one must have a complete grasp of the explicit and implicit premises upon which they are based and from which they are proceeding.

*There is no proper discussion of "logic" without having an understanding of the premises upon which it is based. This is especially true when we attempt to illustrate "logical thinking" by giving examples of the thinking or actions of people in different cultures.*

A more lighthearted example may be seen in the case of some Turks living in Istanbul, and is best considered in two parts.

**Part 1:** One day a neighbor, Morodeen, went to borrow a big cooking pot from his friend Falatuck. When this neighbor had not yet returned the pot several weeks later, Falatuck sent a messenger to inquire about it. Morodeen quickly brought it back, with an apology. Morodeen began to make his departure when Falatuck noticed that there was a smaller pot inside the big pot, and he could not understand why it was there. He turned to Morodeen and questioned him about this. The neighbor said: "Your big pot had a baby pot. That is yours too." Falatuck was overjoyed, and thanked his neighbor profusely for bringing back the big pot and its baby pot.

**Part 2:** Some time later Morodeen came to borrow the big pot again, and of course Falatuck was happy to lend it. When the big pot had not yet been returned a month later, Falatuck inquired about it. The neighbor said: "I am sorry I will not be able to return your big pot." Falatuck asked why. The neighbor explained: "It died."

For the person who is only aware of Part 2 of the story, the neighbor's comment appears illogical. For the person who is aware of both Parts 1 and 2 of the story, the neighbor's statement may be seen as logically resting on the premise which both parties agreed to, by implication, in Part 1, i.e. "Pots are living things."

### Evaluating the Logic of the Natives in their own Environment

A person entering a new culture may often feel that the natives are acting "illogically", when in fact they are not. More likely, they are applying logical methodology to move forward from premises which they consider valid. Since the foreigner is unaware of these premises, he assumes that these premises are the same as those shared by the members of his own background culture. This results in his conclusion that their procedures are "illogical", when in fact it is just that their stated (and unstated) premises are different.

Among the Chinese there is often some misunderstanding of the value, function, and purpose of logic. The Chinese writer Lin Yu-tang frequently praised "reasonableness", but was critical of logic. In *The Importance of Living* he maintained that the logical man always thinks he is right, and therefore is "inhuman" or without "human-ness", while the reasonable man, "in suspecting that perhaps he is wrong, is therefore always right."

Certainly there is more to Mr. Lin's remarks than a mere attempt to be witty. Unfortunately, he has done the Chinese reading public something of a disservice in misrepresenting the "logical man", by equating him with the man who considers himself too wise to make any mistakes. In fact the logical man insists on one essential premise: if someone is trying to prove a point, then the evidence which they are using for proof should be examined thoroughly. Logic shows us the way to examine evidence. To be logical and reasonable at the same time is not contradictory, as Mr. Lin suggests. Turning toward the end of Chapter 2 of *Chwang Tsu*[a], we see the following words:

> Suppose you and I argue. If you win and I lose, are you indeed right and I wrong? And if I win and you lose, am I right and you wrong? Are we both partly right and partly wrong? Are we both all right or both all wrong? If you and I cannot see the truth, other people will find it even harder.
>
> Then whom shall I ask to be the judge? Shall I ask someone who agrees with you? If he already agrees with you, how can he be a fair judge? Shall I ask someone who agrees with me? If he already agrees with me, how can he be a fair judge? Shall I ask someone who agrees with both of us? If he already agrees with both of us, how can he be a fair judge? Then if you and I and others cannot decide, shall we wait for still another? Waiting for opinions to change is like waiting for nothing. Seeing everything in relation to the heavenly cosmos and leaving the different viewpoints as they are, we may be able to live out our years.

To the westerner, it appears that Chwang Tsu is placing the topic of "debate" (or argument) into a vacuum, and attempting to dissect it, or weigh its merits as a philosophical exercise. He concludes that there is no way to determine right and wrong, hence there is no point in debate. The flaw in his argument is that he has ignored either side's stated "reasons", and the supporting evidence which can be offered. The choice of a fair judge is most properly made by selecting someone who will, in an objective and unbiased manner, examine the evidence which the two sides present as the reasons for their beliefs. This is where logic comes in: we are concerned with logic when we give reasons for any of our convictions, beliefs, or points of view. When presenting these reasons, we are reasoning. Reasoning is either logical or illogical.

In discussing logic and the Chinese classics, one foreign scholar of my acquaintance made an insightful remark by saying that nowhere in Confucius's works does one find the type of statement, which is comparatively common in Plato and Aristotle, asserting "No, this does not logically follow from that." Although some may say that this just a stylistic difference, we suspect that the explanation goes much deeper. It may be asked: "What are the premises which the Chinese consider valid and which might have some influence on their exercise of logic?"

Important Premises for the Functioning of Chinese Logic

The search for harmony is certainly one major premise which affects the functioning of logic. After long residence in China some foreigners of impressive academic credentials have made the observation that "the Chinese would rather be all wrong in a harmonious fashion than all right in a non-harmonious one." While I would not attempt to propose this as an universal axiom applicable in all situations, nevertheless it does appear to have enough validity to give it a place of prominence in a list of the Top Ten Chinese Psychological Peculiarities.

---

a. 莊子

A historical fact is that although China has known periods where debate was encouraged, in practical terms the influence which this has had on the thinking and actions of common man has been minimal, or at best has been largely cancelled out by influence of other doctrines. Thus it is not uncommon to hear French, Germans, Poles, and other Europeans, even those who speak the Chinese language fluently, letting out a long drawn sigh when the subject of "friendly debate" is mentioned, as in "What has been your experience in having a friendly debate on some topic with the Chinese people?" They often remark that compared with their cultures, the Chinese have "no history of debate", and we may take this as a valuable point of reference for discussing the use of logic in present-day Chinese society. Without debate, even in calm, slow, and measured tones, logic does not have room to function.

"My dear Watson, I cannot agree with those who rank modesty among the virtues. To the logician all things should be seen exactly as they are, and to underestimate one's self is as much a departure from truth as to exaggerate one's own powers." [1]

—— Sherlock Holmes

A further concern to us here is that the Chinese have a high sense of integration between the concepts of "self-confidence" and "arrogance", with little attempt to distinguish between the two, thus placing them both in direct opposition to the highly praised Oriental virtue of "modesty" or "humility". The man who tries to win an argument by advancing logical rationale in a self confident manner is seen by the Chinese as arrogant, and therefore not-humble. The quick conclusion is that "he has a lot to learn," and they have no desire to continue the discussion.

The comment in Sun Tzu's *Art of War* (circa 500 B.C.) is notable in this connection as well: "When you surround an army, leave an outlet free." The Chinese do not consider it polite for you to "push someone into the corner" with your stated points of view, even though you have hard evidence to disprove all of what the other party says. In the name of propriety, you should "leave a stairway for them to descend" (in a figurative sense), so that they may go on their way with their "face" intact. This attitude also appears to pose serious obstacles for the true exercise of logic. The disclaimer that you are not expressing "personal views in a subjective sense" but are rather trying to present "logical views in an objective sense" is worth very little. The Chinese rarely try to make an active distinction between these.

Another important premise to the functioning of Chinese logic is their feeling that **"custom" represents rationality.** The Chinese rarely question "custom", with the stated

---

1. Reference: *The Adventures of Sherlock Holmes,* "The Greek Interpreter".

## Custom

A teenage child newly arrived in the United States was noted to have a peculiar habit whenever she wanted to be seated. First she would grab hold of the back of the chair and rock it backward and forward, forward and backward, and then sideways. After this she would walk around to the front of the chair and kick it with moderate force once in each leg. Only at this point would she position herself and gradually begin to lower her bottom in the direction of the chair seat, an action which she also performed in a very slow and deliberate manner. The whole procedure took nearly ten seconds, and each and every time she sat down in any chair she went through it entirely.

The child was asked "Why do you do this? What is the reason?"

She replied that she did not know. Discussing the entire issue, it was found that this sort of ritual was part of "sitting down" in her idea. Her mother had always sat down in this way, and she had never thought of sitting down any other way.

This situation intrigued several members of the local community, and they went to find the mother. She was seen to go about the action of sitting down in the same fashion, and when questioned about it, she merely stated that that was the way her mother had always sat down. She had never thought of sitting down any other way. "That is our custom," she replied.

The grandmother was located in a town in Central America. When questioned about this way of sitting down, the grandmother thought for a long time, and then said: "When I was little we lived in a remote area of South America that was infested by small termites. They would bore into furniture and eat it from the inside. If you just sat down, often as not the chair would collapse under you. So we would always rock the chair back and forth several times to make sure it was solid, kick it in the legs a few times for good measure, and then sit down very very slowly."

This story is a good illustration of the origin and force of "custom".

Additionally, this type of situation tends to verify what most westerners feel about "custom" — it is something that was unquestionably valid at one time, however in the present era it may no longer be valid. To accept it unquestioningly just because "that is our custom" often strikes the westerner as being a very dubious premise.

---

assumption that "Any ideas, ways of thinking and behavior, etc. left to us by our ancestors, and which have survived down to the present day, are inherently correct." Hence, this tends to be the starting point when the Chinese sit down to discuss philosophy, yet when the westerners talk about philosophy, this kind of assumption is the first thing that is thrown out the window. Rudolph Flesch[1] hinted at this when he said "Creative thinking may mean simply the realization that there's no particular virtue in doing things the way they always have been done."

---

1. Rudolph Flesch (1911–    ), received his Ph.D. from Columbia University in 1943. Among his many books are *How to Make Sense, The Art of Clear Thinking, Say What You Mean,* and *How to Write, Speak, and Think More Effectively.*

Hence, we often see that in regard to any mode of behavior, if the Chinese agree that "That is our custom", there is, in their minds, no need to look for further reasons, or to examine the "logic" of the action in question. It is assumed valid by definition. The reader may refer back to our remarks on Rationale Weight Indexing in Chapter 9 to review some of the more common ramifications of this attitude.

## Autocratic Hierarchical Logic

As has been outlined previously, the Chinese have their own definitions of what constitutes naturalism and natural moral law, of what constitutes the proper scope and functioning of sympathy, politeness, hospitality, face, respect & obedience, indirectness, etc., and all of these, in addition to many Buddhist, Taoist, and Confucianist teachings, serve as important premises for their logic. Hence, different results will be obtained in analyzing many situations, i.e. different from what the westerner would consider "logical".

If however we were asked to isolate one major trend or current in Chinese logical thinking, we would first point to the strong authoritarian/autocratic bias. It is with the hope of clarifying this particular aspect that we have advanced the concept of "Autocratic Hierarchical Logic".

### Suspected Contradictions, Apparent Non-Sequiturs, and Seeming Inconsistencies

We may look further into the nature of Autocratic Hierarchical Logic by noting one particularly strong bias which people using this logic appear to have. It is the lack of a highly developed sense of "logical contradictories", and/or lack of a sense that these kinds of contradictions are unacceptable.

**Example 1.** Closed?

At the gate of a park, public monument, cemetery, or other area, Party V (Visitor) is stopped from going in by Party A (Attendant).

Party V: Is it closed?
Party A: No, it is not closed.
Party V: If it is not closed, then it must be open.
Party A: No, it is not open.
Party V: That is contradictory.
Party A: Oh, is that so.

**Example 2.** Available?

In a library, periodical center, government information office, or other locality that deals with the public, Party V (Visitor) inquires about some figures or other data with Party A (Administrator).

Party V: Is this information classified?
Party A: No.
Party V: Is it available to the public?
Party A: No.
Party V: May I get a copy of it?
Party A: Perhaps you should go somewhere else.

**Example 3.** Obey Whom?
In the school, the children are told that to obey their parents and teachers is a virtue.
Teacher : Students, you must remember never to cross the street against the light, litter in public places, ride your bicycle on the sidewalk, kill endangered species of animals, etc.
Student S goes with parents on a picnic a few days later.
Parents: Just throw the trash over there behind that bush, it doesn't matter.
Student S: My teacher said that was wrong.
Parents: Don't argue, that is not virtuous. We are going home now, let's cross the street quickly.
Student S: But the light is red.
Parents: It doesn't matter. Don't argue.
(Note: The student in this example is not necessarily in Elementary School, he/she could be junior high school age or above.)
The premise here in the first two examples is autocracy or at best authoritarianism, and consequently Party V has only those rights which Party A chooses to give to him at the moment. The two parties have a hierarchical relationship, not an equal one. Party A is in the superior position, and the logic of the situation develops from the premises he has established. This is abundantly clear in the 3rd example as well.

Extrapolated Origins of A.H.L.
Where is the starting point for the development of such a logical orientation? Some observers would say it begins from a lack of ability to communicate. The first party says do it my way, or don't do it. Another person proposes another method, and asks: "Why is your way better than mine?" The first party may have some reasons, but he is unable to formulate them in any presentable fashion. His easiest mode of response is to adopt and authoritarian stance, and say: "Because I said so." Additionally, we could say that such a logical orientation is a direct outgrowth of the five human relationships: between sovereign and subjects, father and sons, husband and wife, among brothers, and among friends. These are essentially based on one person being in the leading position and another person following: superior to subordinate.Except possibly in the situation of friends, they are not relationships between equals.
**Striving for Synthesis:** The authoritarian bias in much of the interaction in the family and society, the underlying force of the group mentality, combined with the heavy em-

## Synthesis

In his paper "Synthesis in Chinese Metaphysics", published in 1967, Wing-tsit Chan stated:

Chinese philosophers, both ancient and modern, have been interested primarily in ethical, social, and political problems. Metaphysics[1] developed only after Buddhism from India had presented a strong challenge to Confucianism. Even then, basic metaphysical problems, such as God, universals, space and time, matter and spirit, were either not discussed, except in Buddhism, or discussed only occasionally, and then always for the sake of ethics. Discussions have been unsystematic, seldom based on hypothesis and logical analysis, for Chinese philosophers have always shunned abstraction and generalities and have always been interested more in a good life and a good society than in organized knowledge. If in our search for a world perspective in philosophy we rely chiefly on theoretical foundations and logical subtlety, Chinese philosophy has little to offer.

But if we are interested in a synthesis[2] of philosophies, it will be worthwhile to look into what has taken place in Chinese philosophy, for one of the outstanding facts in the history of Chinese philosophy has been its tendency and ability to synthesize.

Dr. Chan's viewpoint is valuable, however the force of his comments is to say that in China metaphysical problems have been treated unsystematically, yet with a tendency to synthesize, or syncretize. The outcome of this is that the Chinese have an unsystematic synthesis, and to the westerner this is something of a contradiction in terms. Also troubling to the westerner is the idea that a good life and good society can be had without organized knowledge, for this would tend to deny science, medicine, engineering, and many other fields of endeavor. Knowledge must be organized so that future generations can add to it and contribute to continuous benefit for civilization, indeed civilization itself appears to be constructed upon systematic organized knowledge.

phasis in the Chinese schools on memorization, and minimal attention given to the individual's own interpretation, certainly helps to mold a citizenry which does not question contradictions too thoroughly, and which strives more toward synthesis than analysis.[3] The fact that this "synthesis" may only be superficial or temporary is not questioned too closely. The populace seeks to accomodate itself to the varying demands placed upon it (by government, philosophy, religion, etc.) and maintain a mental equilibrium through the locating of complements or points of juxtaposition, and mak-

---

1. Metaphysics: **The branch of philosophy that deals with first principles and seeks to explain the nature of being or reality (ontology) and of the origin and structure of the world (cosmology). It is closely related with a theory of knowledge (epistemology).**

2. Synthesis: **The putting together of parts or elements so as to form a whole, as opposed to analysis. In philosophy: deductive reasoning, from the simple elements of thought into the complex whole, from cause to effect, from a principle to its application, etc.**

3. Among schoolchildren, any attempts at analytical thinking are quickly thwarted by the herculean effort required to learn and remember several thousand Chinese characters, over 90% of which defy systematic analysis of any sort. In a typical intuitive-perception-of-knowledge stance, the parents and teachers tell the student "Memorize and then you will know." Using such a methodology, any knowledge and synthesis which the student does achieve is intuitively felt, and incapable of scientific dissection or explanation.

ing efforts to correlate rather than to polarize.

The ancient idea of *yin* and *yang* has further served to bolster this striving for synthesis, and this acceptance of the status-quo. Whatever *yin* and yang may be, they are not a struggle between good and evil, (a major theme of western civilization), but are merely viewed as equally important elements in the universe, a kind of dynamic interplay between polar opposites — indeed a "unity of opposites". Thus we see that the westerner's religious background of a perceived conflict between good and evil has given him a preference for viewing things in strict **either/or** terms: good or bad, right or wrong, life or death. The Chinese, lacking this background, ten to view things as **both/and**. With this emphasis on the whole and not the parts, contradictions are allowed to exist side-by-side. A Chinese might think to himself "If there is an explanation to be had, certainly I will not be able to arrive at it before I am very well advanced in years, because the elderly are the wisest. It is best to be obedient and unquestioning."

In Chinese style polytheism, the pantheon of gods is open, whereas in western monotheism it is closed.[1] Western religions are mutually **exclusive**, for example a person is a Methodist, Mormon, or a Catholic, but he cannot simultaneously be all three. In China however, religions are viewed as **inclusive**, and a person may commonly be a combination of Buddhist, Taoist, and Confucianist, with some other elements thrown in as well. Chinese tend to look for a "god" that can solve a specific problem at an immediate time, and to fill a particular need. They visit a variety of temples and shrines to give offerings. When the westerner inquires as to which idols or images in the temple are representative of which religion(s), it is most likely none of the Chinese in attendance knows. Chinese style polytheism does not search for a consistent body of ideas and explanations. In fact, the notion that there is a need for a coherent theology is a western idea, and an outgrowth of monotheism.[2]

Any number of contradictory maxims may be collected when examining various Buddhist, Confucianist, and Taoist texts, and the Chinese do not serously question the problems thereby raised.[3] They are happy to live within the polytheistic religious maze, and they accept it for what it is. When word-of-mouth advice received from friends and relatives states that god w can solve any sort of problem, they go see god w when anything comes up. To the extent that god x can offer help for financial difficulties, they go see god x when they get in financial straits. If god y seems more reliable for a child's illness, they go visit god y when their child get sick. If god z is reputed to take good care of travellers, they go to see god z before they go on a trip. The westerner asks "What is the relation between god w, god x, god y, and god z?" After some

---

1. And has been closed for thousands of years.
2. The combining of differing beliefs in religion, philosophy, etc., so called "syncretism", is not opposed by the Chinese.
3. As a basic point of reference, many observers have noted that the Chinese tend more to follow Confucian norms in work and society, and Taoist norms in private life.

thought, the Chinese reply "No doubt there is no relation."[1] The westerner asks "Do their scopes of power and influence conflict?" The answer received is "Probably not." The westerner inquires "Have you seriously researched your theology?" The answer comes back "No, that is not our custom."[2]

Different Orientations toward Facts and Sarcasm

The lack of comprehension which many Chinese show to uses of western style sarcasm also gives the impression that they are advancing rationale that are "illogical". For example, five westerners in their 20's and 30's were having an informal dinner with several of their Chinese friends one warm evening. As is common in many domestic Chinese meals, no beverages were served. One of the westerners asked if there was any ice water which he could drink with his food, since his throat was dry. The Chinese were surprised at this, and one of them said "It is not a good idea to drink ice water." The dry-throated individual asked why this was so. The Chinese stated "It is bad for your stomach and it will cause your insides to shrink-up so you will not grow and develop properly." Another westerner in the group glanced around the table and noted that the body-builds of the westerners seated were substantially taller and more muscular than their Chinese friends, and indeed this was the situation he commonly encountered in Chinese society in general. He made the quick retort: "Yes, that makes sense, most of the westerners I see are shorter and weaker than the Chinese of the same age group!" The other foreigners all laughed at this comment, (one fell off of his chair), however the Chinese, apparently taking it at surface value, merely looked at each other and nodded their heads.

Inquiries among Chinese parents, school teachers, and others do reveal that there is a common feeling that "cold beverages will stunt one's growth." When the Chinese person eating at the dinner table with these westerners advanced this "common sense" proposition, his countrymen nodded in agreement. It did not occur to them to examine the body builds of those present, or to reflect on the body builds of the people they frequently saw in the streets, and reformulate their "common sense" on that basis. Such an attitude certainly appears to be an acceptance of a great deal of authoritarianism, and shows a willingness to acquiesce to tenets advanced by parents, elders, teachers, etc. without additional contemplation.

---

1. The gods of Chinese polytheism may have a general sense of a hierarchy in heaven, however it is difficult to determine or define specific relations between most of them.

2. The present chapter has not specifically treated Buddhism in our discussion of **Opposing Explanations and Varying Worldviews.** One main reason for this is the non-doctrinal nature of so much of the Chinese populace's religious thinking. It has been the author's experience that it is comparatively easy to lead Chinese people into a discussion of the main schools of Chinese philosophy, since they are taught this in the educational system, and very difficult if not impossible to engage in a coherent discussion of Buddhism as such, unless one specifically searches out a monk or other Buddhist religious official. Hence while research into Buddhism and comparison with the Chinese thinking will certainly show the foreigner that much Buddhist thought has dovetailed nicely with traditional Chinese ideas, the exact element of "purely Buddhist input" is more difficult to quantify.

As a further consideration, one suspects that if medical evidence could be shown to support the truth of the Chinese's claims about cold beverages, the westerners might be persuaded to modify their stance. However, if the medical evidence pointed to no correlation between drinking cold beverages and stunted growth, one doubts the Chinese would be so easily convinced, and they would probably fall back on some maxim such as "Oh, this is what we Chinese believe."

In a similar fashion, the Chinese people will often deny the value of "progress", such as when they point out that "Harmony is desirable, and if progress contradicts with harmony, then I want harmony." The westerner quickly clarifies for them that by making such a statement: "You have just forfeited your right to wear mass-produced clothes, shoes, socks, etc., or to buy prescription eyeglasses, or to travel by train, supersonic jet, or hydrofoil, or to use the telephone, watch TV, etc." At this juncture they quickly say that such considerations are not the main issue, and that is not what they meant, or that the westerner is impolite for speaking to them in this tone of voice.

Inevitably, the culture within which we live shapes and limits our imaginations, and by permitting us to do and think and feel in certain ways makes it increasingly unlikely or impossible that we should do or think or feel in ways that are contradictory or tangential to it.

——— *Margaret Mead*

*Different Orientations toward Theory vs. Practice*

The use of autocratic hierarchical logic is also frequently the cause of a major discorrelation between theory and practice. Consider the following:

Premise 1. **We want to promote honesty in society.**

Premise 2. **Policy C will promote honesty in society.**

(Democratic E. Logic) Conclusion: **We want to enact Policy C.**

(Autocratic H. Logic) Determination: **We do not necessarily want to enact Policy C.**

Autocratic hierarchical logic may reject the initial Conclusion for a number of reasons. These include "That is not our custom", "We have other more pressing concerns at the moment", "We prefer to adopt a more indirect approach", or the handy rejoinder "We do not like your attitude in making this kind of ultimatum." Further notions such as "This conflicts with other traditional considerations which we feel are more important" could easily fall into the realm of of "unstated premises" as discussed above. While making this Determination, the users of autocratic hierarchical logic still feel themselves free to go on stating Premise 1 on any and all occasions: "We want to promote honesty in society."

It is easy for the reader to see how the same technique could be applied in order to deny (or at least overlook) suggestions for promoting traffic safety, raising sanitation standards, reducing pollution, increasing democratic reforms, cracking down on bribery and corruption, liberalizing trade and tariff policy, eliminating counterfeiters, etc. while at the same time announcing these as primary goals of the people in power.

Premise 1. **We want to promote modern business practices.**

Premise 2. Measures F,G, and H will promote modern business practices.

D.E.L. Conclusion: We want to enact Measures F,G, and H.

A.H.L. Determination: We do not necessarily want to enact Measures F,G, and H.

Again, the reasons given for this Determination (by the officials in power) could be "We have other more urgent concerns on our schedule at the moment", "We currently have a manpower shortage in this department", "We have decided to call a moratorium on this issue until further studies can be done", all the way to "The direct approach used by these measures is not 'the Chinese way'", etc. The next time the officials are interviewed, whether by the local or international press, of course they will state: "We want to promote modern business practices, and we are doing our best to see that such practices are implemented."

**Survey Work:** Hence it may appear to outsiders that those with this logical orientation are "saying one thing and doing something else." This is also frequently apparent when westerners take surveys of the local populace to determine their attitudes on a multiplicity of issues. For example, some foreign scholars are interested in finding out attitudes about nepotism, child-rearing practices, certain aspects of the requirements of parental obedience, future life goals, employees' views toward contractual relation, etc., and they often devise elaborate surveys and questionnaires to research such topics. However, what the surveyors generally fail to realize is that results tabulated do not necessarily reflect the actions which the people surveyed will actually take in the future when and if confronted with these or similar situations.

This occurs because when the questions on the survey are posed to a local person, he/she gives an answer from what is essentially a "hierarchical vacuum". In other words, at the time respondent answers the questions, he/she is not currently subject to any hierarchical pressure in regard to the issue(s) at hand. When the respondents are confronted by a similar situation in their real lives, it may often happen that the demands of teachers, parents, elders, or other superiors are simultaneously brought to bear, with the result that the person (after some consideration) feels it best to follow along with the wishes or dictates of those higher in the hierarchy. The tendency of the Chinese away from individualism, and more toward a group orientation also supports this kind of conclusion.

The Route from B to E

Among those of a similar logical orientation, in discussing the adoption of various strategy or methodology, what is also missing in an A.H.L. Determination is attention to **process.** There is a beginning, an end, but no middle. The present situation is the beginning (B), the realization of the stated goals is the end (E), and the means of moving from B to E is the process. As in the above examples of promoting honesty in society, promoting modern business practices, etc., the process is often being ignored, severely downplayed, or specified in only a vague manner, as if it were some trifling technicality. Overtones of such fatalistic thinking[a] "Man cannot control nature", "One's fate

---

a. 宿令論

is in the heavens", etc. are also evident, as is a bias toward intuitive perception of knowledge, and the lack of a systematic research mentality.

In China there is a widespread notion of an "ideal horse"[a] as one which is 1) strong and lean, 2) plump and pretty, and 3) does not consume grass, straw, etc.[1] These three qualities would indicate that it is a strong worker and tireless runner, comes from a prosperous family and has a generous owner, and can be maintained at a very low cost. The fact that this ideal contains contradictory elements is not seriously debated, nor is there an active discussion among the populace, or among Chinese horse breeders, as to the process of how such a horse might be raised. The ideal is apparently not viewed as a goal which we should work toward, but as something divorced from reality. (Moving away from the strict literal application to raising horses, this ideal is often used in a much wider sense, where "horse" can refer to any person or organization. Indeed, this is one way of explaining why so many Chinese regulatory bodies, research organizations, and other entities are traditionally under-budgeted.)

The Chinese will often make claims such as "We will overtake the Japanese in X-number of years"[2], "Chinese will be the world-language of the next century", "In ten years we will bring our efficiency and quality control (in some area) up to developed country standards", etc., and these types of remarks elicit energetic applause, if not standing ovations, at Chinese academic, cultural, political and other meetings. At the same time neither the speaker, nor undoubtedly any native Chinese in the audience, is able to lay forth any comprehensive plan of action where this type of goal can be realized in a gradual step-by-step progression within the announced time framework. In a typical autocratic hierarchical logic stance, they would of course not consider their goal invalid just because they can formulate no way of achieving it. It is logical and valid because they say so, similar to an "Imperial Decree".

**Challenges:** This brings us to consider a further lack which the A.H.L. Determination reflects, namely an absence of the "challenge" mentality. The users of autocratic hierarchical logic who advance various statements will not accept a challenge: "Prove what you say is valid (reasonable, fair, just, etc.)" Indeed the people using this formulation are rarely able to prove many of their contentions. Their autocratic opinion is right because they say it is, or at least until such time that someone more powerful than they are (i.e., of a higher position in the hierarchy) says differently. Overtones of "maintenance of pride" and "desire to keep face" are clearly evident.

A foreigner was talking to a Chinese mother who had a new baby. He asked if the mother wanted her new baby to grow up big and strong, and she replied that she did. He then inquired why she was feeding the baby rice soup and some salty vegetables,

---

1. Horses were traditionally only fed these items.

2. This claim is especially curious, since it appears to imply that research and development efforts in Japan are currently at a standstill.

a. 理想的馬

since certainly the nutritive content of these items was not very high, and the family could afford better. The mother thought that these foods did contain abundant nutrition, and was surprised that he would make such a statement. He dropped the matter at the time, but a few weeks later when he heard another Chinese mother make a similar claim, he challenged her. The next day he brought a selection of nutrition reports from the library, and pointed out what better menu selections she could make for her baby's meals. Result: Of course the mother continued feeding the baby what she had previously been feeding him.

We would be wrong to jump to the conclusion that the Chinese are consistently out to give the foreign-born, or foreign-educated, a quick rejection or snub-off in all such situations. Rather, from the dozens of examples that I have collected, I begin to see that the Chinese do not accept the broad daily use of the technique of trying to prove a point or assert one's belief by "making a challenge." In regard to differing data or opposing points of view, they do not even appear to understand why they are being challenged, or "taken to task" in regard to various aspects of their thought or behavior.

Chinese are not adverse to gambling, yet we must keep in mind that they have no expression which corresponds to the English "Put your money where your mouth is." Also, the westerner, in offering a challenge, is approaching the issue in a direct manner, which is the only one he considers reasonable or efficient, but the Chinese prefer to deal in an indirect manner. Interestingly, the Chinese do not consider their unwillingness to take up a challenge as a lack of sincerity, or lack of truly felt belief for their original assertion.

### Logical Viewpoints toward Good and Bad

In the writings of George Washington, Thomas Jefferson, and other American Founding Fathers, we find references to logic as "the rules of correct thinking". This is quite a generalized definition. More specifically, many scholars say that logic begins with the Law of Identity, and as such it may be stated that logic is "the Law of Identity and its various corollaries", or in less technical language, logic is "the art or skill of non-contradictory identification". It is within the scope of this definition to recognize that the logic of mathematics is more rigorous and exacting than the logic of philosophy, and this is even more finely elaborated than the logic of human relations. However, this definition still overlooks the issue that logic is extrapolated from certain underlying premises, and when we change the premises, the result of our "logical thinking" will be different. We may further illustrate this with an example from the sport of baseball, by considering the words ball and strike. Let us deal with the proposal to eliminate these words from our vocabulary, and refer to them as being "good" or "bad" balls. Logically speaking, should a ball be considered a "good ball" or a "bad ball"? What about a strike?

A chart may be drawn as follows.

**From the pitcher's point of view**

| definition | | | reason |
|---|---|---|---|
| ball | = | "bad ball" | With four balls the batter may advance to 1st base. |
| strike | = | "good ball" | With three strikes the batter is out. |

**From the batter's point of view**

| definition | | | reason |
|---|---|---|---|
| ball | = | "good ball" | With four balls I can advance to 1st base. |
| strike | = | "bad ball" | With three strikes I am out. |

Depending on which point of view we take, it may be logical to call a strike a "good ball" or a "bad ball", and likewise a ball is also eligible for either of these two appellations. How are we to decide the issue? Certainly we need to determine whether we want to use the pitcher's view or the batter's view. In the Chinese rationale, the pitcher's view represents the opinion of the majority of the players on the playing field at any one time, and is therefore indicative of the Group Mentality. Thus it is the choice they would invariably consider correct.[a]

## Logical Viewpoints toward Up and Down

Consider the following circumstances which offer opposing viewpoints of "up" and "down".

**Physical Movement**

**Situation 1:** Billy Hwang and Mary Lee are on the 5th floor.
    The elevator is on the 1st floor.
    They want to leave the building.
    Looking at the buttons on the wall, Billy says "We should push the UP button."
    Mary says "We should push the DOWN button."
    Speaking from a logical standpoint, which person is correct?

**Situation 2:** Billy Hwang and Mary Lee are on the 9th floor.

---

[a.] 以投手的立場爲準

The elevator is on the 16th floor.
They want to visit their friend on the 14th floor.
Looking at the buttons on the wall, Billy says "We should push the DOWN button."
Mary says "We should push the UP button."
Speaking from a logical standpoint, which person is correct?

Examining the thinking of Billy and Mary, we see that they have considered different facts to be critical. Billy regards the current location of the elevator to be most important. His preference is to push the button that denotes the direction of travel which the elevator must take in order to meet him at his present position in the building. Hence, in Situation 1, he opted for the UP button. In Situation 2, he opted for the DOWN button. We may call this the "Current location style of elevator button-pushing."

Mary considers the direction of her own desired movement to be most important, and ignores any consideration of the elevator's current location. Hence, in Situation 1, her preference was to push the DOWN button. In Situation 2, she wanted to push the UP button. We may call this the "Desired movement style of elevator button-pushing."

Both viewpoints make sense from a logical standpoint, and are equally valid. However, from a practical standpoint, people with long experience in riding elevators recognize that elevators were designed to operate in the style which corresponds to Mary's reasoning. If Billy wants to promote his point of view, he will have to found his own elevator company.

In an advanced Post Industrial Revolution society where the populace has grown up "in an age of elevators", most people will use the "Desired movement style of elevator button-pushing" instinctively. However, in a newly industrialized or non-industrialized society where elevators are a fairly recent introduction into the lifestyles of the people, we may find the preferences of the populace evenly divided between the two styles.

Movement in Time

Let us suppose that today is Saturday, July 15th, and we are considering the proposal to eliminate the words next and last from our vocabulary. We will replace them with the words "up" and "down". Logically speaking, should next Monday be considered "up Monday" or "down Monday"? What about last Monday?

A chart may be outlined as follows.

Revision Style 1.
If last = "down", and next = "up"
Today is Saturday, July 15th. Up Monday is July 17th. Down Monday is July 10th. Up month is August. Down month is June.

**Revision Style 2.**

If last = "up", and next = "down"

Today is Saturday, July 15th. Down Monday is July 17th. Up Monday is July 10th. Down month is August. Up month is June.

To the western mind, Revision Style 1 is the most appealing. We often tell someone to "get up and get on with it" when we want them to do something. Action is seen as going forth, and we have to "stand up" in order to get moving. We speak of our children as "growing up", and say that when a person gets promoted he has "moved up in the organization". In all of these instances "up" is associated with a forward movement in time.

However, some familiarity with the Chinese language quickly allows us to see that the overwhelming Chinese preference is for Revision Style 2. The word "up" is *shang*.[a] The word "down" is *hsia*.[b] Next Monday is considered down Monday. Last Monday is considered up Monday. Next month is down month. Last month is up month.

Speaking from a logical standpoint, which Revision Style is more valid? That depends on our premises. Certainly it is not an exaggeration to say that the Chinese view history as a decline from some envisioned utopia in the past, whereas westerners view history as an ascent toward some envisioned utopia in the future. In this regard the Chinese and the westerners are clearly operating from different premises. Overviewing the development of the Chinese language, we may want to consider whether it was these premises which served to influence the form of the language, or the language which influenced the form of these premises. An answer to that is quite difficult to determine. No doubt the premises partially served as both cause and effect, and the same is true for the language in its earliest stages of development.

## Logical Viewpoints toward Medical Treatment

If a westerner has a pain in the lower spine, he may rub some cream or other medicine on the area. If he has an earache he may buy some drops to put in his ear. If his knee hurts he may put some salve on it and bandage it up. Chinese people trained in traditional medicine are often puzzled by such medical techniques, even though the westerner explains their rationale as "common sense". Indeed, the Chinese acupuncturist will offer treatment in a different fashion: for a lower spine pain he often concentrates his insertion of needles in the wrist, for an earache he will place needles in the feet, and for a knee discomfort he may insert needles in the toes and upper leg. Which method of treatment is more logical? Of course it depends on your premises. Clearly the Chinese acupuncturist has dealt with the perceived flow of *chi* through the body and organizes

---

a. 上    b. 下

574

Bases for Action and Non-Action

## RECOGNITION TEST OF CHINESE CHARACTERS OF THE PICTOGRAPH TYPE

Many Chinese characters in modern usage bear a real resemblance to the object which they represent. Put on your thinking cap and determine which Chinese character most likely represents the English word in question for each of the ten entries below. Write the number of your selection in the small box provided at the left. Scoring: 10 points each. (Ask your Chinese friend or the headwaiter at your local Chinese restaurant to determine your score). If you have never studied Chinese before and can still get seventy points or more, congratulations! You may qualify for admission to first grade in the Chinese elementary school of your choice under the "early acceptance" program.

Chart 10-1

| Label | 1 | 2 | 3 | 4 | 5 |
|---|---|---|---|---|---|
| Man | 呆 | 人 | 本 | 方 | 京 |
| Water | 朋 | 兆 | 巡 | 水 | 形 |
| Moon | 雲 | 月 | 口 | 日 | 介 |
| Cow | 無 | 趁 | 牛 | 字 | 聲 |
| Mountain | 當 | 琴 | 凸 | 焚 | 山 |
| Rice | 米 | 品 | 三 | 零 | 蕊 |
| Knife | 上 | 投 | 金 | 象 | 刀 |
| Pig | 獲 | 樂 | 鳥 | 豕 | 商 |
| Horse | 筷 | 馬 | 猴 | 盜 | 起 |
| Rabbit | 兔 | 黃 | 兑 | 魚 | 公 |

his treatment in a different way from that of the western doctor, but his methodology is logical when understood from that basis.

## Arbitrary Logic

In my many years of studies of Chinese language, and discussions of the peculiarities of the Chinese language with foreigners, I have often found it useful to introduce the concept of "Arbitrary Logic". Many people say that this is oxymoronic, a contradiction in terms. How can something be logical and also arbitrary? I agree with their analysis, but I find since many people lack this concept on the theoretical level, they are unable to deal with it in practice either. It is worthy of being introduced, and the accompanying chart, or quiz, will serve the purpose of doing so.

Any Chinese language textbook will tell us that the translation of these ten English words are all Chinese characters of the pictograph type. We are told that the character for water "looks like water", the character for moon " looks like the moon", the character for man "looks like a man", etc. and therefore the writing of Chinese characters is logical. Granted the Chinese characters have gone through some changes over the millennia, and all the characters show here are the modern, unsimplified versions. Yet when I give this test to foreigners who have just begun to study Chinese, whether using the more ancient characters or the modern script, most only get a score of 30 or 40. I am sure that if I were to give 25 possible character choices for each English word, there would not be one of these beginners in a hundred who would get a grade as high as a 20.

However, any Chinese person will be happy to point out the correct answer in each case, and also to go into a long discussion about why that is the one and only logical choice: the character for mountain "looks like a mountain", the character for knife "looks like a knife", etc. The beginning student who has taken this quiz first may stop and think: "From what perceptual basis are you saying that the character for man looks like a man? Is that the same perceptual basis you are using when you say the character for mountain looks like a mountain?"

We may draw many different squiggles on the paper and say that they represent something. However, that is not logical. In order for our squiggles to mean something logically, there must be a continuity of perceptual basis in the way in which we form or devise them. What we find in this quiz is that the correct answer in every case is logical in terms of one particular perceptual basis (structural analysis, pictorial condensation, etc.), but the perceptual basis is different in each case. This is a perfect example of Arbitrary Logic. Having learned how to write (and pronounce) these ten Chinese characters, we are still at a loss to determine how an eleventh might be written if a number of choices are offered. If we are given a second quiz on ten more Chinese characters, it is unlikely we would get a higher grade than we did on the first, despite all the explanations we have been given in the interim. I do not deny that Chinese characters are very interesting, however I fail to see how their written form can be called "logical". A much better way of describing the formation of the characters is to say that they are "assigned". This being the case, we have effectively merged our language discussion back into our main topic — Autocratic Logic.

Note: By comparison, the spelling of English words represents more of a Systematic Logic. We must keep in mind however that modern English spelling reflects the pronunciation of the 15th rather than the 20th century.

## Conclusion and Summary

The Closed? and Available? examples above would not classify as "logic" if considered from a formal mathematical or even philosophical standpoint. If these were isolated incidents, it might hold some validity to say that Party A is "acting illogically". But when A's behavior is the norm in society rather than the exception, to make such an assessment with regard to the people of an entire culture certainly defeats our purposes in acculturology. It is in this regard that the aforementioned definitions of Democratic Equalitarian Logic and Autocratic Hierarchical Logic have been given. They are intended to be conceptual tools to help us in our study of acculturation.

**Democratic Equalitarian Logic** also includes the idea of individualism, but states that the individual is not free to obstruct the freedom or impinge on the rights of others. As such it recognizes some sense of objectivity, realizing that what is good for society as a whole, (measures necessary to maintain social order, for example), and actions which may be beneficial for the society over the long term, may perhaps be bad for particular individuals. That is unavoidable. Democratic equalitarian logic stresses weighing the evidence, and thus has a strong undercurrent of what some would call scientific logic. In its own eyes it is rational.

**Autocratic Hierarchical Logic** stresses sacrifice of the individual to group interests, thus severely downplaying the concept of "self". It recognizes a great deal of subjectivity, and does not pay much attention to the establishment of bad precedent, thus by trying to satisfy the demands of differing groups, it tends to lose a sense of proper direction for the society as a whole. In stating that the views of those in the higher hierarchical position(s) are "right", it is a non-scientific logic, since it tends to regard evidence contrary to its stated point of view as a nuisance, and unworthy of consideration. However, in its own eyes it is rational.

Undoubtedly there are other types of logic in the acculturological sense. These two appear relevant to our present discussion.

As a final note, we must reiterate that: One's premises are very important in discussing what constitutes a logical thought process. Bearing in mind all of the above, one supposes that in attempting to discuss the subject of logic with the Chinese, we are well advised to reflect upon the words of Thomas Paine, who said "Time makes more converts than reason."

## Syllogisms and Illogic

Most westerners try to develop the ability to think in a logical manner, and yet oftentimes they lack in formal logical training. Many Chinese do not like logic, and will criticize it. Once there was a informal gathering of Chinese and westerners at an after-dinner discussion, and the subject of logic came up. A Chinese who had studied in the United States remarked that he did not think too highly of logic, and much preferred reasonableness. Even more to his liking were 1) sympathy/sentiment, 2) reason, 3) law, in that order. He offered the following comment: "Here is an example of your logic —

(1)    *Your father is a man.*
       *I am a man.*
       *Therefore, I am your father."*

He asked any of the westerners present if this was not indeed a logical argument. They said "Structurally, it appears to be logical."

"Yet the conclusion is clearly at odds with the facts," the Chinese stated.

"Yes," they agreed, "that is so."

"Well then, please refute it from a 'logical' point of view, or point out its 'logical flaw'."

This they were unable to do. As a result, all the Chinese present agreed that "the western idea of logic is not worth much".

Refutations

In fact, there are a number of ways to refute the "argument" which this Chinese person has stated. Some westerners have suggested this reply:

"Your statement is as logical as saying —
(2)    *Whales eat seaweed.*
       *Chinese eat seaweed.*
       *Therefore, Chinese are whales."*

However, such a reply is more in the way of verbal sparring, and does not serve to fully clarify the issues involved. It is therefore not the optimal response.

A more proper reply involves considering the philosophical underpinnings of deductive logic, and the rules which apply to the formulation of premises.

Categorical Propositions

Traditional syllogistic logic is chiefly concerned with categorical propositions. It is important to recognize that categorical propositions assert or deny relationships bet-

## Categories

In his paper "Epistemological Methods in Chinese Philosophy", published in 1967, E.R. Hughes stated:

> In China the development of systematic categorical thinking came a little slowly and was hampered by the Confucianists' tendency toward authoritarianism and by the Taoists' tendency toward a denial that any categorical statement can be more than relatively true.
>
> Thus we do not find in Han philosophy anything comparable to Aristotle's analysis of the Greek language and its underlying categorical abstractions, nor do we find a parallel to the syllogistic logic which he built on his categories.
>
> There was, from Han times on, the category of the *yin* and *yang*, and alongside it, more or less dovetailed into it, the five hsing [1], i.e. the five physical forces operating in the universe. As if that were not enough, a school of so-called Confucianist thought took the diviners' cabalistic [2] figures of divided and undivided lines and linked them by a sort of science of symbolism to the *yin* and the *yang* and the five *hsing*. For many minds this symbolism was the key to the march of history. For others it was an epistemological [3] method, a sure guide to all possible forms of knowledge. The correlation of these abstract categories with the other more universally recognized abstractions was never, as far as I have been able to discover, successfully made.
>
> Chuang Tsu sowed in Chinese thinkers' minds the unceasing suspicion that all categorical thinking, by very reason of its being categorical, was in the very nature of a tentative experiment into the mysterious hinterland of knowledge. What is true today may easily be untrue tomorrow.

To the westerner, abstract thinking often involves the formulation of hypotheses which then need to be tested by further research and experimentation, and there is a pronounced orientation toward the future. However Mr. Hughes points out that in the writings of the Chinese thinkers one constant recurrent characteristic is an appeal to history.

> In other words, one indispensable method of achieving reliable knowledge was the historical method. It was as if a man's contemporaries said to him, "Speculate, theorize, as much as you like, but check up on your speculations by finding out what has happened in the past."

Clearly the tendency to think in abstract categories, in terms of actions or precepts which are outside of direct sensory perception or experience, and representing ideas which (at the moment) have no direct correspondence in physical reality, has not been highly developed. Abstract thinking plainly falls outside of practical and situation-centered Chinese ethical concerns.

---

1. Five hsing: the five elements of **metal, wood, water, fire, and earth.** Such an orientation of "fundamental elements" seems to have been largely discarded in the west with the advent of the Renaissance in the 1500's and the scientific revolution of the 1700's, although it still exists in some branches of astrology.
2. Cabalistic: **secret, mystic.**
3. Epistemology: **the study or theory of the origin, nature, methods, and limits of knowledge.**

Analogy is milk for babes, but abstract truths are strong meat.

——— Martin F. Tupper

ween classes.

In a syllogism, the first line is the major premise, the second line is the minor premise, and the third line is the conclusion. The following is an example of a valid syllogism —

(3)  *All men are mortal.*
*All Chinese are men.*
*All Chinese are mortal.*

Of course we must pay special attention to the usage of any and all words. In this example "men" is used to refer to "members of the human race", and not to "men" as distinct from "women".

A categorical syllogism is an argument that has **two premises** and a **conclusion.** Each of these must be a categorical proposition.

Each proposition has a subject term and a predicate term, however there are only three distinct terms in the entire syllogism. How do we determine which term is which? This may be done by first referring to the conclusion, where we delineate a subject term and a predicate term, abbreviated as S and P respectively. The third term is a middle term, abbreviated as M, which occurs once in each premise. Of course both the S and the P also occur in one of the premises.

In syllogism (3), we see that "Chinese" is the S term, and "mortal" is the P term, hence   The major premise is of the form M_P
The minor premise is of the form S_M
[The conclusion is of the form S_P]

There are four general kinds of categorical propositions, or statements. We must use one of these types in each of our premises. Let us use the imaginary word "forp" to denote one class of objects, and "gork" to denote another class of objects. (If the reader finds these terms tiring, he may replace them with the letters F and G instead.)

| Kinds of Categorical Propositions | Abbreviation |
|---|---|
| 1. Universal affirmative propositions. Example: *All forp are gork.* | A |
| 2. Universal negative propositions. Example: *No forp are gork.* | E |
| 3. Particular affirmative propositions. Example: *Some forp are gork.* | I |
| 4. Particular negative propositions. Example: *Some forp are not gork.* | O |

At this point we may refer back to the original "argument" advanced by the Chinese party, and see a number of logical flaws. Clearly its "premises" do not express relationships between classes. Furthermore, its premises are not categorical propositions, because neither of them corresponds to one four kinds we have outlined.

The original statements do not lend themselves to rephrasing in the form of categorical

propositions, however we can rephrase them in a simpler manner, as follows.
> *Your father is a member of the human race.*
> *I am a member of the human race.*
> *Therefore, both your father and I are members of the human race.*

This type of logical argument is not very advanced, but it is logical nevertheless.

However, syllogism **(2)** still appears valid to us from a structural logic standpoint. Mentally adding an "All" to the major and minor premise and the conclusion, it would appear that each represents a universal affirmative proposition. Hence we will have to delve further into the structure of deductive logic in order to show its non-validity.

**Figure and Mood:** We must start by further clarifying the concepts of figure and mood in logic.

There are four acceptable ways in which the three terms (S, P, and M) may occur in the two premises of a syllogism. These are called the four figures.

| 1. | 2. | 3. | 4. |
|---|---|---|---|
| M—P | P—M | M—P | P—M |
| S—M | S—M | M—S | M—S |

The mood is specified by indicating which type of proposition occurs as major premise, minor premise, and conclusion. For example, syllogism **(3)** is AAA. There are sixty-four moods.

| | | | |
|---|---|---|---|
| AAA | EAA | IAA | OAA |
| AAE | EAE | IAE | OAE |
| AAI | EAI | IAI | OAI |
| AAO | EAO | IAO | OAO |
| AEA | EEA | IEA | OEA |
| AEE | EEE | IEE | OEE |
| AEI | EEI | IEI | OEI |
| AEO | EEO | IEO | OEO |
| AIA | EIA | IIA | OIA |
| AIE | EIE | IIE | OIE |
| AII | EII | III | OII |
| AIO | EIO | IIO | OIO |
| AOA | EOA | IOA | OOA |
| AOE | EOE | IOE | OOE |
| AOI | EOI | IOI | OOI |
| AOO | EOO | IOO | OOO |

Combined with the four figures, this yields 256 distinct syllogistic forms. However, not all combinations of figure and mood produce valid syllogisms, and this was recognized in ancient times. Out of 256 forms, only nineteen are consistently valid.

|   | Figure for major and minor premise | Valid Moods for premises and conclusion |
|---|---|---|
| 1. | M__P<br>S__M | AAA, AII, EAE, EIO |
| 2. | P__M<br>S__M | AEE, AOO, EAE, EIO |
| 3. | M__P<br>M__S | AAI, AII, EAO, EIO, IAI, OAO |
| 4. | P__M<br>M__S | AAI, AEE, EAO, EIO, IAI |

Referring back to syllogism (2), we see that whales is the predicate, and Chinese is the subject. Looking at our two premises, we see that they fall in the pattern of P__M, S__M, and this is figure 2. The mood is AAA, and this is not a valid mood for this figure, hence we should not be surprised that we have reached a nonsense conclusion.

It is not expected that the reader will be an expert on formal logical analysis after reading this brief introduction. We have not delved into related considerations such as existential import, the square of opposition, Venn diagrams, distributed terms, undistributed terms, binary predicates, ternary predicates, propositional calculus, first order predicate calculus, and myriad other important concepts in the realm of logic, which are all covered in a good logic course in any university. However it is interesting to pause and consider the entire structure we have briefly presented here, which starts from a basis of 256 forms, and builds from there. It is not an exaggeration to say that this is as complex, or more complex, than the Chinese *Book of Changes*, which has only 64 diagrams. In order to discuss either of these fields of learning in a coherent fashion, we should do some research in the library first, or inquire with an expert.

## Psychological Peculiarities

Listed below are the author's candidates for "The Top Ten Chinese Psychological Peculiarities (As Perceived by Westerners)". All of these attitudes, feelings, desires, etc. go into forming the Chinese psychological makeup, and appear to have wide ramifications in many areas.

1. *Having a complex combination of the feelings of extreme pride and extreme inferiority, constantly interacting.*

*Comments:* The Chinese are taught to be extremely proud of their 5,000 years of history and culture. At the same time they realize that in many areas they are behind the west, not only in technology, but also in educational levels and modes-of-thinking.

The excessive concern with face appears directly related to this Peculiarity. When someone is shown to be less competent, knowledgeable, irreplaceable, wealthy, generous, etc. than they wish to appear, the mask is broken, and their inferiority is shown, hence they "lose face".

2. *Too practical to believe in religion, and too superstituous not to.*

*Comments:* The Chinese tend to have a wide variety of "religious" beliefs, which may be an amalgam of those of many different sects. If remedy to the problem at hand (however defined) can supposedly be obtained by worshipping at a Buddhist shrine, then this worship is performed. If poor results are achieved, then a visit to a Taoist temple is clearly warranted, and then to the temple of the local earth god, the ancestral graves, and on and on through a host of local and not-so-local gods, saints, images, idols, as well as necromancers, geomancers, the general run of fortune tellers, etc. An acceptable solution may sometimes be attained somewhere along this route, or one's funds and the funds of one's family members, relatives, and friends may be totally and utterly exhausted.

Stories of Chinese Christians who continue to worship and make offerings at ancestral shrines, Buddhist temples, etc. are too numerous to mention. Nevertheless, the exact determination of what any one Chinese person's religious beliefs include, and what they do not include, is often difficult to ascertain.

3. *Possessing a strong desire for very small gains, but not concerned with small amounts of money.* [a]

*Comments:* The "very small gains" refer to income or inflow of money or goods, and the "small amounts of money" refer to outflow or expense. This Peculiarity must be understood in regard to an Agricultural Society Reward/Effort Relationship, and in relation to the Oriental idea of mutual dependance, hence gifts offered for no apparent reason may not be accepted.

The Chinese may ask a foreigner to do a piece of work or other job *for free* (thus obtaining this benefit), and yet present him/her with gifts, pay taxi fares, meals, etc. (in "repayment") all of which adds up to substantially more than what the foreigner would have charged. Yet the suggestion that the work or undertaking be viewed as a straight monetary proposition is considered "improper between friends" and "too practical".

The tendency not to differentiate between business and personal afairs certainly complicates this entire matter.

4. *Tending to regard reality, when it differs from theory or postulation, as irrelevant.*

*Comments:* These types of often heard rationale seem to offer evidence of the existence of this Peculiarity:

---

a. 貪小便宜，不計較小錢

1) *That* has nothing to do with this.
2) We are in a transitional period.
3) Chinese were traditionally _____, so we are _____ by definition.

Directly or indirectly we often see the claim that another party's "practice" is most properly compared to the Chinese "theory", since the Chinese feel that due to temporary distortions or other transitional factors, their present "practice" is not true practice, and therefore not real reality. Thus when comparing foreign political systems to the Chinese ones, the Chinese ones are better, because the Chinese compare foreign political "practice" with Chinese political "theory". When asked to compare foreign political practice to Chinese political practice, they claim that due to China being in a transitional period, present practice does not clearly represent the true picture. Comparisons of foreign and Chinese big business, educational institutions and methods, organization of the family, operations of any companies in the service sector, enforcement of law, operations of the police and other official agencies, etc., are often approached in this same way.

5. *Preferring to be all wrong in a harmonious fashion, than all right in a non-harmonious one.*
Comments: The reader is free to extract examples from the previous pages of this volume.

6. *Generally lacking the ability, desire, or strength-of-convictions to validate or legitimatize their own actions.* [a]
Comments: The story is told of the German missionary who came to China and researched much medical knowledge found in ancient Chinese texts. One technique which he found particularly useful was Chinese foot massage, and using the methods described he was able to improve the health of all body organs. Much success was even made in dealing with patients with paralyzed limbs, liver ailments, gall stones, and a wide range of maladies. He applied with the Chinese Government for a license to open a clinic using this technique, and was told that such a license could not be granted, since no department, bureau, or institute had the authority to grant it.

Returning to Germany, he presented his case to the German medical community, and after some period of time was granted a license by the German government to use this Chinese foot massage technique. Upon his return to China, he presented this internationally recognized license to the Chinese government, and was at last able to obtain official certification to give Chinese foot massage.

In general, the lack of a great deal of Chinese medicine to gain acceptance in the west is due to the inability of the Chinese to establish its validity in internationally acceptable terms; surprisingly the same situation exists domestically as well. Traditional Chinese medicine as engaged in by this group of practitioners is not recognized by that group, much less by the western oriented Chinese medical community.

---

a. 常常無法肯定自己

In a related issue, several decades ago the Food & Nutrition Board of the U.S. National Academy of Science, a non-governmental organization, established full data on Recommended Daily Allowances of Vitamins and Minerals, and they continue to update this information every five years. In China, we find no similar data available for the Chinese physique, (a Chinese RDA), nor any commonly available, authoritative analysis of the nutrient components of various Chinese herbs and spices.

Turning to language, a new Chinese dictionary is published which claims to give the correct writing of the strokes of all characters, as well as the correct usage of characters in all idiomatic phrases (an issue of high concern to all, since Chinese is a language of homonyms). However if a student in school follows this dictionary's usage and is marked wrong by his teacher, producing the dictionary is unlikely to help his case, since the teacher can disregard it. If the editors of the dictionary are called in to prove what they claim (in light of the teacher's counter-claim), it would be extremely rare for them to agree to do so, because "that would produce disharmony".

Hence, "the (modern-era) authoritative or definitive textbook or reference work accepted by all" (in any particular field) is very hard, if not impossible, to find, and the lack of preciseness which this lends to many scholarly pursuits is significant. Certainly the excessive Chinese concern with modesty is directly related to this, as is the "non-action" doctrine of Lao-tse.

In the business sphere, Chinese in a wide variety of enterprises and other endeavors who need design, marketing, research knowledge and know-how, etc. prefer to use 1st) foreign personnel trained in foreign techniques, 2nd) local personnel trained in foreign techniques, and 3rd) local personnel trained in Chinese techniques.

Many Chinese also recognize that many of their prizes, awards, commendations, etc. are without an objective basis, and tend to be given to those who "follow the prescribed line", "conform with announced policy", etc. Hence, one award or commendation from a western organization is often seen as giving the holder more status than ten such awards from domestic organizations.

7. *Often willing to give more weight to comments and directions of parents, teachers, or elders than to expert opinion.*

Comments: The reader may find a number of examples in the pages of this volume.

8. *Able to accept criticism given by fellow (Chinese) countrymen, but often not the same criticism offered by others.*

Comments: Many types of critical statements are more easily accepted (by the public or masses) when a local "mouthpiece" is used. Hence there is a distinct need to locate and groom a local secretary, spokesman, colleague, or other confidant who will support one's (the foreigner's) point of view in a discussion, negotiation, or argument, and be willing to speak in your behalf, while you sit by the side and smile calmly in an unpreturbed manner.

9. *Little realization or examination of the subconscious, little attention to Freud, or to the post-Freudians (e.g. Carl Jung, Erich Fromm, Wilder Penfield, Eric Berne, and others).*

*Comments:* In the west the entire field of psychiatric treatment, both formal and informal, is traceable directly to Freud's work, since he recognized man as having a multiple nature, and saw that warring factions exist in the unconscious. He defined psychoanalysis as a **dynamic conception which reduces mental life to an interplay of reciprocally urging and checking forces.** The usage of many terms or expressions such as "neurosis", "psychosis", "repression", "latency", "sublimated libidinal energies", "erotic impulses", "paranoia", "renunciation of instinct", etc. in English (and German) have distinct Freudian overtones.

Books on Transactional Analysis have been big sellers in the west; most of their theoretical underpinnings are from Freud, although they have expanded, adjusted, or otherwise clarified his premises.

The Chinese have different explanations for people's fears and anxieties, and generally make little effort to recognize psychic disorders in others, or attempt to minimize their development in children. The concept of *jen* 仁 puts an emphasis on interpersonal transactions, and does not consider the individual psyche's deep cores of complexes and anxieties. The Chinese rationale is that any person's individual behavior is most properly viewed or contemplated in terms of how well it conforms to the interpersonal standards of the society/culture.

10. *Lacking completeness in many concepts, and failing to see the lack.*

*Comments:* The Chinese concept of cleanliness and sanitariness is the first thing that most foreigners note as being "strange", yet in reality the Chinese spend much time talking about such concerns. The discrepancy between talk and action in this case lies in the fact that the Chinese idea of what constitutes cleanliness is incomplete. As one foreigner stated: "They wash the inside of the wok, but not the outside." Other examples in the realm of cleanliness are too numerous to mention.

The Five Relationships model is incomplete.

The excessive Chinese concern with morality does not include or attempt to define business morality, and essentially only deals with those of high official rank, or the "scholar" subclass. Immanuel Kant wrote: "Confucius teaches in his writings nothing outside a moral doctrine designed for princes."

"Racial discrimination" as a moral issue appears almost completely lacking in Chinese ethics, however it is a major concern of present day morality in the west.

Man is considered to be a rational[a] animal, but the Chinese concept of rationality is so different from the western one (based on Greek philosophy) as to be almost unrecognizable; certainly the Chinese concept has multitudinous areas that are off limits to questioning or inquiry.

Classical Chinese architecture exists, however the Chinese appear unable to define or develop modern Chinese architecture. The design of apartment buildings, office

---

a. 有理性

buildings, schools, etc. is often strikingly similar to structures built in large cities in Africa, South America, Europe, etc., and without a sense of "Chineseness".

Classical culture includes values and concepts from the the aristocracy, from the peasants, but none from the middle class. Present day Chinese "common-line culture" appears mainly imported from the west. This is easily seen in 98% of Chinese wallpaper shops, where everything is available except *Chinese wallpaper*, i.e. wallpaper with Chinese motifs. All the designs are western.

Etc., etc.

World harmony is a stated goal of much of Chinese philosophy, but no systematic way is outlined to achieve it, nor does the government generally accept suggestions which would serve to promote this goal. "Non-action is action" or "the indirect approach is best" are the accepted rationale.

# PART 5 Coping with Non-Western Behavior

## Chapter 11 Strategies and Responses

### Introduction to Chinese Negotiation

After considering a number of strategies for dealing with problems raised by the considerations we have outlined in the preceding chapters, we feel that one of the most basic is the Black Face/White Face Strategy. We will want to examine this technique in some detail before we can examine any subsidiary or related techniques.

Diagram 11-1

In this diagram, the man, who is already inside the entry-culture, is holding his rope-lashed log raft as the lake waves roll in to engulf him. The lake represents the problem with which he is now confronted, and the raft represents the strategy he is using to stay afloat during his upcoming journey. His goal is to reach the shore on the other side in one piece. Many perils await him on his trip across the lake, including the possibility that his raft may come loose at its bindings, or disintegrate due to some other structural imperfection. Additionally, some unexpected current, wind shift, or creature from the deep may catch him off guard and seriously disrupt his progress, or in the worst case sink him altogether.

A large degree of patience will be necessary for him during his journey, as well as the ability to develop a certain sense of equanimity. As with all effective person-to-person strategies for dealing with the Chinese, certain underlying tenets are essential:

1. Remain calm and undisturbed. Retain an evenness of mind and temper. Be composed.

2. Many writers on human relations over the ages have stressed the adage: When you are angry, count to ten before you make a reply. If you have trouble putting this into practice, always count to ten before you say anything, no matter what mood you are in.

3. The Chinese sense of fair play does not rest primarily on reason, but rather on sympathy/sentiment, emotion, and face. Remember: it is often not as important what you say as how you say it. Retain a pleasant attitude.

4. In regard to the unacceptable points of your opponent's stance, enumerate upon them as an insect alights upon the screen and then flies off, don't bring them up with the force of a brick in order to smash the window. Speak slowly. Sympathize with the other side's point of view, do not satirize it, or call it ridiculous.

5. Approach the problem with the idea that you and your "adversary" are already good friends, and that you will want to settle your differences amicably, so that you will remain friendly in the future. Adopt a friendly tone of voice, smile, and attitude.

6. Consider that you have an "on-going mutually beneficial relationship" with the other party. It may be possible to convince the Chinese side to give you "a break" now, in return for your oral promise of further business, or some other benefit or special terms, in the future.

7. Downplay the concept of your "legal rights". The Chinese are not legally oriented. You are perhaps best advised to act unaware of the true nature of the situation, and innocently state: "I did not know you were allowed to do that."

8. Add the necessary overtones of misfortune, poverty, ill health, etc. to your case where necessary, to elicit sympathy.

9. Praise the other side's competence and good intentions. There is a tendency in Chinese reasoning to say that actions which were not done intentionally, according to that side's explanation, are not their fault. (Homocide is certainly an exception.) Likewise for natural calamities such as rainstorms, bridge collapses, wind or dust storms, etc., which have caused the job to go uncompleted. These may be regarded as "fate" by the Chinese, without any consideration that planning, insurance, contingency measures, etc. could have made up for them.

10. Consider the possibility of postponing a decision or resolution to another date or time. However, to be effective, this must be suggested well before the two sides reach an actual impasse.

## Negotiation Types: Front-end and Rear-end

Negotiation itself may be compared in many respects to leading a cow up a hill. It is always preferable to have a firm hold on its nose than to be grasping its tail. While this concept is often difficult to put into practice in daily encounters, it nevertheless remains an ideal which we may work toward. We should calculate our moves so that we are in a commanding position, and be able to seize the opportune moment to advance, while remaining aware of when we must retreat. If we are "being dictated to" as opposed to "dictating", we have lost much of our bargaining power, and will soon be forced into a corner.

In practical terms, the assumption of "equality between the two sides", in regard to both parties' exercise of legal rights, is seriously hampered by the lack of a basic contractual mentality among the Chinese populace. In some relatively simple situations it must be replaced by direct requests for "sympathy and favoritism", and in more complicated situations by indirect requests for such. Whichever side can present a more convincing case that sympathy should be extended to its point of view will tend to have the outcome tilted in their favor, unless the other side is in a more powerful position.

Sources of power will vary, however the ability to retreat at any given moment, so as not to be trampled, or backed up against a wall, is often regarded as a basic safety measure, and can be considered a fundamental source of power. The ability to retreat[1] is of course related to having other viable alternative options for action. With these options in the wings, one can take a firmer stand in the negotiations, and if one's terms are not met, the negotiations may be abandoned, and more promising activities commenced. Certainly the ability to abandon the negotiations and let the present situation develop onward unchecked, or "let nature take its course", is another aspect of this, and affirms that one holds a more powerful position in the negotiations.

For example, if we are leasing an office, and an engineering check of the building reveals that there are violations of various health, safety, and other standards on the premises, this a problem. The building may be full of tenants, however their true "legal status" may not be evident from superficial appearances. Building violations may result in the foreigner being unable to register his company address at this location, since "the building is unsafe." (The Chinese have their own ways of handling such difficulties.) Our best move is to first have the Chinese landlord negotiate with the building committee to have these violations rectified before we sign the lease. Our line of retreat is: we can give up consideration of leasing this location and go somewhere else if our terms are not met.

If we have already signed the lease when these problems are discovered, our line of

---

1. The proper steps for conducting a retreat are 1) small, 2) slow, and 3) unpredictable.

retreat may have been cut off[1].

## The Black Face/White Face Strategy [a]

In Chinese society, the Black Face/White Face Strategy begins in the household at an early age. This is denoted by the expression *yan fu sz mu* [b] which means "strict father, kind mother". In other words, the Chinese father maintains a very strict posture, while the mother is more kind and forgiving. For example, after a child was scolded or slapped by his father, the mother might hold him and say some sympathetic remarks, while explaining the correct type of behavior which in the future will not make father angry. The child is given the impression that while his behavior should be changed, there is no need for rebellion, because there is someone on his side. In this mode, the father is the Black Face and the mother is the White Face.

This formulation is used in society as well, such that whenever two parties are at odds in a discussion or negotiation, some people will move into the middle and, while maintaining the posture of the group they represent, will nevertheless display more of a benevolent or sympathetic attitude, in hope of lessening the conflict, bringing the issue to a resolution, maintaining peaceful relations, and saving face.

Let us take the example of a local artist, Mr. Wu, in an Asian country who has an exhibition of paintings. One gentleman, Mr. Grant, desires to buy one painting which is marked $200,000 in local currency, however he feels that perhaps $50,000 would be a fairer price. The artist maintains that $200,000 is a reasonable price, since he spent many years in contemplation and travelled many places before coming up with the inspiration for this work. Mr. Grant remarks that it is a wonderful painting, and he would love to own it.

Off to the side, Mr. Grant's secretary then engages Mrs. Wu in a discussion, and points out that her boss is very appreciative of fine art. He knows that the picture is well worth the asking price, however it is just a problem that this figure exceeds his budget. She asks if there is any way that it would be possible for her boss, with his love of art, to be able to appreciate this picture on a more permanent basis, and adds that she knows Mr. Wu respects people who truly enjoy his work.

It is quite possible that there will be no immediate conclusion to the negotiations between Mr. Grant's secretary and Mr. Wu's wife. It may be the case that both "sides" want to get to know each other better, and they may want to have dinner, go out to nightclubs or other social functions, go on a combined weekend vacation, etc. Naturally the party initiating the negotiation (Mr. Grant in this case) will want to pick up the

---

1. There may be various service companies dealing in handling all the details involved with company registrations, and some may be able to assist in these situations. Have your secretary check the classified section of the Chinese newspapers.

a. 黑臉、白臉　　b. 嚴父慈母

tab for all of this. Very little mention of the deal at hand will be made during these social and recreational activities. Mr. Wu may even suggest "Let the ladies handle all that, let's talk about other things", and lead the discussion into business, fine arts, language, politics, etc. Hence Mr. Wu retains a Black Face posture on this issue, but otherwise is very amicable and harmonious in his contact with Mr. Grant.

During the course of the behind-the-scene negotiations, it is to be expected that Mr. Wu will be said to fervently maintain his demand for $200,000. He is the Black Face. His wife, who is more amenable to adjustment of the stated terms, is the White Face. The other party, Mr. Grant and his secretary, is initiating the negotiation, and is trying to get the price reduced. As such, the negotiation is being carried on by the representative of the Initiators and the other side's White Face. With this strategy it is possible in the end that a successful negotiation can be concluded for considerably less than the $200,000 figure.

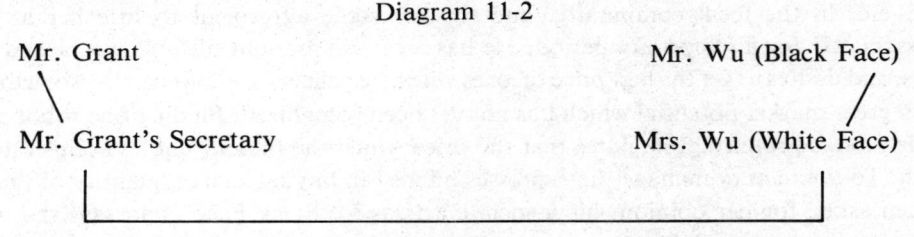

Diagram 11-2

Mr. Grant                                      Mr. Wu (Black Face)
    \                                                /
     \                                              /
    Mr. Grant's Secretary              Mrs. Wu (White Face)
            |_____|

Nevertheless, Mr. Wu maintains that he never has, nor never will, capitulate for a lower than originally stated figure, and that he is a man of strong principles, and this is agreed to by all in the negotiations. The fact that his intermediary did accede, and the same result was obtained (as if he had capitulated) is not mentioned, and he saves his face.

In this example, Mr. Grant worked through his secretary, although it is possible that he could approach or deal with the "White Face" of the other side person-to-person. Since the other side's White Face was a woman, the situation was greatly facilitated by Mr. Grant's female secretary acting as go-between.

The following points are notable:

1) This is an instance of essentially "Elective Negotiation". The parties can negotiate, or the person who desires to make the purchase may go somewhere else. It is not a situation where "a conclusion must be reached", as would be the case in a contract violation, damage claim, etc., This latter type would fall more into the realm of "Necessitated Negotiation".

2) The White Face of the other party was quickly located. In some instances, the locating of the other party's White Face may entail considerable effort.

3) The Initiators endeared themselves to the other side by acting in a very generous manner, treating to dinners, nightclubs, etc.

4) The party which was selling adopted the White Face/Black Face posture. This

is by no means always the case; sometimes the buying party is the Black Face/White Face. The key point as to which side may effectively use this Strategy is "the other party's desire to make a transaction". If there is no desire to do business, it is unlikely this Strategy will be effective in negotiating better terms and conditions.

5) The way that the negotiations have developed here could be described as SINGLE-SIDED MODEL, since only one side acted out the Black Face/White Face roles.

## THE OPPOSITION MODEL (also called THE DOUBLE-SIDED MODEL)

In some situations, in order to deal with the multiple demands of highly involved bargaining, it may happen that both sides in the negotiation have some personnel adopt the Black Face posture, and some adopt the White Face posture.

We may consider the buyer from a large western import firm at an International Toy Show. Travelling alone, the buyer locates a western girl who is currently living, studying, etc. in the local community, and reaches some agreement to hire her as his "associate" for a temporary period. He has a certain amount of money to spend on toys, and desires to get the best price on ones which he believes are "sleepers"—something with great market potential which has not yet been recognized. Finding one robot doll which looks promising, he notes that the price which the factory quotes seems rather high. To the factory manager he expresses interest in buying a large quantity of these. When asked for her opinion, his associate acts as a "Black Face" and says that she feels they have very little market potential, therefore she is not willing to back their purchase, or support their marketing in the discussion in the home office.

After carrying on this way for some time, the associate may say that she wants to look at other exhibits, and wander off. The buyer is then in a position to ask the factory for their lowest possible price, and to say that he will try to "convince" his associate that they should buy these toys.

The next day he and his associate may return, and in light of the low price now quoted, reexamine these dolls and reconsider their purchase. If the price is still felt too high, a re-enactment of the previous day's ploy, with the associate saying she feels they have very little market potential, etc. may be undertaken.

However, many times this type of Strategy will countered by the other side's adopting a similar technique. One person on the factory staff, perhaps Mr. P, will say that he would of course like to reduce the price further, however another executive in the company, Mr. Q, objects. In this fashion, Mr. P has set himself up as the White Face, while rendering Mr. Q as the Black Face. The development of closer personal relations with Mr. P and his associates might be useful at this juncture, after which some special terms could be requested "as a personal favor".

Further points are notable:

1) The true nature of the Black Face/White Face Strategy being a ploy for "sympathetic treatment" has become more apparent in this example. Each side's White Face often strives to cast himself in an unfavorable position in his own organiza-

tional/family/employment structure, and attempts to convince the other side that his plight should be recognized, and hence that his view toward a reasonable settlement of the negotiations be accepted.

2) For effective use of this Strategy, and in order to deal with the other side's possible countermoves, a negotiating party of two or more people is desirable.

3) Although this example has assumed an Opposition Model of one Black Face and one White Face on each side, this would only occur in the simplest situation. Either party could well have multiple Black Faces, and multiple White Faces.

4) Although the buyer's associate, acting the part of the Black Face, stated her opposition to the offered items and terms directly, this need not always be the case. Often times the White Face will claim that his associate/coworker/boss/relative objects to the terms, (hence "setting him/her up" as the Black Face) whereas when the person in question shows up on the scene, he/she politely denies this. Since the Chinese are aware of many aspects of indirect communication, this politeness (of the Black Face) is interpreted as a face-saving gesture, and the White Face's explanation of his associate/coworker/boss/relative's real objection is generally accepted regardless.

5) In international diplomacy, during formal meetings and other conferences, the Black Faces could maintain a largely unchanging attitude, while the White Faces of the two sides deal with most of the real terms of negotiation behind the scenes, and in this way everyones' faces are saved.

## THE SINGLE-SIDED ROTATING MODEL

In many types of discussions, an advanced variation of the above technique, with the more "talented" side adopting a Rotating Black Face/White Face Strategy, can also prove very effective. We may consider the example of a well known singer, who is negotiating for a tour contract. Since most Chinese entertainers of this type do not have agents, it is most likely that a relative or close friend will act as go-between, while in the case of many female singers the mother usually acts as "agent". In order to deal most effectively with the tour promoters, the mother and daughter may adopt a more involved and indirect formulation, whereby one acts as White Face, and one acts as Black Face, but they rotate the roles continuously. When the tour promoters talk to the singer, she agrees to various stipulations, says that she will have to think about others, and says that her "agent" is adamant about certain other terms, although she (the singer) of course is more inclined to go along with the tour promoters' ideas. In this way the singer has established herself as the White Face, while setting up her "agent" as the Black Face.

When the "agent" meets with the promoters, he/she agrees to various stipulations, says that certain others will necessitate discussion with her principal (the singer), and says that the singer is adamant about certain other terms, although of course from their personal viewpoint (the agent's), he/she is inclined to agree that the promoters' demands are quite reasonable. In this manner the "agent" has established that he/she is the White

Face, while the singer is the Black Face. The roles have been reversed.

This Rotating posture may be employed, re-employed, and otherwise "acted out" as many times as necessary to bring the negotiations to a sucessful conclusion, or until an impasse is reached, and the negotiations are abandoned. In this example we may view the tour promoters as the Initiators of the negotiations, and the singer and her agent as the "Faces". Since the Initiators have not brought forth any similar countermoves, we may view this as a typical Single-Sided Rotating Model.

Notes of interest:

1) We notice that the Faces' statements such as "I will have to think about it" or "I will have to discuss it with my partner" may have various implications: they may indicate indirect refusal, or they may be stalling tactics; the effect is certainly to eliminate these items from discussion at the moment. The negotiation of some terms thereby having been "temporarily put on the back burner", it is quite conceivable that these may come up again as part of either Black Face's untractable conditions (as stated by the White Face). When either the principal or agent acts the role of White Face, they are still free to directly deny that that is their own posture, and can always blame it on their partner.

2) The naive westerner will point out to all present that the principal's and agent's statements of each other's positions are at a distinct variance. This shows an unawareness of the true nature of their negotiating postures and the importance of saving face. In fact, if either Face is confronted with such a statement (i.e., that his demands are in reality more strict or more involved than he says they are), a polite denial would be the expected response.

3) It appears in this example that the principal and agent have met with the other party at separate times, however this need not always be true. The agent and principal can meet together with the other party, and the elder Face (generally the agent) would best do most of the talking. One of the Faces (principal or agent) may want to leave early so that more effective negotiation may be done.

4) The principal and agent should never dispute their real position in front of the other party, however they may dispute their "assumed position" for dramatic effect.

5) Although this example has dealt with a principal and an agent, this need not always be the case. Someone acting the part of the principal's agent and someone acting the part of their close relative could employ the technique equally well, while the principal was off somewhere else and involved in other projects.

It is easily seen that if the other party countered with a similar Strategy, this would result in an DOUBLE-SIDED ROTATING MODEL.

In dealings between two organizations, the changing of personnel during a negotiation may also occur, as new people assume positions of authority in either organization, and original personnel are transferred or retired, or as a tactic used in order to deliberately obfuscate the on-going bargaining. We refer to this as a personnel shift, and say that the element of shift has been introduced into the negotiations. Used in conjunction with the Black Face/White Face Strategy, and combined with our previous versions, three more possibilites immediately become apparent:

THE SINGLE-SIDED SHIFTING MODEL would be the simplest formulation, and if this shift tactic was adopted by the other side, we would have THE DOUBLE-SIDED DOUBLE-SHIFTING MODEL.

Introducing the element of rotation, we would have THE SINGLE-SIDED SHIFTING ROTATIONAL MODEL or THE DOUBLE-SIDED DOUBLE-SHIFTING ROTATIONAL MODEL which would only be seen in the most highly complex negotiations, and which would clearly give the impression of being used for the express purpose of stalling or otherwise thoroughly befuddling the proceedings, while still attempting to save face. We leave the consideration of specific examples of these as exercises for the reader.

Good-Guy/Bad-Guy

Some books on negotiation have discussed a similar strategy to that described here, known as the good-guy/bad-guy routine, or the hardhearted partner routine. In response to our demands, the other side says "Your stipulations are perfectly reasonable, and I agree with them. But my partner absolutely refuses to go along, even though I have tried my best to explain your position." Westerners tend to feel that perhaps by getting this person's agreement, preferably in writing, it may be possible to speak or deal directly with the hardhearted partner. However, this appears to assume that the members of any one team have equal authority in the negotiation, and have banded together to combine talents, so to speak. This is often not the case in Oriental society, which is oriented more toward the group.

In the Single-Sided Model above, for example, the wife of the artist might agree to Mr. Grant's overtures (as expressed through his secretary), but she would never put her feelings in writing. Often times we will see that the typical White Face is in such a position that he/she may influence or persuade the Black Face on his/her own side, but can hardly be said to have much real authority in final determination of what terms will be accepted.In dealing with many Oriental individuals, or family-run organizations, final authority for acceptance of the terms offered may rest with some elder who is not even present at the negotiations.

The same considerations are true when we are dealing with the more complex models, as well as when the elements of rotation and shift are introduced, and even when multiple members of each Face color, in many and varying hues, appear on the scene.

## The Sunglasses Incident (continued)

To consider a basic example of the use of the Black Face/White Face Strategy, we will return to the Sunglasses Incident presented in Chapter 4. We will want to examine the way the merchandiser attempts to resolve this conflict and learn what techniques are effective in such situations.

After some polite inquiries about each other's recent business and family situations, the head of this factory in Taichung, a Mr. Lin, says that he is sorry that there seems to be some confusion in the price for the sunglasses with the pouch. However, he states that he asked his assistant to call SSS up a few days ago, and he hopes the correct price is now clear. The merchandiser says that unfortunately SSS telexed the price to a US buyer, and even before Factory G had notified them of the discrepancy, the US buyer had FAXed acceptance at the original terms.

Mr. Lin: That is a problem. Did you telex the buyer back and explain the situation to him?

Merchandiser, Mr. Chang: We tried to contact him but the telex lines broke down.

Mr. Lin: Were you able to contact him later?

Merchandiser: Yes, but the Purchase Order had already been mailed out, and when we came to the office in the morning there was a FAX informing us that he had already opened the LC.

Mr. Lin: Have you found a factory that can manufacture at the $5.00 price?

Merchandiser: We were hoping to work out some agreement with your factory along those lines.

Mr. Lin: I don't think that is possible, the prices of raw materials have all gone up recently. Even at the $5.20 price our profit is negligible.

Merchandiser: I think you will agree that we have given you a great deal of business in the past.

Mr. Lin: We certainly appreciate that, but you know our production line is very busy now, and my factory manager has advised me it would be best not to take the order unless the buyer will accept the $5.20 price.

Merchandiser: My manager, Mr. Jones, and I certainly understand your position, but our customer does not. If we ask the buyer for a higher price, it will cause us a serious loss of face.

Mr. Lin: This is of course a problem, and I want you to know we are trying to be reasonable on this, but I think as human being to human being you should try to understand our factory's point of view.

Merchandiser: Well, you know I am in serious trouble here too, and as you say human beings are human beings, I was hoping as a personal favor you could help me save face with my boss. Otherwise I might be fired. He thinks I made a mistake in the price calculation.

Mr. Lin: It was just a clerical oversight on our factory's part.

Merchandiser: I understand that, but my manager does not. If you will help me out with this, I will see to it as a personal favor to you that you get some big orders from our company in the future. Between you and me I think it is quite possible that the price of those orders can be adjusted upward somewhat, to make up for any inconvenience you might suffer now.

Mr. Lin and Mr. Chang went out to dinner, but this business discussion was not mentioned during the meal.[1] After dinner, Mr. Lin escorted Mr. Chang to the train station by taxi, and they concluded their discussion. The final result was that SSS would be given the 50,000 pairs of sunglasses in pouch at the $5.00 price.

Observations:

1) The strict legal interpretation that since the mistake or oversight was made by Factory G, as represented by its personnel, and so therefore "they were responsible for it" was not mentioned. The issue of "responsibility" was not debated.

2) The discussion was conducted in a calm manner, both parties speaking slowly, and each waiting for the other party to finish talking before beginning their own remarks.

3) No discussion of honesty, morality, or other related philosophical concerns was attempted. No attempt was made to clarify different Perceptions of Value, or decide on what Perception of Value should be used in this or similar cases.

4) Each party gave the other party respect, even to the point of demonstrating generosity, and no attempts at sarcasm or belittling were made.

5) The merchandiser has effectively used the Black Face/White Face Strategy, employing what we might call a Single Sided Double-Tiered Model. He has set himself up as the White Face, while introducing the overseas buyer and his own boss as two levels (i.e., two tiers) of Black Faces, both seemingly direct adversaries to himself, and his position.

A touch of the general overall Oriental concept of "losing face" has been employed to add weight to this line of presentation.

6) Although the parties had a meal together, and drank some liquor, however discussion of business matters over the meal was kept to a minimum or avoided entirely. Family matters and other small talk were engaged in with the intent of building up a friendlier relationship.

7) According to the factory, fulfilling this order will cause them to suffer a financial loss. Hence, the merchandiser has made a promise to enable them to make up the amount of this loss on some future orders.

8) The merchandiser emphasized his relation with the Factory head on a personal level, thus emphasizing an assumed high degree of integration between Business Relations and Personal Relations.

9) Throughout the discussion, a relation between the two firms as "long term" and "continuing into the future" was implicit and assumed.

---

1. In order to avoid any problems with indigestion.

10) The fact that if the factory did not accept the order at the US$5.00 price the trading company would cancel all further dealings with them was implied, but not openly stated.

Questions asked by westerner observers:

**Q:** The promise of future orders to the factory was made in a rather non-concrete manner I think, and the statement that the price on future orders could be adjusted upward, to make up for the present inconvenience, sounds rather dishonest to me, or at best a gross exaggeration.

**A:** The Merchandiser recognizes that the Factory holds the RR Perception of Value. He therefore uses the same Perception of Value in dealing with the Factory. Thus the value of promises such as "we will place big orders with you in the future", "you may adjust the price upward on future orders", etc. is subject to the RR Perception of Value when the subjective considerations of SSS's position change. The Factory personnel certainly understand this unstated assumption to "go with the flow",[a] and adjust to a situation as new circumstances arise.

The "intention" here stated is to give the Factory more orders in the future, however we may assume that no firm decision one way or the other has actually been made in SSS headquarters. By not making a firm decision, but only indicating an intention, use of the RR Perception of Value in regard to promises allows the Merchandiser to skirt the issue of his own honesty altogether.

**Q:** Are you suggesting that every dispute of this kind can be brought to this type of successful conclusion?

**A:** No, certainly we are not. Our intention is present a general type of negotiating stance for reference of westerners who find themselves in these types of situations. Some insight into non-western methods of problem resolution can certainly be gained in this manner.

Referring back to our statement "it is better to be leading the cow by the nose than holding on to its tail", we should look closely at the item or items which serve as a source of bargaining power in the negotiations. The merchandiser is clearly using the promise of future orders as a major bargaining ploy. If the Factory is not desirous of having any further relations with SSS Trading Company, and is willing to walk away from the negotiations and suffer any consequences which might result, this approach will fail. However, the factory does indeed seem interested in maintaining long term relations.

**Q:** I believe there is a Chinese expression which says "Long-term pain is not as good as short-term pain."[b] By pushing the resolution of this pricing problem into the future you are opting for long-term pain, and you have failed to confront the issue of which

---

a. 聽其自然　　b. 長痛不如短痛

side is responsible for the "mix-up". Is there not a lesson to be learned here? In the view of accepting short-term pain and getting it over with, I think the factory would be best advised to confront the loss now, and to realize that the way to avoid similar problems in the future is to train their personnel properly.

A: You have forgotten that even better than short-term pain is no pain, which is possible if we can shift some or all of the responsibility for our actions onto the other party. In any event, according to the Chinese conception of pricing as discussed in Chapter 3, if the factory was in the position of suffering a loss in fulfilling this order, it would be unfair to hold them strictly to their original spoken or written price quote. From the economic standpoint of wanting to maintain order in the marketplace, whether this type of attitude represents a *long-term view* (i.e., having long-term beneficial effects, albeit perhaps some temporary unpleasantness and conflict) or a *short-term view* (i.e., having short-term benefit, especially in terms of promoting harmony, albeit perhaps some detrimental effects when considered over the long run) is open to debate, although the Chinese tendency for sympathy is usually equated with a short-term view.

In *Morals and Conduct,* John Dewey said:

> Liability is the beginning of responsibility. We are held accountable by others for the consequences of our acts. They visit their like and dislike of these consequences upon us. In vain do we claim that these are not ours; that they are products of ignorance not design, or are incidents in the execution of a most laudable scheme. Their authorship is imputed to us. We are disapproved, and disapproval is not an inner state of mind but a most definite act. Others say to us by their deeds we do not care a fig whether you did this deliberately or not. We intend that you shall deliberate before you do it again, and that if possible your deliberation shall prevent a repetition of this act we object to.

These remarks certainly represent a western-style direct approach to the entire issue of responsibility, however the Chinese are much more accustomed to an indirect approach.

## Task Completion

### William and His Temper
### A Study in Task Completion

One year in March, William was hired by a large quasi-governmental Chinese organization to do several days of work in organizing and editing some English language materials. After completing the job, he was paid the previously-agreed upon daily rate, minus taxes. He signed a slip for receipt of the funds, and assumed that was the end of the matter.

Eight months later, early one morning, William received a call from the Accounting

Department of the organization. Did he remember that he had worked for them several days the previous March? Yes, William assented that he did. The Accounting personnel then asked for William's local address, noting that they needed that information to complete their tax filing procedures at the end of the year. William said this was no problem, and stated that he lived on the 3rd Floor, #38, Lane 14, Alley 36, Ta Hsin Road.

The Accounting personnel thanked him for this, but said that they also needed the "community", "neighborhood", and "district" designations for their paperwork. William said he was sorry, he did not know those. The Accounting personnnel asked him to try and find out, and said they would call back later.

Over the next few days, William made a number of investigations and inquiries. He looked on the official address plaque on his building, and noted that the the "community" and "neighborhood" designations were not listed, although the "district" was. That was one down, and two to go. He happened to run into several neighbors, however since they were new in the city, they were unaware of these two other bits of information. He asked his landlord, but since the landlord was himself subletting the apartment from the original landlord, (thus acting as "second landlord" in renting out the apartment to William), he was unaware of these details. The original landlord (the owner) lived in a distant community, and he came to town infrequently. The second landlord had forgotten where he had put the owner's telephone number.

Several days went by, and one afternoon William was in his apartment when the Accounting personnel called again. William said that he had determined the "district", but was unable to be of any help with the other details, as several days of inquiries had produced no results. The Accounting Department urged him to continue his investigation, since they truly needed this information. William grudgingly accepted their advice.

Further research proved unsuccessful however. Inquiry with a foreign resident nearby who had an Entry Visa and a Residence Certificate showed that the specific "community" and "neighborhood" information was not included therein. William ran into the postman one day, but since his mail deliveries covered a large area, he was unaware of the specific details of each alley or lane, or how the demarcation lines were drawn. Indeed the addresses on 99% of the mail did not contain such data. Inquiry with a company on the main road revealed that their Accounting girl was out sick, and she was the only one who would possibly know that information.

Two days passed, and late one afternoon William had just come in the door with one of his friends, when the telephone rang. The Accounting personnel asked if he had now determined the "community" and "neighborhood" information. William said that repeated inquiries had failed to yield any results in this regard. The Accounting personnel asked if he would please continue in his research, perhaps by visiting some local government offices. William thought for a moment, and then replied "No, I am quite busy, so I will not be able to do that. I have already spent much time on this wild goose chase, and I am not willing to spend any more."

The Chinese could not understand what chasing wild geese had to do with the matter, so William rephrased his statement. However, when they had realized his meaning, they said "But you seem to have misunderstood. We have to have this information."

"I am sorry," William said, "but that is your problem. I do not want to be bothered by it anymore."

An argument ensued. William's friend asked to take the telephone, and William handed it over. Explaining his relation with William, the Chinese friend, Chris, apologized for the trouble, and asked what the specific problem was. After some discussion, Chris agreed to go with William to the District Government Office, and ask for this information.

The next day Chris and William made a visit to that Office. After being shuffled from one bureaucrat to another for twenty minutes, they finally came to someone who seemed to be in possession of such specifics, and William passed over his Chinese address for reference. The official in charge looked William over carefully and then inquired "Why do you need this information?"

William replied calmly "What business is it of yours?"

The official seemed greatly surprised at this remark, and said "I just want to know why you are requesting this information."

William said "Look, is this information public or classified? If it is public, then I want it, and I am not required to answer any questions. If it is classified government information then I will be happy to go back home without it."

Some unpleasantness ensued. However William insisted that he was not going to answer a lot of questions to obtain unclassified government information, since that represented a violation of his basic rights. After Chris apologized to the official, he and William left the building, empty-handed.

Two days later when the Accounting personnel called again, William was terse and to the point. He had visited the District Government Office, and they had refused to give him the information. He therefore recommended that the Accounting personnel contact them, or other appropriate authorities, by themselves. He did not have the time or energy to conduct any more inquiries in this regard, and after considering the entire situation he felt it strange that the Accounting personnel thought he was "required" to do so. He added a closing remark to the effect that he did not want to be bothered any further by this matter, and suggested in the strongest terms that they should stop calling him on the telephone.

Not five minutes after the conclusion of that telephone call, the head of the Accounting Department called. He seemed to be quite upset. William repeated his feeling that he had completed the required duties in his job the previous March, and had been paid. If there was any required paperwork in connection with that payment, it should have been brought up at the time, and stated as a pre-condition of payment. However, no such requirement had been made. He had wanted to help in the spirit of friendliness, and had done his best to locate the "community" and "neighborhood" designations when the request for these was brought up at this late date. He had failed. Now it was the problem of the Accounting personnel, and they could handle it however they saw fit. He refused to discuss it any further. Thanking the man for his time, he hung up.

William did not answer the phone in his apartment during daylight hours for two weeks, and this entire incident seemed to have blown over. In March of the following year William received another request to work in the same organization, and they mentioned the excellent job he had done the previous year. He went and did that work. On the last day, he asked his supervisor if there were any accounting problems in dealing with foreign personnel. His supervisor said that except for the deduction of the required taxes, he was unaware of any. At any rate the Accounting Department was on another floor, and he was unaware of their operations, although of course he had heard that they employed a lot of part-time help at the end of the year to deal with all the required government paperwork.

*What went wrong?:* The above story is worthy of serious discussion. The acculturatized foreigner will be able to indicate the exact point where William went wrong in his dealings, where a minor change in technique could have brought the entire issue to a more harmonious conclusion in the Chinese style. That "point" is certainly well before the encounter in the District Government Office. However we will temporarily leave consideration of this matter alone until we have looked at the following similar circumstances.

### Vicki and Her Forgetfulness
### A Study in Task Completion

A group of teachers and office personnel were under contract, through an outside company, to perform teaching services in a large Community Cultural Center in a major Chinese city. Investment in the Cultural Center was primarily by a local newspaper. The newspaper frequently reported details of the classes being offered, as well as providing interesting details of the goings-on therein.

Since the editors of the newspaper were busy with other projects, and unable to gather the necessary news tidbits, they requested that the office personnel submit one article per week describing some interesting, informative, or humorous aspect of happenings between students and teachers every week. The length specified was between 200 and 300 Chinese characters. Manuscript fee for such a piece, if published, would ordinarily have been a minimal amount of money (approximately enough to buy two cans of sodapop). However, this was considered an internal organizational matter, and no manuscript fee was to be paid.

Ronald was an American teacher who had many classes in the Center, and since his Chinese was pretty good, he was frequently asked to try to compose these short essays, and indeed he wrote, or helped to write, several of them. As the weeks went by he began to run out of ideas however, and the Chinese staff often had no suggestions either, since they were generally too busy with their salaried administrative duties to attend to this matter. As such, the completion of a suitable essay every week became a source of some irritation in the office.

A further peculiarity of this arrangement was, in Ronald's opinion, that there was no feedback at all from the editorial office to their administrative office which coordinated teaching activities. Although the editorial department would call on the telephone once or twice a week to ask when the essay would be submitted, after it was submitted there was no further word on it, until the call came requesting submission of the following week's essay. Indeed, often as not, it was not even printed. Some informal inquiries as to the status of essays that had not been printed proved useless. The editorial personnel who called had no power to decide what actually went into the newspaper, and the chief editor, who had final say over the content of the newspaper every day, was rarely in the office. When he was in, he was far too busy to bother with such minor inquiries.

Ronald assumed that if an essay was not printed one week, it could be put in a holding file, and considered for publication the next week, but this was apparently not being done. Also since there was no feedback from the editorial department, it was impossible to determine what style of essays they preferred, or in what ways the essays submitted in the future could be improved so as to better meet their requirements.

Ronald asked the head of the administrative people in the office, Miss Peng, if submission of the essay every week was a specific requirement of their contract. Miss Peng, who had lived in Europe for several years, said that it was not mentioned in the contract, and clarified that the Chinese preferred to sign contracts which were formulated in broad general terms, leaving the discussion of specifics as a matter for later determination. In that way the stronger party, meaning the party which had least to lose by cancelling the contract altogether, could dictate its views, and demand that they be accepted, in a typical Chinese authoritarian stance. She suggested that Ronald, having studied Chinese for only six years, and with his western democratic background and legally based ideas of fairness and propriety, was at a decided disadvantage in trying to understand Chinese negotiating strategy. In response to Ronald's statement "Why don't you just refuse to write it, saying that you are not required to do so?" Miss Peng sighed slowly, and stated that since there was much professional jealousy among the different departments in a typical Chinese organization, that kind of refusal would certainly be seen as creating disharmony in the group and not giving face to the editorial department. This would infuriate many people, and it could be expected that they would use this to cast contempt not only on her department's cooperative spirit, but also on their administrative competence, teaching program design, teachers' qualifications, etc. In fact, a list of allegations, real or imagined, could easily be compiled at any time, and having created disharmony in the organization you were effectively "guilty until proven innocent". Hence, Miss Peng stressed, refusing a request of this nature was highly inadvisable.

Adopting a very commendable stance, Ronald politely said that he would not involve himself in the matter any further, and was willing to view the future developments on this essay problem purely as an unbiased and impartial observer. Miss Peng said "Of course, that is all that is required of you. You are a foreigner."

Over the next few weeks Ronald saw that completion of the required essay every week was delegated to a new Chinese employee in the office named Vicki. Commenting on Vicki's personality, Ronald noted that she appeared very bright and cheery, and frequently giggled. Since she came from a large family, her other family members would occasionally come to meet her after work. She was recently graduated from a local commercial college, and was also often in contact with a large number of her classmates, sharing their joys and sorrows. When the weekly calls from the editorial department came, Vicki handled them, and Ronald heard from her tone of voice that she was very cooperative and happy to be of service. Many times she completed the essays, but then again many times she did not, and she apologized to the editorial personnel in the most heartbreaking terms when they pointed this out, stating that she had had to visit a classmate's mother in the hospital, go to a relative's funeral, leave town to go to a friend's wedding, or attend to other pressing family matters. The editorial department, rather than being angered by such statements, were most sympathetic to Vicki's plight.

Sometimes Vicki simply forgot to complete the essay, and when the editorial call came at the last minute, she would apologize profusely, and scold herself for her forgetfulness and incompetence, while telling the caller in a cheery and optimistic manner that she would interview all the teachers on her own time and write an especially good essay for the following week. Often as not she would then go on to forget the following week's essay as well, and then copy some joke or other humorous item out of some books on American humor which she found laying around the office, only changing the names and locations. In her hurry to meet some classmates after work to discuss their problems she often forgot to take these down to the editorial department altogether. She was continually cheery and cooperative when these oversights were pointed out by the editorial people, and asked for forgiveness in a polite and yet helpless manner, giving the impression of sincerely wanting to do better in the future. This endeared her to everyone in the editorial department, who gradually began to give her wide leeway in the specified time frame for completing the essays, and rarely called on the telephone. Other offices in the building continued to receive ultimatums from the editorial people that their essays were to be completed on a weekly basis however, and the no-feedback, no constructive-criticism, publish-at-our-discretion policy was still very much in effect.

*Comments and Analysis:* Since harmony is so important in Chinese relationships and social dealings, it is always advisable to avoid "confrontation" in any and all situations. Some of the techniques which are useful for avoiding confrontation in China may strike the foreigner as unusual at first consideration, since they represent non-western approaches to problem resolution.

Many westerners, when asked to fulfill some task or run some errand, and when a completion date is specified, assume that only two alternatives are open to them:

i) On the one hand, they can agree to do it, and then do it. This represents a non-confrontative attitude and compliance with the request.

ii) On the other hand, they can refuse to do it, and then not do it. This represents a confrontative attitude and non-compliance with the request.

Since we have specified a time completion date, we will temporarily disregard the issue of employing stalling or delaying tactics, however it is certainly true that these are a viable option in many types of discussions over some proposed course of action to be taken. Even with this in mind, the two possibilities given above are only "two extremes" in dealing with task completion, and two other possibilities are still available to us, as the following diagram clearly shows. Our two extremes merely represent options (A) and (D).

For clarity of discussion, let us refine our terminology by speaking of the Requester who makes the demand, and the Requestee of whom the demand is made.

| Requestee's behavior in response to a demand by any Requester | Brief explanation in plain language |
| --- | --- |
| A. Non-confrontative Compliance | No argument before doing the task. |
| B. Confrontative Compliance | Arguing first, then doing the task. |
| C. Non-confrontative Non-compliance | No argument before not doing the task. |
| D. Confrontative Non-Compliance | Arguing first, and not doing the task. |

Ordinarily we would expect to see the (B) option in the event that the Requester was finally able to convince the Requestee that he should indeed do the task outlined. After some initial argument or objection, the Requestee completes the task.

The third option is often overlooked by many westerners in China however. As a result of this, much conflict (i.e. "disharmony") is created in society, when it could have easily been avoided.

The "technique" which William has employed in the above example is clearly the (D) option. By contrast, Vicki has, deliberately or non-deliberately, successfully used the (C) option.

Hence the juncture at which William stated "No, I am quite busy, so I will not be able to do that . . . ", thus indicating that he was adopting a confrontative stance, is the exact point at which he went wrong in his dealings with the Accounting personnel.

Nevertheless, his visit to the District Government Office would have gone much more smoothly if he had downplayed his concepts of rights, and acted in a meek and incomprehending manner. When asked why he needed the information, he could have replied slowly, and with some hesitation, saying something to the effect that since he was applying to the Ministry of Education for a special scholarship, he needed his complete address for the official paperwork, but there seemed to be no way to locate it. Expressing his desire to continue with his Chinese studies, he could then have rather shyly asked the official if he knew anywhere that this type of information could be located, etc., etc. Adopting this or a similar approach would have no doubt quickly produced the desired data.

Perhaps if he had not been so abrupt on the phone, all of this unpleasantness could have been avoided. Examining his telephone manners, we see that he would have been better advised to agree to the other party's requests completely, make an effort to locate the requested information, and scorn his own incompetence when he could not find it. Agreeing to ask the neighbors for example, he could then claim that the neighbors had gone on vacation to some distant locality. Agreeing to ask the mailman, he could then state that he had not run into the mailman. Agreeing to go to the District Government Office, he could have then stated in a helpless manner that he was unable to find that Office, and/or the relevant department therein, or that having found it, he was unable to get his meaning across. Consideration of the statements Vicki used in her situation also suggest many additional respcnses. The allegation that William was not sincere in his offer to help would never be forthcoming, since that would be not giving face.

In this manner, each telephone call that William received could have been kept to a length of one minute or less, and all parties involved would have been able to maintain their mental equilibrium. Eventually the Accounting people would have realized that William was incompetent to complete this type of task, and they would have consulted the proper reference books, or made other inquiries, to complete the task themselves. The staff in the Accounting Department would then have stopped bothering William, and the situation would have solved itself, while allowing everyone to keep their faces intact and maintain harmony.

Reservations and Clarifications

No doubt some points about the above stories should be clarified. Certainly William and Vicki were not involved in life or death situations. Nor did their failure to act have any serious effect on their standing in the community, or maintenance of law and order, or the maintenance of their own legal position, including matters relevant to William's visa status. With these qualifications in mind, we believe that the westerner is well advised to fully familiarize himself with the local behavior patterns, and put them into practice to his own advantage, all the time remembering that "the wise man acts foolish".[a] The westerner is advised to act as the guest, act as the unaware new arrival, throw efficiency to the wind and "comply".

---

a. 大智若愚

Further Uses

Non-confrontative Non-compliance may also be useful in a wide variety of more common daily dealings. If we are eating, often times some fatty meat will be served. When the westerner cuts off the fat, and just eats the lean meat, many Chinese will comment "The fatty part tastes the best." To this the westerner may reply "Thank you" or "Oh, really?", while continuing to place the fatty meat on the side and eat in the originally preferred fashion. No disharmony is created by using this method.

One of my Australian friends felt strongly about the subject of ants, since his grandfather had been eaten alive by them in the outback some years previously. In China, when asked what his hobby was, he replied "Killing ants." Whenever he went on camping or sightseeing trips, he would frequently go out of his way to pour a kettle of boiling water on any large collections of ants he noted in the vicinity. This seemed to bother many of his Chinese acquaintances, who would see him begin to pour the scalding water and then say "Killing ants is bad." Rather than enter into a discussion on the matter, he simply replied "Thank you" and went on pouring. Certainly the Buddhists in the crowd did not enjoy his attitude, however he at least succeeded in keeping disharmony to a minimum.

Clearly the use of this technique requires some discretion, however when employed appropriately it can prove to be invaluable.

## Proper Replies and Responses

It is important for the westerner to remember that much of Chinese officialdom will make small talk with foreigners or other applicants and inquirers for various services. Such talk, when it is not directly relevant to the issue at hand, is best treated in a casual manner, and certainly not in a confrontative one. The foreigner (who is not charged with a crime) may generally cast aside the assumption that the officer, by his questions, is trying to trap the foreigner into some sort of reply that will compromise his position.

Tax Office Official: What do you usually do in your spare time?

Foreigner A: I like to go fishing. You know that there are many excellent fishing poles made in China, and I wrote to all my friends back home and told them what wonderful fishing poles you make.

Foreigner B: I like to go fly kites. You know that the Chinese make the best kites. I frequently go to the park and watch the people fly them, sometimes I even try myself, but it is not easy to fly the big ones.

Police Station Official: I see from your passport that you have not been home in several years to see your parents.

Foreigner C: Well, you know my parents came over here for a vacation just six months ago, and we had a wonderful time touring around.

Foreigner D: My father is retired now and was thinking of coming over here to study the language and learn about the people, do you think that is a good plan? Or maybe it is better to go to Europe?

Department of Foreign Affairs official: Have you ever visited the Soviet Union?

Foreigner E: Is that the big country next to Finland? I always thought it must be very cold over there. If I was going that far north, I think would go to Sweden.

Foreigner F: Oh, no, I usually spend my vacations in Hawaii. The New Siberian Islands never appealed to me. My feet are too big, I cannot buy snowshoes in my size.

**Analysis:** Chinese officials often like to engage in offhand conversation with various applicants, in order to fill up some of the empty time when dealing with various documents or inquiries. The Chinese feel this is a polite way to treat a foreigner, and so the foreigner is best advised to reply in a generalized fashion, and attempt to keep the conversation going in a smooth and harmonious manner. This will certainly promote good feelings in the department involved.

The foreigner may even turn the situation around, and ask the official about his/her home life, family, marital status, travel experiences, etc., and this will be considered very nice, while never being regarded as "overly personal".

In dealing with all Chinese people, offering congratulations and best wishes on a promotion, a wedding in the family, a new baby, etc. are always appreciated.

## Behavioral Modification Exercise

The foreigner may want to try the following Behavioral Modification Exercise for 1) one day, and 2) seven days in a row.

**A.** Say nothing to offend anyone. Make no sarcastic remarks. Exhibit patience in all situations.

**B.** If you are asked for assistance or help in any project, if you desire to become involved, you may say so. If you do not desire to become involved, say anything you feel proper but do not make a direct refusal. (Delaying or stalling tactics may of course be used.)

**C.** Go along with the group in any given situation, and play down your own feelings, instincts, and prerogatives.

**D.** Do not complain. Follow the determinations of your superiors, or the group consensus. If you are given conflicting instructions, follow the ones which were received more recently.

**E.** Do not stress your own knowledge, and do not point out inconsistencies or lack of intelligence in others' actions.

*By following this Behavioral Modification Exercise for a period of time, the westerner will be able to intuitively grasp many important aspects of the Chinese habits of speech and expression, and determine their real meaning.*

## Steps In Project Management

There once was an essay contest I saw in the Chinese papers on the topic of "Bosses": the term in Chinese denoting the head of a company. Many essays were submitted and published on such titles as "My Favorite Boss", "My Most Memorable Boss", "My Father's Boss" etc. There was even one written by a foreigner describing his impression of Chinese bosses in general, and his experiences in meeting and working with them.

Due to the fact that small and medium sized businesses predominate in China, the foreigner in the normal run of social, business, neighborly, and other relations tends to come into contact with more "bosses" and "preparatory bosses" (or "soon-to-be bosses") during his stay in China than he perhaps ever did when living in his home country among his own people.

Many of the thinking processes of "bosses", even in different cultures, will be similar, especially on the most basic level, for example in relation to something like "Project Initiation" and "Project Management". However, to many foreigners who have not had much daily exposure to dealing with "bosses" even in their own cultures, there is often some room for confusion. Added to this is the Chinese penchant for informal working arrangements, which means that much part-time, and even to some extent full-time work is ordinarily arranged without any sort of employment contract, and often times the foreigner is running around in circles trying to decipher what his best reaction in any one situation should be.

To refresh our memory on the normal flow of "Project Management", we may analyze the flow into three major stages: conceptualization, undertaking, completion. However, a more accurate analysis, more in the line of the way a "boss" would be likely to view the problem as a cooperative effort among two or more parties, would include many more stages. Twelve possible stages are: **1.** Discussion of project, **2.** Agreement on terms and specifications, **3.** Promise to participate, **4.** Confirmation of the promise, **5.** Contractual discussions, **6.** Contractual agreement, **7.** Begin Work on the project, **8.** Further discussion with possible readjustment and rescheduling, **9.** Finish work and inspection, **10.** Agreement to pay, **11.** Payment by check, **12.** Bank clearing of the check. Many "bosses" will point out that before the twelfth step is accomplished (the actual receipt of funds), the preceding eleven steps are not worth a whole lot.

This analysis, rudimentary as it may be, is useful, because we find that the foreigner often fails to understand the nature of a "promise" as given to him by a person from another cultural background. A promise may be defined as **a written or spoken understanding, agreement, or accord, to do, or not to do, something.** It is generally made between two parties: the giver of the promise, and the receiver of the promise. Yet there are many factors such as the giver's social standing, his influence in the community, the generally recognized availability of access (or non-access) to certain types of information, and the known business and social practices of our own home country, which give us clues to evaluating the "possibility of fulfillment", in some sort of general percentage terms, when promises are being made between people of our same social and cultural background. The majority of this basic data is missing when we deal with people from another culture. Thus the foreigner must consider the dilemma of "When is a promise not a promise"? Or put in another way, "When can I reasonably expect a promise to be fulfilled, and when should I not get my hopes up?"

There is no simple answer to this question. Those of us with an abundance of real business experience will realize that a number of the best intentioned "promises" will fall through, even in our home countries, but people with less exposure to wheeling-and-dealing will perhaps not realize this.

By way of illustration of the complexities involved, consider those types of large real estate sales and other undertakings, where even a commission of a few percentage points would be an amount of money so vast that the average person could immediately retire. In Japanese these are called "3/1000 business". Examples would be the consultancy arrangement to locate and refurnish a suitable group of buildings to house an enormous consumer products company, or to find a tract of land suitable for the building of a massive factory and production complex, or construction of a major international hotel with golf course.

After locating a site, the work involved in the project, from the Real Estate Agents' point of view, would consist in convincing the company's Board of Directors, and possibly the stockholders, that this is indeed the best location, and is more desirable than any of the other competing offers. At this point, the commission on the actual sale of the property is still a long way off.

The validity of the Japanese type of nomenclature is fairly evident, especially to people with experience dealing in such ventures. What is meant is that if you are involved in 1000 of such schemes, then you have good prospects that perhaps three of them will eventually bring in the Mother lode. Most of us will quickly see that that is a long way from even a .3333 batting average, (which would be 333 out of 1000). Yet many of these dealings may get as far as stage 7, (or further), which is well past the preliminary, secondary, etc. rounds of assurances and promise-making, before they reach a snag. We may say that the promises given were perhaps not empty, but they did not produce any final results either, and in terms of performance that amounts to about the same thing.

In the realm of everyday routine dealings, due to the basic Chinese tendency toward indirectness, they will often tend to describe reality in warmer or more favorable terms than the facts would merit, and some number of promises are often as quickly made as "a conversational expedient" as they are forgotten about. Due to the concept of face, it is seldom that one Chinese takes another to task for not fulfilling a oral promise alone (betrothal and the lending of money do present special complications), or even for non-fulfillment of the oral promises accompanying written ones, both sides preferring to just let the matter evaporate into thin air, and to allow harmony to be achieved in this go-with-the-flow fashion. (Written promises often fare little better.) Extenuating circumstances regarding non-fulfillment which might appear to the foreigner as "excuses", the Chinese will generally calmly accept as "rationale", nor will the receiver question the giver's sincerity in making the original promise, now that it remains unfulfilled, for that would be not giving face.

## Go Roman Strategy
### When in Rome, What Should You Do?

Recently I happened to pick up a newsmagazine which has extensive Asian coverage, and saw a number of interesting articles. A western woman and her son had been arrested for buying hashish in one Asian capital, given a lengthy prison term and heavy fine, while the local person who sold it to them was punished with a small fine and a warning. A foreign gentleman residing in one country had applied to open a nightclub, and was told that such nightclubs must be locally run, foreign ownership is not permitted. Some European travellers took a bus ride into the interior of another country and were picked up by the police, who stated that the area was off limits to tourists. Some Americans were introduced to blackmarket traders in one country to change money, and were handcuffed by undercover police agents on the spot, while the blackmarketeers went on about their business. Other stories of foreigners being arrested and stiffly fined for visiting unregistered brothels, unlicensed gambling establishments, or underground nightclubs, while the native patrons continue going on about their dealings, also turn up in the international press with surprising regularity.

There is an old adage to which many people strongly adhere, to wit: "When in Rome, do as the Romans do", which we will abbreviate as WRDRD, and which is often attributed to St. Ambrose, who lived in the 4th century. This may be roughly rendered as "When in an area (or country), do as the local people do," however to suppose that this is a universal rule of correct conduct when travelling or living abroad strikes our study group as rather naive. This "rule" seems to assume that "local people" and "foreigners" are treated equally, but casual reference to the international news media over a period of months and years will turn up a large number of situations where that is definitively not true, and we suspect that the "unequal treatment" situations which do not make the papers are far more numerous than those that do.

"Conform your actions to those of the locals"[1] is another way of putting it. This may be referring to customs, standards, laws, habits, etc. However many times it may be extremely difficult to determine what the local standards are, since in many countries, in many fields of activity, what the locals do and what the law allows are at a distinct variance. In many cases the foreigner who behaves in a similar manner to the natives will be arrested. The reader may think back to our discussion of TV Shooting in France, and contemplate what would have been the outcome if the situation had been reversed, with a French film crew coming to China and carrying-on in a similar manner.

---

1. Generally translated as 入境隨俗.

### The English and the Africans

A passenger jetliner was flying over southern Africa on its way back to England, and due to a bomb scare was forced to make a landing in the bush. A lengthy multiple-hour inspection was undertaken of the craft. The passengers waited under the shade of some nearby trees, and a number of bushmen gathered in the distance. Food and drinks from the airplane's stores were brought out and served. One passenger was familiar with the local bush language, and offered himself as interpreter for any of the others who wanted to engage in cross-cultural communication with the scantily clad, spear-toting bushmen. One passenger wanted to offer the natives some food, but when this was translated they declined the offer. It was then asked if they had any objection to the foreigners (the passengers) eating this food. This also received a negative reply.

The significance in this situation is that while the foreigners were consuming fried chicken, hamburgers, beefsteak, and a wide variety of other food and beverages, the natives did not disapprove of this, even though the items were not part of their local diet. Thus another curious aspect of strict adherence to WRDRD is illustrated, in that many times the natives will have no objection to the foreigner ignoring local preferences, and carrying on in exactly the same way as he did in his own country. Also we feel that WRDRD is a tenet that clearly falls in the nativist camp, and we have discussed the general inapplicability of this stance in a previous essay in Chapter 6.

Of course in terms of cross cultural male-female relations, marriage rites, death rites, geomancy, etc. it is not hard to imagine a multitude of situations where the natives could be quite adamant that their views be respected. In China for example, most people think it unwise to marry or to move house in the seventh lunar month, the so called "Month of Ghosts", and most likely the foreigner living in China will be expected to follow along with this cultural aspect. There may be superstitions regarding certain locations which should be observed, such as when the Chinese say that if a man and his girlfriend visit a certain temple they will surely fall out of love, or that if someone serves a certain combination of foods many of the guests will die. On the first day of the Chinese New Year, it is stipulated that no housecleaning of any sort should be done, since "sweeping the good fortune out the door" would be considered very inauspicious for one's circumstances in the coming year. However, in regard to such concerns as bathing, sanitation, toiletry habits, and many other issues, the foreigner who settles in one area may be able to establish a "middle of the road approach" that satisfies his own desires, and by no means irritates the natives. Clearly, accomodation should be viewed as the key concept, not total assimilation. As such, we do not expect that the fully acculturated individual can truly claim to be bicultural, unless he defines this term very loosely. After lengthy in-country experience, many foreigners will tell us that becoming totally bicultural is not a realistic or practical goal anyway. For example, it is often seen that new methods in management, accounting, sales organization, research, medical treatment, sanitation, quality control, etc. are more desirable than old-style procedures, and this is recognized by educated people in the local community, although not by the majority of the local population, who continue to engage in traditional practices.

### Dealing with Local Attitudes

To the foreigner who is still undecided on how to deal with the local ways of doing things, and hopes to avoid making any big blunders, some bewilderment will no doubt be encountered, as he searches for understanding. He may well express his feelings by saying: "If you want me to follow your customs and not violate your taboos, I will certainly try my best. Where can I buy a complete listing and summary of them in book form?" The answer to this in most cases is "Such a book is not available. Experience is the best teacher."

In light of all the above facts, we feel that WRDRD does not have wide enough applicability to be put forth as the supreme guide to cross-cultural conduct. A related phrase "When in Rome, Act as a Guest of the Romans" (WRAGR) is much better advice, and a much better yardstick for behavior when we are travelling in another region, which is different from our homeland. In other words, when in a another country, each foreigner should act as a guest, realizing that he/she is different and not equal, and make an effort to try to adjust to the surroundings. More specifically, the best advice for the foreigners is to direct their energies into researching the science of acculturology. This science we have defined as: **the study of the process and rationale whereby one may become adapted or adjusted to new cultural patterns; primarily, the study and accumulation of knowledge relevant to living in another country, as a foreigner, and maintaining peaceful, productive relations with the local inhabitants.**

Many times it is even possible for the foreigner to do things in a humorous fashion that will serve to ingratiate him to the local populace, and they may come to enjoy and appreciate many of his differences.

## A Short Course in Human Relations

Expressing sympathy for the other person's position is often a useful starting point for discussions in potential conflict of interest situations. For example, in our homes it is often necessary to have deliveries made of furniture, appliances, gas-cylinders for cooking, etc. When the delivery man agrees to come at 10:00 am, and finally shows up at 2:00 pm, thus resulting in much delay in our scheduling for the day, and assorted other secondary problems, we have two obvious choices for our comments, to wit:

1. Why are you so late? I thought you said you were coming at 10:00. We have been waiting a long time, and have been severely inconvenienced.

2. You must be tired after climbing up the stairs. Are you delayed in your deliveries today? We were afraid something might have happened, or there had been an accident or something. Please sit down and have some tea.

The second alternative is certainly much better received by the delivery man. It also represents an application of Whither-To Reasoning, which is the Chinese preference in most situations. The foreigner who adopts this approach is more likely to achieve an overall favorable outcome, and we believe this is fully in keeping with a proper application of the doctrine of WRAGR, in that one is acting as a guest/visitor in the country and not being too overbearing.

The reader may pick other appropriate replies from the following collection:

*When some important machinery parts are delivered late.*
1. We have been waiting for these for hours. Where have you been? Do you know what time it is?
2. Is it very difficult to locate these parts? Did you have to look a long time? I am sorry for the trouble. I was afraid something might have happened that caused you to be unnecessarily delayed.

Obviously one's comments should be made in a concerned (and not sarcastic) tone of voice.

*When an agreement to run an advertisement on a particular day is cancelled by the newspaper.*
1. What is this? I already made a down-payment to have the ad run on this day. Where do you get off telling me that I will have to wait for some space availability on another day?
2. I think you must have come up against quite a big difficulty in order to make this decision. It is not easy to coordinate all the advertising that you handle in this department. I know that there are a lot of people who have to be given some special consideration.

After an amicable basis for discussion is established, the main point of "I hope you can help me out with this . . . ", reiterating that one's boss was counting on this advertising space, etc. may be initiated, in the typical Black Face/White Face Strategy.

*When a withdrawl from the bank must be made in an exact amount of specific denomination bills, but the bank personnel say that they do not have enough of these in their drawers, and the girl in charge of the safe has gone out to lunch.*
1. Well, who is in charge when she is not available? I need my withdrawl in this exact combination of bills, and I don't see why I should have to wait, or come back later! Don't you advertise "Attention to Customer Service" on your brochures?
2. Is it possible one of the other cashiers or tellers has some of these bills? Perhaps you could change with them. Or maybe some of these other depositors are bringing in adequate amounts of cash? Maybe if I waited a minute or two, it might be easier for you.

The bank personnel are more inclined to help when approached in this fashion, and the harmony thus maintained will insure that one's next visit to the bank proceeds smoothly too.

The preceding examples all fall into the general pattern of a service-requester dealing with a service-fulfiller, although the following one is a slight variation on this.

*When a speaker's statements of fact, as quoted from history, literature, science, etc. are in error.*

1. Excuse me, you are mistaken on that one. I happen to know that the correct data is different from what you have presented here. I did a report on this in college, so there is no room for error, I am 100% sure of the facts.

2. The points you have raised are very interesting. However, I am a bit confused. I remember that one of my teachers in high school always told us that the situation was somewhat different from what you have introduced here. I think you make a very good presentation, but I hope that we could get together and check this out again before any final conclusions are reached.

By pushing the issue of "who has real expertise" off on someone else, such as a teacher, colleague, famous statesman, etc., (as opposed to presenting oneself as having authority in the matter at hand), we avoid appearing arrogant. A low-key approach to the whole situation also saves quite a bit of face for the speaker.

If we consider the person listening to the speech or presentation as the service-requester, and the person giving it as the service-fulfiller, this of course still falls into our pattern.

In the **Insults in the Night Market** essay in Chapter 1, we advised on the frequent use of the expression *dui bu chi*,[a] and the reader may want to review those comments, especially as they relate to the matter of "who is at fault". In the way of further extrapolation on this, in general we see that when two Chinese are involved in situations such as those above, the service-requester may start off by making some remarks to the effect "I am really sorry for the mixup". This type of statement does not mean that the service-requester is admitting fault; it is a statement of essentially neutral connotation.

Nonetheless, by beginning one's comments in this manner, and then proceeding to delineate (and/or apologize for) some minor issue connected with this or previous dealings with the service-fulfiller, we place him in a much better frame of mind, and the discussion of our current difficulties may then advance in a more calm, rational, and mutually-sympathetic manner. The foreigner dealing with Chinese people in a wide variety of situations may modify or expand upon these Human Relations techniques as the need arises.

> The music that can deepest reach,
> And cure all ill, is cordial speech.
> —— *Ralph Waldo Emerson*

---

a. 對不起

## Let the Police Handle It

**Case 1.** A foreigner is walking on the sidewalk. An unlicensed street vendor is blocking the sidewalk by displaying a large quantity of his ceramic wares on a large blanket, and offering these wares for sale. The foreigner accidently stumbles and steps on a piece of ceramic ware with a substantial value.

*Observations:* There are a number of possible resolutions to this kind of problem. First would be to pay the vendor for the value of the broken merchandise. Second would be to pay the vendor a portion of the value for the broken merchandise. Neither of these solutions readily appeals to most westerners, because in their analysis the street vendor is displaying his merchandise on the sidewalk illegally and therefore at his own risk. Contrastingly, the pedestrian has broken no law.

The Chinese analysis would say that you should have sympathy on the vendor's plight. Such subjective reasons as "he is trying to earn a living to support his wife and children", "He has elderly parents to attend to", etc. would be offered as rationale. Therefore it is expected that the pedestrian would pay him for the value of the broken merchandise. To disregard the vendor's circumstances would be seen as lacking benevolence. Since the street vendor has suffered a loss and is upset, the dictates of maintaining harmony would also dictate that the party suffering the loss should be paid regardless of who is legally at fault.

It is then apparent that the thinking of the foreign pedestrian and the street vendor are miles apart. Thus it would be of little use to have any discussion or debate whatsoever about the issue at hand. In fact, debate could easily lead to argument, and this could perhaps get out of hand, or become a shouting match, with a strong possibility of the foreigner being rough-handled by the street vendor and other members of his working group.

In light of this, a more suitable course of action could be proposed as follows: 1) Express that you are sorry at having broken the item(s) in question. Maintain a friendly attitude. Offer the vendor a cigarette if you have one. 2) Praise the street vendor on his other merchandise, acting as if interested in perhaps buying some other pieces, thus giving him the impression that he may be able to recoup his "loss" on the sale of other items. 3) If the vendor is disinclined to let you go on your way, you will want to call the Police "to come and translate" because you will want to say: "I cannot understand". If the Police can be contacted, then by all means have someone contact them, or go with the vendor to the Police Station. Your reason for going to the Police Station should not be to settle your differences, (because you have no "differences" at this point, having engaged in no discussion or debate on the matter), but because you have stated through words or sign language that you are too stupid to understand, i.e. that your language skills are insufficient for communication. (This is the correct approach even if your Chinese is fluent.) 4) Attitude is very important, and you should not get irritated. Feigned ignorance may often be useful. For example, when you are asked to speak, you calmly say to the Police officer: "I did not know that China's law allowed vendors to display and sell things on the sidewalk. In my country that is not allowed."

By maintaining a composed attitude, not accusing the other party of any wrongdoing, not finding fault with his point of view, and maintaining a general air of innocence, many times the Police will tell you to go on your way, and they will sort it out with the vendor on their own time.

**Case 2.** A foreigner is driving a vehicle when a Chinese motorcyclist swerves in front of him. Unable to stop in time, he hits the motorcyclist, knocking him over.

*Observations:* At this point the motorcyclist and/or his motorcyle may be damaged. If the damage is moderate, the typical Chinese handling of this situation is often to pay the motorcyclist a cash settlement on the spot. However, if this does not seem feasible, or if the motorcyclist asks for an exorbitant sum, some other strategy may be called for.

Some Chinese motorcyclists in fact may ask that the driver accompany them to a particular "private clinic" for treatment, or to return home to consult with their family members on how to best handle the situation. As a further complication, the motorcyclist may have been carrying some medicinal bottles filled with strange liquid, which are now broken. He may then claim that these contained a very valuable potion for the cure of one of his parent's ailments, etc., and that this represents a severe financial loss, etc.

The foreigner should maintain a pleasant attitude during all of these discussions. However, the best advice is to go with the injured party directly to the Police Station, and sort the matter out there as well as possible. Certainly it would be unwise to go to the injured party's home at this point, or a clinic of his designation, since being surrounded by his cohorts would not put one in a very good bargaining position.

**Case 3.** A foreigner is riding in a taxi which has an accident.

*Observations:* In any type of situation which may lead to the filing of a damage claim, the more evidence which can be assembled the better. If the foreign passenger is severely injured or incapacitated in this accident, or rendered unconscious, of course there is little he can do. If the circumstances are less serious however, and he is still able to function, it would certainly be advisable to note the cab number and/or license plate, color, etc., as well as the time of day, and the location of the accident. If names and addresses of several witnesses could be jotted down, this might prove useful later in corroborating certain details of the entire situation. Chinese judges and arbitrators have far more faith in the accuracy of medical bills from large public hospitals, or church-affiliated hospitals, so going to one of these facilities is certainly preferable to going to a small private clinic for treatment of any injuries. Receipts for all expenditures should be obtained of course. Photographs of the crash, or crash site, could also prove valuable for future reference, although if one did not have a camera handy, some other arrangements would have to be made.

It is advisable to file a report with the local Police as quickly as possible after the crash, expecially if injuries have been sustained. This will serve as a further official record of the entire incident. If a damage claim is to be brought against any other parties, such an official record would lend much to the solidness of one's case. As a first line of inquiry, the foreigner should ask his own insurance company how to deal with the entire matter.

If the crash is merely of the fender-bender variety, it is within the dictates of propriety to get out of the cab, pay the taxi driver an amount of money sufficient enought to cover the expense of the trip so far (don't ask for change), and leave the scene promptly.

*Afternote on these three cases:* Many knowledgeable observers have stated that in China when one contacts the Police in taking care of these kind of difficulties, it is a good idea to note the name and/or badge numbers of the officers, judges, and other personnel involved. After the circumstances have been resolved, a call to these people by phone or in person is most always appreciated, and this will result in the foreigner building up a useful network of social relations in these departments, which could prove helpful in later dealings. This is a thoughtful approach which recognizes that even inside a society that operates with group mentality norms, individual achievement should be acknowledged. If the Police or other government officials were particularly helpful in any dealings, a letter written to their department head, or someone else higher up in the hierarchy, expressing appreciation for their assistance, will certainly be warmly received. This will insure that future relations with the departments involved go very smoothly.

## Zip the Lip

A long time resident of China who returned to the west for several months noted that, in many types of encounters, there is one technique which the foreigner can use in China, but which does not work so well in his homeland. This technique is: *Maintaining silence, saying nothing.*

In many sorts of encounters where the other side has become perturbed, some angry question such as "Why did you do that?" or "Why are you doing that?" will be asked. Often the best reply to such queries is no reply. Thomas Carlyle said "Silence is more eloquent than words." In many situations this is more true in China than it is in the west.

If you have made a mistake, and this has now been pointed out, clearly you have lost face. Everyone can see that. For you to offer some snappy retort (no matter how fluent your local language skills are), does not help the problem to reach any final resolution.

Added to this is the fact that you are the foreigner, you are not a native. It would be reasonable in many cases to say that "You do not know." and "You are not expected to know." The other people present at the time also realize this, or it will soon dawn upon them.

That the perturbed party will press you by saying "What is the matter with you, can't you talk?" is generally inconceivable. That is satire. That is backbiting. That is not giving face.

Speaking of one of his friends who was able to keep disharmony to a minimum in many types of awkward situations, Oscar Wilde admiringly commented "He knew the precise psychological moment when to say nothing."

Not only can the foreigner effectively use this elemental strategy in many situations, but he will be admired for it as well. The Chinese idiom *da jr rwo yu*[a] clarifies that "the wise looks dumb", because he never shows off.

> I have often regretted my speech, never my silence.
> ——— Syrus

## Building-Up Company Culture

The type of management style which the foreign manager of a Chinese staffed organization adopts will depend on many factors. Among these are the educational levels of the employees, their work experience, the type of service or product in which the company is dealing, the marketing and sales policy used, the manager's actual distance from, and degree of contact with the the rank and file, etc. In some large organizations of several hundred employees or more, where the foreign manager is buffered by one, two, or more levels of local supervisors, and employs a full time Personnel Chief, it may be true that various manifestations of the Chinese tendency not to separate personal and business affairs may cause few problems for management. However, in some smaller organizations of a few dozen local employees or less, the problems generated in this fashion may become a source of daily irritation, and/or periodic surprises. When difficulties do develop, company morale may be hurt significantly.

The following guidelines, rules, or suggestions, have been formulated to aid foreign managers who are assuming control of, or setting up, Chinese staffed organizations, and may serve as a basic framework for employee relations in the workplace, until more specific policies may be established. This list may be amended as fits the particular situation, and posted or otherwise promulgated in whatever fashion is considered suitable. It is important to build-up company culture. These guidelines may serve as a starting point.

### Employee Guidelines

1. Personal and business relations are separate. All employees should complete their duties to the best of their ability. All company information, including suppliers,

---

a. 大智若愚

customers, personnel records, internal documents and correspondence, etc., belong to the company. The information therein may not be communicated to outsiders without management permission.

2. Suppliers, customers, and our employees are forbidden from having any financial dealings among themselves, including borrowing money, loaning money, or the taking of commissions.

3. Contact between suppliers, customers, associates, etc. and our company employees, whether during office hours or after work, are all regarded as representing the company and not as individual dealings.

Our employees must inform the management in writing of any gifts or presents received from suppliers, customers, associates, etc.

4. The management does not approve of employees raising money through use of the *hui*. *Hui* related activities, such as organization of participating members, collection of funds, etc., shall not be done in the office or other company premises. Employees are not allowed to engage in gambling, or any gambling related activities.

5. Employees should respect each other. Employees should take an active interest in studying English. Employees should give kind and warm service to our suppliers, customers, and associates.

Gifts, presents, or other items exchanged between employees at weddings, funerals, birthday parties, births, Chinese New Year's, and on other occasions and holidays. should not exceed US$_____ equivalent, (local currency _____ 元 ), as a principle. Gifts and presents should not be exchanged between employees separated by more than two levels.

6. Eliminate thinking "the more you do, the more possibility you have for making mistakes".[a] Plan carefully and try new alternatives.

7. The salaries, bonuses, and commissions of all employees are all company secrets, never to be revealed to outsiders. Each employee's financial remuneration is a matter for concern of the company management and the employee in question, and no other employee is entitled to that information. No comparison or other discussion of different employees' financial remuneration is permitted. Any dissatisfaction with financial remuneration should be reported directly to the supervisor.

8. No company documents should be left on desks, tables, etc.. where they may be seen by outsiders. Employees should put away all important papers when they are not working on them.

9. Employees who wish to be excused from work on a particular day should apply in writing one week before the proposed absence.

A. Sickness: each case will be viewed on its own merits

B: Other types of leave: A full explanation should be given

Provisions for resigning
       (to be specified)

---

a. 多做多錯

Employees who leave the company are not entitled to take any internal company data with them without specific management permission.

10. The management encourages employees to suggest programs for employee training, including attendance in instructional or informative courses in other schools, institutes, or organizations. If approved, the cost for such instruction will be paid for by the company from the Employee Educational Fund.

Some commercial Chinese shipping companies have employee rules which are more strict than those promulgated by the Chinese Navy. For example, requirements that female employees come to work 30 minutes earlier than male employees in order to straighten up the office, or requirements that women employees assume the duties of pouring tea when guests arrive, are all seen as compatible with the Chinese cultural background, and can serve as a part of company culture if desired.

Western writers in business management have stated that the dominance and coherence of culture is an important quality in truly excellent companies. Ideally, a great deal of company culture should be directed toward the marketplace, but for the westerner who is running a Chinese staffed organization in China, some in-house ground rules are also necessary.

In an established organization, any significant change in company rules or regulations will often be greeted with a number of employees expressing their desire to quit. Continued discussion after this juncture, or any sort of debate on the reasonableness of the new policy measures could often result in a loss of face for many employees. In regard to these expressions of intention to leave the company, the foreign manager is best advised to state "I would prefer that you do not make a decision now. Think it over for one week and then let me know." If the employees make no further mention of the matter, then the manager need not bring it up either.

## Trademark Imitation Headaches

Over the years I have heard a number of stories from lawyers who have had their share of problems in dealing with various "Catch-22isms" in the local laws of Asian countries, and listened to them describe the difficulties this often presented when trying to undertake certain legal action. The case of trademark infringement of a wide variety of consumer items is illustrative, although some certain background information must first be given.

**Background:** Westerners often forget that in countries that do not employ a language based on Roman lettering, trademark recognition often does not rest on the word(s) in the trademark in particular, but rather in style of lettering, the colors of labelling, and the so-called trade dress in general. For example, if the western company registers a certain artistic style of lettering, enclosed in a green and blue hexagon, spelling out the letters BORN-A-STAR, as a trademark, on first glance this may appear very distinctive from the point of view of the original equipment manufacturer (OEM) in the western country. By promoting the use of this trademark in the marketplace for many years, and stressing high quality, an excellent reputation may be built for products with this trademark.

Figure 11-1

OEM Packaging (identical to trademark registration)

A manufacturer in an Asian or African country (Country Z) may want to jump on this bandwagon, so he may apply for registry of a trademark he thinks would be good, perhaps DORN-A-STOR, in a somewhat different graphic layout. After this is approved by the Bureau of Standards in his country, he can proceed to do some crafty business, closely copying the overall trademark BORN-A-STAR design very closely on his product packaging and labelling, although spelling it DORN-A-STOR.

Figure 11-2

Country Z manufacturer's trademark registration

By using a minimal capital outlay, ignoring quality, and keeping prices low, it is quite possible that a substantial export market can be developed for the DORN-A-STOR trademarked merchandise. This is because a Chinese, Sri Lankan, or Egyptian may be essentially unable to tell BORN-A-STAR from DORN-A-STOR in the marketplace. Moreover, this latter merchandise will generally have a higher mark-up for the retailer, many third country retailers would prefer to stock it. In many countries that do not have a language based on Roman lettering, the "competing" trademarks which have highly similar patterns or designs (i.e., identical in color scheme, graphic layout, bordering, style of lettering, etc.) may be virtually indistinguishable to the common man. Local legal problems in the country of manufacture are largely avoided if the factory involved concentrates its sales on the export markets, where they are so much more difficult to trace.

When the OEM finds that various markets are being flooded with seemingly counterfeit copies of his merchandise, he may launch and investigation and find the factory in question. Upon further inquiry he will quickly learn that they are manufacturing under their own registered trademark, and therefore locally employed legal counsel will offer the advice: "Technically speaking, they are not counterfeiting. Examination of their trademark registration in the Bureau of Standards here shows that their product markings are in substantial conformity with it."

Figure 11-3

Country Z manufacturer's packaging label

DORN-A-STOR ☆

Hence, it is highly advisable for the OEM to register not only the name in his trademark, but also to complete the paperwork for the other elements of the design as separate trademark registrations. This includes the graphic design, the artistic lettering style, and any other notable points. Such trademark registrations should be made in all countries that have the industrial capability to make this type of merchandise. This renders it much more difficult for would-be counterfeiters to compete with a similar packaging or labelling scheme.

**Catch-22:** Difficulties often arise with procedural evidentiary problems in the countries in question, making enforcement of anti-counterfeiting measures extremely difficult. In the case of China, suppose that we have not quite established that some locally manufactured merchandise is in actuality infringing on our trademark. We continue to assemble all relevant evidence. Through our overseas contacts in Abu Dhabi, United Arab Emirates (UAE), we learn that the suspect merchandise has shown up there, in Mullah Brothers Stores, and was packed in cartons identifying Fong & Fong of a certain Chinese city as the exporter. Our trademark and all of its component parts are registered in the UAE, so we believe that based on this we will be able to have future shipments stopped.

When we bring this case to court in China, Fong & Fong counters by saying that certain unnamed parties are trying to frame them, and in actuality they have never sold DORN-A-STOR merchandise to the UAE. The courts feel this is a reasonable defense, and request that further documentation be produced before any final judgment can be made. What is needed at this point are copies of the Letters of Credit from the relevant Export Bank in the province where Fong & Fong are located. The local Chinese bank, acting under bank secrecy laws, normally refuses to turn over any records unless the requesting parties obtain a subpoena. Going back to the local Chinese court, we are then told that before a subpoena can be issued, one has to prove to the satisfaction of the court that the records or documents sought do indeed exist and are indeed in the possession of the party upon whom the subpoena is to be served. This essentially puts the burden of proof on the applicant, and seems tantamount to requiring to show the court a copy of the documents sought. Of course if one had such copies, there would be no need in having a subpoena to obtain second copies.

Next our legal staff makes inquiries in the UAE, and some investigation reveals that

Mullah Brothers use a particular bank there. An appointment with the general manager of the bank is obtained. This man says that although he would like to help, nevertheless he is bound by the bank secrecy laws of the UAE from turning over copies of the documents without the permission of Mullah Brothers. This seems impossible. However, after consultation with friends in banking circles, we are able to persuade the UAE bank to write us a simple letter of the following content.

> Al Ful Sultanate Bank
> One Billion Oilwell Place
> Abu Dhabi
>
> American & Western Law Associates
> Washington, D.C.
>
> Dear Sirs,
>
> In response to your request I regret to inform you that due to the bank secrecy laws of the UAE, and without an order from a UAE court, or personal instructions from the Sheik, we cannot turn over copies of the documents you requested unless we receive the permission of our customers, Mullah Brothers, 11 Drydock Road, Abu Dhabi.
>
> This is also to inform you that our confirming bank in China for all Letters of Credit opened with this financial institution for merchandise imported from all ports in China is the Middle Kingdom Export Bank.
>
> Sincerely yours,
>
> *Doolah Al'fool ah*
> Gen. Manager

Although seemingly innocent, this type of letter can be very helpful when returning to deal with the Chinese courts. The initial paragraph of the letter is adequate to prove the existence of the documents we are seeking. The second paragraph establishes that these documents are in a particular bank in China. With copies of our original inquiry letter and this reply, we are then able to get a subpoena for the bank, recover copies of the Letters of Credit, and to obtain prosecution in the case of the infringing merchandise, finally including a revocation of the cunningly similar trademark.

## Simple and Successful Negotiation

The following comments on Negotiating Techniques are not made with any hope for their successful use in any western countries. Hence, we would not be able to advise on their applicability in North America, Europe, etc. However, among the members of our study group, we have found these tactics and orientations useful in China.

THE "TAKE THE REMAINING QUANTITY" TECHNIQUE

An important consideration which may be useful in some negotiations is the idea that the buyer who purchases all of the remaining quantity, of some particular merchandise, is entitled to a higher than normal discount.

This is easily seen in the Chinese fruit market. If the banana salesman offers bananas for $15 per kilo, some simple negotiation may get a 10% to 20% reduction on this price. At this discounted price, if the value of the remaining bananas for sale is $345, it is quite possible that by buying all these at once, a price of $250 to $275 could be negotiated, with the reason given "I am buying all of them." This of course effectively results in a further discount.

The same technique is generally applicable to stock lots of other food items and/or manufactured merchandise when buying from wholesalers or factories, and oftentimes even from retail outlets.

In terms of buying fruit, of course if one is buying in some quantity it is certainly worthwhile to seek out the wholesale market in the city, where the fruit is originally brought in directly from the countryside. Fruit is sold by the case/carton in these markets, and prices are often substantially lower than what one would pay in shops, street markets, or other locations.

THE "DEDUCTION OF THE DISPUTED AMOUNT" TECHNIQUE

A mistake which many consumers and other buyers often make is trying to have the original purchase price refunded, because the merchandise was found unsatisfactory. In many cases, especially when dealing with family-run enterprises, or with very conservative management, this will only result in argument.

A simple change in tactics can often be more effective in such situations. Suppose we buy a jar of instant coffee (of a brand name with which we are familiar), and upon opening it find that the coffee has gone stale. When we make a cup, it is very bitter. We go back to the store and make a complaint. Instead of asking for our money back, we may pick out an additional selection of other merchandise, with a total value exceeding the amount which we paid for the coffee. When settling the bill, we ask the manager to deduct the price of the coffee, (which is the disputed amount), and we give him the difference. To use some imaginary figures, suppose the coffee was $500. Upon returning to the store to complain, we pick out an additional quantity of merchandise, with a total value of $715. When we go to pay the bill, we then ask that the Manager deduct the disputed amount, and we give him $215.

To refund the price of the item in question outright can be seen as very detrimental to the store's "business fortunes" for the day. By contrast, the Deduction of the Disputed Amount Technique saves a certain amount of face for the store personnel, and results in an additional inflow of money to the store's coffers, which is seen as additional business generated. Good fortune and good luck are hence maintained.

The customer should stress that he does (or will) do a lot of shopping in this store, because he lives close, works close, or feels it is the best store in the neighborhood. Avoiding placing blame for the bad merchandise directly on the store personnel also saves them much face. It may be stated that this was the supplier's or distributor's fault, the fault of the factory, of other middlemen, etc.

In addition to a wide range of use in domestic dealings, this technique is commonly used when doing import/export business. When merchandise was found faulty on the last shipment, the western buyer asks that some allowance for this be deducted from the next order. The assumption of an on-going business relationship is of course implicit in this formulation. If one refused to have any further dealings with the store/factory/wholesaler in question, then negotiations for refund of the disputed amount would have to proceed on some other basis.

## THE "FIRST CUSTOMER" TECHNIQUE

My Chinese friend Charlene recently visited a newly opened shop of women's handbags and other accessories. There were many floral wreaths on the sidewalk outside the shop, and it was apparent that they were having their grand opening. A sign to that effect was posted on the door, saying that the formal opening would be at 11:00 am. As per the Chinese custom, it would be expected that many fireworks would be shot off before the formal beginning of business.

When Charlene happened by, it was approximately 9:45, but of course there were many employees both inside and outside the shop involved with various decorating and other preparatory activities. Charlene walked in the door and began looking at handbags. The manager seemed happy to have a customer so early in the morning, and appeared in no hurry to have her leave. Charlene finally selected one handbag which was marked for the equivalent of US$100. She had been to Hong Kong and Japan recently and seen the same handbag offered for between US$125 to US$140, so she felt that this price was reasonable.

The Manager asked if she would like to buy it, and she replied: "That is not possible, I only brought $25. Perhaps I will come back later." She started to walk out the door, but the Manager called her back. Smiling warmly the Manager said: "Since you are the first customer, I will let you have it for $25." She wrapped it up, and Charlene gave her $25. As she left the other employees applauded and cheered.

A visit by some of Charlene's friends to the shop over the next few days confirmed that that style of bag was being sold for $100, and the lowest price the store personnel would bargain for was $95.

This represents another interesting aspect of the Chinese attitude toward good luck and good fortune. Traditional thinking holds that the "first customer" must be sold, even if it involves giving a substantial discount. The possibilities for turning this attitude around, and effectively using it as a negotiating technique, are certainly worthy of serious investigation and experimentation by the interested buyer.

The first customer may be defined in many ways. In terms of a ranking, I would offer the following: 1) The first customer on the first day of business of a new enterprise is of immense importance. 2) The first customer on the first day of business after Chinese New Year is also highly significant. 3) The first customer on any regular business day is also of some consequence, although probably less than either of the above two types.

As a final comment it must be added that: If you are the first customer and no agreement can be reached between you and the shop personnel on the price of the item(s) you select, it is considered basic business etiquette to select some other small item(s) and buy them. In this way the shop still gains "fortune" by not failing to sell something to the first customer.

## Indirect Stalling and Refusal Techniques for Persistent Salesmen

Occasionally the foreign manager will be confronted with overzealous local country salesmen and saleswomen of a variety of types. Sometimes ten minutes of explanation will not be as effective as some other simple ten second strategy in convincing these people that their products or services are not required.

This was once illustrated to me when an American friend of mine, George, dramatically convinced a salesman of some new types of off-brand cleansing products that he was "not interested". Adopting an indirect approach, with the idea of saving the salesman's face, George admired the packaging of the products, and said "I think that I would like to purchase some of these for use around here. We do quite a bit of cleaning." He then asked the salesman to step with him into a back room for a moment, and when they came out ten seconds later, the salesman offered his thanks, packed up his sample case and left.

I asked George what technique he had used to have this energetic salesman leave the premises in such an amicable manner. George took me in the back room and showed me. On a shelf in a corner of the storage room some sixty bottles of various types of cleansing solutions were neatly arranged. Whenever the salesmen come George shows them all these bottles, and states: "We purchased these from a friend who went out of business. As soon as we finish using them I will give you a call." At this point the salesmen promptly leave.

In terms of "Endearing Oneself to the Chinese People" on a scale of 0 to 10, with

10 being the highest rating, most indicative of maintaining harmony and promoting mutual friendship, and 0 being the lowest rating, most likely to generate permanent bad feelings and cast suspicion on the intentions of all westerners, I would give this technique an 8. It has the advantage of casting one's own motives in a clear light, and offering a reasonable and coherent rationale as to why the intended sale cannot be made. No argument or conflict is generated, and the entire flow of events is brought to a swift and, from the foreigner's point of view, successful climax.

Essentially irrelevant is the following afternote: George told me that he always saves all of his old used containers which have cleansing solution labels, and then keeps them filled with water in case of temporary plumbing problems in the building, or other occasions when there is a water shortage. Most of the bottles in the storage room are of this variety, although a few of the ones in the front are "the real McCoy". Naturally, it would be a loss of face for George if the salesmen were to question or doubt the integrity of this "display", and recognizing this, none of them ever do. This is a typical example of the **Exaggerated Display Diversion.**

## Magazine Advertising

Another friend of mine, Mr. Smith, was frequently hounded by a representative of a monthly magazine, published in English, which was distributed domestically in a wide variety of commercial and tourist outlets. Since he felt that the advertising would not be advantageous, and questioned the firm's efficiency, he used the following techique to convince the advertising executive (commonly called "A.E.") that he was not interested in placing an advertisement therein. At that time he was being urged to buy space in the June issue. First he asked the A.E.: "When foreign people come here in July and pick up a copy of your magazine, which issue do they expect to pick up?"

As would be expected, the A.E.[1] replied: "Of course they want to look at the July issue."

"Yes," Mr. Smith reiterated, "no one is very interested in looking at the June issue in July, because it is considered out-of-date. Everyone wants to look at the current issue for the month, and their first assumption is that in July they should be reading the July issue."

"Of course," the A.E. assented.

"So let's consider it this way," Mr. Smith continued, "if I buy an advertisement in the June issue, what I am buying is thirty days of advertising, June 1st to June 30th. If the magazine is late in being printed and distributed, and does not get out until the 6th, I have lost five days of advertising, or 5/30 of the price I paid for the ad. Let's add a clause in the advertising contract to the effect that you must mail me, by registered

---

1. In some contexts A.E. is construed to mean Account Executive.

special delivery, a copy of the magazine when it comes out, and I will pay the postage for that. Considering the postmark as valid, for each day past June 1st that the magazine is mailed out, I will deduct 1/30 of the price we agree upon for the ad. After I receive the magazine however, I will write out a check and pay you in full for the remaining amount due.''

The A.E. said that he would check with his boss about this stipulation, however since the magazine was newly established and could not be sure of getting out on time every month, they were unwilling to agree to these conditions. The A.E. of course stopped calling. Mr. Smith's ploy here could be called the **Full Value for the Money Paid Stipulation.**

*Rating and Comments:* In terms of "Endearing Oneself to the Chinese People" on a scale of 0 to 10, I believe this technique is barely a 5. Its overly legal and some would say nit-picking approach clearly ignores the need for sympathy and a mutually forgiving attitude in business relations, which is so important to the Chinese. It would be expected that under normal circumstances the magazine might reach the newsstands on the 16th, due to unavoidable delays in production, but the full advertising price would of course fall due regardless. The advertiser would be expected to sympathize with the magazine's circumstances, in the Chinese viewpoint.

Nevertheless, some foreigners have used this, or similar techniques, successfully in analogous types of dealings.

Another stance to adopt when approached by repeated requests for advertising support of various magazines and newspapers, in which one has no interest, to ask the publishers or the company representatives for "solid distribution figures". In the west many types of publications are proud of their large circulations, and some types of journals even take pride in their small circulations, since they are considered highly prestigious. In contrast, most Chinese-run periodicals are hesitant to release any audited statements of circulation whatsoever, although of course they frequently do publish highly exaggerated figures in their literature and on their mastheads. In the case of many types of periodicals which are being mailed overseas, (many of which advertise local products, services, merchandise for export, etc.) the A.E. will state that their overseas mailings every issue amount to so many tens of thousands. The foreign manager may want to reply: "Fine, but before we talk any further, please bring in the postal receipt for the postage paid on your last mailing, so that I may verify that figure." Since such periodicals are mailed at the bulk rate, such a receipt will commonly show the quantity mailed, the postage rate for each, and the total amount paid.

This is the **Solid Distribution-Figure/Demographic-Data Stipulation.** Most, but not all, periodicals are hesitant to let their advertisers know "the real picture", so this stance usually brings a halt to any further discussion.

*Rating and Comments:* This technique may rate as high as a 6. It is quick and to the point, and cloaks the foreigner's attitude in an air of concerned sensibility, without the necessity of coming out and stating the true facts of the matter, "I do not want to advertise", which would be overly direct. Frequently the A.E. will counter with the statement that showing the advertiser the postal receipt "is not our custom". Rather than argue this point, it may be best to divert the issue: "An audited statement by any of the internationally recognized accounting firms, or the local accountants rated as 'A' grade by the local Banker's Association of American and European banks will be equally acceptable."

Recruitment and Re-recruitment

Many of the export-advertising periodicals and trade journals may employ large staffs of A.E.s who call on potential advertisers (exporters, factories, etc.) continually. Since the major sources of "leads" for locating such potential advertisers are the pages of other similar journals, it may happen that a company which has already placed an advertisement in "New Export News" and some other publications, frequently receives additional visits or calls from A.E.s of "New Export News" asking the company to place an advertisement. This may strike the foreign manager as unusual, since he has indeed already placed such an advertisement.

This situation arises for one major reason: None of the A.E.s ever reads his own publication. Moreover, the publisher has no other organized system to inform A.E.s of who is already advertising in their own publication, and who is not. The A.E.s comb the pages of other journals, and call whatever companies seem promising.

A possible technique for dealing with this type of problem is to tell the A.E., upon signing of the advertising contract, that calls of this nature will be regarded as harassment, and that monetary compensation will be required for each advertising solicitation call received from other A.E.s of the same organization. It may be specified that such a clause be written into the advertising contract. This is the **Non-Harassment Stipulation.**

*Rating and Comments:* This technique is really stooping rather low, and I would have to give it a 3 or 4, depending on how it was employed. I have known a number of publications to agree to this stipulation in principle, and then allow their own personnel to violate it in practice, thus resulting in the advertiser's anger. At this point, the Chinese publisher could not understand why the advertiser could not accept a simple apology for the oversight, (sometimes two or three apologies a week), and insisted on carrying out the terms of the agreement. The Chinese felt that this put them in an unfair position, since they had not deliberately intended to violate the stipulation, and hence felt that their predicament should be sympathized with. To the foreigner who insists on taking the contractual stipulations at surface value, it would be expected that the Chinese would regard this stance as unreasonable.

Payment for Non-Contracted Advertising

Still another situation which may arise is where the A.E. has already placed the advertising without notifying the company beforehand (this is usually done by copying the advertisement which the company has placed in another journal). When the A.E. arrives on the scene to ask for advertising support, he/she shows the foreign manager the ad which has already been run, as evidence of his/her goodwill and concern for the company. (Newly founded journals frequently use this tactic.) The entire situation is easily dealt with as follows: 1) if the A.E. is a member of the opposite sex, and attractive, the foreign manager should offer to take them out to dinner. If this is not feasible, then 2) the foreign manager should thank them very much, and say that although advertising budget is rather tight right now, nevertheless when plans are made for the new year, some consideration will be given to advertising in this publication, etc. By maintaining a pleasant demeanor, and diverting the discussion to side issues (including the A.E.'s educational background, family & relatives, future job prospects, or other popular news topics), few problems will develop.

Other ways of handling various types of salesmen's calls may be formulated and put into practice as the need arises. The preceding comments can serve as useful guidelines as to how the entire issue may be approached.

## True Intentions

In dealing with cultures whose members are oriented toward the group, or tribe, and with historical autocratic leadership patterns, it is often true that individuals who are questioned about their plans or intentions may express a preference for handling certain affairs one way, however in the group context they later go along with a decision to handle the affairs some other way with little or no comment.[a] We can talk of their action in this regard by introducing the concept of "remelioration".

Let us first define TOPIC as: **Thoughts, Opinions, Plans, Ideas, and other Considerations.**

Remelioration: **the reformulation of TOPIC to coincide with needs and desires newly recognized at the time when action is taken; when these needs and desires seem more preferable than those TOPIC expressed at an earlier date.**

Clearly this is related to the Retroactively Readjustable Perception of Value.

Homework

A certain Mrs. Lee was once asked "Is it honest for children to copy each other's homework?" She replied "No, certainly not. That is not honest." Some weeks later another co-worker Miss Jwang, who had no children of her own, visited the Lee's household. In a small room in the back of the house, the elder son and two of his classmates were busy studying, and upon closer inspection it was noted that they had divided up several portions of the homework assignments, and then copied each other's

---

a. 説歸説・做歸做

work to save time. When this was mentioned to Mrs. Lee, she remarked "Yes, sometimes they have more homework than one student can do alone, so this seems to be the only way to complete it on time." Miss Jwang said that she thought she remembered that Mrs. Lee had previously stated opposition to this practice. Mrs. Lee sighed, and said "Under the circumstances, there is no other method."

Many foreigners teaching English have noted that in a language class of 20 or 25 Chinese students, when the homework is to write sentences using certain key words, or write out short descriptions of various things, there may only be a total of four or five "versions" among all the homework papers collected. Interestingly, the teacher can often recall that many of the students had voiced their objection to any such copying activities on previous occasions during classroom discussion.

Incidents of this sort are significant, since they remind us that rather than speaking of what the the members of any cultural group state as their views of acceptable, allowable, or justified behavior in any particular instances (i.e., TOPIC), it is often more helpful for us to speak of what their actual behavior really is, and to see what this denotes about their TOPIC in practice, i.e. after remelioration. Certainly this is of far greater reference value for the foreigner, and it will serve as a much sounder base on which to extrapolate other aspects of the local people's behavior. However, this type of information is perhaps not easily collected, except from lengthy observation. It would rarely come to light in data collected from various types of survey or questionnaire sampling techniques, which might tend to be overly abstract, theoretical, and short-term oriented.

Several kinds of data may be differentiated, in a type of progressive order of real-world relevance: t, e, a, and r. In most information from scholarly studies, opinion polls, sampling surveys, etc. we are presented with a two-step analysis:

> *original TOPIC data as collected*      ***t data***
> *behavioral predictions Extrapolated*
>      *from t data*      ***e data***

More helpful would be the following:

> *data collected in Actual situations*      ***a data***
> *TOPIC, after Remelioration*      ***r data***

From the point of view of acculturology, t data and e data are theoretical, and not finalized. In fact, they may be very misleading. What we desire is r data, which is a much truer picture of what some researchers thought they had when they collected the initial t data.

### Superficial Western Influence

In China, many members of the populace, especially those exposed to western thought, literature, philosophy, language, economic organization, etc. to some degree, may take stances on many issues which correspond fairly closely to western norms. However, when various types of social and group pressure come into play, they may submit to the tendency to remeliorate their feelings and hence to uphold many traditional Chinese notions, even though this is contrary to their originally announced stance.

For example, we may ask "Do you think that the leaders in your company (school, trade association, nation, etc.) are 'right' by definition?" The Chinese will answer "No, of course not." Later, when some new policy enactment by the leader seems of questionable benefit, and perhaps even of some detriment, we ask "Did you go on record as being against this? Did you stand up and voice your objection?" Generally we are given the answer "No, I thought that since everyone else seemed willing to go along with it, there was no point in my making trouble. If I were to say something, it might be taken to denote disloyalty, jealousy, ungratefulness, or regarded as promoting confrontation, advocating an overthrow of the present system, etc."

In this instance we say that the Chinese party has remeliorated his/her views on the issue of whether "the leader is 'right' by definition". The original stated opinion may be regarded as one facet of the personality, the actual behavior remains as another facet which, in the western viewpoint, is seemingly unrelated to the first. However, given the Chinese preference for seeking harmony in the group, and a tendency toward indirectness, this is not illogical.

TOPIC and Organizational Behavior

Given the Chinese value system, several notable ramifications in the realm of management may be outlined. These will be of reference to the foreigner who is in a managerial position in a Chinese organization, and dealing with people both lower and higher in the hierarchy.

We may say that over time, there tends to be remelioration of the views of Chinese people in a Chinese organization to the effect that

1. The leader should be respected.

*Ramification:* If anyone questions the leader's policies, decisions, or strategies on any issue, it is equivalent to questioning his ability to lead, or the appropriateness of his continuance in the leadership position.

Comments: High position equals high morality in the traditional Chinese conception. Therefore the leader, by definition, "does not make mistakes".

This also dovetails with the view that the Chinese maintain a high integration between "criticizing" and "cursing", i.e. they often do not attempt to distinguish these clearly. Unfavorable comments are regarded as cursing.

Studies of leadership positions in all levels of Chinese society have found that the typical leader has a marked preference for hearing only information that supports his established point of view. Other comments seem to be viewed as threatening the leader's position. Historically, unfavorable comments which common citizens made about the officials in power might commonly be replied to by the statement "Oh, you are trying to overthrow the government", whereupon the citizens would be arrested and jailed.

In summary, it is often felt that to question the leader's policies is to be in need of "re-education".

2. Positions of leadership should be occupied by the elders.

*Ramification:* If you appoint a director or manager of a department who, although excellently qualified and trained, is younger than most people in the department, a stalemate will often develop. Many Chinese have a hard time subordinating themselves to anyone who is younger than they are.

Comments: The phrase "Respect the elderly and respect the wise",[a] although firmly entrenched as a Chinese adage, nevertheless in practice only the elderly seem possible of being termed "wise".

Western writers have often noted that the leaders in most Chinese governmental and private organizations tend to be advanced in years, and in in the international news media we see frequent references to these people in terms of "the ruling gerontocracy".

3. Bonuses should be awarded on the basis of seniority.

*Ramification:* In a department of people of different ages, where bonuses are awarded on the basis of competence or outstanding performance, the elder members may feel it very unfair, and tend to cause problems if they are frequently or consistently outperformed by younger members, and hence receive less in the way of bonuses.

Comments: This is related to the view that the elders should be respected. If they receive less money, they may feel that they are not being respected. The greater disparity there is between ages of employees in any department, the more chance there is of this problem developing.

However even within the Chinese value system, paying bonuses on the basis of seniority is not without its problems. In some smaller organizations, some employees may feel "It is not fair for Joseph to get a bigger bonus, after all we do the same work he does."

With the belief that definition of the problem is half of the solution, these three points have been outlined. Each manager may need to devise techniques for solving them according to his own particular style of management.

## Differing Management Orientations

**Orientation 1.** Boss tells managers "Your job is to solve problems which come up and report to upper management on the results obtained."

**Orientation 2.** Boss tells managers "Your job is to explain problems which come up, and report to upper management on the difficulties encountered in dealing with them."

In dealing with planning, accounting, administration, sales or production of an

---

a. 尊老敬賢

established product, many foreign bosses stress 70% Orientation 1 and 30% Orientation 2.

In dealing with high technology, engineering, research and development, many foreign bosses stress 30% Orientation 1 and 70% Orientation 2.

Clearly in Orientation 1 the stress is more on "Results", while in Orientation 2 the stress is more on "Reaction".

## Managing Your Way Through the Chinese Holidays

The three most important Chinese holidays, when gifts are given, are 1st) Chinese New Year, 2nd) Mid-Autumn Festival, 3rd) Dragonboat Festival. For the foreign manager of a Chinese staffed organization, especially a newly founded organization, there should be a policy statement on how these holidays will be handled.

**Chinese New Year.** Some basic policy on New Year's bonuses[a] (paid before the vacation starts) must be established, such as "Two months bonus will be paid as a general management policy." This wording indicates that the bonus may be more than two months salary if the company has been especially profitable. New employees are paid an equivalent percentage. In this example, an employee who worked a full year would be entitled to a two month bonus. An employee who was hired five months before the Chinese New Year would only receive 5/12 of two month's salary as a bonus.

Gift policy for building managers, building guards, custodians, etc. should be formulated.

Some consideration should be given to how the first day back in the workplace after Chinese New Year will be treated. In a factory, using the first two hours as a "friendship time" with refreshments such as punch, soft drinks, simple snacks, etc. is often appropriate, however in an office this may not be necessary.

Some factories or offices may come back one day earlier than normal for the purpose of "starting work"[b] in the new year. Activities included in this day are turning on all machinery and doing basic inspection, general clean-up and straightening-up around the workplace, shooting of fireworks, etc. A meeting may be held to discuss the performance of the past year and plans for the new year. Upon conclusion of this the employees usually go home early, after the management passes out red envelopes containing a small amount of "good luck" money.

**Mid-Autumn Festival.** Oftentimes management gives each employee a gift of some sort at this time. Single men or women employees over the age of 50 can be given an extra gift, and this will promote good relations in the workplace. The Personnel Chief

---

a. 年終獎金　　b. 開工

or Head Secretary may pass these out, and this is viewed as giving much face.

Gift policy for building managers, building guards, custodians, etc. should be considered.

**Dragon Boat Festival.** Some procedure may be formulated. This holiday is less important than the other two. Some companies may have no special celebration or gift-giving, others may only put up some decorations in the workplace.

Notes: The dictionary defines "bonus" as **1) anything given in addition to the customary or required amount; gift or something extra. 2) an extra dividend paid out of accumulated profits.** Hence, some westerners would say that the decision made very early in the year to pay out "two months bonus" at the end of the year as a general management policy is not a "bonus" at all, but rather a part of each employee's "expected salary", i.e. the employees are being paid fourteen months salary every year instead of twelve. To be something *extra*, the bonus should be calculated at the end of the year, and based on all the data of the company's performance during the year, especially as regards each individual's performance in the organization. However the Chinese tendency is to pay "bonuses" on an equal "percentage" basis throughout the organization, admittedly with some allowed differentiation based on seniority.

Certainly the entire issue of bonuses is a very sensitive matter among employees, and hence is one which causes much consternation among foreign managers. It is especially complicated by the fact that Chinese employees will openly discuss salary levels, commission payments, and bonuses among themselves, and actively compare how much everyone got, or is getting. If this is not desired, some statement should be made to this effect early on: see item 7 on our list of Employee Guidelines. Such a statement will certainly not eliminate the "problem" entirely, but it does keep it down to more manageable proportions.

Indeed many western companies do not pay across-the-board bonuses in their home environments as a general management policy, and only pay year-end bonuses based on individual performance. Evaluation of the pros and cons of the suggestion "Why not just eliminate these so-called bonus payments in China altogether, and spread the entire year's earnings for each employee more equitably over twelve months?" is beyond the scope of this text. However the Chinese style bonus system does have a basic problem in that a great deal of employee turnover is concentrated into the period following the Chinese New Year. Employees who are unsatisfied with their working conditions often just fail to come back to work. Adoption of this "equitable spread" suggestion would appear to mitigate this, however without the approval and cooperation of the Chinese government authorities it would appear a very difficult suggestion to put into practice throughout society.

Certainly the amount of "bonus money" which the employee brings home before the Chinese New Year is highly related to his "face" in the family/clan.

## Positive vs. Negative Financial Reinforcement

In many organizations, the problem of employee motivation, adherence to company rules & regulations, and other related matters often cause much consternation, especially in jobs that are very procedurally oriented. Many westerners adhere to the doctrine of a clear differentiation between "reward" and "punishment", with the result that they would recommend "If the employees are late to work, fail to come to meetings, do not turn in their reports on time, or break other rules, we should make a deduction from their salary."

Unfortunately, with the Chinese concern for face, sympathy, harmony in the group, etc., this type of negative reinforcement often generates much in the way of bad feelings, and produces a very high rates of personnel turnover. A reversal of this technique is often effective however, and will be summarized here for the reference of managers who are dealing with Chinese employees and formulating salary policy.

### The Hundred-fold Bonus Technique

In this formulation, each employee is given an extremely low basic salary, however nearly every activity which he/she must complete during the normal pay period (usually one month) is associated with a bonus of varying amounts. The total amount of salary which the employee may earn by accumulating all of these bonuses in addition to his/her basic salary is calculated to exceed the salary earned by similar individuals serving in similar positions in similar companies in the area. (Chinese employees assume that working for a foreign company will be more highly paid than working for a local Chinese-run firm.)

Certainly different firms will have different requirements. However, some possible categories are suggested here:

Arrival on time for work every day is a daily bonus of $ _____ .

Arrival on time for work for the entire month is an additional one time bonus of $ _____ .

No leave taken during the month (annual leave excluded) is an additional one time bonus of $ _____ .

No early departure from work is a daily bonus of $ _____ .

No early departure from work for the entire month is a one time bonus of $ _____ .

Completion of all reports is a daily bonus of $ _____ .

Prompt arrival at weekly meetings, and attendance to the end is a weekly bonus of $ _____ .

Correct and timely maintenance of all machinery is . . .

No breakage, spillage, damage, to production (or not to exceed a specified percentage) is . . .

No faulty registration of data is . . .

The manager is free to use his creativity to develop further categories which more closely fit the situation in his organization. If employees are paid by the hour, or on a commission basis, certain variations of this technique may be employeed as well, with the goal of having a large number of bonus categories.[1] Sometimes these may have to be changed, revamped, or added to over time, as new eventualities emerge.

This type of arrangment would be practical for line employees, but it is probably not feasible to the same degree for higher level executive type positions. Although the "accounting" or "record keeping" which this so-called Hundred-fold Bonus Technique entails may seem a bit troublesome in theory, office work in China tends to be labor intensive, and so this is nothing unusual. The effect of this formulation is that the errant employee is not directly penalized for incorrect action, but rather indirectly penalized, since he/she merely fails to receive the relevant bonus. The goal of providing proper motivation is often achieved where other methods have proved less successful. Experimentation with this will yield many varieties of application.

Many foreign executives suggest employing Chinese managers to manage Chinese staff and workers. While we feel this is excellent advice, we still believe it is useful for the westerner to be aware of basic Chinese attitudes in the workplace, so that he may enter into a discussion of all the relevant issues, in preparation for the enactment of various new policies, as the need arises.

## Uninvited Guests

Due to the maintenance of agricultural society norms in the present era, many Chinese people will drop in uninvited and without previous appointment to visit their foreign friend in the workplace. If this happens just when the foreigner is busy with several other projects, it can be difficult to deal with. Some guidelines for handling this type of situation would be: 1) Give the acquaintance/visitor tea or coffee, and ask them to sit down. 2) Offer a few sentences of greeting, and inquire about their recent circumstances. 3) Say "I am quite busy now, but I estimate that I will be free in _____ hour(s)." 4) Suggest that you meet together in a nearby coffee shop or refreshment stand at that time. 5) If the acquaintance says that this is not necessary, or not feasible, get his/her telephone number and say you will give him/her a telephone call later.

For the foreign manager who has a full time Chinese secretary, most of these problems may be left for her to deal with.

---

1. A local accounting firm may be consulted to determine whether or not these bonuses are to be considered as wage income for calculating employee withholding taxes.

### Ridiculous and Stupid

Both of these words are much more severe in their negative connotation in Chinese than in English. In a discussion or negotiation, using them to refer to the other side's statements, plans, ideas, etc. is ill advised. Rather than saying "That is ridiculous!"
      Say "I think this way would be wiser." Then outline what you feel is a better methodology.

Rather than saying "That is a stupid suggestion!"
      Say "I think this suggestion would be better." Then offer your own suggestion.

Of course, ridiculous [a] has many synonyms (most notably: **nonsense**) and stupid [b] has many synonyms (most notably: **dumb**) which are best used with extreme caution as well.

### Indirect Recommendation

In a choice of two methods A1 and B1, if we say "I was stupid and used the B1 method before, but I failed", this is an acceptable use of the term "stupid" because it indicates my own humility. At the same time it becomes an indirect recommendation of the A1 method.

## Telephone vs. Letter

Lengthy observation tends to suggest that telephone calls to various Chinese government agencies for rectification of various abuses (e.g. for assistance in towing away abandoned rusting vehicles, fixing broken high-voltage wires that are hanging in the street, repairing broken street lights, clearing illegal obstructions off sidewalks, covering open holes near construction sites, etc.) are often difficult to bring to a successful conclusion. Many officials appear to be expert at "kicking the ball", whether deliberately or non-deliberately. The telephone caller is often routed and rerouted through endless layers of bureaucracy, many times ending up just where he started at the beginning. To an extent we suspect that this situation arises because the job duties and areas of authority of the differnt bureaux and departments are not as well defined as similar agencies in western countries, hence many times the Chinese officials do not know how to deal with anything much outside the realm of routine matters. In any event, such a situation can be very frustrating for the foreigner.

    Our advice is: Write a letter. If you feel most comfortable writing in English, then do so, but be sure to make it neat and legible, or use a typewriter if at all possible. Much weight is added to your case if you enclose photos of the problem. Mail your letter to the Chinese government department you think is in charge of the area in question, and if you do not know then send it to the Mayor or County Magistrate. Of course it is a good idea to put the address and other data on the envelope in English and Chinese, that way the mailman will have an easier time, and your letter will be delivered more promptly.

---

a. 廢話、可笑的、荒謬的    b. 笨、愚蠢的、愚昧無知的

# Chapter 12 Cross-Cultural Model Building

## Making a 3-D Model

One Chinese artist, Mr. Chen, was asked by a construction engineer to design a 3-D model of his new housing project which was rapidly nearing completion and scheduled to go on the market, with much fanfare, July 18th. Mr. Chen was given a tour of the site, and many pictures were taken for reference. He spent two weeks, with an assistant, designing and constructing the model, which was approximately 15 square feet in size. On July 17th, Mr. Chen delivered the 3-D model to the company showroom, and as per previous agreement, expected to be paid his entire fee in cash the same day. However, the construction engineer was out of the office at that time, and could not be located. The secretaries in charge were not aware of what exact arrangement the boss had made with Mr. Chen, but they assured him that everything would be alright, and that the boss would call him as soon as he came back. They helped Mr. Chen set up the 3-D model on a large table in the middle of the showroom.

Mr. Chen tried to contact the construction engineer over the next few days, but he was always out. Finally, on July 21st, the last day of the new construction exhibition, the engineer was located. After some discussion, he said that he was not very satisfied with the 3-D model, and had decided that he did not want to buy it after all. He asked Mr. Chen to stop by and pick it up at his convenience.

At this point Mr. Chen was in a very bad negotiating position. The company was not willing to pay for the model they had ordered, and no written agreement had been signed. However, regardless of the existence or or non-existence of a written contract, Mr. Chen could have avoided this situation in several ways: 1) He should have stipulated 20% of the agreed upon price as a downpayment. If the construction engineer thought this was unreasonable, or complained that he had no "proof" that the job would be completed if this sum were given, Mr. Chen could have politely refused the work. 2) An additional 50% of the price should have been stipulated as due when the model was half finished. If the engineer did not pay this additional money upon half-completion of the model, Mr. Chen would be free to devote his time to other projects. 3) Upon delivery of the completed model, if it happened that the engineer was not present, and no preparation for paying the outstanding balance had been made, Mr. Chen should have taken the model back home and waited for further developments.

Using this strategy, or a similar one, a more successful outcome might have been obtained, or an unsuccessful, unpromising project stopped in its early stages. In general, this is the same stance used in the interior decorating business in China, the street-wise interior decorator will separate the price of the entire job into units, and may ask for payments in blocks of 10% or 15%. Thus, when X % of the job is done, X % of the total price (or more) is due. If it is not received, then work is stopped. The westerner may want to adapt this type of bargaining strategy to his own field of endeavor as applicable.

Of course, the above comments are only intended as suggestions. For the intelligent foreigners who find themselves in a position similar to that of Mr. Chen, some might feel it is desirable to get half of the money after the project has been half completed, some might feel otherwise. There is certainly room for debating various initial postures and stipulations, and we would not want to suggest that there is only one way of looking at the entire issue.

In terms of concluding the transaction, perhaps the engineer will be present on the premises when the final model has been brought over, and yet will have forgotten to bring along the necessary funds, as originally agreed upon. At this point the designer could specify that a receipt be written out, clarifying the object received and the amount owed in payment, and accept this as showing good faith. Certainly the designer is well advised to call on the telephone first or send a messenger to reconfirm the exact payment arrangements.

Let us now turn our attention to developing more broadly based conceptual models and charting methods for overviewing and understanding some important aspects of Chinese thinking.

## Yes You May, No You May Not

Living in Chinese society, one is struck by the amount of things which are not clearly stated as being permissible, or non permissible. You do not have to know many people in the TV industry for example, to hear of a constant stream of new government pronouncements as to what can be spoken or acted out on the air, and what cannot. This week short skirts are in, next week they are out. Story lines involving prostitutes were O.K. last year, but now they are forbidden. Incidents of police corruption surface in the Chinese newspapers at various times, but a TV series on such a topic which was in the advanced planning stages is now ruled as unacceptable, by a new official in the relevant government bureau, with the reason given that "that only happens in western countries". In a similar manner, sitting in a Chinese newspaper office for a few days, one is aware of a constant flow of government pronouncements as to how to best handle the news, even to the point of saying such and such a story should not be printed. As would be expected in this kind of environment, investigative reporting for the TV or the newspapers often tends to be rather limited in scope, since no one wants to take responsibility for what might happen if something were printed that upset some influential officials or their relatives, and they decided retroactively that "that is not allowed to be said".

Why not have a clear set of regulations as to what anyone can and cannot say, or print, or act? Discussion with many private Chinese citizens in many different age groups reveals an interesting conceptual peculiarity in this regard. In general the Chinese feeling is that it is impossible to devise a set of all inclusive regulations, that will cover every possibility, and that will serve as a fair standard for everyone to follow.

A story from my high school days is convenient for illustrating the difference in Chinese and western thinking on this issue. I attended a private high school in Massachusetts; coats and ties were standard classroom wearing apparel. One hot June afternoon, I was taking a final exam in algebra with over seventy other students in a large basement classroom. Realizing that the combined pressure of the exam and the heat were difficult for the students to bear, the professor in charge had stated that we could remove our coats and loosen our ties. This was welcome news to all those seated, and it gave everyone a chance to cool off.

One fellow named Douglas was particularly cool, for he had cut the entire back out of his shirt, and since he was not wearing an undershirt, after taking off his sportcoat his entire back was revealed. Several of the students seated nearby began laughing at this sight, and even though Douglas was seated at the back of the room, it did not take the professor long to discover the source of their amusement. Walking over to Douglas's side, he nodded several times, and then said "Well, what have we here?"

"Nothing, sir," Douglas replied.

"Oh, but it appears you have forgotten to wear a shirt," the professor said, "and that is against school regulations."

"Oh, I am sorry sir, there must be some mistake. I am wearing a shirt." As he spoke, Douglas turned to face the teacher full-front, and indeed from that angle his apparel did look perfectly normal.

"No," the professor rejoined, "what you are wearing does not qualify as a shirt."

"I am very sorry, sir. I was not aware of that. Does it say that in the Blue Book?" Reaching into his coat pocket, Douglas handed the professor a copy of the School Rule Book. This booklet had a blue cover, and was commonly referred to as the Blue Book by the student body.

The professor glanced through it briefly. As was well known to all the students present, the wearing of shoes, socks, pants, sportcoat, and tie were fully required for all students. "Shoes" were specifically defined, as were "pants" and "sportcoat". However, the term "shirt" was not defined. In order to bring the matter to a swift conclusion, the professor said "Well, we will talk about this after the examination."

Douglas and the professor did speak about it after the examination, but as I and many other students who followed the development of this "incident" over the next few weeks gradually realized, no action was to be taken. The School Board had briefly touched on the matter at one of their monthly meetings, however it was verified that the student's statement was correct: nowhere in the Blue Book was the term "shirt" specifically defined, hence the student's feeling that he had broken no rule was, on the basis of the objective evidence, valid. There was some discussion as to whether this oversight in the Blue Book should be corrected the the following year's issue, but nothing ever came of it. The School Board felt that this had been an extremely rare situation, and it appeared that Douglas was just having some innocent fun. They were content to let the matter drop. I should add that no one among the student body was particularly surprised at this course of events.

Moving back to China, we find that the Chinese attitude toward this type of "encounter" is a bit different, and indeed many elderly Chinese are puzzled by the outcome that was achieved in the original example, quite frankly it offends their moral sense. "What," they ask, "happened to 'Respect for Elders'? What happened to 'Respect for Teachers'? The rulebook may not have specifically defined 'shirt', however that is essentially irrelevant. Everyone knows what a shirt should be, and the professor's statement that what Douglas is wearing does not qualify as a shirt carries the most substantial weight. When the School Board meets to discuss the incident, they need only concern themselves what is appropriate disciplinary action for Douglas, since he has been disrespectful and discourteous to his teacher."

The westerner may analyze this Chinese reaction from any number of angles. Perhaps it is significant to note that many Chinese hope that their country can institute democratic reforms, and thereby become increasingly democratic. They are however generally unable to answer the question "Where is democracy, or increased democratic reform, supposed to start?" In the west it would appear that there is much democracy in the school system, in China considerably less so. One important prerequisite for democracy would seem to be a clear-cut statement of rules and regulations, so that students, citizens, workers, etc. know at all times what their rights and obligations are. As has been stated above, we may establish a first premise that "The Chinese populace generally accepts the point of view that a clear-cut all-inclusive statement of rules and regulations cannot be made." As this case of the open-backed shirt illustrates, we may establish a second premise that "Many Chinese are unwilling to accept the consequences of such a set of rules if they are made, because they often feel those consequences are not correct." This of course is fuel for the fire in adding support to the validity of our first premise. Hence, what we commonly find is that the Chinese do not try to to formulate a specific set of rules and regulations in most areas, indeed they prefer to make the regulations vague enough to give themselves

## Contradictory Regulations
## Getting Permission from the Owners

A non-partisan (i.e. a member of the opposition party) legislator in Taichung wanted to hold a speech to talk about his political views. According to the law, such political speeches must be held during a specified two to three week period before the actual election, however application for permission to conduct such speeches must be made two weeks or more before this. The actual conditions necessary for approval to have such a speech are not-specified in law, but rather up to the discretion of the regulatory body. As if this were not enough, most often it is the case that after application is made, no further word is heard one way or the other. The candidate must go check the status of his application, and unless he has some pull, he may not be even able to find out anything, or by the time he finds out the "problems" with his application, and attempts to solve them, the registration period is already past.

This non-partisan candidate decided to have his speech in the parking lot of a large public cemetery near National Tung-Hai University. When he was finally able to find out about the status of his application, the authorities said this would be alright "if he could produce documentation from the landlord(s) of the property giving their approval." Since it was a public cemetery, the only possible definition of landlord(s) would be (A) the government, i.e. the current party in power, (B) the people buried in the cemetery. He was unable to obtain such documentation of course, and the period for registration of such speeches elapsed.

wide leeway in interpreting them.

In summary we might say that the Chinese do not like the idea of people getting away with something of which the officials in power disapprove just because of a loophole or other oversight in some set of regulations. This offends the Chinese moral sense.

A further example which comes to mind is in the mass-media field — a TV program which was about a boy who had been born in one city by a mother who abandoned him, raised in another city by a stepmother until the age of twelve, and when a downturn in this family's finances meant that they could no longer support him, he had gone to live with another family during his teens and early twenties. After his military service he had made the decision to "go back home and live with his mother", but he did not know which mother he should go back to. Finally he decided to return to his third mother, since he felt closest to her.

When this script was submitted to the relevant Chinese authorities for script review and approval, it went through several layers of bureaucracy and screening before some official noted that this turn of events was unacceptable to the Chinese moral sense. A child owes his greatest debt to the mother who gives him birth, for without her, he would not exist. He must therefore go back and live with his first mother, in keeping with the Chinese doctrine of respect for parents and filial piety.

If there was a rule among a comprehensive set of Regulations for Writing TV Scripts which was precise to the point of saying that "The Chinese moral values must be upheld", and then even specifically noted the virtues of "Respect for parents and filial piety", one supposes there would still be room for debate in a case such as this, where a boy effectively had three mothers. If this were to be shown on television, it might cause a bad influence in society, and some important officials' moral sense might be offended, in which case the government organization in charge of making such regulations would get a tongue lashing. How much better it is then to only have vague regulations, and to handle everything on a case-by-case basis.

Dovetailing with a preference for vague regulations is the promulgation of contradictory regulations, since they also serve the purpose of enabling the people in power to say: "Make an application and we will consider it", thus handling each application on a case-by-case basis. Either of these formulations is at odds with a clear-cut methodology.

Five reasons for having no clear-cut regulations for the performing arts, for completion of the many types of licensing necessary for the establishment of a business, or for the holding of public rallies, meetings, etc. might be given as follows. A Chinese government organization tends to have the following desires and needs in dealing with an application:

1) It desires to be able to do what it wants. The Chinese people like to be able to have a say over a wide variety of affairs. Thus, with no clear-cut regulations, the organization is free to make this application its business, or say that it is someone else's business, however they see fit at the moment, and depending on how they read the current flow of government thinking.

2) It desires to give people jobs, and to make these jobs have the appearance of being busy. The less clear-cut the regulations, the more people who will be involved in determining the suitability of any application, and the more meetings and discussions which can be held when differences of opinion arise within the organization itself. This not only provides employment, but also activity. ("Power" of course rests at the top of the hierarchy.)

3) It desires to instill a sense of its loftiness and a respect for its authority among the populace. If people must beg the relevant department officials in order to have their applications approved, and the officials are free to heed these pleas or reject them as they see fit, then the people will hold the officials in some degree of reverence.

4) It desires to maintain the ability to use its control however it sees fit, especially in the form of granting special favors, and making exceptions to the general rulings for friends, relatives, etc.

5) It desires to maintain a sympathetic posture, so that unusual considerations may be contemplated and weighed regarding the handling of any application, and the interests of special individuals, special causes, or other matters may be carefully and subjectively deliberated at any time.

## THE PRIVATE SWIMMING POOL CLUB MODEL of Chinese Authoritarianism

In something so complex as a society, it is hard to draw any simple parallels, but I am often intrigued by the possibilities of comparing some important aspects of the Chinese concept of authority and regulation to the operation of a Private Swimming Pool Club. In this Club, you are welcome to come in and swim, if you obey the rules. Americk, being a typical American guy, agrees to do this and comes with his Chinese friends for a swim. Americk is told before going that the Pool authorities want to keep the Pool clean, so they require all swimmers to wear a swimming cap. He assumes this refers only to girls, and so when he goes he does not have a cap. This causes a minor problem with the lifeguard, but Americk agrees that the mistake was his own, and so he goes and buys a swim cap. Coming back to the pool, Americk jumps into the water in the doubled-up fashion, rear end first, and sends the water splashing in every direction, as well as soaking a number of his friends and other swimmers who are both in and out of the pool. Americk finds this to be good clean fun, and something that always startles the girls, so he jumps in a few more times. At this point the lifeguard comes over and says to the Chinese people, "Please tell your friend that that kind of jumping is not allowed."

Americk considers: "We all came to the pool to have fun, and we are having fun. Where does it say that I cannot jump in the water?"

To this the lifeguard replies: "Do not jump in the water in that way."

Americk shruggs his shoulders and walks off to the deep end to practice some diving. He is the only one at that end of the pool at this time, and is enjoying himself bouncing up and down on the diving board. The lifeguard says: "It is not allowed to jump up and down on the diving board in that way. You are supposed to jump up and then dive in the water."

Americk replies: "Where does it say that I cannot jump up and down on the diving board until I get the proper feel of it?"

The lifeguard says: "Do not jump on the diving board in that way."

Americk shruggs his shoulders, dives in the water, and swims around for awhile.

After resting briefly on the bleachers, Americk notices an unused inner-tube by the side of the pool, so he throws it in and dives in after it, and starts to play around. The lifeguard blows his whistle and says: "That inner tube is for exclusive use of the lifeguards. You are not allowed to play with it."

Americk asks: "Where does it say that it is for the exclusive use of the lifeguards?"

The lifeguard replies: "That is the rule."

Noticing an inflated beachball seemingly abandoned nearby, Americk asks if he can play with the beachball in the water with his friends? Also, whether he can teach his friends diving from the side of the pool in the shallow end, whether swimming is allowed across the pool or only up-and-down, whether it is permitted to wear swimfins, mask, and snorkel, or if only swimming trunks are allowed in the pool, whether boys and girls may hold hands in the water, etc. The lifeguard gets a pained expression on his face and walks away.

A hour or so later Americk leaves with his friends, and on the way out he makes a thorough inspection of the walls for any notices concerning Pool Regulations. He finds these at the entrance to the locker room area. In addition to noting times when the pool opens and closes, and the fact that no beverages or edibles may be taken into the pool, along with the stipulation that swimcaps must be worn, no other specific rules are stated.

However it is understood that Americk is wrong because he created disharmony in the organization. He "made waves", both in a figurative and literal sense.

**Overview:** This example shows us a number of interesting points about Chinese use of authority, and which many observers have seen borne out by examination of much Chinese family and social organization. First, there is the presence of a large number of unwritten rules and regulations, some of which may be made up seemingly on the spur of the moment. The people affected are of course expected to follow these regulations without question.

Second, while discussion of a decision or regulation is allowed, nevertheless dispute or debate is not, because that is seen as being disrespectful to one's elders.

Third, there is no requirement that a complete set of specific rules be listed now or in the future. The rules will continue to be what those persons in authority say they are.

Fourth, people in authority are not responsible for their decisions to those affected by those decisions. For example, if the lifeguard says Americk may bring his swimfins next time, and Americk does so but is told by another lifeguard that swimfins are not allowed, that is Americk's problem. There is no responsibility implied by the authority figure making the first statement, hence he owes the questioner, or applicant, nothing (not even an explanation) if his pronouncement is later overruled by a person of higher authority.

Fifth, there is no requirement that the people in charge be consistent in their rulings, nor is there any requirement that they follow what appears to be the precedent set in an earlier case. They may state the rules as they see fit. If, for example, bikinis are suddenly labeled as being representative of foreign decadence, they are free to impose a ban on bikinis immediately, without making any changes in posted rules, or going through any process of obtaining the assent of pool users, etc.

Resolution of Differing Opinions

In this situation, if Americk has a dispute to resolve with the lifeguard on any issue, a number of avenues are open to him, none of which relies very heavily on what one might see as "the facts of the matter", "who is right and who is wrong", or an attempt to objectively determine "what is fair" from the regulatory or legal standpoint. Americk's best solution is an indirect one: to use his social contacts to persuade the lifeguard in question to adopt a different view. (Since the youth in society rarely have any social contacts who have any real power, this kind of formulation of course assures that "power" is maintained in the hands of the elders.)

Nevertheless, if Americk were in a situation where a very good friend of his was the President of the Private Swimming Pool Club, it might be easy to invite this gentleman out to dinner, and after the required small-talk, to try to convince him that he, Americk, should be allowed to do activities X,Y,Z, in the Pool, which are of course not specifically excluded by the rules. If this President agrees, he may then make a simple call to the lifeguard to clarify his private agreement with Americk, and in the future Americk would receive special treatment.

Someday in the future at the swimming pool, if someone else sees Americk doing something out of the ordinary, and asks the lifeguard why he can do that, the person will be informed that Americk is a special case, and/or to mind his own business. When asked how he can apply to be a special case too, the person will of course be told that it is not possible, (since anyone who asks so stupid a question probably has no connections).

If Americk knew someone who knew the father of the lifeguard, that also might be a possible route to pressure the lifeguard into seeing his point of view on any and all situations. If Americk's relative owned the Swimming Pool, he could perhaps have the lifeguard fired or transferred at his whim, and future lifeguards might get the hint to leave Americk alone. If Americk wants to do something which conflicts with government policy on swimming pool use (whether long-standing or recently promulgated policy), it would probably be extremely difficult for him to "negotiate", unless his contacts were of the highest caliber.

In some ways then, we may gain a glimpse of the use of authority in Chinese society merely by constructing the Private Swimming Pool case study as above. If the foreigner can understand these kinds of goings on in a Private Swimming Pool, he will perhaps better be able to understand what posture he should take when he encounters a related situation in society. If he uses the western approach of standing up for his rights, he will find that the Chinese citizenry will rarely sympathize with him. We note again for the Nth time that it is apparently inconceivable to the Chinese that one set of all inclusive rules be made up, voted upon, amended as necessary, ratified and posted for all to use, and which would serve as a strict basis for what can and cannot be done, therefore eliminating any need for argument between swimmers and the lifeguards. The Chinese prefer to avoid argument by telling those not in a position of authority to "do what you are told". This also explains a view that many Chinese have of their place in society, which tends to fall in one of three categories: 1) I am giving orders, 2) I am taking orders, 3) I have no opinion.

## Press Interviews

Keeping in mind this example of the Chinese application of authority, let us look at another situation which occurred a number of years ago involving foreigners and the local Chinese press. One Chinese daily newspaper with a circulation of approximately 250,000 per day decided, during one of its editorial meetings, that they would interview a large number of foreigners on their impressions of China, and write this up as a series to be published in the newspaper. Several reporters were picked to begin doing these interviews along with their regular reporting assignments. The reporters began inquiring with various schools, organizations, clubs, etc. where foreigners were known to congregate, as well as with foreign invested corporations.

The reporters, many of whose foreign language skills were minimal, began their series of interviews. Using the typical Chinese approach, when they could not fully handle an interview in English for example, they would either take along a friend or former classmate who had the requisite level of language skills to act as a free translator, or else prepare a written set of questions in English before they went, go over these with their fellow reporters who had more capability in English to be sure they were reasonably clear, and merely use a tape recorder to tape the foreigner's replies. In this case they could again go find someone with the necessary language skills to help them go over the tape (for free), and write up their interview from there.

Some of the foreigners were students of the Chinese language however, and could conduct their interviews directly in Chinese. As a matter of fact a number of these China scholars in addition to possessing language skills, were also versed in Chinese history, government, society, and other issues, and in giving their "impressions of China" would often make comparison with other Asian countries, pointing out the good and bad of each. I talked to several of the interviewed individuals a month or so later, and they informed me that they had tried to give a "balanced account", by pointing out the strengths and weaknesses of China and the Chinese way of thinking and doing things, as opposed to what other people in other countries were doing. Since they were speaking in Chinese, it seemed unlikely that their remarks could have been thoroughly misinterpreted.

Nevertheless, when the interviews were printed, there were some interesting omissions, namely: all the major complaints they had made about China and the Chinese way of doing things had been left out, but their complaints about other countries' practices had for the most part remained. Their praise for China and the Chinese way of doing things were clearly stated, although all the praise which they had given other countries' practices, customs, or attitudes had disappeared, or been severely downplayed.

Knowledgeable foreigners had of course not been caught in this trap, since they knew from experience to keep the tone and content of their interviews light and down to earth. They had limited their remarks to the difficulty they had had using chopsticks when they first arrived, famous blunders they had made with the Chinese language, their enjoyment of Chinese food, the intricacy and beauty of Chinese arts and crafts, the warm hospitality of the Chinese people, etc. This is what we might call the friendly approach to an interview situation, and it is a suitable approach for the foreigner who cares for nothing more than to see his name in the paper and get a nice comment or two from his Chinese co-workers.

For the foreigner who desires to make more of a truthful comparison, and expects his remarks to be printed, there are some other considerations which should be stipulated. In all fairness it must be stated that there are a few Chinese authors who adopt more of a critical, or objective, stance to the goings-on in their society, and are not interested in presenting a wholly "one-sided" viewpoint. Therefore, if given the opportunity to have an interview with a Chinese periodical, it would be reasonable to ask the Chinese interviewer if he is interested in both good and bad impressions, or just the good. The interviewer will undoubtedly say that he is interested in both types, at which point the foreigner may ask for samples of his work (if the foreigner is prepared to invest the time in going over the Chinese with another friend, and judging this interviewer's writing style), or consent to the interview directly with the stipulation that it must be done objectively. Since oral promises mean nothing, and since the reporter in a Chinese news organization generally has no power, perhaps some written form from the Editor specifying that the writing up of the interview will be done in an objective manner, should be obtained. Obviously this type of stance will not endear you to the Chinese newspaper or other media people. Nevertheless with an agreement of this kind, and a recorded copy of the interview for your own reference, you would be free to write a letter of complaint to a major foreign news organization if the editor did not keep his part of the bargain.

The situation with interviews is very tricky indeed, and it is generally true that the foreigner needs much experience in dealing with the Chinese media before he can really become comfortable working with them. His ability to read the Chinese newspaper or magazine that is writing about him may also often affect his impression of their impending treatment of his comments. We feel that it is not possible to make a broad statement like "No criticism is allowed", because the amount of criticism in the Chinese press tends to be directly related to a number of factors.

## THE SKYSCRAPER & WINDOW WASHERS MODEL of Newspaper Reportage

We can perhaps relate the workings of the reporters in a news organization to the window washers on a hanging platform outside a large skyscraper. This may be summarized in the following way:

Every office in the skyscraper represents a government or quasi-government agency, which is involved with regulating or overseeing one or more issues in the society. Every office has a window. Hence, as we look in the windows, we may grasp the totality of what control is being exercised over the society. The society, which we may call "the masses", are at the bottom of the skyscraper and surround it. On the deck of the hanging platform itself is a set of controls by which it can be manuevered (these are the manual controls), however the main control booth is on the roof of the building, and staffed by certain individuals. The job for the newspaper reporters is to wash off the windows and report on what they see, so that the masses, which are their readers, may be better informed about any and all decisions or events which may affect their lives.

In any society, there may be various offices whose windows are locked, whose windows cannot be cleaned with any amount of wiping and rubbing, or whose curtains are closely drawn. Some windows may be open, and the window washers may be free to go in and take a look around. Some windows may be open today, but curtained and locked tomorrow.

Of course it is true that the window washers also go down into the society and report on goings-on there. Nevertheless they constantly ruminate on the conversations they have had with, and the bulletins they have received from the people in the offices of the building, as well as what knowledge they have picked up (from various sources) of the conversations that other window washers have had with, and the directions other window washers have received from these office people.

In China however, the following peculiarities are apparent:

The movement of the platform up, down, right, and left is controlled by a team of salaried building managers (in the main control booth on the roof), who are in constant touch with all the people of authority in all the offices in the building. They are free to leave the movement of the platform on "manual", letting the reporters control its movement as they see fit, until at whatever time they (the salaried building managers) are instructed to do otherwise.

If any of the people in the offices object to the window washers cleaning their windows and looking in, they will generally engage the window washers in pleasant conversation, and make some statements about the correct point of view that should be taken in observing the going-on in their offices. The window washers will heed this advice of course, for not to do so would risk word being passed on to the building managers in the main control booth, who then might jerk the platform to the extent that the window washers would fall off.

Whenever the window washers (reporters) move to a location on the skyscraper where they are not welcome, their controls are quickly overridden by the managers in the main control booth, who have presumably just been notified by the authorities in charge to take such action. The window washers will of course never be given a specific list of which windows should never be washed or looked into, but they will come to have a feel for such things with experience in the job, and by talking to other window washers.

No special tricks or apparatus may be used to peer behind curtains or to catch a glimpse into seemingly closed offices, since the window washers' final consideration is their own job safety and security, and to overstep the guidelines indirectly laid out for them would be to risk the wrath of the authorities in the various offices, who might instruct the managers in the main control booth to cancel their job status, and perhaps blacklist them from other jobs as well.

The reportage which the masses see everyday is, in many ways, indirectly controlled by the officials throughout the building.

In the United States, the following peculiarities are apparent:

The movement of the platform up, down, right, and left is controlled by the Head Engineers of the Window Washing Co., (in the main control booth on the roof), which is to say, by the Editors of the newspapers. After assigning the window washers their duties, they tend to give them quite a bit of freedom in manipulating their controls to reach the windows which they deem appropriate.

If any of the people in the offices object to the window washers cleaning their windows and looking in, they are free to voice their complaints to the window washers or to the Head Engineers, who are also free to point to the situation of their employment, which is essentially an independent contract. One of the Head Engineers may then pass word on to them to the effect "You do your job and I will do mine."

Whenever the reporters move to a location on the skyscraper where they are not welcome, they usually get the hint very quickly, and then make arrangements to come back some other time for a better look.

The reporters are free to use whatever means are at their disposal in order to find out the real story, including technologically advanced listening and viewing apparatus, since their final responsibility is to the Head Engineers, who are in turn responsible to the public.

The reportage which the masses see everyday is quite directly controlled by the window washers and the Head Engineers.

Paper and No Paper

In practical terms, a government monopoly on the import of newsprint (i.e., rolls of newspaper) is also effective in exercising indirect control of local news content.

Government official: I don't know if you have heard that there is some shortage in the availability of newsprint in the world markets recently.

Publisher A: I was not aware of that.

Government official: Yes, I am afraid the supply of rolled newsprint to your organization will be cut substantially.

Publisher A: That is surprising. I have recently been talking to publishers of some other local newspapers, and they didn't mention anything about this.

Government official: Oh, they are not affected.

Publisher A: I see. Well, is there some way I can become unaffected?

Government official: I suppose something could be worked out. Perhaps we could meet for dinner . . .

## Taking Responsibility

Several management studies of Chinese firms over the years have confirmed that there is a low tolerance for failure in the management of most Chinese enterprises. Contrastingly, many best selling books on international management have noted that in excellent firms, the tolerance for failure is high.

The traditional Chinese reticence to delegate authority is to some large degree based on this low tolerance for failure. Several Chinese language phrases reflect this thinking, most notably: "The more you do, the more chance you have of making an error"[a], "The less you do the less chance you have of making an error"[b], "Doing one thing more is not as good as doing one thing less"[c], etc. The Chinese feeling is that by doing what you are told, the other (superior) party then effectively takes responsibility for your actions. If you take the initiative to do anything, you of course will be quickly charged with making an error if something goes wrong. If you try something new, you may be accused of disloyalty, since that is not the normal procedure, which has already been approved by those in power. Therefore it is better not to take the initiative. This is further impressed on the consciousness of the lower level officials by seeing that when someone oversteps the bounds of his normal duties, and achieves a good result, the officials higher in hierarchy always take credit for this.[d] If he fails, he bears the full blame.[e]

The ramifications of this kind of attitude are often seen in the Chinese bureaucracy. Any other than the most routine request (and sometimes even those), are passed on to another level or another department of the bureaucracy for their recommendation and decision. As these requests make their rounds of the various departments, they eventually meet with some sort of bottleneck, and get to the stage where they sit in limbo. Reasons for this are many. One significant reason is that at any one of these points, the person in charge is often without a clear set of statements regarding the scope of his job duties. The organization tends to feel that if the subordinates understand the leader's thoughts, they will be able to deal with all situations in the proper manner, without elaborately detailed instructions. This is directly related to the Confucian idea that the leader leads through displaying a high moral character.

Hence, no one has the authority to deal with most applications which are at all out of the ordinary, and these unusual requests are generally handled through the cultivation of Close Personal Relations (CPR). If the requester is on good relations with a fairly notable figure in the hierarchary, Mr. M, or perhaps knows the friend or relative of Mr. M, then Mr. M may be indirectly persuaded to take up the cause as a personal one, and to move its "approval" through the different departments, offering assurances that no problems will develop, etc. If not, it could easily die a slow death through inaction.

---

a. 多做多錯    b. 少做少錯    c. 多一事不如少一事
d. 功由上賞    e. 罪由下當

## Differing Harmony Models

The following diagrams have been formulated to show different views of Harmony in viewing the relations A) between Regulatory Agencies and those who are regulated, B) Superiors and Subordinates, etc.

| | **Harmony 1**<br>Procedurally Weighted<br>*"Follow the Rules and You Will be Alright"*<br>One Objective Standard, Same For All<br>Harmony 1 = Following Procedures and Regulations | | **Harmony 2**<br>Results Weighted<br>*"Don't make Waves and You Will be Alright"*<br>Subjective Standard, Not the Same For All<br>Harmony 2 = Keeping Your Superiors Happy | |
|---|---|---|---|---|
| Results<br>Rows | + | − | + | − |
| 1) →   1 2 3 4 5 | Harmony | Harmony | 1 2 3 4 5   Harmony | Disharmony |
| 2) →   1 2 3 4 − | Disharmony | Disharmony | 1 2 3 4 −   Harmony | Disharmony |
| 3) →   1 2 3 − − | Disharmony | Disharmony | 1 2 3 − −   Harmony | Disharmony |
| 4) →   1 2 − − − | Disharmony | Disharmony | 1 2 − − −   Harmony | Disharmony |
| 5) →   1 − − − − | Disharmony | Disharmony | 1 − − − −   Harmony | Disharmony |
| 6) →   − − − − − | | | − − − − − | |

Explanation of the Differing Harmony Models represented in these diagrams:

With harmony as a goal for social dealings between superiors and subordinates, especially in regard to the relations between regulators (those regulating) and regulatees (those being regulated), this diagram essentially shows the different results achieved through different views of what "harmony" is. Harmony 1 is Procedurally weighted. Harmony 2 is Results weighted.

On the far left side of the diagram are "Relevant Requirements Complied With, a Total of Five". For the purpose of discussion and illustration, we have assumed the necessity of complying with five requirements, steps, or regulations, or the need for obtaining five approvals in order to undertake (not necessarily "complete") any project, which is indicative of dealings between superiors and subordinates, and/or within some sort of regulatory framework. Such a project could be 1) a consumer's application for a loan with a bank, 2) a new restaurant owner's application for a business license, health certificates, and other relevant approvals in order to start operations, 3) a factory manager's application for a business license, safety inspection, and other relevant approvals in order to begin production, etc.

For example, in order to grant a loan request, the bank will first have the customer fill out a loan application, provide credit references, provide collateral, prove income sufficient to repay the loan, etc. The bank must then check to see that all the information provided is true, make a determination that the loan is a good risk, etc. All of these items amount to steps or requirements which must be completed before the loan may be granted.

Our analysis will only consider action which is actually taken, i.e. the event where the loan was granted, the restaurant owner did indeed commence business, the factory did begin production, etc. We will not consider the event where the applicant did not proceed with his undertaking.

In the first row, all five requirements have been complied with.
In the second row, only four requirements have been complied with.
In the third row, only three requirements have been complied with.
In the fourth row, only two requirements have been complied with.
In the fifth row, only one requirement has been complied with.
In the sixth row, no requirements have been complied with.

Under the Harmony 1 section, we have two columns + and -. Under the Harmony 2 column we also have two columns + and -. These columns indicate "results". For example, if a bank officer grants a loan request, the loan may be repaid (+) or defaulted upon (-). If a new restaurant is opened, no complaints may be received from the populace (+), or some people may get food poisoning (-). If a new factory is opened, no problem may develop in the community (+), or the factory may have an industrial accident, chemical explosion, its products may be found dangerous to health, etc. (-).

## The Loan Approval Example
### Harmony 1.
*Procedurally Weighted, "Follow the Rules and You Will be Alright", One Objective Standard, Same For All*
Harmony 1 is one view of what "harmony" consists of.

If all the relevant requirements are followed, and the loan is repaid, we are in row 1 of the + column. Harmony has been achieved.

If the loan is defaulted upon, we are in row 1 of the - column. Since all relevant regulations were complied with, certainly this was unexpected, and the organization (the bank) recognizes this. The person who completed the case (the loan officer) is not scolded or demoted for this unexpected event. The organization takes responsibility, and harmony is maintained.

If one of the relevant regulation or requirements was not followed, but the loan is repaid, we are in row 2 of the + column. Since regulations were not followed, disharmony is the result. Whether the loan is repaid or not is seemingly a secondary consideration in this Procedurally weighted environment, indeed the organization is willing to deal with either eventuality.

### Harmony 2.
*Results Weighted, "Don't make Waves and You Will be Alright", Subjective Standard, Not the Same For All*
Harmony 2 is another view of what "harmony" consists of.

If all relevant regulations are followed, and the loan is repaid, we are in row 1 of the + column. Harmony has been achieved.

If the loan is not repaid, we are in row 1 of the - column. The lack of repayment will anger the high officials in the hierarchy, and the loan officer will be accused of dereliction of duty. Charges will be brought up showing that he was incompetent and irresponsible in his supervision of this case. Disharmony has been the result.

If one of the relevant regulations or steps is not followed, and the loan is repaid, we are in row 2 of the + column. Any lack in the requirements or procedures is quickly forgiven if the loan is repaid in this Results weighted environment, so harmony is the result. If the loan is not repaid, we are in row 2 of the - column. The organization will use this failure to complete one requirement as the crowning point in their accusation that the loan officer was acting in an incompetent and irresponsible manner in handling this case, and should be demoted or fined. Disharmony has been created.

## The Restaurant Example
### Harmony 1.
*Procedurally Weighted, "Follow the Rules and You Will be Alright", One Objective Standard, Same For All*
The restaurant begins business. If all the relevant requirements have been followed, and no complaints of any serious nature are forthcoming from any people with power and influence in the society, we are in row 1 of the + column. Harmony has been achieved. If the restaurant has a fire and burns down, along with damaging several other

buildings in the community, we are in row 1 of the - column. Since all relevant regulations were complied with, certainly this was unexpected, and the organization (the relevant government bureaus) recognize this. The people who finalized approval of this case (the relevant government officials) are not scolded or demoted for this unexpected event. The organization takes responsibility, and discussion is undertaken as to how to improve regulations so as to avoid similar situations in the future. Harmony in the regulatory organization is maintained.

If one of the relevant regulation or requirements was not followed, but no complaints are received from citizens' groups, important officials and their relatives, etc., we are in row 2 of the + column. Since regulations were not followed, disharmony is the result. Whether accidents occur, complaints are lodged, other protests made, etc., (thus putting us in the - column), are seemingly secondary considerations in this Procedurally weighted environment, indeed the regulatory agency is willing to deal with either eventuality. In reviewing the restaurant's paperwork, the lack of the completion of all necessary procedures calls for quick remedial action by those in charge.

**Harmony 2.**
*Results Weighted, "Don't make Waves and You Will be Alright", Subjective Standard, Not the Same For All*
The restaurant begins business. If all relevant regulations are followed, and everything goes smoothly, we are in row 1 of the + column. Harmony has been achieved. If the restaurant serves spoiled food to several customers and they go to the hospital, the newspapers will cover this story, moving us into row 1 of the - column. This will anger the high officials in the regulatory hierarchy, and the bureaucrats who handled the restaurant's case will be accused of dereliction of duty. Charges will be brought up showing that they were incompetent and irresponsible in their supervision of this case. Disharmony has been the result.

If one of the relevant regulations or steps is not followed, and the restaurant operates smoothly, we are in row 2 of the + column. Any lack in the requirements or procedures is quickly overlooked if no problems develop in this Results weighted environment, so harmony is the result. If the restaurant building collapses and crushes several people, this will take us into row 2 of the - column. The regulatory agency will use this failure to complete one requirement as the crowning point in their accusation that the bureaucrats who gave the final go ahead in this case were acting in an incompetent and irresponsible manner, and should be demoted or fired. Disharmony has been created.

Further Evaluations
By examining the complete diagram, the reader will be able to see how evaluations of Harmony or Disharmony are reached in a Procedurally weighted or Results weighted orientation, where no problems develop (the + column), or where some problems do indeed develop (the - column), and in the event two of the requirements were not com-

plied with, three of the requirements were not complied with, four of the requirements were not complied with, etc. The situation where none of the five requirements was complied with, Row 6, seems highly unlikely, hence we leave it as undefined.

**Procedurally Weighted Harmony**
*OBSERVATIONS*

1. The subordinate completes his responsibility through the performance of specific duties or requirements.

2. If a difficulty develops, the Group protects the individual if he has done his duties. The Group exists for the protection of the individual. The Group is not assumed to be a "perfect" entity.

3. Requirements are specifically defined, and harmony is evaluated in terms of following procedures, with each individual doing his job. Unwritten regulations are very rare.

4. There is a comparatively high tolerance for failure, if regulations are followed.

5. Rules and regulations are specified in detail first, and situations which develop are handled in accordance with these rules.

6. Rights which are not specifically excluded are granted by definition.

**Results Weighted Harmony**
*OBSERVATIONS*

1. The subordinate completes his responsibility through obtaining successful results.

2. If a difficulty develops, the individual will be "sacrificed" to protect the integrity and assumed perfection of the Group. The individual is required to protect the Group; Group interests are superior.

3. Requirements tend to be loosely defined, and harmony is evaluated in terms of getting successful results; keeping the Group out of trouble. Unwritten regulations abound.

4. There is a comparatively low tolerance for failure, even if regulations are followed completely.

5. Rules and regulations tend to be made up as situations develop, as opposed to being established first.

6. Rights which are not specifically granted are excluded by definition.

7. The "man controls nature" orientation is predominant. There is an attempt to control the flow of events through advance planning and established procedures.

7. The "nature controls man" orientation is predominant. "Go with the flow" is a basic concept, and various stopgap or temporary solutions are advanced as problems arise. There is little advance planning.

8. Being procedurally oriented, there is a stress on long term thinking, and on the formulation of methodology.

8. Being results oriented, there is a stress on short term thinking, and not on methodology.

9. Harmony is viewed objectively through established standards. There is a stress on Rule by Law.

9. Harmony is viewed subjectively, through maintenance of good relations with superiors. There is a stress on Rule by Man.

10. There is a uniform enforcement of regulations, and no laxity in enforcement due to other "over-riding concerns".

10. There is selective enforcement of regulations, and laxity in enforcement due to other "over-riding concerns": such as national security, maintenance of party-in-power's position, desire to avoid citizens' confronting government with demands for welfare payments, etc. Hence there is much laissez faire in allowing citizens to earn a living if no big problems develop.

**Conclusions:** Of course it is hard to create a theoretical model that will apply in 100% of all real world situations. However, many observers have stated that Chinese management, regulatory control, etc. tends to follow the Results weighted Harmony Model, while western management tends to follow more of a Procedurally weighted Harmony Model.

That the Chinese organizations and bureaucracies do tend to follow the Results weighted Harmony Model is supported by the following considerations:

*Assumption of Responsibility*

The power in a Chinese organization tends to be concentrated at the top, and lower level bureaucrats or functionaries often hesitate to take action or make a decision in handling many kinds of situations, as if wanting to go to great length to avoid "taking responsibility". With the lack of truly objective standards in dealing with a wide variety of issues, the Results weighted Harmony Model is "damned if you do, and damned if you don't", i.e. the lower level bureaucrat is always held responsible by those higher in the hierarchy if something goes wrong, regardless of whether or not originally specified regulations were complied with.[1] Numerous "unwritten rules" are always being brought up to "justify" this type of procedure.

*Primary Sympathetic Orientation*

Additionally we see that the Chinese prefer to deal with all types of official and even private social dealings by avoiding a strict "legal" interpretation of relevant rules and regulations, and using more of a sympathetic orientation. Hence, the applicants to the regulatory agencies tend to request sympathy in asking that those agencies be exceedingly flexible in application procedures, and equally lenient in enforcement of all relevant rules and regulations. In keeping with the traditional Chinese view that "Laws are without Sympathy" and that Sympathy is more important than law, these requests also frequently tend to be granted, especially to those with close personal connections (CPR) in the relevant government departments. This is again the outcome that would be expected in the Results Weighted Model.

*Illegal Businesses*

Other supporting evidence is found by noting the large number of underground factories, unregistered and unlicensed restaurants, dance halls, small hotels, shops and stands in any Chinese city. Observation and investigation reveals that unlicensed private bus lines serve many outlying communities, houses of ill repute operate openly in some back alleys, small restaurants and shops freely violate health regulations, etc. To the extent that no problems are caused for the superiors in the relevant regulatory agencies, i.e. no pressure from other people higher in the hierarchy, no serious public protests, etc., harmony is considered to be maintained. If problems of any fashion develop, including public or legislative outcry, or various types of accidents, then disharmony is immediately apparent, and must be dealt with by use of various temporary or stopgap measures, or other acts which appear to knowledgeable outsiders to be mere tokenism. When the "problems" have blown over, harmony is again restored (thus conforming to the cyclical view of natural action), and it is back to regulation in the original "Go with the Flow" fashion.

---

1. One clever way of avoiding this "responsibility" is of note. This occurs when many citizens are seriously injured or killed, and the head of the government regulatory agency involved moves to relieve himself of blame by submitting his resignation. Often as not, after a period of time has elapsed he is persuaded to stay at his post by other government ministers, or transferred to another equally impressive position, and his department is back to "laissez faire regulation" as usual. The entire incident is swept under the rug in this fashion.

## Problem Solving

When facing difficulties, one needs to define the problem and think how to create alternatives to choose from. Having compared the pros and cons of the alternatives, one makes the decision and implements it efficiently, and the problem is either solved or more thoroughly befuddled.

In any field of knowledge, there is the necessity of establishing a classification system in order to accomplish the effect of describing present phenomena. We have chosen to define various Perceptions to provide an organized structure whereby many facets of Chinese and western thinking can be examined and compared.

Some scholars have defined and discussed different types of problems encountered in organizations. We may look at these in regard to an individual from a particular background culture who deals with problems in the entry culture.

An "unstructured problem" refers to one which has not been encountered in quite the same form before and for which no predetermined and explicit set of ordered responses exists in the foreigner.

A "developmental problem" refers to one which involves the search for, and perhaps construction or synthesis of, instruments which yield a course of action that is better than any available at the time.

An "evaluative problem" refers to one in which the alternative courses of action are completely specified in advance and the solution consists of selecting the "best" of these.

Through our acculturological study we hope to turn unstructured problems into developmental problems, and then to turn these into evaluative problems.

## Implementation vs. Excuses

It is often difficult to state precisely the relationship between the existence of a set of criteria and their need for implementation. It is also sometimes difficult to see where non-implementation represents non-sincerity in carrying out the true goals of the criteria. This is because after implementation begins, the other side presents us with excuses, which somehow seem to bear some degree of weight as being valid reasons why their hands are tied in moving ahead with more vigor.

After we arrange a series of meetings to deal with the problem the other side has presented, implementation is begun again, only to hit another snag a short time later. This results in more meetings, and further efforts to clarify that **what is needed is for them to more properly coordinate their own administrative departments.** Implementation may be begun again, and then continued in this *go-, stop-, go-, stop-* manner indefinitely. Of course this is an issue which not only bothers foreigners, but often local people as well, and we do find a descriptive phrase in Chinese which addresses it, to wit: "When the head hurts you treat the head, when the foot hurts you treat the foot."[a] This is light-hearted and yet to the point, and may be used in speaking of procedures taken by an organization. It carries distinct overtones of being "insincere" and "unsystematic", while tending to indicate a lack of thoroughness in planning.

More significantly, the following logical framework may be of some reference value in dealing with the initial conceptualization of activity, and before such problems are encountered. At each level, two options are given. One is justifiable in light of the announced initial starting point, the other is not. It may then be easy to lead the opposite party to a more rational evaluation of the facts, and their own actions, if this step-by-step analysis is employed. At each level one choice must be made.

Chart 12-1

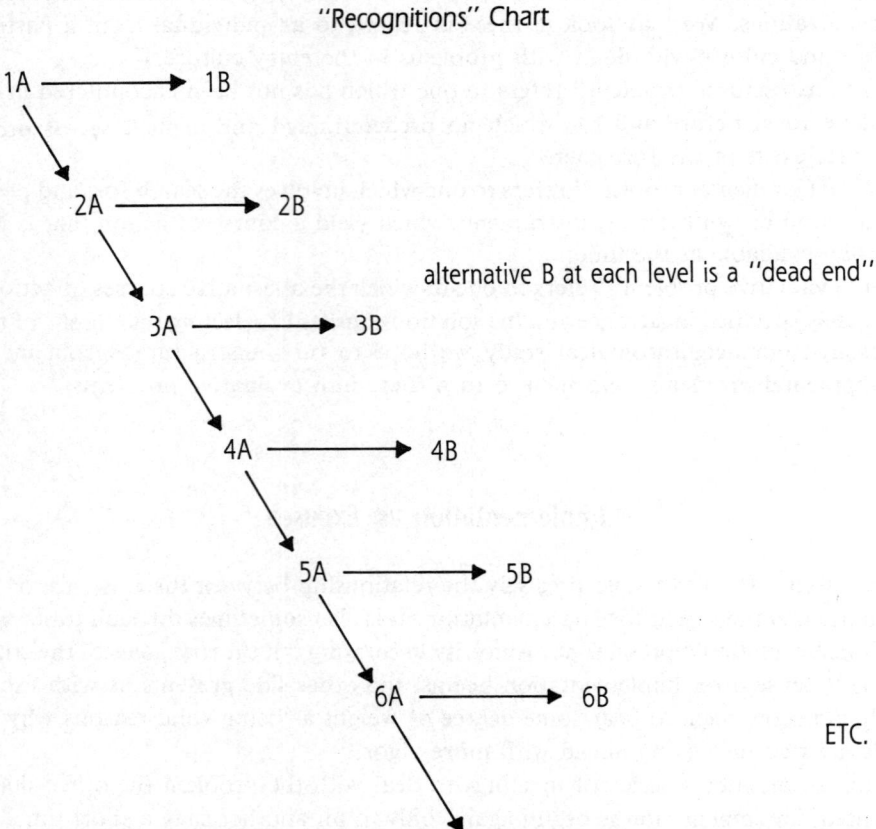

"Recognitions" Chart

```
1A ─────▶ 1B
  ↓
  2A ─────▶ 2B
    ↓                    alternative B at each level is a "dead end"
    3A ─────▶ 3B
      ↓
      4A ─────▶ 4B
        ↓
        5A ─────▶ 5B
          ↓
          6A ─────▶ 6B
            ↓                                                    ETC.
```

Let us consider the situation of a western government diplomatic delegation from Country Alpha that desires to convince another country's officials in Country Zina that they should take a certain course of action. After lengthy talks, the officials of Country Zina agree to the proposal.

---

a. 頭痛醫頭，脚痛醫脚

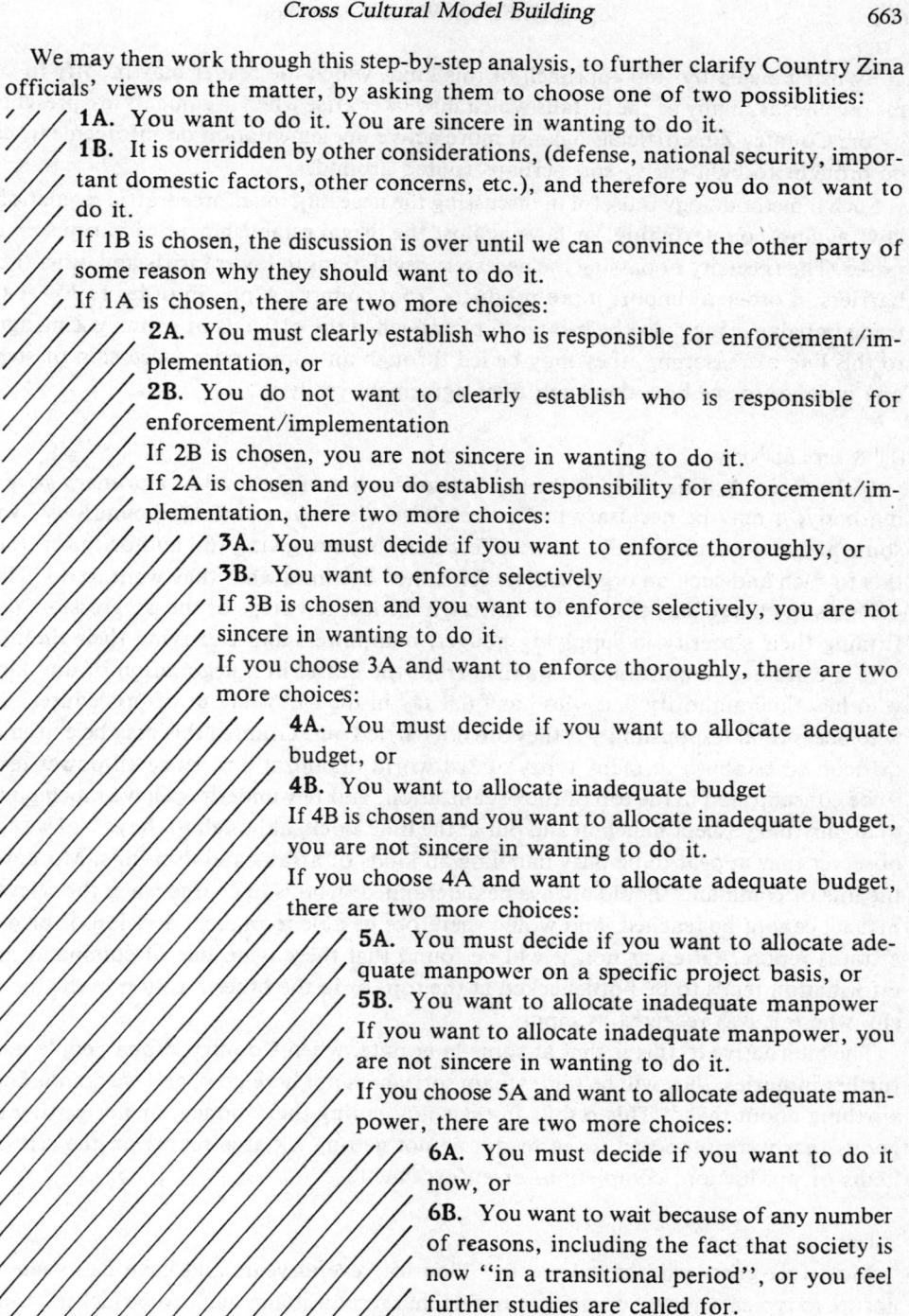

We may then work through this step-by-step analysis, to further clarify Country Zina officials' views on the matter, by asking them to choose one of two possiblities:

**1A.** You want to do it. You are sincere in wanting to do it.

**1B.** It is overridden by other considerations, (defense, national security, important domestic factors, other concerns, etc.), and therefore you do not want to do it.

If 1B is chosen, the discussion is over until we can convince the other party of some reason why they should want to do it.

If 1A is chosen, there are two more choices:

**2A.** You must clearly establish who is responsible for enforcement/implementation, or

**2B.** You do not want to clearly establish who is responsible for enforcement/implementation

If 2B is chosen, you are not sincere in wanting to do it.

If 2A is chosen and you do establish responsibility for enforcement/implementation, there two more choices:

**3A.** You must decide if you want to enforce thoroughly, or

**3B.** You want to enforce selectively

If 3B is chosen and you want to enforce selectively, you are not sincere in wanting to do it.

If you choose 3A and want to enforce thoroughly, there are two more choices:

**4A.** You must decide if you want to allocate adequate budget, or

**4B.** You want to allocate inadequate budget

If 4B is chosen and you want to allocate inadequate budget, you are not sincere in wanting to do it.

If you choose 4A and want to allocate adequate budget, there are two more choices:

**5A.** You must decide if you want to allocate adequate manpower on a specific project basis, or

**5B.** You want to allocate inadequate manpower

If you want to allocate inadequate manpower, you are not sincere in wanting to do it.

If you choose 5A and want to allocate adequate manpower, there are two more choices:

**6A.** You must decide if you want to do it now, or

**6B.** You want to wait because of any number of reasons, including the fact that society is now "in a transitional period", or you feel further studies are called for.

If you want to wait, you are stalling, and are not sincere in wanting to do it. If you want to do it now, then it is time to get started.

By using a step-by-step approach of this kind, which the reader may modify to suit his own needs, many of the pitfalls which may later arise when arguments are presented by the Country Zina officials against more active implementation or enforcement, can be brought to light early, and perhaps routed around.

Such a methodology is useful in discussing the necessity to enforce traffic regulations, laws against counterfeiting, or laws against the illegal establishment of various enterprises. The necessity of passing the necessary regulations to lower tariffs and other trade barriers in order to import more products from country Alpha in order to lower the trade imbalance may also be brought up, and when the officials of country Zina agree to this line of reasoning, they may be led through an appropriate succession of steps, one by one, to see how thorough their agreement really is.

## Full & Final Authority

If the Country Zina party in the negotiations is not of the level of a primary governing body, it may be necessary to first establish a similar set of "'recognitions'" with some higher governing body, to the effect that they are giving full authority for doing this to such and such an organization. This then becomes what they want to do. Their officials-in-charge may then be lead through the last few steps of the progression, confirming their sincerity in supplying budget, manpower, and clarifying their timing.

It is extremely important to establish from the outset in a negotiation of any kind, who has final authority and who has final say in the carrying out of procedures, and who bears final responsibility if they are not carried out. Granted this may be extremely difficult to establish in many types of 3rd world organizations, since all power tends to be concentrated in the top of the organization, and few underlings have much power to do anything except punch in and out at the time clock, although to the casual western observer they appear to be busy handling all kinds of affairs and decisions. Moreover, the line of command should always be determined: who is in charge when the relevant official cannot be reached, and would therefore be able to make a decision or provide a status report? Often as not, it will be found that there is no line of command, and information tends to be bottlenecked at the top, or in the other position in the hierarchy where it was received as input.

The alternative to this is that at some later date, when Country Alpha people make further inquiries, they will be told: "I am sorry he is not here now, and we do not know anything about that." This results in their not getting their money, or not getting the goods that were supposed to be ready, or not getting a status report on the relevant items of production, completion, or enforcement.

## Stalling and Extensions

Most foreigners who have lived in China for several years and have had some exposure to typical Chinese organizations feel that responsibility tends to be kicked around like a hot potato. Thus, if you have the power and/or the pull or foresight, penalties should be stipulated for failure to comply with any terms which you are stating in a contract or other agreement. This is because, whether deliberately or non-deliberately, the Chinese ability to play "the stall game" is so far advanced over the westerners as to put it in another category of games altogether. The Chinese can redefine organizational goals and reallocate manpower without so much as a surface ripple, and the westerner innocently thinks "nothing has changed", whereas in fact, the original stipulations and promises have now taken on secondary (or worse) place to other more pressing problems. If Country Zina's interests are jeopardized, they might play the stall game deliberately, if not, they might still play it accidentally, due to complex bureaucratic procedures which they see and accept as unchangeable, and expect you to see the same way. This appears a normal outcome of "Group Mentality" thinking processes.

It should always be one's goal in a negotiation to have some sort of commanding position at all stages. For example, you may want to require that evidence of compliance be presented to you by a certain date. The experienced foreigner often recognizes that aside from a number of classical Chinese philosophical tenets, the Chinese hold very few things as "absolute", therefore they naturally believe that something as unfeeling as a piece of paper covered with stipulations (a contract) cannot be without exceptions to its terms. If their interests are jeopardized, they may try using the sympathy tactic at the last minute, to ask for an extension. Therefore one would be wise to be very specific in stipulating that any requests for extensions be prepared in exactly what sort of manner, and that they include what sort of documentation, or what penalities will fall due for non-compliance.

"Communications Pipelines"

Negotiations with a large organization must consider the totality of the organizational structure.

Chart 12-2

The ZZ Organization
Organizational Chart

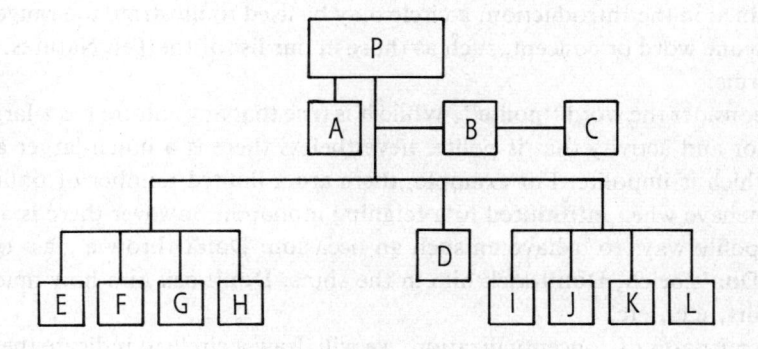

```
                    P
                    |
        A --------- B --------- C
        |           |           |
    ┌───┼───┬───┐   D   ┌───┬───┼───┐
    E   F   G   H       I   J   K   L
```

In this diagram, the Head or President of the organization (in country Zina), labelled P, has many subordinate divisions, committees, and departments under his direction. He may agree to a certain course of action, however the implementation must be done by the person(s) to whom he assigns the task. The AA organization in country Alpha which desires to deal with ZZ successfully will use a task-force approach: in addition to initial contact and agreement to "go ahead" which is received from P, additional contact will want to be maintained with one or more persons next to P (i.e. A, B, or C) as well as at least one subordinate on a much lower level, such as I, J, or K.

The establishment of formal and informal "communications pipelines" in this fashion will greatly facilitate much of the dealing between the two organizations. Essentially, if contact and coordination is achieved with B and J, then both of these can act as continuing "internal sales" (of AA's product, idea, good intentions, etc.) within the ZZ organization, with B working down through the levels of the organization to persuade all people of the advisability of cooperation with AA, and J working from the bottom up. As problems or snags arise, they may be informally communicated to the AA task-force members via B and J. In this manner many difficulties and bottlenecks may be dealt with in the early stages and resolved before they reach unmanageable proportions.

The needs of B and J should be considered, and when the AA organization can provide them help and assistance they will certainly feel more motivated to work together in fulfilling AA's goals. This is in keeping with the Chinese view that relationships are mutually beneficial. For example, B or J may need documentation, research reports, statistical data, etc. for one of their own projects in the ZZ organization, and AA can assist in assembling these. Other personal concerns, such as assisting in the paperwork involved for a child to study in the west, arranging competent language lessons and counseling, etc. are also possible types of help which can be offered.

## Spectra Charts

As outlined in the Introduction, a circle may be used to illustrate the range of meaning of any one word or concept, such as those in our list of the Ten Natures, and other related terms.

Let us consider the word "polite". While it is true that any culture has a large amount of behavior and activity that is polite, nevertheless there is a much larger amount of activity which is impolite. For example, there are a limited number of polite ways to talk and behave when introduced to a reigning monarch, however there is a very long list of impolite ways to behave on such an occasion: Don't throw a glass of water in his face, Don't belch, Don't kick him in the shins, Don't ask him how much he paid for his shirt, etc., etc.

For the purposes of conceptualization, we will draw a circle to indicate the collection of positive values, and a much larger oval to indicate the collection of negative values. This is illustrated for the case of "politeness" in figure 12-1.

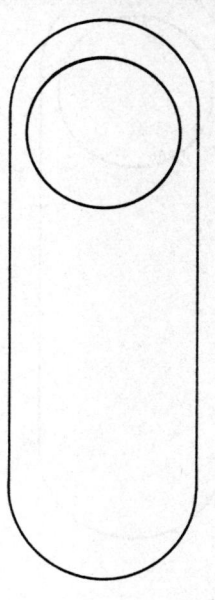

Figure 12-1

We will call this type of diagram a Spectrum Chart, and in this case "a Spectrum Chart for Politeness ". Behavior which is considered polite may be represented by a point in the politeness area. Behavior which is considered impolite may be represented by a point in the impoliteness area. The area which lies beyond the borders of the impolite area we refer to as "outside the politeness/impoliteness spectrum".

If we do an addition problem, and get an answer, someone may ask "Is that considered polite or impolite?" However, the adding up of numbers is not usually associated with a sense of politeness. If we wanted to illustrate this on our Spectrum Chart for Politeness, it would be a point outside, as illustrated in figure 12-2.

The Spectrum Chart is referred to by its positive value, so this is a Spectrum Chart for Politeness. We will speak of *diagramming* a point, *charting* a concept, and *compiling* a comparative example list.

Representing the Conceptions of Different Cultures

By taking one concept such as Politeness, we may draw a Spectrum Chart for the prevalent value system in the **Entry Culture:** the region where the foreigner has come to reside. This is the E chart, and it has three areas: the positive, the negative, and the outside. We will denote these as $E+$, $E-$, and $Eo$.

In a similar fashion, we may draw a Spectrum Chart for the prevalent value system

Figure 12-2

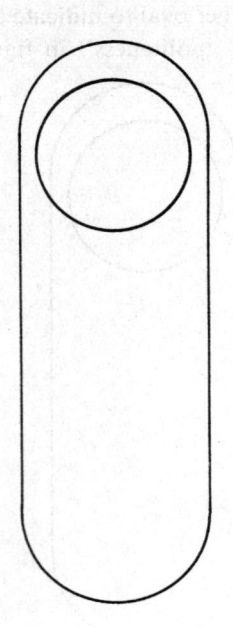

in the **Background Culture:** the region from which the foreigner has come. This is the B chart, and it also has three areas, which we will denote as B+, B-, and Bo.

Superimposing the B chart on the E chart, to indicate the foreigner's arrival into the Entry Culture, we have a complete Spectra Chart. This illustrates that in different societies the range of meanings and scopes of relevance for any one concept are similar but not the same.

***Example:***

| China<br>(Entry Culture) | U.S.A.<br>(Background Culture<br>of the acculturator) |
|---|---|
| E | B |

Confucius said: "At seventy I could follow whatever my heart desired without transgressing the rules of correct conduct."[a] Hence many Chinese would maintain that it is much too early to enter into a thorough discussion of the demands of politeness if

---

a. 論語 II，4：七十而從心所欲，不踰矩。

Figure 12-3

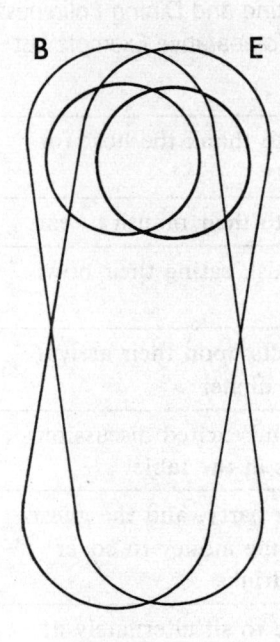

Spectra Chart

we have not reached the age of 70. Nevertheless I will try to present the following analysis in a coherent manner, and hope that the reader will bear with me for any oversights which are due to my relatively young age, (which happens to be approximately half of the figure which Confucius mentioned).

In dealing with Politeness, our + will indicate "polite" (the positive value), our - will indicate "impolite" (the negative value), and our o will indicate "unrelated to politeness" (outside consideration of the positive or negative value). E will indicate "as seen by the Entry Culture", B will indicate "as seen by the Background Culture". Hence,

- **E+** the positive value, as viewed by the Entry Culture
- **E-** the negative value, as viewed by the Entry Culture
- **Eo** outside consideration of the positive or negative value, as viewed by the Entry Culture
- **B+** the positive value, as viewed by the Background Culture
- **B-** the negative value, as viewed by the Background Culture
- **Bo** outside consideration of the positive or negative value, as viewed by the Background Culture

Nine examples from the realm of eating have been collected for reference.

## Eating and Dining Politeness
## Comparative Example List

| *examples* | | | *conclusion* |
|---|---|---|---|
| 1. The guests make a point to thank the host for his/her excellent hospitality | E+ | B+ | agreement |
| 2. A person lifts their bowl to their mouth to eat | E+ | B− | disagreement |
| 3. A person takes care to finish eating their bowl of rice | E+ | Bo | disagreement |
| 4. The hosts kiss or hug guests upon their arrival at a TV & Movie Awards dinner | E− | B+ | disagreement |
| 5. Guests engage in a loud and excited discussion of differing political views at the table | E− | B− | agreement |
| 6. Mr. R holds a going-away party, and the guests are asked to contribute some money to cover the cost of the food and drinks | E− | Bo | disagreement |
| 7. Men and women take care to sit alternately at a formal dinner | Eo | B+ | disagreement |
| 8. A person agrees to come to a friend's banquet, and then does not show up (or telephone) | Eo | B− | disagreement |
| 9. A guest is asked if he wants orange juice, and replies that he prefers water | Eo | Bo | agreement |

Using the symbol ∩ to denote "intersects", "intersects with", or "intersecting with", many different areas on our Spectra Chart may be named, such as E+ ∩ B+, E− ∩ Bo, etc. In our cross cultural studies, if we want to examine an action which we feel is polite, we may diagram it as a point on a Spectra Chart for Politeness, and determine where it lies in any one of nine regions. The above nine situations are diagrammed as figure 12-4 or figure 12-5.

The Chinese say that "Over-politeness is not a fault,"[a] however this clearly depends on how you define politeness. As our Spectra Charts would indicate, "over-politeness" to some (i.e., being very very polite) might be regarded as "impoliteness" to others, especially in cross-cultural dealings.

---

a. 禮多人不怪

Figure 12-4

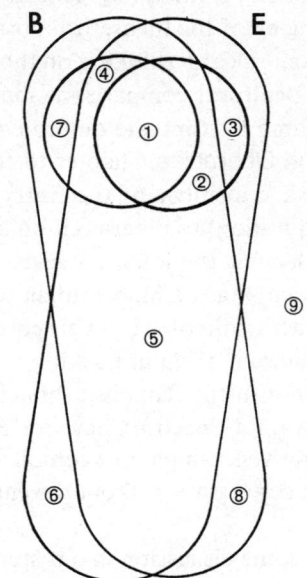

```
     B         E
      ④
   ⑦  ①  ③
         ②


        ⑨
    ⑤


  ⑥    ⑧
```

Figure 12-5

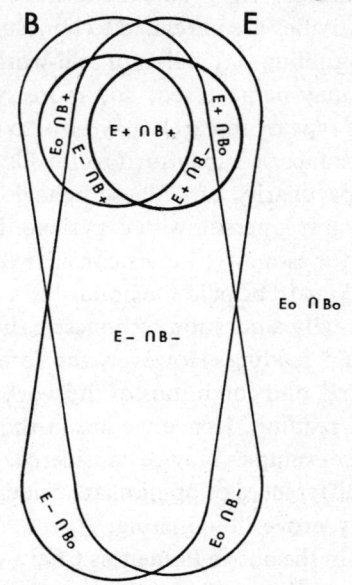

```
     B         E
   Eo∩B+   E+∩Bo
     E+∩B+
    E-∩B+  E+∩B-

        Eo∩Bo
       E-∩B-


    E-∩Bo   Eo∩B-
```

*Notes:*

I. These are general models which are presented to aid conceptualization of some of the different outlooks involved in cross-cultural encounters. Many variations are possible. In a previous essay we saw that the concept of "face" is much larger in China than in the west, which perhaps indicates that on a Spectra Chart for "Maintenance of Face" the E+ area is perhaps best rendered as a bigger size/quantity than the B+ area. However, since our primary intention is to diagram points and not quantities in this kind of Spectra Chart model, we need not be overly worried about this, unless we are engaged in highly advanced analysis. In any event, the general structure and utility of Spectra Chart composition remains the same.

II. We do not mean to suggest that the people of E Culture have no differences of opinion among themselves, or that the people of B Culture are in total agreement on all issues. However, we do address our focus of attention to concrete examples upon which there is a wide consensus of opinion.

III. Spectra Charts may be drawn and Comparative Example Lists compiled for the many and myriad terms which need further clarification in cross-cultural dealings. If we look at a Spectra Chart for Honesty, we immediately see that some activities which the Entry Culture typically views as outside the honesty/dishonesty spectrum (i.e., "unrelated to honesty"), are considered by the Background Culture of the foreigner to be honest, while some are dishonest. Other times there is indeed agreement that certain activities are unrelated to honesty. By examining all of the theoretical possibilities, and compiling actual lists of real-world examples, some clearer thinking on the relevant issues may be achieved, and more systematic cross-cultural comparisons made.[1]

This type of research may also be made into a game to stimulate our conversation. For instance, we may turn to the Opportunities and Obstacles Chapter to ferret out some peculiarity of Chinese behavior, and then ask a member of the Entry Culture (preferably a person with experience in the area in question) to diagram it on a Spectra Chart for Honesty. Let us consider the example of leaving the job after seven months, and asking to be paid the bonus for a full year's service. Many Chinese might say "This is not really a question of honesty, there are other factors involved." This corresponds to an Eo reading. However, the foreigner may maintain "You are asking to be paid for work, and conditions of the work, that you did not fulfill. That is dishonest." This is a B- reading. Hence we are in the Eo ∩ B- area on a Spectra Chart for Honesty.

Other examples may be considered, and a Comparative Example List compiled. When some differences of opinion are evident, an in-depth conversation about the entire matter may prove illuminating.

IV. In the above Politeness Chart, there has been some discussion in our study group of the possible confusion involved with an E − ∩ Bo determination. For example, sticking one's chopsticks straight up in a bowl of rice when going to make a phone call could easily be viewed in this category, as well as turning over a fish (to eat the other side) when dining on a boat. The differing attitudes here are complicated by certain superstitious beliefs held among the members of one or the other cultural groups. In dealing with these issues, the foreigner is certainly well advised to investigate all the oddities of usage in regard to the native eating implements, plates, bowls, etc. and peculiarities regarding the consumption of various types of food, drink, etc. in the Entry Culture.

Nevertheless, in light of the standards commonly held in the larger background culture from which this foreigner has come, it would appear that an E − ∩ Bo determination is valid.

Another interesting item involves the habit of many Chinese in a banquet situation to toast someone with a big glass of liquor, and then demand that the other party "bottoms up"[a] with them. Foreigners more adhere to the practice of "you drink your liquor and I will drink mine", and see no need for toasting every drink, or forcing others

---

a. 乾杯

1. In many accounts written by foreigners in China we may read many stories and come across conclusions such as "The Chinese are very honest." In another book we read other stories, with a conclusion "The Chinese are very dishonest." Such conclusions are reconcilable if we realize that the former author spoke of an activity which would fall in the E+ ∩ B+ area on a Spectra Chart for Honesty. The latter spoke of an activity or action that quite possibly falls in Eo ∩ B−.

to "bottoms up" in this manner. Hence many foreigners soon come to regard such activity as impolite, (thus giving a B- reading), and question their Chinese friends about it. The Chinese frequently say "This is not really a question of politeness, this is just our custom", (hence giving an Eo reading). Clearly we are in the Eo ∩ B- area on a Spectra Chart for Eating and Dining Politeness. Resolution of this difference of opinion may prove difficult.

V. In this essay we have dealt with the concept of politeness (more specifically: Eating and Dining Politeness), and more briefly the concept of honesty. Additional concepts may also be charted, including our Ten Natures, Acculturologically Sensitive Terms (introduced in the Appendix), and others.

# Appendix

## Confusing Terms
### Foreign, Native, Western, Chinese, American

As touched upon in the Introduction, many terms have some potential for confusion in our cross-cultural discussion. For example, the use of terms such as "native culture" and "foreign culture" are perhaps best avoided, unless it can be carefully clarified to which culture these terms refer. Consider: **a)** To the native of the Entry Culture, the acculturator's culture is the foreign culture. **b)** To the acculturator, the Entry Culture is the foreign culture. In this volume we have used foreigner to refer to "non-Chinese", hence we would tend to view the acculturator's (foreigner's) culture as the "foreign culture", as per definition a).

Foreigners in China may often obtain alien registration documents. From the geographical standpoint of China (the entry culture), clearly it is the non-Chinese who is the alien. This is the viewpoint of the acculturological sinologist, and hence the viewpoint which I have adopted in this volume. To the foreigner, the entry culture is the alien culture however, hence one sees that such terms as these have the potential to become confusing if not used with one consistent perspective in one's writing and speaking.

When someone wants to introduce new ideas into the entry culture, it is often desirable to identify from where these ideas have come, and this is called the source culture. In times of war people speak of the entry culture and invading culture.

This volume, written originally in English, has deliberately taken an uncommon perceptual basis in the use of some terms, since the concern of the discussion is the foreigner living in China. Thus, where not otherwise specified,

| | |
|---|---|
| local | = the place of residence in China |
| native | = Chinese |
| domestically | = in China |
| imported | = imported into China |
| exported | = exported from China |
| entry culture | = China |
| native culture | = China |
| foreigner | = 1) westerner, 2) non-Chinese in general |

Further confusion over the terms "foreign" or "foreigner" may be generated in talking about a "foreign language institute". Again, with the point of view of Chinese being the native culture (and entry culture), such a language institute would, in the simplest analysis, be any that taught English, Japanese, German, or some other "foreign" language. Ownership could be local (Chinese), foreign, or a cooperative venture.

When speaking of many concepts, and comparing them to Chinese concepts, we are forced to attach the term "western", although this at first seems a bit unusual to English speakers. Hence we speak of western liquor, western food, western medicine, and western morality.

By "westerner", we are primarily speaking of members of the most populous linguistic and cultural groups in North America, England, and Western Europe. However, the author being American, and with the collected comments of many other Americans appearing in this volume, there is a reasonable justification for saying that the "westerner" herein indicated is primarily American.

By "western food", we are primarily speaking of food from the three regions stated above. By "western medicine", we are primarily speaking of medical techniques originally developed and practiced in these regions. Western food and western medicine have obviously now spread to other regions of the globe.

Where comments or comparisons specifically relevant to Japanese or Koreans have been made, they have been clearly noted.

The sense of what "foreign" (*wai gwo* 外國) or "foreigner" (*wai gwo ren* 外國人) means may not always be easily determined. An example is when westerners are in a western country and speaking to Chinese people in the Chinese language. From such a point of reference, we believe either party could reasonably be called "foreign". We have rarely come across this situation in the events described in this volume, which is more concerned with life in China proper.

In speaking of "overseas Chinese" (especially those in possession of a foreign passport) who have come to China, the question of whether they are foreigners or natives often arises. The situation is complicated by the fact that while the USA, Canada, England, France, etc., are countries, they are rarely regarded as "races", while China/Chinese represent both a country and a race. Additionally, China has long recognized dual nationality, or dual citizenship. Thus if a Canadian obtains USA citizenship, he ceases to be Canadian. If a Chinese obtains French citizenship, he does not cease to be Chinese however.

In reality, there tends to be no objective rule for determining the overseas-Chinese person's status upon his "return" to the ancestor-land. In some cases he will be considered a Chinese, and in others a foreigner. If this results in a disparity in financial compensation, he/she may often be forced to grin and bear it. In this volume we have generally taken the Chinese view that "overseas Chinese" (the common appellation for a person of the Chinese race who holds a non-Chinese passport) does not immediately equal "foreigner"; indeed this person's status is in something of a gray area.

From the point of view of many Americans and Europeans, all Chinese practicing medicine are Chinese doctors, all Chinese making garments are Chinese garment manufacturers, all Chinese publishing books are Chinese publishers, etc. However, to avoid vagueness and possible misinterpretation, we have found it necessary in this volume to be a bit more specific. Considering the term "Chinese doctor", any of the

following could be the intended meaning (in China):
  A) A doctor of Chinese nationality practicing Chinese medicine
  B) A doctor of *non-Chinese nationality* practicing Chinese medicine
    01. overseas Chinese (racially a Chinese)
    02. non blood-related Chinese (racially a non-Chinese)
  C) A doctor of Chinese nationality practicing western medicine

In this volume we have used "Chinese" primarily in the sense of **A)**, thus indicating a Chinese person engaging in Chinese activities. Secondarily, our meaning is **B)**, especially to extent that this person of non-Chinese nationality (i.e., the holder of a foreign passport) is an ethnic Chinese, the so called "overseas Chinese", (listed as subcategory **01**). Non-ethnic Chinese practicing Chinese medicine would be the next consideration, (listed as subcategory **02**).

Doctors of Chinese nationality practicing western medicine in China we have generally considered as western doctors, or native western doctors. Thus when we say that "Much of the medical establishment in China tends to be monopolized by western doctors", the exact meaning of this remark is rendered much more precise.

By using the same formulation, it will be clear what is meant by Chinese musicians, Chinese horticulturists, Chinese chefs, Chinese lawmakers, Chinese painters, and other occupational titles.

By "native American" we are primarily indicating someone who was born and raised in the United States of America.

Westernization

It should be noted that the remarks and descriptions of thought patterns in this volume are primarily descriptive of non-westernized Chinese. In other words, we are talking about Chinese in China. Chinese in the west are, due to their environment, exposed to a multitude of western influences. Chinese in China are primarily exposed to Chinese influences, although this is tempered somewhat if they work for a foreign organization and associate with foreigners every day. However, if their foreign organizations or branch offices are staffed by Chinese, they may still be exposed to primarily Chinese influences on and off the job.

In fact, many western influences which reach China have been considerably filtered or watered down. If a Chinese person has spent considerable time living and studying in the west, and associating with westerners in a "non-Chinatown environment", and in a variety of situations, we would expect that he/she will have become westernized in many respects. If not, he/she may be westernized in only a very superficial fashion.

In many international conferences, especially those on legal issues, when the Chinese and western parties try to iron out their differences, it is often rewarding for the western delegates to find that the Chinese participants share many of their viewpoints. However, it should be remembered that the Chinese participants in such conferences are often very westernized, and their views do not always represent the views of the majority of the more traditionally oriented Chinese populace. In another consideration, with regard to the concept of face, it could be true that the Chinese participants are making various statements with the specific intention of "pleasing the guests", since guests are preeminent in Chinese society.

## Caution with Terminology

*Before I discuss anything with you, you must define your terms.*
— *Voltaire*

From the point of view of acculturology, it is important that certain words be used carefully, and accurately qualified. If this is not done, our attempts to deal with many concepts will be considerably muddled. This is especially true since our mission is to explain a point of view existing in one culture to a person who is a non-native, or to otherwise deal in communicating concepts cross-culturally.

Words are units of language serving as labels for objects and ideas, and undoubtedly few people can give a dictionary or technical definition of any given word. However, agreement as to the sense of what a word means, or what conduct qualifies to be adjectively described in any particular way, could be expected to be far more widespread among the members of one cultural group (intra-culturally) than among members of different cultural groups (inter-culturally).This is especially worthy of note in regard to the following words, which I regard as being "acculturologically sensitive".

In this listing I will abbreviate the word "culture" as C.

common sense, *lack of common sense*
    Common sense is certainly related to the belief systems which the people hold, and these often differ in different Cs. One C's common sense is another C's lack of reasoning.

courteous, courteous, *discourtesy, discourteous*
    What is courtesy in one C may be discourtesy in another, also it may frequently be seen that many gestures, whether meaningless or well-intentioned, may imply discourtesy to members of another C. Statements which one C considers straightforward honest comments may be regarded as a total lack of courtesy in another C.

ethics, ethical, *unethical*
    Different Cs have different ideas of what constitutes ethical and moral behavior in specific situations. (See "virtue") There is not always a direct correlation between law and ethics. In some C's which hold to old traditional value systems, legal interpretations of right and wrong, or enforcement of the law in many situations may be viewed by the populace as unethical. Conversely, many activities, endeavors,

requests, demands, etc. which are forbidden by law, or without any legal basis, may be viewed by the populace as fully ethical. This shows the existence of a legal/moral gap. In a C which has a large legal/moral gap, the view that "you will be respected for obeying the law" is frequently invalid.

fair, fairness, *unfair, unfairness*

A sense of what constitutes fairness is assimilated from the C, and rarely taught as a specific subject in the schools. Determinations that are seen as fair in one C may be seen as unfair in another.

goodness, good, *bad*

Goodness needs to be defined in relation to some stated considerations, underlying beliefs, or goals, and different Cs may see different goals as important.

honest, honesty, *dishonest, dishonesty*

The concept of honesty as an ideal of human conduct is easily cancelled out by other more important considerations in some Cs, such as the ideal of maintaining harmonious human relationships, respecting elders and teachers, etc. The demands of honesty in different Cs are frequently dissimilar, and the idea that "you will be respected for being honest" is not always true, especially in societies that place much emphasis on indirectness and saving face. Additionally, some activities or behavior which one C regards as dishonest another C may regard as outside the realm of honesty/dishonesty altogether.

integrity, *lack of integrity*

Integrity may be used in reference to to the damage to mental or physical integrity arising from torts. It may be used in a different sense to indicate the integrity of beliefs, especially belief in the existence of basic human rights, such as the freedoms of speech, religion, association, publication, etc., or belief in what are men's most important and inviolate virtues. The statement that a particular person is a man (or woman) of integrity could easily be taken to mean, especially in translated form, that he had no physical infirmities or handicaps. In the other sense, beliefs or virtues which are important to one C may be unimportant, or even unknown, in another C, thus lending considerable inspecificity to the idea of what integrity is. In the west, many people associate integrity with honesty, but the demands of honesty may vary in different Cs. (See "honesty") Some people may feel that integrity means that "what one says" and "what one does" are the same, but this type of definition is not shared by all Cs. Integrity to some people means making the choice of right instead of wrong, all the time. This sense of "right" is related to truth and virtue, which are also acculturologically sensitive. (See "truth", "virtue") Integrity is also often associated with loyalty. (See "loyalty")

just, justice, *unjust, injustice*

Different Cs may have highly variant views of the demands of justice, or of what type of behavior is viewed as just, righteous, upright, etc. in any given situation. Such variant views may easily arise due to the influences of differing religious, social, and philosophical doctrines, as well as dissimilar notions as to what types of actions fall within the scope of a discussion of morality and virtue, and what types of actions do not.

logic, logical, *illogical*

Looking at any particular situation, different Cs may see different elements as being important, therefore the premises for their logic may not be the same. Dissimilar results and conclusions are therefore easily reached.

loyalty, *lack of loyalty*

Loyalty must exist in relation to its object: a person, government, cause, duty, etc. Some Cs may feel that loyalty to one object, one's employer for example, is overridingly important, some may feel that loyalty to the family/clan is more important than this. Different Cs could be expected to have different rankings of loyalty preferences.

morality, moral, *immoral*

Action which is considered moral by members of one C may be considered to be without the slightest relation to morality by members of another C. In some situations what is generally regarded as moral behavior in one C may even be viewed as immoral behavior in another. (See "ethics", "virtue")

natural, naturalism, *unnatural*

Actions, behavior, and thinking which one C regards as natural may be regarded as unnatural by another C, and perhaps seen as barbaric, primitivist, immoral, going against prevailing religious and philosophical tenets, social doctrines, etc.

polite, politeness, *impolite, impoliteness*

Politeness in one C may be seen as inappropriate behavior in another. Likewise, what one C regards as impoliteness may be regarded by another C as living up to the demands of honesty or sincerity. Sometimes, what one C regards as impolite gestures or expressions may have little or no no significance whatsoever in the viewpoint of another C.

principle, principled, *unprincipled*

What values and beliefs are seen as principles may vary from C to C. The concept of principle being inviolate is not common to all Cs; principle could be less important than the requirements of politeness for example.

propriety, proper, *improper*

Proper behavior in one C may be improper in another. The demands of propriety, and the sanctions for a lack of propriety, may vary from C to C.

rational, *non-rational, irrational*

In order to talk about what is rational, we have to talk about what is reason. Some Cs may make no distinctions between reasoning and excuse-making; some may. Some Cs may try to reason objectively, and consider all evidence, some may have a strong subjective bias and consider only what evidence supports its established point of view. In some Cs "custom" may be considered equivalent to reason or reasoning, and

rarely be open to debate.
rationale, *lack of rationale*
   Comments which one C views as rationale may be regarded as nonsense by another. The weight attached to various specific rationale, or types of rationale, can vary from C to C due to different patterns of thinking.
rules of reason, reasonable, *unreasonable*
   What is reasonable conduct from the point of view common to one C may be unreasonable from the point of view common to another, and may be classified as selfish, immoral, stingy, or otherwise unacceptable.
sincerity, sincere, "in good faith", *insincerity, insincere*
   Behavior that appears as sincerity in one C may appear as a condescending, obsequious, or superficial in another. Some behavior which one C regards as insincere another C may regard as outside the realm of sincerity/insincerity altogether.
true, truth, *falsity*
   In some Cs that stress belief over proof, some definition of or attempt to establish objective truth may be of little weight. Additionally, truth is often derived from ideology, and different Cs have different ideology.
virtue, virtuous, *not virtuous*
   Activity which is considered virtuous in one C may be considered without the slightest relation to virtue in another, or sometimes even perhaps as highly unvirtuous. The rankings of the virtues in order of importance may vary widely as well.

Any nouns, adjectives, or other parts of speech related or closely associated to these would also best be used with regard to their "vagueness potential" or "confusion potential" when used cross-culturally. Relevant here are possibilities for **a)** differing interpretations due to varying philosophies, **b)** differing allowed and expected degrees of discorrelation between "theory" and "practice", **c)** difficulty of exact translation into another language, etc. This is because these words have meanings, connotations, comparative degrees of importance, and understood scopes of relevance that are quite dissimilar among people with different cultural backgrounds. Hence we refer to them as being acculturologically sensitive.

One example comes to mind which will illustrate this dissimilarity. Several years ago, I came across an article in an English language Economics journal published in China, which described a meeting held between representatives of the local Chinese manufacturing, trading, and publishing industries and a visiting US Trade Delegation. The issues of trademark counterfeiting, patent infringement, invasion of copyrights, and other topics were discussed. One US delegate made the statement: "I do not think we have a problem here. We can solve our differences if everyone will agree to the principle of honesty."

In such an intercultural setting, one is intrigued by this reference to honesty as a "principle". Honesty, to the American mind, calls up thoughts of "Honesty is the best policy".

However I find it easy to imagine that in more traditional societies, there might be other ethical considerations which are more important, if and when some conflict of interest situation arises, than "honesty". As to what constitutes "honesty" in any particular situation, I suspect that the American and Chinese representatives to the meeting might even have difficulty deciding on the "honest" price of a plate of fried rice in a restaurant, if a problem arose with the personnel of the establishment. How much more difficult it is to make a determination of what constitutes honesty in the case of an intangible and abstract concept like "copyright invasion"!

"Principle", to the American mind, suggests something that is a fundamental truth, or a rule of correct conduct. However it may not carry such strong connotations as these in another language.

Added to this is the problem that even if we can reach agreement on what these terms mean and how they are to be used, the people in some cultures may try to be objective, and strive to bring this theory and practice together, whereas people in some other cultures may be so subjective as to see very little relation between theory and practice at all, and be willing to accept "saying one thing, and doing something else," especially when the consideration of face is involved.

Thus when such remarks are spoken directly to members of another culture who understand our language, or translated into their language for their ease of comprehension, some difficulties may arise. Even if we receive their indication of assent or agreement, they may in fact be agreeing to something quite different from what we thought we said.

It will be helpful in the study of acculturology if, when using terms such as those listed above, we attempt to clarify from what point of view we are using them.

## Considerations of Phraseology in Dealing with Cross-Cultural Topics

I have felt it advisable in this book to consciously avoid saying that anything is a "principle", "an important principle", "a basic principle", etc., because in Chinese and English the force of the term "principle" is quite widely separated. (It appears that the principles the Chinese adhere to most closely are concrete ones, especially those which dictate personal relationships, whereas many of the principles which the westerners adhere to are based on abstract concepts.) Such loose usage of the sensitive terms above, such as "It stands to reason that . . . ", "logically speaking we can see that . . . ", "the demands of morality would require that . . . ", etc. have also been avoided. The expression "at face value" has been replaced with "at surface value". The words "reasonable", "fair", "proper", etc. and other related terms such as "reasonable demands", "fair play", "proper conduct", etc. which give an implication of value-judgments, have been used only after first attempting to define or illustrate the perceptual basis on which they were resting. Although I have tried to be careful in usage of the words "nature", "natural", and "naturalism", one flaw in this regard has been the often rather casual use of the term "naturally", which I regret to have found largely unavoidable, since in English it is often employed in the loose sense of **as one might expect, of course**, etc., without being literally related to nature, or some natural doctrine. A separate essay has outlined differing views on "Naturalism", and should serve to clarify the issue to a suitable degree.

It is the first business of mind to be "realistic," to see things "as they are."

———— *John Dewey*

With the desirability of avoiding any casual usage of the words listed above, we have still needed some sort of base-line for our thinking, and in this study we have chosen the following.

objective, *subjective*

For the purposes of discussing various cross-cultural issues, we are regarding the words "objective" and "subjective" to be of minimal acculturological sensitivity.

**Objective: 1) of or having to do with a known or perceived object as distinguished from something existing only in the mind of the subject, or person thinking, hence, 2) being, or regarded as being, independent of the mind; real; actual.**

**Subjective: 1) of, affected by, or produced by the mind or a particular state of mind; 2) of or resulting from the feelings or temperament of the subject, or person thinking, rather than the attributes of the object thought of.**

It is further felt that "objective" contains some idea of acting or striving to act for the greatest good of the greatest number, an ethical thought from the utilitarian school, however with bases as far back as the writings of Aristotle. In addition, the ramifications of our actions are to be considered over the long term, and they are judged in regard to their continued benefit or detriment to the populace.

Admittedly, so called "objectivity" changes over time, but this is due to the very nature of its striving, which causes it to move forward and redefine itself in light of new factors.

It is not our intention to suggest that use of either one of these two words is valid in any context just because the author decided to use it however. Clearly, the terms "objective" and "subjective" must be used in a justifiable manner.

With this in mind one may consider the members of any cultural group, and evaluate certain criteria, including the statements they make, and the beliefs they hold, which would fall under the categories of "reason", "rationale", "principle", "good", etc. and describe them as objective or subjective. No doubt some cultures place more emphasis on subjective reasoning than others.

I hold that man is in the right who is most closely in league with the future.

———— *Henrik Ibsen*

## Types of Definitions

Definitions have frequently been provided for terms or concepts in this volume. At least five types of definitions are relevant to the discussion of cross cultural issues. One's understanding of the meaning of various terminology is greatly facilitated if an appropriate type of definition is used.

*Lexical definitions* attempt to report usage. All good dictionary definitions are lexical, since they state how native speakers employ the words in all of their various senses.

*Stipulative definitions* are those which specify or stipulate the meaning of a word or phrase. Sometimes these involve the introduction of new terms, or the stipulation of new meaning for old terms.

*Extensional definitions* are simply a list of all the things to which the term applies. For example, the term "Chinese Provincial Capital" can be defined extensionally by listing all the capitals of the Chinese provinces.

*Intensional definitions* list a set of properties such that the term applies to all things having that set of properties, and to nothing else. A chemist or geologist might supply us with an intensional definition of the term "gold".

*Ostensive definitions* indicate the meaning of a term by providing a sample of the things denoted. We can define "polite" ostensively by making a listing of polite actions and behavior. The Comparative Example Lists which we use with our Spectra Charts may be categorized as comparative ostensive definitions.

Obviously, ostensive definitions are risky, or unclear, in ways that extensional definitions are not. An extensional definition provides the complete extension of a term or concept, and hence leaves minimal margin for error in interpretation. An ostensive definition furnishes only part of the extension of a term. However, some concepts are so complex that extensional definitions are extremely difficult to formulate.

## New Chinese Idioms

There are a number of unknown and unadopted phrases in Chinese which could be profitably incorporated into the language. The following are the author's choice for the ten English language derived expressions which would be the most useful. A four-character idiomatic Chinese translation is given for each, as well as some English sentence examples.

1. 野雁追踪 a wild goose chase

**a fruitless, futile, or unsuccessful search, exploration, or quest**

A. The girl at the front desk told me to go to Department A, the Department A personnel told me to go to Accounting, Accounting told me to go to Personnel, Personnel told me to see the Division Manager, and I am tired of being on a wild goose chase.

B. After being shunted between many bureaus and ministries in order to find the information, I finally realized I was on a wild goose chase.

2. 排高悬乾 high and dry

**abandoned and seemingly without recourse, alone and helpless, stranded**

A. When the factory closed down and the management disappeared, all the employees who had not been paid for three months were left high and dry.

B. After Pao-lin spent all Melvin's money and moved back in with her family, Melvin was left high and dry.

3. 置蛋一篮 putting all your eggs in one basket

**being short sighted, not making a comprehensive plan, failing to take all possibilities into account, risking all that one has on a single venture, method, etc.**

A. Mary only had one boyfriend all through high school, and he ran off with Alice after graduation. Mary suddenly came to the understanding that she should not have put all her eggs in one basket.

B. After losing all my money in the stock market crash, I realized I should not have put all my eggs in one basket.

4. 最终之草 the last straw

**the last of a sequence of annoyances or troubles that results in a breakdown, defeat, blow up, etc.; the point beyond which one can no longer endure**

A. When Mr. Jones caught his daughter watching cartoons the night before her midterm examinations that was the last straw, and he banned her from watching TV for a month.

B. You are always late for work, take things from the office, and don't complete your reports on time. Today you broke the boss's favorite flower vase, I think that was really the last straw.

5. 履换他足 the shoe is on the other foot

**the situation is completely reversed**

A. All those times I wanted to borrow money and you would not help me out, now you are here asking me. Well, the shoe is on the other foot.

B. My ex-friend Michael laughed at me when I fell and broke my arm, saying that I was clumsy. Now I learn he has broken his pelvis and it is clear that the shoe is on the other foot.

6. 盛不了水 does not hold water

**is not sound, consistent, or coherent, does not make sense, does not stand up to analysis**

A. That is a great theory that you have, but according to my research it does not hold water.

B. We argued for a lengthy period of time, but my friend finally had to admit that his ideas did not hold water.

7. 學繩習索 learning the ropes
**becoming acquainted with the procedures, becoming familiar and oriented to a new situation**
A. I really like my new job, but I am still learning the ropes.
B. He went to a school in Texas. Having never been to a university in the USA before, it took him several weeks to learn the ropes.

8. 腳底生寒 to get cold feet
**to become afraid after starting out with a bold idea**
A. You promised to invest $100,000 in my new company, but you did not come to our new stockholders meeting yesterday. Did you get cold feet?
B. I saw a pretty girl in the restaurant and was about to speak to her, but I got cold feet.

9. 難如取齒 like pulling teeth
**very difficult, because the person in question is not anxious to cooperate**
A. Trying to get him to say anything is like pulling teeth.
B. Getting her to straighten up the house is like pulling teeth.

10. 漆屋陷隅 paint yourself into a corner
**to put yourself in a bad situation, circumstance, or predicament, from which there is no easy remedy, escape, solution, etc.**
A. After agreeing to meet all the requests of my fiancee's family, I realized that I had painted myself into a corner.
B. If you leave this Cartoon Syndicate and go to that other one to draw, you should be aware that the Director over there is very strict. If you lose that job you may find that you have painted yourself into a corner.

Note: The above ten idioms do not exist in the Chinese language at the present time, but it is hoped that they will be gradually assimilated in the near future.

## Acculturology and Other Sciences

The acculturologist is the person who studies acculturology, however he may or may not be an acculturator, meaning that he may or may not be living in another culture, and attempting to acculturate himself.

By way of contrast, we may consider some other sciences which focus on human beings: physiology, psychology, philosophy, history, law, economics, political science, anthropology, sociology, etc. It is often difficult to draw clear cut boundary-lines between these various disciplines, however some specific knowledge of the scope of the latter two is useful for reference in the present studies.

ANTHROPOLOGY is broadly divided in physical anthropology and cultural anthropology.

**1.** Physical anthropology studies homo sapiens as a species, especially as regards tracing our relationships to related species and reconstructing the evolutionary branching and differentiation of the primate order.

**2.** Cultural anthropology is concerned with human cultures or ways of life, both in the present and in the past. Cultural anthropology may be subdivided into three main branches: archaeology, linguistics, and ethnology.

**a)** Archaeology is the study of the life and culture of ancient peoples, especially in regard to cultures now extinct.

**b)** Linguistics is the study of languages. Major divisions are 1) Descriptive or Structural Linguistics, 2) Historical Linguistics.

**c)** Ethnology is the study of contemporary cultures. Major divisions are 1) Cognitive anthropology, 2) Social anthropology, 3) Economic anthropology, 4) Political anthropology, 5) Culture and personality, 6) Cross-cultural studies in religion, folklore, art, music, warfare, etc.

SOCIOLOGY is the study of the history, development, organization, and problems of people living together as social groups. It pays particular attention to all peoples and groups which have become involved with the processes of modernization, urbanization, industrialization, and civilization, with the major focus of attention being a community, ethnic enclave, institution, or other sub-cultural group.

While all of these fields of study are important, and indeed related to the present cross-cultural discussion, yet none specifically addresses the major concern of acculturology — how the foreigner may best orient his thinking and behavior in order to adapt to life in the entry culture society, recognizing that he is a foreigner and not a native, living with a minimum of friction, achieving his own personal, business, scholarly or other goals, and enjoying the best elements that the local expatriate community and the native society have to offer.

## Author

Richard W. Hartzell was born and raised in Dayton, Ohio, USA, and attended Phillips Academy, Andover, Massachusetts, 1966—1969, graduating in the class of 1969. He became interested in Chinese while attending World Campus Afloat in 1971—1972. As a two-semester student aboard the "Floating University", *S.S. Universe Campus,* which was staffed with a Chinese crew, he visited over twenty countries in Africa, Asia, and the South Pacific. After this global tour he continued undergraduate studies at the University of Pennsylvania's Wharton School where he majored in International Business and minored in Mandarin Chinese, receiving his B.S. in Economics in 1974.

Returning to the Republic of China in the Fall of 1975, Richard immersed himself in Chinese language and cultural studies. He chose the Chinese name of 何瑞元. In the summer of 1978 he began a weekly column in Chinese for the local daily Min Sheng News 民生報. He was invited to move his weekly column to the Chinese language United Daily News 聯合報 (daily circulation over 1,000,000 copies) in early 1981, and wrote there for three years. He simultaneously wrote a monthly column for the Chinese language monthly Crown Magazine 皇冠雜誌, and frequently received requests to submit pieces to other newspapers and magazines.

Richard's collected Chinese essays in ten volumes have been published by Crown Publishers, Taipei, 皇冠出版社 and are sold in the mass circulation paperback market. Richard's books in Chinese are:

①見山不是山　②見山又是山　③老外與臭豆腐
④鷹的傳人　　⑤洋洋奇觀　　⑥下海與上陸
⑦美國式接觸　⑧察眼觀色　　⑨山姆叔叔吃皮蛋
⑩洋和尚取經

His status as Chinese language author is unique among westerners in the modern era, and necessitates that he maintain an active schedule of speaking engagements and TV appearances. Beginning in 1981 he served as MC of a 90 minute New Year's TV Special *Foreigners Celebrate the Chinese New Year* for five years.

After laboring for some years to explain the western point of view to the Chinese, Mr. Hartzell has now turned his attention to explaining the Chinese point of view to the westerners, in order to give them a peek under the bamboo veil.

Richard currently serves as Education Director of the Rei Huang Language Institute, 10th Floor, 46 Min Sheng East Road, Taipei, Taiwan 10443, Republic of China. He hopes that this book will serve to promote intercultural understanding between the people of China and the west. Readers who have comments, suggestions, stories, criticisms, different points of view, etc. are invited to write, although due to the volume of Chinese and foreign mail presently received, it may not always be possible to reply to every letter.

Mr. Hartzell promotes cultural exchange programs, in order that the people of China and the west may learn more about each other's culture, language, business practices, negotiating styles, social structure, educational methods, psychological make-up, legal concepts, etc. Richard is also involved in Public Relations activities, for people, companies, and organizations which need to promote and develop their contacts in the Republic of China in every field.

*Appendix*

# Acknowledgements

The number of people who offered advice and comments during the formulation, research, writing, reviewing, and editing of this volume was quite extensive, and included hundreds of Chinese and westerners. It would be difficult or impossible to list all of their contributions. Many afternoon and evening discussion sessions went on for untold hours, and the actual writing of the text required three years. Ms. Annie Chen, a native Chinese who studied management and negotiation in Japan, encouraged me in the initial conceptualization of the work, and offered valuable insight numerous times when gaps in the text needed to be filled out. She made available many of her unpublished studies of liability and damage handling in the hotel industry, introduced me to many leaders in government and private industry, as well as in the art, educational, and literary fields. With her assistance, I had the chance to participate in many negotiation sessions, where cross cultural issues came into play.

Roy Robinson, an Englishman who studied at Harvard and worked in Korea for many years, offered innumerable ideas and proposed many valuable lines of inquiry. My parents in Tennessee reviewed portions of my writing and provided many helpful clarifications. David Wu, a bilingual Chinese-Canadian, assisted with putting my notes in order and composing various essays during the summer of the year before publication. Judy Kokura from Vancouver, B.C., read over the text and suggested improvements based on her experience living in India. Marlene Moilanen, employed by a pharmaceutical importer in China, offered helpful suggestions on nutrition, medicine, and Chinese herbs. Matthew Sarno, a stock-market analyst in a Securities house in China, offered many useful tips on Chinese-style banking and investments, as well as some stylistic considerations in the writing of prose. Haiden Wu, a mechanical engineer employed by the Chinese government in a high-tech research and development institute, offered comments on Chinese bureaucratic organization, government structure, and effective negotiation tactics in the Chinese environment. Tom Howard from the University of Missouri served as English grammar editor. William S. Thompson, employed by an international corporate security consulting firm, offered overviews of property rights protection, commercial fraud inquiries, and other areas of commercial investigation. Several Malaysian-Chinese offered comments on the situation from their point of view. I was privileged to attend a series of lectures on Chinese culture given by Dr. Stephen W. Durrant, of the University of Utah, during the spring before publication. Dr. Durrant's many comments served to reinforce and further clarify much of the information I had assembled. My New York legal and management-consulting contacts have asked to remain anonymous.

Over a period of years the situations in this book were researched and discussed among the many members of my study group, which not only included those people above but also many others, some of whom have now been transferred to Africa, South America, and other remote regions.

## Notes and Analysis

It should be stated at the outset of the Notes that the formulation of Rules, Perceptions, Integration of Concepts, Rationale Weight Indexing, PC Paradoxes, Spectra Charts, Harmony Models and myriad other items in this volume, including the entire introduction of the study of acculturology as a separate social science, are the author's own analysis. To restate my comments in Chapter 6, in the study of acculturology we must endeavor to explain Entry Culture phenomenon using terminology, phraseology, and methodology that the foreigner can understand, yet which may not always correspond to the way the Entry Culture natives would explain their own thinking and actions.

Where it is helpful to analysis of the issues at hand, much terminology has been borrowed from the field of economics: marginal utility, opportunity cost, factors of production, land, labor, capital, entrepreneurial ability, inflation, investment, divestment, division of labor, labor theory of value, exchange rate, trade barriers, trade imbalance, capitalism, socialism, etc.

Chinese behavioral, cultural, and semantic analysis which does exist, and is felt to be noteworthy, has been presented where appropriate. For example, in Chapter 4 the Reward/Effort Relationships are introduced, and this entire discussion has grown out of consideration the the meaning of *bu lao er hwo*, as footnoted on p 141. The legal/moral gap which is mentioned frequently in the text is something of which the Chinese are aware, although I do not find any colloquial phraseology for it in the Chinese language. If there is a better translation than "Empty Talk" for the two types of talk mentioned on p 51, I am unaware of it. Description of thinking, management methods, and scheduling preferences as "go with the flow" is derived from the Chinese idioms footnoted on p 53.

There is something called "the editorial we", and I have frequently used "we" in this sense in the text, since I did to some degree serve as my own editor. More broadly, "we" refers to myself and members of my study group as outlined on p 688, and the consensus that "we" reached. "I" refers to the author's personal view or personal experience. Many insights were gleaned after lengthy discussions with Chinese, Americans, Canadians, Englishmen, Malaysians, French, and others who expressed the desire to remain anonymous. Names of individuals specifically mentioned in the text, pp 1 to 673, (except for quotations), have been changed in order to offer some anonymity to those who were involved in the various situations.

There was some disagreement in our study group as to whether or not "western" should be written as "Western", and whether "westerner" should be rendered as "Westerner", and to some degree these have been used interchangeably. Although the many countries and communities of North America and Europe do have cultural differences, it appears that they have enough similarities to speak of "Western culture" as distinct to itself, and as contrasted with "Chinese culture". Likewise it seems reasonable to speak of a "Westerner" as contrasted with "Chinese". Therefore there may be some rationale to saying that where the capitalized form is used in the text, it is with the attempt to place a bit more stress on the cultural aspect.

"Chinese" is used in two senses in this volume: 1) Chinese people, 2) Chinese language. In the first sense, the verb employed is plural: "have", "are", "tend to", etc. In the second sense the verb used is singular:, "has", "is", "tends to". Some examples of this are on p 81, and other pages.

Benevolence is an important concept in Confucianism. The reader should pay special attention to all places in the text where this "key word" is mentioned, including the Law vs. Benevolence Questionnaires. A differing western viewpoint is footnoted on p 214, and the lack of Biblical references is footnoted on p 517.

It is unfortunate that not every original or translated edition of the *Analects* has the same Chapter and verse numbering, although in my experience the variation has generally not been too large. Most commonly it is in the range of +1 to -1 verse number in different editions. Nevertheless the reader should be aware of this potential discrepancy when cross-checking my references. If English translations are consulted, it is generally advisable to compare the wording in several versions, so that the true significance of the lines may be more fully grasped.

The following are more Notes on specific items in the text. The initial number followed by a colon refers to the page number in this volume. Bracketed [ ] numbers refer to books or articles in the accompanying Bibliography. Abbreviations used are "p" for page, and "pp" for pages.

## Chapter 1

One of the major points of the initial essay on pp 1 to 14, and in other essays throughout Chapter 1, is to clarify that the Group Mentality of the Chinese finds its basis in the way that the Chinese eat their meals. Indeed this Group Mentality orientation is reinforced everytime the Chinese eat.

To review this I will give the following example: when several Chinese are seated in a restaurant eating a meal, the dishes are usually placed in the center of the table, and everyone eats from these common dishes. If a friend happens to show up (without prior arrangement), he is immediately brought into the group and may begin eating at once. It would be rare at the conclusion of the meal that he would be asked to pay for the portion he ate. Conversely, when several westerners go to a restaurant, they generally each order their own meal selection, and then consume it individually. If a friend happens to join them (without prior arrangement), he must wait for his meal selection/portion to come, and it is most likely that the others will continue eating while he waits. At the end of the meal it would be expected that he pay for the portion he ate. This again shows that the Chinese are more oriented to the Group, and the westerners are more oriented to the individual.

The allocation of money among friends and relatives follows similar patterns to these in many respects, in that the Chinese do considerable more "dividing", "sharing", and even "giving away" than is common among westerners. Further insights are in Chapters 4, 5, and 7.

029: Myrdal's comments appear in [60], page xxiv.

067: The footnote here is not intending to imply that the Chinese never seek revenge. Indeed they may do so if they feel that they have been wronged.

## Chapter 2

078-080: I originally did much more research into cross-cultural color comparisons than what is presented here. After several years of collecting examples it appeared to me to be an endless task, hence it was necessary to put some limits on my search. As a result, comments relevant to food and drink were retained here, other interesting items were moved to Chapter 9, and the additional ones I rather reluctantly discarded. All references to colors or color-related items in this volume are listed in the index under "colors".

082: "Man shall not live by bread alone" is from Luke 4:4. The Chinese evaluation of the meaning of this verse (as suggested here) is of course a misinterpretation.

086-100: The examples of English and Chinese idioms presented in these pages were collected from a wide variety of sources, including dictionaries, textbooks, speeches, newspaper and magazine articles, and the author's own personal experience. It is hoped that this listing will be of some reference value to all westerners who are formulating written or oral remarks to be presented to Chinese people.

097-098: I have heard stories from people travelling in various Chinese provinces that in some localities there are some shops which produce certain types of bread, breadsticks, buns, or cakes that sell very briskly. It is possible that in those areas there may be a close local equivalent to the western phrase "selling like hotcakes". There appears to be no close equivalent in common use throughout all of China however, hence I regard this as (U).

## Chapter 3

101: By way of contrast, in politics a "conflict of interest" is a circumstance where a public officeholder's personal interests (such as investments) are being affected by his/her official actions, duties, or influence. However, the definition of "conflict of interest" used in acculturology is different from the one used in politics.

109: Attention to weights and measures is stressed in *Analects* XX, 1, however in the present era the Chinese are known to have a lack of uniform standards in this area.

122: It is my observation that the Chinese prefer Whither-To Reasoning in most conflict of interest situations.

126-127: Jevons' work is discussed in [19], pp 401 to 402, 517 to 519, and 528 to 530.

## Chapter 4

137: Heston's experiences in the acting profession are given in [37].

146: This linguistic analysis was perhaps first pointed out by Smith in [79], p 59.

150: The Chinese pattern in regard to expenditures is further outlined in Chapter 8, pp 326 to 327.

157: It has often been said that Chinese immigrants to the west are more frequently duped, cheated, or otherwise swindled by other Chinese than by westerners.

158-163: The differing views of westerners and Chinese toward "contractual relation" are attributable to religious history to some extent. This is discussed in the Sympathy essay in Chapter 10.

161: The blanket statement "There is no honest businessman" can only be understood if viewed in a Pre Industrial Revolution agrarian society context. Viewed in this way, it gives a strong implication that the only (or the greatest percentage of) honest sellers of merchandise are the producers themselves. In selling (directly to consumers) the goods which they themselves produce, they earn income for the physical labor they have exerted. "Businessmen", who must be construed here as "non-producers", are seen as obtaining profits by dealing in merchandise produced by others, and this is viewed as reward without effort. Such a view may have had some validity in a society where where sales, marketing, promotion, and related planning activities were not highly developed. Additionally, in such an Pre IRAS era where communications were poor, businessmen could easily spread false information about supply and demand in order to gain unfair profits. It is assumed that the producers themselves would not do this.

193: One additional undercurrent of the TV Shooting in France story is that the film crew's plans are constantly changing. This of course reflects a go with the flow scheduling preference.

199-202: Some foreign students do enroll in Chinese elementary schools without the problems that this family encountered. Refer to the explanation on p 202: "In reviewing these . . . " However, a child with no legal father can find it nearly impossible to register in Chinese schools, even if the child is racially 100% Chinese.

200-201: The two tenets mentioned here are from the *Analects*: XV, 39, and XII, 5.

202: These maxims are also from the *Analects*. "All men . . . " is from XII, 5, and "Is it not . . . " is from I, 1.

210-213: I have not discussed other Chinese methods of raising funds privately, since a number of them fall into what the westerners would loosely call "numbers rackets". In the United States and China such schemes are generally illegal in the private sector, although they are organized by state (or provincial, or national) governments under special legislation.

## Chapter 5

216: The reader will not have to look far to determine which religious practices are spoken of here: see the title of the essay beginning on p 259, with related remarks on pp 295-296, etc.

226: The conclusion reached here surprises some westerners, but rarely surprises the Chinese. Indeed such a conclusion is a basic ramification of the Chinese thought processes and value system.

228: A person's knowledge, education, communication skills, attitude toward the proper allocation of time, etc., to a large degree also reflect his/her economic background.

230: With regard to footnote 3, paragraph 1, some people tell me this is what is known in Africa as "jungle justice".

232: For further comments on objective right and wrong, see p 376.

237: The discussion in Part V, and the Debate Topics presented here are attempting to further clarify the comments on p 232, especially the latter part of the first paragraph, beginning with: "In many conversations, I have . . ." Debate Topic #3 on p 525 brings up this entire problem for discussion once more.

## Chapter 6

243: The definitions of "culture" and "subculture" are taken from [71], pp 24 and 33 respectively.

245: In the second paragraph I say " . . . We may then turn back to focus our attention on the Mainland and see the goings-on there with a clearer eye." It is my impression that many reporters for the international news media who cover Mainland Chinese affairs are unable to distinguish between which attitudes, behavior, sentiments, beliefs, etc. are Chinese, and which are communist. One's ability to differentiate these can certainly be improved by reading this volume, which deals with present day non-communist Chinese society, and can therefore serve as a basic point of reference.

For a discussion of whether it is the communist or non-communist society that yields a better life for the working classes, please review pp 127 to 128.

245-248: This summarizes some of the major points in [38], pp 44 to 100.

253: In old China, books, songs, essays, poems, and other literary creations were considered "belonging to everybody", and quite a bit of the influence of this attitude has carried over into present day Chinese society. Even in those few cases where royalty fees were paid, China's long history has resulted in a vast body of writing which is now fully in the public domain. My footnote here outlines some of the practical ramifications of this for the publishers of today.

## Chapter 7

265-266: The point of writing out these Revisions of Historical Documents is to illustrate the disparity between Chinese and western thought. It is by no means an exercise in satire. When the Revisions I have made here are presented to the Chinese, the great majority finds them perfectly acceptable. Please refer to my discussion of Naturalism in Chapter 10 for further clarifications of Chinese-westerner conceptual differences.

Point of reference: In regard to all the peculiar incidents and situations presented in Chapter 7, beginning on approximately p 268 and going on to the end of the Chapter, please refer again to p 146, Note 2, and p 237, item V.

Also refer to *Analects* IV, 18: "In serving his parents a son should mildly remonstrate with them; but should he find that they will not listen, he should still not fail in respect for them nor disregard their wishes; however much anxiety they might give him, he should never complain." Further comments on filial piety are widespread in the *Analects*, particularly notable are I, 7, and II, 5.

278-279: The Chen and Wu genealogies are as described. The charting method used is my own invention. Different styles of type and levels of indentation are used for different generations. Arrows with internal dots add further emphasis. This seemed more convenient than any of the other methods which I considered.

284: For further comments on work in this field since Moore, see the Introduction of [73], page v, and indeed all the other essays in that 786 page volume. I spent over a year reviewing these before I began my research on *King Lear*.

285-288: I have tried here to summarize the excellent treatment of this entire topic in [20], pp 9 to 79.

290: My use of connectives and logical notation is partially borrowed from the dBASE programming language. For example, I am using .OR., .NOT., .AND., .T., .F., etc.

290-291: The essay here on Objectivity is summarized from Carl Wellman's article "Emotivism and Ethical Objectivity" in [73], pp 276 to 287.

291: The misspellings in the original autobiography have been retained.

296-298: Thomas Jefferson said: "A lively and lasting sense filial duty is more effectually impressed on the mind of a son or daughter by reading *King Lear*, than by all the dry volumes of ethics, and divinity, that ever were written." Whether the Chinese would agree with this statement is something the reader may judge after reading all of Chapter 7.

301: The reason or cause sought by these behavioral scientists can only be found by re-investigating the basic tenets of Confucianism. Refer to p 300, paragraph 3, which begins "Historically, the Chinese . . . " Also see related comments on p 653.

303-304: Data on child abuse is in [50], pp 18 to 21.

## Chapter 8

308: From the viewpoint of national economic development, the promotion of the custom of using real money to buy "paper money" which is then burned as an offering to various spirits, seems highly inadvisable. It is a gross misallocation of financial resources.

317: Dr. Chan's paper is collected in [58], and these comments are taken from p 49.

330-331: If Mr. Ching had married a westerner, I wonder if she would have been able to handle the entire situation as deftly as Mrs. Ching has done here.

337: The German social historian has cast a questioning eye on the real significance of "5000 years of history and culture." Aside from the items he mentioned, he has overlooked a wide variety of other barbaric customs traditionally practiced in China, and which we suspect would still be practiced today, if it were not for western influence. One example: when burying a deceased husband to also bury alive the wife (or wives), concubines, servants, etc.

338: Butterfield has made related comments on nationalism: see [08], p 24.

340: As with other terminology not specifically footnoted or attributed to other sources, "Inter Group Face Conflict Cycle" is my own analysis.

343: See Psychological Peculiarity #3, p 582.

362: Li is defined in most books which discuss Chinese philosophy, and in many newspaper articles, especially in the English language press in Asia. I have attempted here to provide a compilation of the various definitions offered in [08], [13], [14], [20], [58], and [90], and various newspapers.

The importance of having (or developing) a sense of shame is mentioned several times in the *Analects*, perhaps most notably in II, 3, and XIII, 20.

365: This type of bad weather situation has happened more than once, see another version in [08], pp 54 to 56.

366: Related comments on indirectness are in [79], pp 65 to 73.

371: The reader will see that in numerous chapters I have correlated many aspects of Chinese thinking and behavior to norms found in a Pre Industrial Revolution subsistence agricultural society.

376: The discussion of justice and righteousness here must be considered in relation to the comments in the Introduction, page vii, diagram C. The words in English and Chinese simply do not imply the same things. The analysis I have presented here does not shock the Chinese, although some westerners are quite surprised by it. Refer to the discussion of moral obligation on p 183 for one application of this.

## Chapter 9

380: The misspellings in the original essay have been retained.

393: A comparison of cognitive meaning and emotive meaning is given in [45], pp 185 to 187.

394: Further remarks on being conservative are given later in this text on p 408.

396: The lack of coordination is also very apparent in Chinese medical circles, as per the comments in Chapter 1, pp 15 to 22.

399: Related comments on privilege appear in [08], pp 76 to 77.

401: Many scholars maintain that historically speaking, "creativity" is another term which is Neutral Plus to Good in English, but has carried essentially Bad Emotive Content in the Chinese language. With a state religion of ancestor worship well established for thousands of years, "creativity" has not been just frowned upon, it has been considered heresy. The Chinese people have always idealized the past and the ways of the ancestors (cf. p 573). They have always stressed carrying on beliefs and practices of the ancients, without trying to improve upon these practices or exceed them (cf. p 555 ff). However, due to western influence, this rather negative approach to "creativity" has been somewhat modified in the last seventy to eighty years, so this term has not been formally included in our listing on p 401.

411: The relation between task fulfillment and loyalty is discussed in [78], pp 177 to 178.

413: For a discussion of Confucianism's encouragement of students to ask questions see [58], p 109, in an essay by Hu Shih. Also refer to the *Analects* XIX, 6. Contrasting comments on intuitive perception of knowledge are on p 538.

414: This is based on the dBASE programming language.

418: My discussion of inner-mode and outer-mode in language is based on the comments in [02], pp 34 to 36.

422: Scholars have traditionally interpreted *Analects* XIII, 3, as calling for a "rectification of names".

428-432: Chinese Proofreading Marks are not categorized in any encyclopedias or other reference materials that I have consulted, so I have been forced to compile my own listing. If the reader has any questions on this, he may consult his Chinese friends and associates.

## Chapter 10

501: This quote is from Arthur H. Smith in [79], p 190.

502-503: Please also refer back to the comments on relationships on p 223.

503: The westerners tend to think in abstractions. The Chinese attitude often is "It does not exist, so what is the point of discussing it?" or "Let's worry about it when it happens." See additional comments on p 521, as well as pp 658 to 659.

512: In [42], p 213, Hsu says "Corruption in the Chinese government is really another aspect of the basic Chinese pattern of mutual dependence."

513-515: Reference is made to the remarks in [79], pp 194 to 216.

517: I have consulted nearly a dozen reference works, concordances, and Bibles, yet I fail to find any instances of the word "benevolence" in the Old Testament. The King James Version of the New Testament does have one instance in 1 Corinthians 7:3, to wit: "Let the husband render unto the wife due benevolence", however in the American Standard Version this is merely rendered as "her due". Scholarly commentary on this passage states that it refers to marital duty, conjugal rights, or the duty of cohabitation. As such it bears little or no relation to the "benevolence" in Confucianism.

529-532: I welcome readers' comments on their experiences using the Sympathy and Legality Test.

535-536: Thoreau's comments largely dovetail with the American viewpoint expounded upon by Hsu in [42], p 88.

538: Many assertions on "sudden intuition" may be found in the writings of Wang Yang-Ming. I researched [15], among other studies. Other possible renderings of this term are "sudden enlightenment", "sudden realization", or "instantaneous apprehension".

542-543: Questions 1, 2, and 3 are based on the statements in [48], pp 66, 76, and 121.

543-544: See [80], Book 1, Chapters 1 and 2. This is further summarized in [26], pp 40 to 53, and in [38], pp 281 to 286.

549-550: Much of this is based on a summary of the material in [38], pp 44 to 100.

549-556: I have done some research in comparing Chinese views to those of the Catholic Church, although that analysis is not included in this volume. Both certainly place a strong stress on traditional values, customs, and orthodoxy, while disapproving of heterodoxy.

551-552: The remarks on Copernicus' and Newton's work are summarized from [26], pp 130 to 142; 152 to 162.

554: See Toffler's comments in [85], p 327.

554-555: The discussion of schools and textbooks here also serves to clarify the results obtained in my conversation with the college students in Chapter 1. This was presented on p 17, beginning with the first sentence of the first paragraph: "At this point . . . . "

559: What one does find in Confucius is a dislike of "eloquence". See *Analects* V, 5, and XVI, 4.

564: Dr. Chan's comments are in [58], p 132.

577, 579-581: Much of the material on syllogisms is based on the analysis in [45], pp 188 to 223, although the examples given here are my own.

578: Hughes's paper is collected in [58], and this section is on pp 78 to 79.

584-585: Much information on the theories of Freud is contained in [04], [06], and [36], although it is not specifically compared to the outlook of Confucianism and Chinese philosophy in these three works. Freud's work is also discussed in [26], pp 174 to 185.

585: See additional comments by Kant in [18], [46], and [47].

## Chapter 11

590-595: The Black Face/White Face behavior seems to come naturally to many Chinese, and I suspect they do not really regard it as a "strategy". To the westerner it is one however, and I have analyzed it here as such. The discussion and formation of its many different styles or "models" is also my own analysis.

595: See additional comments on negotiation in [30], especially pp 136 to 149.

619-621: For a further discussion of building up company culture, see [65], pp 75 to 80, 103 to 106, and 319 to 320.

## Chapter 12

661: These remarks on problem solving are adapted from [01] and [57].

670: The intersecting areas on my Spectra Charts employ the same formulation as used in the branch of mathematics known as set theory.

## Appendix

683: My attempt here has been to define the term "definition". This is a modified summary of the contents of [45], pp 176 to 185.

685-686: My initial research into the differences between these various sciences began with the remarks in [02] pp 5 to 10, and in [49] pp 2 to 5.

## Index

An index typically lists only items and page numbers. As a slight improvement on this, I have taken an extra step and introduced some general categories, with the relevant items and page numbers listed under these. In this way certain elements of the same category can be listed together. Colors, holidays, oxymoronic phraseology (i.e. "a contradiction in terms"), and unsystematic thinking are four examples of this listing method. Abbreviations employed in the index are as follows:

"ff" following the page number indicates that the item in question is in a footnote on the page indicated.

"cf/" in front of any page number(s) is used to mean "confer", or "compare with". Although this item is not specifically mentioned on the indicated page(s), nevertheless it is very relevant to the discussion at that point in the text.

"nr." in place of a page number indicates that no references to this specific item exist in the text, pp 1 to 688.

"Ch." means Chapter.

"&ww" means that in addition to the page numbers listed, this item is also very widespread in the text.

Some items in the index are phrases. Although normal practice would be to arrange these with the most important noun first, some flexibility has been used where it was felt that the adjectives or other accompanying words were significant.

# Bibliography

[01] Ackoff, R.L., *Scientific Method: Optimizing Applied Research Decision*. (New York: Wiley, 1962.)
[02] Barnouw, Victor, *Ethnology*. (Homewood, Ill.: The Dorsey Press, 1978.)
[03] Berstein, Richard, *From the Center of the Earth*. (1982.)
[04] Bocock, Robert, *Freud and Modern Society*. (New York: Holmes & Meier, 1978.)
[05] Bond, Michael H., *The Psychology of the Chinese People*. (Hong Kong: Oxford University Press, 1986.)
[06] Brown, James A.C., *Freud and the Post-Freudians*. (New York: Penguin Books, 1983.)
[07] Bueler, William M., *Chinese Sayings*. (Tokyo: Charles E. Tuttle Co., 1972.)
[08] Butterfield, Fox, *China: Alive in the Bitter Sea*. (New York: Times Books, 1982.)
[09] Cahn, Edmond, *The Predicament of Democratic Man*. (New York: Macmillan Co., 1961.)
[10] Capra, Fritjof, *The Tao of Physics*. (New York: Bantam Books, 1984.)
[11] Carnegie, Dale, *How to Win Friends and Influence People*. (New York: Pocket Books, 1940.)
[12] Carroll, Lewis, *Alice's Adventures in Wonderland*. (New York: New American Library, 1960.)
[13] Chai, Chu, *The Humanist Way in Ancient China*. (Taipei: Chinn Shan Books, 1969.)
[14] Chan, Wing T., *A Source Book in Chinese Philosophy*. (Princeton: Princeton Univ. Press, 1963.)
[15] Chang, Carsun, *Wang Yang-Ming*. (New York: St. John's Univ. Press, 1970.)
[16] Chao, Lilian, *Worth Remembering*. (Taipei: Students' English Digest Assn., 1974.)
[17] Chen, Spring, *Chinese Idioms and Their English Equivalents*. (Hong Kong: University of Hong Kong, 1981.)
[18] Ching, Julia, *Chinese Ethics and Kant*. (Honolulu: "Philosophy East & West", 28, 1978, University of Hawaii Press.)
[19] Chisholm, Roger K., *Principles of Economics*. (Glenview, Ill.: Scott, Foresman and Co., 1978.)
[20] Chu, Tung Tsu, *Law and Society in Traditional China*. (Cambridge: Institute of Pacific Relations, 1965.)
[21] Commins, Saxe, *The Social Philosophers*. (New York: Pocket Library, 1954.)
[22] Confucius, *The Analects*. (various editions.)
[23] Covell, Ralph R., *Confucius, the Buddha, and Christ*. (Maryknoll, N.Y.: Orbis Books, 1986.)
[24] Darwin, Charles R., *Origin of Species*. (London: 1859.)
[25] Delfgaauw, Bernard, *Twentieth Century Philosophy*. (Dublin: Gill and Macmillan, 1969.)
[26] Downs, Robert B., *Books That Changed the World*. (New York: New American Library, 1956.)
[27] Einstein, Albert, *Ideas & Opinions*. (New York: Outlet Book Co., 1954.)
[28] Eitel, Ernest J., *Feng Shui*. (Singapore: Graham Brash, 1973.)

[29] English, Jane, *Chuang Tsu Inner Chapters*. (New York: Vintage Books, 1974.)
[30] Fisher, Roger, *Getting to YES*. (Cambridge: Harvard Negotiation Project, 1981.)
[31] Fisher, Tadd, *Our Overcrowded World*. (Macfadden-Bartell Corp., 1971.)
[32] Forman, James D., *Capitalism*. (New York: Dell Publishing Co., 1974.)
[33] Friedman, Milton, *The Tyranny of the Status Quo*. (New York: Pelican Books, 1985.)
[34] Friedman, Milton, *Free To Choose*. (New York: Penguin Books, 1985.)
[35] Geneen, Harold, *Managing*. (New York: Avon Books, 1985.)
[36] Harris, Thomas A., *I'm OK, You're OK*. (New York: Avon Books, 1973.)
[37] Heston, Charlton, *The Actor's Life*. (New York: E.P. Dutton, 1978.)
[38] Hobsbawm, E.J., *The Age of Revolution 1789—1848*. (New York: New American Library, 1962.)
[39] Hoffman, Mark S., *World Almanac and Book of Facts*. (New York: Scripps Howard Co.)
[40] Hospers, John, *Human Conduct*. (San Diego: Harcourt, Brace, & World, 1961.)
[41] Hsia, C.T., *The Classic Chinese Novel*. (New York: Columbia University Press, 1968.)
[42] Hsu, Francis L.K., *Americans and Chinese*. (Honolulu: Univ. of Hawaii Press, 1981.)
[43] Ibsen, Henrik, *Ibsen Plays, vol. I & II*. (New York: Methuen Inc., 1981.)
[44] Johnson, David L., *A Reasoned Look at Asian Religions*. (Minneapolis:Bethany House, 1985.)
[45] Kahane, Howard, *Logic and Philosophy*. (New York: City Univ. of N.Y., 1973.)
[46] Kant, Immanuel, *Critique of Practical Reason and Other Works*. (London: 1909.) reprint: New York, Bobbs Merrill.
[47] Kant, Immanuel, *The Groundwork of the Metaphysics of Morals*. (London: 1909.) reprint: New York, Harper & Row.
[48] Kearny, Edward N., *The American Way*. (Englewood Cliffs: Prentice-Hall, Inc., 1984.)
[49] Keesing, Roger M., *Cultural Anthropology*. (New York: Holt, Rinehart and Winston, 1981.)
[50] Kempe, C. Henry, *Child Abuse*. (Suffolk, England: Fontana, 1983.)
[51] Lang, Olga, *Chinese Family and Society*. (New Haven: Yale University Press, 1946.)
[52] Leys, Simon, *Chinese Shadows*. (New York: Penguin Books, 1977.)
[53] Lin, Yu Tang, *Famous Chinese Short Stories*. (New York: Pocket Books, 1952.)
[54] Loss, Myron, *Culture Shock*. (Winona Lake, Ind.: Light and Life Press, 1983.)
[55] McCormack, Mark H., *What They Don't Teach You at Harvard Business School*. (New York: Bantam Books, 1986.)
[56] Mencius, *The Book of Mencius*. (various editions.)
[57] Mintzberg, H., *The Structure of Unstructured Decision Processes*. (Ithaca: "Administrative Science Quarterly", 21, 1976, Cornell University.)
[58] Moore, Charles A., *The Chinese Mind*. (Honolulu: University of Hawaii Press, 1967.)
[59] Motte, Andrew, *Sir Issac Newton's Mathematical Principles of Natural Philosophy & His System of the World*. (Westport, Ct.: Greenwood Press Inc., 1962.)
[60] Myrdal, Jan, *Report from a Chinese Village*. (New York: Signet Books, 1966.)
[61] Needham, Joseph, *Science and Civilisation in China, vol. 1*. (London: Cambridge University Press, 1985.)
[62] Nierenberg, Gerard I., *The Art of Negotiating*. (New York: Cornerstone Library Inc., 1981.)
[63] Peale, Norman V., *The Amazing Results of Positive Thinking*. (Englewood Cliffs: Prentice-

Hall, 1959.)

[64] Peter, Laurence J., *Why Things Go Wrong*. (New York: William Morrow & Co., 1984.)

[65] Peters, Thomas J., and Waterman, Robert H. Jr., *In Search of Excellence*. (New York: Harper & Row, 1982.)

[66] Peters, Thomas J., and Austin, Nancy K., *A Passion for Excellence*. (New York: Random House, 1985.)

[67] Rand, Ayn, *Philosophy: Who Needs It*. (New York: Bobbs-Merrill Co., 1982.)

[68] Rand, Ayn, *For the New Intellectual*. (New York: Random House, 1961.)

[69] Reischauer, Edwin O., *Japan Past and Present*. (Tokyo: Charles E. Tuttle Co., 1973.)

[70] Ruby, Lionel, *The Art of Making Sense*. (London: 1968.)

[71] Samovar, Larry A., *Understanding Intercultural Communication*. (San Diego: Wadsworth, Inc., 1981.)

[72] Saret, Laura, *Data Processing Logic*. (New York: McGraw-Hill, 1984.)

[73] Sellars, Wilfrid, *Readings in Ethical Theory*. (New York: Meredith Corp., 1970.)

[74] Seward, Jack, *Japanese in Action*. (New York: Weatherhill, 1969.)

[75] Shakespeare, William, *King Lear*. (London: 1606.)

[76] Sherrill, Wallace A., *Heritage of Change*. (Taipei: East-West Eclectic Society, 1972.)

[77] Sidgwick, Henry, *The Methods of Ethics*. (New York: The Macmillan Co., 1907.)

[78] Silin, Robert H., *Leadership and Values*. (Cambridge: Harvard University, 1976.)

[79] Smith, Arthur H., *Chinese Characteristics*. (Shanghai: 1894.) reprint: Telegraph Books, Norwood, Pa.

[80] Smith, Adam, *The Wealth of Nations*. (1776.)

[81] Storr, Anthony, *Jung: Selected Writings*. (Suffolk, England: Fontana, 1983.)

[82] Sun, Tsu, *Art of War*. (various editions.)

[83] Swift, Jonathan, *Gulliver's Travels*. (1726.)

[84] Thoreau, Henry David, *Walden*. (1854.)

[85] Toffler, Alvin, *Future Shock*. (London: Pan Books, 1971.)

[86] Vanderbilt, Amy, *Everyday Etiquette*. (New York: Bantam Books, 1981.)

[87] Watson, Burton, *The Works of Han Fei Tzu*. (Taipei: Confucius Publishing Co., 1984.)

[88] Wolf, Margery, *Women and the Family in Rural Taiwan*. (Stanford: Stanford Univ. Press, 1972.)

[89] Worsley, Peter, *Modern Sociology*. (New York: Penguin Books, 1978.)

[90] Wright, Arthur F., *The Confucian Persuasion*. (Palo Alto: Stanford University Press, 1960.)

[91] Yohannan, John D., *A Treasury of Asian Literature*. (New York: New American Library, 1956.)

# INDEX

abacus 237, 363
Ability-to-Pay 229-235
absolute 665
absolute knowledge 493
absolute statement 187, cf/369
abstract 61ff, 61, cf/133, 141, 189ff, 224, 455ff, 503, 521, 578, 579, 681
academies, private 177-180, 324
acceptability, minimum standards of 114
acceptance, blind 536
accident 203, 226-228, 235
acculturation i, 240-245
acculturative knowledge iv, v, vii, 240
acculturologists 227
acculturology 242-245, 613, 632, 677, 681, 685-686
accuracy, unfailing 485
acetify 89
Acting Work 134-139
acupuncture 401
Adams, J. 233
advertisement mistake 103-104
advertising 139-141, 349-350, 628-631
advertising, false 188, 347
Aesop's fables 88
Africans 612
agent, purchasing 118-121
agreement, written 212
agricultural ideas 162
agriculture 245-247
agriculture, subsistence 229, &ww
alien 674
allegations, list of 603
alphabetic vs. character 470-472
alteration, superficial 98
altruism 314, 500
altruist 314
altruistic heroism 499
American, native 676
*Analects* 361-362
*Analects* (I,9) 283; (II,4) 668; (IV,10) 299; (VII,1) 555ff; (IX,4) 299; (IX,24) 227; (X,8) 415ff; (X,10) 20; (XII,2) 227; (XII,10) 227; (XII,22) 227; (XIII,18) 376; (XV, 39) 201; (XVIII, 8) 299; (XIX,21) 227
analysis, transactional 585
analysis, where is the 478
ancestors; ancestor worship 302, 308, 327-328, 345, 398, 408-409, 517, 523, 537
ancestors 254-304, 536
ancestry, mixed 398
Anglo-American legal system 510
angry 317ff
anthropology 686
anti-creativity bias, cf/Ch. 9, cf/Ch. 10
anti-individualism bias, *see* Group Mentality
ants 607
AO Perception of Value 105-124

AP Perception of Liability 229-237, 505
Appalachia 229
apple pie 3, 38, 87
Aquinas, T. 214ff
architecture 585-586
argue 503
aristocratic ideas 250
aristocratic thinking 361
Aristotle 112, 284, 290, 295, 410, 503ff, 518, 559, 578
art 252, 262
art museum 455-458
art objects 360
Art of War 560
artist 50-51, 271, 590, 640-641
artistic 443-444
arts, performing 645
artwork 321
AS Perception of Injury 217-220
AS Reward/Effort Relationship 141-149, 179, 190, 194, 196, 452, 457, 505
assenting 358
auction of land 281
authoritarian; authoritarianism 411ff, 492, 555, 563, 566, 603, 646-648
authority, delegate 653
authority, full and final 664

baby: bury alive 273
babysitting 263
backdoorism 515
bad debt allowance 197
baking 43-45
balance sheet 222ff
banking 150, 153-158, 200-202, 218-219
bankruptcy, deliberate 213-214
barter 447
bartering 224ff
bathroom 48
beauty and perfection 359-360
beer gardens, illegal 184
behavior 498
behavior, children's 345-346
behavior, forbidden 237
behavior, organizational cf/133, cf/181-186, cf/196, cf/300-301, cf/515, 633-636
behavior, organizational *see* Ch. 10, 11, 12
behavioral modification 608
beheading 356
belongings, careless with 199
benefit, fringe 340-343
benevolence viii, 111, 120, 214, 230, cf/235-236, 517, 523, 537ff, 539, 543, 616
benevolence, *see* sympathy
benevolent; benevolently 156ff, 237ff, 522
Berlin 259

beverages, cold 566
bias, grammatical 82, 432-435
biased and conservative 404
Bible 58-60, 268, 269, 312, 362, 515-517, cf/537
bicultural 443, 612
bicycle 226
big eats little 237ff
bilingual 443
black, see colors
Black Face/White Face 587-599, 614
blackmarket 100, 611
blasphemy 541
blood lines 282
blood relation 274
blood ties 223
blood, mixed 398
Bonaparte, N. 367
bones, small 34
bonus, monthly 209
bonus, year-end 214
bonuses 332-333, 634-638
Book of Changes 547-548, 581
Book of Rites 286
bosses 609
both/and 565
bottlenecks 85, 666
bottoms up 672-673
bourgeoisie, see 1) middle class; 2) capitalists
box meals cf/35, 118-120
Boxer Rebellion 316
bread, grains, and pastries 97-98
bribe 69
British seapower 351
broken promises 132
Browning, R. 177
Buddhism 474, 565-566
Buddhist; Buddhists 15, 254, 474, 562, 582, 607
budget problems 205-208
budget, adequate 663
budget, no 455
budget, tight 631
budgeting estimates 202-203
buffet 7
bug holes 124
building, jump off 261-262
bull-frogs 152-153
bureaucracy, see organizational behavior
bureaucratic rigidity 515, cf/653
business organization 3
businesses, illegal 660
businesses, small 609
businessman, no honest 161


Cake, chocolate 30-32
cakes 366
calligraphy 443-444

capital 150-151, 162, 224, 544
capitalism 541, 543, 549
capitalist cf/128, cf/541-543, cf/549
capitalist system 128
capitalization 106, 484
card, send a 9, 25
Carnegie, D. 309
case-by-case 645
catch-22 623
categories, abstract 578
categories, six 463
Catholic 407
Catholic Church 551-552
cattle 92-93
censorship 395, 497, cf/537-538
chairs 106-107
challenges 569-570
change 117-118, 554
Changes, Book of 547-548, 581
channels, indirect 206
characters (CDL) 485
characters, Chinese 253, 574-576
characters, number of 486-487
chauvinism 406
chauvinistic attitude 335
check borrowing 218-221
checks, post dated 218-219, 336, 447
chemical elements 489
chemists 331
cherry pie 38
chi 443ff, 573
child abuse 303
children, successful 310
Chin Dynasty 556-557
chinaware 269
Chinese eating, rules of 11, 27, 29
Chinese language study orientations 480, 490
Chinese New Year, see holidays
Chinese, overseas 675
Ching Dynasty 254, 553
chops 323
chopsticks 38, 56-57, 67, 71, 649
Christian 407
Christianity and Confucianism 537ff
Chwang-tse (Chuang Tsu) 317, 559, 578
church and state 296
circus 94
City Councilman 329
civilization 350, 536
cleverness, assumed 385
clothing 320-321
coffee 78, 109, 625
coffee shop 31
collateral 155, 213, 222-223, 281
colors & related terms
—Black Face/White Face 587-599, 614
—black 22-23, 79, 81, 92, 94, 95, 403

—blackmarket 100, 611
—blue 392
—brown 78-79
—gold, golden 11, 90, 100, 267, 473, 520, 521
—gray 675
—green 77, 79, 81, 124, 403
—orange 81, 272-273, 290
—pink cf/41 (rare meat)
—purple 81
—red 79, 81, 149-150, 319, 394, 526, 545, 563
—red envelope 120-122, 327, 394
—silver 78-79
—tan 78
—white 78, 81, 94, 95, 150, 403, 417
—yellow 79-80, 81, 89, 316, 407
commission 449
common sense 677
common-line culture 359-360
communication 164, 253, 383-386, 438-440, 470-472, 476-478, 488, 616
communication problems vii, viii
communication, basic 170, 473
communication, indirect 451, 593
communication, see Ch. 2, Ch. 9
communications pipelines 665-666
communications, wireless 361
company manuals 148
compass 351
competence 316, 411
complaining 38-46, cf/633
completeness, lack of 585-586
component cost 106, 114
composition in Chinese 446, 491
computer industry 165-167
computer, Chinese mode 486-487
condensing 491
condiments 98
conference, international 339, 456-458
conflict of interest 101-124, 179-180
conflict resolution 103, cf/353, cf/597-598, cf/605, cf/616-618
conflict, avoidance of 348
conformists 555
conformity cf/314, cf/318, 394, 536, cf/554-555
confrontation 604-607
Confucian doctrine 332
Confucianism 295-296, 301, 303ff, 537ff
Confucianism cf/112ff, cf/161-162, cf/193, cf/585, 653
Confucianism, see benevolence
Confucius 283, 288, 338-339, 361-362, 422
Confucius, see Analects
confusion 385-387, 674
connections 182-186
consequences, everyone share 113, cf/122, cf/343
conservative 394, 404, 408
consultant, hotel 205-208

consulting 168-171
consumer movement 103, 347, 353ff
Continental Law System 533-535
contract 168-171, 179, 224, 550, 603
contractual relation 138-139, 144-145, 146, 147, 220, 225, 345, 516-518, 537ff, 568
contractual stipulations 630
control, indirect 652
conversation, a Chinese cf/472-473
conversation, point of 440
cooking, white boiled 37
coordination, lack of 661
Copernicus, N. 294, 301, 551-552
copyright laws cf/181, 253ff
corpse, complete 541
correctness, level of 449-450
corruption 400, 641
cosmology 564ff
count, generation 248-249
counterfeit merchandise 181, 621-624
counterfeiters 567
courtesy 677
courts, backlogged 512
covenant 516-517
CPR 184, 497, 653
creative energy 549
creativity 24, 64-66, 357, 411, cf/555ff
credibility 212
credit 177
credit arrangements 153-158
credit information 213
credit rating 183
credit record 148, 148
critical mass 102
criticism 128-130, 538, 584, 650
criticism, constructive 199, cf/492
crusade mentality 22, 503ff
cultural background 453
cultural differences 228
cultural gap 384-385
cultural similarities 228
cultural understanding 193
culture ii, vii, 20, 225, 242-245, 481
culture, background 242-243
culture, classical 586
culture, common-line 359-360
culture, company 619-621
culture, entry 242, 674
culture, foreign 674
culture, guilt 362
culture, invading 674
culture, native 674
culture, new 242
culture, shame 362
culture, source 674
culture, target 242
curb market 155

custom cf/23, 69, 70, 72, 73, 199, 269, 280-281, 304, 326-328, 415-416, 453, 489, 514, 560-561, 566, 630, 673
customs and traditions 23-25, cf/237, 294, 302
cut down another person 67

damage compensation, multiple 218
Darwin, C. 552
data 632
daughter, unmarried 327-328
daughters-in-law 513
death certificate 450
debate 559-560, 647
debate topics 237-238, 525
debates, political 322
decadence, foreign 647
decision, postponing a 588
definition, acculturological 243-244
definitions 61, 683
deliberate acts and behavior 519-520
deliberately 630
democratic 603
democratic reform 245, 643-648
deodorant 348-349
departmentalism cf/324-325, 405
dependence, mutual cf/9, 220, cf/258, 447, 545
description, structural 472-473
destiny 404, 540
Dewey, J. 539, 599, 682
dialect 405
dictionary 96, 176, 476, 485-486, 545, 584
diet, balanced 16
dieting 35-37
diets, different 85-86
different ideas 189-190
Differing-Economic Background 228
difficulties and solutions 70-76
dinner for two, romantic 40
direct and indirect 363-376
direct refusal 365, 368
direct vs. meaning 453
directions, new 163
directness 370-371
disasters, natural 501
discorrelation 162, 567
discount 119-120
discrimination, racial 585
discussions, amicable 517
disharmony 340, 603, &ww
disloyalty 653
diversionary tactic 79
do nothing 195
do nothing, see non-action
doctor 675-676
doctrine 503
dogma 395, 550

double standard 18
dowry cf/263, 495
dozen 403
dragon 394
Dragon Boat Festival, see holidays
dragonflies 418
dramatic 406-407
draw the line 297, 517-518
drinking 70, 311-312, 313, 319
drinks, toasting 70
drowning babies 303
dui bu chi 69, 615
Dutch treat 342
Dynasties 285-288

eating 1-76, 670
eating and dining 329-331
eating, style of 35
economic affluence 234
economic background 228
economic criminal cf/213
economic disadvantage 505
economic growth 337, 351
economic health 224
economic levels 310
economic livelihood 131
economic loss 170
economic reality 113, 229
economic standpoint 128, 350
economic support 273-276
economic trends 255
economic welfare 156ff
economics, Ph.D. 326
economy, stimulate 197
Edison, T. 350-351, 555
education 254-258, 293-294, 413, 554-555
education, goal of 464
Education, Ministry of 89, 202-203, 324, 510
educational achievements 331-332
educational methods 91
educational structure 463
educational system 406
effort, intangible 190
eggs 39
eggs, putting in one basket 90, 174
egoism 314
egoist 313-314
Einstein, A. 507, 509ff
either/or 565
elementary school, Chinese 199-203
elevators 571-572
embarrassment 313-319
embezzlement 3
embroidering 197
Emerson, R. W. 317, 554, 615
emotional attachment 553

emotional extremes 361
emotive content 393-403
Emotivism 290-291
Emperor 254, 300, 375, 556
empiricism 550
employing the locals 143-149
employment agencies 147-148
empty talk 51
enforce 663
enforcement, erratic 180-181
enforcement, no 546
enforcement, selective 506-507, 534
engineering, mechanical 246
enlightenment 550
entrepreneurial ability 224
epistemology 564ff, 578ff
equality 112, 273-275, 589
error, admission of 522-523
ethical concerns 578
ethical thought cf/264-266
ethics 180-186, 268-304, 677-678
ethnocentric 544
etiquette vs. good fortune 55-57
etymological divinations 490
exactness, mentality of 442
exception 181-182
excluding from choices 4
exclusive 565
excuses 32, 412, 528
Exodus 516
expense, goodwill 197-198, 205, 207
expenses, intangible 189-190
expertise 316
eye test 184


face 283, 306-363, 374, 399, 415, 442ff, 503, 522, 526, 560, 569, 593, 594, 595, 597, 603, 606, 610, 615, 626, 627, 636, 671, 677, 681
facial expressions 424
factory system 246-247
facts and sarcasm 566
facts vs. suppositions 111-113
facts first 363
facts vs. emotions 521
facts, at odds with 338
facts, at variance with 321
facts, unshakable 18-19
fair; fairness 109-110, 144-146, 281, 376, 516, 517, 647, 678
fair play 588
fair solution 274
false advertising 347
false solution 97
family relations 92
family run 102, 106
famine 87

fat 395
fate; fatalism 220, 317, 360, 404, 539, 545, 568
favoritism 340-343, 375
fears, ungrounded 99
fees, separate collection of 202-203, 205-207
feet, cold 419
ferry-boat 204
feudalism 223, 249
filial 258-304
filial piety 344, 514, 537-538, 644-645
Filial Piety Classic 272-273, 288, 348ff
financial base 156
financial independence 275
financial reinforcement 637-638
financial responsibility 275
financial reward 458ff
financial stability 223
fine, small 49, 204
fines, cancellation of 222
firepot 4
FIRPTA 158
fish and seafood 95-97
fish, eating 55
fishing 52-54, cf/95-97, 324
five elements 578ff
five relationships 315, 494-503, 563
flattery 94
Flesch, R. 561
flexibility 4-6, 299-301, 353
flowers 24, 469
fluency; fluent 194, 227, 481-484
fluency, total 441-443
fluency-level, target 444-445
food & pricing 104-126
food groups 15-16
food science 15-17, 330
Ford Motor Co. 264
Foreign Relations Committee 363
forgetfulness 602-607
France 171, 191-193, 611
Franklin, B. 273, 298
frankness 366
fraud 111
free and independent 538
free enterprise 541
free market 113, 512
freedom 313-316
freedom to sell 102
freelancer 49-50
freelancing 194-196
freeloading 40
French 10, 38, 356-357
French lady 6, 357
French Revolution 549-551
Freud, S. 584-585
friends come from afar 202
frontier 542, 552

fruit; fruits 72, 87-88, 109-110, 625
funeral expenses 212
funerals 260-304, 327

Galileo 551
gambling 142, 570
game, pinball 240
games 458-463
genealogy 278-279, 282
Geneen, H. 18
General, successful 225
generation count 248-249
generic compounds 18
generosity 26-29, 198, 330, 340, 341, 353
geographic mobility 108, cf/115, 117-118, cf/202, 251, cf/283, 519
gerontocracy, ruling 634
get even 120
Ghosts, Month of 612
ghosts, unworshipped 282
gibberish 492
gift giving cf/23-25, 512
gifts 336
girlfriend 335
gloves 335-336
gluttony 36ff
Go Roman Strategy 611-613
go with the flow 53, 179, 484, 540, 660
goat, black 22-23
God 407, 496, 537
Goethe 545, 551
gold, see colors
Golden Rule 11, 520-521
good 284, 402
good and bad 570-571
Good Guy/Bad Guy 595
good luck 626-627
good, common 543
good, intrinisic 284
goodness 678
gourmet 33
government, overthrow the 634
GRAD 521
grammatical bias 82, 432-435
grease, drain the 44
green, see colors
gregarious 315, 404-405
group 315, &ww
Group Mentality 2-4, 15, cf/28, 113, 225, 256ff, 263, 277, 314-315, 333, 342-343, 471ff, 540ff, 563, 665
Group Mentality, see kinship, patrilineal
growth 165-168
growth, industrial 246-247
guanxi 151
guanxi, see CPR

guarantors 155, cf/222-223
guest is first 526
guests 6, 26-27
guests, uninvited 638
guidelines, employee 619-621
guilty until proven innocent 603
Guinness Book 490

habeas corpus 512
hands, holding 647
handwritten data 490
handyman 347
harassment 122, 181, 236, cf/281
harm a child 303
harmonious social relations 133
harmony 22, 155, 348, 407, 500, 532-533, 539, 559, 567, 586, 616
harmony models 654-660
Hartzell, R. W. cf/153-154, cf/266-267, 686-687
Hathaway, K. B. 318
Hawthorne, N. 552
head hunters 147-148
Health Dept. 157, 331
hepatitis 47
herbal medicine shop 348
hierarchical relationships 112, 498, 500, 563
hierarchical vacuum 568
Hippocrates 270
Hippocratic Oath 336-337
historical documents, revisions of 264-266
historical overhang 248-249
holidays
—April Fool's Day 74
—Chinese New Year 198, 333, 467, 612, 635
—Christmas 5
—Dragon Boat Festival 198, 333, 636
—Easter 5, 76
—Father's Day (USA: 3rd Sun./June, China: Aug. 8th) nr.
—Groundhog Day 100ff
—Halloween 472
—Lantern Festival 467
—Mid Autumn Festival 198, 333, 635-636
—Mother's Day (2nd Sun./May) nr.
—Riddle Day 467
—Thanksgiving 5, 25, 41
—Valentine's Day 9
Holmes, S. 560
homesick; homesickness 2, 346, 394, 411
homework 491, 631-632
homogeneous 102, 118, 398
homogeneous race 65ff
homonyms 475, 489
homophones 487
honest 678

honesty 50, 58-62, 111, 251, 325, 339, 342, 370, 373, 519-520, 567, 598, 631-632, 671, 672, 680-681
Hong Kong 305-306, 511
honor 312-319, 410
Hoover, H. 297
horse, ideal 569
horses 94-95
horticultural research 13
hospitable 189
hospitality 29-30, 525-528, 650
hotel 54-55, 185, 205-208
house rules 215
hui system 210-213, 225
human relations 330-331, 503, 518, 570, 588, 613-615
humanism 541
humanity 21, 230ff, 232ff
humble 442ff
humility 300, 410
hunting and gathering stage 20
hypothetical models 146

Ibsen, H. 682
Iceberg Model 523-525
iconoclastic 401
idealism 359-360
identity, law of 290, 570
idioms, new Chinese 683-685
idolatrous practices 537
idolatry 396
ignorance, feigned 616
illegal beer gardens 184
illegal businesses 660
illegal factories 344, 509
illegal food stalls 353
illegal gambling parlors 355
illegal hostels 355
illegal hotels 185
illegal obstructions 639
illegal restaurants 184
illegal supermarkets 182-183
illiteracy, widespread cf/251, 519
image 317
imitation 94
immigration 356-357
implementation vs. excuses 661-666
import tax 222
inaction 373-374
inclusive 565
income statement 222ff
independence 411
independent 2, 542
independent pronunciation 489
index, no 468

Indians, Ten Little 353
indigenization 241ff
indirect, indirectness 6, 145, 325, 349, 363-376, 586, 610, 633
—channels, indirect 206
—communication, indirect 451, 593
—control, indirect 652
—investment, indirect 373
—penalization, indirect 638
—recommendation, indirect 639
—refusal, indirect 594, 627-631
—speech, indirect 251-252
—stalling, indirect 627-631
Individual Mentality 342
individualism 405-406, 411, 545, 550
individual vs. unit pricing 124-126
Industrial Revolution 107-108, 115-118, 245-252, 360ff, 549-551
inexactness 162, 369, cf/485
inflation 113
influence, western 632
inheritance 274
innovation 398
innovation, see creativity
inscrutable v
insecticides and pesticides 124
inside and outside 361, 367
insincere 662, &ww
insults 66-70
insurance industry 156, 214
insurance settlement 238-239
insurance, liability 231-232
insurance, not carry 203
intangible 189-190
integration 143, 297, 326, 342, 502, 560, 597, 633
integration of concepts 143, 409-412
integrity 678
intellectual property 181
Inter-Group Face Conflict Cycle 340
Interest Orientations 314-315
interior decorating 641
introducer 403
intuitive perception 538-539, 569
inventions 350-351
inventive intelligence 351
investment 149-153
investment in goodwill 198
investment, return on 224
irrational 346
IS Perception of Injury 217-218
IS Reward/Effort Relationship 141-149, 190, 196
isolationist 241-242
Italians 5
itch, dry 34-35

Jackson, A. 14

Japan 12, 27, 45, 63-64, 161, 165, 166, 206, 271, 344
Japan, catch up with 167
Japan, overtake 569
Japanese 57ff, 438, 610
jealous; jealousy 88-89, 140, 215, 355, 603, 633
Jefferson, T. 233, 542, 570
jen 303ff, 361-362, 517
Jevons, S. 126
Johnson, A. 471
joint venture partner 167-168
jokes 76
judiciary, independent cf/294, 506, 508
juice vs. drink 82
Jung, C. 315, 544, 584
justice 227, 237ff, 376, 410, 678-679
justice and jeopardy 216-239
justice, sale of 512

Kant, I. 301, 585
Kepler 551
keyboard, computer 165-168
king of the castle 27
kinship 494-496
kinship, patrilineal 201, cf/274
kite 273, 346, 607
Korea 22-23, 64, 161
Korean 57ff, 388ff

labor 223-224
labor, better life for 127-128
labor, division of 543, 544
labor theory of value 126-128, 224
laissez faire 659
lamb 272
land 223, 224, 260
land holdings, disputed 281
language, see Ch. 9
language institute, foreign 674
language lessons, free 178-179
language schools 177-180
language, international 171
language, organization of 252-253
language, teaching 171-174
Lao-tse, (Lao-tsu) 541, 547-548
laundry, Chinese 196-199
law and ethics 180-186
law and filial piety 282, 285-288, 285-288
law enforcement 511, 526
Law of Identity 290, 570
Law vs. Benevolence Questionnaire 48-49, 204
law, above the 230ff, 232ff, 296, 399
Law, Anglo-American 510
Law, Continental 533-535
law, ignorance of 519

law, rule by 103, cf/122, 510-512
law, universal 301
Lawrence, D. H. 315
laws 237
laws, unfair 506-512
LD Perception of Liability 229
leader 633
leader deification 522-523
leadership 634
Lee, R. E. 366
legal complications 182-185
legal fees, high cost of 512
legal reality 146
legal rights 296, 588
legal terminology 456-457
legal/moral gap 146, 147, 230, 282, 302, 345ff, 509
lessons, memorize 514
li 362
liability 226-239, 599
liberalism 550
license, business 222
license, operating 183-186
lied 518
lighting 39-40
Lin, Y. T. 558
Lincoln, A. 556
line, dividing 237
line, draw the 297, 517-518
lines, blood 282
linkage 481
liquids 98-99
lists, ordered 468
literal translation 453
little 403
little eats big 237ff
loan guaranteeing 222-223
logic 290, 301, 556-581, 679
logic, conversational 415-416
long term 682
loss leader 105
loss management 199
loyalty 411, 679
Luther, M. 552


machines 245-247
magazine advertising 628-630
magical powers 489-490
magnetism 548
maintenance 249-250
male heirs cf/263, 282
man and God 496
management orientations 634-635
management style 619-621
manual labor 3, cf/249-250, 335, 347
manual system 476ff

marginal utility 126-127, 439
mark-up, the 208-210
market economy 115-118
market strategy 106
market, free 113, 512
marriage 327
marriages, late 539
marriages, polygamous 496
married, pressure to get 501ff
marry 261-262, 275
Marshall, A. 127
martial arts 335-336
Marx, K. 126-128
master and apprentice 501
matchmaker 368, 373
materialism cf/21, 224, 225, 327
maturity 275
maxims, contradictory 565-566
May 4th Movement 553
Mead, M. 567
Mean, Doctrine of the 410
meaning, intended 473-474
measurement, units of 84-85, 109
meat buns 62-63, 93
meat, rare 41
meats 93-95, cf/109
medical conference 445
medical research 22
medical terminology 435-438
medical treatment 573
medicine 436-438, 583
medicine and health 19-22
medicines, prescription 189
memorization 514, 555, 564
memorize it 463
Mencius 156ff, 282, 303ff, 494, 511ff, 554
Menger, K. 126
mental flow 465-466, 477
mental telepathy 159
menus and signboards 454-455
mercury 331
metaphysics 564ff
Mid-Autumn Festival, see holidays
Middle Ages 315
middle class 229, 370-372, 549
middle class values 250
miracles in Bible 312
miraculous cures 20-21
misrepresentation 519-520
model building 640-673
modest; modesty 326, 330, 370, 560
money 25, 131-132, 570
money markets 104
money, marginal utility of 127
money, spend all the 143
monopoly 652
monopoly licenses 538

monopoly rights 400
moonlighting 396
Moore, G. E. 284
moral obligation 183
moral standards, raise 161
moral standpoint 185
morality 170, 193, 250, 585, 679
morality, see Ch. 3, 5, 7
morally speaking 170
More, T. 308-309
Mormons 537
Mother's boy 393
mothers, three 644-645
motion picture industry 452
motorcycles 222, 250
Movie Work 134-139
MSG 37
museums 360
mutual dependence cf/9, 220, cf/258, 447, 545
mutuality 502
Myrdal, J. 29

naive 397
Nanking, Treaty of 247, 511
nationalism 338
native 432-433
natives vs. non-natives 481
nativist 241-242, 612
nativization 244
natural 314, 679
natural course 250
natural order 2
natural value orientation 105-118
naturalism 105-108, 113, 535-544
Nature controls man 221, 540, 659
nature, lack of sympathy to 515
naval power 541
negligence; negligent 97, 230
negotiating 138-139, 447
negotiation 104, 140-141, 321, 587-639, 640-641, 662-666
nepotism 375, 394, 568
nest, leave the 543
new directions 163
newsletter 369
newspaper 484
newspaper essays 602-604
newspaper offices 642
newspaper reportage 322, 649-652
newsprint 652
Newton, I. 301, 551
nightclub singer 464-465
non-action 42, 373, cf/538-539, 541, 546, 586
non-evidential bias cf/71, cf/321-322, cf/325, cf/338, cf/363, cf/539
—"unfilial" children 285-286

—right vs. wrong, view of 112-113
—saving face 330-331, &ww
non-exact cf/162, cf/369, 485
non-materialism 327
non-sequitur 410
noodles 55
not bad 397
nuclear power plant 479
numismatics nr.
nutrition; nutritious 15-17, 251, 316, 569-570, 584
nutrition and medicine 17-19

Obedience vi, 258-304
obedient, being 528
obey 261
objective; objectively 181-182, 185, 290-291, 347, 352, 525, 682
objective standards 180
objective standards, *see* respect
objectivity 290-291
objectivity, lack of cf/57, 375
obligation 52-54, 183, 358
obstructions, illegal 639
officials 499ff
old 396
Old Testament 515-517
OM Perception of Value 119-122
ontology 564ff
OP Perception of Value 119-122
open 390-391, 403-404
opera 338
Opera, Peking 311
Opium War 247, 316, 511
opportunism 398
opportunist; opportunistic 96, 341
opportunity cost 220
opportunity, equality of 542
opposite meanings 387-392, 491-492
order in society 110
order in the family 287
ordering 468-469, 476, 486-487
original 404
orthodoxy 549-556
osmosis 538
overhang, historical 248-249
oxymoronic phraseology
—abstract sympathy-based theory 521
—arbitrary logic 575
—legalized corruption 400
—locality of non-registration 433
—non-similar similarities 391-392
—unity of opposites 565
—unnatural naturalism 542
—unsystematic synthesis 564

pain 262
Paine, T. 577
paintings, purchase of 590-592
palindromes 467
paper 9, 351, 652
paper tiger 95
parochialism 405
parties, political 508
partner, joint venture 167-168
patience 406
patriotic reaction 312
patronizing 69
PC Paradox 128-130, 235, 272, 490
peace, disturbance of 260
peace, promote 101
Peale, N. V. 545
peanuts 100, 356
peasant class cf/29, 250-251
Peking Duck 40-41
Peking Opera 311
penalize, indirectly 638
people's livelihood 1-14
people, different types of 239
Perception of Injury 217-218
Perception of Liability 229
Perception of Obligation 52-54, 358
Perception of Value 105-124, 141
perception, intuitive 538-539, 569
perceptual basis 575
perfection 359-360
perfectionism 454
permissible and non-permissible 641-652
personal favor 139, 142, 455
personal relations 142
personnel shift 594-595
Ph.D., double 442
pharmaceutical companies 17-19, 348-350
pharmaceutical technology 297
philately nr.
philosophy, moral 301
philosophy, moral *see* Ch. 7
philosophy, well-developed 227
phonetic rendering 475
phonetic value 462-463
phonics 477-478, 488
photographs 196, 617
photography 325-326
phraseology 681-682
pig in a crate 23-25
pigs 43
Pilgrims 552
ping pong 408
planning, central nr.
planning, lack of 8, 32, 659
plans 134
Plato 284, 295, 503ff, 542, 559
Plautus 540

poetry 2, 252-253, 443
poetry, translating 174-177
point, press the 32
point-of-sale 102-124
police 616-618
polite 74-75, 666-673, 679
polite race, a 338
politeness 42-43, 68-69, 250, 667-673
politeness, see Ch. 7
politician 404
pollution 321, 515, 567
polytheism; polytheistic 396, 540, 565
Pope 64
popular 401
porcelain nr.
positiveness 544-549
poultry 89-92
power 589, 598, 648, 659
practical 224, 401-402, 582
praise 492, 588
Pre Industrial Revolution 249-252, &ww
Pre Newtonian world 539
premises 557-581
press interviews 649-652
press, Chinese 156-158, 366
press, foreign 303, cf/652
press, freedom of 245
preventative maintenance 249, cf/347
price, fair 107, 114
price, quoted 118
price, unit 124-125
prices and pricing 43, 104-128
prices, marked 115-118
pricing and value cf/449-452, 454-455
pricing problem 520
pricing: Chinese notation 125-126
pricing, minimum 105-108
pricing, natural 115-118
pride 312-319, 401, 581-582
pride, empty 350
Primary Sympathetic Orientation 146, 194, 216-217, 226, cf/577, 660
primitivism 539
principle 124, 503, 518, 591, 679, 680-681
principle, ethical 287
printshop 423
privacy 408
privacy, right to 260
privilege 399-400
problem 303, 412
problem solving 376, 661
problem, defining the 303
process 568-569
production cost, below 105-107
production, factors of 126, 224
profit sharing 209-210
progress 408, 539-540, 543, 550, 567

project management 609-611
proletariat cf/127-128
promise 173-174, 325, 358, 609, 610
promise, cancellation of a 358
promise, not following up on a 133
promises, empty 54-55
pronunciation 322, 381-383
proofreading 425-432
propaganda 395
propriety 679
prostitution 306-308
Protestant 407
Protestant Reformation 552
proverb, East European 1
proverbs 161
provincialism 405
purchasing agent 118-122
psychiatric treatment 585
psychological conditions 247
psychological peculiarities 581-586
public or classified 563, 601
publishing house, Chinese 253ff
purchasing power 128


Quality and value 449-452
quality control cf/21, 160, 166-168
quality, inconsistent 449
question it, don't 463-464
questions, ask 413-414


R.S.V.P. 6
races 398
racial conflict, history of 102-103
racial discrimination 118, 156, 585
radical, metal 478
radicals, Chinese 465-466
radio 312
railway system 549
rational 111, 294, 550, 679-680
Rational Group Interest 314-315
Rational Self Interest 314-315
rationale 680
Rationale Weight Indexing 413-416
rationality 342, 560-561
raw vegetables 7
razor 349
reaction, negative 69-70
reason, ability to 214ff
reason, rules of 680
Reasoning, Where-From 122-123
Reasoning, Whither-To 122-123, 412
rebel and revolutionary 553ff
receipt 239
recommendation, indirect 639
Rectification of Names 422

red, see colors
red envelope 120-122, 327, 394
redundant 95
references 166-168
Reformation, Protestant 552
reforms, democratic 245
refugee policy 515
refusal to sell 102, 123
refusal, direct 6, 328-329, 364-365, 368
refusal, indirect 594, 627-631
refusals 225
regulations, clear-cut 642-645
regulations, contradictory 416-417, 507, 644
regulations, unwritten 206, 658-659
regulations, vague 643-645
relations, personal 121
relations, public 102
relationship model 112
relationship: based on money 223
relationship: go sour 223, cf/330
relationship, special 118-119
relationships 494-503
Relationships 6 and 7 513-515
relationships, mutually dependent 9, cf/220, cf/258, 447, 545
relatives 2, 26, 223
religion 582
religious history 515-517
remelioration 631
renting an office 447
renting a room 142-143
reorganization 397
reporting, investigative 642
respect 259, 314, 317, 321, 363, 410, 441-443, 493, 540, 597, 633, 643, 644-645
respect and obedience 265, 271
respect and worship 259
respect for elders cf/60, cf/287, cf/290ff, cf/293, cf/297-298, cf/302, 537-540
respect for law 509
response, inadequate 99
responsibility cf/196, 519-20, 547, 597, 599, 653, 659, 660, 664
responsibility for care 269
responsibility, not accept 234
responsibility, bi-directional 258
responsibility, organizational 133, cf/188
responsible 647
restaurants, illegal 184
resumes 451-452
retreat 588
Reward/Effort Relationships 141-149, 452, 457
Ricardo, D. 544
rice 7, 10, 43, 45, 78, 82-83, 171
rice pudding 44
rice, fried 104-105
ridiculous and stupid 639

right and wrong 112, 250, 287, 301, 503
right and wrong, objective 232ff, 505, 525
right, doing things 455
right, in the 682
righteousness 223, 376
rights & obligations 520
rights & obligations, balance of 110-112
rights, constitutional 510-511
rights, standing up for 648
Rites, Book of 286
ritual 63-66, 265
rituals, pagan 540
role, fit the 501, cf/536
Roman dictate cf/21, 189
Roman lettering 621-622
Rome 611-613
roots, forget your 398, 411
RR Perception of Value 105-124, 146, 342, 598, 631
rule by law 103
rule, standard of 185-186
rules 643, 646-647
rules are unnecessary 300
rules, lack of 488-489
rules, make up 8
rules, unwritten 122, cf/647, cf/658


Salary 332-333
sales, below cost 105-106
sandwiches, club 31
sanitary cf/3, 46-48, 585
sarcasm cf/63-68, 566-567
satisfaction 188
saying what you mean 51-52
scholar-ethic 347
school, elementary 199-203
schools and textbooks 554
science 251
scientific methodology 538
scientific revolution 550
screen door 267
seating arrangements 8-9
secretary cf/25, 447, 638
secrets 139
see again 400
self, concept of 315, 317
self confidence 22, 410
self, denial of 263ff
self determination 537
self interest 544
self reliance 545, 554
self sacrifice 268
selfish; selfishness 112, 224, 314, 412
sentiment 504-505
sentimentalistic orientation 120
sexually liberated 408

shadow boxing 335-336
Shakespeare, W. 296, 298, 309, 362, 420ff, 471
shame, sense of 362
Shanghai 248
share the consequences 113, cf/122, 343
shares in an enterprise 149-151
shares, anonymous complimentary 151, 186
sharing 28
shave 349
Shaw, G. B. viii, 344
sheep 272, 288, 376
sheep and goats 80, 92
Shepard, O. 556
shipping companies 621
shirt 642-643
short term 106, 108, 114, 217
shove it 527-528
side effects 17, 297
silence, maintaining 618-619
sin 421
sincerity 138, 342, 370, 663-664, 680
Singapore 27, 479
singer 593-594
singing 352-353, 464-465
sloganeering 533
Smith, Adam 543-544
society, order in 110-112
society, place in 648
society, subsistence agricultural 249, &ww
sociology 686
soft 508
sold out 102
something for nothing 186-189
Soul, Ladder of the 214ff
South America 20
space exploration nr.
speak indirectly 251-252
spectra charts 666-673
speculation 398
speed of speech 379
spontaneous manner 538
spontaneously 301
sports 354
spread the blame cf/113, 122, cf/343
staffing 160
stalling 605, 608, 663, 664-665
stalling tactics 594
stalling, indirect 627-631
standard 397
standard, a fair 510-512
standard, objective 290
standardization; standardized 21, 472, 474-475
statesman 404
status quo 550, 565
statutes, contradictory 508
Steinbeck, J. 555
stereotyping 501

Stevenson, C. L. 290-291
Stevenson, R. L. 270
stingy 40, 198
storks 24
strategy, strategies 407, 587-639
Strategy, the P.I. 205-208
straw, last 517-518
street vendors 182
subconscious mind 416
subculture 243
subjective; subjectively 180, 182, 290, 320-321, 352, 682
subpoena 623-624
subscripts, translation of 452
succession questions 362-363
sudden intuition 538
suicide 263, 344
sunglasses 158-163, 595-599
supermarkets, illegal 182-183
superstitious beliefs 672
supply and demand 458
Supreme Being 295
surgery 348
surveys 568
swimming pool model 646-648
syllogisms 577-581
sympathetic nature 132
sympathetic note, strike a 198
sympathetic posture cf/220, 645
sympathy 192-193, 199, 224, 323, 323, 503-532, 588-594, 616-617, 660
synthesis 563-566
Syria 438-439
Syrus 619
systematic analysis 463
systematic descriptive structure 487
systematically 539


Tai Ping Rebellion 553
Taiwan, R.O.C. 128, 149-150, 245, 248ff
Taoist 15, 562
task completion 599-607
task-force approach 666
taxes 150, 154, 158, 192, 399
tea 34, 65, 73, 78, 83, 170-171, 243
tea, cup of 98
teachers 332, 333
teaching language 168-171, 171-174
TEFL 168
telephone 599-602, 606
telephone vs. letter 639
telephone, use of 487-488
Ten Natures v, iv, vii
ten parts 214

ten, seven, three, four 213-214
Tennessee 14-15, 266
Tennyson 410
TESL 168
testing 383, 503, 514, 555
textbooks 16, 202, 332
textile industry 163-165, 196
theology 565-566
theory and practice iii, v, 162, cf/202, 567-568
thick skinned 399
thinking, Industrial Rev. era 247-249
Thoreau, H. D. 535-537
threats 281
throat, dry 566
time confusion 434-435
time is money 452
time limit 358
time relation 146
tips 42
title disputes 222ff, 281
titles 363
toasting drinks 192, 319, 672-673
TOEFL 383
Toffler, A. 554
togetherness and sharing 9
tokenism 502, 660
tolerance 332, 406, 502
tolerance for failure 354, 653
tongue in cheek 419
Top 40 List 21-22
TOPIC 631
toy show 592-593
trademarks 621-624
trading, international 158-168, 208-210
tradition 337-339, 536, 552-553, &ww
tradition, break with 401
tradition, change of 397-398
traffic 500
traffic safety cf/250, 293, cf/509, 567
translation 445-458, 474-475
translator, free cf/455, 649
transliteration 474-475, 488-489
travel overseas 538
treaties 511-512
tributes 326
true statement 159
trust 187
truth 680
truth is your best defense nr.
try my best 402
tuberculosis 269-271, 293
tuition 254-257
TV production 139-141
TV Scripts 644-645
TV Shooting in France 191-194, 611
TV Work 134-139
typewriter story 526-527

Uncoordinated 396, 405
underarm odor 348
undercapitalized 225
underdog 505, 521
undifferentiated terms 420-424
unfilial 264-304
unionism cf/264, 315
Universe, structure of 547-548
unknown and unadopted 85, 417-419
unscientific bias, see language 491-493
unsympathetic 193, &ww
unsystematic thinking
—coordination, lack of 661
—rules, lack of cf/300, 488-489
—rules, unwritten 122, cf/647, cf/658
—when the head hurts 662
unsystematic thinking, origins of
—characters, Chinese 462-464, 574-576
—intuitive perception, sudden intuition 538-539
—lack of coherent theology 565
—lack of descriptive structure 473, 487
—lack of standardized ordering system 468-469, 486-487
—polytheism 565-566
—spontaneous action in the Universe 301, 547-548
up and down 571-573
US Presidents 233
utilitarian 682
utilitarianist questioning 550
utility 126-127
utopia 308-309, 573


Vacations 2
value of merchandise 126-128
value system 48-49, 204
value, labor theory of 126-128, 224
vegetables 43, 124-125
vegetables, raw 7, 41
vehicle 228, 236-237
venture capital 225
verb tenses 146, 323, 434-435
victory 354
view, long term 106, 110-111
Villemin, J. A. 270
vinegar 89, 98
violence 230ff
virtue 680
virtue, Aristotle's view of 284
virtue, superior 300
virtues, one hundred 268
virtuous conduct 300
visit 238
vocabulary, specialized 445
vocation, denial of 544
Voltaire 677

wage income 128
Washington, G. 233, 570
watches 339
we eat everything 45
wealth 228, 543
wealthy 310, 403
wedding 314, 320
wedding dinner 327, 345-346
weddings 194-195
weights, units of 109, 112
Wellman, C. 291
West Orange, N.J. 350-352
western 675
westernization 676-678
what am I being paid for? 134, 136-137, 194-196
white, *see* colors
why? 261, 542
Wilde, O. 619
window washers model 650-652
winter coats 103
word meanings 369
work, intangible 190

work, investigative 364
working capital loans, temporary 221-222
world harmony 338
World War II 337
worship 254-304
wrong, can do no 523

Xenophobia cf/511-512

Yahweh 516
yarn, new 163-165
yellow, *see* colors
yellow journalism 407
yin and yang 16, 547-548, 565, 578
you don't get something for nothing 114
you get what you pay for 113-114, 233
yuan fen 30

Zip the lip 618-619

敦煌書局
CAVES BOOKS, LTD.
公司：(02)5371666 • 中山店：(02)5710732
中：(04)3265559 • 台　南：(06)2296347
：(07)5615716 • 全省連鎖為您服務